*First Print Edition [1.0] -1433 h. (2012 c.e.)*

Copyright © 1433 H./2012 C.E.
**Taalib al-Ilm Educational Resources**

**http://taalib.com**
**Learn Islaam, Live Islaam.**<sup>SM</sup>

All rights reserved, this publication may be not reproduced, stored in a retrieval system, or transmitted in any form or by any means, electronic, mechanical, photocopying, recording, scanning, or otherwise, except with the prior written permission of the Publisher.

Requests to the Publisher for permission should be addressed to the Permissions Department, Taalib al-Ilm Educational Resources by e-mail: **service@taalib.com**.

Taalib al-Ilm Education Resources products are made available through distributors worldwide. To view a list of current distributors in your region, or information about our distributor/referral program please visit our website. Discounts on bulk quantities of our products are available to community groups, religious institutions, and other not-for-profit entities, inshAllaah. For details and discount information, contact the special sales department by e-mail: **service@taalib.com**.

The publisher requests that any corrections regarding translations or knowledge based issues, be sent to us at: **service@taalib.com.** Readers should note that internet web sites offered as citations and/or sources for further information may have changed or no longer be available between the time this was written and when it is read.

We publish a variety of full text and free preview edition electronic ebook formats. Some content that appears in print may not be available in electronic book versions.

*ISBN EAN-13:*          978-1-938117-01-5    [Soft cover Print Edition]
*Library of Congress Control Number:*    2012933378

**From the Publisher**

GOLDEN WORDS UPON GOLDEN WORDS…FOR EVERY MUSLIM.

"Imaam al-Barbahaaree, may Allaah have mercy upon him said:

**May Allaah have mercy upon you! Examine carefully the speech of everyone you hear from in your time particularly. So do not act in haste and do not enter into anything from it until you ask and see: Did any of the Companions of the Prophet, may Allaah's praise and salutations be upon him, speak about it, or did any of the scholars? So if you find a narration from them about it, cling to it, do not go beyond it for anything and do not give precedence to anything over it and thus fall into the Fire.**

Explanation by Sheikh Saaleh al-Fauzaan, may Allaah preserve him:

'Do not be hasty in accepting as correct what you may hear from the people especially in these later times. As now there are many who speak about so many various matters, issuing rulings and ascribing to themselves both knowledge and the right to speak. This is especially the case after the emergence and spread of new modern day media technologies. Such that everyone now can speak and bring forth that which is in truth worthless; by this meaning words of no true value - speaking about whatever they wish in the name of knowledge and in the name of the religion of Islaam. It has even reached the point that you find the people of misguidance and the members of the various groups of misguidance and deviance from the religion speaking as well. Such individuals have now become those who speak in the name of the religion of Islaam through means such as the various satellite television channels. Therefore be very cautious!

It is upon you oh Muslim, and upon you oh student of knowledge individually, to verify matters and not rush to embrace everything and anything you may hear. It is upon you to verify the truth of what you hear, asking, 'Who else also makes this same statement or claim?', 'Where did this thought or concept originate or come from?', 'Who is its reference or source authority?'. Asking what are the evidences which support it from within the Book and the Sunnah? And inquiring where has the individual who is putting this forth studied and taken his knowledge from? From who has he studied the knowledge of Islaam?

Each of these matters requires verification through inquiry and investigation, especially in the present age and time. As it is not every speaker who should rightly be considered a source of knowledge, even if he is well spoken and eloquent, and can manipulate words captivating his listeners. Do not be taken in and accept him until you are aware of the degree and scope of what he possesses of knowledge and understanding. As perhaps someone's words may be few, but possess true understanding, and perhaps another will have a great deal of speech yet he is actually ignorant to such a degree that he doesn't actually posses anything of true understanding. Rather he only has the ability to enchant with his speech so that the people are deceived. Yet he puts forth the perception that he is a scholar, that he is someone of true understanding and comprehension, that he is a capable thinker, and so forth. Through such means and ways he is able to deceive and beguile the people, taking them away from the way of truth.

Therefore what is to be given true consideration is not the amount of the speech put forth or that one can extensively discuss a subject. Rather the criterion that is to be given consideration is what that speech contains within it of sound authentic knowledge, what it contains of the established and transmitted principles of Islaam. As perhaps a short or brief statement which is connected to or has a foundation in the established principles can be of greater benefit than a great deal of speech which simply rambles on, and through hearing you don't actually receive very much benefit from.

This is the reality which is present in our time; one sees a tremendous amount of speech which only possesses within it a small amount of actual knowledge. We see the presence of many speakers yet few people of true understanding and comprehension.' "

*[The eminent major scholar Sheikh Saaleh al-Fauzaan, may Allaah preserve him- 'A Valued Gift for the Reader Of Comments Upon the Book Sharh as-Sunnah', page 102-103]*

❧ *Is not He better than your so-called gods, He Who originates creation and shall then repeat it, and Who provides for you from heaven and earth? Is there any god with Allaah?  Say: 'Bring forth your proofs, if you are truthful.'* ❧-(Surah an-Naml: 64)


*Explanation:* ❧ *Say: "Bring forth your proofs..*❧ This is a command for the Prophet, may Allaah praise and salutation be upon him, to rebuke them immediately after they had put forward their own rebuke. Meaning: '*Say to them: bring your proof, whether it is an intellectual proof or a proof from transmitted knowledge, that would stand as evidence that there is another with Allaah, the Most Glorified and the Most Exalted*'. Additionally, it has been said that it means: '*Bring your proof that there is anyone other than Allaah, the Most High, who is capable of doing that which has been mentioned from His actions, the Most Glorified and the Most Exalted.*' ❧*...if you are truthful.*❧ meaning, in this claim. From this it is derived that a claim is not accepted unless clearly indicated by evidences."

[Tafseer al-'Aloosee: vol. 15, page 14]


Sheikh Rabee'a Ibn Hadee Umair al-Madkhalee, may Allaah preserve him said,

'It is possible for someone to simply say, "*So and so said such and such.*" However we should say, "*Produce your proof.*" So why did you not ask them for their proof by saying to them: "*Where was this said?*" Ask them questions such as this, as from your weapons are such questions as: "*Where is this from? From which book? From which cassette?...*" '

[The Overwhelming Falsehoods of 'Abdul-Lateef Bashmeel' page 14]


The guiding scholar Imaam Sheikh 'Abdul-'Azeez Ibn Abdullah Ibn Baaz, may Allaah have mercy upon him, said,

'It is not proper that any intelligent individual be mislead or deceived by the great numbers from among people from the various countries who engage in such a practice. As the truth is not determined by the numerous people who engage in a matter, rather the truth is known by the Sharee'ah evidences. Just as Allaah the Most High says in Surah al-Baqarah, ❧ *And they say, "None shall enter Paradise unless he be a Jew or a Christian." These are only their own desires. Say "Produce your proof if you are truthful."*❧-(Surah al-Baqarah: 111) And Allaah the Most High says ❧ *And if you obey most of those on the earth, they will mislead you far away from Allaah's path. They follow nothing but conjectures, and they do nothing but lie.*❧-(Surah al-'Ana'an: 116)'

[Collection of Rulings and Various Statements of Sheikh Ibn Baaz -Vol. 1 page 85]

Sheikh Muhammad Ibn 'Abdul-Wahaab, may Allaah have mercy upon him, said,

'Additionally verify that knowledge held regarding your beliefs, distinguishing between what is correct and false within it, coming to understand the various areas of knowledge of faith in Allaah alone and the required disbelief in all other objects of worship. You will certainly see various different matters which are called towards and enjoined; so if you see that a matter is in fact one coming from Allaah and His Messenger, then this is what is intended and is desired that you possess. Otherwise, Allaah has certainly given you that which enables you to distinguish between truth and falsehood, if Allaah so wills.

Moreover, this writing of mine- do not conceal it from the author of that work; rather present it to him. He may repent and affirm its truthfulness and then return to the guidance of Allaah, or perhaps if he says that he has a proof for his claims, even if that is only a single statement or if he claims that within my statements there is something unsupported, then request his evidence for that assertion. After this if there is something which continues to cause uncertainty or is a problem for you, then refer it back to me, so that then you are aware of both his statement and mine in that issue. We ask Allaah to guide us, you, and all the Muslims to that which He loves and is pleased with.'

*[Personal Letters of Sheikh Muhammad Ibn 'Abdul-Wahaab- Conclusion to Letter 20]*

Sheikh 'Abdullah Ibn 'Abdur-Rahman Abu Bateen, may Allaah have mercy upon him, said,

'And for an individual, if it becomes clear to him that something is the truth, he should not turn away from it and or be discouraged simply due to the few people who agree with him and the many who oppose him in that, especially in these latter days of this present age.

If the ignorant one says: *"If this was the truth so and so and so and so would have been aware of it!"* However this is the very claim of the disbelievers, in their statement found in the Qur'aan ❰ ***If it had truly been good, they would not have preceded us to it!"*** ❱-(Surah al-Ahqaaf: 11) and in their statement ❰ ***Is it these whom Allaah has favored from amongst us?"*** ❱-(Surah al-Ana'am: 53). Yet certainly as Alee Ibn Abee Taalib, may Allaah be pleased with him, stated *"Know the truth and then you will know it's people."* But for the one who generally stands upon confusion and uncertainty, then every doubt swirls around him. And if the majority of the people were in fact upon the truth today, then Islam would not be considered strange, yet by Allaah it is today seen as the most strange of affairs!"

*[Durar As-Sanneeyyah -vol. 10, page 400]*

# *Statements of the Guiding Scholars of Our Age Regarding Books & their Advice to the Beginner Seeker of Knowledge*

*With Selections from the Following Scholars:*

Sheikh 'Abdul-'Azeez Ibn 'Abdullah Ibn Baaz
Sheikh Muhammad Ibn Saaleh al-'Utheimeen
Sheikh Muhammad Naasiruddeen al-Albaanee
Sheikh Muqbil Ibn Haadee al-Waadi'ee
Sheikh 'Abdur-Rahman Ibn Naaser as-Sa'adee
Sheikh Muhammad 'Amaan al-Jaamee
Sheikh Muhammad al-'Ameen ash-Shanqeetee
Sheikh Ahmad Ibn Yahya an-Najmee
*(May Allaah have mercy upon them.)*

&

Sheikh Saaleh al-Fauzaan Ibn 'Abdullah al-Fauzaan
Sheikh Saaleh Ibn 'Abdul-'Azeez Aal-Sheikh
Sheikh Muhammad Ibn 'Abdul-Wahaab al-Wasaabee
Permanent Committee of Scholastic Research
& Issuing of Islamic Rulings
*(May Allaah preserve them.)*

With an introduction by:
**Sheikh Muhammad Ibn-'Abdullah al-Imaam**

Translated & Compiled by:
Abu Sukhailah Khalil Ibn-Abelahyi al-Amreekee

# Table of Contents

## *1. Guidance for Every Male and Female Muslim*

## 2. Golden Advice That Benefits the Beginner Regarding Acquiring Knowledge

### 3. Beneficial Guidance for Female Students of Sharee'ah Knowledge

## 4. Guidance from the Scholars Regarding Important Books to Acquire for Seeking Knowledge

### 5. The Warning of the Scholars from the Books of those who have Deviated from the Sunnah & Warnings Regarding Ways of Going Astray

## 6. Clear Statements from the Advice of the Scholars
## Regarding Memorizing Knowledge

## 7. Issues Related to the Verifiers of Books in our Age

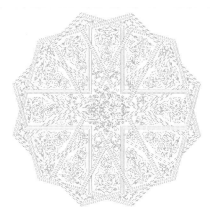

**Images of handwritten original introduction of
Sheikh Muhammad Ibn 'Abdullah al-Imaam (may Allaah preserve him)**

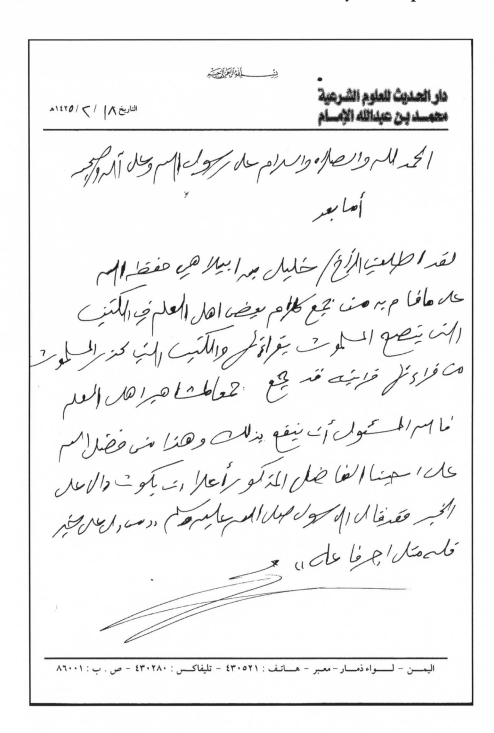

# Images of handwritten original introduction of
# Sheikh Muhammad Ibn 'Abdullah al-Imaam (may Allaah preserve him)

# Introduction of Sheikh Muhammad Ibn 'Abdullah al-Imaam (may Allaah preserve him)

All praise is due to Allaah, may Allaah's praise and His salutations be upon the Messenger of Allaah, his family, and Companions.

As for what follows:

The brother Khalil Ibn-Abelahyi, may Allaah preserve him, has shown to me that which he has undertaken in gathering the speech of some of the people of knowledge regarding the books the Muslims are advised to read, as well as those books that the Muslims are warned against reading.

After reading it, I see that he has compiled a collection from the statements of well-known people of knowledge, and he has selected well and brought forth good for the Muslims in what he presents to them in this blessed book. How can this not be so, when the foundation of every good is in reading the book that possesses benefit and in having a righteous teacher? As the scholars have mentioned, "*The one who carefully selects his teacher and his book has protected his religion with the best of safeguards.*"

Sheikh Ibn al-'Utheimeen, may Allaah have mercy upon him, was asked, "At whose hands should we take knowledge?' He replied, "*From the one of correct beliefs, sound methodology, and the proper goal and objective.*" Likewise, the author of the 'Risaa'il al-Islaah' stated, "*The rectification of the Muslim nation is through the correction of its deeds and endeavors, and the correction of its deeds and endeavors is based upon the rectification of its branches of knowledge, and the rectification of its branches of knowledge lies in the reliable transmitters of its knowledge.*" Consider what Ibn Taymeeyah has said regarding Abee Haamed al-Ghazaalee: "*The book ash-Shifaa' caused him to become afflicted...*" (Majmu'a al-Fatawaa, Vol. 10, Page 552). Meaning that the illness of Abu Haamed originated from the reading and studying the book ash-Shifaa' of Ibn Sinaa, due to what it contains of deviations that lead one outside of Islaam. May Allaah be generous to the one who said:

*We ceased our brotherhood with those*

    *who became diseased from the Book Ash-Shifaa'*

*And how many times have I said, oh people you are*

    *on the very edge of the cliff because of the book Ash-Shifaa' '*

*When they dismissed our warning to them*

    *we return in death, back to Allaah with Him being sufficient for us,*

*Yet they then died upon the religion of Ibn Rustaalas!*

    *while we lived upon the way of the chosen Messenger.*

                           *(Majmu'a al-Fatawaa, Vol. 9, Page 253)*

Therefore from the completeness of a Muslim's protection from harm and trials is that he does not acquire a book or choose it for reading or study until he inquires about that book from someone whom he knows is reliable in both his religion and his knowledge.

How many diseases of our Muslim nation are caused by reading books that are not truly reliable when judging according to the guidance of the Sharee'ah! Therefore as a statement of ample warning regarding every book in which its harm is known to be greater than its good, it is not permissible to publish it, read it, or give it as a gift.

As for the books of the sects of the Raafidhah, the Sufeeyah, the people of philosophical argument and false rhetoric- then it should be known assuredly that their evil and harm is significantly greater than any good within them. So from the completeness of a Muslim's protecting himself from harm and trials is that he does not acquire a book or choose it for reading or study until he inquires about that book from someone whom he knows is reliable regarding his religion and knowledge.

Written by

Muhammad Ibn 'Abdullah al-Imaam

# Compiler's Introduction

*In the name of Allaah, The Most Gracious, The Most Merciful*

Verily, all praise is due to Allaah, we praise Him, we seek His assistance and we ask for His forgiveness. We seek refuge in Him from the evils of our souls and the evils of our actions. Whoever Allaah guides, no one can lead him astray and whoever is caused to go astray, there is no one that can guide him. I bear witness that there is no deity worthy of worship except Allaah alone with no partners. And I bear witness that Muhammad is His worshipper and Messenger.

❴ *Oh you who believe, fear Allaah as He ought to be feared and do not die except while you are Muslims.* ❵–(Surah Aal-'Imraan:102)

❴ *Oh mankind, fear Allaah who created you from a single soul and from that, He created its mate. And from them He brought forth many men and women. And fear Allaah to whom you demand your mutual rights. Verily, Allaah is an ever All-Watcher over you.* ❵–(Surah an-Nisaa:1)

❴ *Oh you who believe, fear Allaah and speak a word that is truthful (and to the point) - He will rectify your deeds and forgive you your sins. And whoever obeys Allaah and His Messenger has achieved a great success.* ❵–(Surah al-Ahzaab:70-71)

As for what follows:

The best speech is the book of Allaah, and the best guidance is the guidance of Muhammad, may Allaah's praise and His salutations be upon him. And the worst of affairs are newly invented matters in the religion, and every newly invented matter in an innovation, and every innovation is a going astray, and every going astray is in the Fire.

Certainly, every Muslim hopes for success and happiness in this world and the Hereafter. Our Lord has taught us to ask Him for guidance in the "Mother" of al-Qur'aan, Surah al-Faatihah, where He explains to us exactly which path is the true path to contentment and the true way of success. The guiding scholar Sheikh 'Abdul-'Azeez Ibn 'Abdullah Ibn Baaz, may Allaah have mercy upon him, comprehensively described this path to happiness:

*"…the path to happiness and the path to success is the path which was taken by the first believers, the Companions of the Prophet, may Allaah's praise and His salutations be upon him, and those who followed them in goodness. As Allaah, the Majestic and the Exalted, says,* ❴ *… this is my straight path. Follow it and do not follow the other paths as they will separate you from His path. This is what he has ordained for you, in order that you may become righteous.* ❵–(Surah al-Anaam: 153) *The path of Allaah is knowledge, this truly is His path, this truly is guidance, this truly is Islaam, this truly is goodness, and this truly is the fear of Allaah.*

*Regarding this, Allaah, Glorified and Exalted, says in Surah al-Faatihah,* ❴ **Guide us to the straight path.** ❵ *Our Lord has instructed us to ask for this; instructed that we ask from Him guidance to His straight path. And His straight path is that knowledge that was brought by His Messenger, as well as acting according to that."* [1]

The hadeeth scholar Sheikh Hamaad Ibn al-Ansaaree, may Allaah have mercy upon him, explained the meaning this verse, ❴ **Guide us to the straight path** ❵ which is recited by all of us in our ritual prayers:

---

[1]    From our sheikh's comments upon "Understanding of the Religion' by Sheikh Saaleh al-Fauzaan

*"The meaning of ❦ **Guide us to the straight path** ❧ is: Our Lord whom we have praised by means of what You have taught us. We ask You and supplicate to You by this supplication, which You have taught us, that You guide us to the straight path. And the meaning of ❦ **Guide us to the straight path** ❧ is: Teach us that which will benefit us, and then grant us success to act in accordance with that which benefits us."*[2]

Indeed, from the greatest means to achieving this foundation of success and happiness; is the seeking of beneficial knowledge and acting according to it. As was mentioned by Sheikh al-Islaam Ibn Taymeeyah, may Allaah have mercy upon him:

*"The seeking of Sharee'ah knowledge is generally a communal obligation upon the Muslims together collectively, except for that which has been specified as an obligation for each and every individual. For example, the seeking of knowledge of what Allaah has commanded everyone in general and what He has forbidden for them. The obtainment of that type of knowledge is considered an obligation upon every individual. As it has been narrated in the two 'Saheeh' collections from the Prophet, may Allaah's praise and His salutations be upon him, that he said,* {**The one whom Allaah intends good for He gives him understanding of his religion.**}*"*[3] [4]

The guiding scholar Sheikh Ibn Baaz, may Allaah have mercy upon him, explained the meaning of "Sharee'ah" knowledge:

*"Knowledge is known to possess many merits. Certainly the noblest field of knowledge which the seekers can strive towards, and those who aspire can endeavor to reach, is gaining Sharee'ah knowledge. While the term 'knowledge' is used generally to refer to many things, within the statements of the scholars of Islaam what is intended by 'knowledge' is Sharee'ah knowledge. This is the meaning of knowledge in its general usage as expressed in the Book of Allaah and in the texts of the Sunnah of His Messenger, may Allaah's praise and His salutations be upon him. This is knowledge of Allaah and His names and attributes, knowledge of His right over those He created, and of what commands He legislated for them, Glorified and Exalted is He. It is knowledge of the true way and path, that which leads and directs toward Him, as well as its specific details. It is knowledge of the final state and destination in the next life of all those beings He created. This is Sharee'ah knowledge, and it is the highest type of knowledge. It is worthy of being sought after and its achievement should be aspired to.*

*Through this knowledge one understands who Allaah, Glorified and Exalted, is, and by means of it you are able to worship Him. Through this knowledge you understand what Allaah has permitted and what He has prohibited, what He is pleased with and what He is displeased with. And through this knowledge you understand the destiny of this life and its inevitable conclusion. That being that a group of the people will end in Paradise, achieving happiness, and the rest of the people, who are indeed the majority, will end in Hellfire, the abode of disgrace and misery."*[5]

---

[2]   Risaa'il feel-Aqeedah: page 22

[3]   This hadeeth {*The one whom Allaah intends...*} is found in Saheeh al-Bukhaaree: 71, 3116, 7312/ Saheeh Muslim: 1037/ Sunan Ibn Maajah: 221/ al-Muwatta Maalik: 1300, 1667/ Musnad Imaam Ahmad: 16395, 16404, and other narrations/ Musannaf Ibn Abee Shaaybah: 31792/ & Sunan al-Daramee: 224, 226/- on the authority of Mu'aweeyah. And it is found in Jaame' al-Tirmidhee: 2645/ Musnad Imaam Ahmad: 2786/ & Sunan ad-Daaramee: 270, 2706/- on the authority of Ibn Abbaas. And  it is found in Sunan Ibn Maajah: 220/ & Musannaf 'Abdul-Razzaaq: 30851/- on the authority of Abee Hurairah. It was declared authentic by Sheikh al-Albanee in Saheeh al-Aadab al-Mufrad: 517, Silsilat al-Hadeeth as-Saheehah: 1194, 1195, 1196, Saheeh at-Targheeb at-Tarheeb: 67, as well as in other of his books. Sheikh Muqbil declared it authentic in al-Jaame' al-Saheeh: 9, 3123, 4650, may Allaah have mercy upon them both

[4]   Majmu'a al-Fatawaa: vol. 28/80

[5]   From a lecture given by the eminent scholar at the Islamic University in Medinah on 3/26/1404

Therefore, it becomes clear that this desired goal which leads to true success, as has been mentioned, is only possible through the seeking of beneficial knowledge, meaning Sharee'ah knowledge, from its carriers- the scholars. Similarly, what is meant by the term 'scholars' are those people of knowledge from the saved and victorious group of Muslims who have always remained upon the guidance of the Messenger, may Allaah's praise and His salutations be upon him and his Companions, inwardly and outwardly, in every generation and age. They are the people of true guidance, the well-grounded scholars of Ahlus-Sunnah wa al-Jama'ah from the early generations, the later generations, and our present day scholars.

We must recognize them and affirm their position, defend their honor, and strive to assist and cooperate with them because they carry and preserve the inheritance of the Messenger of Allaah, may Allaah's praise and salutations be upon him. Sheikh al-Islaam Ibn Taymeeyah mentioned in his book, '*Lifting the Blame*', Page 10:

> "*It is obligatory upon the Muslims after loyalty to Allaah the Exalted and His Messenger, to have loyalty to the believers, as is mentioned in the Qur'aan. This is especially true in regard to the scholars, as they are the inheritors of the prophets and are those who have been placed in a position by Allaah like the stars by which we are guided through the darkness of land and sea.*
>
> *The Muslims are in consensus regarding their guidance and knowledge. Since in every nation before the sending of our Prophet Muhammad, may Allaah's praise and His salutations be upon him, their scholars were indeed the worst of their people, until the time of the Muslim Ummah; as certainly the scholars of the Muslims are the best of them. They are the successors of the Messenger, may Allaah's praise and His salutations be upon him, in his nation, and they give life to that which has died from his Sunnah…*"

It is necessary that every Muslim understand the importance of the role of the scholars and their position in our lives, being connected to them, and listening to their advice and guidance. Thereafter, it is upon us to maintain as strong connection and relationship to them as possible. Additionally, it is necessary for us to be aware of the deception, delusions, and falsehoods of those who strive to separate or distance the Muslims from our scholars, specifically coming from those people of division and group partisanship who falsely accuse the scholars of not understanding the current situation of the world, among their other false claims. They are the ones who fail to give the scholars their proper position among the people nor acknowledge their rights upon the people. The guiding scholar Saaleh al-Fauzaan, may Allaah preserve him, stated in his book, '*The Obligation of Confirming Affairs and Honoring the Scholars and an Explanation of their Position in this Ummah*' (Page 45):

> "*Specifically, we hear this in our time and age from those who speak attacking their honor and who falsely accuse the scholars of ignorance, short-sightedness and a lack of understanding of current affairs, as they claim; and this is a very dangerous matter. Because if we are deprived of the reliable ones from the Muslim scholars, who will lead the Muslim Ummah? Who will be turned to for rulings and judgments?*

*And I believe this to be a devised plan from our enemies. This is a plan which has deceived many who do not properly understand matters and those who do possess an intense love and strong enthusiasm for Islaam, but which is only based upon ignorance. So they have intense love and strong enthusiasm for Islaam, but the matter is not that simple. Since the most highly honored position in this Ummah is that of the scholars. It is not permitted to disparage them or accuse them of ignorance and short-sightedness, or with seeking the pleasure of the rulers or to describe them as the 'scholars of the rulers' or other such descriptions. This is extremely dangerous, oh worshiper of Allaah! So let us fear Allaah in regard to this matter and take caution. Clearly, it is as the poet said,*

> *Oh scholars of the religion, oh 'salt' of the land,*
>
> > *What will rectify our affair, if the 'salt' itself is corrupt?' "*

Therefore this connection and relationship between the Muslim and the scholar is a necessity for every Muslim and especially for the beginning student of knowledge. The esteemed major scholar Sheikh Muqbil Ibn Haadee al-Waadiee, may Allaah have mercy on him, stated in '*Tuhfat al-Mujeeb 'alaa Asilaat al-Hadhar wa Ghareeb*' (Page 181-182):

*"...So the cure is in returning to the Book of Allaah and the Sunnah of the Messenger of Allaah, may Allaah's praise and His salutations be upon him and his household, and then by returning to the scholars. As Allaah says,* ❖ **And when there came to them a matter concerning (public) security or fear, they announced it to the people. But if only they had referred it back to the Messenger or to those charged with authority amongst them, those who have the ability to derive a proper conclusion from it would have understood it.** ❖ *–(Surah an-Nisaa:83) Therefore it is an obligation upon us to turn to the scholars in our affairs:* ❖ **These are the parables that We send forth to the people, yet no one (truly) understands them except those with knowledge.**' ❖ *–(Surah al-'Ankaboot: 43)*

*But what you see is some of the people merely memorizing three or four subjects and then taking that to the masjids, thrusting themselves forward and confronting others. Then his companions designate him 'Sheikh al-Islaam'! Is this to be considered knowledge?!?*

*Rather, the matter of knowledge is sitting upon a mat with your legs beneath you, being patient with the necessary hunger and poverty that comes with seeking knowledge. Consider the state of the Companions of the Messenger of Allaah, may Allaah's praise and His salutations be upon him and his household, and what they were patient in the face of.*

*In addition, the people of knowledge- they are the ones who put matters in their proper places, as established in the previous noble verse where Allaah, the One free from imperfection and Exalted says,* ❖ **Verily, in that is a reminder to those who possess knowledge.** ❖ *–(Surah ar-Room: 22)'"*

In summarizing what has been mentioned of the importance of this relationship between the worshippers of Allaah and the guiding scholars, the major scholar Sheikh al-Fauzaan, may Allaah preserve him, said in his book, '*Explanation of the Mistakes of Some Authors*' (Page 18):

*"Oh Muslim youth! Oh students of knowledge! Connect yourselves to your scholars, attach yourselves to them, and take knowledge from them. Attach yourselves to the reliable scholars well known for the correctness of their beliefs and the soundness of their methodology, in order that you may take knowledge from them and establish your connection with your Prophet, may Allaah's praise and His salutations be upon him, as your pious predecessors did. The Muslims have never ceased receiving this knowledge from their Prophet, through their scholars, generation after every generation."*

And if one were to ask: "Who are the reliable well-known scholars?' meaning by this those well grounded in knowledge? Imaam Ibn-Qayyim, may Allaah have mercy upon him, stated:

*"The one who is well grounded in knowledge; if he is confronted with uncertain matters as numerous as the waves of the ocean, his certainty and steadfastness is not affected nor diminished, nor is he afflicted by doubt. As he is steadfast and well grounded in his knowledge, he is not disturbed by such uncertainties and doubts. Rather, what occurs with one such as this is in fact the repulsion of doubts due to his being safeguarded by his knowledge and the disturbances are thus bound and subdued...."* [6]

Certainly, Allaah facilitated for me the compilation of some of the statements of advice from the scholars regarding seeking knowledge and beneficial books, as well as their warnings against books containing misguidance. Initially, this was simply to remove ignorance from myself and the members of my family, and then afterwards also for my brothers and sisters who are also seeking knowledge. This is in order that we all are able to strive to proceed with correct methods and manners in our seeking of beneficial knowledge. This was accomplished only with the assistance of Allaah, the Most Generous.

I ask Allaah the Majestic to make this effort purely for His sake, and to accept it from me. I hope that this will be a beneficial book in this subject and area, for the one who seeks adherence to the religion of truth through the learning of beneficial knowledge -wherever they may be in the world. As was mentioned by Sheikh al-Islaam Ibn Taymeeyah, may Allaah the Exalted have mercy upon him, understanding the nature and source of beneficial knowledge is essential to obtaining it:

*"...As for which books can be utilized and relied upon in the various areas of knowledge, then this is an extensive matter. Additionally, this differs according to the differences among the young people within a certain land. Since what has been made easy for them in some lands, from knowledge, its path, and its study; has not been made possible for others in different lands. But, gather whatever goodness is possible by turning to Allaah, the Most Perfect, for assistance in acquiring the transmitted knowledge from the Prophet, may Allaah's praise and salutations be upon him. As this is what is truly entitled to be called knowledge.*

*As for other matters besides that, either it is knowledge but it is not truly beneficial, or that which is not actually knowledge but only mistakenly considered to be. Indeed if it actually was beneficial knowledge, then undoubtedly it must be from that which springs from the inherited guidance of Muhammad, may Allaah's praise and salutations be upon him. As there is nothing that can serve in its place as an alternative or substitute, from that which is considered similar to it or seen by some to be better than it.*

---

[6]　Miftah Dar as-Sa'dah: vol. 1 page 442

*Therefore, if his purpose and intent is to understand the goals and objectives of the Messenger of Allaah within everything that he commanded and that which he forbade, as well as in the rest of the Messenger's statements; and if his heart becomes satisfied with this understanding and the explanation of the rulings, this is the aim and objective of the Messenger's guidance.*

*...It is not possible to set straight or rectify the relationship between him and Allaah, the Most High as well as the relationship between him and the people, until he is capable of possessing this understanding. So struggle in every area of the various areas of knowledge to adhere to the foundation and fundamental knowledge which is transmitted directly from the Prophet, may Allaah's praise and salutations be upon him"* [7]

**This collection has seven general sections and three appendixes:**

| | |
|---|---|
| The first section: | *Guidance for Every Male and Female Muslim* |
| The second section: | *Golden Advice That Benefits the Beginner Regarding Acquiring Knowledge* |
| The third section: | *Beneficial Guidance for Female Students of Sharee'ah Knowledge* |
| The fourth section: | *Guidance from the Scholars Regarding Important Books to Acquire for Seeking Knowledge* |
| The fifth section: | *The Warning of the Scholars from the Books of those who have Deviated from the Sunnah & Warnings Regarding Ways of Going Astray* |
| The sixth section: | *Clear Statements from the Advice of the Scholars Regarding Memorizing Knowledge* |
| The seventh section: | *Issues Related to the Verifiers of Books in our Age* |

| | |
|---|---|
| *First appendix:* | Categorized List of Books Recommended within the Scholars' Statements Gathered in this Work |
| *Second appendix:* | Index of Questions and Issues Organized by Scholar's Name |
| *Third appendix:* | Telephone Numbers for some of our Scholars |

---

[7]   Majmu'a al-Fatawaa: Vol. 19, page 119

## Guide to the Symbols for Different Types of Texts or Citations Used with the Book

❴ ❵- (...) indicates a verse of the Qur'aan and the source surah of that verse.

{...}-(…) indicates a narration of the Messenger of Allaah, may Allaah's praise and salutations be upon him, or a narration from one of the first generations or one of the scholars.

The second set of brackets -(...) is where I have in a basic format referenced and indicated some but not all, of its sources as well as its similar supporting narrations, as many times these were not present in the original printed or audio sources. All stated rulings of authenticity are from Imaam al-Albaanee or Imaam Muqbil, may Allaah have mercy upon both of them, according to my limited ability. Similarly I have sometimes mentioned other relevant statements about the referred to narrations from these two distinguished scholars which I found in their books. Lastly, long source citations according to narrator have been separated from the text as numbered footnotes to facilitate reading. It should also be noted that the numbering systems of editions vary widely, and in newer printed or electronic editions the enumeration may differ.

[...] indicates an incorrect statement found among some of the common people or from the callers to falsehood whether from a book or tape.

((... )*-*) indicates the summarized or complete name or description as found in the text being quoted as a book accepted and recommended by the scholars. In some instances I have translated the title if the work is available in English or for another benefit for the English reader. Immediately following this is a number indicating the book's category and individual number within the list of books I have compiled at the end of the work. That list has further book information such as the title, author, and which scholars within this work have recommended it. I generally only translated the book titles when it was necessary for understanding the scholars statement or in some cases that the book was available in English under that title.

The reader should take note that the citations in the list are restricted to the explicit recommendations of the scholars found within these compiled texts. Without doubt, there are other book recommendations from these same scholars in other sources, as well as valuable recommendations from other scholars which should also be accepted and benefited from where ever found.

[[...]] indicates the name, whether in summarized or complete form, or description of a book which has been criticized and spoken about with a warning from the people of knowledge to turn away from its use and to not rely upon it for Sharee'ah knowledge.

## Important Note:

The third time I presented this compilation to him in order that he might further review it, I requested of Sheikh Muhammad al-Imaam, may Allaah preserve him, to add any necessary comments that he considered appropriate. He replied, may Allaah preserve him, that the words of these scholars are not in need of any comments from him. It is upon the reader to note that I have attempted to carefully select, type in, and organize the words of the scholars from a number of different sources to facilitate the subjects presented to the beginning student of knowledge like myself. This compilation is not intended only for the new Muslim, convert, or revert, but for anyone who wishes to truly better understand how Islaam has been studied and practiced throughout the centuries, as both a belief and a way of life sent as a blessing, and mercy from the Creator to His creation.

Yet as was mentioned by Ibn 'Abbaas, may Allaah be pleased with him, *"Verily about a single matter I used to question thirty of the Prophet's Companions, may Allaah's praise and salutations be upon him."* [8]. And without doubt, the aim of clarifying the correct path of seeking knowledge is more worthy of endeavoring and striving to take from many sources and of greater importance in the life of the worshipers of Allaah than obtaining correct knowledge regarding a single secondary issue. Therefore one must be aware that there are many other clarifications and statements of advice from the scholars of our time and other ages in different beneficial forms that I did not have the ability to include in this compilation.

But know, oh noble reader, may Allaah direct you towards goodness, that although the writings, statements, and authored works of the people of the Sunnah are vast in number, and varied in their many areas of knowledge, they all still carry the same belief and methodology. This was mentioned by Sheikh as-Sama'anee in his letter to the major scholar Sheikh Sadeeq Hasan Khaan al-Qanoonee al-Bukhaaree, may Allaah have mercy upon them both:

*"As-Sama'anee stated: 'And from those things which indicate that the 'people of hadeeth' are upon the truth is that certainly if you were to bring all of their authored works - the first of them to the last, the oldest of them and the newest, along with the differences in their lands and ages, the distances between where they reside, and that every one of them resided in a different country, is that in regard to their belief and methodology they are upon a single path and way, and upon a single methodology. You find that they are upon a single path that none of them deviate from and none turn away from.*

*Their hearts in this are like a single heart, and their transmission of knowledge is unified such that you do not see true differing or true separation in any matter which they have stated. Rather, if you gather everything which has come from their tongues and what they have transmitted from the first generations, you would find that it is as if it has originated from single heart, and come from a single tongue. Is there in truth, anything which is more evident than this?"* [9]

So I advise the reader to refer back to every source of the statements of the affirmed scholars that you have access to in order to further elucidate, confirm, and clarify any unclear matter or question discussed in this work.

---

[8]   Seyaar 'Alaam an-Nubalaa': 3/334
[9]   A Guide for the Student Towards the Superior Pursuit' Imaam Sadeeq Hasan Khaan al-Qanoonee al-Bukhaaree: page 58

Accordingly, whatever it contains that is correct is from the grace of Allaah, the Most High and the Most Exalted, and anything it contains that is in error or is deficient is from myself or from Shaytaan, the accursed. I ask Allaah to remove my mistakes, and I ask that anyone who wishes to indicate a mistake which is present in this book specifically to write an explanation of the mistake along with the evidence and send it to the following internet address: *kitaabaqwaal@taalib.com*- so that it may be verified and corrected in the next update of the work.

## Note regarding Translation (English edition only)

The esteemed Sheikh Saaleh al-Fauzaan, may Allaah preserve him, states in his book: '*Illuminations from the Fiqh Rulings of Sheikh al-Islaam Ibn Taymeeyah Related to Correct Belief* (Vol. 1, Page 407):

*"Guidelines Regarding Translation: "The sheikh states concerning translation- the meaning of which is the conveying or communicating the meaning of expressions or statements from one language to another language; He (Ibn Taymeeyah) said, "Translation and explanation have three levels:*

*One of them is the translation of just basic expressions, such as conveying the meaning of one single expression by using another expression having a similar meaning. With this level it is necessary to comprehend that which is specifically understood through this second expression with those it is directed towards. This is accomplished by giving consideration to the specific meaning conveyed by this expression among those people. Therefore, this is beneficial knowledge when many of the people hold a specific meaning for a specific term; as such he should not exclusively abandon use of these terms completely.*

*The second is the translation or explanation of the meaning of a statement by illustrating its meaning to the one you are speaking to. This illustration of its meaning to him and enabling him to understand the statement requires a higher ability than just the translation of single expressions. This case is similar to when a book in the Arabic language might be explained to an Arab, and although he hears the Arabic terms and expressions within it he does not comprehend their full meaning, nor understand them completely without further explanation. The comprehension of their meaning comes through conveying the particular meaning or characteristics of a specific term or expression to him. When a term carries a composite meaning- composed of individual words used together- then the one being addressed should come to understand the combined concept or illustration that is referred to in its comprehensive meaning either by specification or an approximate meaning.*

*The third level is the explanation of the level of correctness of that first meaning or initial concept and verifying it by mentioning evidences and making analogies which will substantiate and confirm that meaning."'*

Sheikh al-Islaam Hafidh Ibn Hajr, may Allaah have mercy upon him, states in his book 'Nuzhat al-Nathr':

*"As for narrating hadeeth by their meanings, without strict adherence to transmitting the specific wording, then the differing regarding this is clearly acknowledged. The majority hold that it is permissible. Additionally, from the strongest proofs of this is the consensus of the Ummah regarding the permissibility of explaining the laws of the Sharee'ah to non-Arabs in their languages by one who is knowledgeable of their languages.'*

Commenting on this passage in his recorded notes upon this work of Ibn Hajr, our father, Sheikh 'Abdul-'Azeez Ibn Baaz, may Allaah have mercy upon him, stated:

*"This is through translation; translating the meanings of the verses of the Qur'aan and hadeeth of the Messenger of Allaah to non-Arabic speakers in their own languages, by bringing forth the meaning of the verses and the meaning of those hadeeth of the Messenger to those non-Arabic speakers. As what is intended for them is its meaning and acting according to it."*

In this text I have translated the original Arabic expression which is transliterated as, *'salla Allaahu aleihi wa sallam'* in reference to the Messenger of Allaah Muhammad Ibn 'Abdullah, according to the explanation found with the scholars of Ahlus-Sunnah wa al-Jama'ah. Its' meaning is explained in the compilation *'Salafee Selections from the Explanation of Aqeedah al-Waasiteeyah'.* Sheikh al-'Utheimeen, may Allaah the Most High have mercy upon him, stated on pages 114-115,

*"As for the meaning of "salla Allaahu aleihi" the most accurate of what has been stated regarding this is what has been related from Abu Aleeyah, may Allaah have mercy upon him: 'It is Allaah's praise and commendation of him among the highest gatherings and assemblies in the heavens.'*

*…And as for the meaning of "sallam" for him, within it is a statement of his being preserved from errors and shortcomings, and in the statement of "salat" upon him is an affirmation of his realization of the good characteristics and traits… So the single sentence with: "salat' and "sallam' contains an expression that informs but whose meaning is in fact one of asking or requesting by the speaker, as what is intended is supplication to Allaah.'*

Sheikh al-Fauzaan, may Allaah preserve, commented on page 116 of that same work:

*"And the statement "salla Allaahu aleihi" linguistically carried the meaning of supplication; and the most authentic of what has been stated regarding the meaning of the "salat" from Allaah upon His Messenger is what Imaam al-Bukhaaree mentions in his Saheeh collection from Abu 'Aleeyah that he said: 'It is Allaah's praise and commendation of him among the highest gatherings and assemblies in the heavens.'… and the "sallam" means: salutations of honor or mention of his soundness and freedom from faults and failings'*

Therefore within this book its most common transliterated form, *"salla Allaahu aleihi wa sallam"* has been translated as: may Allaah's praise and salutations be upon him, and *"salla Allaahu aleihi wa alaa ahlehe wa sallam"* has been translated as: "may Allaah's praise and salutations be upon him and his household'.

## Words of Thanks and Appreciation

I thank Allaah, Glorified and Exalted, for every blessing He has given me. I ask for good mention and prayers and blessings be upon the Prophet of mercy and the Messenger of guidance Muhammad and his family. I wish to thank our esteemed Sheikh Abu Nasr Muhammad Ibn 'Abdullah al-Imaam, may Allaah preserve him, as I occupied his valuable time on more than one occasion, seeking his assistance in the affairs of my deen. This blessing was like what was mentioned by Imaam al-Laalikaaee:

*"Ayyub said, 'Certainly from the success of the youth and the non-Arab is that of Allaah guides him to association with a scholar from Ahlus-Sunnah."* [10]

I also thank him for appointing our brother Abu Sufyaan az-Zaylaee' (Dar al-Hadeeth Ma'bar) to supervise the completion of (the original Arabic compilation) this work after his review and introduction. I thank my beloved wife Umm Mujaahid for her assistance to me and constant support which, if Allaah wills, shows the truth of the statement of Allaah's Messenger, may Allaah's praise and His salutations be upon him: *{The whole world is a provision, and the best object of benefit of the world is the pious woman.}*- (Saheeh Muslim: 1467). As Allaah willed that it would not have been possible to complete this continuing effort, by the permission of Allaah, the Most High, the Exalted, without her encouragement, patience, and many other contributions.

I also must thank my beloved brothers in Islaam, Abu Sufyaan az-Zaylaee' and several others for their assisting me in so many matters. Certainly the one who is not thankful to the people is not thankful to Allaah. There is no doubt that their brotherhood is a blessing from Allaah as was narrated by Imaam al-Lalikaaee:

*"Ibn Shuwdhab said: 'Certainly from the blessing of Allaah upon a striving youth is that he gives him a brother as a companion who adheres to the Sunnah who assists him upon that.' "* [11].

Lastly, I thank those brothers from among the students of knowledge in Dar al-Hadeeth in Damaaj, who helped with corrections, proof reading, reviewing, clarifications, and various advices which assisted me in the improvement of this book.

I ask Allaah, Glorified and Exalted, to place me and every Muslim and Muslimah upon the path of beneficial knowledge and righteous actions, and to enable us to walk in the truly successful path as our pious predecessors did so that our knowledge a proof for us and not against us. May Allaah's praise and His salutations be upon our Prophet Muhammad and upon his family and Companions, and all those who follow his guidance until the Day of Judgment. And all praise is due to Allaah, Lord of the Worlds.

*Written by Abu Sukhailah Khalil Ibn-Abelahyi al-Amreekee*
*Yemen- Dar al-Hadeeth Damaaj*
*The fifteenth day of the month Of Rabee'a ath-Thaanee*
*In the year One thousand four hundred and twenty seven*
*Of the Hijrah of the Chosen Messenger*
*Allaah's praise and salutations be upon him.*

*[Corresponding to the May 13th of 2006 C.E.]*

---

[10]  Sharh Usul al-'Itiqaad Ahlus-Sunnah wa' al-Jama'ah: number 30
[11]  Sharh Usul al-'Itiqaad Ahlus-Sunnah wa' al-Jama'ah: number 31

# UIDANCE FOR EVERY MALE & FEMALE MUSLIM

*Isma'eel Ibn Bashr Ibn Mansoor and Ishaaq Ibn Ibraheem al-Sawaaq both narrated that 'Abdur-Rahman Ibn Madhi narrated to us on the authority of Mu'aweeyah Ibn Saaleh on the authority of Dhamarat Ibn Habeeb and the authority of 'Abdur-Rahman Ibn 'Amr as-Salamee that he heard al-'Irbaadh Ibn Saareeyah who said:*

*{Allaah's Messenger gave us an admonition which caused our eyes to shed tears and the hearts to fear, so we said, "Oh Messenger of Allaah (may Allaah's praise and salutations be upon him) this is as if it were a farewell sermon, so with what do you counsel us?" So he, may Allaah's praise and His salutations be upon him, said:*

*"I have left you upon clear guidance, its night is like its day; no one deviates from it except one who is destroyed.*

*And whoever lives for some time from amongst you will see great differing; so stick to what you know from my Sunnah and the Sunnah of the rightly guided caliphs.*

*Cling to that with your molar teeth, and stick to obedience even if it is to an Abyssinian slave since the believer is like the submissive camel; wherever he is led, he follows."}*

(Narrated through various narrations in *Sunan Abu Dawud*: 4607/ *Jaame' al-Tirmidhee*: 2676/ *Sunan Ibn Maajah*: 42, 43, 45/ & *Musnad of Imaam Ahmad*: 16692, 16693, 16695/ -on the authority of al-'Irbaadh Ibn Saareeyah. It was declared authentic by Sheikh al-Albaanee in *Silsilat al-Hadeeth as-Saheehah*: 937, (his verification of) *Mishkaat al-Masaabeh*: 165, *Saheeh at-Targheeb at-Tarheeb*: 37, *Dhelaal al-Jannah*: 33, 45, *as-Saheeh al-Jaame'a' as-Sagheer*: 2539, 4369, as well as in others of his books. Sheikh Muqbil declared it authentic in *al-Jaame'a' al-Saheeh*: 3249, and he did not state any difference with the ruling of authenticity given by Haafidh al-Haakim in his own verification of *al-Mustadrak alaa Saheehayn-*'*Pursuing the Errors of al-Haakim which adh-Dhahaabee Did Not Mention*' regarding hadeeth numbers 329, 331, 332.)

**(1) The Eminent Guiding Scholar 'Abdul-'Azeez Ibn 'Abdullah Ibn Baaz, may Allaah have mercy upon him, from 'Collection of Rulings and Various Statements': Vol. 6, Page 232**

*Writings of Sheikh Ibn Baaz to Others: To the Youth who are Part of Today's Revival of Islaam*

I direct my letter to all of the youth whom Allaah has granted success in holding firmly to this religion, understanding it, and inviting to it in all of His lands. I advise them to fear Allaah and to confirm matters and proceed carefully in their affairs avoiding hastiness. Similarly, I advise them to devote themselves to the Noble Qur'aan, its recitation, its contemplation, its memorization, and its review and study.

Likewise I advise them to adhere to the Sunnah of the Messenger of Allaah, may Allaah's praise and His salutations be upon him, memorizing its texts, giving attention to it and studying it well. In the same manner, to study the books of sound authentic beliefs, the beliefs of the people who cling to the Sunnah and the body of the Muslims who are united upon the truth. For example, *((Kitaab at-Tawheed)06-01) ((Thalaathatul Usul)06-02)*, and *((Kashf ash-Shubahaat)06-04)* of Sheikh Muhammad Ibn 'Abdul-Wahaab may Allaah have mercy upon him. Also the books *((at-Tadrumeeyah)06-07)*, *((al-Hamaweeyah)06-06)*, *((al-Aqeedatul-Wasateeyah )06-05)* of Sheikh al-Islaam Ibn Taymeeyah, may Allaah have mercy upon him. And such as *((al-Qaseedat an-Nooneeyah)06-15)*, *((as-Sawa'iq al-Mursalah)12-04)*, *((Ighathatul al-Lahfaan min Makaa'id as-Shaytaan)12-05)*, *((Zaad al-Ma'ad Fee Haadee Khair al-Ebaad)09-05)*, *((Ijtimaa' al-Jawaish al-Islaameeyah)06-16)* from the major scholar Ibn al-Qayyim, may Allaah have mercy upon him. And the book, *((Lama't al-Itiqaad)06-13)* from Muwafiq Ibn Qudaamah may Allaah have mercy upon him, and *((al-Muqadamah)12-06)* of Abee Zayd al-Qeeruwaanee al-Maalikee, may Allaah Have mercy upon him. As well as similar works from books of correct belief written by the scholars well known for their knowledge, merit, and true beliefs. Additionally, for example the book *((Kitaab at-Tawheed)06-36)* of Ibn Khuzaymah, may Allaah have mercy upon him, and *((Kitaab as-Sunnah)06-22)* from 'Abdullah Ibn Ahmad Ibn Hanbal, as well as other books similar to them.

I advise them with concern for the call to Allaah, enjoining the good and forbidding wrong with wisdom, excellent behavior, and good speech. They should proceed not with harshness and severity, but rather with gentleness and insight, as Allaah, Glorified and Exalted says, ❡*Invite (mankind, Oh Muhammad) to the Way of your Lord (i.e. Islaam) with wisdom (i.e. with the Divine Inspiration and the Qur'aan) and fair preaching, and argue with them in a way that is better.*❡-(Surah an-Nahl:125). And He, Glorified be He, said, ❡*And by the Mercy of Allaah, you dealt with them gently. And had you been severe and harsh-hearted, they would have broken away from about you.* ❡-(Surah Aal-'Imraan:159)

I advise them to avoid hastiness in every matter. Rather, they should ascertain matters carefully, consult others, and cooperate upon goodness until they understand the religion properly, as the Messenger, may Allaah's praise and His salutations be upon him, said, *{The one whom Allaah intends good for He gives him understanding in the religion}* [1].

Indeed hastiness leads to tremendous harm. Thus, it is an obligation to verify matters and give attention to the Sharee'ah evidences, and to always frequent the sittings of knowledge of those people of knowledge well known for their uprightness and sound beliefs.

### To the Scholars and Students of Knowledge

I advise the scholars and the students of knowledge collectively to fear Allaah, and be concerned with the verification of issues of knowledge through Sharee'ah evidences, not through simply blindly following this person or that person. And I advise all of you to devote yourselves to the Book of Allaah and the Sunnah of the Messenger, may Allaah's praise and salutations be upon him, and to refer back to the clarifying words of the scholars, until you comprehend the truth by its evidences, not merely by unconditionally accepting the speech of this individual or blindly following that person.

Likewise, I advise the students of knowledge to continue to strive to understand this religion, to derive knowledge from the Sharee'ah evidences, as well as to cooperate upon goodness and the fear of Allaah and advise others to hold to the truth and be patient upon that. I advise them to spread knowledge among the people in the masjids as well as outside of the masjids in other locations, in their sermons, lessons, sittings of knowledge, in the schools and universities- in any place they may be. I ask Allaah to grant all of us success, and to rectify both our intentions and our actions.

---

[1]   Narrated in Saheeh al-Bukhaaree: 71, 3116, 7312/ Saheeh Muslim: 1037/ Sunan Ibn Maajah: 221/ al-Muwatta Maalik: 1300, 1667/ & Musnad Imaam Ahmad: 16395: 16404, and other than these two/ Musannaf Ibn Abee Shaybah: 31792/ & Sunan ad-Daaramee: 224, 226/ - on the authority of Mu'aweeyah. And it is found in Jaame' al-Tirmidhee: 2645/ Musnad Imaam Ahmad: 2786/ & Sunan ad-Daaramee: 270, 2706/-on the authority of Ibn 'Abbaas. And it is found in Sunan Ibn Maajah:220/ & Musannaf 'Abdul-Razzaaq: 30851/-on the authority of Abu Hurairah. It was declared authentic by Sheikh al-Albaanee in Saheeh al-Aadab al-Mufrad: 517, Silsilat al-Hadeeth as-Saheehah: 1194, 1195, 1196, Saheeh at-Targheeb at-Tarheeb: 67, as well as in other of his books. Sheikh Muqbil declared it authentic in al-Jaame' al-Saheeh: 9, 3123, 4650, may Allaah have mercy upon them both.

**(2) The Eminent Guiding Scholar Muhammad Ibn Saaleh al-'Utheimeen, may Allaah have mercy upon him, from 'Islamic Revival- Guidelines and Guidance': Page 221**

*Question: The revival of Islaam that we are witnessing: is it simply a reaction to the present societal corruption and far from Allaah's true way, as some have portrayed it? Or is it based and well-founded upon that which will produce true results, if Allaah wills?*

Answer: That which is apparent to me is that this revival has two causes. The first cause is the sincere desire to return to the religion of Islaam; and this is what is found among the majority of those who are known as Islamic thinkers. Certainly the intelligent person, when he views the state in which the majority of people find themselves today- and this state is not only present among the Islamic or Arab nations but is a general condition among the nations of the world- he sees the deterioration of life, general confusion, unrest and unease, and people's weariness. It becomes clear that there is no solution to this except to adhere to the Sharee'ah of Allaah, Glorified and Exalted, as it is that which Allaah, the Exalted, revealed as a guiding light for the creation, to guide them in their lives in both principles and practice. Regarding this, Allaah the Exalted says, ❋ *Oh mankind! Verily, there has come to you a convincing proof from your Lord, and We sent down to you a manifest light -this Qur'aan*❋-(Surah an-Nisaa':174).

A person will perfectly understand this fact if he establishes a firm connection with Allaah, Glorified and Exalted. This results in a contentment of the heart, and the presence of tranquility and light within it, that will not be found in the one who is averse and turns away from guidance, as Allaah the Exalted says, ❋ *Whoever works righteousness, whether male or female, while he is a true believer verily, to him We will give a good life (in this world with respect, contentment and lawful provision)*❋-(Surah an-Nahl:97) So these intelligent and discerning individuals see that that which is commonly found amongst the people, or the majority of the people, from deterioration of morals, weakness in holding to agreements and contracts, and the general misuse of the intellect- are all matters driving the people towards ruin. Then they realize and see that is necessary for humanity to have a clear reference and guide by which it can be directed in life. So they are returning to Islaam, and this is something which it is hoped will bring about good, because these individuals have returned to Islaam based upon conviction, study and insight.

The second cause is blind following, as some of the people inevitably blindly follow others. Like a young man who sees his brother, his cousin, his neighbors or friends directing him towards a correct way or practice from Islaam, and he follows that. Then this blind following of another takes root within his heart and he becomes content and satisfied with it; and so it remains and becomes settled. Then Shaytaan may deviate him away from this, such that the conviction he had about the correctness of this approach wanes and so he veers towards some other way or course. These are what I believe to be the causes behind this revival.

However, after acknowledging this, we must strengthen the efforts to consolidate and firmly establish this revival, as well as strive to guide it from the direction of its knowledge and understanding as well as in respect to its actual endeavors and efforts. This is because although some of the people have benefited and increased in knowledge tremendously from this revival, from the viewpoint of the extent of proper methodology, education and cultivation upon the truth, correct ways and procedures, it certainly has deficiencies and shortcomings.

Indeed sometimes one is hasty in his efforts, due to the love of good that is within his heart and the desire to make the people firm upon the religion of Allaah. He then proceeds in an extremely impatient manner and does not correctly assess the conditions of the people; nor does he understand how their conditions will truly be rectified, as the sensible way is that which is encompassed within the Sharee'ah. We see that when Allaah, Glorified and Exalted, sent Muhammad, may Allaah's praise and His salutations be upon him, to the creation, He did not reveal the complete Sharee'ah in a single week, a single month or even a single year. Rather, the Messenger, may Allaah's praise and His salutations be upon him, remained in Mecca thirteen years, and from the pillars of Islaam there was only made obligatory upon them the two testimonies of faith and the ritual prayer. Whether zakaat was obligatory at that time is differed upon by the scholars. After these two pillars, fasting was then prescribed in the manner in which they had the choice to fast or eat if they wished to eat. Then at a later time, the limits and regulations of fasting were specified, and lastly those of Hajj were established. Hajj was not made an obligation until after the conquest of Mecca, as after the surrender it was no longer difficult for the people to be able to travel to Mecca.

In any case, the one who recognizes the wisdom of Allaah, Glorified and Exalted in the gradual revelation of the Sharee'ah understands that the people will not be able to understand and implement it in the period of half a day, nor immediately change from what they are upon of incorrect matters to those which are acceptable and suitable. If a person understands this, then it is possible that, through what Allaah has guided him to of knowledge, he may then guide the people toward goodness with wisdom and a good reminder, and with patience and deliberateness. As for the one who desires or intends that the people become steadfast upon the religion in a single day, then he has challenged and called into question the wisdom of Allaah, Glorified and Exalted, and contradicted the Sharee'ah. It is obligatory upon the people to weigh and assess matters correctly and not imagine that every person is like himself, so that it actually becomes possible to rectify that which has been corrupted among the various life affairs of the worshipers of Allaah.

**(3) The Eminent Guiding Scholar Saaleh Ibn Fauzaan, may Allaah preserve him, from 'A Selection of Islamic Rulings': Vol.1, Page 408**

*Question: "Islamic revival" is a term which is common in these days, such that we find it generally used to refer to the increase of religious practice and the people returning back to judging by the Book of Allaah and Sunnah of His Messenger, may Allaah's praise and salutations be upon him. What do you say concerning this and with what do you advise the youth?*

Answer:  The phrase "revival" which is circulating upon the tongues of the people in these days, is a phrase which needs careful consideration, especially in this land of Saudi Arabia which has never left, and will not leave- by the permission of Allaah- a strong adherence to Islaam. It was never heedless of it, nor "sleeping', such that later it awoke and was revived. So this expression is correct in relation to some of the societies, but it is not correct when used in reference to Saudi society, which rules by the Book of Allaah and the Sunnah of His Messenger, may Allaah's praise and salutations be upon him, and which enjoins the good and forbids wrongdoing. It is an upright nation that is attentive, alert, and dutiful in regard to Islaam. And all praise is due to Allaah.

As to that which we advise the youth; it is to learn beneficial knowledge from the hands of the scholars and to avoid hastiness in relation to rulings in the religion. Also, we advise them to avoid accepting concepts and statements without thoroughly examining them and scrutinizing them carefully, including what they embody and contain within them. Indeed, it is upon them to verify, and then to ask the scholars, and not to act hastily. They should also keep away from acting emotionally, with blind enthusiasm which will lead them to fall into a state of error. Likewise, I advise them to be far from association or affiliation with anything which distances them from the methodology of the Book and the Sunnah and the way of the people of the Sunnah and the Jama'ah. As Allaah, the Most High says, ❴*...and hold fast to the rope of Allaah altogether and do not divide.*❵-(Surah Aal-'Imraan:104) and He says, ❴*And obey Allaah and His Messenger, and do not dispute (with one another) lest you lose courage and your strength depart, and be patient. Surely, Allaah is with those who are as-Saabirin (the patient ones, etc.).*❵-(Surah al-Anfaal:46). Indeed, joining and gathering upon the truth is a mercy, and separation from the truth is an affliction.

**(4) The Eminent Guiding Scholar 'Abdul-'Azeez Ibn 'Abdullah Ibn Baaz, may Allaah have mercy upon him, in 'Collection of Rulings and Various Statements': Vol.8, Pages 232-233**

*Question: There is spreading throughout the Muslim world a blessed Islamic revival which all Muslims welcome and are pleased with. However, we see that this revival does not place sufficient concern and emphasis on the correct understanding of Sharee'ah matters, nor upon the fundamentals of the correct beliefs of Islaam. What is your advice, esteemed scholar, in relation to this revival?*

Answer: My advice to all of the Muslims- the Muslim youth as well as to the elders, the men and the women- my advice to all of them is to give attention to the Book of Allaah, the Noble Qur'aan. Focus upon its recitation, its contemplation, thinking about it and acting according to it, and asking about any matter they do not understand. Also that they refer to and read the reliable books in the field of explanations of the meaning of the Qur'aan, such as the books of *((Ibn Jareer)01-04)*, *((Ibn Katheer)01-01)*, *((al-Baghawee)01-07)*, and other reliable books from the works which explain the Qur'aan. This is in order that they will be able to understand the meanings of the Word of Allaah and be steadfast upon that which the Book of Allaah guides to from the matters of worshipping Allaah alone without partners; have sincerity towards Him alone, establishing all its requirements or affairs, and leaving that which negates it. Along with this, one should give attention to the books authored regarding the beliefs held by the first three generations of righteous Muslims such as *((Kitaab at-Tawheed)06-01)*, *((Thalatatul-Usul)06-02)*, and *((Kashf as-Shubahaat)06-13)* by the Sheikh Muhammad Ibn 'Abdul-Wahhab, may Allaah have mercy upon him. Also *((al-Aqeedat al-Wasatiyyah)06-05)* of the Sheikh Ibn Taymeeyah, *((Lama't al-Itiqaad)06-13)* of Imaam al-Muwafiq Ibn Qudaamah and *((Sharh at-Tahaweeyah)06-09)* of Ibn Abee al-Izz, and written works similar to them which are well known to proceed upon the methodology of the people of the Sunnah.

Additionally, the summarized books of hadeeth narrations such as *((Arba'een an-Nawawee)02-27)* and *((the supplement)03-09)* which completes it by Ibn Rajab, *((Amdatul-Hadeeth)02-29)* by Sheikh 'Abdul-Ghanee al-Maqdasee, and *((Bulugh al-Maraam)02-34)* by Ibn Hajr. Haafidh Ibn Hajr also has a beneficial work related to hadeeth science terminology, *((Nukhbat al-Fikr)04-01)*, as well as *((his own explanation)04-02)* of this book. Similarly in the principles of jurisprudence, or deriving the understanding of the texts, refer to the book, *((Rawdhat an-Naadher)08-08)* of Muwaafiq Ibn Qudaamah.

So what is intended by all of this is giving attention to the fundamentals in the subject of correct belief, to the fundamentals of the science of deriving the correct understanding from the source texts, and the fundamentals of the hadeeth sciences and terminology. These would benefit them, and it is these fundamentals that the various areas of knowledge are built upon.

Likewise in the area of compiled works of fiqh rulings, *(('Amdat al-Fiqh)07-03)* of Muwafiq Ibn Qudammah, *((Zaad al-Mustaqna')07-01)* of Hajaawee, and *((Daleel at-Taalib)07-23)*. These books benefit and are useful to the student of knowledge, in as far as they will help him comprehend various issues, their related evidences, as well as the sources or references which are relied upon. All of these are matters of importance for the student of knowledge.

(5) THE EMINENT GUIDING SCHOLAR MUQBIL IBN HAADEE AL-WAADI'EE, MAY ALLAAH HAVE MERCY UPON HIM, IN 'THE STRUGGLE': PAGES 100- 106

### *My Advice to the Youth of the Revival of Islaam*

What is considered the present Islamic revival in this age should in reality be considered a sign from the signs or proofs of the truth of the Messenger's prophethood, as its presence is despite the fact that the conditions of our age have weakened the efforts of those who truly call to Allaah. And from those affairs which in the recent past have harmed and greatly diminished the efforts towards implementing Islaam are:

1- Wars and internal conflicts among the Muslims within their lands.

2- The neglect of the rulers of the Muslims to give priority and true importance to Islaam.

3- The occupation of many of the scholars and the Muslims with worldly gains; and their preoccupation with this rather than true concern for knowledge and teaching.

4- Dangerous ideological trends originating from the enemies of Islaam which are directed towards us, and which turn people away from the religion and belittle those who hold steadfastly to it, asserting that they are people who wish to return to the past and are backwards. Allaah alone frustrated their aspirations and made their deceptions and plans ineffective and fruitless, as the hearts of the Muslims are accepting Islaam and turning more towards Islaam and acknowledging the guidance of our Prophet Muhammad, may Allaah's praise and His salutations be upon him and upon his family.

In view of this one may recall that which is narrated by Imaam al-Bukhaaree where he mentioned that Abdullah Ibn Abee al-Aswad narrated to us, that Yahya informed us from Isma'eel, that Qais narrated to us that he heard al-Mugheerah Ibn Shu'ba say: I heard the Messenger of Allaah, may Allaah's praise and salutations be upon us, say, *{A group of my Ummah will remain victorious until Allaah's Order (the Hour) comes upon them while they are still predominant victorious.}* [2]. And Imaam al-Bukhaaree, may Allaah have mercy upon him, also mentioned that al-Humaidee narrated to us, that al-Waleed narrated to us, saying: Ibn Jaabir narrated to me saying, Umair Ibn Haanee narrated to me that he heard Mu'aweeyah say: I heard the Prophet, upon him and his household be Allaah's praises and the best of salutations, saying,

[2]    Narrated in Saheeh al-Bukhaaree: 3640, 7311, 7459/ Saheeh Muslim: 1921/ & Musnad Ahmad: 17779, 17701/ -from the hadeeth of Mugheerah. Declared authentic by Sheikh al-Albaanee in Silsilaul-Hadeeth Saheehah: 1955, and by Sheikh Muqbil in al-Jaame' as-Saheeh: 4, 528, 2385, 3358.

*{A group of my Ummah will keep on following Allaah's Laws strictly and they will not be harmed by those who will abandon them nor by those who stand against them until Allaah's Order (The Hour) will come while they will be in that state...}* [3]. *Umair said: Maalik Ibn Yukhamer said: Muadh said: And they are in Shaam. And Mu'aweeyah said: Maalik asserts that he heard Muadh say: They are in Shaam (the land directly north of the Arabian peninsula).*

This hadeeth is also narrated by Imaam Muslim and narrated from a group of the Companions, may Allaah be pleased with them. From them is Imraan Ibn Hussein, whose narration is found in the collection 'Sunan Abu Dawud', with a chain of narration that conforms with the conditions of Imaam Muslim, as well as the narrations of Thawbaan, Jaabir Ibn Samara, Jaabir Ibn 'Abdullah, and Abdullah Ibn 'Amr Ibn 'Aas found in 'Saheeh Muslim'. Also the hadeeth of Qirat Ibn Eyaas in 'Sunan at-Tirmidhee' regarding which Imaam Tirmidhee says, *"This hadeeth is hasan saheeh"*. And from them is the narration of Salama Ibn Nufeel as-Sakuunee found in the Musnad of Imaam Ahmad and the book 'at-Tareekh' of Imaam al-Bukhaaree. I have mentioned these in their entirety with their chains of narration in my book *((as-Saheeh al-Musnad min ad-Dalaa'il an-Nabuwwah)06-44)* and all praise is due to Allaah.

As for my advice to the youth of the Islamic revival than I have mentioned that within my book, *((al-Makhraaj min al-Fitnah)11-21)*, and I will summarize it here and supplement it as is necessary.

1- To have fear of Allaah. Allaah, the Most Perfect and the Most High says: *◆Oh you who believe! If you obey and fear Allaah, He will grant you a criterion to judge between right and wrong, or a way for you to get out from every difficulty, and will expiate for you your sins...◆*-(Surah al-Anfaal:29).

2- To consider every Muslim upon the earth your brother, and to direct your enmity towards the one who truly merits it- the enemies of Allaah from the Jews, the Christians, the Communists, the Ba'athists - anyone who strives to obstruct from the path of calling to Islaam. Be wary of becoming someone constrained and shackled to the leaders of one of the various groups or affiliating yourself with one group restrictedly, as Allaah, the Most High and the Most Exalted, says, *◆The believers are nothing else than brothers ...◆*-(Surah al-Hujaraat: 10) and He says, *◆And hold fast, all of you together, to the Rope of Allaah (i.e. this Qur'ân), and be not divided among yourselves...◆*-(Surah *Aal-'Imraan*:103). and He says: *◆And do not dispute (with one another) lest you lose courage and your strength depart...◆*-(Surah al-Anfaal:46). And Allaah mentions the state that may arise in which conflict and differing occur, saying, *◆And in whatsoever you differ, the decision thereof is with Allaah...◆*-(Surah al-Shura: 10) and He said, *◆(And) if you differ in anything amongst yourselves, refer it to Allaah and His Messenger, if you believe in Allaah and in the Last Day...◆*-(Surah an-Nisa:59)

3- To seriously strive towards uniting the Muslims under one leader who will

---

[3]   Narrated in Saheeh al-Bukhaaree: 3641, 7460/ Saheeh Muslim: 1037/ & Musnad Ahmad: 16485 -from the hadeeth of Mu'aweeyah, and in Saheeh Muslim: 1920/ & Musnad Ahmad: 21897 -from the hadeeth of Thawbaan Ibn Bejjaded. And in Jaame' al-Tirmidhee: 2192/ Sunan Ibn Maajah:6/ & Musnad Imaam Ahmad: 19849 -from the hadeeth of Qurra Ibn Eyaas. It was Declared authentic by Sheikh al-Albaanee in Silsilaul-Hadeeth Saheehah: 1957, and by Sheikh Muqbil in al-Jaame' as-Saheeh: 2384.

have the characteristic of being from the Quraish. As the Prophet, may Allaah's praise and His salutations be upon him and his household, said, {*Our leaders are from the Quraish*} [4]. al-Haafidh Ibn Hajr in his commentary, 'Fath al-Baaree', stated, "*This has been narrated from the Prophet, may Allaah's praise and His salutations be upon him and his household, from approximately forty Companions.*" In addition, he should be from the people of the Sunnah, as the sect of the Raafidhah are from those with the greatest enmity towards Islaam, and the Shee'ah are the most ignorant of the people of Islaam. It is not suitable to have someone from an ignorant or foolish group lead and guide the Muslim Ummah. What good could possibly be found with those who say, [Being occupied by the communists is preferable to us than being dominated by the Wahaabees.]?? And they label as "Wahaabees" anyone who calls to the book of Allaah and the Sunnah of the Messenger of Allaah, may Allaah's praise and His salutations be upon him and his household. All praise is due to Allaah, now these Raafidhah here are like the dead to us; unknown and extinguished in Yemen as people claiming Islaam. The call to the Sunnah through the works ((*A Garden of Paradise in Refutation of the Enemies of the Sunnah*)11-18), ((*The Guidance Regarding the Fading of the Tribulation from the Extremist Worshipers from the Rawaafidh in Yemen*)11-17), and ((*The Disbelief of Khomaynee in the Land of the Two Holy Sanctuaries*)11-19) exposed them. And all praise is due to Allaah, all of these books have been printed. These finished off their insignificant existence, and I watched over and oversaw this destruction. And the thanks for this is to Allaah alone.

4- To open the door for jihaad in the path of Allaah; as Allaah, the Most Perfect and the Most High says, ◆*And fight them until there is no more fitnah (disbelief and worshipping of others along with Allaah) and (all and every kind of) worship is for Allaah (Alone).*◆-(Surah al-Baqarah:193) and in the hadeeth of Ibn Umar on the Prophet, may Allaah's praise and His salutations be upon him and his household, {*If you engage in 'Enaah' and hold onto the tails of cows, becoming pleased with agriculture, and so abandoning jihaad, then Allaah will place a disgrace upon you that will not be raised until you return to your religion*} [5]. Jihaad in the path of Allaah is struggling against the disbelievers until the word of Allaah becomes supreme above all others. However, the majority of the fighting today is between the Muslim rulers simply for the sake of positions of worldly power, even though it is not permissible for the Muslim to fight his brother for the aim of seizing the position of leadership held by so-and-so; indeed your most valuable resource is your own life! How excellent is the one who said,

---

[4]    Narrated in Musnad Ahmad: 11898/ -from the hadeeth of 'Anas Ibn Maalik. It was Declared authentic by Sheikh al-Albaanee in Irwa' al-Ghaleel :520, Saheeh at-Targheeb wa at-Tarheeb:2188, and in his comments upon hadeeth number 784 in Silsilatul-Hadeeth Saheehah he states: " '*Our leaders are from the Quraish...*' *this is a continuously narrated hadeeth of the highest level of authenticity, as was mentioned by al-Haafidh Ibn Hajr.*".

[5]    Narrated in Sunan Abu Dawud: 3462/ & Musnad Ahmad:  4810, 4987 -from the hadeeth of 'Abdullah Ibn 'Umar. It was Declared authentic by Sheikh al-Albaanee in Silsilatul-Hadeeth Saheehah :11, in Saheeh at-Targheeb wa-al-Tarheeb: 1389, as well as in other of his works.

*I will never kill a man who prays*

    *for the sake of another ruler of the Quraish*

*Upon the ruler is the accountability for his authority and upon me is my own sin.*

    *We seek refuge in Allaah from ignorance and recklessness*

*Do you wish me to kill a Muslim who has committed no crime?*

    *Surely, never in my lifetime will that bring me any benefit*

5- That you restrict yourself to only acting upon evidence from the Book of Allaah or from the authentic Sunnah of the Messenger of Allaah, may Allaah's praise and His salutations be upon him and his household, as found in the statement of Allaah, Glorified and Exalted, **Follow what has been sent down unto you from your Lord, and follow not any Auliyaa' besides Him (Allaah). Little do you remember!**-(Surah al-'Araaf: 3) and the statement of the Most High **Whatsoever the Messenger (Muhammad) gives you, take it, and whatsoever he forbids you, abstain (from it)...**-(Surah al-Hasr: 7)

6- That you abandon revolting against the rulers and authorities except in the case of witnessing from them open and indisputable disbelief regarding which you have a clear proof from Allaah, as is mentioned in the hadeeth of 'Ubaidah which is found in both the collections of Imaam Bukharee and Imaam Muslim. This is in view of the consequences that generally result from revolting against them such as triggering and instigating severe trials and the killing of innocent people. Allaah, the Most Perfect and the Most High, says, **And whoever kills a believer intentionally, his recompense is Hell to abide therein, and the Wrath and the Curse of Allaah are upon him, and a great punishment is prepared for him.**-(Surah an-Nisaa:93). And the hadeeth of Abee Bakara, may Allaah be pleased with him, also found in the two well known 'Saheeh' collections wherein he says, *{I heard Allaah's Prophet saying, 'If two Muslims meet each other with their swords then (both) the killer and the killed one are in the HellFire.}* [6].

7- To avoid having an inclination or partiality towards those who are unjust, due to the statement of the Most High, **And incline not toward those who do wrong, lest the Fire should touch you...**-( Surah Hud:113) as well as the statement of the Most High, **And had We not made you stand firm, you would nearly have inclined to them a little. In that case, We would have made you taste a double portion (of punishment) in this life and a double portion (of punishment) after death. And then you would have found none to help you against Us.**-(Surah al-Isra'a:74-75). And Imaam Ahmad narrates in his collection of hadeeth, his 'Musnad', on the authority of Jaabir, may Allaah be pleased with him, that the Messenger of Allaah, may Allaah's praise and His salutations be upon him and his household, said, *{Oh Ka'b Ibn 'Ujrah! Seek refuge in Allaah from the disgraceful rulers.' He said, "Who are the disgraceful rulers, oh Messenger of Allaah?" He said, "Those rulers who will come after me but will not*

---

[6] Narrated in Saheeh al-Bukharee: 31, 6975/ Saheeh Muslim: 2888/ Sunan Abu Dawud: 4268/ Sunan an-Nasaa'ee: 4125, 4126, 4127, 4128, 4129/ & Musnad Ahmad: 19926, 19959, 19980/ -from the hadeeth of Abu Bakrah. And in Sunan an-Nasaa'ee: 4123, 4124/ Sunan Ibn Maajah: 3964/ & Musnad Ahmad: 19093/-from the hadeeth of Abu Moosa al-'Ashar'ee. It was Declared authentic by Sheikh al-Albaanee in Saheeh Sunan Abu Dawud and in Saheeh Sunan an-Nasaa'ee.

*adhere to my Sunnah and not be guided by my guidance. As for those who affirm their lies and deceptions and assist them upon the injustice they commit, then these people are not from me and I am not from them, and they will not approach the cistern on the Day of Judgment. Those who do not affirm their lies and do not assist them upon the injustices they commit, then these people are from me and I am from them, and they will come to the cistern on the Day of Judgment.}* [7]. And I have mentioned this Hadeeth with its chain of narration in the second edition of the book *((as-Saheeh al-Musnad min ad-Dalaa'il an-Nabuwwah)06-44),* and its complete discussion can be found there.

8- To emigrate from that land in which it is not possible for the Muslim to establish his religion, or one in which he fears he will be placed in a prison of the unjust rulers -who are truly "terrorists"- and may be possibly be tortured beyond what he could bear.

9- To make supplications that Allaah shake the feet of the unjust rulers and that He place the best of those from amongst the Muslims in authority over them.

10- To stay away from the causes of separation and differing. From the greatest causes of separation is the arrogance of some of the groups over others and their spreading of wicked statements among people. Allaah the Most Perfect and the Most High says, *And say to My slaves that they should (only) say those words that are the best. (Because) Shaytaan verily, sows disagreements among them. Surely, Shaytaan is to humanity a plain enemy.* -(Surah al-Isra':53). And He said, *The good deed and the evil deed cannot be equal. Repel (the evil) with one which is better (i.e. Allaah ordered the faithful believers to be patient at the time of anger, and to excuse those who treat them badly), then verily! he, between whom and you there was enmity, (will become) as though he was a close friend.* -(Surah Fusilat:34). Also from the causes of division is arguing and disputing based upon falsehood, as is seen in that which Imaam at-Tirmidhee narrated in his well known hadeeth collection on the authority of Abee Umaamah, may Allaah be pleased with him, where he said, The Messenger of Allaah said, *{A people have not gone astray after being guided except that they entered into the practice of disputing.' Then he recited the verse, They quoted not the above example except for argument. Nay! But they are a quarrelsome people.'}-(Surah Zukhruf: 58).}* [8]. Imaam at-Tirmidhee stated that this hadeeth was authentic.

11- To free yourself from the following of desires. Allaah, the Most Perfect and the Most High says, *But if they answer you not, then know that they only follow their own desires. And who is more astray than one who follows his own desires, without guidance from Allaah? Verily! Allaah guides not the people who are wrong-doers.* -(Surah al-Qasas: 50).

---

[7]  Narrated in Musnad Ahmad: 14860/ -from the hadeeth of Jaabir Ibn 'Abdullah, which was Declared authentic by Sheikh al-Albaanee in Saheeh at-Targheeb wa al-Tarheeb: 2242; & Musnad Ahmad: 17660 -from the hadeeth of Ka'ab Ibn Ujrah, and Sheikh Muqbil stated was acceptable level of authenticity in Saheeh al-Musnad min Dala'il an-Nabuwwah page 562. Likewise Sheikh al-Albaanee stated in Dhelaal al-Jannah: 759 regarding the hadeeth of Hudhaifah– *'It's chain of narration is good'*.

[8]  Narrated in Jaame' at-Tirmidhee: 3253/ Sunan Ibn Maajah: 48/ & Musnad Ahmad: 21660, 21701/ -from the hadeeth of Abu Imaamah Sadee Ibn 'Ajlaan, which was declared it of a acceptable level of authenticity by Sheikh al-Albaanee in Saheeh at-Targheeb wa al-Tarheeb: 141, and he stated that it was authentic in his checking of Mishkaat al-Masaabeeh: 180, and Sheikh Muqbil declared it authentic in al-Jaame' as-Saheeh: 116, 3783, 4288, 4523.

12- To seek beneficial knowledge, and to travel to the scholars of the Sunnah, and to understand the source texts as the first generations understood them. Proceed upon this endeavor by benefiting from two tremendous books, the first of which is the book, ((Jaame'a Bayaan al-'Ilm wa Fadhlihee)12-01) of Hafidh Ibn Abdul-Bar, and the second book is ((ar-Rihlah)12-08) by al-Hafidh al-Khateeb. Then your understanding will be built upon what you have read from the understanding of the first generations of Muslims. This is in order that you stand in a position of safety from slipping, as the people involved in ways of innovation usually slip into error, or from the weakening and compromising in your affairs, as many of the modern callers have weakened and compromised theirs. I ask Allaah for guidance for them and us, ameen.

13- To separate yourself from falsehood and its people, with the exception of interacting with them for the purpose of calling them to Allaah. Indeed the believer who mixes with the people and is patient with what he suffers from them is better than the one who does not mix with them and so is not patient with what he will suffer from them, as is affirmed on the Prophet, may Allaah's praise and His salutations be upon him and his household.

14- That you love for the sake of Allaah and hate for the sake of Allaah. Allaah, the Most Perfect and the Most High says, *Oh you who believe! Whoever from among you turns back from his religion (Islaam), Allaah will bring a people whom He will love and they will love Him; humble towards the believers, stern towards the disbelievers...*- (Surah al-Maidah:54). And the evidences related to loving for the sake of Allaah and hating for the sake of Allaah are numerous. Our brother Muhammad Ibn Saeed Ibn Salim al-Qahtanee has encompassed most of them in his worthy book, ((al-Walaa' wa al-Baraa' Fee al-Islaam Min Mafaahem Aqeedatul as-Salaf)12-38). I advise the reading of this book and benefiting from it.

15- I warn them against those who are actually scholars of evil, so that such individuals are not able to disguise and conceal from you the true nature of their behavior and conduct, as Allaah, the Most Perfect and the Most High said, *Oh you who believe! Verily, there are many of the (Jewish) rabbis and the (Christian) monks who devour the wealth of mankind in falsehood, and hinder (them) from the Way of Allaah*-(Surah at-Tawbah:34).

16- Be warned against the regulating and the influencing of the endeavors to call to Allaah by the rulers and those scholars who receive salaries; as the rulers actually seek to diffuse and dissolve the various calls related to Islaam, fearing for their own power and authority. Yet those acquainted with those who truly call to Allaah know that they are not interested in taking positions of authority but only give importance to rectifying the people of the Muslim Ummah as well as their leaders.

17- I advise them to revisit and reconsider the issues or conflicts that stand between each other and review their statements and writings regarding each other, and to consider carefully their behavior in regard to the problems that they face among themselves. The enemies of Islaam may seek to promote a specific individual from the ranks of the people of the Sunnah or the one who is affiliated with them, if they do not heal and reconcile the wounds or problems that exists between them.

18- To warn against the people of falsehood according to the limits of your ability and expose their falsehoods, whether this is within the various forms of media or through writing about it. And we consider both of these acts from us a defensive effort and from those which defend Islaam.

So these are quickly offered brief points of advice to the youth of the Islamic revival. I had previously written it in the fourth issue of the magazine [[al-Bayaan]], and it was entitled, ((*My Advice to the People of the Sunnah*)12-13). Additionally, I had written it and supplemented it in an article entitled, ((*This Is Our Call and Our Belief*)12-17). And all praise is due to Allaah both of these are printed. I also sent it to the magazine 'al-Istiqaamah' as ((*My Advice to the People of Hadeeth*)12-39). I hope that you will read these three advices, as each of them complements the others. I also have written in the last section of ((*The Sharp Sword against the Apostasy of the Disbelieving Communists*)11-02), my recommendations to the Muslim rulers. And the books ((*The Exit from the Tribulation*)11-21) and ((*The Sharp Sword...*)11-02) both encompass my various advices for the students of knowledge. And Allaah is the one who grants success. We trust in Allaah that these efforts put forward for His sake, He will not allow them to be squandered nor wasted.

(6) The Eminent Guiding Scholar Muqbil Ibn Haadee al-Waadi'ee, may Allaah have mercy upon him, from 'Bridling the Resistant One': Page 385

*Question: What is the correct and sound position to be adopted by the scholar, the student of knowledge, and the caller to Allaah in relation to the modern day groups, parties, and Islamic organizations?*

Answer: The position of the scholar, the caller to Allaah, and the student of knowledge- indeed the position of every Muslim- is that it is obligatory upon him to remind these groups to remember Allaah, the Most Perfect and the Most High, and to warn them about the consequences of separation and differing. They must also warn them about the deviations which have occurred among the youth due to these various groups and parties. Indeed from the present complaints is that there is such and such group, which is established and calls to itself. Then there is this other party which is established and calls to itself, and another which is established, and also calls to itself. So this leaves a young person confused, not knowing whom he should follow- and more than one of our brothers has complained to us of this. Therefore, it is necessary for the students of knowledge and the callers to Allaah to make clear their freedom and disassociation from these various parties and groups.

All praise is due to Allaah, we have an audio cassette which is entitled '*My Advice to the Scholars & Disassociation from Partisanship*'. In addition, from the blessings of Allaah related to this audio lecture is that it was heard by some of the righteous scholars of Najd in Saudi Arabia; and they declared themselves free from group division and partisanship and turned themselves away from it. And perhaps what may have occurred is that they had forgotten or had become accustomed to the prevailing conditions, as otherwise its evidences certainly would have the effect of causing them to act upon them previously.

It has now become apparent that the people of partisanship and separation are ashamed that one of them might openly say, [I am a person upon partisanship to this group.] And at times some of them actually swear and go to the length of saying, [By Allaah! I am not a person of group partisanship!] But he is one who travels from Sana'a to Ma'rib for the purpose of calling to his group, and then from Sana'a to Aden calling to his group, and from Sana'a to Hadhramaut- still calling to his group. And I do not know the extent of how much deception and trickery has occurred here in Yemen through this statement, [By Allaah! I am not a person of group partisanship!] Or perhaps he does not understand the true meaning of partisanship. In actuality, the people are only divided into two groups: into the party of ar-Rahman, The Merciful, and into the party of Shaytaan.

And all praise is due to Allaah that the significant and respected scholars have come to truly understand the seriousness of the partisanship. So that it is said: 'Those scholars who ceased following the correct methodology which we invite you towards- even their students have left them, such that you will see that he is now alone with no one left to teach!'

This is a clear trend among them. In any case, all praise is due to Allaah, many of the youth now perceive and understand the danger of partisanship.

As for the issue of disassociation from it and those upon it, then this is a required matter, as they are considered people upon innovation in the religion. The Messenger of Allaah, may Allaah's praise and His salutations be upon him and his household, said, *{…every innovation is a going astray.}* [9].

And he said, *{Allaah is separated from the repentance of every person of innovation in the religion until he abandons his innovation.}* [10].

So the nature or level of the deviation of innovating in the religion is that it stands on the verge of reaching the level of disbelief in the religion itself. Therefore, if one has allegiance solely for the sake of a group or party or has enmity and disassociation solely for the sake of a group or party, then we fear that he may eventually fall into greater disbelief. As Allaah says, *Verily, your Wali (Protector or Helper) is Allaah, His Messenger, and the believers; those who perform as-Salaat, and give zakaat, and they bow down.*-(Surah Maidah: 55)

Indeed after all this that has preceded and been made clear, I do not truly know where the intellects of many of the today's youth are! The people of partisanship and separation have been repeatedly exposed and uncovered time and time again, but we still see that some of the youth follow after and remain with them. And this can only be for some worldly benefit, not truly for the sake of the religion. And from Allaah alone we seek assistance from this unfortunate state.

[9]  Narrated in Saheeh Muslim: 876/ Sunan an-Nasaa'ee: 1579/ Sunan Ibn Maajah: 45/ Musnad Ahmad: 13924/ & Sunan ad-Daaramee: 206- from the hadeeth of Jaabir Ibn 'Abdullah. And it is in Sunan Abu Daawud: 4607/ Sunan Ibn Maajah: 42/ Musnad Ahmad: 16694, 16695/ & Sunan ad-Daaramee: 90/-from the hadeeth of al-'Irbaadh Ibn Saareeyah. Declared authentic by Sheikh al-Albaanee in Silsilatul-Hadeeth Saheehah: 2735, and in Saheeh at-Targheeb at-Tarheeb: 37.

[10]  Narrated in Sunan Ibn Maajah: 50/- from the hadeeth of 'Abdullah Ibn 'Abbaas, by Sheikh al-Albaanee judged it to be an unacceptable narration in Silsilatul-Hadeeth adh-Dha'eefah: 1492, but authenticated a different but similar narration from 'Anas Ibn Maalik "*Indeed Allaah is shielded or separated from the repentance of every individual upon innovation in the religion until he abandons his innovation*" in Saheeh at-Targheeb at-Tarheeb: 37.

**(7) The Eminent Guiding Scholar Ahmad Ibn Yahya an-Najmee, may Allaah preserve him, from 'The Distinct Guidance in Explaining the Book, 'Explanation of the Sunnah' by al-Imaam al-Barberhaaree': Pages 35-36**

*Examine, may Allaah have mercy upon you, everything you hear from the people of your age.*

His statement: "*Examine, may Allaah have mercy upon you, everything you hear from the people of your age, particularly. Do not be hasty and do not enter into a matter until you ask and investigate: have any of the Companions of the Prophet, may Allaah's praise and His salutations be upon him, spoken about this matter, or have any of the scholars....*'" Up until the end of what he stated in this section.

So I say: May Allaah have mercy upon the author, as he has guided the people to benefit with this statement, and commanded that one act cautiously and with deliberation when entering into newly developed or arisen affairs in the religion. If you hear someone inviting and calling to the methodology of the group known as the "Muslim Brotherhood", then do not be hasty in accepting it, and do not simply accept his praise of this methodology. If you hear someone calling to the methodologies of the followers of Muhammad Suroor, or the followers of Sayyed Qutb, or the group known as 'Jama'at at-Tableegh', then do not be hasty in accepting their methodologies and entering yourself into adopting these ways until you ask, investigate, and research.

You should consider carefully and research either with someone who has an understanding of that methodology but who has not actually embraced it, or from one who previously accepted that way and then turned away it, or with one who has read sufficiently about them so that they can clarify to you the reality of that group. For if you act hastily, you will find yourself in a difficult situation and within the web of group affiliation and partisanship which only wants to take possession of you by entering you into their ranks or organization. After this, you would then stand as one who innovates in the religion and as one who defends those who innovate in the religion. So I say: from Allaah we come and to Him shall we return! How many have been sacrificed to these methodologies by hastily entering into them, how many have been victimized within their dangerous trap before they understood their errors and deficiencies!!

Certainly this is what occurs to individuals in these organizations and groups. Due to this I clearly warn you, just as the author of this text, meaning the author of the book *((Sharh as-Sunnah)06-58)*, has warned you. I warn you against hastily entering these groups and parties, and I call you to act carefully, cautiously, and to investigate beforehand. Take and read from the books authored in criticism of these groups and parties. Take from such works, meaning these investigative works, and read about these groups and parties before you enter into any of them. And if you find the truth in these works, then do not give preference to anything above it. Indeed, your call and way as a Muslim is not correct- and before this, your Islaam is not correct - until it is truly supported and born witness to by the message of testifying that Allaah alone is to be worshipped.

Moreover, you are not personally responsible for this person or that group; rather fear Allaah regarding yourself first, and be wary of falling victim to the harmful effects of these groups and parties. Indeed, you will regret what comes from joining them, sooner or later. It is not enough for you to work to heal and rectify your state and condition after the damage and harm has already occurred and you have already been severely harmed or ruined though them. No by Allaah! As Allaah the Exalted has said,

❧*By al-'Asr (the time). Verily! Man is in loss, Except those who believe and do righteous good deeds, and recommend one another to the truth, and recommend one another to patience.*❧-(Surah al-'Asr: 1-3). And the success is from Allaah.

(8) The Eminent Guiding Scholar Saaleh Ibn Fauzaan, may Allaah preserve him, from 'An Explanation of the Mistakes of Some of the Writers': page 222 )

### *Proceed with caution, oh you who call to the 'renewal' of the religion!*

We continually hear in recent times, from here and there, calls for renewal in the religion from those who do not possess the knowledge and understanding of the true sphere, principles, or the acceptable scope of renewal in Islaam- they specify matters or areas for renewal in the religion which are not suitable. Renewal or revival in the religion is indeed something desired from the qualified people of knowledge. They return to the religion its prominence and nobleness by removing from it the distortions or false attributions that have been placed upon it by the ignorant, those who desire to alter the religion, or by the false concepts of the disbelievers. Indeed the Prophet, may Allaah's praise and salutations be upon him and his household, gave glad tidings that Allaah would bring forth at the beginning of every century- someone from the Muslim nation who would revive this religion.

But as for the 'renewal' in the religion which means bringing forth innovations and new matters within the religion which are not originally part of it- then this type of 'renewal' is refused and rejected from the one who claims it -as is stated in the narration of the Messenger. It should be said first of all, that the renewal which is desired cannot be carried out except by those practicing, active scholars, those who strive diligently and who possess patience. In view of this, from which of the two classes of people do you think today's callers to 'renewal' are from, since they are clearly not from those scholars who specialize in the area of Sharee'ah knowledge? They are in fact individuals whose specializations are in the fields of knowledge such as chemistry, physics, medicine, or engineering.

As for the renewal that they are calling for, then it is a so-called 'renewal' of the religion by inventing a new modern understanding and interpretation of laws and guidelines -as they have stated- because the old understanding and interpretation- as they claim- is not suitable for this age in its present form and implementation. They call for this 'old understanding' to be substituted with what they term the 'modern understanding of present day affairs'.

We have heard some of them state in their lectures, openly calling within them, to a 'renewal' in the fundamental understanding of the religion and in its general thought and principles by saying, [The religion is the revealed laws the Sharee'ah as well as its practical implementation. So the Sharee'ah from is the Book of Allaah and the Sunnah and these two cannot accept being renewed; as for the practical implementation of the religion, then it capable of being renewed.] How free is Allaah from all imperfections! From where does the understanding and implementation of the religion come from? Is it not derived and taken from the Book of Allaah and the Sunnah?! Indeed, it is the actual and full explanation and correct understanding of the Book and the Sunnah!

And is it possible that specific derived understandings or derived rulings differ from the sources of the Book of Allaah and the Sunnah? Yes, there exists historical cases where derived rulings from scholars differ with the two sources, and it is obligatory to not accept or act upon this class of rulings. However, in their general nature such rulings still agree with the way of the Book of Allaah and the Sunnah in an important way- in that they came about by being derived from the efforts of the people of the transmission of knowledge and understanding from the scholars of the Muslim Ummah. So who is the one who will then replace such scholars and bring forth these new rulings and understandings? Is it to be the graduate of the College of Engineering, or Pharmacology, or the graduate of the College of Education, or a physics or chemistry professor? Certainly not.

If one of the scholars of the sciences of the Sharee'ah was to speak regarding their (these so-called scholars) fields of medicine, physics, or any other field- meaning in an area that was not his own specialization and training related to the affairs of this world and its events, and these others rebuked him for that, they would be right in doing so. Therefore, how can they then allow themselves to enter into a realm which is not from their own area of speciality and training?!?

Moreover, if the specific issues that these individuals raise in relation to the call for renewal are those which they see as part of the present inferior position of the Muslims- and this situation has undoubtedly occurred- then they must believe that the reason for this condition is adherence to the 'old' understanding and implementation of the religion. This belief of theirs is actually claiming that Allaah is ignorant of the correct diagnosis of the illness as well as of the knowledge of its cure!

But in reality, the cause of the inferior position of the Muslims is due to their failure to adhere to the correct understanding, implement it, and practice it, as well as its substitution by many Muslims with human conceived systems and human designed laws. Thus, the reason for their position is that they have abandoned it, not that they are holding onto to it! As is said,

*We blame the times we are in but in reality the fault lies with us,*

*The only deformity in our time is our own selves.*

We do not deny the presence of modern situations that require study and deliberation; however the remedy for this is not that we produce a new understanding or reject the old system of practically understanding and implementing the religion. The remedy is that we submit it to the previously established correct system of understanding the religion, its principles, its flexibility, and its completeness. It is capable, with Allaah's permission, of bringing these difficult cases to a successful state of resolution if it is undertaken by the people specifically qualified for this from the scholars of the Sharee'ah.

I do not say this to diminish those who are not from those scholars specializing in the Sharee'ah, but only as a mercy for them to preserve them from entering into a domain that is far outside of their training and specialization. Yes, it is their right to say, "*What has occurred among some of the Muslims requires a remedy, so it is requested from the scholars to investigate these present problems.*" But it is not their position to seek to bring forth a new system of principles and derived rulings and abandon the previous system of principles and rulings. Because the practical meaning of this would necessitate the separation of the present generation of the Muslim Ummah from the past generations of the Muslim Ummah and the turning away from its legacy and tremendous storehouse of knowledge; as well as the opening of this important area to trespassers in the area of established knowledge and understanding ho would then begin to make reckless changes and substitutions.

Through this statement I do not wish other than the offering of sincere advice. ❈*I only desire reform so far as I am able, to the best of my power. And my guidance cannot come except from Allaah, in Him I trust and unto Him I repent.*❈-(Surah Hud:88)

I also understand that the majority of those involved in developing this perspective- this unguided call for renewal- only desire good for the Muslims and a lifting of our bitter circumstances. However, it is not to be found in the means or method which they have stated; rather it lies in connecting these matters to the people truly capable of resolving them. As the Exalted said:

❈*When there comes to them some matter touching public safety or fear, they make it known among the people, if only they had referred it to the Messenger or to those charged with authority among them, the proper investigators would have understood it from them directly .*❈-(Surah an-Nisa:83)

The guiding scholar Sheikh Ibn Saa'dee stated in his explanation of the Qur'aan: "*And in this there is evidence for a social and ethical principle that when you encounter a dilemma from your affairs it in necessary that it be directed towards the people who are specifically related to that domain and field- to place it with those people related to that area and not to take matters into their own hands. This is closer to what is proper, and more suitable for the rectification of the problem.*"

Additionally, I say: The opening of this field of putting forth rulings in the religion to other than those who specialize in this branch of knowledge is the source of facilitating the sporting and playing with the religion of Allaah by anyone who simply has the ability to read or study, such as those who have now filled the world with mistaken rulings and assessments that they call 'new understanding of the religion'.

This affirms what the Prophet, may Allaah praise and salutations be upon him, informed us of; that if we are deprived of scholars then the general people will take as leaders the ignorant who issue rulings without sound knowledge- so they are astray and they also send others astray. This also informs us that in that later ages there will be many speakers but few scholars of understanding. Those who read books today are numerous; however those with sound understanding from among them are few. What is given consideration in possession of true understanding and comprehension of the religion is not simply extensive reading and self study.

It has reached the level among some of them that they actually boast that they are not graduates of the Islamic University! That they have not studied with a scholar, but each educated himself by himself and is the student only of his books. When such individuals hear about this call to 'renewal' and that this domain is now open for them, strange statements begin to pour forth from each and every one of them! What has come of this situation is as has been said:

*She become so lean, such that from this leanness, her state of protection was lost,*

*Thus she was humiliated by every worthless one who approached.*

As these individuals do not see anything standing between one of them and his becoming a 'scholar' except that he has a library and that he reads one or two books and then can proceed forth in giving rulings, teaching, and authoring works. But proceed with caution, oh you who call to the 'renewal' of the religion! Act with care towards your Ummah. May Allaah have mercy upon the one who understanding his own abilities and their limits. I end here with assalamu aleikum.


(9) THE EMINENT GUIDING SCHOLAR MUHAMMAD IBN SAALEH AL-'UTHEIMEEN, MAY ALLAAH HAVE MERCY UPON HIM, FROM 'COLLECTION OF THE SHEIKH'S ISLAMIC RULING': VOLUMES 3 & 9, QUESTIONS 435, 459, 484, 485)

*Four questions regarding the terms "Islamic thought" and "freedom of thought'" The esteemed Sheikh was asked about the correctness of the statement of an individual: "I am free."*

He replied: If that is stated by a person who is indeed free in his legal status, and he intends by this that he is free from slavery to the creation; than yes it can be said that he is free from slavery to the creation. But if he intends by this that he is free from the requirement of the slavery of chosen submission through the worship of Allaah, the Most High and the Most Exalted, then he has a false understanding of the meaning of worship. Moreover, he does not understand the meaning of freedom, as submission and worship to anything or anyone other than Allaah is indeed true slavery. But the submission to and worship of an individual directed towards his Lord, the Most High and the Most Exalted- then this is true freedom. Certainly if he is not subservient to Allaah then he will inevitably become subservient to something or someone other than Allaah. So therefore he is simply deceiving himself if he says: "I am free", meaning by this that he is separated from or not bound by the need to obey Allaah and establish obedience to Allaah's guidance.

*The esteemed Sheikh was asked: We hear and read the expression "freedom of thought," which is a call or invitation to complete freedom of belief; what are your comments regarding this?*

He responded by saying: My comments upon this are that the one who makes it permissible for someone to have absolute freedom- meaning that, regarding his beliefs, he holds that one can choose whatever he wishes from the various religions and ideologies- then he is a disbeliever in Islaam. This is because every individual who believes that someone is allowed to worship Allaah by following a religion other than the religion of Muhammad has disbelieved in Allaah, Most High and the Most Exalted. This requires his repentance; he should repent or the authority in the Muslim lands in which he resides should seek a court decree for corporal punishment.

The various revealed messages from Allaah are not simply thoughts or concepts; rather, they are the revelation which Allaah, the Most High and the Most Exalted, sent down upon His Messengers to facilitate guiding His servants to Him. But as for this expression, specifically the term "fikr" or "thought" by which they intend the path of Islaam, then it is required to remove it from the dictionaries or vocabularies used within Islamic books, as it guides to this corrupt understanding-the understanding that Islaam is simply an ideology or concept, just as Christianity or Judaism is an ideology or concept. It is particularly the focus of the Christians, who call and consider themselves the people of Jesus the Messiah. They undertake this in order to make Allaah's revealed laws on par with or on a similar level with other worldly ideologies that anyone may turn to if they so wish. In truth, the origin of what are seen as the 'heavenly religions' is that they are originally divine messages from Allaah, the Most High and the Most Exalted, which man turns to due to the fact that they are indeed revelation from Allaah by which His worshipers can properly worship Him. Therefore it is not permissible to categorize them as simply ideologies, concepts, or systems of thought.

So in summarizing this response: the one who believes that it is permissible for anyone to worship Allaah in any form or fashion, and that he has complete freedom to worship Allaah in any manner; then he is a disbeliever in Allaah, the Most High in the Most Exalted. As Allaah, the Most High says: ❨*And whoever seeks a religion other than Islaam, it will never be accepted of him*❩-(Surah Aal-Imran:85) And He says: ❨*Truly, the religion with Allaah is Islaam.*❩-(Surah Aal-Imran:19). So it is not permissible for anyone to believe that any religion or way other than Islaam is acceptable to Allaah, or that Allaah has made it permissible to worship Him through some other way. Rather, if he believes this then the people of knowledge have explicitly stated that he is not a Muslim, because this is clear major disbelief that removes one from the ranks of the Muslims.

*The esteemed Sheikh was asked about the terminology 'Islamic thought' or 'Islamic thinker'.*

He replied: The term 'Islamic Thought' is from the expressions that have been warned against, as it requires that we place or consider Islaam in the same context as other opposing ideologies and systems of thought, for possible acceptance or rejection. This is extremely dangerous and is a matter which has been slipped in among us by the enemies of Islaam from a direction that we did not perceive.

As for the term 'Islamic thinker' then I do not know it to be of any harm, as it is simply a description of a Muslim individual, and a Muslim individual is someone who thinks and considers.

*The esteemed Sheikh was asked: It was stated in your previous ruling regarding expression 'Islamic thought'- that it is an expression that is not permissible to use because its purpose is to place Islaam on the same level with the other various ideologies, meaning that perhaps it is right, and perhaps it is not, and so forth. At the same time, you stated that, in general, the expression 'Islamic thinker' is permissible, as an individual's personal thoughts may change or vary, and may be correct or the opposite incorrect. However, the individuals that employ this terminology 'Islamic thought' state: "What we intend by this are concepts and understandings held by individuals and we do not speak about Islaam in its entirety  or restrict its meaning to the Sharee'ah of Islaam." So, in light of this, is this terminology 'Islamic thought' acceptable according to this understanding or not, and what about alternative terms?*

He answered by saying: It is affirmed that the Prophet, may Allaah's praise and salutations be upon him, said: *{Indeed, I judge according to that which I hear.}*[11]. We do not give rulings about individual situations except as they appear and become known. So if it is said: "Islamic thought" then the intent is clearly to mean related to Islaam as a concept, or ideology. If a speaker using this expression means the understanding or thoughts of just a Muslim individual, then he should say: "the understanding or thoughts of a Muslim individual" or  "the Islamic thinker". Additionally, instead of us saying "Islamic thought", we even should say "Islamic governance' since Islaam is about governing and judgment, as the Noble Qur'aan contains either information of the past nations or information about governing, rulings, and judgments. Allaah the Most High said: *And the Word of your Lord has been fulfilled in truth and in justice. None can change His Words. And He is the All-Hearer, the All-Knower.* -(Surah al-'Anaam).

---

[11]  Narrated in Saheeh al-Bukhaaree: 6967, 7169/ Saheeh Muslim: 1713/ Sunan Abu Daawud: 3583/ Sunan an-Nasaa'ee: 5424/ & Musnad Ahmad: 25952, 26078, 26177- from the hadeeth of Umm Salamah.

(10) The Eminent Guiding Scholar Saaleh Ibn 'Abdul-'Azeez Aal-Sheikh, may Allaah preserve him, from 'Knowledge and Speculative Thought': Page 12

### The Difference between Knowledge and Speculative Thought

Knowledge has tremendous benefits, the first of which is the rectification of one's worship. And "Islamic thinkers", as they have said, desire through their efforts to lead the people to a state of piety or to place them, as they say, upon a correct Islamic image or model; but this is not a guaranteed result. Rather this goal of theirs, in most cases, is not attained by them. However, true knowledge does indeed lead to the rectification of worship and towards piety.

This is because knowledge which is taken according to its principals, evidences, and fundamentals, upon the methodology of the first generations of Islaam, does guide to the rectification of one's worship, the establishing of firm and correct beliefs, and the correction of one's behavior and perspective in one's various dealings and interactions with the people, as well as in all newly occurring circumstances or situations.

As for speculative thought and opinion, then it changes constantly. Due to this, when the people do not have clear knowledge to direct and guide them, they frequently discuss and deliberate various matters at length such that new concepts begin to appear in their thoughts and speech. Ten or twenty different ideas or concepts are introduced at the same time, with each individual legitimizing and supporting his view, such that numerous differences and divisions then appear at a single gathering, with perhaps four people holding four separate and distinct views.

Likewise, one may hold a view and yet change it later, taking a differing view because speculative thought and opinion stands as the fundamental source or origin of that view. However, when we place knowledge as the fundamental reference, then the differing will be reduced and limited; it will be restrained such that the people will eventually reach the correct way of worship and the proper understanding.

From the greatest benefits or results of knowledge is that knowledge unifies while speculative thought causes separation. This fact was indicated in the statement of the former head religious authority of the country of Saudi Arabia, the exemplary scholar Sheikh Muhammad Ibn Ibraaheem, may Allaah have mercy upon him. In his time, he noticed the people drifting toward various cultural ideas and abandoning knowledge, and this was even before these different parties, groups, and organizations were known in this land- but close to the end of his life. So he made the following statement to some of the prominent individuals and some of the students of knowledge:

"*I advise the people with knowledge, as knowledge unifies and speculative thought and unrestricted cultural ideas separate between you and cause disunity.*' This is something true, which we have witnessed. Knowledge is that which unifies while unrestricted cultural ideas and concepts separate and lead to disunity. Consider that if you differ with someone on an issue and the fundamental source of reference for you both is knowledge. Everyone initially accepts his own understanding, saying, "*By Allaah, what is clear is that the ruling in this is such and such*' while another says, "*No. It is clear that the ruling in this is such and such.'* However after this they refer back to a scholar, eventually coming to unanimously agree on the correctness of his statement and judgment. Thus they are united after being previously divided in their views over this issue. And differing in relation to specific minor issues in understanding the religion is an easy matter. But how will the situation be if they were to differ in a serious issue- an issue related to the general welfare of the Muslim Ummah, or to the domain of calling to Allaah, or to the rectification of the matters through command and prohibition related to the struggle in the path of Allaah, or significant issues similar to these? In such a situation differing, if it occurs without referring back to the people of knowledge, leads to evil and separation.

The Muslim Ummah has taken a covenant that it would follow the Messenger of Allaah, may Allaah's praise and His salutations be upon him and his household, just as those who came before us followed their messenger or messengers, prayers and good mention be upon them all. As Allaah the High and Exalted says regarding the Christians: ❆*And from those who call themselves Christians, We took their covenant, but they have abandoned a good part of the Message that was sent to them. So We planted amongst them enmity and hatred till the Day of Resurrection...*❆-(Surah al-Mai'dah:14) Meaning a covenant was taken from them that they would adhere to knowledge and abandon the opinions which they had conceived. Ibn Shihab az-Zuhree stated, "*The Jews and Christians did not go astray except through opinions.*"

We see that there was taken from the Christians a covenant that they would adhere to knowledge; yet they partially adhered to that which they were given and in part they followed their own opinions. Thus, what happened is that they eventually separated and divided, and this separation is considered a punishment from the punishments of Allaah, as Allaah, High and Exalted, said, ❆*And from those who call themselves Christians, We took their covenant, but they have abandoned...*❆ meaning they left or turned away from it ❆*they have abandoned a good part of the message that was sent to them*❆ meaning from knowledge. Then they turned towards adherence to their opinions and their desires and so separated from each other. Allaah, High and Exalted, said, ❆*So We planted amongst them enmity and hatred till the Day of Resurrection..*❆-(Surah al-Mai'dah:14)

This separation is not simply minor differing, but division which leads to hatred and enmity. Hatred emerges from it, and then envy emerges from it, and then more hatred which is outwardly or on the surface for Allaah's sake, but which is actually hatred resulting from this separation and division. The cause of their separation is the failure to adhere fully to knowledge from the very beginning, and their following of their own opinions, as what is truly knowledge brings unity, while unrestricted cultural ideas and concepts, and speculative thought causes separation. This is something readily apparent in the past history of the Muslim Ummah as well as in our modern history from what has occurred of the various types of division and disunity of concepts and ideologies among the various groups and societies, such that there is enmity between the various thinkers and writers. Thus it has progressed to the emergence of different schools of thought and distinct methodologies.

So we summarize by saying about the difference between knowledge and speculative thought, and what distinguishes between knowledge and speculative thought, is that knowledge is comprised of various types of evidence which are categorized and structured. As was mentioned by Qaraafee in his book ((al-Usooleeyah)08-10), there are thirteen types of evidence which are recognized, and in their detailed categorization, twenty types. This is opposed to speculative thought, whose evidences are neither categorized nor structured. Speculative thought may proceed in one case upon evidences of a specific thinker taking its origin in historical events, who then makes a determination or ruling derived from those past events upon other occurrences which are occurring in our time. But when can history itself be considered evidence? For example, a specific thinker states that the people from one specific land of the various lands, as is mentioned by the historians, the people of this land abandoned it due to the scarcity of sustenance or because of the harshness of the weather or a similar reason. They put this forth as a convincing demonstration or example, this being a principle from among their principles- the acceptability of the Muslims undertaking the same action. So then they derive from these examples evidences for their idea or opinion.

However, this idea or claim cannot be sound, nor is this opinion valid, because it was derived from an historical example as well as speculative thought which is not founded upon proper structured guidelines. So speculative thought is in fact unsystematic. Perhaps one person may make a statement and derive from that statement a result or conclusion. But the statement does not actually contain any valid evidenced explanation or support of that derived opinion. However, the statement will still be considered a correct and accepted explanation.

Another thinker comes and falsely concludes that the people who adhere to the hadeeth narrations are people who abandon commercial industry and turn away from entering into the various intellectual fields. They state that in the history of the Muslims these "people of hadeeth" did not produce anything worthwhile in the past or present, nor make any discoveries, nor contribute to literature- claiming these "accomplishments" were only produced by the intellectuals, meaning those who give precedence to intellect over revealed knowledge. They state that these intellectuals are the ones who promoted industry and furthered modern ideas and brought many advances to society, and it is their efforts which brought forth modern medicine and mathematics and so on, and none of this is known to have come from the people who adhere to the hadeeth narrations. In their view, this is proof that the way of thinking held by the "people of hadeeth" is incapable of leading the Muslim Ummah, and the methodology of the first three generations is incapable of guiding and directing the Muslim Ummah. Yes, they concede that in relation to limited "religious" rulings they are suited to bring forth their opinions. However in relation to what would truly benefit the people- they hold that the people most suitable for that would be the people like the Mu'tazilah. Thus they believe that the Mu'tazilah are those truly suitable and capable of guiding the Muslim Ummah in the past and in the present age. They believe that the understanding of such "intellectuals", who give primary precedence to the role of the intellect is that which will actually enable the Muslim Ummah to advance. As for the people who adhere to revelation and hadeeth narrations or the scholars who explain the detailed rulings of the religion, then such people believe that their role is simply religious preaching.

Yet the historical assessment and analysis through which they derive this conclusion is reached through rejecting an essential fundamental from the foundations of correct belief in Islaam and through rejecting an evidence from the related evidences. This is that the group which the Messenger stated would be the continually "successful group" from among the Muslim Ummah is indeed those people who hold to the Sunnah of the Messenger of Allaah, and the Jama'ah -meaning those Muslims who remain united upon his guidance and those people of Sharee'ah knowledge. Such Muslims are indeed present today, and their people of knowledge assess every contemporary issue or problem, judging whether such and such matter in question is acceptable or not. Similarly, the true people of knowledge do not in any way prohibit manufacturing and production of goods, nor do they prohibit the various aspects of knowledge related to civilization.

If anyone did prohibit these, it would be due to a deficiency in his understanding or his distance from the correct understanding of the goals of the Sharee'ah. In fact it is only for the scholars to make such determinations for society, as they are also the doctors for our hearts, enabling the true advancement of the people toward the next life. Who else is available to establish the affairs within the Muslim Ummah related to this worldly life, as well as to consider the various aspects of civilization, manufacturing, medical and engineering discoveries, and the principles of chemistry, astronomy, and physics and so on? They are the ones who will actually rule upon an endeavor which may possibly be undertaken by the Muslims: is this endeavor correct or incorrect? Furthermore, we do not merely mean from what has been mentioned that they are from one of the important foundations of society. Rather, the essential and prominent foundation of the religion is certainly the people of knowledge.

As such, the intellectual conclusions by this movement and its methodology of thinking are not based upon sound guidelines and principles, but are derived from merely viewing some aspects of history while at the same time rejecting a fundamental principal of the foundational beliefs as understood by the Sharee'ah. There has always been and will always be a group of Muslims present who are successful in understanding and practicing Islaam. Despite this deficiency there are some who have become satisfied with that false conclusion and circulate their beliefs concerning this issue.

Secondly from the important distinctions is that knowledge has set principles by which matters are assessed and weighed, and speculative thought lacks such principles by which questions and issues can be assessed. If an individual speaks regarding a knowledge-related issue, then we are able to judge whether his statement is acceptable or not acceptable. Are his statements strong or weak? But as for speculative thought, what then are its fundamental guidelines? What are its principles? If someone, meaning one of the general people, wishes to assess the statement of an intellectual thinker, with what standard can they assess it?? He is not able to refer it to accepted authorities to make a judgment or assessment.

However true knowledge in Islaam has such recognized authorities. In contrast, speculative thought is not established upon clear guidelines and principles nor does it have established authorities by which concepts can be evaluated, except by submitting itself to true knowledge. True knowledge acts as the judge and authority over speculative thought. Additionally, knowledge has as one of its essential characteristics that it is worthy of being commended and praised and that its people are worthy of commendation and praise. But as for speculative thought, it is simply various ideas and opinions, and the overall nature of opinion as held by the scholars is that it is condemned and censured. Indeed, this is a tremendous difference and fundamental distinction between these two matters.

(II) The Eminent Guiding Scholar 'Abdur-Rahman Ibn Naaser as-Sa'adee, may Allaah have mercy upon him, from 'A Delight for the Accepting Hearts and a Pleasure for the Noble Eye in the Explanation of a Collection of Narrations': page 65

### An Explanation of a Tremendous Hadeeth

On the authority of Mu'aweeyah, may Allaah be pleased with him, who said that the Messenger of Allaah, prayers and good mention be upon him and his household, said, {Whoever Allaah intends good for He grants him understanding in the religion.}[12]. This hadeeth narration contains an explanation of one of the greatest benefits of knowledge: the indication that the bestowing of beneficial knowledge upon one is from the signs of the success of a worshiper, and a sign that Allaah intends good for him. This mentioned understanding in the religion encompasses understanding of "Emaan" the fundamentals of faith, "Islaam" the pillars of Islaam and their rulings, and "Ihsaan" the realities of virtuous character and deeds. As the religion encompasses all three of these, as is found in the hadeeth of Jibreel when he asked the Prophet, prayers and good mention be upon him and his household, regarding "Imaan" and "Islaam" and "Ihsaan". And he answered him, prayers and salutations be upon him and his household, clarifying their boundaries and characteristics.

He explained "Emaan" by indicating its six fundamentals, and he explained "Islaam" by indicating its five pillars, and he explained "Ihsaan" by saying that it is that you worship Allaah as if you see Him, and if not as if you see him then certainly aware that He sees you.

And what enters into this is the understanding of correct beliefs, as well as understanding the way of the first generations in the matter of beliefs, and making this understanding a reality inwardly and outwardly. In addition, it includes understanding the way of those who have opposed this, and the explanation of their

---

[12] Narrated in Saheeh al-Bukhaaree: 71, 3116, 7312/ Saheeh Muslim: 1037/ Sunan Ibn Maajah: 221/ al-Muwatta Maalik: 1300, 1667/ Musnad Imaam Ahmad: 16395: 16404, and other narrations/ Musannaf Ibn Abee Shaybah: 31792/ & Sunan ad-Daaramee: 224, 226/- on the authority of Mu'aweeyah. And it is found in Jaame' al-Tirmidhee: 2645/ & Musnad Imaam Ahmad: 2786/ & Sunan ad-Daaramee: 270, 2706/- on the authority of Ibn "Abbaas. And  it is found in Sunan Ibn Maajah: 220/ Musannaf 'Abdul-Razzaaq: 30851/- on the authority of Abu Hurairah. It was declared authentic by Sheikh al-Albaanee in Saheeh al-Aadab al-Mufrad: 517, Silsilat al-Hadeeth as-Saheehah: 1194, 1195, 1196, Saheeh at-Targheeb at-Tarheeb: 67, as well as in other of his books. Sheikh Muqbil declared it authentic in al-Jaame' al-Saheeh: 9, 3123, 4650.

contradiction with the Book of Allaah and the Sunnah. What also enters into this is knowledge of how to implement and realize the religion-both its fundamentals and its branches, as well as its rulings regarding worship, general affairs, serious transgressions and other matters.

Additionally, what enters into this is the understanding of the realities of "*Emaan*", comprehending what is the correct behavior and conduct towards Allaah, and conformity with everything that the Book of Allaah and the Sunnah guide towards. Also entering into this is studying all the detailed means that enable one to achieve understanding in the religion such, as the sciences of the Arabic language and its different areas.

So the one who Allaah desires good for, He blesses him with understanding in these matters while enabling him to realize them. And from the comprehensive meaning of this hadeeth is an indication that if someone turns away completely from these various aspects of knowledge, this implies that Allaah does not intend good for him, as He has closed such an individual off from the causes and means which would lead him to these forms of good and enable him to achieve a state of happiness.

(12) THE EMINENT GUIDING SCHOLAR MUQBIL IBN HAADEE AL-WAADI'EE, MAY ALLAAH HAVE MERCY UPON HIM, FROM 'AN OFFERING OF ANSWERS TO SOME OF THE QUESTIONS IN HADEETH TERMINOLOGY': PAGES 8-12

### *Regarding Knowledge: its Merits, and which Knowledge is Considered Obligatory*
All praise is due to Allaah, Lord of all the worlds, may Allaah's praise and His salutations be upon our prophet Muhammad, the Truthful, and upon his family and all of his Companions. And I bear witness that there is none worthy of worship except Allaah alone Who has no partner. And I bear witness that Muhammad is His worshiper and Messenger. To proceed: The subject which has been selected is the subject of knowledge. Knowledge is considered the cure for all of our illnesses and afflictions. Our prophet Muhammad, may Allaah's praise and salutations be upon him and his household, was ordered by his Lord to ask for an increase in knowledge.

Allaah, the Most Perfect and the Most High, said, ❖*Say: "My Lord! Increase me in knowledge.*❖-(Surah Ta-Ha: 114). And the Lord of Might has explained the condition of the scholar and the condition of the one who is ignorant when He says, ❖*Shall he then who knows that what has been revealed unto you from your Lord is the truth be like him who is blind? But it is only the men of understanding that pay heed.*❖-(Surah ar-Ra'd:19).

And our prophet Muhammad, may Allaah's praise and salutations be upon him and his household, said, in what is narrated in the hadeeth of Mu'aweeyah, may Allaah be pleased with him, transmitted by both Imaams Bukharee and Muslim in their two authentic collections of hadeeth: *{Whoever Allaah intends good for He grants him understanding in the religion.}* [13].

And the Lord of Might motivates many in His creation, and He says in a verse from His book, *Verily, in that are indeed signs for men of sound knowledge.*-(Surah ar-Rum: 22) and the Exalted says, *And these similitudes We put forward for mankind, but none will understand them except those who have knowledge (of Allaah and His Signs, etc.).'*-(Surah Ankabut: 43). The Lord of Might gives preference to the dog with training over the dog that does not have training, making permissible the hunted game caught by the trained dog when the name of Allaah is mentioned, as it is sent to hunt. Then the Most Perfect and the Most High says, *They ask you (Oh Muhammad) what is lawful for them (as food). Say: "Lawful unto you are all kind of good foods which Allaah has made lawful. And those beasts and birds of prey which you have trained as hounds, training and teaching them to catch in the manner as directed to you by Allaah*-(Surah al-Ma'idah: 4)

Indeed, Allaah, the Most Perfect and the Most High, informed us that when the hoopoe bird presented his excuse to Sulayman he said, *I have grasped (the knowledge of a thing) which you have not grasped and I have come to you from Saba' (Sheba) with true news.*-(Surah al-Naml: 22)

Our Prophet Muhammad, may Allaah's praise and salutations be upon him and his household, encouraged his Ummah towards knowledge, and encouraged the Muslim Ummah towards the best type of knowledge, which is the memorization of the Book. The people of philosophical argumentation and false rhetoric say, [Certainly, the best branch of knowledge is the science of philosophical argumentation, as it discusses Allaah and His characteristics.] This is due to their ignorance of the Book of Allaah and the Sunnah of his Messenger, may Allaah's praise and His salutations be upon him and his household.

Imaam Shaafa'ee, may Allaah have mercy upon him, said, "My ruling on the people of philosophical argumentation and false rhetoric is that they should be confined in prison cells and struck with whips,' and he said, "This is the penalty for the one who takes a substitute for the Book of Allaah, or for the one who turns away from the Book of Allaah.' It is clear that the best type of knowledge is the learning of the Book of Allaah and Sunnah of the Messenger of Allaah, may Allaah's praise and His salutations be upon him and his household. Allaah says, *Allaah will exalt in degree those of you who believe, and those who have been granted knowledge.*-(Surah al-Mujadiah: 11) and, *It is only those who have knowledge among His slaves that fear*

---

[13] This hadeeth is found in Saheeh al-Bukhaaree: 71, 3116, 7312/ Saheeh Muslim: 1037/ Sunan Ibn Maajah: 221/ al-Muwatta Maalik: 1300, 1667/ Musnad Imaam Ahmad: 16395: 16404, and other narrations/ Musannaf Ibn Abee Shaybah: 31792/ & Sunan ad-Daaramee: 224, 226/- on the authority of Mu'aweeyah. And it is found in Jaame' al-Tirmidhee: 2645/ Musnad Imaam Ahmad: 2786/ & Sunan ad-Daaramee: 270, 2706/- on the authority of Ibn 'Abbaas. And it is found in Sunan Ibn Maajah:220/ & Musannaf 'Abdul-Razzaaq: 30851/- on the authority of Abu Hurairah. It was declared authentic by Sheikh al-Albaanee in Saheeh al-Aadab al-Mufrad: 517, Silsilat al-Hadeeth as-Saheehah:1194, 1195, 1196, Saheeh at-Targheeb at-Tarheeb: 67, as well as in other of his books. Sheikh Muqbil declared it authentic in al-Jaame' al-Saheeh: 9, 3123, 4650, may Allaah have mercy upon them both.

*Allaah.* ❊-(Surah al-Fatir: 28).

The best knowledge is the memorization of the Noble Qur'aan, as our Prophet Muhammad, may Allaah's praise and His salutations be upon him and his household, said in the narration of Uthman, may Allaah be pleased with him, found in Saheeh al-Bukhaaree: *{The best of you are those who learn the Qur'aan and teach it.}* [14].

He also said, as found in Saheeh Muslim in the narration of 'Umar, may Allaah be pleased with him, *{Certainly Allaah elevates by this Book some people and lowers and disgraces others by it.}* [15].

From our scholars in the first centuries, may Allaah have mercy upon them, there were those who specialized in the study of the Qur'aan, and those who specialized in the study of the Sunnah of the Messenger of Allaah, may Allaah's praise and His salutations be upon him and his household, as well as those who specialized in the Arabic language. And in most cases the one who specialized in one field or area also had a basic proficiency of the other branches of knowledge. However, there were also those like Hafs Ibn Sulaymaan, who was a leader in the branch of the science of recitation of the Qur'aan, as he was one of the well known seven scholars in the science of recitation; yet in the area of hadeeth and its narrations he is rejected as a narrator. There would also be one who was a leader in the science of the hadeeth narrations, but who would make grammar mistakes in simple matters, such as Uthmaan Ibn Abee Shaaybah the blood brother of both Qaasim and Abee Bakr Ibn Abee Shaaybah. He was a leading scholar in the sciences of hadeeth but would commit mispronunciations in the recitation of the Qur'aan. Even though Haafidh Ibn Katheer denies this about him in his well-known book on the science of hadeeth, *((Mukhtasir Ulum al-Hadeeth )04-24).*

From our scholars from the first centuries of this Ummah were those who specialized in the Arabic language; and indeed the knowledge of Arabic has several branches and areas. There were those who specialized in grammar, which is related to the structure of statements; and those who specialized in linguistic morphology, which is related to the various forms of words; as well as in other areas of the language. There were also those who combined proficiency in more than one area of knowledge. An example of this is Imaam Shaafa'ee, may Allaah have mercy upon him, who was a leading scholar in the field of language, such that he presented arguments by means of his expert knowledge of Arabic. However, he was also a leading scholar in the knowledge of the Sunnah of the Messenger of Allaah, may Allaah's praise and salutations be upon him and his household, such that he was given the title, "One who brings victory to the Sunnah". Two of the books he authored, *((Mukhtalif al-Hadeeth )04-25)* and *((ar-Risaalah )08-03)*, both prove that indeed he was worthy of being given the title "One who brings victory to the Sunnah," as he refuted the people of unrestricted opinions, the sect of the Mu'tazilah, as well as those who

---

[14]  Narrated in Saheeh al-Bukhaaree: 5027/ Sunan Abee Dawud: 1352/Sunan at-Tirmidhee: 2907/ & Musnad Ahmad: 414, 502/ from the hadeeth of 'Uthmaan Ibn 'Afaan. Declared authentic by Sheikh al-Albaanee in Silsilatul-Hadeeth Saheehah: 1173, and in Saheeh at-Targheeb wa at-Tarheeb: 1415, as well as in other of his works.

[15]  Narrated in Saheeh Muslim: 817/ Sunan Ibn Maajah: 218/ Musnad Ahmad: 233/ & Sunan ad-Daaramee: 3360/ -from the hadeeth of 'Umar Ibn al-Khattab. Declared authentic by Sheikh al-Albaanee in Silsilatul-Hadeeth Saheehah: 2239, Saheeh al-Jaame'a as-Sagheer: 1896, as well as in other of his works.

slandered and defamed the Sunnah of the Messenger of Allaah, may Allaah's praise and salutations be upon him and his household.

So knowledge has a distinguished and prominent position; and due to this there is rarely an author or compiler who does not include in his work a section generally related to knowledge. In the book Saheeh al-Bukhaaree there is the "Book of Knowledge', and in the book Saheeh Muslim there is the 'Book of Knowledge', and in the work al-Jaame'a at-Tirmidhee there is the 'Book of Knowledge'. Additionally, the people of knowledge have authored works individually devoted to the subject of knowledge, such as al-Haafidh Ibn 'Abdul-Bar Yusuf Ibn 'Abdullah, as he compiled a priceless book which is equal to the value of this entire world, entitled, *((Jaame'a Bayaan al-'Ilm wa Fadhlehe)06-44)*. Within this book he mentions the merit of the scholars, the merits of knowledge, and discusses the issue of blind following. And blind following is not from knowledge, as has been stated, "*The scholars have agreed upon the fact that it is not proper to claim that one who blindly follows is from the people of knowledge.*" And the Lord of Might says in His book, ◈ *Follow what has been sent down unto you from your Lord, and follow not any protectors and helpers, besides Him (Allaah). Little do you remember!* ◈-(Surah al-Araaf:3) So, this worthy book begins with a discussion of the obligation of knowledge, and then proceeds to the hadeeth, *{Seeking knowledge is an obligation upon every Muslim.}* [16] and then he, may Allaah have mercy upon him, indicates that he has judged this narration to be weak. However, Imaam as-Suyootee, may Allaah the Exalted have mercy upon him, stated, "This narration has fifty different complementing routes of transmission,' and therefore judges that the narration was authentic.

### What is the knowledge that is considered obligatory?

The knowledge that Allaah requires you personally to learn is the knowledge that is considered obligatory upon you as an individual. Included in this are the basic beliefs of Islaam, and these are obligatory upon every Muslim to learn, as is indicated in the Book of Allaah and the Sunnah. It is prohibited that one be ignorant of the basic beliefs of Islaam, whether that be related to the names of Allaah or His characteristics. It is obligatory to believe and affirm our creed regarding Allaah's names and attributes, just as they appear in the Book of Allaah, and as they appear in the Sunnah of the Messenger of Allaah, may Allaah's praise and salutations be upon him and his household. Such as stated clearly by the slave girl who was a shepherdess over a flock of sheep as found in the narration of Mu'aweeyah Ibn al-Hakim, may Allaah be pleased with him, when he came with a slave girl in order to free her. He said: *{ "Messenger of Allaah, I wish to grant her freedom.' He (the Messenger of Allaah, may Allaah's praise and salutations be upon him) said to her, "Oh slave girl, where is Allaah?' She said, "He is in the heavens." He said, "Free her as she is a believing woman."}* [17].

[16]  Narrated in Sunan Ibn Maajah: 224/ -from the hadeeth of 'Anas Ibn Maalik. Declared authentic by Sheikh al-Albaanee in Saheeh al-Jaame'a as-Sagheer: 1173, in Saheeh at-Targheeb wa at-Tarheeb: 72, as well as in other of his works.

[17]  Narrated in Saheeh Muslim: 537/ Sunan Abu Dawud: 930, 3283/ Sunan an-Nasaa'ee: 1219/ & Musnad Ahmad: 28818, 28819, 28820/ -from the hadeeth of Mu'aweeyah Ibn Hakim. And in Sunan Abu Dawud: 3283/ & Musnad Ahmad: 7836, from the hadeeth of Abu Hurairah, Declared authentic by Sheikh al-Albaanee in Dhelaal al-Jannah: 489, and in Mukhtasir al-'Uluu, pg. 75.

So it is obligatory upon every Muslim to believe that Allaah is in the heavens in a manner befitting His Majesty, and that Allaah the Most Perfect and the Most High is with each of us in His complete knowledge, and through His protection, preservation, and granting of victory to the believers. It is obligatory upon us to believe in this fully, as Allaah says, ❮*Do you feel secure that He, Who is over the heaven (Allaah), will not cause the earth to sink with you, then behold it shakes (as in an earthquake)?*❯- (Surah Mulk: 16) and ❮*The Most Beneficent rose over the Mighty Throne in a manner that suits His Majesty.*❯-(Surah Ta-Ha: 5). There is a valuable book written on the subject that I advise my brothers in Allaah to read. That beneficial book is the work *((al-Uluu Lil Aalee al-Ghafaar)06-44)* by Haafidh adh-Dhahabee, may Allaah have mercy upon him. It was summarized by Sheikh Naasiruddeen al-Albaanee, may Allaah the exalted preserve him. Those among the students of knowledge who have the ability to verify works should try to acquire the original book, and one who does not have that ability should acquire the *((summarized version)06-44)* by Sheikh al-Albaanee. And if you are able to acquire both of them, then this is best, as one of them does not remove the need for the other.

(13) The Eminent Guiding Scholar Saaleh Ibn 'Abdul-'Azeez Aal-Sheikh, may Allaah preserve him, From 'Explanation of The Merits of Islaam': Pages 2-3

### The Important Place of Knowledge within an Individual's Practice of the Religion

Islaam is indeed the most important matter which an individual should commit himself to and adhere to. It is the most important matter he should struggle for and strive within himself towards realizing its reality. However, that is not possible except through knowledge. Indeed, beneficial knowledge is that which rectifies one's heart, and corrects one's actions and deeds. Indicating this, Allaah, the Most Perfect and the Most High, said,

❮*This is my way; I invite to Allaah upon insight, I and whosoever follows me*❯-(Surah Yusuf:108). The meaning of "upon insight' is upon and with knowledge.

As insight for the heart is knowledge which clarifies the reality of matters and shows what is correct within them. Allaah, the Most Perfect and the Most High, has said, ❮*He who was dead without faith through his ignorance and disbelief and We gave him life by knowledge and faith and set for him a light (of Belief) whereby he can walk amongst men.*❯-(Surah al-Ana'am:122)

The people of knowledge state: "This 'light' is Islaam, which is both beneficial knowledge and righteous deeds. Due to this Allaah, the Most Perfect and the Most High, did not command His Prophet, may Allaah's praise and salutations be upon him, or his Ummah after him, to seek an increase in any matter except for an increase in knowledge. Allaah, the Most Perfect and the Most High, said in Surah Ta-ha: ❮*Say my Lord increase me in knowledge.*❯ Allaah has raised the people of knowledge over the rest of the believers due to what they have attained of knowledge. As He, the Most Perfect and the Most High, says, ❮*Allaah raises those who believe from among you, and those who been given knowledge, by degrees* ❖-(Surah al-Mujadalah:11) So every believer has been raised by Allaah, the Most Perfect and the Most High, by his belief in Allaah, and, in addition to this, from within the ranks of the believers every true person of knowledge is further raised by his correct knowledge, such that the person of knowledge has been raised additional degrees over the others. This is from the blessings of Allaah the Most Perfect and the Most High upon the people of knowledge. If the student of knowledge pursues knowledge, and pursues this path of seeking knowledge, then Allaah makes easy for him the path to Jannah. As the Messenger of Allaah, may Allaah's praise and salutations be upon him, said in an authentic narration: *{Whoever goes forth upon the path of seeking knowledge, Allaah makes easy for him the path to Jannah.}* [18].

This is because the path to Jannah is realized by rectifying one's belief as well as by correcting one's deeds. And the rectification of one's beliefs is not possible except through knowledge. Likewise, the correction of one's actions is also only possible through knowledge. The statement, *{Whoever goes forth upon the path of seeking knowledge...}* means knowledge of the worship of Allaah alone, as well as knowledge of how to implement and practice the religion, and of the permissible and prohibited; consequently, *{...Allaah makes easy for him the path to Jannah.}* Since from the reasons of entering Paradise are the correctness of one's deeds, and the soundness of one's beliefs.

From the blessings of knowledge upon the scholar is that all of Allaah's creatures seek forgiveness for him, even the fish in the depths of the oceans. This is because he glorifies Allaah, affirms that there is none worthy of worship other than Him, extols Him, exalts and praises Him, and strives to follow and obey Him through Muhammad, may Allaah's praise and His salutations be upon him; all this with certainty, knowledge, and understanding. By this that completion which is possible for creation may be attained. He becomes from amongst the highest of creation in merit, stature and closeness to Allaah, the Most Perfect and the Most High.

So by this we understand some aspects of the merit of the student of knowledge and the worth and position of the scholar, as all of Allaah's creatures seek forgiveness for him, even the fish in the depths of the oceans. Because all of these created things which Allaah, the High and Exalted, did not make responsible for their actions, comprehend the merit and blessing of the scholar who teaches the people good and the one who cultivates within the people the love of Allaah, the High and Exalted, and knowledge of His names and His attributes, and what is His right, High and Exalted is He, in terms of worshiping Him alone without partners and glorification of Him, and what is the right of His Prophet, may Allaah's praise and salutations be upon him, in relation to loving him and following him and knowledge of his Sunnah and adhering to it. When he becomes from those who spread the love of Allaah, High and Exalted, throughout the world, then by all this he surpasses the remainder of creation in merit. Because of this, every created thing seeks forgiveness for him,

---

[18]  Narrated in Saheeh Muslim: 2699/ Sunan at-Tirmidhee: 2945/ Sunan Ibn Maajah: 225/ & Musnad Ahmad: 7379- from the hadeeth of Abu Hurairah. Declared authentic by Sheikh al-Albaanee in Saheeh at-Targheeb wa al-Tarheeb: 69, 89, as well as in other of his books.

being pleased with the actions he puts forth, such that the angels lower their wings upon the student of knowledge due to their pleasure with his efforts, and due to the significance of his actions.

From this we see that, if one acts upon even some of these matters, then certainly he will receive a tremendous benefit from knowledge in relation to memorization, teaching, the attendance of circles of knowledge, as well as in understanding. Because no one desires these except the believer who has correct faith, and no desires to be far from these except every individual of separation and distance from the truth. Every person who struggles with himself in seeking knowledge, truly struggles in rectifying his heart and correcting his actions. Thus, the scholar or the student of knowledge if they fall into error, then their seeking forgiveness is not like the seeking of forgiveness of others. When they seek forgiveness, they are doing so upon knowledge and clarity, and the understanding of Allaah, the Most Perfect and the Most High, and what He requires from them, and understanding their own deficiencies, what they have indeed done and where they have fallen short in that.

So we see that the leader of the scholars of the Muslim Ummah after its Prophet, may Allaah's praise and salutations be upon him, Abu Bakr as-Siddeeq, may Allaah be pleased with him, was taught by our Prophet, may Allaah's praise and salutations be upon him, to supplicate in his prayers by saying, *{Allaah, certainly I have committed many injustices against my own soul, and there is no forgiveness of transgressions except through You, so forgive me as you are the One who Forgives, the Merciful.}* [19].

This supplication was for Abu Bakr as-Siddeeq, the most perfect follower in relation to his knowledge, deeds, behavior, characteristics, and his love and precedence in following the example of the Prophet, may Allaah's praise and His salutations be upon him! The Prophet taught him this supplication, which contains an extraordinary seeking of forgiveness and repentance from the standpoint of the significance in the acknowledgement of one's transgressions: *{My Lord, certainly I have committed many injustices against my own soul, and there is no forgiveness of transgressions except through you.}* [20].

Therefore, every student of knowledge and scholar, to the degree of his knowledge about Allaah, and his actions for the sake of Allaah, the High and Exalted, and his knowledge of the details of the Sharee'ah, and his knowledge of the rights of Allaah related to beliefs, is increased in his awareness of his sins and transgressions. So much so that he sees deeds of his as requiring the seeking of forgiveness, whereas another lacking that insight would not consider them matters which require the asking of forgiveness. For this reason, the level of the student of knowledge or the scholar is raised and increased according to the degree of knowledge they attain of the correct understanding of worshiping Allaah alone, and knowledge of the significance of

---

[19]  Narrated in Saheeh al-Bukhaaree: 834, 6326, 7387, 7388/ Saheeh Muslim: 2705/ Sunan at-Tirmidhee: 3531/ Sunan an-Nasa'ee: 1303/ Sunan Ibn Maajah: 3835/ & Musnad Ahmad: 8, 29/ -from the hadeeth of Abu Bakr as-Saddeeq. Declared authentic by Sheikh al-Albaanee in Saheeh al-Jaame'a as-Sagheer: 7850, as well as in other of his books.

[20]  Narrated in Saheeh al-Bukhaaree: 811, 5977, 6975/Mustradraak al-Haakim: 2419, & other collections/-on the authority of Abu Bakr. And it is found in  Saheeh Muslim: 1330/ Saheeh Ibn Hibaan: 2743/ & other collections -on the authority of Alee Ibn Abee Taalib. It was declared authentic by Sheikh al-Albaanee in al-Kalimah at-Tayyib, 172, Saheeh al-Jaame'a: 1821, 2069, Mukhtasir ash-Shama'el al-Muhammadeeyah: 198, and in other of his works.

their seeking forgiveness and repenting to Allaah, High and Exalted is He.

And in this age perhaps we may see that many people have mistaken ideas regarding knowledge from one perspective- or, actually, from several perspectives. They hold a mistaken idea regarding knowledge in that some think that knowledge does not possess benefits or rewards equal to what one sacrifices in its pursuit or in achieving it.

And there are those who hold the mistaken idea regarding knowledge that if you do strive for knowledge, at the end of your efforts you will still be just like any other person, not having obtained any significant results equal to your difficulties encountered in obtaining that knowledge. Then there are those who hold the mistaken idea regarding knowledge that the most important priority nowadays is calling and guiding the people, striving in this area, and similar efforts, believing that seeking knowledge does not have any significant effect or does not produce true results like these activities of calling and similar endeavors do. Additionally, there are those who hold the mistaken idea regarding knowledge that its attainment does not bring to the one who has acquired it any importance or significance in his status.

Rather, they believe that true importance is held by the people of worldly concerns, or those of the various other approaches and perspectives in this life.

All of these matters are actually from having mistaken ideas or concepts regarding the Sharee'ah itself, as knowledge is the Sharee'ah. So it is obligatory upon the student of knowledge to correct his understanding regarding Allaah, Glorified and High, to correct his thinking regarding acting according to knowledge, to correct his thinking regarding both knowledge and deeds collectively, and that he undertake all of this. How excellent is the saying of Ibn Qayyim, may Allaah have mercy upon him:

> Ignorance is a mortal disease which is healed,
>> with two complementary sources combined,
>
> A text from Qur'aan or from the Sunnah
>> and the doctor overseeing this cure is the guiding scholar.
>
> Knowledge is divided into three, not having a fourth,
>> the truth that which is contained in these two cures.
>
> Knowledge of the description of His Loftiness and Ascendency and His actions,
>> likewise of the names of the One who Judges after the Final accounting
>
> As well as the commanding and forbidding as found in His religion,
>> The reminding of the first separation death, as well as the second-
>> that of the Day of the Hereafter
>
> and every matter from the Qur'aan and Sunnahs
>> which came to the one sent with the true criterion
>
> By Allaah no eloquent one speaks from other than these two sources-
>> except for the one who is confused or simply delirious .

Additionally, one of the scholars said in ordered poetical verses, or rather composed poetry related to this, saying:

*Do not have a bad opinion about knowledge, young man,*

*As bad suspicion about knowledge certainly leads to your ruin.*

Indeed, this is the truth, as we have experienced and seen that every individual who has a mistaken or incorrect concept or idea regarding knowledge and so strays away from the path of traveling and seeking knowledge, and thus abandons it without continuing to seek knowledge- he does not achieve completeness. As knowledge is that which perfects the soul, and by it one's belief is perfected, and by it one's deeds are completed, and by it the ease and pleasure of the hearts is completed, and by it one's view and perspective of matters is perfected, and by it one completes the hope to do every matter according to the standards of the Sharee'ah. The people of knowledge mention that from the causes of the misguided people going astray within this Muslim Ummah is that they went astray because they were not established upon correct knowledge. This is because correct knowledge is a reason from among the reasons for the protection from trials and from the causes of misguidance and separation, as well as being a protection from other matters that are from the effects of abandoning knowledge.

Therefore I advise you and myself to preserve knowledge and preserve the memorization, examining, and carrying of knowledge, and that an individual should commit himself to studying it. Also, that he approaches what he does not know by taking knowledge of that matter from scholars about whom is known the reliability of their understanding of knowledge and their implementation of it. As through this, if Allaah, the Exalted wills, the rectification of the individual and of his actions will be realized. I ask Allaah, High and Exalted, to increase us and you in guidance and knowledge, and that He make us from truthful worshipers upon purity of intention for His pleasure alone, and that He forgives us our sins, as certainly He is free from all faults, the Bountiful, the Generous.

(14) The Eminent Guiding Scholar 'Abdur-Rahman Ibn Naasir as-Sa'adee, may Allaah have mercy upon him, From 'A Delightful Collection of Benefits and a Pursuit of Clarifications': Benefits 33 and 65

### The Prophet Sought Refuge from Knowledge which does not Benefit & Knowledge is of Two Types

He, may Allaah's praise and salutations be upon him, sought refuge from knowledge which does not benefit, and this encompasses several matters:

From them: Harmful types of knowledge that are completely damaging; the evil they bring is much greater than the good, such as the sciences of magic, and learning falsehood without ever discerning the truth.

And from them: Becoming occupied with branches of knowledge which preoccupy the worshipper from more beneficial endeavors, even if the area of knowledge is itself acceptable.

And from them: Knowledge of the Sharee'ah which the one who possesses it does not act upon, understanding what is good but turning away from acting upon it and understanding what is evil and harmful but still foolishly rushing into it.

And from them: Being occupied with areas of the natural sciences if they cause the one involved in them to turn away from the branches of science of the religion. As restricting his participation in them is an obligatory matter for the one who has become confused and misled in his study, as well as the one who likewise becomes conceited against the acceptance of truth in relation to his personal understanding or practice, as is often witnessed in the one who occupies himself with purely modern areas of knowledge, while he is neglectful of the sciences of the religion.

As for the beneficial branches of knowledge: These are the sciences of the religion, as well as those areas of knowledge which support them such as knowledge of the Arabic language and its various branches. Encompassed within this is that which rectifies one's religious affairs, one's worldly affairs, one's character, or any of the various aspects of life- with the condition that the religion takes the position of precedence, acting as the foundation, and everything else follows this and is defined and structured by the religion.

The branches of knowledge are of two types: Beneficial areas of knowledge which assist people in becoming righteous, to develop good character, to correct ones beliefs, and through which righteous actions and deeds result and are produced. These are the sciences of the Sharee'ah, and what is related to and assists it from areas of knowledge such as the sciences of the Arabic language.

The second type: the branches of knowledge whose goal is neither the development of righteous character nor the correction of one's beliefs and deeds. Rather, what is intended through them is simply a worldly benefit, such as manufacturing from the various commercial industries. These vary in estimation of their value, depending on the worldly benefit they produce. So if a general good is intended through them which is connected to the strengthening of faith and the religion, then these worldly sciences actually become sciences of the religion. Yet if one's involvement with them is not intended to generally benefit the religion then they become solely areas of knowledge related to the worldly affairs, with no noble goals attached to them. Rather, their goal is only the lowly and deficient passing life of this world, and they may potentially harm the people involved with it from two directions:

First: It becomes the reason for their worldly distress, their actual ruin, and being made examples of, as is often witnessed in these times. Such that it becomes from the most harmful examples of knowledge which has been newly invented, as are the new devices and dangerous weapons which are a tremendous evil upon their creators and upon all others.

Secondly: Those involved with this knowledge become people of arrogance, pride, and self amazement due to their worldly knowledge; as this goal of achieving renown and prominence becomes the intended objective of every effort, so that they show disdain and contempt for all others except themselves. So much so, that when the knowledge of the Messengers is brought to them, and it is clearly beneficial knowledge, they reject it and are arrogant towards it, being only pleased with their physical sciences by which they have become distinguished among the people. Indeed, these people conform to what is found in the statement of the Most High, ❰ *Then when their Messengers came to them with clear proofs, they were glad and proud with that which they had of the knowledge of worldly matters: And that at which they used to mock, surrounded them i.e. the punishment.* ❱-(Surah Ghaafar: 83). So we seek refuge in Allaah from knowledge which does not benefit.

**(15) THE EMINENT GUIDING SCHOLAR SAALEH IBN FAUZAAN, MAY ALLAAH PRESERVE HIM, FROM 'AN EXPLANATION OF THE MISTAKES OF SOME WRITERS': PAGES 10-12**

### *The Categories of Knowledge and the Rulings Regarding Them Knowledge is of Two Categories: Beneficial Knowledge and Harmful Knowledge*

Beneficial knowledge is itself divided into two categories. First is that knowledge which is tremendous in its benefit, as it benefits in this world and continues to benefit in the Hereafter. This is the religious Sharee'ah knowledge. Second is that which is limited and restricted to matters related to the life of this world, such as learning the process of manufacturing goods. It is a type of knowledge related specifically to worldly affairs.

And Sharee'ah knowledge is further divided into two types: Firstly, knowledge of how to worship Allaah alone without associating anything with Him in that worship, which is the foundation. Secondly, the knowledge which springs or comes from this foundation, and it is the correct understanding of how to implement and practice the religion and everything related to it.

As for harmful knowledge, these are subjects such as knowledge of magic and of astrology, which is knowledge of prediction of the future and fortunes. Sheikh al-Islaam Ibn Taymeeyah mentioned that Yahya Ibn Umair stated:

"*The branches of knowledge are five:*

*1. First is that knowledge which is the life of the religion, this is the knowledge of tawheed, meaning the worship of Allaah alone without associates or partners.*

*2. Secondly, there is that knowledge which nourishes the religion, this is the knowledge of reminding one of the meanings and the understanding of the Qur'aan and hadeeth narrations.*

*3. Third, there is that knowledge which is a medicine and healing for the religion, this is for situations that come upon the worshipper where he will need to turn to someone to help him*

*4. Fourthly as was said by Ibn Mas'ood, "There is knowledge which sickens the religion and that is innovated speech.*

*5. And there is knowledge in which there is the destruction of the religion and that is the knowledge of magic and what is similar to it.'*

### The Ruling of Learning these Various Branches

1. The ruling regarding the acquisition of Sharee'ah knowledge is divided into two types: that which is an individual obligation and that which is a collective obligation. As for that which is an individual obligation to learn, it is the knowledge which no one should be ignorant of and without which one cannot properly practice his religion. This includes matters such as the knowledge of worshiping Allaah alone and encompasses understanding the right of Allaah over His worshipers to worship Him alone without partners, and what it is necessary to affirm regarding His Names and Attributes, as well as the understanding of those matters which we must declare Him free of from defects and deficiencies.

Similarly, learning the rulings of how to perform the acts of worship properly, without which one's worship will not be correct, and from these are the salaat- the ritual prayer, zakaat, the fasting of Ramadhaan, and the obligatory pilgrimage. That which is a collective obligation to learn includes those matters that go beyond this foundation, examples of which are the ruling on everyday dealings, inheritance, marriages, crimes, and other similar matters. As for the second category, if its requirements are established sufficiently by it being learned by some individuals, then any sin of neglecting that obligation is removed from the remainder of the people.

And so continuing to study and learn these areas sufficiently is from the best types of supplemental worship. Additionally, connected to religious knowledge are those subjects which will assist one in establishing the religion, such as the knowledge of Arabic grammar, Arabic language, history, and mathematics.

2. As for the learning of worldly knowledge, such as knowledge of manufacturing, then it is legislated to learn whatever the Muslims have a need for. If they do not have a need for this knowledge, then learning it is a neutral matter upon the condition that it does not compete with or displace any areas of Sharee'ah knowledge. Additionally, it can not be training or instruction in the manufacture of prohibited products such as musical instruments, products with forbidden images, knowledge related to the production of music, and so forth.

3. As for harmful knowledge, then it is forbidden to learn it. Indeed, it may be an act of disbelief, such as the learning of magic. As Allaah the Exalted says, ❴*...but the Shayaateen (devils) disbelieved, teaching men magic*❵-(Surah al-Baqarah:102)

**(16) THE EMINENT GUIDING SCHOLAR SAALEH IBN FAUZAAN, MAY ALLAAH PRESERVE HIM, FROM 'A SELECTION OF ISLAMIC RULINGS': VOL.I, PAGE 320**

*Question: Certainly in these days many associate themselves with calling to Allaah, making it necessary that we know who are truly the recognized people of knowledge; those who are in fact engaged in guiding the Muslim Ummah and its youth upon the true and proper way. Therefore, who are those scholars that you advise the youth to strive to benefit from, to follow and hold to their regular lessons and audio tapes, and to take knowledge from them, and who are those who we should refer to in significant issues, any dilemmas or difficulties that occur, and during times of tribulation and confusion?*

Answer: The endeavor of calling to Allaah is a matter which is indeed necessary and required, as the religion was established upon calling to it and striving in Allaah's path after the obtaining beneficial knowledge. Allaah says, ❨*Except those who believe and do righteous deeds, then they shall have a reward without end.*❩-(Surah at-Tin: 6). Here what is meant by '*believe*' is the knowledge of Allaah, the Most Perfect, the Most High, His names and attributes, and His worship. Likewise, righteous actions are considered a branch of beneficial knowledge, as it is required that actions be based upon knowledge.

So calling to Allaah, enjoining good, and advising and spreading advice and good counsel between the Muslims are all desired matters. However, not everyone is suitable for carrying out these duties. They cannot be carried out properly except by the people of knowledge and by the people possessing a properly developed perspective, because these are significant and important affairs. They are not actually established except by the one who is qualified to do so.

Truly, from the trials of our time is that the door of undertaking the call to Allaah has been flung wide open, such that anyone and everyone enters into it. Then these individuals become known for "calling' and are recognized, even if they are ignorant and not qualified for the endeavor of calling to Allaah. They corrupt more than they rectify, and being enthusiastic, they enter into various affairs hastily and with recklessness. From such actions more harm is produced than good, until the harm is even greater than that which they wished to rectify.

Indeed, perhaps a person becomes someone who is known for and associated with calling to Allaah, and actually he has other aims and objectives he wishes to achieve- so he calls to them indirectly and wants to reach them at the expense of the call to Allaah. He ends up causing confusion in the minds of the youth, all of this being done in the name of calling to Allaah and the claim of having concern for the religion. Yet it is likely that their true goal was different than this result, such as perhaps seeking to have the youth to turn away and separate themselves from their society or from their rulers or from their scholars.

But they come forward apparently from the direction of "giving advice' and through the path of "calling to Allaah', just as is the case and situation of the hypocrites of this Ummah; those whom clearly desire evil for the people yet bring it forth in the form of a supposed good.

I will make an analogy for you with the example of those people who were connected to what is known as 'Masjid Dhiraar' or the 'masjid of harm' in the time of the Messenger of Allaah, may Allaah's praise and salutations of upon him. Certain individuals built a masjid which outwardly and apparently was a righteous deed. Then they invited the Prophet, may Allaah's praise and salutations be upon him, to pray within it so that the people would afterwards wish to come to this masjid and be pleased with it.

However Allaah knew the unstated intentions of the people who built this masjid and that they actually wanted through this endeavor of theirs to harm the Muslims and to harm Masjid Qubaa, the first masjid established upon the fear of Allaah, and that they wished to split the unity of the Muslims. For that reason Allaah exposed to the Messenger of Allaah their scheme and plan.

So then the following statement of the Exalted was revealed: ❮*And as for those who put up a masjid by way of harming the Muslims and disbelief, to disunite the believers, and as an outpost for those who fought against Allaah and His Messenger aforetime, they will indeed swear that their intention is nothing but good. Allaah bears witness that they are certainly liars. Never stand you therein. Verily, the masjid whose foundation was laid from the first day on piety is more worthy that you stand therein (to pray). In it are men who love to clean and to purify themselves. And Allaah loves those who make themselves clean and pure.*❯-(Surah Tawbah:107-108)

This tremendous account clarifies to us that not every effort which outwardly seems good and appears to be a righteous endeavor actually is. Indeed, perhaps the goals of those behind this endeavor is in fact the opposite of its apparent aim.

Consequently, it is clear that among those who associate themselves with calling to Allaah today are some who actually misguide others. They intend to cause the youth to go astray, they desire to turn the people away from the true religion, and split the unity of the Muslims, to bring down upon them trials and tribulations. And Allaah the Most Perfect, the Most High warned us from these individuals, saying, ❮*Had they marched out with you, they would have added to your efforts nothing except disorder, and they would have hurried about in your midst spreading corruption and sowing sedition among you, and there are some among you who would have listened to them. And Allaah is the All-Knower of the wrongdoers.*❯-(Surah Tawbah:47).

Therefore what is to be given true consideration is not the mere affiliation to the efforts or endeavors of calling to Allaah or simply one's outward appearance. Rather, what should be taken into account is the reality and what is actually produced and results from these affairs.

It is required that you examine all those individuals who affiliate and attach themselves to the affair of calling to Allaah. Where did they study? Where did they take their knowledge? What is their origin or initial development? What are their beliefs?

Next, look at their deeds and actions and their effect upon the people. What good do they produce? Do the results of their work and endeavors bring about rectification and correction of affairs? It is obligatory to carefully study their condition before one is simply captivated by their eloquent statements and their outer appearances. This is an essential matter that must be undertaken. Especially in this age and time, when there are many individuals who are actually only callers to trial and tribulation.

Certainly, the Prophet, may Allaah's praise and salutations be upon him, described the callers to tribulation as people who would have our familiar and recognized appearance and outward characteristics, as well as speaking with statements and speech that we recognize. And from the hadeeth of Hudhaifah Ibn al-Yamaan, may Allaah be pleased with him, the Prophet, may Allaah's praise and salutations be upon him, when he was asked about the trials said, {*...people who will invite others to the doors of Hell, and whoever accepts their invitation to it will be thrown into it by them.*} [21]

Take note; he explicitly called them and labelled them as "inviters" or "callers"! So it is upon us to take heed of this, and not simply consider as part of the endeavor of calling to Allaah anyone and everyone, or to blindly accept every person who simply says "*I call to Allaah*", or "*This group calls to Allaah.*"

What is necessary is that one look carefully into the reality of the matter, and it is necessary to investigate the true state of these individuals as well as these groups and organizations. As Allaah the Most Perfect, the Most High, has limited and defined what is calling to Allaah by what calls to the path of Allaah; the Exalted said, ❴ *Say, this is my way; I invite unto Allaah...* ❵-(Surah Yusuf:108)

This verse following clearly indicates that they are indeed people who call to other than Allaah. Allaah, the Most High, has informed us that the disbelievers invite us to the Fire, saying, ❴*And do not marry women who commit shirk until they believe. And indeed a slave woman who believes is better than a free woman who commits shirk, even though she pleases you. And give not your daughters in marriage to those who associate others in worship with Allaah, till they believe in Allaah alone and verily, a believing slave is better than a free man who associates others with Allaah, even though he pleases you. Those who associate others in worship with Allaah invite you to the Fire, but Allaah invites you to Paradise and forgiveness by His Leave...* ❵-(Surah al-Baqarah:221)

As Sheikh al-Islaam Muhammad Ibn 'Abdul-Wahhab, may Allaah have mercy upon him, said regarding the following verse, ❴*This is my way; I invite unto Allaah...*❵-(Surah Yusuf:108): "*It refers to purity of intention, as many of the people actually call to themselves, and do not truly invite to Allaah, the Most High, The Most Exalted.*"

---

[21] Narrated in Saheeh al-Bukhaaree: 7084/ Saheeh Muslim: 1847/ & Sunan Ibn Maajah: 3979/- from the hadeeth of Hudhaifah Ibn Yamaan. Declared authentic by Sheikh al-Albaanee in Silsilatul-Hadeeth Saheehah: 2739, and in his verification of Mishkat al-Masabeeh: 3358

**(17) THE EMINENT GUIDING SCHOLAR SAALEH IBN FAUZAAN, MAY ALLAAH PRESERVE HIM, EXCERPTED FROM 'BENEFICIAL ANSWERS TO QUESTIONS ON NEW METHODOLOGIES': PAGE 243**

*Question: What are the Sharee'ah guidelines which enable the Muslim to preserve his adherence to Islaam, to hold closely to the methodology of the first three generations of believers such that he avoids straying from it, and protect him from being influenced by foreign ideologies of misguidance?*

Answer:    Those Sharee'ah guidelines should be understood by way of all the statements which have proceeded this question. That being: firstly, that an individual always refers back to the people of knowledge and insight in the religion; learning from them and seeking their assessment and opinion regarding ideas and concepts he may have wandering in his mind which may eventually lead to some harm.

Secondly: To carefully consider matters, avoiding hastiness, and to avoid rashness in judging people. Instead, what is required upon you is verification. Allaah the Exalted says, *Oh you who believe! If a rebellious evil person comes to you with a news, verify it, lest you harm people in ignorance, and afterwards you become regretful to what you have done.* -(Surah al-Hujuraat:6) And Allaah, the Most Perfect, the Most High says, *Oh you who believe! When you go to fight in the cause of Allaah, verify the truth, and say not to anyone who greets you by embracing Islaam: "You are not a believer'; seeking the passing goods of the worldly life. There are much more profits and bounties with Allaah. Even as he is now, so were you yourselves before till Allaah conferred on you His Favors, therefore, be cautious in discrimination. Allaah is Ever Well Aware of what you do.* -(Surah an-Nisa':94). We explain this as meaning: verify that which you are informed of by others.

Once you have verified a situation, then approach the matter in a way which ensures its rectification, not in ways that are harsh and severe, or in ways which may cause further disorder or increase confusion. The Prophet, may Allaah's praise and salutations be upon him, said, *{Facilitate things for people, and do not make it hard for them.}* [22]. So in all circumstances, these matters are resolved through wisdom and careful consideration. They are not rectified by anyone and everyone placing themselves into the matter or situation while not having the proper way of dealing with and approaching them.

---

[22]   Narrated in Saheeh al-Bukhaaree: 6124/ Saheeh Muslim: 1732/ Sunan Abu Dawud: 4835/ & Musnad Ahmad: 19200/- from the hadeeth of Abu Musa al-'Asha'ree. And in Saheeh al-Bukhaaree: 69/ Saheeh Muslim: 1734/ 'Abad al-Mufrad: 488/ Musnad Ahmad: 11924, 12764/ -from the hadeeth of 'Anas Ibn Maalik, Declared authentic by Sheikh al-Albaanee in Silsilatul-Hadeeth Saheehah: 712, 992, 1375, Mishkat al-Masaabeh: 3722, & Saheeh al-Jaame'a' as-Sagheer: 35, 246, 8086, 8087. He also said, *{You have been sent to make things easy and not to make them difficult}* - as narrated in Saheeh al-Bukhaaree: 220, 6128/ Sunan Abu Dawud: 380/ Sunan at-Tirmidhee: 148/ Sunan an-Nasaa'ee: 56, 330/ Musnad Ahmad: 7214, 7740- from the hadeeth of Abu Hurairah  Declared authentic by Sheikh al-Albaanee his verification of those three Sunan collections (Abu Dawud, an-Nasaa'e, at-Tirmidhee), Saheeh at-Targheeb wa at-Tarheeb: 2673, Mishkat al-Masaabeh: 491, & Saheeh al-Jaamea' as-Sagheer: 2350. Additionally, he said to some of the noblest of his Companions, *{Some of you make people dislike good deeds. So whoever among you leads the people in prayer should shorten it because among them are the weak, the old and the needy.}*- as narrated in Saheeh al-Bukhaaree: 702, 704, 6110, 7159/ Saheeh Muslim: 466/ Sunan Ibn Maajah: 984/ Musnad Ahmad: 16617/ & Sunan ad-Daaramee: 1259- from the hadeeth of Abu Mas'ood 'Uqbah Ibn 'Amr al-'Ansaaree d, Declared authentic by Sheikh al-Albaanee in Mishkat al-Masaabeh as '*agreed upon*' & in Saheeh al-Jaamea' as-Sagheer: 7868.

Thirdly: From these guidelines is that a person should strive in gaining and increasing in knowledge by sitting with the people of knowledge and listening to their views, by reading the books of our righteous predecessors, and by reading the biographies of the scholars and the those who corrected and rectified the affairs of this Ummah. How did they rectify matters? How did they encourage and remind the people? How did they enjoin the good and prevent wrong doing? How did they judge and weigh matters?

All of this is recorded in their biographies and life histories, as well as in the narrations and historical accounts of those who came before us of the people of goodness, the people of uprightness and truthfulness. Allaah, the Most Exalted, says, ❈ *Indeed in their stories, there is a lesson for men of understanding.*❈-(Surah Yusuf:111)

Consider that the Muslim individual is but one person from within the Muslim Ummah; however, the Muslim Ummah is every Muslim from the emergence of Islaam until the establishment of the Hour of Judgment. This is the entire Ummah. So the Muslim must refer to our righteous predecessors from the first generations and their narrations and accounts of their circumstances in order to see how they rectified their affairs, and see their guidance in such matters, so that he follows and proceeds upon their path and example. Do not turn towards the statements of those who are hasty, or the ignorant assertions of those individuals who lack sound judgment who incite and merely stir up the people heedlessly.

Today, many writings, lectures, and articles stem from ignorance of the Sharee'ah issues and only inflame the people's emotions. They direct and encourage the people towards matters which neither Allaah nor His Messenger, may Allaah's praise and salutations be upon him, commanded them. Even if this originates from a good or sincere intention, what is given true consideration of worth and significance is that which actually stands as correct and true; with the truth always being that which agrees with the Book of Allaah and the Sunnah, as understood by the first generations of Muslims. As the people in general, except for the Messenger of Allaah, may Allaah's praise and salutations be upon him, sometimes they are wrong and sometimes they are correct. Therefore, accept what is correct from them and abandon every mistake or error.

(18) The Eminent Guiding Scholar Muhammad Naasiruddeen al-Albaanee, may Allaah have mercy upon him, from audio lecture no. 382 of the 'Guidance and Light' Audio Tape Series

*Question: May Allaah reward you with good. In Imaam Shaatibee's book 'al-Muwaafiqaat' he has the following statement. He says, "The ruling given by the scholar in relation to the common person who is aware of it, is like or has the similar standing of the evidence which is known to the scholar who is capable of deriving independent rulings from the sources, meaning it must be followed.' So we need a clarification of this statement. Is the common person sinning if he deliberately differs from the ruling given to him by a leading scholar, just as it is known that a scholar is considered to have transgressed if he contradicts the clear evidence from the sources which he is aware of?*

Answer: Undoubtedly, I say the same thing as Imaam ash-Shaatibee. There is no doubt that the common person who opposes the ruling of the scholar who issues a ruling for him without a valid excuse from the Sharee'ah, then firstly he is following or adhering to his desires, and secondly he contradicts what is required and obligated from the statement of our Lord the Blessed and the Most High, ❨*Ask the people of knowledge if you do not know*❩-(Surah an-Nahl:43). Our Lord, the Blessed and the Most High, has clearly commanded the general people in this verse to ask the people of knowledge. So do you think that anyone who has been given understanding by His Lord, the Blessed and the Most High, of what He has commanded in this verse: ❨*Ask the people of knowledge if you do not know*❩-(Surah an-Nahl:43) can then say that what is intended is that after a common person asks a scholar for a ruling, he is then free to chose to follow or act upon what the scholar directed him to or free if he wishes to not follow or act upon it?!!

Is there anyone who holds such an understanding or is the correct understanding of the verse ❨*Ask the people of knowledge if you do not know*❩-(Surah an-Nahl:43) that one must act upon and comply with the rulings which the people of knowledge give you? Is there anyone who differs that indeed this is correct understanding of this verse? Certainly, this is its correct and proper meaning.

If the common person asks a scholar and he gives him a ruling, then it is obligatory up on him to comply and act upon this ruling, except for in the case where he has some significant doubt about the accuracy of the ruling. And this is something which happens often, especially in these later times, when those who are taken as people of knowledge are often actually people of ignorance as was indicated would occur by the Prophet, may Allaah's praise and salutations be upon him, in his saying as found in the hadeeth of 'Abdullah Ibn 'Umar Ibn al-'Aas, which is found in both the collections of Imaam Bukharee and Imaam Muslim when he says: The Messenger of Allaah, may Allaah's praise and salutation be upon him and his household, said,

*{Verily, Allah does not take away knowledge from people directly; rather, he takes away the scholars and consequently takes away (knowledge) along with them and leaves amongst persons the ignorant, as their leaders who deliver religious verdicts without knowledge and themselves go astray and lead others astray.}* [23].

So if the common person is tested and put to the trial by asking an individual he believes is a scholar, yet that individual gives him a questionable ruling, similar to the ruling given by Tantaawee that it is permissible to save your money in a saving account of a bank. If a common person is put to trial through the likes of this questionable ruling which was issued by this Egyptian, meaning Tantaawee, and he then has doubts about the validity of the ruling; then in this case he should not act upon it until he has asked several other people to see if they have knowledge of other statements from the scholars, and he is personally satisfied and his heart is comfortable that a specific ruling is indeed sound; then it is obligatory to act according to that ruling he is confident is sound.

But as for the situation where he does not have any doubts or reservations about what he is informed of in a ruling from a scholar, then the situation is what we have previously stated of what the mentioned verse: ❈*Ask the people of knowledge if you do not know* ❈-(Surah an-Nahl:43) intends and correctly means. Thus, this understanding indicates to us the validity and soundness of that significant statement made by Abu Ishaaq ash-Shaatibee, that the ruling given- in relation to the common person- is like the evidence presented to other individuals who are from the people of knowledge. Otherwise the deen simply becomes a situation of chaos, and likewise becomes simply the following of one's desires. And there would be no true benefit in statements of Allaah the Exalted, such as ❈*Ask the people of knowledge if you do not know*❈-(Surah an-Nahl:43).

Therefore I would like to take this opportunity to direct our attention toward the way of some of our brothers, meaning those who stand upon our same methodology and path of acting upon the Book of our Lord and the Sunnah of our Prophet and the way of the first three righteous generations, who go to extremes when they make it obligatory upon all the various general Muslims, who are both incapable and lack this ability; they make it obligatory upon the common Muslims to know the evidence of every matter and issue. They even claim that it is not permissible for someone, meaning every single Muslim, to accept a ruling of the scholar regarding what is permissible, prohibited, or obligatory, except that it is put forth along with its relevant evidences.

---

[23]  Narrated in Saheeh al-Bukhaaree: 100, 7307/ Saheeh Muslim: 4829 / Sunan at-Tirmidhee:  2576/ Sunan Ibn Maajah: 51/ Musnad Of Ahmad: 6222, 6498, 6602/ & Sunan ad-Daaramee: 239 from the hadeeth of 'Abdullah Ibn 'Umar Ibn al-'Aas.

This is going to extremes and exceeding what is correct by making obligatory upon the common people that which has not been made obligatory for them. And from here we come to a point of having to turn our attention to the necessity of stating that important condition or qualification which has always being the focus of our call, that it is not sufficient to only call to the Book of Allaah and to the Sunnah of the Messenger of Allaah alone. We must join and connect along with that the condition "*according to the way and methodology of the righteous predecessors from the first three generations.*" This is because their methodology will clarify for us a significant number of matters and issues which are not clear to the majority of the people of knowledge, especially the students of knowledge. And as such this especially applies to those people below the students of knowledge even more so. So this issue should be approached from this perspective.

Indeed, what is found by the one who researches the historical narrations from the first three generations of Muslims in those instances- for example when someone who requires a ruling would ask for one from 'Abdullah Ibn 'Umar or 'Abdullah Ibn Mas'ood or from someone else who was from the Companions of the Messenger of Allaah, may Allaah praise and salutations be upon him. In these cases did the scholar give the ruling according to his position and efforts of independently reasoning and then say "*...and its evidence it such and such.?*"

No, although this does sometimes occur. They did not always adhere to this practice. Due to this we understand that, as this reality from them is transmitted to us in a way that there is no doubt concerning, that it is not from the methodology of the first three generations to be required to give rulings to the general people in that way.

Take, for example, a case related to the inheritance which is to be divided between the remaining inheritors. They would say so and so receives a third and so and so receives a fourth and so on. I swear by Allaah, I confess that I personally am not able to fully grasp even until today, the various evidences regarding these various detailed divisions- so how about the common people from among the Muslims, who are clearly not capable of comprehending the evidences of those detailed divisions?!

But the first generations did not act or follow this extreme way, meaning that every ruling given by every scholar who issues rulings must be accompanied by his evidence. And that it is upon every individual who asks the scholars regarding a matter that he requests the specific evidence for everything he desires a ruling about. This is the point that I wanted to direct your attention to.

And I think that now we should stop for a while, because I see that our brothers have begun to get drowsy, and are rubbing their eyes. So we will move on to other subjects, especially since the forehead of our companion seems to be sweating. So we will break for a while.

*The questioner: May Allaah reward you with good, perhaps we can pray Salat al-'Isha' during this break?*

Sheikh al-Albaanee, may Allaah have mercy upon him: This is the best thing for us, please go ahead and call the adhaan.

(19) The Eminent Guiding Scholar Muhammad Ibn Saaleh al-'Utheimeen, may Allaah have mercy upon him- Ruling from the Radio Program: 'Nur 'Alaa ad-Darb'

*Question: Indeed, Allaah hears our supplications, may Allaah bless you. A listener from Pakistan says, "Esteemed Sheikh, please inform us about the concept of 'ijtihaad', and the concept of 'taqleed'. What is meant by 'taqleed' and what is meant by 'ijtihaad'? Was the practice of 'taqleed' present in the age of the Companions and the generation after them, that of the Successors to the Companions? Did the some of them make 'taqleed' of others from among them in Sharee'ah rulings or not?'*

Answer: As for the meaning of 'ijtihaad', it is putting forth the effort required to independently arrive at the correct Sharee'ah ruling directly from the Sharee'ah evidences found in the Book and the Sunnah, as well as using consensus and correct analogy. This is what is generally known as 'ijtihaad' and it is well known that it is not proper for someone to undertake making 'ijtihaad' except for the one who is knowledgeable of the methods and proper way of doing so, as well as also possessing both sufficient knowledge and proper comprehension, such that it is possible for him to have reached the level of being able to derive the proper rulings from the evidences of the sources and what they actually indicate.

As for 'taqleed', it means to accept the statement or ruling of a scholar who has independently derived a Sharee'ah ruling, without you having personal knowledge of its evidences. Rather you blindly accept that from him due to your holding his knowledge-based statements as being reliable. And 'taqleed' in reality was something which occurred in the time of the Companions of the Messenger of Allaah, may Allaah be pleased them all. As indeed Allaah said, ❊*Ask the people of knowledge if you do not know* ❊-(Surah an-Nahl:43).

There is no doubt that among the people in the age of the Companions of the Messenger of Allaah, may Allaah be pleased them all, up until this very age that we live in- there were and are those individuals who do not have the ability to reach the proper rulings by themselves, due to their ignorance, shortcomings, and being occupied with various affairs. Such an individual simply has to ask one of the people of knowledge about a matter. Moreover, this asking the people of knowledge requires that he accept what they inform him of regarding the ruling in such and such a matter. And this accepting of a ruling by him from a scholar is clearly blind following.

Therefore based upon this we say that the one who does not have the necessary knowledge and understanding needed to arrive at the truth of a Sharee'ah ruling himself, then it is possible to reach the needed Sharee'ah ruling by blindly following someone else who is from those people of knowledge whom he has been commanded to ask, since he is not a scholar himself.

However, if it is asked by the common person "*Who then, should I blindly follow?*" then the response is that it is obligatory that you blindly follow the one whose positions and rulings you believe are closest to the truth. The people of knowledge are like doctors; indeed they are the doctors of people's hearts. Just as if one of us were to become physically sick, and there are within our land many different doctors; then he would choose the one who is the most skillful and knowledgeable in the field of medicine, its various treatments, and the remedies used. Likewise, it is not sensible that someone would knowingly go to a less qualified doctor, when there was another available to him who is more qualified and experienced than the first, except if forced to do so by necessity.

In the same way, concerning the matter of blind following, one should select the scholar one sees as being closest to the truth in his statements and rulings, due to him being more knowledgeable of the Sharee'ah, and having more fear of Allaah the Most High and the Most Exalted. Then in this way you stand as having properly complied with and obeyed the command of Allaah, the Exalted in His statement *Ask the people of knowledge if you do not know* -(Surah an-Nahl:43).

(20) The Eminent Guiding Scholar Saaleh ibn 'Abdul- 'Azeez Aal-Sheikh, may Allaah preserve him, in, 'From the Fruits of Knowledge' Question 3

*Question: What is intended by the statements of the scholars of the fundamentals of the religion: "The general person should blindly follow the people of knowledge." Is the meaning of this that it is obligatory upon the general Muslim to follow one scholar in every one of his rulings, or does it mean something else? I hope for a clarification of this.*

Answer:      The meaning of 'taqleed' is blind acceptance and following of a statement by someone, when it is not considered one of the fundamental sources of the religion. It is acceptable by the agreement of the people of knowledge in its place with certain conditions. From these is firstly, the situation of the general person who has a question, but being a general person he does not understand the evidences nor the various derived rulings. Therefore it is obligatory for him to ask, as the Most Exalted and most High said, *Ask the people of knowledge if you do not know* -(Surah an-Nahl:43). So if he does not know the ruling of Allaah, Most Exalted and Most High, in a certain matter, then it is an obligation upon him to ask regarding it. And the general people are not all of the same type or description; rather, they are of different levels. One might be a student of knowledge, but is considered from the general people in regard to certain issues, as he does not know the rulings of these issues. So he must ask the people of knowledge regarding those and then act upon the rulings they guide him to in those issues.

As for the common person when asking, he should ask one of the people of knowledge whom he knows is reliable in his knowledge and religion. He should search in his land and ask others about who has the most knowledge and understanding, or he may find someone who he knows. Such that he says to himself, "*I am confident of this scholar's knowledge and practice of the religion.*" Then he should ask him whatever is necessary and act upon his advice. But it is not a fundamental concern nor required, meaning it is not an obligation upon the scholar, that he mention the evidence of his answer to the common person who asks him.  This is the way of giving rulings proceeded upon by the Companions, may Allaah be pleased with them. They issued rulings without always presenting the related evidence. Similarly, this way is reported from the practice of the leading scholars of Islaam, such as Imaam Maalik in his body of rulings, and Imaam Shaafa'ee in different issues, and Imaam Ahmad in various issues narrated from him. They gave rulings without mentioning the evidence; and this is something clear. Because it is an obligation to ask and inquire, but Allaah, The Most Exalted the Most High, did not make obligatory upon the people of knowledge to present the evidence, meaning to make clear the evidence to the one taking the ruling from him.

The second category of those who can blindly follow are the scholar and the student of knowledge; meaning that they accept the statement of one of the scholars without explicit evidence. If one needs to utilize such a statement because he does not have the time to investigate independently what the correct understanding in a specific issue is, and he is assured of this scholar's knowledge and his practice of the religion, then it is permissible to blindly follow him. So by agreement of the scholars, it is acceptable due to a situation where there is lack of time. Such as someone saying, *"Do I pray now or not pray? What should I do?"* So he asks one of the students of knowledge or a scholar who says to him: *"Pray now."* Then it is permissible upon him to blindly follow in this situation because of the absence of time to investigate, whether the one asked is a scholar or a student of knowledge. And the scholar can blindly follow the one who is more knowledgeable than him. This occurs frequently among the scholars of Islaam. Imaam Shaafa'ee would blindly follow Imaam Maalik in certain issues and then later change his stance, and Imaam Ahmad would blindly follow Imaam Shaafa'ee in a certain issue and than later change his position, and so on, as is well-known.

So if there is a situation where one's time is restricted but it is necessary for him to act, then he should not leave the matter to his own desires- that which he is inclined to do, or that he finds himself leaning towards without having the guiding words from a scholar. This includes an individual referring to what he has memorized from the knowledge based texts which explain how to practice the religion; such as what one might have memorized from *((Zaad al-Mustaqna')07-01)* and so forth.

Or one knows for a fact that a specific scholar has given a ruling in the issue that is being asked about, whether this is in an issue of purchasing, companionship, establishment of rights, or prayer. He is aware of the ruling but does not know from what evidence it is derived. Or perhaps one only remembers a scholar's statement in a knowledge-based text regarding the issue. Then one acts according to this recollection due to the condition of the limited time to verify and confirm the statement of the scholar because he has limited time available to research and what is correct in this issue, and related matters. So regarding the issue of blind following and the blind following of the common person, then the levels of independent investigation have several distinctions, and the levels among the common people vary greatly, so its discussion requires distinguishing between the people. This is presented to give a basic explanation, as discussing the details requires a considerable amount of time.

**(21) The Eminent Guiding Scholar 'Abdur-Rahman Ibn Naasir as-Sa'adee, may Allaah have mercy upon him, in 'A Delightful Collection of Benefits and the Pursuing the Desired Distinctions': Benefit III**

*I was asked by one of the people of knowledge, "What is my obligation in regard to my behavior with the scholars of Najd? Do they have distinctive merit that is greater than the rest of the believers?"*

So I said to the questioner, "Why did you restrict the scope of your question? Why didn't you ask about the scholars of the entire kingdom of Saudi Arabia? Or even ask about the scholars of all the various lands of the world?"

*The questioner replied, "What you have said is not less than what I intended, but I had hoped to lessen what was required from you in response. Additionally, these scholars are those who in general we know the most about. Similarly, if an answer is given regarding them, then the proper way to be taken with all other scholars is the same of the way required for them. Moreover, it is not required that questions be all-inclusive in nature, rather many responses from detailed or specific questions are more clarifying and more enlightening than answers from those which are comprehensive or all-inclusive."*

Thus when I understood his intent, or rather when I am made to understand what was intended I replied:

"The response to this, and we ask Him for support and from Him is all success, is: Oh my brother, know that what is obligatory upon you is to support, have allegiance to, and love all of the scholars of Najd, and to seek closeness to Allaah through this. In addition, one must recognize their distinction over the majority of the believers, because of what Allaah distinguished them with of knowledge, faith in Him, efforts of teaching, calling to Allaah, and establishing many of those necessary collective obligations which they have undertaken on behalf of all of the Muslims. Indeed this is a significant number of reasons. You must focus upon these aspects of their distinction and characteristics of merit placing them before your eyes; while knowing along with this that they, like the rest of the people, are human and there will be experienced from them those mistakes which one experiences from the rest of humanity. Place whatever you come to know of from them that could be correctly criticized, even though in most cases this criticism is not valid, place that in comparison to all that which comes from them of clear goodness and benefit and it will make those other things of little consequence. Make every effort to alleviate or remedy anything you may hold within yourself against one of them, with that which would cure and heal it from love for them, their praise, and supplications for them, seeking in your efforts to come closer to Allaah, establishing that which is obligatory regarding this, and striving towards the highest possible degree of completeness in it.

Know, all praise is due to Allaah, that all of these scholars are upon the methodology of the righteous predecessors of the first three generations of Muslims, standing in agreement upon what is affirmed by Allaah and His Messenger from the attributes of Allaah, the Exalted and Most High, without exception, understanding them in a manner that is appropriate and befits His transcendence and majesty; Similarly, they negate everything which Allaah and His Messenger negated from Allaah in terms of deficiencies, equals, associates, and comparisons. These scholars also stand in agreement upon the essential issue of inviting towards the two fundamental affirmations of bearing witness sincerely to Allaah's absolute right to be worshiped alone sincerely, as well as the true following of His final Messenger sincerely.

If there occurs a mistake in some issues from one of these scholars, yet he believes and affirms this essential foundation of faith, then his mistake will be forgiven by Allaah, and his error is overlooked as he has striven to reach the correct conclusion. He stands as someone whom we hold a good opinion and impression of. Rather, his general acknowledged state of soundness upon knowledge is something well-known and established with us. They are those who correctly believe that which has been mentioned sincerely with their hearts, invite toward it, and acknowledge its truth, while denouncing and criticizing all those who are deniers and rejectors of this, just as they denounce and criticize all those who are deniers of the affirmation of Allaah's sole right to be submitted to, obeyed, and worshiped. Additionally, all of them stand in agreement that an act of intentionally and knowingly directing any action from the different categories of worship towards other than Allaah, regardless of which aspect of creation it is directed towards- (whoever does this) is considered a disbeliever, associating partners to Allaah. This is the boundary or limit of the major category of association of others with Allaah in worship which takes one outside the boundaries of Islaam.

So if you understand what has been mentioned to you regarding these scholars, and yet you still have some doubts regarding this, then ask one of those knowledgeable people who are not from those who are motivated by vain desires or a desire for material wealth. Those who understand that it is obligatory upon them to distinguish these scholars with their support, love, praise, as well as the spreading their merits, suppressing those who oppose them, and the giving of advice to the ones who have suspicions regarding them which conflict with what we have mentioned regarding them. Make this your way, the path which you yourself proceed upon, as it is the Straight Path that is in agreement with the Book of Allaah and the Sunnah as well as the principles and foundations of the Sharee'ah.

Additionally, know that in this land of Najd there are four individuals from the people of knowledge who are responsible for its religious affairs, who are distinguished over others. They are distinguished regarding their knowledge, efforts of teaching and calling, and general benefit to the people. And there comes from them and through their hands tremendous good and enormous benefit. So distinguish them, oh brother, as those deserving your love, acknowledge their ability, increase your supplication for them and your praise of them, and your spreading of their virtues, seeking closeness to Allaah through this. Know who they are specifically and inform others about them, and our mentioning their characteristics is more essential then mentioning their names. Joining with these four individuals is a fifth person through whom Allaah has brought blessings. And he, even if he is less than them in his degree of knowledge, he has achieved by his efforts much benefit for this religion through teaching that has not been achieved through others. Some of the areas of the kingdom show some bias regarding him; so may Allaah guide those regions and change them so that they accept the way of the predecessors of the first generations, and increase the numbers of the people of knowledge present among them. Indeed, if Allaah blesses them with knowledge, there will proceed from that tremendous good. And this fifth individual is from the stronger callers to Allaah and to His religion. As such, it is obligatory to support, assist, commend and defend him, just as is obligatory in regard to the other four as well as for other than them from the scholars of the Muslims. Furthermore, be cautious, dear brother, about hearing one of them defamed or listening to one of them being criticized except that you refute that speaker and give advice to the one saying this, explaining to them the high position and status of these scholars. Do not be deceived because many of the people abandon the implementation of this right, which is from the most clearly established rights of the Muslims. Indeed, by doing this the worshiper receives tremendous good and reward, and he brings about many aspects of both the specific and general overall benefit for the people."

This was the response which I mentioned to him. And even if the subject was that part of the country in which the question came from, and this specific time in which we answered the question, then it applies comprehensively to all of the scholars of the Muslim countries from those who are known to have knowledge and a sound practice of the religion. In addition, it encompasses all the various ages and eras, and the first and foremost of those people who are included in the following supplication: *Our Lord! Forgive us and our brothers who have preceded us in faith, and put not in our hearts any hatred against those who have believed. Our Lord! You are indeed full of kindness, the Most Merciful.*-(Surah al-Hashr:10) and His statement, *So know that none has the right to be worshipped but Allaah, and ask forgiveness for your sin, and also for the sin of believing men and believing women. And Allaah knows well your movements, and your place of rest in your homes.*-(Surah Muhammad:19) The first and the most important of those who are included within this supplication are the Muslim scholars of every time and place. Just as in regards to the descriptions of goodness and completion, the declarations about rewards, then the most worthy of those who enter into all these and those to whom they most truly apply are the people of knowledge and faith. This is because they possess the highest degree of every merit and distinction, and they are those leaders and guides toward every matter of good.

(22) The Eminent Guiding Scholar Ahmad Ibn Yahya an-Najmee, may Allaah preserve him, excerpted from 'Decisive Rulings on the Methodologies of Calling to Allaah': Vol.2, Page 18

*Question: Who are those individuals in our land of Saudi Arabia upon the call to follow the methodology of the first three generations of Islaam from whom it is befitting that we seek knowledge at their hands?*

Answer: Those scholars upon the call to the methodology of the first three generations of Muslims, who are the ones who it is proper that you listen to their lessons are such as Sheikh 'Abdul-'Azeez Ibn 'Abdullah Ibn Baaz, Sheikh Saaleh Ibn Fauzaan al-Fauzaan, Sheikh 'Abdul-'Azeez Ibn 'Abdullah Aal-Sheikh, and Sheikh 'Abdullah Ibn 'Abdur-Rahman al-Ghudyan, as well as all of the scholars of the Council of Major Scholars. Similarly, the scholars in Medina, and the scholars who it is clear that they support the truth, and stand in opposition to the people of divisive partisanship. As the endeavors of these scholars indicate that they are from those who adhere to the way of those who follow the methodology of the first generations. Therefore, it is suitable and fitting that you sit with them, listen to their lessons and audio lectures, and sit in their gatherings of knowledge. This is what is appropriate and fitting.

(23) The Eminent Guiding Scholar Muhammad Ibn 'Abdul-Wahhab al-Wasaabee, may Allaah preserve him, from our trip to Hudaydah, Yemen in the month of Shawwal in the year 1425

*I asked our sheikh for general advice, as well as to inform me of who the guiding scholars of our present time are. He answered on audio cassette:*

All praise is due to Allaah Lord of the worlds. I bear witness that there is none worthy of worship except Allaah alone, having no partners. And I bear witness that Muhammad is His worshiper and Messenger, may Allaah's praise and salutations be upon him and his family. As for what proceeds: We praise Allaah, the Most Glorified and the Most Exalted, who has favored us with following of the Book of Allaah and the Sunnah. The call of the people of the Sunnah is a call of purity and clarity. It does not have within it divisive partisanship, nor innovation in the religion, nor the following of whims and desires. The call of the people of the Sunnah is based upon the Book of Allaah, upon the Sunnah, and upon the methodology of the predecessors of the first three righteous generations. They call to the Book of Allaah and encourage people towards it. They call to the Sunnah of the Messenger of Allaah and encourage following and adhering to it. Additionally, they encourage the people to adhere to the understanding of the first three generations.

The people of the Sunnah and the Jama'ah warn the people away from innovation in the religion and from those matters which conflict with the guidance of Islam. They warn against adherence to one's desires and clinging to weak narrations and unreasonable or harmful opinions, while they encourage the gathering around and establishing closeness with the scholars upon the Book of Allaah and the Sunnah. The call of the people of the Sunnah and the Jama'ah does not legitimize having multiple groups or organizations, or secret allegiances; nor does it include the practice of rebelling against the Muslim rulers. This practice of rebelling against the Muslim rulers is from the call and way of the sect of the Khawaarij, as well as that of the sect of the Mu'tazilah. And these divisive groups and organizations are considered to be people innovating in the religion and simply pursuing their own desires. But as for the call of the people of the Sunnah, then it encourages the people to unite the voices of the Muslims, and calls them towards cooperation with the Muslim authorities upon every matter of truth, upon the guidance of the Book of Allaah and the Sunnah, and upon goodness and the fearing of Allaah. Allaah, the Most High says, ◈*Help you one another in goodness and the fearing of Allaah; but do not help one another in sin and transgression.*◈-(Surah al-Maidah:2) And narrated on the authority of Abee Ruqayyah Tameem Ibn Aws ad-Daaramee, may Allaah be pleased with him, that the Messenger of Allaah, may Allaah's praise and salutations be upon him, said, *{"The religion is giving advice and well wishing." So we said, "For whom, Messenger of Allaah?" He said, "For Allaah, His Book, His Messenger and for the leaders and the general Muslims."}* Therefore the people of the Sunnah are established upon giving advice to the general Muslims and the leaders of the Muslims, as well as upon the offering of sound guidance with wisdom and a good admonishment. As Allaah says, ◈*Invite to the Way of your Lord with wisdom and fair preaching, and argue with them in a way that is better.*◈-(Surah an-Nahl:125) Additionally, the people of the Sunnah and the Jama'ah are free from the way of elections, as well as the way of terrorist explosions and activities, and free from revolutionary methodologies and efforts adopted to overthrow the leaders and those responsible for the affairs of the Muslims. As the Messenger of Allaah, may Allaah's praise and salutations be upon him, said, *{Listen to the leader of the Muslims and carry out his legitimate commands; even if your back is flogged and your wealth is taken from you.}* [24].

The religion is giving advice and well wishing, and is not malice and gloating over the difficulties of others. It is giving advice and well wishing, not flattery and the seeking of favor. The religion is giving advice and well wishing, not treachery, deceptions, and plots against the Muslim authorities and the general Muslims. Rather, it is the giving of advice and offering of good counsel through "*Allaah has said*" and "*The Messenger of Allaah, said*" praise and salutations be upon him. As such, the people of the Sunnah and the Jama'ah do not declare the Muslims to be disbelievers, they only rightly consider as disbelievers those whose disbelief is indicated by Allaah and His Messenger according to Sharee'ah evidences. So the Muslim who correctly worships Allaah alone does not declare the Muslims as disbelievers and does not consider them disbelievers due to their committing an act which is a sin, except if the act they commit is of a type that obligates the ruling of disbelief.

---

[24]  Narrated in Saheeh Muslim: 1837/ -from the hadeeth of Hudhaifah Ibn al-Yamaan. It was declared authentic by Sheikh al-Albaanee in Silsilat al-Hadeeth as-Saheehah: 2739 where he stated, "*This tremendous hadeeth is from the signs and evidences of prophethood of the Messenger of Allaah, may Allaah's praise and salutations be upon him, and from his giving advice to his Ummah. How significant is the need of the Muslims for this guidance in order to free themselves from the division and biased partisanship towards groups which has separated their united body, split their unity, and taken away their might and power. And this division and splitting is from among the reasons for the domination of their enemies over them...*".

Additionally, they consider an act which is disbelief as an act of disbelief, but do not necessarily judge the one who does that act as being a disbeliever, until all of the conditions for the ruling of disbelief upon that person are fulfilled, and all the barriers that would prevent that ruling from being applied are lifted or removed. So they differentiate between the disbelief of the act itself and the one who commits the act, between the disbelief of the statement itself and the one who makes the statement. A statement may be disbelief or an action may be disbelief, but the one who made the statement is not a disbeliever if the conditions for that ruling upon him are not fulfilled and the barriers to that ruling are not removed or lifted from him.

The people of the Sunnah and the Jama'ah are devoted to beneficial knowledge, and the people of the Sunnah encourage the general people to seek knowledge and to gain understanding of the religion. The people of the Sunnah and the Jama'ah do not defend the people of falsehood, nor the people who practice innovations in the religion. The people of the Sunnah do not defend those who innovate in the religion such as Muhammad Suroor, 'Abdur-Rahman 'Abdul-Khaaliq, or Sayyed Qutb, and those similar to them from the people of innovations and desires. The people of the Sunnah and the Jama'ah warn against the people of innovation and desires and they do not praise and venerate the innovators. They do not praise the people of innovation and desires, nor the innovators, nor the people of division and partisanship who stand upon falsehood.

So I advise the Muslims to have fear of Allaah, the Most Glorified and the Most Exalted, and to hold firmly to the religion, and to refer back to the people of knowledge and to return and refer to the guiding major scholars, and to keep far away from division and partisanship, and to remain distant from the scheming, repulsive, hateful groups of division and partisanship. Allaah, the Most Glorified and the Most Exalted, said, *And hold fast, all of you together, to the Rope of Allaah, and be not divided among yourselves*-(Surah Aal-'Imraan:103) And the Most Perfect and the Most High, said, *And be not as those who divided and differed among themselves after the clear proofs had come to them. It is they for whom there is an awful torment. On the Day when some faces will become white and some faces will become black.*-(Surah Aal-'Imraan:105-106). So be steadfast upon the Book and the Sunnah, and be cautious concerning the people of innovations and desires. Muhammad Suroor is not to be considered from the scholars, those who are referred to for rulings or whose statements or positions are to be adopted. Indeed the correct assessment is that he is merely to be considered from the students of knowledge. And one does not refer the important and essential issues and matters to any of the students.

On the contrary, you should return to the scholars, those guiding scholars who are clearly upon the correct methodology. Similarly, 'Abdur-Rahman 'Abdul- Khaaliq has many errors and contradictions which have been indicated, and indeed these have been refuted. The people of knowledge have refuted his errors, so do not be someone who still falsely follows these clear errors. Rather, you should refer to the statements of the scholars such as Sheikh Ibn Baaz, may Allaah the Exalted have mercy upon him, to his books, writing, and audio lectures. And the likes of Sheikh al-Albaanee, may Allaah have mercy upon him, and the likes of Sheikh Muqbil, may Allaah have mercy upon him, and the likes of Sheikh al-'Utheimeen, may Allaah have mercy upon him, and the likes of Sheikh Fauzaan, may Allaah have mercy upon him, and the Permanent Committee of Scholars in the Kingdom of Saudi Arabia, the likes of Sheikh 'Abdul-'Azeez Ibn 'Abdullah Aal-Sheikh, and Sheikh Muhammad Ibn Ibraheem Aal-Sheikh, and Sheikh as-Sa'adee. These are all from the guiding scholars who educate the people upon the Book of Allaah and the Sunnah, and encourage the people to hold fast to the Book of Allaah and the Sunnah. They do not call to divisive partisanship, or to Islamic organizations, or to ugly bigotry or bias towards a group. On the contrary, they teach the people the Book of Allaah and the Sunnah, and warn them against innovation, sins, and opposing guidance. Know, oh worshiper of Allaah, that the Messenger of Allaah, praise and salutations be upon him, said, "This Ummah will divide into seventy-three sects, all of them in the fire except one." Therefore it is obligatory upon the Muslim to search for the truth and follow the truth, and to be among this single successful group. They should not be one of those who follow one of the other seventy-two sects, as these seventy-two are liable to enter the fire, and we seek refuge in Allaah from that.

So fear Allaah, of worshiper of Allaah, and hold steadfastly to the religion, and adhere to the Book of Allaah and the Sunnah. Give importance to seeking knowledge, and be cautious from hearsay and speculative talk, and be cautious of wasting time, and hold to affairs of goodness and benefit. Call the people to Allaah; do not call them to groups and parties. As Allaah, the Exalted, and Most High says, ❖*Invite mankind (Oh Muhammad ) to the Way of your Lord...*❖-(Surah an-Nahl:125); and He said, ❖*And who is better in speech than he who invites to Allaah, and does righteous deeds*❖-(Surah Fussilat:33); and the One Free from Imperfections said, ❖Say, "*This is my way; I invite unto Allaah with sure knowledge, I and whosoever follows me. And the Most Glorified and the Most Exalted be Allaah. And I am not of the idolaters.*❖-(Surah Yusuf:108)  The true call is not to division and partisanship, nor to innovation in the religion, nor to an organization or group; rather, it is to the Book of Allaah and to the Sunnah of the Messenger of Allaah. I ask Allaah, the Most Glorified and the Most Exalted, to unite the voices of the Muslims upon the Book of Allaah and the Sunnah, and to unite them upon the truth, and to distance them from the differing groups, and to distance them from innovation in the religion, and to distance them from trials and tribulations whether apparent or hidden. And may Allaah's praise and His salutations be upon our Prophet Muhammad, and upon his family.

This being stated on the fourth day of the week in the month of Shawwal in the year 1425 from the Hijrah, in the city of Hudaydah. I ask Allaah, the Most Glorified and the Most Exalted, to establish truth and nullify falsehood and to make the Muslims victorious and to warn the disbelievers and those who associate others with Allaah, and to unite the voices of the Muslims upon the Book of Allaah and the Sunnah. And certainly my Lord hears the prayer to Him. May abundant peace and complete praise, salutations and blessing be upon His worshiper and Messenger, our prophet Muhammad and upon his family, and his Companions.

(24) The Eminent Guiding Scholar 'Abdul-'Azeez Ibn 'Abdullah Ibn Baaz, may Allaah have mercy upon him, excerpted From 'A Collection of Rulings and Various Statements': Vol.5, Page 48

*Question: We would like you to explain the meaning of Allaah's statement, ‹Verily those who fear and have reverence of Allaah the most from His worshipers are the scholars›*

Answer: This is a tremendous verse, and indicates that the scholars of Allaah, of His religion, of His exalted Book, and of the Sunnah of His noble Messenger are the strongest of the people in standing in awe and reverence of Allaah, and those most complete in fearing Him, the Most Free from Imperfections. Its meaning is that those who have awe and reverence for Allaah in a true and complete manner, they are the scholars of Allaah, who know their Lord by His names and attributes, and who exalt and magnify Him. They are those who consider carefully the matters of his Sharee'ah, and those who understand the bounty that will be found with Him from happiness for those who fear Him, as well as the punishment for those to turn away from Him and His guidance and commit sin and transgression. And they are those who, due to the comprehensiveness of their knowledge of Him, are the strongest of the people in having true reverence of Him and the most complete of the people in having fear of Him.

At the head of them are the Messengers and the Prophets, upon them all be praise and salutations, as they are the most complete of the people in standing in awe and reverence of Allaah, the Most Free from Imperfection, and in glorifying Him. After them, then those who succeeded and followed them, meaning the scholars of Allaah and His religion. And the people are categorized according to different levels, as the verses do not mean that others who are not scholars do not fear Allaah, as every Muslim and Muslimah, every believing man and believing woman fears Allaah the Most High, the Most Exalted. Rather, it is that the fearing of Allaah among them is in varying degrees, and whenever the believer is more perceptive and conscious of Allaah and the more knowledgeable about Allaah and His religion, then his fear of Allaah will increase. Whenever his knowledge and perception decreases, then his fear of Allaah, reverence and awe of Allaah, the Most Perfect also decreases.

So the people vary greatly in regard to their levels, such that even the scholars are of different levels in their reverence and awe, as was discussed. So whenever they are increased in knowledge then their awe of Allaah increases and likewise, whenever their knowledge decreases this diminishes their awe and reverence of Allaah. And due to this the Most High and Most Exalted says,

❧*Verily, those who disbelieve from among the people of the Scripture and those who associate others with Allaah will abide in the Fire of Hell. They are the worst of creatures. Verily, those who believe and do righteous good deeds, they are the best of creatures. Their reward with their Lord is 'Adn Paradise, underneath which rivers flow, they will abide therein forever, Allaah Well-Pleased with them, and they with Him. That is for him who fears his Lord.*❧*-*(Surah al-Baiyyinah:6-8) And Allaah, the Most High, says, ❧*Verily! Those who fear their Lord unseen, theirs will be forgiveness and a great reward*❧*-*(Surah al-Mulk: 12). And the verses with this meaning are many, and from Allaah is the success.

(25) THE EMINENT GUIDING SCHOLAR 'ABDUR-RAHMAN IBN NAASIR AS-SA'ADEE, MAY ALLAAH HAVE MERCY UPON HIM, FROM 'LIGHT OF THE PEOPLE OF INSIGHT AND THE MEN OF UNDERSTANDING': PAGE 64

### Regarding the Right of the People of Knowledge

The greatest of the obligatory rights after the rights of the Messenger of Allaah are the rights of the educating scholars who are the connection between the Messenger of Allaah and his Ummah in conveying the religion and Sharee'ah he was sent with. Those whom, if they were not present, the people would behave as though they were animals. The rights of the scholars upon the Muslim Ummah are greater than the rights due to fathers and mothers, as they educate and cultivate the hearts and souls of the worshippers through beneficial forms of knowledge and sound insights. They are the guides of the Muslim Ummah in both the foundations of their deen and its branches. They are the ones who are turned to for the rulings regarding the rights and affairs of the people, just as they are the ones referred to in the matters of worship. Through them the Book of Allaah and the Sunnah are established, clarifying the truth from falsehood, guidance from misguidance, the permissible from the impermissible, what is good from what is evil, and that which is healthy from that which is corrupted.

In this they are upon different levels, according to what they establish from their knowledge and teaching, as well as the abundance of or lack of benefit that they bring to others. Indeed, their right upon the Ummah is tremendous, and their position is significant. It is therefore essential that the people love them, have a high regard for them, honor them, acknowledge their merits and good qualities, and, due to all these matters, thank them with the finest thankfulness. In addition to this, one should pray for contentment for them as well as for us, and seek to become closer to Allaah through loving them, praising them, spreading their good qualities, and ensuring that one's heart and tongue overlook their errors and faults which, if brought forward, would cause the belittling of their good qualities and knowledge.

You should seize the opportunity to benefit from their presence, drinking from the fountain of their knowledge, and being guided by their light. And know everything which would help to things comfortable and easy for them and commit yourself to assisting them, in consideration of the fact that they are occupied with their important duties which are ordinarily considered to be their most important priorities. These are teaching the ready and willing students and being dedicated to their well being, guiding the general people, giving rulings on questions which are brought to them, judging in the different affairs between the people and settling their disputes, as well as many other matters that they have upon them which cannot be fully estimated and counted. Therefore the people are compelled to refer and turn to them, and so their rights as scholars from a detailed aspect, cannot be fully counted.

(26) The Eminent Guiding Scholar Saaleh Ibn Fauzaan, may Allaah preserve him, From 'Beneficial Answers To Questions on New Methodologies': Page 251

*Question: What is the description of those scholars whom we should be guided by?*

Answer: The description of those scholars you should be guided by is that they are the people who possess knowledge of Allaah, the Most Perfect, the Most High. They are those who have the understanding of the Book of Allaah and the Sunnah of His Messenger, may Allaah's praise and salutations be upon him, and are distinguished by beneficial knowledge as well as by righteous actions. Those who you should truly follow combine both these aspects, joining beneficial knowledge and righteous actions. So do not follow the scholar who does not act by his knowledge, and do not follow the ignorant one who does not possess knowledge. Only follow the one who combines both of these aspects: beneficial knowledge and righteous actions. And in relation to those who you should follow in this land of ours, those whose audio lectures you should make use of, then they are numerous. And all praise is due to Allaah, they are well known to the people. No one is ignorant of them, not the city dweller nor the man of the desert, neither the young nor the old. They are constantly engaged in giving religious rulings, judging, teaching, and other activities. From them you clearly perceive knowledge, the reverence and fear of Allaah, and piety. At the head of these scholars is the Sheikh 'Abdul-'Azeez Ibn Baaz, may Allaah the Exalted preserve him. He is an individual whom Allaah has blessed with abundant knowledge, good works, efforts in calling to Allaah, as well as purity of intention and truthfulness. And it is not hidden from anyone that he, all praise is due to Allaah, is the source of tremendous benefit from his books, general writings, audio lectures, and regular lessons.

Similarly, those scholars who give rulings for the radio program *"Light upon the Path"*. And all praise is due to Allaah, we also know that sound rulings and beneficial statements come from them. They are his eminence Sheikh 'Abdul-'Azeez Ibn Baaz, and the esteemed Sheikh Muhammad Ibn Saaleh al-'Utheimeen, and their brothers in faith from the honorable judges. As no one is occupied with such judicial matters and has had the people come to rightfully rely upon them regarding these matters of familial issues, financial disputes, and matters related to marriage, except that their knowledge can be relied upon.

These individuals have made considerable effort in calling to Allaah with purity of intention, as well as refuting those who wish to turn the efforts to call to Allaah in a way which deviates from the straight path, whether this straying be intentional or not. Their statements show that they are experienced and well-tested; and that they show deliberation and careful consideration of matters, distinguishing between what is sound and what is deficient. It is an obligation to promote their audio lectures and regular lessons and to benefit from them, as clearly in them there is tremendous benefit for the Muslims. Therefore every scholar who has not been seen to have significant errors and that we do not see deviation in his understanding or his conduct, then knowledge should be taken from him. Moreover, it is not permissible to take from the ignorant even if they are teachers; or to take from those who have deviated in their beliefs by associating others with Allaah in worship or who negate Allaah's names and or attributes. Neither should we take from those who have innovated in the religion or gone astray from what is correct, even if some of the people consider and refer to them as scholars.

So there are these three types of people: the people of beneficial knowledge and righteous action, the people of knowledge who have not acted according to their knowledge, and the people whose actions are not based upon knowledge, are all mentioned by Allaah the Exalted in the end of Surah al-Faatihah. Allaah has commanded us to ask Him to guide us to the path of those of the first description and to distance us from paths taken by those of the last two descriptions. Allaah the Exalted says, ❖*Guide us to the straight path, the way of those on whom you have bestowed your grace, not the way of those who have earned your anger, nor those who went astray.*❖-(Surah al-Faatihah:6-7) Only the people of the first category are those who have been blessed to be truly guided by Allaah. Those of second category have earned Allaah's anger and the people of the third category went astray from the correct way. These last two categories are illustrations of the deviated groups present today, despite that fact that they attribute themselves and associate themselves to Islaam.

(27) The Eminent Guiding Scholar Muhammad Ibn Saaleh al-'Utheimeen, may Allaah have mercy upon him, in 'Explanation of Riyadh as-Saaliheen': Vol. 4, Page 8

### *Who are the people who truly fear Allaah?*

The people who have true reverence and awe of Allaah are the scholars; those scholars who have knowledge of Allaah, His names, attributes, actions, and rulings. They are those who understand what is due to Allaah, the Most High and the Most Magnificent, from the ruling by and being pleased within His decrees and what He has legislated. He, the One free from any imperfection, the Most High, is perfect in every aspect, and there cannot be found in His actions or His rulings any deficiency. So due to understanding this they possess reverence and awe of Allaah, the Sublime, the Exalted. This is an indication of the merit of knowledge, and that it is considered to be from the means of attaining reverence and awe of Allaah. If someone is granted success in attaining reverence and awe of Allaah, he is better safeguarded from committing sins. And if he commits a sin, he characteristically seeks forgiveness and repents to Allaah the Most High, the Most Magnificent, due to his possessing reverence and awe of Allaah, fearing Him, and exalting Him.

Then after this, what should be mentioned are the relevant hadeeth narrations, beginning with the hadeeth of Mu'aweeyah Ibn Abee Sufyaan, may Allaah be pleased with him, that the Prophet, may Allaah's praise and salutations be upon him, said: *{Whoever Allaah intends good for He grants him understanding in the religion.}* [25]. Allaah, the Most High, the Most Magnificent, wills for His creation what He wishes from the good and the bad. However, He wants for them good, and as for what He decrees for them then this contains good and bad. Every decree of His is good, but as for the actual realization or fulfillment of that decree then it contains both good and evil. And the people are like vessels; from them are those whom Allaah, the Exalted, has given knowledge of good within their hearts and they have been made successful, and from them are those whom Allaah, the Exalted, has only given them knowledge of evil in their hearts and they have been deserted or abandoned by Him, and we seek refuge in Allaah. Allaah, the Exalted, said, ❖ *When they turned away from following guidance, Allaah turned their hearts away from guidance*❖-(Surah as-Saf:5). Allaah did not turn their hearts away from guidance except after they first chose misguidance, intended evil, and would not conform to that which was good. But as for the one who Allaah has given knowledge of good in their hearts, then they agree with and conform to it. So when Allaah places within the heart of an individual knowledge of what is good, then indeed He intends for that person good. And when he intends for that person good, He gives him understanding of the religion, and gives him knowledge of His Sharee'ah which is not given to just anyone from the people. And this indicates that it is necessary for the individual to aspire

---

[25]  Narrated in Saheeh al-Bukhaaree: 71, 3116, 7312/ Saheeh Muslim: 1037/ Sunan Ibn Maajah: 221/ al-Muwatta Maalik: 1300, 1667/Musnad Imaam Ahmad: 16395: 16404, and other than these two/ Musannaf Ibn Abee Shaybah:31792/ Sunan ad-Daaramee: 224, 226/- on the authority of Mu'aweeyah, and  it is found in Jaamee'a al-Tirmidhee: 2645/ Musnad Imaam Ahmad: 2786 /Sunan ad-Daaramee: 270, 2706/- on the authority of Ibn 'Abbaas, and  it is found in Sunan Ibn Maajah:220/ Musannaf 'Abdul-Razzaaq: 30851/- on the authority of Abu Hurairah. It was declared authentic by Sheikh al-Albaanee in Saheeh al-Aadab al-Mufrad: 517, Silsilat al-Hadeeth as-Saheehah: 1194, 1195, 1196, Saheeh at-Targheeb at-Tarheeb: 67, as well as in other of his books. Sheikh Muqbil declared it authentic in al-Jaamee'a al-Saheeh: 9, 3123, 4650.

toward understanding of the religion with a strong desire, because if Allaah, the Most High, wishes a matter, then He facilitates the causes or reasons for its achievement. And from the causes of attaining understanding is learning and studying, as well as striving to reach that high level. Allaah intends for you good, so strive to attain an understanding of the religion of Allaah.

Moreover, understanding of the religion is not simply knowledge alone; rather, it is both knowledge and deeds. For this reason our predecessors from the first generations warned about the condition of the Muslims having many speakers but few people of understanding. 'Abdullah Ibn Mas'ood, may Allaah be pleased with him, said, "*How will your condition be if you have many speakers but only a few people of true understanding among you?*" So a person who has knowledge about a matter from Allaah's Sharee'ah, but does not act upon it, does not have a true "understanding" of that. Even to the degree that he memorizes the largest book of jurisprudence that one might be able to grasp and understands it; however, he does not act according to it. Then he is not called a "faqeeh" a person of understanding, rather simply a reader; but he is not considered truly a person of understanding. The person of understanding is the one who acts upon the knowledge he has learned. First he learns, and then he acts according to what was learned. This is the one who truly has understanding of the religion. As for the one who has knowledge but does not act according to it, then he is not known as a "faqeeh" or a person of understanding. So we call this having information, but not truly "understanding". Due to this the people of the prophet Shu'ayb said to him, ◈ *We do not understand much of what you say...* ◈-(Surah Hud:91) This was because the evil within their hearts barred them from the goodness of knowing Allaah. So strive to attain knowledge and make every effort to act according to it, so that you may be amongst those whom Allaah intends good for. I ask Allaah, the Exalted to make me and all of you from those whom He grants understanding of the religion of Allaah, and makes us from those to act according to it, and those who benefit others and are benefited ourselves.

(28) THE EMINENT GUIDING SCHOLAR 'ABDUR-RAHMAN IBN NAASIR AS-SA'ADEE, MAY ALLAAH HAVE MERCY UPON HIM, FROM 'ISLAMIC RULINGS OF SHEIKH SA'ADEE': PAGE 21

### The Way of the People of the Sunnah and the Jama'ah in Relation to Knowledge and Deeds

The people of the Sunnah and the Jama'ah believe in and act upon the truth that there is no path to Allaah or to the honor which He gives except through beneficial knowledge and righteous deeds. Beneficial knowledge is that which the Messenger of Allaah came with of the guidance of the Qur'aan and Sunnah. They strive to comprehend its various meanings and to gain understanding of its foundations and branches. They pursue all of the specific paths to accomplish that, including studying those textual evidences that are in conformity with each other, those textual evidences which are comprehensive in intent, as well as those textual evidences that indicate the ruling of obligation. So they exert their strength in understanding all of these according to the level of ability and understanding given to them by Allaah. They believe in and consider all of these to be from the beneficial branches of knowledge, as well as everything which is derived from them of accepted categories of knowledge and from the suitable insightful statements, in addition to every area of knowledge that supports and assists them in this. This is considered Sharee'ah knowledge. Conversely, every type of knowledge which contradicts it or conflicts with it is considered false and rejected. So this is their methodology regarding knowledge.

As for their way in relation to deeds, certainly they seek to increase in closeness to Allaah, the Exalted, through the affirmation of the truth, and complete acknowledgment and thankfulness. They have "emaan" or faith, which is free from doubts, regarding the fundamental beliefs of the religion as they are the basis and foundation for all acts of worship. After this they seek to increase in closeness to Allaah through performing the obligatory deeds He has ordered in connection to establishing the rights that are due to Allaah as well as the rights that are due to the creation. In addition to this, they are those who engage in an abundance of the additional non-obligatory acts of worship; they pursue goodness to the creation through every available means, and abandon the forbidden and disapproved matters, thus worshiping Allaah the Exalted. And they know that Allaah does not accept any action except the one done purely for His sake alone, and whose performance adheres to the way and guidance of the Noble Prophet. So they seek the assistance and support from Allaah by way of all of these beneficial paths which are from the beneficial knowledge and the righteous deeds leading to every form of good, success, and happiness, both in this world and the next.

These tremendous principles are merely an essential foundation gathered in this response in summarized form, presented as a suitable overview of them. And if we elaborated in detail and specified all of its matters mentioning their evidences, this would require lengthy explanation and comprise a large book. And Allaah knows best, peace and prayers be upon the Messenger of Allaah, his family and Companions.

(29) The Eminent Guiding Scholar Muhammad Naasiruddeen al-Albaanee, may Allaah have mercy upon him, excerpted From 'Clarification and Cultivation and the Need of the Muslims for Them': Pages 14, 29-31

### The Sole Remedy is Returning to the True Religion

So I say: how do the Muslims return to their religion? Indeed the remedy stated by the Messenger, upon him be the praise of Allaah and best of salutations, is that it is necessary for them to undertake the removal of the affliction that is upon them, which otherwise cannot be lifted. And he said, *{When you enter into forbidden 'eenah transactions, and hold on to the tails of cows, being pleased solely with agriculture, and abandon jihaad in the path of Allaah. Allaah will place a disgrace upon you that will not be lifted until you return to your religion}* [26]. Accordingly, there is only one cure, and that is to return to the religion...

A return to the religion is a return to the Book and the Sunnah. These two are the essence of the religion by agreement of all the leading scholars of the Muslim Ummah. These two are what protects the people from going astray and slipping into misguidance. Therefore the Messenger, upon him be Allaah's praise and salutations, said, *{I leave among you two things which you will not go astray if you follow, the Book of Allaah and my Sunnah, and they will not separate from each other until they return to my pool on the Day of Judgment.}* [27]. And we have given some examples which show the obligation upon the people of knowledge today to return to an understanding of the religion from the two mentioned foundations: the Book of Allaah and the Sunnah, so that the Muslims do not make permissible matters that Allaah has forbidden, mistakenly believing that to be something which is permitted by Allaah.

My closing words regarding the return to the religion are: If we desire the glory and honor which comes from Allaah, Blessed and Exalted, that He lift us from this disgraced position, and gives us victory over our enemies, then it is not sufficient simply to undertake what we have indicated from the obligation of correcting our understandings and removing the various opinions by which many of the people of knowledge and specialized jurisprudence wrongly interpret the legitimate Sharee'ah evidences. There is also an additional matter which is essential. It is the heart and core which is directly related to correcting one's understanding. And that being taking firm knowledge to deeds and actions, as knowledge is the means to deeds. If a person learns, and his knowledge becomes pure, that is, having clarity, but then he does not act according to it, then it goes without saying that his knowledge was neither productive nor useful. So it is necessary and required to join along with that knowledge the action according to it.

---

[26] Narrated in Sunan Abu Daawud: 3462/ Musnad Imaam Ahmad: 4810: 4987/ -from the hadeeth of 'Abdullah Ibn 'Umar. It was declared authentic by Sheikh al-Albaanee in Silsilat al-Hadeeth as-Saheehah: 11, Saheeh at-Targheeb at-Tarheeb: 1389, as well as in other of his books.

[27] Narrated in Mustradraak al-Haakim: 319/ -from the hadeeth of Abu Hurairah. It was declared authentic by Sheikh al-Albaanee in his work 'The Position of the Sunnah in Islaam', Saheeh al-Jamee'a: 2937, 3233, as well as in other of his books. Sheikh Muqbil did not state any difference with the ruling of authenticity given by Haafidh al-Haakim in his own verification of al-Mustadrak alaa Saheehayn- hadeeth number 332; and he declared it authentic in al-Jaamee' al-Saheeh: 2937.

It is an obligation upon the people of knowledge to undertake the cultivation of the new generation of young Muslims upon the light of guidance affirmed within the Book and the Sunnah. It is not permissible to leave the people upon the mistaken understanding and errors which they simply inherited from those before them. Some of these matters are completely false by agreement of all the leading scholars, and there are differences in some of them, as they contain aspects of varying views, opinions, and independent judgments. However, some of these positions of independent judgment and views even contradict the Sunnah. Therefore, after clarifying what is correct and incorrect within these affairs, and bringing to light what it is obligatory to proceed upon, it is required that we educate the new young generation upon this correct knowledge. This education or cultivation is the one which will bring forth for us a true Islamic society, and then the eventual establishment of the Islamic state for us. And without these two foremost foundations: correct authentic knowledge, and proper education and cultivation upon that authentic knowledge, it is impossible, in my belief, to establish the reign of Islaam, the rule of Islaam, or the Islamic state.

(30) The Eminent Guiding Scholar 'Abdul-'Azeez Ibn 'Abdullah Ibn Baaz, may Allaah have mercy upon him, from 'Collection of Rulings and Various Statements': Vol. 5, Page 101

### The Reasons for the Weakness of the Muslims in the Face of their Enemies and the Means to Cure This

All praise is for Allaah Lord of all the Worlds, the final destination of those who fear and revere Him, and praise and salutations be upon His worshiper and Messenger, and the One entrusted with His revelation, the best of His creation, our Prophet, leader, and chief, Muhammad Ibn 'Abdullah Ibn 'Abdul-Mutalib and also upon his Companions and those who travel upon his path and those who follow his guidance until the Day Of Reckoning. As for what follows:

Certainly concern has been shown by the prominent Muslim thinkers and intellectuals, those who are associated with the present Islamic revival, and the individuals who contemplate matters seriously, for the circumstances which the Muslims find themselves in. Without question, they have occupied themselves with this matter a great deal, and considered at length the reasons for the weakness of the Muslims, the causes for their inferior position in front of their enemies, and the reasons for their divisiveness and disunity. In addition, they have contemplated the reasons for the arrogance of their enemies in relation to them, such that they have even taken control of some of their lands. Subsequently, after they have understood the causes and reasons, and these reasons are evident, then importance must be given to determining the cure and solution required to remedy the causes which have inevitably led to our disgrace and weakness. And this solution is also known. However, what is necessary is that it be publicized and explained clearly. This is because recognizing the illness and then determining the cure is from the most significant means leading to successful treatment and health.

The one with an illness, when he understands the illness as well as understanding the cure, is best capable of beginning to utilize the cure and free himself from that illness. And it is natural for the intelligent person who prefers life and freedom from illness to give importance to recognizing the illness and knowing its cure. However, some of the people have been overtaken by the disease and overwhelmed by it until they become satisfied with it, and pleased with it, until their perception and awareness has died. Thus they do not pay attention to the one who explains to them the remedy, as the illness itself has become normal and natural to them. They are comfortable and content to remain in a corrupted state of mind, having a weak perception, along with the domination of their desires over them; their intellects, hearts, and conduct. And this has happened to the majority of people in relation to the illness and deficiency in their practice of the religion and the cure for it. And most people are thus content, preferring to remain in a miserable condition and state of sickness which weakens them and prevents any attempt to truly recognize the illness, its consequences, and what will result from it immediately and long term, as well as preventing efforts to search for a cure, or desiring that, even when it is clearly described and explained to them, and close at hand. They do not give any importance to this. With this comes the worsening of the sickness, the further satisfaction with its presence, the concealment of its harm upon them, and the lack of strong determination to understand the significance of the problem.

And so the causes for the weakness of the Muslims and their present inferior position has been explained by the scholars, the people of intelligence, and the leaders possessing true insight into and knowledge of the nations in this age and the periods preceding it. In addition, they have clarified the means to the effective remedy, its results and outcome, if the remedy is properly used.

So the reasons for the weakness, inferiority, and domination of our enemies return back to a primary cause from which proceed many other causes, and from a single factor from which many other factors spring. The primary cause and single factor is ignorance. Ignorance of Allaah and His religion, and the consequences of this ignorance which have overtaken the majority of them, such that the present state has become one where knowledge is rare and this ignorance widespread. Then from this ignorance stems further causes and factors, such as love of the worldly life and a hatred of death, and the negligence of prayer and the following of desires. From these is the lack of preparation for confrontation with their enemies and being pleased to have their needs supplied by their enemies, and a failure to give high priority to the producing of goods for their essential needs from their own lands and resources. Also stemming from this is division and differing, the lack of having a united voice, and lack of unity and cooperation. So from these dangerous causes and their results has come about that which is seen of weakness in the face of our enemies and our inferiority in every matter except that which Allaah has willed, as well as the devotion to prohibited desires, and becoming occupied with matters that hinder efforts in the path of Allaah and guidance, not to mention the lack of preparing to confront our enemies, either from the aspect of means of production, or in terms of sufficient weaponry that would intimidate the enemy and is needed to fight and struggle against him, and take what is a right from him. In addition, there is the lack of preparing our bodies for jihaad and the failure to use our wealth on what is necessary to prepare in strength of numbers for the enemy, to protect against the harm they may bring forth, and to be able to defend both the religion and the land.

Also proceeding from this sickness is the striving to obtain worldly things by every possible way, and to gather them by every means, so that every individual becomes someone who only gives importance to serving himself and is not truly connected to his land. Through this state of affairs, his religion, or the majority of it, basically fades away. This is in fact the general condition and what is prevalent in most of the states or countries associated with the religion of Islaam today. Rather, it is more accurate that we say that this has occurred everywhere except where Allaah, the Most High, the Most Sublime, decreed that some efforts of preparation and protection are being made; however not in a complete way that fulfills all the desired aspects of rectification.

(31) THE EMINENT GUIDING SCHOLAR AHMAD IBN YAHYA AN-NAJMEE, MAY ALLAAH PRESERVE HIM, FROM 'A GUIDING TREATISE EXPLAINING THE TRUTH REGARDING THE JUDGMENT OF JIHAAD': PAGES 99-106

### Reasons for the Attainment of Victory

We have completed the discussion regarding the ruling of jihaad, having established that it is a collective obligation as opposed to an individual one through clear evidences not opposed by anyone except an obstinate one who turns away from the truth. Therefore, it is necessary that we explain the causes by which victory is reached as explained to us by Allaah, the Most Glorified and the Most Exalted, in His Book, as certainly it has causes. So, with the assistance from Allaah, I begin by saying:

The first reason: It is an obligation that we know the most important cause for success is sincerity of our efforts for Allaah, the Exalted, Alone. We must ensure that the intended goal of our jihaad is to give victory to the religion of Allaah, the Most Glorified and the Most Exalted, over the other ways of belief, the elevation of the Word of Allaah over the ideologies and paths of disbelief, the manifesting of faith in Allaah over disbelief, truth over falsehood, and justice over oppression, until the Sharee'ah of Allaah rules on Allaah's earth and the people of Allaah's religion are empowered and the people of disobedience are humbled. So the one who fights with this intention is the one given victory by Allaah and the one fighting solely for Allaah becomes, through that, deserving of victory from Allaah. Allaah, the Exalted, has said, ❮*Oh you who believe! If you support (in the cause of) Allaah, He will support you, and make your foothold firm.*❯-(Surah Muhammad:7) Allaah, the Exalted, also says, ❮*And fight them until there is no more fitnah, and the religion (worship) will all be for Allaah Alone.*❯-(Surah al-Anfaal:39). And as found in the two Saheeh collections on the authority of Abu Musaa (may Allaah be pleased with him): {*A man* came to the Prophet and said, *"One man fights for pride and haughtiness, another fights for bravery, and another fights for showing off; which of these cases is truly in the path of Allaah?"* The Prophet said, *"The one who fights that Allaah's Word should become superior is the one who fights in Allaah's Cause."}* [28].

Second: Patience; as Allaah, the Exalted, says, *But those who knew with certainty that they were going to meet Allaah, said, "How often has a small group overcome a mighty host by Allaah's leave" And Allaah is with those who are patient.*-(Surah al-Baqarah:249) And the Exalted says, *It is not al-Birr (piety, righteousness, and each and every act of obedience to Allaah, etc.) that you turn your faces towards east and or west (in prayers); but al-Birr is (the quality of) the one who believes in Allaah, the Last Day, the Angels, the Book, the Prophets...* up to the point where Allaah says, *...and who are as-Saabirin (the patient ones, etc.) in extreme poverty and ailment (disease) and at the time of al-Baas* And the meaning "time of al-Baas" is the time of fighting. *...Such are the people of the truth and they are pious.*-(Surah al-Baqarah:177)

Third: Steadfastness in the heat of battle and not fleeing during fighting. Allaah says, *Oh you who believe! When you meet (an enemy) force, take a firm stand against them and remember the Name of Allaah much (both with tongue and mind), so that you may be successful.*-(Surah al-Anfaal:45) And the Exalted says, *Oh you who believe! If you help (in the cause of) Allaah, He will help you, and make your foothold firm.*-(Surah Muhammad :7) *Oh you who believe! When you meet those who disbelieve, in a battle-field, never turn your backs to them. And whoever turns his back to them on such a day - unless it be a stratagem of war, or to retreat to a troop (of his own), - he indeed has drawn upon himself wrath from Allaah. And his abode is Hell, and worst indeed is that destination!*-(Surah al-Anfaal:15-16)

Fourth: Frequently remembering Allaah with both the heart and the tongue. The Exalted says, *Oh you who believe! When you meet (an enemy) force, take a firm stand against them and remember the Name of Allaah much (both with tongue and mind), so that you may be successful.*-(Surah al-Anfaal:45)

Fifth: Sincere faith which produces righteous deeds. Allaah, the Exalted, says, *Verily, We will indeed make victorious Our Messengers and those who believe- in this world's life and on the Day when the witnesses will stand forth*-(Surah Ghafir:51)

Sixth: General good works, as the Exalted says, *Allaah has promised those among you who believe and do righteous good deeds, that He will certainly grant them succession in the land, as He granted it to those before them, and that He will grant them the authority to practice their religion which He has chosen for them. And He will surely give them in exchange a safe security after their fear if they worship Me and do not associate anything with Me. But whoever disbelieved after this, they are the rebellious*-(Surah an-Nur:55).

---

[28] Narrated in Saheeh al-Bukhaaree: 2810, 7458/ Saheeh Muslim: 1904/ Jaame'a at-Tirmidhee: 1646/ Sunan Ibn Maajah: 2783/ & Musnad Imaam Ahmad: 19049, 19134: -on the authority of Abu Moosa al-'Ash'aree. It was declared authentic by Sheikh al-Albaanee in Saheeh Sunan at-Tirmidhee.

Seventh: Legislated righteous actions; and these are what was commanded by Messenger of Allaah, upon him be the best praise in the heavens by Allaah and His angels and the best salutations, not innovations and desires. Due to this, the verse which comes before it in which Allaah promises to make as successors the believers who work righteously, is itself preceded by a verse which encourages obedience to the Messenger of Allaah, upon him be the praise in the heavens by Allaah and His angels and the best of salutations, and followed by a verse which encourages obedience to the Messenger of Allaah, upon him be the best praise in the heavens by Allaah and His angels and the best of salutations. In the verse that precedes it, the Exalted says, ❖*Say: "Obey Allaah and obey the Messenger, but if you turn away, he is only responsible for the duty placed on him and you for that placed on you. If you obey him, you shall be on the right guidance. The Messenger's duty is only to convey (the Message) in a clear way.*❖-(Surah an-Nur:55). Then, afterwards, He says, ❖*Allaah has promised those among you who believe and do righteous good deeds, that He will certainly grant them succession in the land,*❖-(Surah an-Nur:55) up until he says after it: ❖*And perform the salaat, and give the zakaat and obey the Messenger that you may receive mercy.*❖-(Surah an-Nur:54-56). So the sequence of these verses indicates that the meaning of righteous deeds is those which were commanded by the Messenger of Allaah, upon him be the best praise in the heavens by Allaah and His angels and the best of salutations. As for those things which were invented after him from innovations in the religion, then it is not correct that they be described as righteous. Within the hadeeth of Irbaadh Ibn Saareyah that the Messenger of Allaah, may Allaah's praise and salutations be upon him, said, *{...So stick to what you know from my Sunnah and the Sunnah of the rightly guided caliphs. And beware of newly invented matters, as every newly invented matter is an innovation, and every innovation is a going astray.}* [29]. So as innovation is a going astray then you cannot build upon it victory nor succession upon the earth. The person of innovation claims that their innovation is a worship that is good and that it is a seeking closeness to Allaah, but actions are weighed and judged according the Sharee'ah, not according to opinions of the people. So what is considered righteous in light of the Sharee'ah, then it is considered righteous, and that which is considered a matter of deviation or going astray is considered as such.

---

[29]  Narrated in Jaame'a at-Tirmidhee: 2676/ Sunan Ibn Maajah: 42/ & Musnad Imaam Ahmad: 16692, 16694, 16695/ and within other collection- on the authority of al-'Irbaadh Ibn Saareeyah. It was declared authentic by Sheikh al-Albaanee in Silsilat al-Hadeeth as-Saheehah: 937 as well as in others of his books. Additionally Sheikh Muqbil declared it authentic in al-Jaame' al-Saheeh: 3249.

Eighth: Righteous deeds in general, which means the performance of the obligatory actions, as well as compulsory and recommended ones. These are deeds such as the establishment of obligatory prayer, and the paying of the zakaat from one's wealth, the fasting of the month of Ramadhaan, the obligatory and recommended pilgrimages, kind treatment of your parents, the maintaining of family ties, good behavior towards one's neighbors, the fulfilling of the trust, enjoining the good and forbidding evil, and good treatment of close relatives, orphans, and widows, to show mercy towards the poor, to stand for the night prayer, to often give charity, to offer the non-obligatory prayers, to practice the non-obligatory fast of three days every month and other fasts. Likewise, to leave the forbidden matters such as drinking intoxicants, using wealth earned through interest-based transactions, unjustly using the wealth of orphans, personally using the charity given to the Muslims, using wealth obtained through prohibited ways, such as that obtained through accepting bribes, deceptions, forcing others to give you their wealth and other similar things, the delaying of obligatory prayers from their appointed times, smoking cigarettes and tobacco water pipes, and chewing Qat leaves, and the mocking of the Muslims, treachery towards the Muslims, spying upon them, and pointing out their weaknesses, imitation of the disbelievers and those who deny Islaam, the production of images of living things, as well as other prohibited matters. You must the abandon what you are capable of leaving from the disapproved matters, and leave doubtful and suspicious matters due to piety. All of these actions of performance or abandonment encompass righteous deeds.

Ninth: To have trust and reliance upon Allaah, and to hold fast to and seek refuge in Him, while placing yourself fully in His hands, as the Exalted has said, ❧*Those to whom the people said, "Verily, the people have gathered against you, therefore, fear them." But it only increased them in faith, and they said, Allaah is Sufficient for us, and He is the Best Disposer of affairs." So they returned with grace and bounty from Allaah. No harm touched them; and they followed the pleasure of Allaah. And Allaah is the Owner of great bounty."*❧-(Surah Aal-'Imraan:173-174)

Tenth: To turn away from self satisfaction, abandoning being impressed by yourselves and your courage, your numbers and equipment. To leave all of that and rely upon Allaah alone, trusting fully in Him while recognizing your weakness. As the Exalted says, ❧*Truly, Allaah has given you victory on many battlefields, and on the day of the battle of Hunaayn when you rejoiced at your great number, but it availed you naught and the earth, vast as it is, was straitened for you, then you turned back in flight. Then Allaah did send down His sakinah, his tranquility, on His Messenger, and on the believers, and sent down forces which you saw not, and punished the disbelievers. Such is the recompense of disbelievers.*❧-(Surah Tawbah:25-26)

Eleventh: Drawing near to Allaah through devotion, frequently supplicating to Him, and disregarding seeking victory through numbers, as Allaah says, ❁*Remember when you sought help of your Lord and He answered you saying: 'I will help you with a thousand of the angels'*❁-(Surah al-Anfaal:9). And the Exalted says, ❁*So they routed them by Allaah's leave and Dawud (David) killed Jalut (Goliath), and Allaah gave him (Dawud) the kingdom after the death of Talut and Samuel and al-Hikmah (prophethood), and taught him of that which He willed. And if Allaah did not check one set of people by means of another, the earth would indeed be full of mischief. But Allaah is full of bounty to the `Alamin (mankind, Jinn and all that exists).) These are the verses of Allaah, We recite them to you (Oh Muhammad ) in truth, and surely, you are one of the Messengers (of Allaah.)*❁ and the Exalted said, ❁*And your Lord said, "Call upon Me, I will answer you. Verily, those who scorn My worship they will surely enter Hell in humiliation!*❁-(Surah Ghaafer:60)

Twelfth: To stay away from wrongfully taking from the spoils of war. Ibn Hajr brings forth in his book, "al-Mutaalib al-Aleeyah fee Zawaid al-Musanid al-Thamaneeyah" under the section entitled, "*The Seriousness of Wrongfully Taking from the Spoils of War*", Volume 2, Page 190, a hadeeth narration on the authority of Abee Dhar, may Allaah be pleased with him in which he says, "I heard the Messenger of Allaah, upon him be the best praise in the heavens by Allaah and His angels and the best of salutations, say, { *My Ummah will not be subjugated and its enemies will never be established as conquerors over it.*} [30]. Abu Dhar said to Habeeb Ibn Muslimah, "Is it confirmed that the conquered enemies of Halab have sheep?" He replied, "Yes, and several sheep that are very fine." So Abu Dhar said, "Then chain and secure them, by the Lord of the Ka'abah..."

Thirteenth: To keep far from committing sins, both those which are seen as insignificant and those which are deemed significant, and from disputes which will lead to your failure. The Most High said, ❁*And Allaah did indeed fulfill His promise to you when you were killing them (your enemy) with His permission; until (the moment) you lost your courage and fell to disputing about the order, and disobeyed after He showed you what you love. Among you are some that desire this world and some that desire the Hereafter. Then He made you flee from them, that He might test you. But surely, He forgave you, and Allaah is Most Gracious to the believers. And remember when you ran away without even casting a side glance at anyone, and the Messenger was in your rear calling you back. There did Allaah give you one distress after another by way of requital, to teach you not to grieve for that which had escaped you, nor for what struck you. And Allaah is Well-Aware of all that you do.*❁-(Surah Aal-'Imraan:152-153). These two verses were revealed regarding specific archers who had been ordered by the Prophet, upon him be the best praise in the heavens by Allaah and His angels and the best of salutations, to remain upon the mountain. And he said to them {*Do not leave your positions until I send for you...*} -(Narrated in Saheeh al-Bukhaaree: 2892)

---

[30] Narrated in Mu'jam al-Awsat of at-Tabaraanee: 8339/ & al-Mutaalib al-'Aleeyah: 2123/- from the hadeeth of Abu Dhar. It was declared weak by Sheikh al-Albaanee in Silsilat al-Hadeeth adh-Dha'eafah: 5169 as well as in Dha'eef at-Targheeb at-Tarheeb: 843.

Then when the victory began to become obvious they descended and disobeyed their commander, 'Abdullah Ibn Jubayr. And when they abandoned their mountain positions, the enemy cavalry of those who associated others with Allaah came at the Muslims from the rear and disrupted the Muslim ranks, killing many of them. Additionally, Shaytaan shouted out that Muhammad had been killed, at a time when the enemies from those who associate others with Allaah where very close to defeat.

The meaning of: ❴*And Allaah did indeed fulfill His promise to you*❵ means, through granting them victory. ❴*When you were killing them...*❵, meaning fighting and slaying them, ❴*with His permission*❵, means by your domination over them, ❴*... until (the moment) you lost your courage and fell to disputing about the order...*❵ that is, the command which was given to them by the Messenger of Allaah, upon him be the best praise in the heavens by Allaah and His angels and the best of salutations,❴*and disobeyed after He showed you what you love.*❵-(Surah Aal-'Imraan:152) meaning turned away from the command of your Prophet and abandoned the position on the mountain.

So be a witness, that if what happened to the Companions of the Messenger of Allaah, upon him be the best praise in the heavens by Allaah and His angels and the best of salutations, occurred simply due to a single sin they committed; then what would be the situation of the Muslims if they confronted their enemies while they were persisting in disobedience to Allaah without any limits! Therefore it is an obligation upon the Muslim army to purge themselves of frequent sins as well as those committed rarely before confronting the enemy, and to repent to Allaah so that hopefully Allaah will accept their repentance and grant them victory over their enemies.

The meaning of this is not that they will be like angels, not making any mistakes; as making mistakes is something that is common to all mankind. However, what is required of them is that they repent from persisting in sins which have become habitual for them, and that they seek forgiveness for that which occurs from the unintentional sins. Those that do this are then worthy of Allaah's blessing them with victory, and Allaah does not turn back from His promises, yet most of the people do not understand.

# GOLDEN ADVICE THAT BENEFITS THE BEGINNER REGARDING ACQUIRING KNOWLEDGE

'Amr Ibn Qays al Malaa'ee said:

*"If you see a youth initially upon the way of the people of the Sunnah and adherence to the Jama'ah then have hope for his success, but if you see him with the people of innovation in the religion then lose heart about him, for certainly the youth is generally established upon his first orientation."*

('*al-Ibaanah al-Kubra* by Imaam Ibn Batah': no. 45 vol.2 Page 481)

**(32) The Eminent Guiding Scholar Muqbil Ibn Hadee al-Waadiee, may Allaah have mercy upon him, From 'A Defending Mission from Audio Lectures upon the People of Ignorance and Sophistry': Vol. 1, Page 321**

*Question: Should we begin with seeking knowledge or with calling to Allaah?*

Answer: I advise you to begin with knowledge; as if you begin with knowledge then your words will become statements which are accepted. After this we can then proceed to call to Allaah upon clear knowledge. Allaah, the Most Perfect, the Most High says, ❨*Say "This is my way; I invite unto Allaah with sure knowledge, I and whosoever follows me*❩-(Surah Yusuf:108). And Allaah, the Most Perfect, the Most High says, ❨*Let there arise out of you a group of people inviting to all that is good, and forbidding all that is forbidden. And it is they who are the successful.*❩-(Surah Aal-'Imraan: 104) We see from this that one should call to goodness. But the ignorant one cannot not truly know whether he calls to goodness or not. Therefore study, and then proceed to call to Allaah with gentleness and kindness according to the limits of your ability, as gentleness and kindness are the two matters through which Allaah brings forth benefit. As for harshness, then we do not have in our hands the power or authority to fight and oppose those who reject entering into the religion of Islaam, nor do we have in our hands the power or authority to imprison those who deserve the punishment of imprisonment. So the remaining option is the invitation and calling accompanied by gentleness and kindness. We also advise them to sit with the esteemed scholars of all the Muslim lands. And if you are able, then call the people to benefit through lectures, such that if there is a lecture regarding the prayer then it in itself is considered a blow against the deviant sect of the Mukaramah. Or if there is a lecture regarding fasting then it in itself is also considered a blow against the sect of the Mukaramah. Rather, such a gathering of the people itself should be considered a blow against the sect of the Mukaramah.

But you should not say: This lecture did not bring about true benefits because it did not warn against nor discuss the errors of the Mukaramah. No, this is not a requirement, as the Book and the Sunnah both generally refute the Mukaramah. Thus it is not always necessary that you openly say, *"Sayyed so-and-so is astray and leading others astray"*. You simply teach the people the Book of Allaah and the Sunnah of the Messenger of Allaah, may Allaah's praise and salutations be upon him and his family. Then, if you come to have the ability to do so, continue to give them advice by publishing in daily newspapers, magazines, as well as through books and audio cassettes. Be persistent with such publishing, as this disturbs and disrupts them, meaning those such as the Mukaramah.

Moreover, if an individual from the Mukaramah is prepared to debate with us, then certainly we are prepared to debate with him. As they only posses deceit, lies, dishonesty, and striving to conceal of the truth. They do not possess the knowledge of *"Allaah said"* or that of *"The Messenger of Allaah said"*, may Allaah's praise and salutations be upon him and his family. So it may happen that you obtain enough knowledge that it enables you to face one of the Mukaramah. In this case, if he begins to put forth false conclusions and incorrect interpretations, such as the one

117

who says, [The prayer is a phrase meaning one of the "secrets of the sheikhs"]. And he means by this that you do not need to pray; it is sufficient for you to guard the "sheikh's" secret. So if they, meaning their "sheikhs", inform you of it, then this is sufficient to fulfill this. Likewise with the issues of the pillars of zakaat, charity, and fasting; they are considered to be fulfilled by guarding the "sheikh's" secret. Then you should say "Let us refer back to the books of language. Do they state regarding the definition of "prayer" or "prayers" that it is considered to mean memorizing the secret statements of the "sheikhs"?" Additionally, you should refer back to the correct explanation of the meaning of the word "prayer" in the Book of Allaah and the Sunnah of the Messenger of Allaah, may Allaah's praise and salutations be upon him and his family.

Moreover, after this like pecking, they quickly perform the prayer. You might pray two rakaat of prayer, while the individual from the Mukaramah performs twenty rakaat in the same period of time almost pecking toward the ground like a bird! Indeed, they do not have in their prayer any calmness and humility. And Allaah, the Most Perfect, the Most High said, ❖*Successful indeed are the believers; those who offer their Salaat (prayers) with all solemnity and full submissiveness.*❖-(1-2). So it is sufficient that someone perceives from their performance of prayer that they do not possess such submissiveness and humility; and so they are not the successful ones. Similarly, with the issue of the congregational prayer; they do not fulfill it nor see it as an obligation until as they say the "true" Imaam is present. Such that some of their prominent individuals in the city of Sa'ada presently do not pray the Jumu'ah congregational prayer, waiting until the "true" Imaam is present. Yet Allaah, the Exalted and the Most Sublime says in his Noble Book, ❖*Oh you who believe! When the call is proclaimed for the Jumu'ah prayer on the day of Friday, come to the remembrance of Allaah*❖-(Surah Jumu'ah:9). This verse is general in meaning and not linked to the presence of the Imaam. However right now we don't intend to list every matter that they are upon of evil and disbelief, as we have discussed this in two specific audio cassettes. Rather, I advise my brothers in Islaam to seek knowledge, and by this I do not mean seeking knowledge from attending elementary school, and then secondary school, and then high school, and then a college or university, and after this seeking a master's degree and then a doctorate degree, I do not mean this. I mean that you should seek beneficial knowledge; meaning from the Book of Allaah and the Sunnah of the Messenger of Allaah, may Allaah's praise and salutations be upon him and his family. And perhaps after a period of three years, your level of knowledge may be superior to many of the holders of doctorate degrees. And from Allaah Alone we seek help and assistance.

(33) The Eminent Guiding Scholar Muqbil Ibn Haadee al-Waadi'ee, may Allaah have mercy upon him, from 'A Defending Mission from Audio Lectures upon the People of Ignorance and Sophistry': Vol. 2, Page 373

*Question: What are the guidelines of seeking knowledge and what are the means and ways of seeking it?*

Answer: In regard to the principles of seeking knowledge: beneficial knowledge begins with the Book of Allaah and its memorization. As the Prophet, may Allaah's praise and salutations be upon him and his family, stated, *{The one who is proficient in reciting the Qur'aan is associated with the noble, upright, recording angels, and the one who makes mistakes in it, and finds difficulty in it, receives have a double reward}*[31] narrated by both Imaams Bukhaaree and Muslim on the authority of 'Aishah, may Allaah be pleased with her. And the Prophet, may Allaah's praise and salutations be upon him and his family, said, *{It will be said to the reciter of the Qur'aan: Read and beautify your recitation, and your place and status will be equal to the last verse you recite}* [32] as collected by at-Tirmidhee on the authority of 'Abdullah Ibn 'Amr Ibn al-Aas.

And the Lord of Might said in His Noble Book, ❊*Verily, this Qur'aan guides to that which is most just and right...*❊-(Surah al-Isra':9) And He says, ❊*And We send down of the Qur'aan that which is a cure and a mercy to the believers, and it increases the wrongdoers in nothing but loss.*❊-(Surah al-Isra':82). Therefore it is upon the student to start with the memorization of the Qur'aan. As you have also been commanded, begin along with your memorization of the Qur'aan those additional matters which Allaah has obligated upon you. For example, in the area of correct beliefs you should study a basic summarized book, whether this be *((al-Aqeedatul-Wasateeyah)06-05)* by Sheikh al-Islaam Ibn Taymeeyah or *((Tatheer al-Itiqaad)06-30)* by Imaam San'anee. Both of them are simple, easy works, all praise is due to Allaah. Then proceed to study whatever Allaah has required of you and this is the meaning of the statement of the Prophet, may Allaah's praise and salutations be upon him and his family: *{Seeking knowledge is an obligation upon every Muslim}* [33]. So if you intend to pray you should understand how the Messenger of Allaah, may Allaah's praise and salutations be upon him and his family, prayed, as he said, *{Pray as you see me praying.}* [34]. And if you intend to make obligatory pilgrimage of Hajj, you must first understand how the Messenger of Allaah, may Allaah's praise and salutations be upon him and his family, made pilgrimage, as he said,

---

[31] Narrated in Saheeh al-Bukhaaree: 4937/ Saheeh Muslim: 798/ Sunan Abee Dawud: 1454/ Jaame'a al-Tirmidhee: 2904/ Sunan Ibn Maajah: 3779 / Musnad of Imaam Ahmad: 23691, 24113, and others- on the authority of 'Aishah Mother of the Believers. It was declared authentic by Sheikh al-Albaanee in Irwaa' al-Ghaleel: 2598, and in Saheeh Sunan Abu Dawud 1454 and Saheeh Sunan at-Tirmidhee 2904.

[32] Narrated in Sunan Abee Dawud: 1454/ Jaame'a al-Tirmidhee: 2904 /-on the authority of 'Abdullah Ibn 'Amr. It was declared authentic by Sheikh al-Albaanee in Silsilat al-Hadeeth As-Saheehah: 2240 Irwaa' al-Ghaleel: 2598, and in Mishkaat al-Masaabeeh: 2134. Sheikh Muqbil declared it authentic in al-Jaame'a al-Saheeh: 54.

[33] Narrated in Sunan Ibn Maajah: 224 /-on the authority of Anas Ibn Maalik. It was declared authentic by Sheikh al-Albaanee in Mishkaat al-Masaabeeh: 218, in Saheeh al-Jaame'a as-Sagheer 3813,3914, in Saheeh at-Targheeb wa at-Tarheeb 72 and in Saheeh Sunan Ibn Maajah.

[34] Narrated in Saheeh al-Bukhaaree: 613, 5669/ - on the authority of Maalik Ibn Huwayreth. It was declared authentic by Sheikh al-Albaanee in Saheeh al-Aadab al-Mufrad: 216.

*{Take from my actions your rites of pilgrimage.}* [35]. Likewise, this is the case with the zakaat charity and other matters. If you are engaged in the affairs of buying and selling then it is necessary that you understand the rulings of the Sharee'ah regarding buying and selling. And the knowledge of the Book and the Sunnah is simple. As the Lord of might says in His Noble Book, *◈And We have indeed made the Qur'aan easy to understand and remember; then is there anyone who will remember◈*-(Surah Qamar:17) And the Prophet, may Allaah's praise and salutations be upon him and his family, said, *{I was sent with the straightforward Hanafeeyah.}* [36] meaning the naturally simple worship of Allaah alone . What actually ends up making knowledge complicated are the people. From the best sayings is the one who said,

> *If it was not for the worldly rivalry by offering similar books,*
>> *there would not be books named 'Mugnee' or' Amdah',*
> *They legitimize them by claiming that they solves complex issues,*
>> *but in the books which are produces, the problems of complexity simply increased*

And Sharstaanee explained quite clearly his own confusion:

> *I wandered around all the different centers of theoretical or speculative study*
> *passing my sight between their various different teachers,*
> *I did not see except the one who had sadly held his chin in his hand or the frustrated one who gritted his teeth in sorrow and regret.*

Imaam as-Sanaanee came across these two verses of poetry and criticized them, saying:

> *I fear that you failed to travel to the center of the true people of the Messenger*
> *nor those who have allegiance to him from every true scholar,*
>> *For the one who guided by the guidance of Muhammad is not confused*
>> *nor will you see him gritting his teeth in frustration and regret.*

And Raazee said after squandering his years away in philosophy and then later returning back to the guidance of the Book of Allaah and the Sunnah:

> *The end result of the building the intellect upon the unrestricted ideas of the mind is only shackles*
>> *and the inevitable conclusion of that worthless endeavor is nothing other than a false empty accomplishment,*
> *Our spirits became hateful within our own bodies,*
>> *and the end of our worldly life was only destruction and evil consequences*

---

[35] Narrated in Saheeh Muslim: 1297/ Sunan Abu Dawud: 1970/ Sunan an-Nisaa'ee: 3064 / Musnad of Imaam Ahmad: 14208, 14623/- on the authority of Jaabir Ibn 'Abdullah. It was declared authentic by Sheikh al-Albaanee in Hajj an-Nabee: 85, and Saheeh Sunan Abu Dawud.

[36] Narrated in Musnad of Imaam Ahmad: 21788- on the authority of Abu Imaamah Sadee Ibn Ajlaan. It was declared authentic by Sheikh al-Albaanee in Silsilat al-Hadeeth as-Saheehah: 2924.

*We did not benefit at all from this path we took in seeking truth nor the great length of time spent of our efforts,*

*Except that we gathered in that period, only the worthlessness of this one said that and other one said this.*

And Ayyub as-Sakhtiyaanee said, "*From the true success of an individual is Allaah guiding him to the Sunnah from the beginning of his youth.*" But consider the example of the one who passes through a stage of involvement with Sufism, and then moved on to a period of participation in group partisanship and various movements, and then slips from this to involving himself with prohibited entertainments such as movies and other matters which simply waste time, and then finally sucessfully moves on to an attachment to the Sunnah, how much of his time has been wasted and lost?! The Prophet, may Allaah's praise and salutations be upon him and his family, said, *{A servant of Allaah will not move his feet from his place on the Day of Judgment until he is asked about four matters..}* [37] and from them is his time and how he spent it. Yet someone who is granted success to adhere to the Sunnah early on, it is possible that after two or three years of study, with the permission of Allaah, he may become a reviewer, author, a verifier of hadeeth, or whatever Allaah, by virtue of His power, enables him to accomplish. So it is essential that he make his focus upon worldly affairs secondary to seeking knowledge, and does not make seeking knowledge secondary to worldly affairs. Allaah will not allow your efforts to be wasted.

(34) THE EMINENT GUIDING SCHOLAR SAALEH IBN FAUZAAN, MAY ALLAAH PRESERVE HIM, EXCERPTED FROM 'BENEFICIAL ANSWERS TO QUESTIONS ON NEW METHODOLOGIES': PAGE 130

*Question: I ask that you would give us your guiding advice for the beginning students of knowledge.*

Answer: My advice to the beginning students of knowledge is to become students of trustworthy scholars well known for their correct belief, knowledge, and advice. You should begin studying shorter summarized works in the various branches of knowledge and strive to memorize them; taking the explanation of these works from your scholars step by step. Particularly in reference to the educational courses in the institutes of knowledge and the Sharee'ah colleges, as these educational programs have tremendous benefit in that a student of knowledge is taught stage by stage.

Yet if a student is not able to attend these organized schools, then he should remain close to those scholars teaching in the masjids, whether this is to study jurisprudence, or Arabic grammar, or correct beliefs, or something similar. But as for what some of the young men do today, by starting their studies with longer detailed books, which one of them purchases a copy of and then simply sits in his home to read and study- then this is not proper. Indeed, this is not how we truly learn; rather,

[37]  Narrated in Jaame'a at-Tirmidhee: 2417/ & Sunan ad-Daaramee: 537/ -on the authority of Abu Burzah al-'Aslamee. It was declared authentic by Sheikh al-Albaanee in Saheeh al-Jaame'a as-Sagheer: 7300, and he stated in his verification of 'Iqtida'a al-'Ilm al-'Amal, "It chain of narration is authentic"

it is an arrogant self-deception. This is a way which some of the people proceed upon and then they proceed to speak in the matters of knowledge and give rulings in issues without true knowledge. They peak about Allaah without true knowledge, because they were not brought up and established upon a firm foundation. So it is essential to sit in front of the scholars in the circles of remembering Allaah through the study of knowledge, and it is necessary to have patience and endurance, as was mentioned by Imaam Shaafa'ee, may Allaah have mercy upon him:

*"The one who has not tasted the humbleness of learning for even an hour,*
*Drinks from the glass of ignorance for his entire life."*

(35) The Eminent Guiding Scholar Muqbil Ibn Haadee al-Waadiee, may Allaah have mercy upon him, from 'The Final Travels of the Imaam of the Arab Peninsula', by Umm Salamah as-Salafeeyah, Page 233

*Question: What is your advice for the beginner in seeking Sharee'ah knowledge?*
Answer: This is a wide area of discussion, as beginners vary and are on different levels. Among them are those who do not have the ability to write well, therefore it is proper that they begin with learning how to write. But there are those who write well so this will be easy upon them, if Allaah wills. So what remains is that they begin with the fundamentals of knowledge. The Messenger, upon him be the best of greetings and the best mention in the heavens by Allaah and His angels, said when he sent Mu'adh to Yemen, {*Certainly you will be coming to a people from the people of the previously revealed books, so make the first matter that you invite them to be bearing witness that there is none worthy of worship but Allaah alone and that Muhammad is the Messenger of Allaah.*} [38]. It is an issue of proceeding by stages no matter whether that occurs at the beginning of your seeking knowledge or an advanced level. It is not proper that someone study alone a great deal, as this will only leave partial traces of knowledge he has studied. When Imaam Shaafa'ee passed by a teacher of the child of the Muslim ruler he said, "*Do not convey to him the entirety of this branch of knowledge until he has mastered its fundamentals. Because if you transmit this area of knowledge to him as a whole before he has properly mastered it fundamentals, it will leave him with only fragments or portions of the knowledge he has studied.*" So this is one matter. An additional matter, as Imaam Shaafa'ee, may Allaah have mercy upon him states, "*Certainly, memorization and understanding are two gifts from Allaah, the Most Perfect, the Most High.*"

So the people differ in their level of possessing them. If you see a man who is able to memorize two pages a day from the Qur'aan, and you are not able to do that, then we advise you to memorize a single page. And perhaps your understanding of it will be stronger and firmer than the one who memorizes the two pages. And some of the people may be able to memorize an entire thirtieth of the Qur'aan in single day, as this is simply from the blessings of Allaah, the Most High, the most Exalted. And from Allaah alone we seek assistance and support. However, undertaking too

[38] Narrated in Saheeh al-Bukhaaree: 1496, 4347/-on the authority of 'Abdullah Ibn 'Abbaas. And it is found in Saheeh Muslim: 19/-on the authority of Mu'adh Ibn Jabal. It was declared authentic by Sheikh al-Albaanee in Saheeh al-Jaame'a as-Sagheer: 2298 from the hadeeth of Ibn 'Abbaas.

many lessons, and burdening of oneself with what you are not able to bear, will be the cause of your ruin.

(36) The Eminent Guiding Scholar Muhammad Ibn Saaleh al-'Utheimeen, may Allaah have mercy upon him, from 'The Book of Knowledge': Page 149

*Question: I want to seek Sharee'ah knowledge and begin studying; however I don't know how to begin. What do you advise me in this regard?*

Answer: The best methodology for the student of knowledge is for him to begin with seeking to understand the Word of Allaah, the Most Glorified and the Most Exalted, from the reliable books which explain the Qur'aan such as *((Tafseer Ibn-Katheer)01-01)* or *((Tafseer al-Baghawee )01-07).*

After this, he should proceed towards acquiring an understanding of what is affirmed as being authentic from the Sunnah of the Prophet, may Allaah's praise and salutations be upon him, from the reliable books of hadeeth, such as *((Bulugh al-Maraam )02-34)* or *((al-Muntaqaa)12-21)* and the fundamental books of authentic narrations such as *((Saheeh al-Bukhaaree)02-01)* and *((Saheeh Muslim)02-02).*

Then he should proceed to the books of sound belief such as *((al-Aqeedatul-Wasatiyyah)06-05)* from Sheikh al-Islaam Ibn Taymeeyah. Then continue on to the summarized books of jurisprudence for that school of jurisprudence which you consider to be closest to the Book and the Sunnah. In time you will advance to reading the longer books that will increase you in your knowledge.

(37) The Eminent Guiding Scholar Ahmad Ibn Yahya an-Najmee, may Allaah preserve him, from 'Decisive Rulings on the Methodologies of Calling to Allaah' Volume 1, Page 38

*Question: Our esteemed sheikh, may Allaah preserve you, I have a desire to seek Sharee'ah knowledge, and I want for you to clarify to me the correct path for seeking Sharee'ah knowledge- may Allaah reward you with good.*

Answer: In relation to seeking Sharee'ah knowledge, its path is clear. It is that you should seek knowledge from the scholars; those upon the methodology of the predecessors of the first generations of Muslims. You should be cautious and on your guard against of the people of the various new movements, those individuals of newly formed and innovated methodologies. So if you truly want advice, it is that you do not approach or go to these individuals, but that instead that you go to the people of knowledge. Those scholars that teach the Book of Allaah and the Sunnah of the Messenger of Allaah, upon him be the best mention in the heavens by Allaah and His angels and the best of greetings, and the correct beliefs held by the first three generations of believers. You should start with the most important subjects, and then proceed to those matters which are next or follow in level of importance.

(38) THE EMINENT GUIDING SCHOLAR MUQBIL IBN HAADEE AL-WAADIEE, MAY ALLAAH HAVE MERCY UPON HIM, EXCERPTED FROM 'THE FINAL TRAVELS OF THE IMAAM OF THE ARAB PENINSULA' BY UMM SALAMAH AS-SALAFEEYAH, PAGE 273

*Question: For the beginning student of knowledge, for example in America, what is your advice regarding those books which he should begin with and then those to proceed to step by step?*

Answer: If he is able to sit with a scholar and have him instruct and guide him upon the path of seeking knowledge, then this is a good way. Indeed, instruction through the scholars and the influence of the relationship that is between the student and his teacher will help make clear and evident within the mind of the student- what knowledge his sheikh relates to him. This method of instruction is a remarkable thing in terms of what is received and what is given back. So if this is easy then we advise him with this initially, and if that is not something possible for him then we advise him to begin with summarized books such as the book, *((A Beneficial Statement Regarding the Evidences of Tawheed)06-19)* by our brother in Islaam Sheikh Muhammad Ibn 'Abdul-Wahaab al-'Abdalee al-Wasaabee, and likewise the book, *((Thalaathatul-Usul)06-02)* by Sheikh Muhammad Ibn 'Abdul-Wahaab an-Najdee, may Allaah have mercy upon him, and also *((al-Aqeedatul-Wasateeyah)06-05)* by Sheikh al-Islaam Ibn Taymeeyah.

The student should dedicate time to the memorization of the Qur'aan. If he has the ability to memorize, then it is proper that he designates a large portion of his time for the memorization of the Qur'aan. This follows that which we mentioned regarding it. If he is a non-Arab, then we advise him to give importance to learning the Arabic language. This is because our brothers from the non-Arabs are quick to accept and follow the one who has strength in the Arabic language. Many people responded to the false call of Khomaynee, and the majority of those who responded were non-Arabs. Additionally many people responded to the false call of the Qaadeeanees, and many people responded to the false call of the Tijaanee Sufees because they had with them upon their way those who were strong in the Arabic language. Therefore, we advise our brothers from the non-Arabs to give importance to learning the Arabic language, such that if you draw a conclusion regarding a matter of the religion, you will understand whether your conclusion is properly derived or not. However, if one of our brothers is not from the non-Arabs then he should begin with the study of correct beliefs. Additionally, it is also important for the non-Arabs to proceed by small steps, in moderate amounts. We have ended with this part of the advice.

After this, if Allaah wills, perhaps a scholar can educate his students by the study of a single hadeeth from *((Saheeh al-Bukhaaree)02-01)* and benefit them with its proper understanding, as well as studying Imaam al-Bukhaaree's biography, as many scholars were amazed when encountering the biography of Imaam al-Bukhaaree. In this way, the students will benefit from it regarding both in the understanding of the hadeeth and in regards to the text of narration itself. And they will benefit in knowing how to search for information related to the narrators of the hadeeth, and how one is able to reach the assessment that a hadeeth is authentic or weak.

Perhaps only a short period will pass and they will benefit. Additionally, I advise them to specialize. So the one who has the desire to specialize whether it is, as was mentioned, in the study of hadeeth, or if he has a desire to specialize in grammar; then we advise him to settle himself upon that chosen area of grammar. This will allow him to best utilize his free time. So if one has a desire to specialize in hadeeth and the science of hadeeth terminology, then we advise him to do so, and another wishes to specialize in the explanations of Qur'aan or jurisprudence then we advise that he also do so.

In addition to what is mentioned, specializing has a basis in evidence, as Hudhaifah said, "*The people used to ask the Messenger of Allaah, may Allaah's praise and salutations be upon him, regarding good and I used to ask him about evil as I feared that it would come upon me.*" And the Prophet, may Allaah's praise and salutations be upon him, recognized this, even giving him the nickname, 'Holder of the secrets of the Messenger of Allaah', may Allaah's praise and salutations be upon him. From this we see that specialization is a beneficial matter. After this, we advise that you do not jump into too many lessons, as you will have entered into them but will not understand their various aspects properly, and your condition will become, as one person said:

And he proceeded upon his plans and spent the fruits of his youth, but in the end was uncertain and unsure, without have attained clear successes or failures. So do not undertake more lessons than you have the ability to tolerate and comprehend. And even worse than this is that one of you begin to attend lessons in the subject of correct beliefs, but then you say: "*By Allaah, so-and-so is teaching grammar, and by Allaah's decree he is benefiting his students*", so then he says, "*I will study with him!*" So then he studies for a short period of time in grammar, but eventually says, "So-and-so is now teaching hadeeth science terminology, and he is an ocean of knowledge in the science of hadeeth terminology, Allaah has decreed that he is excelling in this. So I will study hadeeth science terminology with him." Then, another comes along and informs him that someone is teaching the book of Imaam Shawkaanee related to jurisprudence. So now this same student then says "*I will go and study with him.*" and he goes and studies with him, leaving what he had begun studying a short time before.

This is truly a pity and a failure, and it has occurred to more than one individual, among those who become bored easily from the students of knowledge. So no, it is necessary as is said,

A man stands with his feet firmly upon the earth,

but the highest of his aspirations are in the stars.

It is necessary that he makes efforts and struggles and has patience with difficulties and hardships, as knowledge is not achieved except through suffering and difficulty, as occurred to our scholars of the first generations, may Allaah the Most High have mercy upon them. And from Allaah we seek help and assistance.

**(39) The Eminent Guiding Scholar Muhammad Ibn Saaleh al-'Utheimeen, may Allaah have mercy upon him, From 'The Book of Knowledge': Page 124**

*Question: With what do you advise the one who wants to seek Sharee'ah knowledge but he lives far away from the scholars, considering however, that he has a collection of books containing both complete books as well as summarized books?*

Answer: I advise him to persevere in seeking knowledge, firstly by seeking the assistance of Allaah, the Most High, the Most Exalted, then, after that, through the assistance of the people of knowledge. This is because a person receiving knowledge from the hand of a scholar lessens the time used in study, compared to the one who goes and reads various different books in which there are differing views and opinions. However, I do not say as some do, [Certainly, it is not at all possible to acquire knowledge except through a scholar or from a person of knowledge.] This is not correct. The reality of the matter contradicts this. However, your studies with a scholar clarify and illuminate the path for you and shorten the length of having to proceed upon it.

**(40) Sheikh 'Abdul-'Azeez Ibn 'Abdullah Ibn Baaz, may Allaah have mercy upon him, excerpted From 'A Collection of Rulings and Various Statements': Vol. 7, Page 243**

*Question: What is your view of the saying found on the tongues of many students of knowledge that, "The one whose teacher is his book, his errors are greater that which he is correct in"?*

Answer: It is well known that the one whose sole teacher is his book, then his mistakes are more numerous than the matters he is correct in. This is the expression which we know, and it is correct, as the one who does not study with the people of knowledge, does not take knowledge from them, and does not understand the path that they have passed upon in seeking knowledge, certainly makes many errors. Also, it may be unclear and doubtful to him the difference between what is right and what is wrong or incorrect regarding specific issues, as he has not fully understood the Sharee'ah evidences, nor the established methods which the people of knowledge have made use of; meaning those which they had utilized and acted upon in making such determinations.

As to whether his mistakes will be more numerous than what they are correct in, then this is something debatable. But in any case he will make many mistakes, as he did not learn from the people of knowledge nor benefit from them. Thus, he does not understand the principles which must be utilized in reaching conclusions, and therefore makes many mistakes. Additionally, he cannot distinguish between mistakes and what is correct within printed and manuscript books, as an error will appear in a book and he does not have the familiarity and ability to recognize that, and so believes it to be correct. He then may give a ruling of permissibility for that which Allaah has forbidden, or declare forbidden that which Allaah has made permissible, because he lacks insight. This occurs simply because of a printing or writing error that he came across in a book.

For example, it may state, "*Such and such is not permissible.*" while what is correct from the original text is that states that it is permissible, as there is may be an unwarranted addition to the text of that printing which is an error. Or the opposite where it says, "*Such and such is permissible*" while what is correct in the original text is that it states that it is not permissible. This would be caused by an omission in that specific printing or line, and this is a tremendous mistake. Similar is the expression: "*...what is correct is such-and-such*", while what is actually correct is that is stated "*... what is not correct is such-and-such*". So he would get confused in this because of his lack of perceptiveness and knowledge and so does not recognize an error that may be present in a book, or situations similar to this.

(41) The Eminent Guiding Scholar Muhammad Ibn Saaleh al-'Utheimeen, may Allaah have mercy upon him, excerpted from 'The Book of Knowledge': Page 153

*Question: With what do you advise the one who begins seeking knowledge when he is older in age? Additionally, if is it not easy for him to take knowledge from and sit often with a scholar, will he benefit from seeking knowledge without a scholar?*

Answer: We ask Allaah, the Exalted, to assist the one whom He has honored by directing him towards seeking knowledge. However, seeking knowledge is itself a difficult matter and requires tremendous effort, and we know that often as a person progresses in age they increase in weakness and decrease in mental ability. So it is necessary that this man who is just now beginning to seek knowledge chooses a scholar whom he knows is trustworthy and then seeks knowledge from him. The reason for this is that seeking knowledge by means of sitting with the scholars is more beneficial, quicker, and easier. It is more productive, because a scholar is considered an encyclopedia of knowledge, especially the one who possesses beneficial knowledge in various areas such as grammar, the explanation of the Qur'aan, hadeeth narrations, jurisprudence, and other areas of knowledge. So compare this to the one studying who needs to read twenty different books! It is easier to receive this from a scholar, and in addition this method requires less time, and brings one closer to acquiring a sound understanding. Perhaps you may rely upon a book and the methodology of the author of that book conflicts with the methodology of the scholars from the first generations of Muslims, whether this be in the method of derivation rulings or even the ruling that is arrived at.

Therefore, we advise this man who desires to seek knowledge at an advanced age to connect himself to a trustworthy scholar and take knowledge from him, as this will be more beneficial for him. Do not give up hope, and do not say, [I am too old for that], as by that you will cut yourself off from knowledge. And it was mentioned that one of the people of knowledge entered a masjid one day after the time of salatul-dhuhr and sat down; then one of the people said to him, "*Stand and pray two rakaats*", meaning for greeting the masjid. So that individual prayed two rakaat. That same day the same person entered the masjid prayed salatul-'asr and afterwards he stood to pray two rakaat. But a man said to him, "*Do not pray, as at this time it is prohibited.*" So he said to himself, "*It is necessary that I strive to seek knowledge, in order to understand these matters."* And he began seeking knowledge until he became a leading scholar. So that ignorance was the cause of him acquiring knowledge. Therefore if Allaah knows that you have a good intention and He then grants you success, you may gather a significant amount of knowledge.

(42) The Eminent Guiding Scholar Muhammad Ibn Saaleh al-'Utheimeen, may Allaah have mercy upon him, from 'Islamic Revival; Guidelines and Guidance': Page 126

*Question: What is the best way to acquire authentic Sharee'ah knowledge in light of the conditions of the age we find ourselves in?*

Answer: Without doubt from the best ways for an individual to begin is with knowledge of the Book of Allaah, and then with what is easy for him from the authentic Sunnah of the Messenger of Allaah, may Allaah's praise and salutations be upon him. Afterwards, he should proceed to what has been written by the people of knowledge in the various rulings and other subjects. However, that which I prefer for the students of knowledge is that they concentrate upon learning the fundamentals and not only the derived rulings. What is meant by this is that they are not from amongst those who only memorize various issues. Rather, that they are from amongst those who give importance to memorizing the fundamentals, principals, and guidelines, such that if there comes to him any smaller matter or issue he has the ability to apply these fundamentals and principles to it. Otherwise, his condition would be as the scholars have mentioned, saying, *"The one who is cut off from the foundations, is deprived of reaching the desired results"*.

You find many students of knowledge who fill their mind with single individual issues and rulings, yet if there occurs something which is outside its specifics, even to the smallest degree, they cannot comprehend anything concerning it. This is because he isn't someone who grasps and understands the guidelines, fundamentals, and principals upon which the rulings of these individual issues are based and derived. And it was mentioned to us at the time when we were students that there was a man who was a student of knowledge. However, he simply memorized without understanding. He had memorized the book *((al-Furu'a)08-11)* which is a book from the school of jurisprudence attributed to Imaam Ahmad Ibn Hanbal. And this book, *((al-Furu'a)08-11)*, is one of the most comprehensive books from the scholars who adhere to this school of jurisprudence. It also contains statements and indications of the positions of the four well known schools of jurisprudence, as well as others. It was authored by Muhammad Ibn Muflih, may Allaah have mercy upon him, one of the students of Sheikh al-Islaam Ibn Taymeeyah. He was distinguished as one of those most knowledgeable of the positions of Sheikh al-Islaam Ibn Taymeeyah in jurisprudence, such that even Ibn Qayyim referred to him regarding the positions of Sheikh al-Islaam Ibn Taymeeyah in jurisprudence. But what is important is that he authored the book *((al-Furu'a)08-11)* .

So it occurred that one of the students memorized it completely; however, he did not understand anything from its meaning. The students of knowledge would come to him as if he was a book. If there was an issue that they needed to investigate, they would say, "*What did Ibn Muflih state in such and such a section, in such and such a chapter?*" He would then recount that to them, even though he did not understand its meaning! So an individual must be concerned with memorizing the rulings, as well as properly grasping the principles; meaning, the principles and fundamentals of deriving rulings from the sources. This is from one of the most important matters there is for the student of knowledge.

(43) The Eminent Guiding Scholar Muhammad Ibn Saaleh al-'Utheimeen, may Allaah have mercy upon him, From 'The Book of Knowledge': Page 181

*Question: Briefly, what is the way knowledge is sought, may Allaah reward you with good.*

Answer:   A summary by points of the ways to seek knowledge is:

*Be diligent in your memorization of the Book of Allaah the Exalted, and designate a specific time every day to review and maintain its recitation, while contemplating it and understanding it. And if a benefit suggests itself to you during your recitation, then write it down.

* Likewise, be diligent in memorizing what is easy for you from the authentic Sunnah of the Messenger, may Allaah's praise and salutations be upon him, and from this is the memorization of the book ((*Amdaat al-Ahkam(02-28)*

 * Be careful to concentrate and reinforce what you learn by not taking just a morsel of knowledge from this area of knowledge, and then another small amount from that area; this will only waste your time and scatter your intellectual strength.

* Start with smaller books by studying and understanding them well, and then proceed to those on the next level above them, until you acquire knowledge step by step, such that you become well grounded and feel assured of your understanding of it. Give attention to understanding the fundamentals and principles behind individual issues and write down every related matter that you come across. And in this light it has been said, "*The one who is cut off from the foundations, is deprived of reaching the desired results*". Discuss issues with your scholar, or with those of your associates who are similar to you whom you are confident of their knowledge and practice of the religion; and if you are unable to debate it with anyone then imagine in your mind that someone is debating it with you.

**(44) The Eminent Guiding Scholar Muqbil Ibn Haadee al-Waadiee, may Allaah have mercy upon him, From 'The Final Travels of the Imaam of the Arab Peninsula' by Umm Salamah as-Salafeeyah Page 254**

*Question: I am a teacher in an Islamic school, teaching boys between the ages of seven and eleven various studies related to Islaam. What do you advise me to teach them? Also, which are the best books for them in the area of fundamental beliefs?*

Answer: A book that is suitable for them in the area of correct beliefs is the book *((A Beneficial Statement Regarding the Evidences of Tawheed)06-19)* by our brother the esteemed Sheikh Muhammad Ibn 'Abdul-Wahaab al-Wasaabee, and likewise *((Kitaab al-Tawheed)06-01)*, by Sheikh Muhammad Ibn 'Abdul-Wahaab an-Najdee, may Allaah have mercy upon him, and the book *(al-Aqeedatul-Wasateeyyah)06-05)* by Sheikh al-Islaam Ibn Taymeeyah. Then after this if you are able, have them memorize the hadeeth narrations which are found in both the collections of Imaams Bukhaaree and Muslim. We advise that they undertake this with hadeeth narrations such as *{The best of you are those who learn the Qur'aan and teach it}* [39], and such as, *{Islaam is build upon five, bearing witness that there is none worth of worship except Allaah, and that Muhammad is the Messenger of Allaah, to establish the obligatory prayer, pay the obligatory zakaat charity, the obligatory pilgrimage of Hajj, and the obligatory fast}* [40]. This is how this version of the narration is structured: *{...the obligatory pilgrimage of Hajj, and the obligatory fast}* with the wording regarding to Hajj coming before that of fasting, but it is also narrated with the wording related to fasting coming before Hajj in some narrations. Likewise, also give attention to those hadeeth that are authentic but not found within the two 'Saheeh' collections of Imaam al-Bukhaaree and Muslim, such as the narration, *{The one who swears by his faithfulness is not from us.}* [41], and similar short hadeeth that will remain in the minds of the students. This is what I advise you with, may Allaah bless you.

Then after this, teach them the Arabic language, as the Arabic language is the language of the Qur'aan. As that which is evil came to many of our brothers from the non-Arabs, some of them accept and follow him such as occurred with Khomaynee the Raafidhee, and some of them accepting and following the Qadeeyannes, and some of them accepting and following the Teejanee Sufees, and some of them accepting and following any astray sect which presents itself to them, simply because they themselves do not understand the Arabic language. So every person who calls them to some way and they consider him to have some knowledge, they follow and

---

[39]  Narrated in Saheeh al-Bukhaaree: 5027/ Sunan Abu Daawud: 1452/ Jaame'a at-Tirmidhee: 2907/ & Musnad Imaam Ahmad: 414, 502, -on the authority of 'Uthmaan Ibn 'Afaan. It was declared authentic by Sheikh al-Albaanee in Silsilat al-Hadeeth as-Saheehah:1173, Saheeh at-Targheeb at-Tarheeb: 1415, Mishkaat al-Masaabeeh: 2109, Saheeh al-Jaame'a as-Sagheer: 5630, and in other works such as Saheeh Sunan Abu Dawud & Saheeh Sunan at-Tirmidhee.

[40]  Narrated in Saheeh al-Bukhaaree: 8/ Jaame'a at-Tirmidhee: 2709/ Sunan an-Nasaa'ee: 5004/ & Musnad Imaam Ahmad: 4783, 5639, 5979/ -on the authority of 'Abdullah Ibn 'Umar. And it is narrated in Saheeh Muslim: 16/ -on the authority of 'Umar Ibn 'Khattab. It was declared authentic by Sheikh al-Albaanee in Irwa' al-Ghaleel : 781,901,971, Saheeh at-Targheeb at-Tarheeb: 350, 737, and in his verification of 'al-Emaan' by Ibn Taymeeyah pg. 4.

[41]  Narrated in Sunan Abu Daawud: 3253/ & Musnad Imaam Ahmad: 22471/ -on the authority of 'Buraydah Ibn al-Haseeb. It was declared authentic by Sheikh al-Albaanee in Silsilat al-Hadeeth as-Saheehah:94, 325, Mishkaat al-Masaabeh: 3420, Saheeh at-Targheeb at-Tarheeb: 2013, 2954, Saheeh al-Jaame'a as-Sagheer: 5436, 6203, as well as in Saheeh Sunan Abu Dawud. Sheikh Muqbil declared it authentic in al-Jaame'a al-Saheeh: 387, 3070, 3280, 4509.

accept that which he calls them to.

So we advise them or advise our brothers to teach their sons the Arabic language. It is essential and it is the language of the Qur'aan. Allaah, the Most Perfect, the Most High says, ⟨*An Arabic Qur'aan*⟩-(Surah Yusuf:2) and He says, ⟨*All praise is due to Allaah, Who has sent down to His servant the Book, and has not placed therein any crookedness*⟩-(Surah al-Kahf:1) The Qur'aan is in the Arabic language, and the Sunnah of the Messenger of Allaah, may Allaah's praise and salutations be upon him, is in the Arabic language, as are the books of jurisprudence. Therefore it is necessary and essential, to teach their sons the Arabic language until they reach a level of understanding where they become safe and protected from someone inviting them to falsehood that they might respond to due to not knowing Arabic. They may even accept the doubts and false ideas presented to them by Christian missionaries or others. Perhaps they may approach them with doubts related to alleged errors within the Qur'aan. But the Qur'aan has been supported and given tremendous attention by our scholars, may Allaah the Exalted have mercy upon them for every service they have put forth. They have discussed these apparent issues, all praise is due to Allaah, in the books that are explanations of the Qur'aan as well as in the book ((al-Mughnee)07-07) of Ibn Qudaamah and other works. So the Arabic language is very important; then after this comes the study of the correct beliefs, and then after this the memorization of what they are able to from the Qur'aan. Next, proceed to the study of what is required to fulfill their need to understand how the Messenger of Allaah, may Allaah's praise and salutations be upon him, prayed, as well as his other deeds and activities. These issues should be given priority over other matters. And from Allaah we seek help and assistance.

(45) The Eminent Guiding Scholar Saaleh Ibn 'Abdul-'Azeez Aal-Sheikh, may Allaah preserve him, from 'Obstacles in Seeking Knowledge'

### Two Significant Obstacles on the Path to Knowledge

Also from these barriers is their saying, [Seeking knowledge diverts from calling to Allaah, and the people today need to be called to Allaah, but they do not have the same need for knowledge.]

This is a very dangerous claim which deadens one's efforts, and I know of many who have been afflicted in this way. These are those who say, [The knowledge of calling to Allaah is more important for us, along with associating with the youth, going with them, mixing and traveling with them to admonish them, or being engaged in some action or activity. As seeking knowledge doesn't bring results, or that the results from seeking knowledge come only after many years.] Indeed, this is a dangerous claim, and a significant barrier which impairs and weakens one's efforts. And it stems from a mistaken understanding regarding knowledge and deeds. The fundamental principle is that knowledge is one aspect or part and calling to Allaah is a separate part. However, knowledge does not come all at once, and calling to Allaah also is not done all at once.

So the student of knowledge, if he studies while also calling to Allaah according to the level of knowledge that Allaah has enabled him to acquire in this area, then he has established himself in knowledge as well as in bringing about good results through calling, to the level of understanding that he is given. But being diverted away from seeking knowledge by being busy with calling to Allaah simply causes one's calls to Allaah to be build upon ignorance. And this is what has afflicted many individuals.

In regard to this, the people have become three types:

Firstly, is one who is exclusively occupied in seeking knowledge, and he does not affect people beneficially at all.

Secondly is the one who turns to calling to Allaah while being ignorant or mostly ignorant of Allaah's religion.

So the first type of person is criticized and the second type is also criticized. This is because knowledge which does not bring good to the one who possesses it nor to others- is not considered beneficial, meaning to the people. As the student of knowledge, when he learns a little and then teaches it, preserves that knowledge with the Muslim Ummah. So if someone acquires knowledge, then his efforts in calling to Allaah should be to that level and degree of what that worshiper of Allaah has been given from knowledge. The endeavor of calling to Allaah is branches from knowledge which is its foundation. It is not possible for a worshipper to call to Allaah without knowledge.

As for the third type of person, he calls to that which he has learned, but he leaves off efforts of calling to those matters which he does not have knowledge of, as in doing that he would simply be like the one who blindly enters into that which he lacks knowledge of. Certainly, the Most High and Exalted says, ❦*Say "This is my way; I invite unto Allaah with 'al-baseerah', I and whosoever follows me*❧-(Surah Yusuf:108). The word '*al-baseerah*' means sure knowledge, ❦*I call to Allaah upon sure knowledge*❧. So it can be seen that knowledge is one necessary part, and similarly calling to Allaah is another additional part. Therefore, if you understand a matter according to its related evidences and it becomes clear to you, then you may call to that matter which you have learned according to what brings benefit to the people.

Some of the people believe that calling to Allaah encompasses nothing other than preaching, or presenting lectures, or travelling to villages, or giving speeches, and similar general activities in which one speaks with the people. But this is not correct. The prophets had the most complete and comprehensive call, and their statements were related to the highest matter of the right of Allaah, the Most High the Most Exalted, and singling Him out for worship alone. So if a student of knowledge teaches people then by this he is calling to Allaah. His teaching the people is in fact calling to Allaah, the Most High, the Most Exalted. He is calling himself as well as other than himself. However, the people have different situations and conditions, and what is facilitated for a person depends on the individual.

Imaam Maalik, may Allaah have mercy upon him, was asked about his exclusive dedication to knowledge, and his leaving of other areas of activity such as jihaad in the path of Allaah. He replied, "*Certainly from the people there are those whom Allaah has facilitated for them prayer, and there are those whom Allaah has facilitated for them the giving of charity, and there are those whom Allaah has facilitated for them the obligatory and non-obligatory pilgrimages, and there are those whom Allaah has facilitated for them striving in the path of Allaah, and there are those whom Allaah has facilitated for them knowledge. Indeed, Allaah has facilitated for me the matter of knowledge and I am pleased with that which Allaah has facilitated for me.*"

This narration remains to this day a reminder of the significant need of the people to remain upon beneficial knowledge.

Still, we should not permit the adopting of this dangerous deception concerning seeking knowledge, which is from the deceptions of Shaytaan: that one should prevent oneself from becoming occupied with knowledge because of the need to call to Allaah in more important. This was said by some of the people who came before us by fifteen years, and this is now twenty years later. When the years passed by, they become weak in their knowledge. They did not excel in seeking knowledge nor did they excel in calling people to Allaah. Knowledge is a weapon in your hand that you truly require and that you fight with, that you clarify and call to the truth with, to the degree of the knowledge Allaah the Most High, the Most Magnificent gives to you as His worshiper....

...Also from the obstacles upon the path of knowledge is the statement of the one who says, [Gaining knowledge requires a long period, dedication, and time, and I don't have the ability to dedicate myself to it or proceed as needed.] This is partially correct. It is true from the aspect that what is required is that knowledge remains with an individual. However, you do not know that which Allaah the Most High, the Most Magnificent will make possible or grant you the patience to accomplish. Moreover every breath of the scholar is in his favor and every step of the student of knowledge is written among his good deeds as he is engaged in a tremendous act of worship. How many people do not recognize within themselves a strong capacity to seek knowledge, then they seek knowledge and are patient in that until after some time they excel?! How many of those who had average or below average grades in school as now students of knowledge, benefitting the people?! While many of those who excelled in school are simply proceeding through life without benefiting anyone. Their previous achievements came to nothing.

The reason for this is as follows. One should know that seeking knowledge is a tremendously praiseworthy form of worship, if you understand that what is sought after is humbleness and the fruits that come from it, then according to the degree of their steadfastness in their continuing efforts- there will be results. Do not consider the time you spend in a gathering of knowledge or listening to a tape with the explanation of a book or a similar endeavor to be time wasted. Activities such as this will endow you with a love of knowledge and its people and will facilitate your acquiring knowledge step by step.

And it was mentioned to you the previous night, as is narrated by al-Khatteeb al-Baghdaadee in his book *((Jaam'ee Ahlaaq ar-Raawee wa Aadab as-Saame'a)04-11)* that one of the people of hadeeth said, *"There was a young man who was seeking knowledge of the hadeeth of the Messenger of Allaah and this became difficult for him. One day he passed by a place where there was a rock or stone, and he observed some water that streamed forth in small amounts, trickle after trickle, which had worn out a depression upon the stone where it flowed. He said to himself: "This is a lesson for you, oh so-and-so. Your heart is not stronger than this stone, and knowledge is not weaker that this flowing water. So he returned and become one of the people of hadeeth and its narrators."* This narration is transmitted authentically.

### (46) The Eminent Guiding Scholar Saaleh Ibn 'Abdul-'Azeez Aal-Sheikh, may Allaah preserve him, From 'From the Fruits of Knowledge': Question 2

*Question: I have been seeking knowledge for some time; however I do not see its results upon myself or upon my family except to a small degree. So what is the reason for this, and what is the remedy for this situation?*

Answer: The fact that a worshipper who is a student of knowledge recognizes his shortcomings is itself from the fruits of knowledge. He recognizes that knowledge has not had a significant effect upon him, and also that it is necessary that he struggle within himself. This is indeed from the fruits of beneficial knowledge. Knowledge is something that must be facilitated for someone and not everyone will have facilitated for him the all various types of knowledge, and not everyone will have a specific type of knowledge made easy for him particularly. Likewise specific actions and deeds are not something which are facilitated for every individual. A man came to Imaam Maalik, may Allaah the Exalted have mercy upon him, and said to him, *"Oh our scholar and leader! We see from you every good matter, except that you do not make jihaad in the path of Allaah." He replied, "Indeed, from the servants of Allaah there are those for whom He has facilitated the matter of prayer, and there are among the servants of Allaah those for whom He has facilitated the matter of fasting, and there are from the servants of Allaah those for whom He has facilitated the matter of pilgrimage to Mecca, and there are among the servants of Allaah those for whom He has facilitated the matter of jihaad, and there are from the servants of Allaah those for whom He has facilitated the matters of knowledge and teaching. I am from those for whom this last has been made easy and I am pleased by that which Allaah facilitated for me."*

The meaning of this is that it is difficult for an individual to establish efforts in every area or type of endeavor, which truly bear fruit and results. This is very difficult, and perhaps the one who was asked to realize this would not be able to fulfill and achieve it, meaning that it is very difficult to successfully seek knowledge in every branch of learning. A student of knowledge who for example, teaches others, always enjoins the good and forbids evil, always fulfills the rights of his parents and those of his children, as well as ensuring at every time to fulfill the general rights others have over him. The fact that these matters are so numerous makes it difficult for them to all be fulfilled by one person from among the people of knowledge. Yet, Allaah, the

Most High the Most Exalted, has designated from His servants those who actually fulfill all of these varied matters. This is the position of the leading scholars, and they are rare in this Muslim Ummah. Their position is that of the revivers of the religion and so it is not proper for someone to place or consider himself at their level.

So if it is due this reason that you say, "I do not see the effects within me", then it is upon you to continue to struggle within yourself and not have disdain for yourself. Do not say, [Knowledge is not benefiting me], or, [I cannot benefit through knowledge], such that you abandon seeking knowledge. No, as knowledge certainly is affected by the performance of the obligatory duties, the abandoning of forbidden acts, studying knowledge, and by beneficial speech. An important factor may only have a small effect; however it will certainly have an effect upon your gaining knowledge. But if knowledge does not have any effect, meaning that the one who has acquired it performs forbidden acts, or falls into major sins, and from this we seek refuge with Allaah, or neglects the obligatory duties, or leaves giving the worshipers of Allaah their rights, or commits injustice against them in regard to their wealth, their possessions, or those prominent among them or something similar; then in this case, it is upon him to repent to Allaah, the Most High, the Most Exalted, and turn to him for assistance. As in this case knowledge brought forth evil results upon him. We ask Allaah, the Most High, the Most Exalted, for health and security.

(47) The Eminent Guiding Scholar Saaleh Ibn Fauzaan, may Allaah preserve him, from 'al-Muntaqaa Min Fataawa': Vol. 2, Page 209

*Question: What is best for the students of knowledge: to devote themselves completely to seeking knowledge, and then afterwards fully dedicate themselves to spreading knowledge among the people, inviting their neighbors and those around them to Allaah? Or is it better to seek knowledge for perhaps a month and then to stop studying, due to the need to engage in calling to Allaah and so proceed according to the limits of the knowledge one has acquired?*

Answer: What is better is that he continues seeking knowledge until he possesses results from his studies as well understanding the fundamentals which he can build upon. As for starting in seeking knowledge and then stopping, this disrupts the proper attaining of knowledge and causes confusion in one's understanding and thinking. Moreover, it is not permissible for him to call to Allaah except after having prepared himself with knowledge. Likewise do not occupy yourself with teaching until after you have completed your studies and have acquired comprehensive knowledge, as one who lacks a thing cannot give to others. There is a well-known wise statement, "The one who neglects the foundation is deprived of achieving the results".

(48) The Eminent Guiding Scholar Saaleh Ibn Fauzaan, may Allaah preserve him, excerpted From 'A Selection of Islamic Rulings': Vol. 2, Page 207

*Question: You have mentioned before about the importance of seeking knowledge and devoting oneself to it. Is the meaning of this that the student of knowledge, in doing so, separates himself from the people and from other beneficial endeavors? I hope that you would clarify this, due to the importance of this issue.*

Answer:  It is required that you give to seeking knowledge what is sufficient for it in regard to time and effort. You should assign it sufficient time, and what is above that you spend in other affairs, such as meeting and interacting with the people in order to bring forth benefit, inviting the people to matters of goodness, as well as other endeavors and deeds. However, giving it the highest priority, you should allocate the largest part of your time to seeking knowledge.

(49) The Eminent Guiding Scholar Muhammad 'Amaan al-Jaamee, may Allaah have mercy upon him, from an audio lecture entitled, 'Twenty-seven Questions Regarding the Methodology of the First Three Generations of Muslims'

*Question: In consideration of your experience and your efforts in seeking knowledge- does seeking knowledge, memorizing texts, occupying oneself in the rulings of various issues, researching, and reading, conflict with the endeavor of calling to Allaah?*

Answer:  I believe that this question does not truly need to be answered. In truth the answer is simple. These matters are from the ways and groundwork for calling to Allaah. Seek knowledge by these means because you are preparing yourself, as seeking knowledge prepares the student of knowledge for the work of calling. Yes through seeking knowledge you are indeed preparing yourself for calling to Allaah. Calling to Allaah is an obligation, but only upon the people of understanding and insight. This way of gaining knowledge and insight into matters is what will benefit and help you become able to call to Allaah. Calling to Allaah is not such a simple matter, such that anyone can leave from his home wanting to call the people to Allaah and to enjoin what is good and forbid that which is wrong, despite the fact that he is ignorant and has not studied, he has not developed himself through these means. Therefore first seek knowledge and then proceed forth to call to Allaah.

(50) The Eminent Guiding Scholar 'Abdul-'Azeez Ibn 'Abdullah Ibn Baaz, may Allaah have mercy upon him, From 'Collection of Rulings and Various Statements': Vol. 8, Page 407

*Question: Some people hold the view that it is necessary that efforts of calling to Allaah only be in the masjids. What is your position regarding this? And which environments and methods are acceptable in the issue of calling to Allaah?*

Answer: In the name of Allaah, all praise is due to Allaah. Calling to Allaah is not limited masjids only. There are clearly other locations and means that are also related to it. There is no doubt that the masjids hold opportunities for calling to Allaah, such as during the day of Jumu'ah sermon, and other sermons, and preaching around the times of the prayers, and circles of learning. So the masjid is the foundation for the spreading of knowledge and the religion. However, calling to Allaah is not restricted to the masjid alone.

The caller to Allaah also invites in places other than the masjids, such as at any suitable gatherings as well as at casual gatherings. So the believers should seize the opportunities to call to Allaah by way of the different forms of modern media, and also by means of written works. All of these are from the ways of calling to Allaah. The intelligent person seizes the opportunities at every time and place where it is possible to call and invite, putting forth as much effort as he is able in calling to Allaah with wisdom, good speech, and excellent behavior.

(51) The Eminent Guiding Scholar Saaleh Ibn 'Abdul-'Azeez Aal-Sheikh, may Allaah preserve him, From 'From the Fruits of Knowledge', Question 6

*Question: What is your view regarding the one who explains the statement of the Messenger, may Allaah's praise and salutations be upon him, "Whoever Allaah intends good for He grants him understanding of the religion", to mean an understanding of which are the best of actions to spend your time upon, and of those which of them possesses the greatest reward that we should give precedence to over other righteous actions, as they are of greater benefit to us in that specific time?*

Answer: This is correct; this is a accurate explanation of the hadeeth, and part of what this hadeeth indicates. Indeed, understanding and teaching the student of knowledge which good deeds have preference and priority is from beneficial knowledge. This means, for example, that such and such action is better and has more reward than this other deed. This requires knowledge and understanding. So if you inform him of that, there is no doubt that he will prefer and incline towards it, as it is better for him. Imaam Ahmad, may Allaah have mercy upon him, when al-Haafidh Abu Zur'ah UbaidAllaah Ibn 'Abdul-Kareem ar-Razee, who was well known, came to him, when he came to the city of Baghdaad, he would discuss and study hadeeth with him. He would discuss and debate with him regarding hadeeth from after salatul-'isha to salatul-fajr, because he only had come for a specific amount of days and he was one of the preservers of hadeeth. They discussed and examined and memorized narrations, distinguishing and recognizing the weak ones from other than them, those with hidden defects, the fabricated ones and so forth.

This benefited the Muslim Ummah tremendously, as during this time Abu Zur'ah was rarely in Baghdaad. Imaam Ahmad said, "*We substituted the praying at night with the sitting and discussion with Abu Zur'ah.*" So he did not stand in prayer those specific nights of the visit, and did not pray these non obligatory prayers as was his custom. So he left his usual practice and only discussed hadeeth with Abu Zur'ah. There is no doubt that this action of his required knowledge and understanding. This is from the understanding of the religion. As *{Whoever Allaah intends good for He grants him understanding in the religion.}* [42]. If a student of knowledge reaches a certain level of knowledge of the religion, he selects the most preferred action from the various preferred actions and the most commendable act from the praiseworthy acts from the various deeds of worship which are possible at a specific time. He chooses the preferred, and selects the most praiseworthy matter from the actions of merit available to him. So there is no doubt that this understanding of affairs is from what Allaah, the Most High, the Most Exalted, gives to some of his worshipers. This situation of priorities frequently reach him during the day and the night, for him this situation of choosing one matter over another is common. For example, the recitation of the Qur'aan before Salatul-fajr in the morning or asking Allaah for forgiveness. Which of these two is preferred?

Presently for many people it is something well known that they usually recite the Qur'aan before salatul-fajr in the morning, holding that this is better than seeking forgiveness. Yet many of the people of knowledge such as Sheikh al-Islaam Ibn Taymeeyah and leading scholars well known for efforts in calling to Allaah give precedence to seeking forgiveness at that time over other deeds, because this is from the guidance of the Prophet, upon him be the best mention in the heavens and the best of greetings. The Prophet, upon him be Allaah's praise and salutations, did not recite Qur'aan between the calling of the adhan of fajr and the call to begin the actual prayer, Also the people who seek forgiveness fall under the general meaning of the statement of the Exalted, *those who pray and seek Allaah's forgiveness in the last hours of the night.*-(Surah Aal-'Imraan:17) and in the general meaning of the statement of the Most High, the Exalted, *They used to sleep but little by night. And in the hours before dawn, they were asking for forgiveness.*-(Surah adh-Dhaariyat:17-18) al-Hasan al-Basree, may Allaah the Exalted have mercy upon him, stated in explaining this verse, "*They would sleep only a little at night, and they would be frightened in the fear of their Lord. So when the morning came they sought His forgiveness having fear that their actions may not be accepted from them.*"

---

[42]  Narrated in Saheeh al-Bukhaaree: 71, 3116, 7312/ Saheeh Muslim: 1037/ Sunan Ibn Maajah: 221/ al-Muwatta Maalik: 1300, 1667/ Musnad Imaam Ahmad: 16395: 16404, and other narrations/ Musannaf Ibn Abee Shaybah: 31792/ & Sunan ad-Daaramee: 224, 226/- on the authority of Mu'aweeyah. And it is found in Jaame'a al-Tirmidhee: 2645/ & Musnad Imaam Ahmad: 2786/ & Sunan ad-Daaramee: 270, 2706/- on the authority of Ibn "Abbaas. And  it is found in Sunan Ibn Maajah: 220/ Musannaf 'Abdul-Razzaaq: 30851/- on the authority of Abu Hurairah. It was declared authentic by Sheikh al-Albaanee in Saheeh al-Aadab al-Mufrad: 517, Silsilat al-Hadeeth as-Saheehah: 1194, 1195, 1196, Saheeh at-Targheeb at-Tarheeb: 67, as well as in other of his books. Sheikh Muqbil declared it authentic in al-Jaame'a al-Saheeh: 9, 3123, 4650.

(52) The Eminent Guiding Scholar Muhammad Ibn Saaleh al-'Utheimeen, may Allaah have mercy upon him, from 'The Book of Knowledge': Page 152

*Question: Should the beginning student of knowledge start seeking knowledge by researching various evidences of different issues or by simply following one of the leading scholars of the four well-known established schools of jurisprudence? Our esteemed sheikh, what is your guidance in this matter? May Allaah the exalted preserve you.*

Answer: It is obligatory upon the beginning student of knowledge to search for the evidence to the extent he is able, as what is desired is that he reach or understand the evidence. Additionally, this is towards the aim of actualizing the practice of seeking the relevant evidences and how to derive them. He will then be proceeding towards Allaah upon understanding and clear evidence. It is not permissible for him to blindly follow except through necessity, such as when he researches but is not able to reach a result or conclusion, or an incident happens to him that requires acting immediately and he was not able to understand the ruling through its evidences before the necessary time would have passed. So if this occurs then he may blindly follow while having the intention that when the evidence of the matter becomes clear to him he will return to it and then follow it. In the case he reaches different possible rulings given by the scholars, then it is said that then you have a choice, some say to take the easier choice as this agrees with the statement of the Exalted,

❖*Allaah intends for you ease..*❖-(Surah al-Baqarah:185)

Yet it has also been said that one should take the more strict of the choices because that would be safer as following the other rulings might leave you with doubt whether he has fulfilled that which was obligatory or not. As the Prophet, may Allaah's praise and salutations be upon him, said, *{The one who fears Allaah in regard to doubtful matters; he has protected and preserved his religion and his honor.}* [43]. However, the preferred way in this situation is that you take that opinion that you believe in most likelihood is closest to what is correct. This is done by considering the one who informed you of it as being more knowledgeable and stronger in piety, and Allaah knows best.

---

[43] Narrated in Saheeh al-Bukhaaree: 52/ Saheeh Muslim: 1599/ Sunan Ibn Maajah: 3984/ & Musnad Imaam Ahmad: 17903, -on the authority of Nu'maan Ibn Basheer. It was declared authentic by Sheikh al-Albaanee in Irwa' al-Ghaleel :2075, Mishkaat al-Masaabeh: 762, Saheeh at-Targheeb at-Tarheeb: 1735, and within Saheeh Sunan Ibn Maajah.

**(53) THE EMINENT GUIDING SCHOLAR MUHAMMAD AL-'AMEEN ASH-SHANQEETEE, MAY ALLAAH HAVE MERCY UPON HIM, FROM 'VARIOUS QUESTIONS', ISLAMIC RULING 9644**

*Question: When there are many issues and various rulings which the student of knowledge must contend, with what is the ideal way for him to correctly comprehend them?*

Answer: The ideal path to obtaining a firm understanding and comprehension of knowledge requires the fulfillment of two matters:

The first matter is related to that which is established between the student and Allaah. It is necessary that the one who desires that Allaah facilitate for him affairs of knowledge, the He grant him success in his understanding, memory, and strength of comprehension establish between himself and Allaah the sincerity of intention that guides the student towards righteousness, and strengthens him upon obedience of Allaah and all good endeavors.

So the first matter I advise the student of knowledge with is to inwardly commit his heart and soul to Allaah Alone, as the one who turns to Allaah with sincerity of intention, Allaah strengthens his heart upon goodness and opens his heart towards obedience and goodness. He also makes knowledge easier for him to the degree of his purity of intention for Allaah alone.

As for the second matter that I advise the student of knowledge with, it is to seek out the causes and means which will assist you in strengthening your knowledge generally, your proficiency within it, as well as your fulfilling its rights upon you. The first of these being, to seek knowledge from its people, as the one who seeks knowledge from the scholars and takes it from them, he connects the chain of transmission of guidance between him and the Messenger of Allaah, may Allaah's praise and salutations be upon him. The nature of this knowledge is that it is received from the people of knowledge, as it is an inherited and transmitted knowledge. Knowledge is the inherited truth. It is that which guides the one who possesses it and by which others than him are also guided. Therefore it is obligatory to search for a scholar who is proficient in his knowledge. If you wish to study the area of correct beliefs, then search for a scholar who is prominent in knowledge of that area.

Similarly, if you wish to seek knowledge of the hadeeth narrations of the Messenger, may Allaah's praise and salutations be upon him, it is necessary to search for a scholar who is distinguished in that area of study and knowledge. If you wish to study jurisprudence and the rulings of matters, then search for someone prominent in these areas of knowledge, someone who has excelled in that field and is now acknowledged by the people of knowledge. If you find such an individual then hold to him firmly with your molar teeth, giving him his right in your efforts to strengthen your knowledge and to attain proficiency. If you attend his sittings maintain the honor of knowledge and the manners of knowledge, so that Allaah does not remove the blessing which can be found in his knowledge.

Be courteous with the scholars when questioning them and select suitable questions and suitable times for asking them. Do not cause difficulty for the scholars and do not cause them harm by seeking them out at inconvenient times, such as their times for sleeping, rest, or traveling. Ensure that your questions are polite and intended to seek the truth, not for the sake of argumentation or disputing. Then if Allaah grants success to a student of knowledge in acquiring knowledge from its people, He adorns him with fear and reverence of Him, making him from the leaders of goodness and acceptance. Then from this the characteristics of the good, noble student of knowledge develop and emerge within his speech, actions, knowledge, and the scholars come too love him.

Moreover, when a student of knowledge is himself loved by a scholar then this brings closeness between them. And when a student of knowledge draws closer to his scholar this facilitates the strengthening of his knowledge and proficiency within it.. As for the paths of interaction between himself and this scholar and what he acquires from him, then it is necessary first and foremost the he resolve and reconcile himself with the struggle, difficulty, and fatigue necessary for achieving knowledge. He should not lose interest, nor become weary, bored, or tired in his efforts. Indeed, if a student of knowledge truly desires knowledge, he must recognize that in seeking it there will be difficulty as well as fatigue. If he sits in a sitting of knowledge and boredom and weariness comes to him, then he should repel them, striving and struggling, drawing closer to knowledge no matter what the circumstances, and no matter what the difficulty.

Additionally, if he encounters circumstances that require sacrifice from him in order to seek that knowledge, he should know that the one who faces extreme distress in the beginning, then afterwards Allaah directs him towards a radiant or brilliant end. He must also be aware that the one who struggles and puts forth effort, then Allaah the Most High will never allows the reward for the best of his works to perish. Therefore, it is required that the student of knowledge utilizes and grasps the specific causes for achieving knowledge. From these is reading the lesson before the time of the sitting of knowledge, one, two, three, or four times.

Secondly, he should attend that sitting of knowledge of which he already possesses a basic understanding of the subject which is being studied or that he wishes to study with the scholar.

Thirdly, he should prepare the questions which he wishes to ask, as well as clarifying the problems he hopes to resolve. If he hears of a lesson, or sits in a sitting of knowledge, he should first consider the level of the scholar; then if he has the ability to gather everything the scholar says then he should do so in both memorization and understanding. Even if he does not have that ability, then he should take the most essential aspects of those statements or a summary of what the scholar has brought forth, knowing with certainty that Allaah the Most Exalted will still give him blessings from that knowledge obtained. He should take from each issue both its ruling and its related evidences, and he should not merely take the understanding of the issue without its evidences. It must be derived from its related evidences, as the evidence is your proof before Allaah the Exalted, which comes from the texts of the Book of Allaah and from the texts of the Sunnah, and from the texts of what is confirmed as the consensus of the Muslims. The evidence of the correct view is that it is based upon or established from the two sources of revelation.

Afterwards, finish up summarizing or compiling what was taught in that lesson, return to your house and slowly go over and review that knowledge. Read it one or two times without becoming bored or weary with it. Know with certainty, that there is not a single letter that reaches you, or a single letter that you hear, or a single letter that you understand except by which Allaah raises your level and position as long as you remain thankful to Allaah, the Most High. Truly, Allaah permits such an increase for the one who is thankful. The one who sits in a sitting of knowledge, taking that knowledge as much as he is able, striving his best with every word of that knowledge; then Allaah blesses him, making him progress and come closer to Him; and there is no change nor strength except through Allaah. As was once said ❬*And Allah has revealed to you the Book and wisdom and has taught you that which you did not know. And ever has the favor of Allah upon you been great.*❭-(Surah an-Nisaa':113)

One person who heard this stood in a sitting of knowledge and said, "*All praise is due to Allaah who taught me what I did not know*". So if you are thankful to Allaah, He blesses you in your knowledge and permits you to increase in that which you take from your scholar. By this, your knowledge would become knowledge that is admirable and blessed. Likewise, it is best and most complete that you select from those students of knowledge who are most reliable in their religion, efforts, exertions, an associate or companion in seeking knowledge. So if that matter is made easy for him, it is upon him to complete this knowledge of a studied subject by what the scholars refer to as a summary or a digest of the subject. He should write a summary of his lesson, and consider this writing of the summary a review for him. This should be done at every available time or period, reviewing and going over what has been studied and looking at it from different aspects until he has completely memorized it, so that it will be a starting point or foundation for his study of other areas of knowledge. Oh Allaah, certainly we ask you to grant us beneficial knowledge and righteous deeds, and that you make that which we have learned and understood something purely for Your Noble face alone and the cause for Your tremendous pleasure.

(54) THE EMINENT GUIDING SCHOLAR SAALEH IBN FAUZAAN, MAY ALLAAH PRESERVE HIM, FROM 'A SELECTION OF ISLAMIC RULINGS': VOL.1, PAGE 396

*Question:   Esteemed sheikh, I love you for the sake of Allaah and I ask Allaah, the Most Glorified and the Most Exalted, to gather us, you, and all of our Muslim brothers all together in Jannah. To proceed: Esteemed sheikh, we hope to receive from you guiding advice for the youth in this city, as there is between them many differences or divisions, each one saying he is upon the truth; and Allaah knows in reality who is upon the truth. So we hope from you guidance and advice as to how they should specifically proceed in beginning their studies or when initially starting to seek knowledge?*

Answer:   In the name of Allaah, the Most Gracious, the Most Merciful. There is no doubt that Shaytaan, Allaah's curse be upon him, desires to cause division between the Muslims. Likewise, his supporters from among humanity also desire to cause division between the Muslims, both the youth and the elderly among them. This is something well known, since Shaytaan was made responsible for this since he said that which Allaah mentions from him, "See this one whom You have honored above me, if You give me respite to the Day of Resurrection, I will surely, seize and mislead his offspring, all but a few!" Allaah said, *❝Go, and whosoever of them follows you, surely, Hell will be the recompense of you all, an ample recompense. And fool them gradually, those whom you can among them with your voice, make assaults on them with your cavalry and your infantry, share with them wealth and children, and make promises to them. But Shaytaan promises them nothing but deceit. Verily, my servants, you have no authority over them. And All-Sufficient is your Lord as a Guardian❞*- (Surah al-Isra':62-65). By this meaning Aadam, peace be upon him.

This is Shaytaan's occupation and profession, and there is no way to oppose him and his supporters except by turning to the Book of Allaah and the Sunnah of the Messenger of Allaah, may Allaah's praise and salutations be upon him, and acting upon that guidance. Along with this is the referring back to the people of knowledge and gaining insight by learning from them and consulting with them. After this, you must be vigilant against the plots and plans which spread through society, from this direction and that direction, all from the hands of those callers to misguidance who wish to break up and cause division in society. However, the society in this land, all praise is due to Allaah, has never ceased to be upon good, distinguished from the rest of the people in other lands. In this land we judge by the laws of Allaah the Most High, the Most Excellent. And its leaders, all praise is due to Allaah, its leaders are believing Muslims. And we do not say that we are perfect in every aspect, or that we do not have deficiencies that could be rectified by means of advising according to the Sharee'ah.

Likewise, this land is founded upon the correct belief that there is none worthy of worship except Allaah. In this land there are no domes or graves that are elevated where others are worshiped instead of Allaah. Nor are there shrines where people associate others with Allaah in worship as is found in other countries and lands. And this is the land of the two esteemed holy cities. It proceeds upon security and peace; security of ourselves, our wealth, and our children, while other societies and lands live in a state of fear. So consider, oh worshipers of Allaah, this tremendous blessing! This blessing which requires our thankfulness. Indeed, if we are not truly thankful certainly it depart from us. Allaah has said, "And remember when your Lord proclaimed: *And remember when your Lord proclaimed: "If you give thanks, I will give you more; but if you are thankless, verily, My punishment is indeed severe*-(Surah Ibrahim:7) So it is upon you, Muslim youth, to remember this blessing and to hold fast to it, making it endure and remain with us; and to rectify those shortcomings which occur in this society by the proper ways and means.

You must also be vigilant and on your guard against the people of corruption who attribute themselves to "calling to Allaah" and Islaam, while in reality they spread animosity and ill-will between the Muslims. They search in murky waters, and hunt for small mistakes in order to exaggerate them until they appear as wrongs that there is no solution for, and there is no way of rectifying, saying that such mistakes are disbelief, and they are this, and they are that, and so on. It is upon us to beware of these types of individuals, as they cloak their actions under the name of "Islaam" and the name of "calling to Allaah". From the characteristics of the true caller to Allaah is sincerity to Allaah Alone, seeking rectification and endeavoring to remove the differences that exist between the Muslims. But as for this "call" which causes separation between the people and disunites them, then this is only a call to turmoil and strife, the exposing of small mistakes, spreading scandals, and discouraging the people regarding the possibility of correcting matters. This is only a call of misguidance. Therefore it is upon us to beware of the likes of such callers, and that we return to our guidance and be thankful for the blessing of Allaah upon us, drawing close to learning beneficial knowledge. We must also remove the differences which exist between us by referring back to the Book of Allaah and the Sunnah of Messenger of Allaah, may Allaah's praise and salutations be upon him. Allaah says,

*Oh you who believe! Obey Allaah and obey the Messenger, and those of you who are in authority. If you differ in anything among yourselves, refer it to Allaah and His Messenger, if you believe in Allaah and in the Last Day. That is better and more suitable for final determination.*-(Surah an-Nisa:59).

**(55) The Eminent Guiding Scholar Muqbil Ibn Haadee al-Waadiee, may Allaah have mercy upon him, From 'A Defending Mission from Audio Lectures upon the People of Ignorance and Sophistry': Vol.2, Page 51**

*Question: What are those matters within the methodology of the people of the Sunnah and the Jama'ah which it is permissible to differ in, while giving advice to each other remains between us; and which matters is it is not permissible for us to differ in? Is it permissible to differ in regards to the basic correct belief, or with the different issues of belief? In what source work can we find a simple clarification of this?*

Answer: Differences are divided into several types: the differences of diversity, such as the differing versions of the statements of 'at-tashshahud' in the prayer, and the different forms of sending praise and salutations upon the Prophet, may Allaah's praise and salutations be upon him and his family, and the difference of raising the hands in prayer to the shoulders or to the edges of the two ears. There are many examples of this type. Sheikh al-Islaam Ibn Taymeeyah stated, "*No one disapproves of or censures someone due to differences of diversity except for the ignorant one.*" Then there are differences of understanding; such as that regarding menstruation- is it pure or impure, as linguistically it can have both meanings. In many issues some scholars hold one understanding and other scholars have a different understanding, and this is from the well-grounded esteemed major scholars. This is considered like the differences of understanding which occurred between the Companions, may Allaah be pleased with them all, at the time when the Prophet, may Allaah's praise and salutations be upon him and his family said to them, *{The one who believes in Allaah and the Last Day should not pray Salatul-Asr except in Banee Qurathah.}*[44]. Some of the Companions said that what was meant was to begin the journey and then to pray on the way. Others, however, differed and delayed praying until they had actually arrived at Banee Qurathah. So this is a difference of understanding. So it is seen that in issues in which there are differences of diversity or differences of understanding there should be no blaming or censuring the other. When someone blames another in an issue related to differences of understanding, certainly he is calling to blind following him.

The third type of differences is the difference of opposition to the truth. This is when someone opposes the authentic, clear, evidence without any authority or proof. You say to him, "*It is forbidden for a man to wear gold jewelry*", and he says, [This is simply for my engagement celebration.] Or you say to him, "*Elections are giving to another the authority that is Allaah's alone, as part of it is the negotiating of which aspects of the guidance of Islaam should be accepted and practiced.*" So he replies, [We are compelled and forced to this.] But the reality is that they are not compelled to it, rather that they have expanded the Sharee'ah allowance of necessity such that in reality they end up abandoning its guidelines. Therefore opposition to the authentic clear evidence without an explanation is that which is considered a difference of opposition the Sharee'ah. It is this differing that it is necessary that we blame and <u>censure the one</u> who falls into it.

[44]  Narrated in Saheeh al-Bukhaaree: 946, 4119/ Saheeh Muslim: 1770/ -on the authority of 'Abdullah Ibn 'Umar.

Additionally, differing in the issues of the correct belief is not permissible, as it is a clear, defined matter and the one who differs in this and produces newly invented principles and beliefs is considered an innovator in the religion. If it is said to him, ❖*The Most Gracious rose over the Throne (in a manner befitting His Majesty and Transcendence)*❖-(Surah Ta-Ha: 5) and he replies,[He is everywhere, in everyplace], then he has a serious error in his understanding and is considered an innovator in the religion. As was stated clearly by some of the preeminent people whom Allaah guided their hand such as Sheikh al-Islaam Ibn Taymeeyah. It was said to Sheikh al-Islaam Ibn Taymeeyah, who was given the title of the 'Nobleman' of his age, "*What do you say about those predecessors of yours from the Asharee sect?*" He replied: "*I say that they were in error, and it is improper that we follow them in their errors.*" Additionally, the people of the Sunnah themselves have differed in some matters, such as the issue of Allaah's descending; does Allaah descend in His essence or by His throne? However, this is considered from the secondary matters, as we believe that Allaah descends to the heaven of this world in the last third of the night, but we do not say it occurs in this way nor say it occurs in that way.

As for the hadeeth: *{Allaah created Aadam upon his image.}* [45]. This is found in Saheeh al-Bukhaaree. It is also found outside Saheeh al-Bukhaaree with the wording *{...upon the image of the Merciful}* [46]. However this is version of the narration is weak. Ibn Qutabah said, "*The people of guidance do not censure the connection of an image to Allaah as they did not originate this statement. The Prophet, may Allaah's praise and salutations be upon him and his family, informed us that in what occurs during the time of resurrection Allaah will come upon his own "image"*. So it is correct to affirm an image to Allaah, the Most Glorified and the Most Exalted - in a way which benefits His Majesty and Transcendence.

---

[45]  Narrated in Saheeh Muslim: 2612/ & Musnad Imaam Ahmad: 7279, 7372, 9646/ -on the authority of Abu Hurairah. It was declared authentic by Sheikh al-Albaanee in Silsilat al-Hadeeth as-Saheehah:862, Mishkaat al-Masaabeh: 3525, and Dhelaal al-Jannah: 519, 520.

[46]   Narrated in Mu'jam al-Kabeer: 13404/ & as-Sunnah of Ibn Abee 'Asim: 529/ & ash-Sharee'ah of al-'Aajooree: 725/ -on the authority of 'Abdullah Ibn 'Umar. It was declared authentic by Sheikh al-Albaanee in Silsilat al-Hadeeth as-Saheehah: 529, Dhelaal al-Jannah: 517.

(56) The Eminent Guiding Scholar Muhammad al-'Ameen ash-Shanqeetee, may Allaah have mercy upon him, From 'Various Questions', Islamic Ruling no. 9698

*Question: What is the proper way for the student of knowledge to act in situations where there is a difference of opinion in knowledge-based issues, in order that unity is maintained between our hearts and conflicts are avoided?*

Answer: In the name of Allaah, all praise is due to Allaah, praise and salutations be upon the best of creation, and upon his Companions, and those who follow them. As for what follows: Firstly, it is necessary for a Muslim to know that he does not speak a word nor give a ruling through a phrase or a sentence in regard to knowledge of this religion except that he is responsible for it in front of Allaah. This knowledge is a trust; so it is required that the one the one who has the responsibility of possessing it- meaning knowledge -imagines the Paradise and the Fire in front of his very eyes. Due to this Imaam Ibn Daqeeq al-Eid said that once when he was acting as a judge, and was serving in Egypt. An opponent in the court once said to him, "*You have oppressed me*", and in some of the narrations they state that the opponent said to him, "*Your statement is not said seeking the face of Allaah!*" or something similar. He replied, may Allaah have mercy upon him, "*By Allaah! I have not uttered a single word in the past forty years except that I have prepared myself to answer for it in front of Allaah.*" So everything a student of knowledge says in debates and dialogues, everything he says when relating rulings, everything he says in matters of knowledge, is fully recorded from him, and he is responsible for it in front of Allaah. However, the questioning about knowledge is not like questioning about other matters. Everything someone says is recorded and he is duly responsible for it. But the questioning regarding knowledge is specific and distinct, as you are attributing it to the religion and to what has been legislated by Allaah. You are stating that the ruling of Allaah in this issue is such and such, or that this specific matter is obligatory, or that matter is merely permitted without reward or punishment, or that this other matter is only recommended. So it is necessary to imagine the Paradise and the Fire in front of your very eyes.

You should not give a ruling nor speak a word except that you have with you a portion of knowledge which you had come across or which was transmitted to you from the Sunnah of the Messenger of Allaah, may Allaah's praise and salutations be upon him. As Allaah says, ❧*Bring me a scripture prior to this or some trace of knowledge, if you are truthful!*❧-(Surah al-Ahqaf:4) Knowledge from the truthful individual is transmitted knowledge; that knowledge which, if a person speaks from it, should originate from the scholars and from the esteemed and honored people of knowledge. Imaam Shaafa'ee, may Allaah have mercy upon him, said, "*I am pleased to have Imaam Maalik as a proof and source for my assertion, between me and Allaah.*" By this meaning that if Allaah asks him, "From whom did you take this knowledge?" He can say, "*I took it from Imaam Maalik.*" So if the issues are ones in which differences exist and those issues which are related to the collective affairs of the Muslims, then you are responsible and a holder of a trust and as such every word you speak -you will be held responsible for it.

So if you are able to firmly establish this then proceed to the second matter. This second matter is that we are those who follow and do not innovate new matters in the religion. We point towards the transmitted knowledge from the past, as was stated by Imaam Maalik, may Allaah have mercy upon him: "*It is an obligation upon every student of knowledge to be upon tranquility, and steadiness, and upon the narrations of those whose have passed before him.*" Therefore, it is a requirement for him to possess this transmitted knowledge from the past. From this point we see that the first matter the successful focused student of knowledge must aim for is that he must not be deceitful in regard to his knowledge. From such a deception in his knowledge is that he acts as one who has the ability to independently derive rulings while he is not from their ranks. From such a deception in knowledge is that he sits to debate with his brother when he has not achieved the level of knowledge necessary to prepare him for such debates or discussions, as well as the possibility that second brother may not be from those whom it is proper to debate with. Also from the ways of deception in one's knowledge is when you bend the texts and force them to hold a specific meaning by your using your opinion and independent reasoning. All this occuring while Allaah is Witness from above the seven heavens that the one doing so doesn't have in his heart a fragment of true knowledge about that specific issue or matter, or that in his heart he does not have a fragment of knowledge regarding that hadeeth, or that he does possess a fragment of knowledge regarding these verses. But he takes these texts and explains the verses of the Qur'aan and explains hadeeth narrations according to his independent thoughts within having any proof for his explanations.

The like of this man knows with certainty that he will be put forward towards the fire of Hellfire. Then at that time let him see whether these actions then seem insignificant or significant to him! This is clear misguidance when a person does not rely upon upon any proof, support or evidence, but is simply grasps at conclusions randomly, debating and arguing, and sitting there stating principles as if he had reached such a high level of knowledge!! This is very dangerous, and an error or lapse that every student of knowledge must seek refuge from. It is required to seek refuge in Allaah from the tribulation of having a false sense of self importance because of one's knowledge. Related to this mistake is the error of leaping too far ahead, especially for the beginning student of knowledge. It is said, "*In the beginning of his affair he jumped too far and in the end he had only achieved anxiety and defeat*", meaning at that he was brought defeat by Allaah, the Exalted.

Therefore it is necessary for the student of knowledge to weigh and assess himself with the scale of true piety, and to know that every verse and hadeeth will be a witness and claimant upon him in front of Allaah if he speaks about them without knowledge. Thus it is necessary that he only speak with a proof, as this makes matters simpler for him upon path and towards his goals. In addition, there is the explanation of verses of the Qur'aan given by one of the Companions, may Allaah be pleased with them all. When you come to the compiled explanation of the Qur'aan by Ibn Abbas, it is an explanation of the entire Qur'aan but is not more that two hundred pages. As they were a people whose tongues were constrained, as they lived in an age of piety and fear of Allaah. So a statement would not leave their mouths except that it was weighed and looked at, considering carefully whether it was based and formed from the light of the Book of Allaah and the Sunnah or not. Furthermore, if within their statement there was anything that was added, then it was something added to the degree that they would not be questioned about it in front of Allaah. In their statements there was no pretentious statements or expressions, no devised phrases, nor words of pretense. The weighed carefully consider word shows hat it is close to the truth, that it is correct in relation to the Sunnah, and that it is suitable to used as a proof, because what it contains from the light from the Light of the Book of Allaah and the Sunnah. Due to this it has been said by the scholars, "*Their speech was brief but tremendous in the blessing it possessed.*" As when it is based upon the Book of Allaah and the Sunnah the student will not debate regarding issues except that he possesses the results of study and acquiring knowledge and a foundation of knowledge that can be built upon.

The third matter: If the student of knowledge arrives at a stage where he has the ability to enter into dialogues, then he should first ask and inquire; as when discussing matters it may be with one who presents himself as someone confronted by a problem and he sits with the students of knowledge to discuss it with them-however, no one among them knows who he is! Know that it is not permissible for you to debate with an individual or discuss detailed or advanced issues while you know that the one in front of you is not a student of knowledge who is from those who it is suitable that he participate in such debates and discussions, as then, if he is not, you are only assisting him upon falsehood. You are helping him upon evil and wrongdoing; upon giving a meaning to the source texts in a manner which is in reality a rejection of the Sunnah. In addition, in any rejection of the Sunnah, one goes astray upon clear misguidance. Oh Allaah Allaah! This will be the cause for the destruction of your brother or for helping Shaytaan against your brother.

If only the students of knowledge satisfied themselves with the provisions they have and restricted themselves to seeking and gathering this knowledge that the first generations were upon! The predecessors of the first three generations were not those who engaged in frequent discussions. But the student of knowledge today perhaps he may have studied only a year or two, except for the one whom Allaah frees in His Mercy from entering into this; and perhaps he has not completed a year or two except that when he sits with his scholar or is with some of the major scholars he seeks to debate and argue. Such that when he comes to ask a question, he does not even know the proper manner of asking questions! Just yesterday he was the most ignorant of the people yet after sitting for a year or two, he comes to view himself as being on the level of the scholars or someone equal with the scholars- and this is clear destruction!

Because this then enters into his intention, enters into his methodology, and enters into his way and path. So it is required that the student of knowledge does not debate except with the one who he sees is from the people suitable for such a discussion, being from its the people from the aspect of capacity in knowledge. Meaning that such a person has sufficient understanding, making him suitable for such discussions and debates. But if you come to know, may Allaah have mercy upon you, that the one in front of you is someone who has little knowledge, or that he is a beginner, then say to him, *"Brother, refrain from saying this."* And advise him with the truth saying to him, *"Brother, those at your level should not discuss these matters, those at your level should seek knowledge and study and then speak."* Say, *"Go and learn then come back and speak regarding this issue."* As he was someone who has not studied, and was not well grounded, and was not firmly established in the knowledge. Then if he returns again and begins to debate say, *"Brother, it is not for someone like you to enter into debating. Indeed I truly feel sorry for you as this task and role of refuting is a serious position and responsibility which refers back to the understandings of the scholars. Within it there are serious difficulties and tremendous exertions are required by it from even the leading scholars capable of debating and discussing the various issues of how to implement this religion."*

The fourth matter: If you are those who are capable of engaging in debates and discussions, then there are matters which it is necessary that you complete before discussing or debating. Firstly, look towards your heart considering carefully what it is that you want to result from this debate. What is it you wish to have come from this dialogue? If you desire the face of Allaah there will not cease to come from Allaah help and assistance by which you will be successful, defended, inspired and guided when your intention is truly made purely for Allaah. Due to this Imaam Shaafa'ee said, *"I have never entered into a debate with anyone except that I hoped that Allaah would make the truth apparent to me through him."* So he has an untainted motive and a completely pure intention with his goal towards Allaah, the Most High, the Most Exalted. This is for any issue, as it may be an issue from among the general people. Therefore it is proper that you as individual weigh the issue by all of these guidelines. Then if you see that the one who is in front of you is from those whom it is suitable to enter into a discussion with, then begin with yourself by ensuring a correct intention, not seeking prominence nor seeking to have him conform to your personal position or view. Surely, this is from the greatest and noblest of characteristics that Allaah grants the people of knowledge. This characteristic is from the tremendous, bountiful, and remarkable blessings, by which we recognize the true scholar. This is that which Allaah has mentioned in the Qur'aan, that the true scholars do not ever seek eminence in the world, ❖*That is the home of the Hereafter, We shall assign to those who do not want to exalt themselves in the land..*❖-(Surah al-Qasas:83) Therefore, there is not any pious scholar being far from reproach, having pure character, conscious of His Lord and fearing Him, whom you would find desiring to become prominent among the people or to demonstrate his support or status among the people. No, this never will be! He knows with sure knowledge that what exists and is established between him and Allaah is sufficient for him, and that if what is between him and Allaah is made purely for Allaah's sake alone and he desires that which is with Allaah, then he is upon goodness, and soundness, but as for anything beyond that then he does not ask about and does not have need of it. Consequently, this is what you find when the esteemed and respected scholars have an individual come to them to debate or discuss, and he is from those suitable for this. You find that the Companions, may Allaah be pleased with them all, debated and discussed and their hearts did not turn against each other, and differences did not appear between them as individuals because they had righteous intentions. Additionally, as some of the scholars have said in general that one does not purify and correct his intention with his dealings with another person in any matter except that then they are blessed with guidance; and two people do not differ or discuss a matter each of them seeking Allaah's pleasure alone except that He guides them to that which is truly correct and best. Therefore, the intention must be given attention before any discussion or debating.

The second point for those who intend to enter into a debate, after the rectification of one's intention, is to establish and confirm ones understanding of the established foundation of the matter under discussion. He should say to the other "*Is the established basis my statement or your statement, as you state that it is obligatory and I state that it is only recommended. So is the basis or foundation that it is an obligatory matter or a recommended one? Or you state that such and such a matter is forbidden and I state that it is merely disliked, so is the foundation that it is forbidden or permissible? If you confirm what the foundation of the issue is, then we say we agree and both affirm this foundation, and then proceed to investigate that which conflicts with that established foundation.*" Therefore if one says: "This is something forbidden", yet the foundation or principle in these matters of general custom is that they are permissible, then we say, "*May Allaah have mercy upon you, bring the evidence from the Book of Allaah and the Sunnah of the Prophet, may Allaah's praise and salutations be upon him, that indicate that this matter is forbidden. If you cannot do so, then it is required that you remain upon the established foundation that these matters of customs as opposed to matters of ritual worship are generally permissible as that is clearly established.*"

Consequently there are principles from the leading scholars of knowledge, may Allaah have mercy upon them with a tremendous mercy, illuminate their graves with radiance, and increase and give them the best of rewards from their efforts for the Ummah of the Prophet Muhammad. From these principles is that we do not leave any matter except that we clarify and explain it even in the secondary issues. As theses present principles, are both well established and strong. And the student of knowledge, if he studies these principles then he understands how to derive a conclusion from the evidences. The methods of deriving rulings themselves have differing levels and categories, every level having its own derived wording and derived understandings.

As for the apparent wording of the text, then first it is derived by its meanings; the meaning of its characteristics, conditions, deficiencies and attributions. Each meaning has a specific degree or level of strength, and possesses evidences that indicate its status as a proof. They also have levels of importance when they contradict other considered factors. They each have a status or level when they stand in conflict to other factors which are based upon transmitted knowledge, as well as if they contradict a factor that is based on an intellectual factor or indicator. Every factor is categorized according to levels, clear principles, and permanent fundamentals of knowledge. However, for the one who simply reads these principles, then he should know that we are not in need of the laying down of new principles ourselves. Rather, what is required for us in relation to dialogues and debates is that we build upon where the people have stopped. This is not building in the sense that we create something new, as they have sufficed us with their legacy of knowledge and way. This is clear, as the Successors built upon the efforts of the Companions, and the Successors of the Successors built upon their efforts and work. In this way some of the Muslim Ummah has always built upon the efforts of the others who came before them. So we ask Allaah the Mighty to inspire us towards the path of those people.

An additional point is that if the evidence becomes clear, and the proof and the path to the proof have emerged, then it is upon the Muslim to fear Allaah and be one who returns to the truth. So if you debate with someone and you learn that the true evidence is that which he presented and the correct way is that which he presented then say, *"The truth is with you in this, may Allaah reward you for what you said. And I am from those who accept the evidence that you mentioned, and I take back that which I had stated."* As returning and submitting to the truth is not a virtue or an act of merit only, as is said, *"Returning to the truth is a virtue."* Rather it is obligatory! It is an obligation upon an individual and a required matter, as well as being a virtue for a Muslim which indicates his nobility and the raising of his level and status, his love for his Lord, and his intention to seek that which is with Allaah of goodness and His Jannah, His abode of Honor. The Muslim must evaluate himself by this affirmed scale and criterion and place the differences in clear boundaries and a clear context. Oh Allaah, Certainly we ask You by your beautiful names, and Your exalted attributes, to guide us to the truth in that which we differ in. Oh Allaah we ask from You what is good and guidance. We ask You, Allaah, for steadfastness upon the truth and what is right and that you make our outcome and end  the conclusion of the people of goodness and guidance.

(57) THE EMINENT GUIDING SCHOLAR MUQBIL IBN HAADEE AL-WAADI'EE, MAY ALLAAH HAVE MERCY UPON HIM, EXCERPTED FROM 'EXCELLENT RESPONSES TO QUESTIONS FROM THOSE PRESENT AND THOSE ABSENT': PAGE 237

*Question: Some of the people of knowledge say, "We advise the beginning student to read in the subject of correct beliefs, the book 'al-Aqeedatul-Wasateeyah' and in relation to fiqh, or the general understanding of how to practice the religion, to study the works of the school of jurisprudence predominantly found within his country. Therefore if the people of the country follow the Hanbalee school of jurisprudence, then study from the book 'Zaad al-Mustaqnaa', and if they follow the Shaafa'ee school of jurisprudence or the Maalikee school of jurisprudence, then study from their relevant books." So what is the proper way to study the branch of knowledge known as fiqh, and which books do you recommend for its study? Also, which scholar's statements are primarily based upon the Book and the Sunnah in this field?*

Answer: All praise is due to Allaah, Lord of all the worlds, and praise and salutation be upon our Prophet Muhammad, and his family, and all his Companions. I bear witness that there is none worthy of worship except Allaah alone having no partner or associate, and I bear witness that Muhammad is His worshiper and His Messenger. As for what follows: The advice to read the book *((al-Aqeedatul-Wasateeyah)06-05)* is advice that is accepted, as it primarily contains verses of the Qur'aan and hadeeth narrations from the Prophet, may Allaah's praise and salutations be upon him. That work, as well as the book *((Beneficial Statements Regarding the Evidence of Allaah's Right Alone to be Worshiped)06-19)*, of Sheikh Muhammad Ibn 'Abdul-Wahaab al-'Abdalee are considered from the best books in relation to the study of correct beliefs. The book *((al-Aqeedatul-Wasateeyah)06-05)* contains an explanation of Allaah's right to be worshiped alone, as well as the correct principles and understanding of his names and attributes, so it is an invaluable book, may Allaah reward Sheikh al-Islaam Ibn Taymeeyah tremendously for authoring it. As for referring to *((Zaad al-Mustaqna')07-01)*, then I hold that one should refer to the Book of Allaah and the Sunnah of the Messenger of Allaah, may Allaah's praise and salutations be upon him. Our Prophet said during his farewell pilgrimage, as found in the hadeeth of Jaabir narrated in Saheeh Muslim, *{Certainly, I am leaving with you two things which if you hold fast to them, you will not go astray; the Book of Allaah..}* [47] and in the narration of Zayd Ibn Arqam, *{I am leaving you with two weighty things. The first of them is the Book of Allaah, as it contains guidance and light, so take the Book of Allaah and hold fast to it...}* [48]. So The Messenger of Allaah, may Allaah's praise and salutations be upon him, encouraged the people to and made them wish to take firm hold of the Book of Allaah.

---

[47] Narrated in Saheeh Muslim: 1218/ Jaame'a at-Tirmidhee: 3786/ -on the authority of Jaabir Ibn 'Abdullah. And it is found in Jaame'a at-Tirmidhee: 3788/ -on the authority of Zayd Ibn 'Arqam. It was declared authentic by Sheikh al-Albaanee in Saheeh al-Jaame'a as-Sagheer: 2458, and in Saheeh Sunan at-Tirmidhee.
[48] Narrated in Saheeh Muslim: 2408/ Musnad Imaam Ahmad: 18780/ & Sunan ad-Daaramee: 3316/ -on the authority of Zayd Ibn 'Arqam. It was declared authentic by Sheikh al-Albaanee in Saheeh al-Jaame'a as-Sagheer: 1351.

Then he said: *{And the people of my family, be mindful of your Lord in relation to my family, be mindful of your Lord in relation to my family, be mindful of your Lord in relation to my family.}* Also the Lord of Might and Glory says in His Noble Book, *⟨Follow what has been sent down unto you from your Lord, and follow not any protectors, besides Him (Allaah). Little do you remember!⟩*-(Surah al-Aaraf:3) He also says, *⟨And follow not that of which you have no knowledge. Verily, the hearing, and the sight, and the heart of each of those ones will be questioned by Allaah⟩*-(Surah al-Israa: 36). And He also says, *⟨And whatsoever the Messenger gives you, take it; and whatsoever he forbids you, abstain from it⟩*-(Surah al-Hashr:7) Our Prophet, may Allaah's praise and salutations be upon him, said, *{..Avoid that which I forbid you to do and do that which I command you to do to the best of your capacity. As the people before you were ruined because they had put too many questions to their Prophets and then disagreed with their Prophets' teachings}.* And in the same hadeeth, *{Completely avoid that which I forbid you from doing and do that which I command you to do to the best of your capacity.}* [49]. Therefore our religion in based upon the verses of the Qur'aan and the Prophetic Narrations.

As you may come across expressions and sayings related to issues of menstruation and issues of divorce in the book *((Zaad al-Mustaqna')07-01)* that will preoccupy you and take your time, which are not based upon evidence from the Book of Allaah or the Sunnah; they are considered to be statements of supposition or speculation. So leave of wrongly thinking that referring to the Qur'aan and Sunnah will require from you a lengthy effort. Indeed, perhaps you may memorize the Qur'aan in a single year and afterwards memorize what you are able to from the Sunnah of the Messenger of Allaah, may Allaah's praise and salutations be upon him, as well as learning the ability to distinguish between what is authentic from what is rejected, and that which has hidden defects from that which is truly healthy. So there is a significant difference and considerable distinction between the Book of our Lord and the Sunnah of our Prophet Muhammad, may Allaah's praise and salutations be upon him, and the expressions and statements found in the work *((Zaad al-Mustaqna')07-01)* or other similar books of fiqh. The Lord of Glory says in His Noble book, *⟨And We have indeed made the Qur'aan easy to understand and remember; then is there anyone who will remember?⟩*-(Surah Qamar:17) Our Prophet Muhammad, may Allaah's praise and salutations be upon him, said, *{I was sent with the straightforward way of worshiping of Allaah Alone.}* [50]. And he said, *{Certainly, this religion is one of simplicity.}* [51].

---

[49] Narrated in Saheeh Muslim: 1337/ Sunan an-Nasaa'ee: 2620/ Sunan Ibn Maajah: 2/ Musnad Imaam Ahmad: 7320, 9890, and other narrations/ -on the authority of Abu Hurairah. It was declared authentic by Sheikh al-Albaanee in Saheeh al-Jaame'a as-Sagheer: 5810.

[50] Narrated in Musnad Imaam Ahmad: 21788/ -on the authority of Abu Amaamah Sidee Ibn 'Ajlaan. It was declared authentic by Sheikh al-Albaanee in Silsilat al-Hadeeth as-Saheehah: 2924.

[51] Narrated in Saheeh al-Bukhaaree: 39/ Sunan an-Nasaa'ee: 5037/ -on the authority of Abu Hurairah. It was declared authentic by Sheikh al-Albaanee in Silsilat al-Hadeeth as-Saheehah: 1161, Mishkaat al-Masaabeh: 1246, Saheeh al-Jaame'a as-Sagheer: 1611, as well as in Saheeh Sunan an-Nasaa'ee.

As knowledge is something simple, and it is the differences that have occurred between the scholars that have preoccupied the students of knowledge away from study of the Book of Allaah and the Sunnah of the Messenger of Allaah, may Allaah's praise and salutations be upon him. Rather, it has even caused some of them to become supporters of separate factions or divisive groups. How excellent is the one who stated:

*If it was not for the worldly rivalry and competition,*

*there would not be such books of debating like al-Mughnee or al-Amad,*

*they legitimize their efforts by claiming to resolve complexities,*

*yet by what resulted, the problem of complexity only increased!*

So through this blessed way of study Allaah may bring benefit in a short period of time, because it is connected to and based upon the Book of Allaah and the Sunnah of the Messenger of Allaah, may Allaah's praise and salutations be upon him. And we discussed the subject of the censure of blind following in the book ((*Establishing the Proof of the Misguidance of 'Abdur-Rahman at-Tahaan)11-22*). Therefore the religion is taken from the Book of Allaah and from the Sunnah of the Messenger of Allaah, may Allaah's praise and salutations be upon him. As for foremost relying upon the statements of this person and that person, and their differences, such that if you follow the Shaafa'ee school of jurisprudence then you consider something to be permissible, while if you were to follow the Hanafee or Hanbalee schools of jurisprudence then you would say that same thing is not permissible This itself is evidence that this concept of restricted closed schools of jurisprudence is something foreign that has infiltrated our understanding of the religion. As the Lord of Might and Glory says in His Noble Book, ❖*Do they not then consider the Qur'aan carefully? Had it been from other than Allaah, they would surely have found therein many contradictions*❖-(Surah an-Nisa'a:82) The Book of our Lord, and the Sunnah of our Prophet Muhammad, may Allaah's praise and salutations be upon him, do not contain contradictions. Rather the differences are from the understanding held by the people of knowledge, and some of the false inclinations and prejudices of a few of the people of knowledge.

Lastly, as for those scholars whom the majority of their speech comes from the Book of Allaah and the Sunnah, then these are those like Imaam al-Bukhaaree and Imaam Ahmad Ibn Hanbal, and Ibn Hazm, while being aware of his misconceptions in the area of belief, and Ibn Qayyim, Muhammad Isma'eel al-Ameer, as well as the likes of ash-Shawkaanee. And all praise is due to Allaah, there are indeed those scholars who the majority of their statements are taken from the Book of Allaah and the Sunnah. Therefore one feels comfortable and confident regarding them and the Muslims from the east and west of this earth have benefited from them.

(58) The Eminent Guiding Scholar Muhammad Ibn Saaleh al-'Utheimeen, may Allaah have mercy upon him, From 'The Book of Knowledge': Page 181

*Question: What characteristics should be found within the one whom you wish to take knowledge from?*

Answer: It is required that you seek knowledge from a knowledgeable and proficient scholar who is also trustworthy, as proficiency in knowledge is strength, and it is necessary to have along with such strength trustworthiness. Allaah, the Most Exalted, says, ❨*Verily, the best of men for you to hire is the strong, the trustworthy.*❩- (Surah al-Qasas:26) Perhaps a scholar may have tremendous understanding and knowledge and the ability to delineate and distinguish the truth of matters; but if he does not possess trustworthiness he may lead you astray from a direction you are not aware of. Additionally, you must know that taking knowledge at the hand of a scholar is more beneficial than from utilizing books from several aspects:

Firstly: Reduction of time required to understand.

Second: It is less difficult.

Thirdly: It is closer to the most proper way, as this scholar has learned and studied and reconciled and gained understanding of these various issues, so when he presents an issue to you its presentation is comprehensive and well rounded. However, he will still train you through additional reading and studying if he is someone who possesses the quality of trustworthiness. As for relying solely upon books, then this requires you to put forth significant effort day and night. Moreover, in reading books which contain comparisons of the various statements of the scholars you find that these scholars steer the understanding of the evidence towards this conclusion, and these others direct the understanding of the evidences to suggest that another conclusion is that which is actually more correct. So one remains confused! Because of this we see that Ibn Qayyim often discusses two differing positions or rulings from the people of knowledge, whether this is from his book *((Zaad al-Ma'ad)09-05)* or *((I'laam al-Muwaq'eyeen)08-12)*. He may discuss the evidence of the first position or a statement from the scholars and then show any weaknesses it may have; thus we might prematurely say to ourselves, "*This is the correct position, and it is not permissible to go against this in any situation that may occur*". But then he continues on in the same discussion to refute that position and comes with an opposing view or position and mentions its evidence and any of its weaknesses, so then we might say, "*Rather, this statement is actually what is truly correct*". So what occurs is that you still have a dilemma and your uncertainty remains. Therefore it is necessary that your reading be with a scholar who is proficient as well as reliable.

(59) The Eminent Guiding Scholar Muhammad Ibn Saaleh al-'Utheimeen, may Allaah have mercy upon him, excepted From 'Islamic Revival- Guidelines and Guidance': Page 122

*Question: Are audio cassettes considered a method from the methods of acquiring knowledge? And what ways, for example, can we benefit from them?*

Answer: As to whether the use of audio tapes is a means or a method from the acceptable methods of acquiring knowledge, then no one doubts that. We do not overlook the blessing of Allaah upon us in audio tapes, as through them we have benefited greatly in regard to the matters of knowledge. They convey to us the statements of the scholars from any land they may reside in. We are able to remain in our homes, and the connection between us and scholar has become easy and facilitated for us. So we are able to listen to his statements by means of an audio cassette. This is from the blessing of Allaah, the Most High, the Most Exalted, upon us. Indeed, they have now become an evidence for us or a proof against us. As certainly, knowledge has been spread extensively by means of these cassette tapes. With respect to how we should benefit from them, this goes back to the specific circumstances of each individual. This is because from among the people is the one who can benefit from them while driving his car, and another who can benefit from listening while eating his midday or evening meal or drinking his coffee. What is important to note is that exactly how they should be used depends on each individual person. Therefore, it is not possible to state any general guidelines regarding this.

(60) The Eminent Guiding Scholar Muhammad Ibn Saaleh al-'Utheimeen, may Allaah have mercy upon him, From 'Islamic Rulings': Vol. 4, Page 284

*Question: I am a young man who wants to be a caller to Allaah, but I do not possess the proper manners necessary for this. Is the publishing and distribution of beneficial Islamic books or an Islamic tapes sufficient for this? Please advise me, may Allaah reward you with good.*

Answer: Yes, there is no doubt that if a person does not have the ability to call to Allaah as an individual, then it is certainly possible for him to call to Allaah through the distribution of beneficial books and tapes. However, because this is being done on the basis of, or because of his not having the ability to call to Allaah as an individual, then he should not distribute books or tapes except after presenting them for examination to a student of knowledge who would be aware of what might be in them from mistakes of errors. This is in order to prevent that person from distributing material that contains mistakes when he has not been advised or become aware of this. Additionally from the methods of calling to Allaah is to come to agreement with a student of knowledge that he produce material that invites to that which is beneficial and good, and that you pay for the expenses of that effort.

**(61) THE EMINENT GUIDING SCHOLAR AHMAD IBN YAHYA AN-NAJMEE, MAY ALLAAH PRESERVE HIM, FROM 'DECISIVE RULINGS ON THE METHODOLOGIES OF CALLING TO ALLAAH': VOL. 1, PAGE 17**

*Question: What is your general advice to the beginning student of knowledge? Which books and audio lectures, that teach the methodology of the first generations of Muslims, are recommended for them?*

Answer: My advice to the students of knowledge, all of them, is for them to fear Allaah, the Most High and Exalted, and to adhere to the path of the Messenger of Allaah, may Allaah's praise and salutations be upon him, and his Companions. This is the path of Salafeeyah, and the Salafee methodology- meaning following the Book of Allaah and the Sunnah as understood by the Salaf- the first three generations of Muslims. I advise them to sit with the Salafee scholars and I advise them to read books explaining Allaah's right alone in being worshiped, books of correct belief, books of hadeeth, and books of fiqh. Likewise, it is required and an obligation upon the students of knowledge that they fear Allaah, the Most Glorified and the Most Exalted. Additionally, they should beware of these false calls of group partisanship and division, which only intend to divide your ranks, break up your unity, and split your united voice. The Prophet, may Allaah's praise and salutations be upon him, warned us against calls that invite to the Hellfire and we seek refuge with Allaah from that. There is no doubt that partisanship contains blameworthy errors, so it is obligatory upon the student of knowledge to beware of it. You should frequent the circles of learning of those scholars who adhere to this way of the first generations of Muslims. You should read those books written by those who follow this methodology and beware of reading the books of the people of division, partisanship, and various groups. Certainly, as is said, within them lies both sweet honey and concealed poison. And the success is from Allaah.

**(62) THE EMINENT GUIDING SCHOLAR MUHAMMAD NASIRUDDEEN AL-ALBAANEE, MAY ALLAAH HAVE MERCY UPON HIM, FROM TAPE NUMBER 806 FROM THE TAPE SERIES 'GATHERINGS OF GUIDANCE & LIGHT'**

*Question: Oh our sheikh, if I have heard from you a response to a specific question directed to you, and at a later time someone asks me this same question. So I answer him knowing that I personally do not possess the knowledge sufficient to answer him, but I answer him based upon your previous answer to this same question or I give the answer of one of the scholars, in doing so have I done anything wrong or sinful?*

Answer: We hope that that this will not be something considered sinful for you, however it is not the best way for you. Rather you should say: "*I have heard from so-and-so such and such ruling or information.*". Because there may emerge from the initially mentioned manner of transmitting, some aspects of harm or corruption that were not intended by the one transmitting the information.

The first of them is that the speaker who becomes accustomed to speaking in manner will himself be harmed. This is something which we presently see today with great sorrow and regret. Such that if you hear from Zayd a ruling and from 'Amr a ruling, and from Ahmad a ruling, and so on, yet each individual who is asked regarding this ruling answers the question without attributing his response or knowledge of the issue to the one of originally responded to it. Such that those who asked you regarding it assume, or make an indirect assumption that you - the one who responded are a scholar- and this false perception is a harm and corruption that you may become accustomed to.

Additionally the scope of this harm continues to spread, as the one you responded to afterwards conveys your words to someone else. In this manner this false practice which the Ummah was previous informed of, spreads. Just as was predicted by the Messenger, upon him be Allaah's praise and salutations in the narration which was narrated by both Imaams al-Bukhaaree and Muslim on the authority of 'Abdullah Ibn 'Amr Ibn al-'Aas, may Allaah be pleased with both of them, in which he stated that the Messenger of Allaah, upon him be Allaah's praise and salutations, said: *{I heard Allaah's Apostle saying, "Allaah does not take away the knowledge, by removing it from the chests of the scholars, but He takes it away by means of the death of the scholars. Until when none of the scholars remains, people will take as their guides ignorant people who when asked will give their own rulings without knowledge. So they will go astray and will lead the other people astray.}* [52]. Therefore due to this we hold that the one who is not a scholar, by rather only someone who is transmitting a matter, that he has a responsibility to mention the source which he is transmitting from.

*The questioner says: This is fine sheikh, and what if you have forgotten the source which you originally heard it from? Is it acceptable if you were just to say I heard from a scholar or read in a book?*

Sheikh al-Albaanee replied: There is no prohibition of only saying this if he has indeed forgotten. But if he only acts as if he has forgotten or pretends not to remember, then transmitting this way is not permissible.

---

[52] Narrated in Saheeh al-Bukhaaree: 100, 7307/ Saheeh Muslim: 4829 / Sunan at-Tirmidhee: 2576/ Sunan Ibn Maajah: 51/ Musnad Of Ahmad: 6222, 6498, 6602/ & Sunan ad-Daaramee: 239 from the hadeeth of 'Abdullah Ibn 'Umar Ibn al-'Aas

**(63)** The Eminent Guiding Scholar 'Abdul-'Azeez Ibn 'Abdullah Ibn Baaz, may Allaah have mercy upon him, from 'A Lecture Discussing the Ideological War' & the First Question following the Lecture

### *The Ideological War: Its Characteristics, Methods and the Required Response to It*

All praise is due to Allaah, and Allaah's praise and salutation be upon the Messenger of Allaah, his family, his Companions, and those who follow their guidance. As for what follows:

The Lord, the Most High and Exalted, sent the Messengers, upon them be Allaah's blessings and salutations, with that which encompasses contentment and success for the world both in this life and the life of the Hereafter. He made them a mercy for His worshipers. He guided them and then guided others through them to the truth; and through them He takes people out of darkness into light. He made our prophet Muhammad the best of them, their leader, and the final Messenger, may Allaah's praise and salutations be upon him. He sent the guidance and the religion of truth so that it may dominate over all the paths, as Allaah, the Exalted and Most High, said in His clear book, ❖*It is He Who has sent His Messenger (Muhammad ) with guidance and the religion of truth*❖-(Surah Tawbah:33)

'Guidance' means that which Allaah sent him with from beneficial types of knowledge, true information, an admonishment which gives life to the hearts, and narrations of past events which remind the worshipers of what will reach the people of faith in Allaah from contentment, and of what will reach the people of disbelief and falsehood from misery, disastrous consequences, and evil. The religion of truth is that which Allaah sent the Messenger with: Allaah revealed laws whose only origin is heaven, the rulings of how to live, and beneficial teachings that guide. He calls to Allaah, the Most High, the Most Exalted, by giving good tidings and warnings, and informing the people of how they may achieve success and happiness while conveying everything to them with a clear explanation. And his Lord did not send him except that His religion would be completed by His Messenger's hand, and that He would perfect His blessing through him, may the best of his Lord's blessings and salutations be upon him.

The subject of the seminar tonight is "*The Ideological War*", and I hope that the noble attendees who undertake consideration of this topic are able to acheive and effectively examination of this subject. We ask Allaah for them, ourselves, and all the Muslims, well-being and success.

The ideological warfare which has been examined and discussed by the scholars, is that which has become pervasive and has spread through the majority of publications, newspapers, and other written works; it encompasses everything that has been spread through the world is that which is clearly related to ideology, concepts, and beliefs. As the enemies of Islaam, when they became infuriated with the continued prominence and emergence of Islaam, and witnessed the people continuing to enter into the religion of Allaah in significant numbers, as well as their seeing the failure of their attempts at military force used to achieve the goal of causing the people to unsure and doubtful about their religion, thereafter in order to further attempt to pull them away from Islaam; then they resorted to different forms and types of ideological warfare by means of various forms of modern media such as television, publications, newspapers, and other written and spoken content produced and developed by those who oppose Islaam. They utilize these in their efforts to hinder and repel the religion of Allaah, and spread uncertainty amongst the people regarding the religion, covering the truth with deceptions and falsehood. This is similar to what Allaah states regarding those who opposed Him from amongst the Jews, where the Most High, Most Exalted says, ❈*And mix not truth with falsehood, nor conceal the truth while you know the truth*❈-(Surah al-Baqarah:42)

The modern forms of media which those who oppose Islaam have established produce damage of every type, and every form of trial and ordeal, while obstructing and hindering every matter related to the truth. They invite to that which is falsehood, while slipping poison within the delightfulness and fullness of what is offered. They have in mind through this way to cause people to have doubts and uncertainties about the correctness of the religion; all in order to pull them out from the light of Allaah and His guidance, towards the darkness of disbelief and misguidance, to turn them away from the truth and encourages them towards misguidance. And what is sufficient initially is that doubt, misgivings, and distance from the truth result from their efforts.

Then they follow up and build upon that with efforts by corrupt and ignorant Muslims, who spread corrupt ideas and mistaken beliefs and ideologies, such that now they, the Muslims, are then surrounded with various forms of falsehood after having been previously prevented from perceiving the truth.

All of this is from what Shaytaan invites to and propagates, as is found in the statement of the Most High, ❈*Surely, Shaytaan is an enemy to you, so take (treat) him as an enemy. He only invites his followers that they may become the dwellers of the blazing Fire.*❈-(Surah Faater: 6). And regarding his party, meaning Shaytaan's- know that the disbelievers of Islaam and every individual who calls to that which obstructs the truth and encourages falsehood- is a supporter of Shaytaan's party.

It is seen that in some instances of their efforts, they would invite to or promote adultery and indecency in its various forms, while at other times they do so through publishing and spreading the images of women.

At other times, they promote the display of women's physical beauty and its exposure in the most beautiful forms in order to push young men and others towards indecency, while at other times, by spreading corrupt beliefs and concepts which negate or remove Islaam.

And at times, they plant doubts about that which the Messengers of Allaah came with, Allaah's praise and salutations be upon them; bringing forth uncertainties that confuse even an intelligent person. All of these matters are part of the call of the enemies of Allaah, and they are the close associates of Shaytaan in his party.

Therefore it is obligatory upon every person of intelligence and every individual who desires safety and protection to look towards the path and way which would distance himself from this current or movement of increasing corruption and from this destructive assault which produces doubt and uncertainties, so that he may stay firmly upon the path of contentment and success in hopes that he will be successful.

This is especially true in our age, in which there are many false ideological calls, and in which there are many forms of falsehood, which have been disseminated and spread, and various types of assaults of corruption and heretical concepts circulated. The world is saturated with writings, which obstruct people from the truth; and those close to the enemies of Allaah have writers engaged in preventing the spreading of the truth by producing such materials for the various forms of print media. Similarly, within the various forms of audio and visual media, there is constantly circulated day and night material which prevents and turns people away from the truth and preoccupies them from that which would benefit and guide them. Anyone who has the most basic understanding of these methods, and what is spread through them by the enemies of Allaah in the newspapers in various languages, know that the lands of Islaam and the Muslims specifically are being attacked by various types of calls and different categories of misguided heretical concepts to turn them away from the path of Allaah. It includes calls to take on aspects of blameworthy or evil character and characteristics and characteristics which Allaah has forbidden His servants to have and possess, and to cause them to hate and turn away from aspects of praiseworthy or good character and righteous actions and endeavors.

So it is a requirement upon every believing man and upon every believing woman to be warned about these deceitful and dangerous methods, either by responding by refuting them or by explaining their falsehood and warning from them. This along with calling the people to turn to and give priority to the Book of their Lord, as it is the foundation of contentment and happiness and the source and well of knowledge. It is the strongest of fortresses for the one who hold firmly to it in protection from the various forms of misguidance. As Allaah, the Most High and the Most Exalted, says in His tremendous Book, *Verily, this Qur'aan guides to that which is most just and right.*-(Surah al-Israa': 9) And the One free from faults says *Say: It is for those who believe, a guide and a healing.*-(Surah Fussilat:44 ) He also says, *This is a Book which We have sent down to you, full of blessings; that they may ponder over its Verses, and that men of understanding may remember*-(Surah Saad:29 ) And the One free from faults says, *And this is a blessed Book which We have sent down, so follow it and fear Allaah, that you may receive mercy*-(Surah al-Ana'am:155) And the One free from faults says, *Verily, those who disbelieved in the Reminder when it came to them shall receive the punishment. And verily, it is an honorable respected Book. Falsehood cannot come to it from before it or behind it. It is sent down by the All-Wise, Worthy of all praise*-(Surah Fussilat:42) As well as of the verses which guide to His tremendous Book, which He has made a guidance and a means of happiness for all of mankind. It is obligatory upon the people of Faith to hold firmly to this book by frequently reciting it and carefully pondering its meanings, as the diseases of the heart, as well as the problems of society, are rectified by this tremendous Book. Along with this, they should produce materials that are related to it, publishing and distributing them by means of various publications, television, and various types of authored works such as small but beneficial introductory or summarized writings which guide to the truth. This is defending Allaah's religion as well as spreading it, and refuting the misguided statements and those writings which plant doubts and uncertainty which are being spread in distributed through every available means by the enemies of Allaah.

In regards to the Sunnah of the Messenger, may Allaah's praise and salutations be upon him, Allaah has made it a source of guidance for the people and the guiding light for the one who holds firmly to it, an explanation to the Book of Allaah, and a clarification to matters which are explained in a basic or simple form in the book of Allaah. Just as Allaah, the Most High and Most Exalted says *We have also sent down unto you the reminder and the advice, that you may explain clearly to men what is sent down to them, and that they may give thought.*-(Surah an-Nahl:44) Allaah, the Most High and Most Exalted, says, *By the star when it goes down, (or vanishes). Your companion Muhammad has neither gone astray nor has erred. Nor does he speak of his own desire. It is only an Inspiration that is inspired.*-(Surah an-Najm:1-4) This is Muhammad, upon him be Allaah's praise and salutations. *Your companion has neither gone astray....* meaning Muhammad, upon him be Allaah's praise and salutations, "...nor has he erred." The one who is "astray" is the one who speaks without guidance, from other than true knowledge. Additionally, the one who "has erred" is the one who opposes knowledge; one who understands but still opposes knowledge, like the Jews, and those like them. Similarly, the evil scholars who comprehend the truth but deviate away from it towards falsehood due to giving preference to their desires, and preference to the world and worldly pleasures. Allaah frees and clears his Prophet from this, may Allaah's praise and salutations be upon him, stating clearly that he is not astray, nor one who has fallen into error; rather he is knowledgeable and guided, may Allaah's praise and salutations be upon him. He is the one who understands the truth, calls to it, and is established firmly upon it. Allaah has made him a noble Messenger who guides and is himself guided; who was a warner away from falsehood for the people and the one who brings the glad tidings of the truth: *Oh Prophet! Verily, We have sent you as witness, and a bearer of glad tidings, and a warner. And as one who invites to Allaah by His Leave, and as a lamp spreading light.*-(Surah al-Ahzab:45-46) May Allaah's praise and salutations be upon him.

He lived in this world after receiving the call to prophethood for twenty-three years, all of which were spent calling to Allaah, teaching, and guiding others by speech and action. All of that time he was striving patiently with his body, and tongue, as well as militarily. Thirteen of these years were within Mecca; calling, guiding, and leading to the truth, being patient with all harm and hardship, guiding the people to goodness by his speech and actions, may Allaah's praise and salutations be upon him. As well as ten years in Medinah, striving militarily and striving with his tongue, and striving through his actions, guiding his companions to goodness, may Allaah be pleased and contented with them, until Allaah completed through them his religion, and perfected His blessing upon them. Therefore it is obligatory upon every individual who wants success and safety, and every individual who wishes for himself honor and desires contentment, to adhere to these two forms of revelation: the Book of Allaah and the Sunnah of the Messenger of Allaah, upon him be Allaah's praise and salutations. He must hold fast to both of them, invite to them, give concern and priority to memorizing them and contemplating them, spreading what they contain of knowledge while acting according to that knowledge and inviting others to act according to it.

Allaah blessed the companions of His Prophet and they held firmly to that and established themselves upon the Book and the Sunnah, may Allaah be pleased with them. They strove in the path of Allaah, and were victorious in many conquests, and founded new cities. They fought against the Romans and the Persians and other disbelieving nations, defeating them and spreading Islaam in their lands. They took the jizyah tax from those Jews, Christians, and Magians who chose not to embrace Islaam. They called to Allaah in speech and action, being patient with the harm and struggle until Allaah raised up His religion, gave victory to His religion through them, elevated His word, and spread the truth through them. This is the way of the companions of the Prophet, may Allaah's praise and salutations be upon him, and the way of the one who proceeds upon their path, the one who shares with them this tremendous struggle and the call to Allaah, the Most High and the Most Exalted. The friends of Allaah and those who support them in the call to Allaah and struggle in His path did not cease their efforts until the conditions changed and there began to enter into Islaam those who were not Muslims. But from the ones who call to falsehood there has occurred what has occurred from the gathering and emergence of various forms of misguidance, until the conditions become like those which we find ourselves within today; evil being predominant with numerous callers to falsehood, and tremendous activity from the direction of the lands of the disbelievers, and weakness in the Muslim states, and their failure to rule by the Sharee'ah except to a small degree. This is because most of them are pleased with the laws devised by men and devised by the enemies of Allaah, while they forsake the Sharee'ah of Allaah. So there has spread in these lands corruption, evil, and misguidance due to their turning away and their inactivity and sluggishness upon the truth; as well as their lack of patience and spreading and calling to the truth, and struggling against those who oppose the truth, until the present situation in which misguidance has emerged and proliferated and is widespread. It is therefore obligatory to call to the most fundamental of foundations: to the book of Allaah and the Sunnah of the Messenger of Allaah, as these two foundations are that which the struggle of the Messenger of Allaah was based upon. Likewise, the noble companions and those who followed them in goodness also struggled upon these two foundations. There is no way to reach contentment and success in the face of this ideological warfare, or victory over our enemies, except by adhering firmly to these two foundations: the book of Allaah and the Sunnah of the Messenger of Allaah, upon him be Allaah's praise and salutations. We must unite upon them, and cooperate in our speech, actions, writings, struggles, and other than that from the various endeavors which give victory to the truth and invite to it, while opposing, suppressing, and exposing misguidance.

They Appeared among the Muslims, and all praise is due to Allaah, in the beginning of this century and in the previous century called and invited to the truth, and made tremendous efforts in calling to Allaah, the Most High and the Most Exalted. There emerged righteous young men who were committed to adhering to the book of Allaah and the Sunnah of the Messenger of Allaah, upon him be Allaah's praise and salutations. They were also supported in that by the scholars and the people of knowledge, and the virtuous people from their elders and their youth, until all praise is due to Allaah, the appearance or manifestation of the success of Allaah's religion. It was given new life against falsehood, and the many people of falsehood. However, their example was stated by the Prophet, may Allaah's praise and salutations be upon him, when he said, *{There will not cease to be a group from my Ummah victorious upon the truth. They are not harmed by those who oppose them, or those that leave them until Allaah's judgment comes.}* [53]. And they, all praise is due to Allaah, are still active, and increase in good; and there has spread through the different countries of the world, to the ends of the earth, the invitation to the truth and guiding the creation. They were graduates from the Islamic University, schools, institutes, and circles of study; and in every location, they spread the truth, calling to it in opposition to the people of misguidance. This situation infuriated enemies of Allaah, and was the reason for them to increase their endeavors of misguidance and the reason for the state of dismay and agitation that we see from them. But we ask Allaah to give victory to His religion and to elevate His word, and that He grant success to all the Muslims, the young and the old, causing them to cooperate and join forces in aiding the truth and to support and assist those who are striving to establish it. We ask that He give victory to them all over the enemies of Allaah, and that He assist them in their striving against Allaah's enemies with the sword and the arrow as well as by the proof and evidence, and to make steadfast the people of the truth upon the truth that is with them. We ask that He guides the Muslim rulers to establish the truth and aid it towards victory, and to rule by the Sharee'ah of Allaah in their affairs until the Supporter grants them victory. We ask that He assist them against their enemies, and that He grants them strength in the goodness they possess, and that they become defended against the plans and plots of Allaah's enemies. As He is the Most High and the Most Exalted, the Bountiful and the Generous.

---

[53] Narrated in Saheeh al-Bukhaaree: 3641, 7460/ Saheeh Muslim: 1037/ & Musnad Imaam Ahmad: 16785/ -on the authority of Mu'aweeyah. And it is found in Saheeh Muslim: 1920/ & Musnad Imaam Ahmad: 21897/ -on the authority of Tawbaan Ibn Bejadded. And it is found in Jaame'a at-Tirmidhee: 2192/ Sunan Ibn Maajah:6/ & Musnad Imaam Ahmad: 19849/ -on the authority of Qurrah Ibn Ayaas. It was declared authentic by Sheikh al-Albaanee in Silsilat al-Hadeeth as-Saheehah: 1957. Sheikh Muqbil declared it authentic in al-Jaame'a al-Saheeh: 2384.

It is an obligation upon every student of knowledge, wherever they are, to make every effort and truly strive to give victory to the truth, and upon every scholar, wherever he may be, to make every effort and truly strive to give victory to the truth. As this age is the age of calling and invitation; this is the age of jihaad by speaking and spreading the truth, of calling to it by writing, calling, sermons, and other methods from the types of jihaad by the pen and the tongue; by striving and working to guide, by giving advice individually and collectively in speeches, as well as other means. In this way, jihaad is established. In this way, the scholar and the student of knowledge, wherever he may be in his land or other than his land, should be among those who spread the truth and call to it, patiently hoping for Allaah's reward, seeking His Face and pleasure and the life of the next world. They should spread the truth by means of the different forms of the media whenever possible, according to what is facilitated for them from deliberateness and surety, with close attention being giving to properly understanding the truth, because speech without knowledge and understanding harms tremendously. So it is necessary to have understanding, and necessary to have knowledge, as Allaah, the Most High says,

❧*Say: "This is my way; I invite unto Allaah with sure knowledge*❧-(Surah Yusuf:108). Indeed, it is prohibited to speak without knowledge. It is upon the scholars and the callers to explain and follow the truth, and to struggle to expose falsehood and suppress it, as well to shield the Muslims from this assault which has been established from many fronts- within publications, television, newspapers, various writings, congregational prayer sermons, marriage sermons, and similar means. This is because every matter is to be opposed by that which is similar to it; so falsehood is combated by that which is similar to it, according to one's capacity, location, and circumstances. Due to this, the scholar, the student of knowledge, and the believer must actively engage in those matters which Allaah has obligated upon him. It is not proper for the intelligent person to see himself as insignificant, as is found in the hadeeth, *{No one should belittle himself, or see something done for Allaah's sake as insignificant, and so not speak..}* [54] or as he actually stated, upon him be Allaah's praise and salutations. It is required that the student of knowledge speak with that which is learned of truth upon understanding, specifically when falsehood has penetrated into every place and the general affairs have become obscure and confused. Allaah, the Most High, Most Exalted, is the One who sent down the Book to clarify every matter. As he, the One free from any defects says, ❧*And We have sent down to you the Book as an exposition of everything, a guidance, a mercy, and glad tidings for those who have submitted themselves to Allaah as Muslims.*❧-(Surah an-Nahl:89) This tremendous book is the Qur'aan, containing both proofs and clarification; a guidance and clarification of the path to contentment, as well as containing a refutation, opposition, and suppression of misguidance. It is not permissible for the scholar to be satisfied with remaining silent, or to be satisfied with doing less than he

---

[54] Narrated in Sunan Ibn Maajah: 4007/ & Musnad Imaam Ahmad: 10862, 11048, 11302, 11458/ -on the authority of Abu Sa'eed al-Khudree. It was declared weak by Sheikh al-Albaanee in Dha'eef at-Targheeb at-Tarheeb: 1387, and in Dha'eef Ibn Maajah. Sheikh Muqbil declared this specific narration to be weak due to having a hidden defect in 'Ahadeeth Mu'alat Dhaaheruha as-Sehah' 155

is truly capable of, regardless of where he is; whether he is in the east, west, north, or south; whether in a car, airplane, or train- in any place he happens to be, and from any direction or way that he may be able to invite and call to Allaah. He should not lose heart and say, [This is something for someone else to undertake.] Nor should he say, [The people do not have any good in them and they will not accept from me.] No! All of these are statements that should not be said. All of these statements are only pleasing to Shaytaan. Rather what is correct is to speak and pronounce the truth, and act in accordance to the statement of the One free from all defects: *Invite (mankind, Oh Muhammad) to the Way of your Lord (i.e. Islaam) with wisdom (i.e. with the Divine Inspiration and the Qur'aan) and fair preaching, and argue with them in a way that is better.* -(Surah an-Nahl:125) The "hikmah" mentioned here is knowledge, meaning "*Allaah said*" and "*the Messenger said*". Allaah has designated or referred to knowledge as "hikmah" because it keeps them and holds them within the proper limits; every word that admonishes, reminds, and draws you away from misguidance and calls you towards the truth contains "hikmah" wisdom.

Then following this is admonition and preaching, as some of the hearts are hard and unyielding and require admonishment. There are hearts which will simply not accept and be guided by knowledge alone. If they hear knowledge, they also require admonition until the hearts are softened and accept the truth and are reminded of Allaah, and of the next life, of Paradise in the Hellfire, that this life is by nature transient and passing away ceasing to be anything of worth, that it is not the place which one remains in and invests in. The place one truly will remain is the one which is ahead of you- either Paradise or the Hellfire. So it is necessary to inspire the desire for the rewards that are waiting with Allaah, and a forewarning of the punishment waiting with Allaah, for the one who remains within the boundaries of Allaah's single path or for the one who calls or invites to anything other than that. Due to this, the Most High, Most Exalted, says, *And who is better in speech than he who invites to Allaah, and does righteous deeds, and says: "I am one of the Muslims."* - (Surah Fussilat:33)

So you, oh servant of Allaah, are responsible according to your capacity and condition. The leading scholar, and the student of knowledge, and the discerning common believer in Islaam who understands what is possible in terms of calling to the path of Allaah, and defending the religion with knowledge- all of us have upon us a portion of this responsibility, and upon each of us is the carrying that part of the obligation which we are capable of. This is done along with studying the truth, along with good manners and behavior which leads to reaching the hearts of those who have not been driven away, along with good dealings and dialogue in the best way through which Allaah gives guidance. This is the way which conveys the truth to the hearts. Knowledge is "*Allaah said*" and His "*Messenger said*", and explanation and clarification of this with good speech, good behavior, and good admonishment, as well as to contend with doubts by discussion in the best manner. If doubts and misconceptions arise then seek to benefit by dispersing or dispelling them and desire to preserve the truth by repelling them; then discuss the matter in the best manner until the truth is made clear to those listening, until the misconceptions are removed and Allaah guides them through that the one whom He had determined would be of the people of success and contentment. The paths and ways available today are different than the ones of yesterday. The paths and ways present today are the numerous means and methods of calling to Allaah which are common and which are generally accepted by the people. Therefore it is obligatory upon the people of knowledge and faith in Allaah to develop them upon goodness and to utilize them for the truth and to oppose misguidance, even monetarily, through spending your money freely towards this. There are newspapers outside Saudi Arabia that are only published for the sake of generating money; but here it is possible, and all praise is due to Allaah, to publish and distribute without the extensive lengths or difficulties that they must go through elsewhere. Such a newspaper may be based in a land that requires considerable money to operate, whereas here if a well-known newspaper requires money we ensure that it receives the funds which are the cause of spreading the truth and inviting to it.

Similarly, publishing requires money, as does translating from one language to another language. All these endeavors require tremendous efforts in the path of Allaah, until the truth is spread and invited to according to the degree of your proficiency in the language you understand, as well your ability to spend your financial resources towards producing translations for other people in those languages you wish. Newspapers also must be given priority, as well is publishing and television. They are present amongst us and used by other people even more than us, so it is necessary that attention be directed towards them. It is necessary that scholars as well as the presenters and broadcasters have concern for this, and examine the errors that are found in our newspapers, as well as that which is stated in various publications which is incorrect, and that they explain and clarify these mistakes.

No one should say, [This is for so-and-so to do.] This is a mistake, as it is upon those amongst the scholars and writers who have the ability collectively to contribute to this effort, and to oppose and combat this assault which has been advanced by the enemies of Allaah and their allies. So it is not for anyone to say, [This is not upon for me], because the one who says that should know that every Muslim has a part of obligation. ❨*Oh you who believe! If you help in the cause of Allaah, He will help you, and make your foothold firm.*❩-(Surah Muhammad:7) ❨*And who is better in speech than he who invites men to Allaah, and does righteous deeds.*❩-(Surah Fussilat:33) ❨*This is my way; I invite to Allaah upon insight*❩-(Surah Yusuf:108). ❨*Indeed in the Messenger of Allaah you have a good example to follow*❩-(Surah al-Ahzab:21). Every one of us has upon us an obligation; every Muslim upon Allaah's earth whether in the East or the West, in every area of the world. Every Muslim, every student of knowledge, and every scholar has upon him an obligation to invite to Allaah's religion, that religion which Allaah has ennobled and honored him by, and repelled doubts from him by, and preserved him from conflicts and misguidance by means of behaviors and paths which are known to be beneficial and lead to the truth, and which encourage the acceptance of the truth and which are known to hold back and prevent falsehood and misguidance.

Indeed from the most significant of trials is when an individual says, [I am not responsible for this.]. This is an error and a mistake; a tremendous, false statement which would not be said by someone of intelligence except in the situation where another has satisfied the need amply or completely, where evil has been removed completely by someone else, or the falsehood has been sufficiently opposed by another. In regard to confronting the opponents of Islaam, then this is accomplished by spreading beneficial statements, and offering beneficial essays to oppose what is being published and televised, and to publish that which brings about benefit in the newspapers. Everyone carries a degree of responsibility until truth is given victory, and until falsehood is repelled and suppressed, and until the proof is established against the opponents of Islaam.

The people of misguidance are now supporting each other. The Communists, Christians, and those astray from the remaining groups of misguidance; all of them stand united in purpose against the truth, while they spend their resources freely while they are upon misguidance and callers to the hellfire. Even to the extent that they travel to remote, dangerous locations in their efforts to invite people to the hellfire! Only inviting to the fire! This is seen from the Communists, the Christians, Qadianees, Bahai's and other people of the hellfire or callers to falsehood. The Raafidhah at this time spread their call towards falsehood in every location, in fact slandering the religion of Allaah in that which they are doing in spreading misguidance. They curse the companions of the Prophet, may Allaah's praise and salutations be upon him, and wrongly accuse the Companions of the Prophet, may Allaah's praise and salutations be upon him, as well as their exaggeration towards the members of the Prophet's family, such as Alee, Hassan, Hussein, and others. All of this is from the forms of misguidance, and it prevents from the true path of Allaah. And this is the way and manner of all of the callers to falsehood and misguidance; all of them are upon this methodology.

The danger and falsehood presented by some of them is clear and readily apparent, such as the Christians, the Jews and those similar to them, and the Communists and those similar to them. However, some of them conceal their reality and nature, such as the Raafidhah and the other known categories of the people of innovation in the religion. For example, the Qaadeeanees, who apparently affiliate themselves with Islaam but falsely claim that their leader and founder, Mirza Ghulam, is the prophet whom revelation was given after Muhammad, upon him be Allaah's praise and salutations; so they call to following him. Similarly, this is the method with the other groups and categories of the people of misguidance. It is an obligation for the people of Islaam from every area of the world to spread the truth in opposition to the falsehood found amongst them. Any place where falsehood is found among them there is an obligation upon the people to circulate the truth and to oppose the falsehood; and that the strength of their confronting falsehood with this guidance be greater than that of the falsehood present, until their land, neighborhood, or tribe becomes cleansed from that misguidance which had spread within it. Undertaking this along with teaching the people the truth, and leading them towards the truth and guidance.

It is required that the efforts to be made by the people of knowledge be divided and apportioned, such that the misguidance that is found in their area is given a portion of their efforts, and the other types or occurrences of misguidance are also given a portion of their efforts. However, they should be stronger and more active in the suppression and removal of the misguidance which is found amongst them in their land, until the Muslim ummah becomes secure from that which they have experienced of evil and falsehood. It is required that the people of the truth be more active than the people of misguidance, and more patient in their efforts. If the people of misguidance are patient to the degree of 100% out of 100%, then it is required that the people of truth be patient to the degree of 400% or 1000%, until they become more active than the people of falsehood. Indeed, the people of misguidance only invite to the hellfire while you invite to paradise and true happiness, as well as receiving a greater recompense and reward from our Lord- and the difference between the two is tremendous. Some of the people of misguidance strive with vigor in their false efforts, believing that they are upon the truth and holding that their way is true, while you are also completely secure that you stand upon the truth, all praise is due to Allaah. Allaah, the Most High, says regarding the reality of the people of misguidance, ❖*Surely they took the Shayaateen as protectors and helpers instead of Allaah, and consider that they are guided.*❖-(Surah al-'Araaf:30) The Christians and those similar to them from the common people believe themselves to be upon guidance, and they are patient and travel to remote areas and unknown lands, inviting to Christianity and so to the Hellfire. They do all this while believing themselves to be guided. Similarly, those who have gone astray from within the Muslims, from the Sufis and other categories of groups which innovate in the religion- the majority of them suppose themselves to be upon guidance; but from their callers and leaders are those who have other objectives and ends in mind. They know they are upon misguidance; however they choose to work towards these other goals and ends in this worldly life. It is therefore obligatory upon the people of truth to be more active, stronger, and more patient in their call to adherence to the following of the Book of Allaah and the Sunnah of the Messenger of Allaah, and proceeding upon the methodology of the companions of the Prophet, upon him be Allaah's praise and salutations.

They must also stick closely to the path of Ahlus-Sunnah wa al-Jama'ah by acting upon everything that Allaah has obligated upon them, and abandoning everything that Allaah has forbidden; directing the people to every matter of truth to be held to, and warning them from every matter of misguidance that is found amongst them, until they are properly guided. Indeed the adviser to the people is the one who directs them to the truth, who directs the one who follows innovated matters towards the true Sunnah, saying to him, "*What you're doing is a mistake, rather, you should do such and such. As Allaah has said such and such and the Messenger, upon him be Allaah's praise and salutations, has said such and such.*" It should be the same way with all the other people of innovation, calling them and directing them towards the truth, hoping that Allaah may guide them from the other ranks of the innovators due to this. And within this month, the month of Rabe' al-Awwal there is an innovation that is widespread in many Muslim lands due to the lack of efforts by the people of knowledge to combat it. That is the innovation of celebrating the Prophet's birthday, may Allaah's praise and salutations be upon him. Additionally, in other lands there are other individual birthdays that are highly esteemed and considered momentous, which the people also celebrate. In these other celebrations there occurs the associating of others with Allaah, aspects of disbelief, and clear misguidance, to a level that only Allaah knows. Similarly in the practices of celebrating the birthday of the Prophet, there occurs from some of its participants associating others with Allaah, and seeking assistance through the Messenger, may Allaah's praise and salutations be upon him, and making supplication to him instead of Allaah, and resorting to that which is the major act of associating of partners with Allaah. And we seek refuge in Allaah from that. This is in addition to what is found within these practices from innovation in the religion, as these celebrations of the Prophets' birthday are a practice which the people invented after the passing of the best generations. Surely, the people before that did not know or practice this innovation of the Prophet's birthday, nor did they in the time of the Prophet, may Allaah's praise and salutations be upon him, nor during the era of his Companions, nor in the age of those Successors to the Companions, and neither was it found in the first second, or third century of Islaam! But it began to be practiced from the fourth century onward, due to the second of the Raafidhah, and those who were ignorant from the people of the Sunnah followed them in that.

It is an obligation upon all of the Muslims to have concern for and to strive to gain understanding of the religion of Allaah, and to gain insight into it, and to seek answers from the people of knowledge regarding their problems and dilemmas; to strive to become close to the Qur'aan and the authentic Sunnah, in order that the student of knowledge understand his religion and stand upon clarity. Also, so that he may be able to convey the correct understanding of the religion to the people found within his community from the general people of his land, region, or from the desert people belonging to his tribe. As information is presently widespread by means of the various forms of media which are being successfully used to spread the truth, just as various statements are spread within the newspapers of this land and others. Similarly, what is being spread by means of publishing the Qur'aan in this land, and what is spread by means of programs (such as radio program *Light upon the Path*). Knowledge is being spread through them, and Allaah has benefited many people through these programs and publications, such as the publications of the Qur'aan, as well is in the statements and writings produced by the scholars of many different lands from Egypt, Sham (the region directly north of Saudi Arabia), the lands of the West- Europe and America.

There are, and all praise is due to Allaah, a group of the people of truth spreading the truth in many places. Some of them are doing that by simply distributing flyers or pamphlets. This is a small effort when compared to those of the enemies of Allaah, and yet Allaah has benefited the people through that. What is imperative is that we increase upon these good efforts. That from the people of knowledge and discernment the one who is not speaking, speaks; and the one who is not writing, writes. And even just doing this is not sufficient for them; they must struggle just as those they oppose struggle and they should produce writings just as their enemies do. They must also closely follow the misguidance that is published in circulars, magazines, various types of publications, televisions, and other formats which are used for publication and circulation of material. They must follow and keep track of them and refute the misguidance found within them, spread the truth, and be patient with the difficulties of that, and the hardships of accomplishing that. This is jihaad. This certainly is jihaad. Calling to Allaah is jihaad, and writing in the path of Allaah is jihaad, and altering works for this is also jihaad.

The Prophet, may Allaah's praise and salutations be upon him, said, *{Strive against those who associate others with Allaah with your wealth, your own selves, and your tongues.}* [55]. So calling to Allaah is jihaad. Hassan Ibn Thaabit was a poet of the Messenger, may Allaah's praise and salutations be upon him, and he used to combat against those associated others with Allaah from Mecca with his poetry. The Prophet, may Allaah's praise and salutations be upon him, said to him, *{Strike against them, by the one who has my soul in his hand, as these words against them are harder that arrows descending upon them.}* [56]. And he, upon him be Allaah's praise and salutations, said, *{Strike against them, as certainly the holy spirit (Jibreel) is with you.}* [57]. Meaning by this the angel Jibreel, upon him be Allaah's praise and salutations. So strive against those who associate others with Allaah by writing and poetry which confirms the truth, and statements in publications, and in sermons. All of these are means by which Allaah gives victory to the truth. Additionally the Messenger of Allaah, may Allaah's praise and salutations be upon him, spent the majority of the effort of his call giving sermons, and through speeches. And then by, upon him be Allaah's praise and salutations, writing letters to the leaders and kings of his time. However, the majority of the efforts of his call, upon him be Allaah's praise and salutations, were primarily through sermons and his statements in the city of Medinah and Mecca, yet his other efforts including his military campaigns were also part of his calling to Allaah. All of his endeavors and actions were calling to Allaah, upon him be Allaah's

---

[55] Narrated in Sunan Abu Daawud: 2156/ Sunan al-Daaramee: 2393/ Mustradraak al-Haakim: 2365/ Sunan an-Nasaa'ee: 4173/ & Musnad Imaam Ahmad: 12029, 13398: -on the authority of 'Anas Ibn Maalik. It was declared authentic by Sheikh al-Albaanee in Saheeh al-Jaame'a as-Sagheer: 3090, Mishkaat al-Masaabeh: 3821, Saheeh Sunan Abu Dawud: 2504, Saheeh Sunan an-Nasaa'ee: 3096.

[56] Narrated in Sunan an-Nasaa'ee: 2896/ -on the authority of 'Anas Ibn Maalik. It was declared authentic by Sheikh al-Albaanee in Saheeh Sunan an-Nasaa'ee.

[57] Narrated in Saheeh al-Bukhaaree: 6153/ Saheeh Muslim: 2486/ & Musnad Imaam Ahmad: 18178, 18203: -on the authority of Bara' Ibn 'Aazab. And it is in Sunan Abu Daawud: 5015/ on the authority of 'Aishah Mother of the Believers. It was declared authentic by Sheikh al-Albaanee in Silsilat al-Hadeeth as-Saheehah: 801, 1970. Saheeh al-Jaame'a as-Sagheer: 3847, 3848, 4287, Saheeh Sunan Abu Dawud, Saheeh Sunan an-Nasaa'ee: 3096. Sheikh Muqbil declared it authentic in al-Jaame'a al-Saheeh: 74, 279, 478, 2563.

praise and salutations.

Therefore the fundamentals are established by what he did through his actions, his behavior and conduct, his standing and his sitting, his sleeping and his waking. Because of this it is obligatory that the scholars make him the foundation and the basis for establishing and organizing, upon him be Allaah's praise and salutations. However in these latter times Allaah has facilitated this matter for them through these new forms of media which have reached the people in every area and location. These various publications and newspapers which are spread throughout the world can be used to transmit your statements. So if they are based upon the truth Allaah will benefit the people through them, as much as He wills, throughout the entire world. Just as if your words are from falsehood, then many people will be harmed by them. This writing could be done in the city of Riyadh and then reach Europe, America, and every other region, spreading through that original composition to every location. They may be used in various types of publications, or in television and then spread to every place, not merely in its original form or instance. But in the beginning it was a limited publication specifically in your country or within the surrounding region. However, today one makes a statement and in one day or one night, rather in a single hour- you make a statement and it is heard by the whole world, from this land and from that land.

Again, if it was a word of truth then the blessing will come from it, and if it was a word of falsehood than what results from it is only harm and offense. And there is no strength or power except in Allaah. As the people must consider- consider and take into account the condition of the people today. One might give a sermon in America and it is heard by the people everywhere. Someone may give a sermon in Egypt and it is heard by many people, or give one in Mecca and it is heard by many people, or in Riyadh and it is heard by many people as well is being heard in other places- regardless of whether it is for truth or for falsehood. For the people, whether calling to guidance or to falsehood, are heard by the people. And the majority of the people are not upon guidance, and indeed there is no strength or power except in Allaah. The majority of people are following their desires. *And if you obey most of those on earth, they will mislead you far away from Allaah's Path. They follow nothing but conjectures, and they do nothing but lie*-(Surah al-An'aam 116) *And most of mankind will not believe even if you desire it eagerly.*-(Surah Yusuf:103). So the majority of humanity are upon their misguidance, wishes, and desires, but not upon the truth. The truth can only be brought to light through the people of insight and understanding, the people of sound intellect, the people of investigation, discernment, consideration, and intelligence; those who possess the ability to distinguish between truth and falsehood, those who comprehend the consequences and outcomes of matters upon faith and sound understanding. However, the majority of the humanity are in a state like that which Allaah, the Most High, Most Exalted, mentioned, saying, *Or do you think that most of them hear or understand? They are only like cattle; nay, they are even farther astray from the Path.*-(Surah al-Furqaan: 44) He has declared them to be more astray than cattle, meaning that some animals are more guided than some of humanity, as they benefit the people. They proceed upon their affair of simply grazing and other activities but do not cause harm or difficulty for the people. But as for the majority of humanity, they are more harmful than the animals; they do not benefit, but instead bring harm to people. We ask Allaah for safety and health. And in this there is a lesson for the person of intelligence to take care such that you benefit and do not bring harm, whether seeking to benefit people by your statements, actions, wealth, power or other matters that benefit- not from matters that would bring harm to the people.

From the trials and tribulations is when someone works, believing that he is upon guidance, believing that he is benefiting in bringing good, when reality is harming the people. Just as Allaah says, *Say: "Shall We tell you the greatest losers in respect of (their) deeds? Those whose efforts have been wasted in this life while they thought that they were acquiring good by their deeds!*-(Surah Kahf:103-104) And this is from a tremendous loss; that one strives diligently with their wealth, time, and the various types of efforts, but in that which in reality does not benefit them, but only harms them. It is from the matters that anger Allaah and which prevent the spread of the truth. So certainly it is one of the tremendous losses and we ask Allaah for safety and health. Therefore the person of intelligence brings himself to account and struggles within himself. He considers carefully and is not silent within himself nor heedless. He considers what it is that he endeavoring upon and what he is sending forth for the next world- thinking and considering carefully. Just as the Most Exalted says, *Oh you who believe! Fear Allaah and keep your duty to Him. And let every person look to what he has sent forth for the morrow, and fear Allaah. Verily, Allaah is All-Aware of what you do. And be not like those who forgot Allaah (i.e. became disobedient to Allaah) and He caused them to forget their own selves, (let them to forget to do righteous deeds). Those are the Faasiqun (rebellious, disobedient to Allaah). Not equal are the dwellers of the Fire and the dwellers of the Paradise. It is the dwellers of Paradise that will be successful*-(Surah al-Hashr:18-20)

So the person of intelligence proceeds and looks and considers what he has sent forward, what has he done for the next world, and his next life! What has he put forward which opposes misguidance, what has he undertaken for the success and contentment of his wife, children, neighbor, and society. Do not be heedless! It is required that he continually and constantly questions and considers. Is he in a state of loss or one of profit and success? Is he content or in misery? Is he upon guidance or misguidance? Consider and evaluate yourself all the time, and make yourself adhere to the truth that you understand- hold fast to the truth by preserving your congregational prayer, by paying the zakaat charity, by good treatment to one's parents, by maintaining family ties, by staying away from the different forms of immoral behavior, and by leaving evil companionship. Similarly, calling yourself to account- so the one who drinks intoxicants calls himself to account and abandons those intoxicants completely, the one who sits with people who are bad or evil companions should call himself to account and distance himself from them. Look carefully at your actions; are they benefiting or harming you? Are you working in that which will benefit you in the next life or acting in a way that will lead to Hellfire? Call yourself to account.

This is an incredibly dangerous age where one sees misguidance everywhere. The radio broadcasts are present, television is present, and newspapers are present all containing evil and harm, the true extent of which is only known by Allaah. You listen with your ears, and see with your own eyes, and write with your own pen, or read; so consider what is achieved from all this. What is actually attained from listening to media broadcasts and watching television, or from reading the newspaper? Have you obtained goodness and benefit or only acquired harm and evil? So if you have only reached harm then be warned and stop. But if you have achieved goodness and benefit then all praise is due to Allaah, continue upon that good, being warned from falsehood and misguidance. Then do not stop only with yourself as an individual, advise your brother, your wife, your father and mother, your child, your neighbor and your friend. Advise them if you witness misguidance that will harm them as it would harm you, as the Muslim is the brother of the Muslim. The Messenger of Allaah, upon him be Allaah's praise and salutations, said, {*One of you does not truly believe until he loves for his brother what he loves for himself.*} [58]. And he said, may Allaah's praise and salutations be upon him, {*"The religion is sincerity and well wishing." Upon this we said, "For whom?" He replied, "For Allaah, His Book, His Messenger and for the leaders and the general Muslims."*} [59].

If the giving of advice before this age or before these new occurrences and developments was an obligation, then today it is now a much greater obligation. If calling to Allaah a hundred years ago or two hundred years ago was an obligation, then today it is a much greater obligation- and so on. As the situation now is that overwhelming evil, as falsehood has dominated and spread. So it is obligatory to double one's efforts to oppose and combat it. All of these are aspects of this ideological war and warfare which are talked about. And it is that struggle which reaches you by means of the television, newspapers, publications, and other authored works; all of these are part of the ideological war, and the war to cause you to abandon Islaam. It is a very damaging war, that harms everyone except the few who are protected by your Lord's mercy. I ask Allaah by His beautiful names and exalted attributes to bless us and you with beneficial knowledge and righteous deeds, and to grant us understanding of the religion and steadfastness upon it and to protect us from the evil of our own selves and from our own evil deeds. And to bless us with the true jihaad against ourselves and that we call ourselves into accounting order that we are firm upon the truth, and leave misguidance.

---

[58] Narrated in Saheeh al-Bukhaaree: 13/ Saheeh Muslim: 45/ Jaame'a at-Tirmidhee: 2515/ Saheeh Sunan an-Nasaa'ee: 5016, 5017, 5043/ Sunan Ibn Maajah: 66/ & Musnad Imaam Ahmad: 12390, 12734, and other narrations/ Sunan ad-Daaramee: 2740/ -on the authority of 'Anas Ibn Maalik. It was declared authentic by Sheikh al-Albaanee in Silsilat al-Hadeeth as-Saheehah: 73, Mishkaat al-Masaabeh: 4961, Saheeh al-Jaame'a as-Sagheer: 7085, 7583, as well as in Saheeh Sunan at-Tirmidhee and Saheeh Sunan an-Nasaa'ee.

[59] Narrated in Saheeh Muslim: 2, 55/ Sunan Abu Daawud: 4933/ Saheeh Sunan an-Nasaa'ee: 4202, 4203/ & Musnad Imaam Ahmad: 16493, 16494, and other narrations/ -on the authority of Tameem ad-Daaree. And it is narrated in Jaame'a at-Tirmidhee: 1926/ Saheeh Sunan an-Nasaa'ee: 4204, 4205/ & Musnad Imaam Ahmad: 7894/ -on the authority of Abu Hurairah It was declared authentic by Sheikh al-Albaanee in Irwa' al-Ghaleel : 26, Mishkaat al-Masaabeh: 4966, and other of his works.

I ask that He bless us and you with excellent companions and righteous associates and that He protect us and all the Muslims from evil companions and harmful associates, and that He grant success to the scholars of the Muslims in every place to spread the truth and establish what is required of them in calling to it, and being patient upon that endeavor. And that He grants success to the Muslim rulers in all parts of the world to be upon a way that He is pleased with. And that He support them in spreading the truth and ruling by the truth, and suppressing falsehood, thus combating falsehood and misguidance and its people wherever they are found. And that He protects them from obeying their desires and Shaytaan, as Allaah, the Most High and Exalted is the Most Giving and the Most Generous.

We ask Him by His noble face to guide our rulers and people of authority to every good, and through them give victory to the truth. And that He assist them in the rectification of these various forms of media and communication until evil and harm are removed from within them and good is firmly established within them, and that they become our tools of goodness and rectification from every aspect and direction, and that Allaah remove from them every harm or tribulation. And that He bless our scholars and the scholars of all the Muslims in every location, to fulfill their obligations and spread the truth, and that He blesses the common Muslims with insight and consideration and steadfastness upon the truth and to be of those who inquire about the truth and abandon misguidance, and to advise with the truth in their various affairs between them. Certainly He is the one who hears and is close to us. And that Allaah's praise and salutations be upon our prophet Muhammad, his family, and his Companions.

*Question: You have mentioned in your presentation that it is upon all the students of knowledge to speak and act for Allaah's religion; and this is true may Allaah reward you with good, as this regard neglect has occurred from the direction of the students of knowledge specifically. However there is also an important point to be made, and it is that it is not permissible for them that they speak except after having received permission, otherwise they will be fall into trials and difficulties. As speaking publicly has conditions, which are not fulfilled by every student of knowledge. Due to this it is necessary that they leave this realm to those who possess the necessary characteristics. What is your opinion regarding this?*

Answer: Such permission is a simple matter and all praise is due to Allaah, as everyone who is known with good then he is given permission. And we do not give the right to speak to just anyone, such that they might speak and invite towards misguidance and spread falsehood- no. But this matter, all praise is due to Allaah, is simple, as the one who is known to have knowledge or has graduated from the college of Sharee'ah, or from the college of "the fundamentals of the religion", or the scholars testify to goodness regarding him- even if it is a single scholar, then he is given such permission, and he can proceed to speak and give sermons, and all praise is due to Allaah.

(64) The Eminent Guiding Scholar Muhammad Ibn Saaleh al-'Utheimeen, may Allaah have mercy upon him, from 'Series of Monthly Meetings': Number 75)

*Question: Esteemed sheikh, the Muslim Ummah is being targeted by its enemies, such that they charge at us from every direction. The latest evil they have directed towards us- and it is the most dangerous of their evils in my opinion- is what is known as the "internet" which attacks our very households. Indeed, internet cafes have opened which are used by both children as well as young men who are not yet reached maturity. Likewise it has been announced that they will open similar ones for women! So what is your advice for us in how we use the internet? Additionally, what is the ruling regarding opening these internet cafes, when the majority of what we see in them are various types of corruption? May Allaah benefit us through you.*

Answer: All praise is due to Allaah, Lord of all the worlds. May Allaah's praise and salutation be upon our prophet Muhammad, and upon his family, Companions, and those that follow them in goodness until the day of Judgment. The Prophet, May Allaah's praise and salutation be upon him and his family, warned against trials with the most severe of warnings. He informed us that trials will appear with increasing severity- one after the other. Meaning that the current trial will make the previous trial seem mild in comparison, due to its own severity and significance. Indeed, this is what has clearly occurred.

Certainly the people have become bored, weary, tired and are now turning away from the satellite channels. Then the "internet" appears and is something which makes it possible for a man to speak to a woman face to face, as well as to view and see whatever he wishes of immorality and corruption. However, I have heard that our government- may Allaah grant it success- have placed a barrier or wall against the spread of that material which is found on the "internet" which corrupts and debases ones' character. This is something which the government should be thanked for, and is from the matters which indicate its concern for providing good protection to its people. Yet even if it is able to prevail from one aspect, clearly it cannot not dominate every aspect of the problem and prevent all the material which is harmful to ones religion or character. Therefore the government's efforts are not to be seen as the complete solution. Isn't that so?

It cannot be considered the complete answer. Indeed it is required upon the people themselves to have fear of Allaah the Most High and the Most Exalted, and to stay away from the harmful material which is published and spread by means of the internet. Every individual is a guardian or shepherd for the members of his household, and responsible for those under his care. By Allaah, if we were to fully practice and act upon this responsibility which we were informed of by the Messenger of Allaah, may Allaah's praise and salutation be upon him and his family, it would rectify the state of the people. As the individual takes his nature from the general disposition of the sons of Aadam around him. So if this person who was in charge of this family rectifies his household, and a second person rectifies his household, and a third rectifies his household, this rectification proceeds forward and progresses and the people's characters are corrected. But the problem is that in these households we have men who are only imitations of real men, rather they are like women. They barely have control over their households and families. Indeed, he is someone who when he comes out in the morning and their family meal is prepared he eats and then returns to bed, or goes to his store or place of business, and doesn't give or direct towards them any true attention. When he comes home in the evening he may find his wife sitting on the couch dressed attractively, and he fulfills he physical need with her, but does not give her any true attention. Is this a man?!

No by Allaah, this one is not truly a man. A man is the one who inspects and reviews his family and considers what are they involved in? What are they doing? From where have they returned? Because he is responsible for them, he is responsible for them, he is responsible for them! Indeed, Allaah, the Most High and the Most Exalted, says: ❖*Protect yourselves and your families against a Fire (Hellfire) whose fuel is men and stones*❖-(Surah Tahreem:6)

We have been commanded to guard our families from the Hellfire. This means that we provide them with an education which will preserve them from the Fire. But with regret, we see that many men are not truly men. Rather they are something close to being men or imitating men, but not true men. For this reasons some of the rulers, after the Ummah began to show divisions and separations, preached to the people by saying: "*Oh you men and those who are not actually men! Oh you men and who are only something like men!*" Because "men" here, means a "man" in the true and full sense and meaning of the word.

Therefore my advice to every individual from my Muslim brothers is to closely supervise his family- both the males and females, because he is responsible for them. If he cultivates and raises them upon a correct sound education, he will benefit from this after his death. They will be righteous people who will supplicate for him after his death.

So the "internet" contains good. We do not say that it is purely evil, rather it contains good also. However, along with that good there are many evils. Evils in relations to beliefs, because being spread through the internet are various innovated beliefs, some of which cause one to leave Islaam and other which incorrect Islamic rulings which can be found. As an individual establishes himself as a "scholar able to give rulings", and he does so without possessing any true knowledge! This is very dangerous for the general people of the Ummah. As the common people are truly upon their name: ordinary and average. As is said: "*The common people are like pests*" Because the common person if someone give a ruling that agrees with his desires, then he then turns away from any other rulings contrary to that. This is very dangerous, and contains harm for one character. Additionally, it is well known that widespread sexual lewdness and immorality and other evils are found on the internet. So the one who takes advantage of the internet and takes from it what is of benefit to them, while protecting themselves from its harms, then for him it is one of the means of gaining knowledge. But are for the one who takes from it what it contains of good as well as its harm, and exposes himself to everything which is available, then this individual stands in a position of significant danger. As for what is related to the question of opening businesses of internet cafes, then this is not something that is to be asked about, as there are specific committees responsible for these things, and they are the ones who should be asked.

**(65) The Eminent Guiding Scholar Muqbil Ibn Haadee al-Waadi'ee, may Allaah have mercy upon him, From 'A Defending Mission from Audio Lectures Upon the People of Ignorance & Sophistry': Vol.2, Page 468**

*Question: What is the Islamic ruling on the use of the television if we have Islamic dialogues with the Christians, and knowledge based lectures that are specifically educational or cultural?*

Answer: As for the television, then it is essential that it not be brought into the home, as it involves worthless speech and music. Moreover, it involves the making of images of living beings and the Messenger of Allaah, may Allaah's praise and salutations be upon him, said, as is found in the two well known 'Saheeh' hadeeth collections from the hadeeth of Abu Talhah, *{The angels to not enter a house in which there is a dog or images.}* [60]. He also refused to enter the room of 'Aishah when he saw that there was a curtain upon which there where figures of living beings. So 'Aishah quickly said, *"I repent to Allaah."* Then the Messenger of Allaah, may Allaah's praise and salutations be upon him and his family, took the curtain and tore it into separate pieces. Also, when he saw two cushions that had images upon them he said, *{Oh 'Aisha! The most severely punished people on the Day of Judgment are those who make such images.}* [61]. And one might say, [This prohibition only applies to three dimensional images.] However the figures mentioned, these being upon a garment, were not three dimensional. Imaam Ahmad narrated in his hadeeth collection "al-Musnad" on the authority of Jaabir, may Allaah be pleased with him, that *{the Prophet, may Allaah's praise and salutations be upon him and his family, when he entered the Ka'bah the day of the conquest of Mecca, found that there were images upon the walls of the Ka'bah. There were images of Ibraheem and Isma'eel divining by arrows. So he called for a rag which was wet with water and wiped them away}*. This is evidence that the images referred to do not have to be that which has a physical form or is three dimensional.

Additionally, television involves worthless speech and music. It is narrated in Saheeh of Imaam al-Bukhaaree on the authority of Abu Aamar al-'Asharee that the Prophet, may Allaah's praise and salutations be upon him and his family, said, *{There will be a people from my Ummah who will make permissible fornication, dressing in*

---

[60] Narrated in Saheeh al-Bukhaaree: 3225, 3322, 4002/ Saheeh Muslim: 2106/ Jaame'a at-Tirmidhee: 2804/Sunan an-Nasaa'ee: 4387, 5349, 5350/ Sunan Ibn Maajah: 3649/ & Musnad Imaam Ahmad: 15934, 27064/-on the authority of Abu Talhah al-Ansaaree. And it is in Saheeh Muslim: 2104/ Sunan Ibn Maajah: 3651/ & Musnad Imaam Ahmad: 24576/-on the authority of 'Aishah. And it is in Saheeh Muslim: 2105/ Sunan Abu Dawud: 4157/ Sunan an-Nasaa'ee: 4281/ & Musnad Imaam Ahmad: 26260/-on the authority of Umm al-Mu'mineen Maymoonah. And it is in Sunan an-Nasaa'ee: 4286/ Sunan Ibn Maajah: 3650/ & Musnad Imaam Ahmad: 8177/ Sunan ad-Daaramee: 2663/ -on the authority of 'Alee Ibn Abee Taalib. It was declared authentic by Sheikh al-Albaanee in Ghaayat al-Maraam 118, Saheeh at-Targheeb at-Tarheeb: 3058, 3058, 3103, as well as in his verification of the four "Sunan".

[61] Narrated in Saheeh al-Bukhaaree: 6109/ Saheeh Muslim: 2107/Sunan an-Nasaa'ee: 5358, 5359, 5365/ & Musnad Imaam Ahmad: 24015, 24035/-on the authority of 'Aishah. It was declared authentic by Sheikh al-Albaanee in Ghaayat al-Maraam 118, Saheeh at-Targheeb at-Tarheeb: 3053, 3055, Mishkaat al-Masaabeh: 119, & Saheeh al-Jaame'a as-Sagheer: 2204, 5892.

*silk, intoxicants, and musical instruments.}* [62]. Television also involves the practice of men looking at women if the announcer or broadcaster is a woman, or the practice of women looking at men if the announcer or broadcaster is a man. This is also something prohibited. Allaah, the Most High, the Most exalted says, ◈ *Tell the believing men to lower their gaze (from looking at forbidden things), and protect their private parts (from illegal sexual acts, etc.). That is purer for them.* ◈ -(Surah an-Nur:30) And He says, ◈ *And tell the believing women to lower their gaze from looking at forbidden things, and protect their private parts from illegal sexual acts* ◈ -(Surah an-Nur:31). In addition to this, is what is narrated by Imaams al-Bukhaaree and Muslim in their 'Saheeh' collections of hadeeth on the authority of Abu Hurairah, may Allaah be pleased with him, that the Prophet, may Allaah's praise and salutations be upon him and his family, said, *{Allaah has written for every son of Aadam a portion of adultery which a man will indulge in without escaping from it, and the adultery of the eye is the lustful look.}* -(al-Bukhaaree: 6243/ Muslim: 2657). Similarly, many periodicals and newspapers also have such immoral images, as well as promoting concepts that are foreign and unacceptable in Islaam. Therefore that which I advise the Muslim who truly wants to receive news, is to suffice himself with the use of a radio. But also to listen to the news from the radio while being aware that these broadcasters are liars and deceivers As whenever I was able to do so, from the beginning of the Gulf crisis up until this very day, I listened to the radio after salaatul-Isha. But all that I heard were deceptions, hypocrisy, deceit, and repeated statements. So we strongly disapprove and censure this worthless speech. And from Allaah we seek assistance.

(66) The Eminent Guiding Scholar Muqbil Ibn Haadee al-Waadi'ee, may Allaah have mercy upon him, From 'A Defending Mission from Audio Lectures upon the People of Ignorance and Sophistry': Vol.2, Page 467

*Question: What is the Islamic ruling on reading daily newspapers, publications, or magazines for the purpose of getting societal, Islamic, governmental, or cultural news in order to understand what is going on around us?*

Answer: That which I advise you is to stay far away from this, as the majority of these newspapers and magazines simply serve the different governments, and deceive and mislead people for the sake of these governments. But let us say that there was indeed a newspaper or a magazine that conveyed the truth. Even after this, every individual only has a limited amount of time to be wasted on this newspaper or magazine. Yet in this 'news' we only see distressing thoughts and statements, and we see in it that which can only lead one to worry and anxiety. Also, perhaps there may be the publishing of insults to Islaam, the criticism of the Muslims, and similar things. But in any case we do not say that it is prohibited to read them; however, we advise the student of knowledge to content himself with the Book of Allaah and the Sunnah, as-

---

[62] Narrated in Saheeh al-Bukhaaree is a mu'alaq narration after hadeeth 5590/ -on the authority of Abu Maalik al-'Asha'ree. It was declared authentic by Sheikh al-Albaanee in Silsilat al-Hadeeth as-Saheehah: 91

*The truly important news is never fails to reach everyone.*

*News reaches you from the one who you did not expect.*

So important news does not hide itself it spreads as quickly as possible throughout the entire area! As for those magazines related to atheist methodologies and concepts, then it is expected that they only promote misconceptions and doubts while causing you to waste your time. Additionally, those managing these various forms of the electronic media and those responsible for the production of newspapers are usually people known to practice deception and hypocrisy. And from Allaah we seek help and assistance.

(67) The Eminent Guiding Scholar 'Abdul-'Azeez Ibn 'Abdullah Ibn Baaz, may Allaah have mercy upon him, excerpted From 'A Collection of Rulings and Various Statements': Vol.5, Page 266

*Question: Some of those who call to Allaah avoid utilizing various types of media because of their rejection of any government controlled newspaper or reject working a magazine which generally relies upon sensational articles to increase their circulation among the people. So what is your esteemed view regarding this?*

Answer:   It is an obligation for those responsible for such newspapers to have fear of Allaah and to guard against those things which harm the people. Regardless of whether this is a daily, weekly, or monthly newspaper. Likewise, the authors should fear Allaah in the material they author. Do not write or publish among the general people except what will benefit them and which invites them to good and warns them against evil. As for the publishing of images of women on the covers of or inside of magazines or newspapers, then this is a tremendous evil, and significant harm, which invites to corruption and misguidance. Similarly, is the publishing of material which call to false socialist ideas or material that invites to sinful behavior, such as adultery, and the exposure of women's beauty outside of proper situations, the using of intoxicants or any matter that Allaah has made forbidden. All of these are tremendous evils, and it is required that those responsible for these periodicals take care to stay away from these matters.

When such things are published they are accountable for the wrongdoing which the people were encouraged towards. As for the responsible individual associated with this periodical which publishes these blameworthy articles, whether he is the editor or an administrator who instructs them with that, he has upon him an equal share of the sins of the people who are misguided by this material and affected by it. Just as the one who publishes that which is good and that which calls to good and beneficial matters receives a reward equal to the one who is affected by it in a good way.

From this starting point, clearly it is obligatory upon the various media organizations which have a tremendous effect and hold upon the Muslims, to ensure that they are free from everything which Allaah has prohibited and that they stay far away from spreading that which undoubtedly harms the society. In view of this, is it an obligation upon these various organizations to make their primary focus and goal that which benefits the people in regard to their religion and worldly affairs. And that they guard against becoming instruments for the destruction of society and the means for its corruption by means of what they publish. Each responsible individual in such a media organization is responsible for this to the degree of his capacity and ability.

And it is an obligation upon the callers that they utilize the opportunities offered by the media to warn against all matters forbidden by Allaah the Most High, the Most Exalted. This is an obligation upon them in their sermons and their gatherings with the people. Every sitting should be a gathering of invitation to good whereever it is. As he is calling to Allaah whether it is within his house, when visiting brothers, or when he gathers or meets with anyone. As it is required from him that he utilize these ways and means, meaning the various forms of media, and spread good through them and not neglect making proper use of them.

(68) THE EMINENT MAJOR SCHOLAR ABDUL-AZEEZ IBN ABDULLAH IBN BAAZ-, MAY ALLAAH HAVE MERCY UPON HIM, FROM 'A COLLECTION OF RULINGS AND VARIOUS STATEMENTS': VOL. 9, PAGE 223

*Question: Clearly, bringing guidance to the people is the result of spreading Sharee'ah knowledge among them, however we see that falsehood is more widely spread over most newspapers and the various types of media, as well as within the education methodologies and curriculums. So what is the position of the scholar and the caller to Allaah regarding this?*

Answer: This reality is something found in every age and the wisdom of this is something Allaah willed just as He states: ❧ *And most of the people will not believe even if you desire it eagerly* ❧-(Surah Yusuf:103) and the Most Exalted says: ❧ *And if you obey most of those on earth, they will mislead you far away from Allaah's Path* ❧-(Surah al-Ana'am:116) However this differs, as in one land it will be greater in degree and in another less, and in one tribe it may be greater and in another less. But in regard to the world in general, then the majority of people are upon something other than guidance- yet this varies for some of the countries, lands, regions, and tribes.

Therefore, it is obligatory upon the people of knowledge to strive vigorously and not let the people of falsehood out strive them. Rather, it is obligatory that they out strive the people of falsehood in their efforts to make the truth clear -calling to it wherever they may be, whether in the street, in a car, in an airplane, in a spaceship, in his home, in any location. It is for them to prevent wrongdoing in the way that is best, and carry this out in the best manner with excellent behavior, gentleness and mildness.

As the Most High and the Most Exalted says: "Invite to the Way of your Lord with wisdom and fair preaching, and argue with them in a way that is better." (Surah an-Nahl: 125) And the One free from all faults says: ❧ *And by the Mercy of Allaah, you dealt with them gently. And had you been severe and harsh hearted, they would have broken away from about you* ❧-(Surah Aal-'Imraan:159) And the Prophet, may Allah's praise and salutations be upon him, said: *{The one who guides to goodness received a reward equal to the who does it..}*-(Saheeh Muslim: 1893) He, prayers and salutations be upon him, said: *{Gentleness in not found with a matter except that it beautifies it and it is not absent from a matter except that this absence tarnishes or taints it.}*-(Saheeh Muslim: 2594) So it is not permissible for the people of knowledge to remain silent and abandon speaking to the sinner, the innovator, and the ignorant one. As this is a tremendous mistake and from the causes of the spread of evil and innovation, the removal of goodness and it being something scarce and the disappearance of the Sunnah.

It is obligatory upon the people of knowledge to speak with the truth and invite towards it and to censure falsehood and warn away from it. And it is obligatory to do this with upon knowledge and insight, as Allaah the Most High, the Most Exalted says: ❧ *This is my way; I invite unto Allah with sure knowledge*❧-(Surah Yusuf:108). And this is after attention being given the means by which knowledge is acquired through studying with the people of knowledge, and asking them regarding ones problems, attending their circles of knowledge, frequently reciting the Noble Qur'aan, contemplating it and reviewing authentic narrations.

This until one benefits and knowledge spreads forth by way of it being taken from its people with evidence with sincerity, a good intention, and humility. It obligatory for them to be diligent in the spreading of knowledge with every vigor and strength, and to not allow the people of falsehood to be more active than them in the spreading of their falsehood, being diligent to benefit the Muslims in their religious and worldly affairs. So this is an obligation upon the scholars, the elders and the young among them wherever they may be, to spread the truth through its Sharee'ah evidences and encourage the people towards it, and turn them away from falsehood and warn them from it in practice, as Allaah the Most High, and The Most Exalted says: ❧ *Cooperate with one another upon goodness and the fear of Allah*❧-(Surah al-Maidah:2) And the statement of the Most High: ❧ *By al-'Asr (the time). Verily! Man is in loss. Except those who believe and do righteous good deeds, and recommend one another to the truth, and recommend one another to patience.* ❧-(Surah al-Asr:1-3)

Likewise, the people of knowledge wherever they are should call to Allah- guiding towards goodness, giving advice to Allaah and His worshipers, with gentleness in that which they command towards, that which the forbid from, and that which they call to -until their call becomes successful and the majority of the people realize a praiseworthy effect and are protected from the plots of our enemies. And from Allaah we seek assistance

**(69) THE EMINENT GUIDING SCHOLAR 'ABDUL-'AZEEZ IBN 'ABDULLAH IBN BAAZ, MAY ALLAAH HAVE MERCY UPON HIM, FROM 'COLLECTION OF RULINGS AND VARIOUS STATEMENTS':VOL. 8 - PAGE 232-234)**

*Question: The youth involved in the revival of Islaam are commonly accused of extremism and "fundamentalism" in some of the various media sources. What is your esteemed view of this?*

Answer: Regardless of this, this is a error which originates from the Western countries from the Christians and Jews, and from the Eastern countries from the communists as well as other than them, from those who want to turn others away from the call to Allaah and those who support it. They wish to stain and slander this call by such accusations or by using the label of "fundamentalism" or this or that term which they label them with. There is no doubt that calling to Allaah is the religion of all the Prophets of Allaah; this was their way and their path. It is obligatory upon the people of knowledge to invite to Allaah and to do this vigorously. Additionally it is upon those young men who fear and have reverence of Allaah, and who hold fast to the truth, that they do not go towards extremism nor negligence.

As some of the young men are ignorant and so the act with extremism in some matters, while others have a deficiency in knowledge and so they are ignorant of their religion. However, it is upon all of the young men as well as others such as the scholars that they fear Allaah and that they investigate and search for the truth of matters by their evidences, by this meaning: *"Allaah, the Most High, the Most Exalted says"*, and *"the Messenger of Allaah, may Allaah's praise and salutations be upon him, says"*. It is also upon them to stay far away from innovation in the religion and extremism and going beyond the proper limits. As well as also staying far away from ignorance and deficiencies in their practice. There is no one among them who is infallible, so there has occurred from some of the people matters of deficiency in the religion, either by adding something or falling short in something. However this is not something all of them can be faulted with, it is only a fault in the specific one from whom it occurs.

The enemies of Allaah from the Christians and others who are upon their same path, use this as a means to strike at and attack the call to Allaah. As well as to cast upon the Muslims the accusation that they are "extremists" or "fundamentalists". And what is the meaning of the term "fundamentalist"? If they are fundamentalist meaning that: that hold firm to the fundamentals of Islaam, and to what Allaah has stated and what the Messenger of Allaah, prayers and good mention be upon him, has stated- then this is in praise of them not censure. Being described with adherence to the Book of Allaah and the Sunnah of the Messenger of Allaah, prayers and good mention be upon him, is certainly praise and is not truly criticism. Rather what is worthy of censure is going to extremes or laxity either through acting in an extreme way by going beyond the proper bounds, or by going to the other extreme through neglect and falling short of what is required. This is what is to be criticized.

As for the individual who holds firmly to the recognized foundations and principles from the Book of Allaah and the Sunnah of His Messenger, prayers and good mention be upon him, then this is not at all blameworthy. Rather it is praiseworthy and from the completion of the religion. This is what is required upon the students of knowledge and the callers to Allaah: that they hold firmly to the foundations from the Book of Allaah and the Sunnah of His Messenger, prayers and good mention be upon him, and what they understand from the principles of deriving the rules of the religion, and the fundamentals of correct belief, and fundamentals of hadeeth terminology in regard to what is used in determining the status of what is accepted as evidence. It is necessary that that they have the understanding of these fundamentals as a foundation that must be relied upon.

So they attack the callers to Allaah with the accusation that they are "fundamentalists", and this statement is intentionally broad without having a corresponding reality, except to throw blame, find fault, and cause fear. As such this label of so called "fundamentalism" is not blameworthy, but in reality is a commendation and statement of praise. If a student of knowledge holds firmly to the fundamentals, has true concern for them, and attends to them carefully- and what is intended by fundamentals is what comes from the Book of Allaah and the Sunnah of His Messenger, prayers and good mention be upon him, and from what has been established by the people of knowledge- then this is not at all blameworthy. But as for going to extremes by innovating matters in the religion, and making additions, and extremism, then this is indeed blameworthy. Or the going to extremes through ignorance and neglect, that is also blameworthy.

It is obligatory upon the callers to adhere to the fundamentals of the Sharee'ah and to hold firmly to them with the moderation that Allaah placed them upon. As Allaah has made the Muslim nation a balanced moderate nation. So it is obligatory upon the callers to: to be moderate between immoderation and inattention, between excess and negligence. And it is upon them to be established upon the truth, and to affirm this by Sharee'ah evidences. Not by excess and extremism, and not by inattention nor negligence. Rather, with the moderation and balance which Allaah has commanded.

(70) The Eminent Guiding Scholar 'Abdul-'Azeez Ibn 'Abdullah Ibn Baaz, may Allaah have mercy upon him, from 'Collection of Rulings and Various Statements': vol. 5, page 77)

*Question: It is well know how much good the Islamic recording distributors have accomplished in the present time and their important role in guiding the people. However some people of evil intent attempt to distort the reputation and state that they are only engaged in making money and other statements that malign them. I hope that, esteemed sheikh, your would clarify this important issue for the people, to protect them from the deceptions of the ones who don't have insight into matters.*

Answer: There is no doubt that the attention given to recording beneficial statements, and sermons, and beneficial speeches. All of this benefits the Muslim nation, and the one who has done so for the benefit of the Ummah then he is thanked. And he should hold to patience and hope for Allaah's reward for those efforts. Even if evil is said about him then he is following the example of Allaah's messengers, may Allaah's praise and salutations be upon them, as well as those excellent predecessors who come before him. So there is no harm in selling audio cassettes of these types of speech, at a affordable price which will not cause difficulty for the people. He can use this money to assist him in his work while benefiting the people by spreading knowledge, and making beneficial material widely available. I advise you to acquire good tapes, and I recommend that the people purchase and benefit from them, if they are beneficial and upright tapes. Yet not every audio cassette is beneficial and upright, and not every speaker is one who truly produces beneficial speech which is actually worthy of recording. Therefore it is obligatory upon the student of knowledge to select audio cassettes which originate from the people of knowledge well known for realizing knowledge, and then benefit from them. He should also play them for his family, his brothers, and friends. And to stay away from those recordings that which will not benefit him or which may harm him.

(71) THE EMINENT GUIDING SCHOLAR MUQBIL IBN HAADEE AL-WAADI'EE, MAY ALLAAH HAVE MERCY UPON HIM, FROM 'EXCELLENT RESPONSES TO QUESTIONS FROM THOSE PRESENT AND THOSE ABSENT': PAGE 139)

*Question: Lastly, what is your advice to us as to how to seek knowledge? Also which books and tapes are needed by the beginning student of knowledge?*

Answer: That which I advise is that he correspond and communicate with the people of knowledge, and that if he has the ability to travel to them that he does so. By this it meant the likes of Sheikh al-Albaanee, Sheikh Ibn Baaz, Sheikh 'Abdul-Muhsin al-'Abaad, Sheikh Rabee'a Ibn Haadee, and Sheikh al-'Utheimeen. Again, if one is able to travel to them he should do so, and if not them he should keep in contact them by means of the telephone and sending of letters. And if there are any eminent scholars found in his own land then we advise him to gather around them. As well as to invite the people to gather around them, with the condition that they do not become a blind bigoted supporter nor someone of group partisanship and division. Certainly the bigoted supporter only calls to his affiliated group or his restricted path, and Allaah has said: ❨*Surely, the religion is for Allaah only*❩-(Surah Zumar: 3). So purity of intention for the religion and in calling to Allaah the Most High, the Most exalted is something required. Allaah says ❨*Let there arise out of you a group of people inviting to all that is good*❩-(Surah Aal-'Imraan:104), and ❨*This is my way; I invite unto Allaah with sure knowledge, I and whosoever follows me*❩-(Surah Yusuf:108), and ❨*Invite to the Way of your Lord with wisdom and fair preaching, and argue with them in a way that is better.*❩-(Surah an-Nahl:125). And here there is a matter that you must be forewarned against. This is that some of the people of group partisanship and division will probably swear to you that they are not a person upon partisanship and separation, but this is because they remain confused about this issue. But if they invite you to participate in elections. or you see them praising others who are known people of group partisanship, receiving, and meeting with them. Then know that he stands in a position of uncertainty and doubt, and it is proper that you be cautious in your dealings with him.

(72) The Eminent Guiding Scholar Saaleh Ibn Fauzaan, may Allaah preserve him, from 'A Selection of Islamic Rulings': vol. 1, page 292

*Question:  Many youth have abandoned reading the books of the first three generations of Muslims and thus correcting their beliefs by them. By this what is meant is such books 'as-Sunnah' of Ibn Abee 'Aasim, as well as other similar books which explain the methodology and position of the people of the Sunnah and the Jam'aah in relation to the Messenger's Sunnah and those who adhere to it, and in relation to the ways of innovation and their people. They have become occupied with reading works of those known as "thinkers" or "callers", those who have in their statements that which contradicts and opposes the contents of books of our Salaf.*

*What is your advice for these youth? Also, which are the books of the methodology of the first generations of Muslims which you advise them to read in order to correctly build their beliefs upon or correct their beliefs by?*

Answer:  This questions stems from the previous one, that being: When we have understood the necessity of giving  priority to having the basic correct belief and studying that as well as learning those matters which are obligatory upon every individual and similar matters then the question arises: What are the sources from which we take this correct belief? As well as who are the people from whom we learn this correct belief from?

The sources which we take the correct belief about the right of Allaah to be worshipped alone and the correct faith from are the Book of Allaah, the Sunnah of the Messenger of Allaah, along with the methodology of the predecessors of first three generations of Muslims. As the Qur'aan explains the correct belief definitively, and explains what differs with it, opposes it, or harms it, and it diagnoses every illness that affects or disrupts it. Likewise the Sunnah of the Messenger of Allaah, prayers and good mention be upon him, the history of his life and his call and the narrations narrated from his are a fundamental source; as is the way of the righteous predecessors, the Successors to the Companions of the Messenger of Allaah, and then those who followed and succeeded them from the chosen generations. These people devoted themselves to the explaining of the Qur'aan and the Messenger's Sunnah, as well as clarifying the correct beliefs within them and explaining and teaching them to the people. So after referring to the Book of Allaah and the Sunnah of the Messenger of Allaah, prayers and good mention be upon him, refer to the statements of the pious predecessors and these are recorded in the books explaining the Qur'aan and the books explaining the hadeeth narrations, as well as being recording in a specific form in the various books of correct belief.

As for whom to take these correct beliefs from, then they are the people who worship Allaah alone without any partners, and their scholars who teach this correct belief in a complete way, instructing the people regarding it . And all praise is due to Allaah they are many of them, especially in this land, the land which realized the worship of Allaah alone. As the scholars of this land specifically, and the upright scholars in general- give importance and priority to the correct belief regarding the worship of Allaah alone, to teaching it, spreading its understanding, clarifying it to the people, and calling them to it. So refer to the people who are upon the worship of Allaah alone without any partners, and their scholars, those whose beliefs are sound and clear. These are the ones from whom you should take the correct beliefs regarding Allaah's right to be worshipped alone without partners. As for the leaving study of correct beliefs to turn to various books of general culture and those of imported concepts and ideologies, then this does not benefit you at all. It is like the saying: "*They have a piece of tough sinewy camel meat found at the top of a mountain which was difficult and rugged to climb!*" These books do not remove or fight ignorance, nor do they benefit you in regard to knowledge.

However the one who strives to attain a good understanding of the areas of knowledge related to the way of worshiping Allaah alone without partners, and the areas of knowledge related to correct beliefs, and the branches of knowledge of the Sharee'ah in general, and who wants to understand them from the aspect of truly comprehending the blessing of Allaah, the most High and the Most Exalted upon him- then he is guided to the correct belief. And this is forbidden from those who busy themselves with idle speech of gossip. As various books and newspapers are full of statements which are fruitless and without benefit, the harm of them being greater that the good within them. Yet this is not an issue, when one only reads that which will benefit him. Therefore it is not permissible for the beginning student of knowledge specifically to occupy himself with such books. Because they will not enrich you, nor satisfy your needs, but simply take away your time, scatter your thoughts and squander your time.

Therefore it is obligatory upon an individual that he selects beneficial books, and useful books. Books which have been enriched from the Book of Allaah and the Sunnah of the Messenger of Allaah, praise and good mention be upon him, and have been explained by the predecessors from the first three generations. As knowledge is what Allaah said and what His Messenger, prayers and good mention be upon him, said. Ibn Qayyim, may Allaah have mercy upon him:

> *Knowledge is "Allaah said" and "His Messenger said",*
>
> *and "the Companion of the Messenger said",*
>
> *As they are the first to have been given understanding.*
>
> *As it is not knowledge that made you foolishly give precedence over*
>
> *the revealed texts to the opinion of so-and-so.*

(73) THE EMINENT GUIDING SCHOLAR MUHAMMAD IBN SAALEH AL-'UTHEIMEEN, MAY ALLAAH HAVE MERCY UPON HIM, FROM 'ISLAMIC RULINGS': VOL. 1, PAGE. 65, NO. 6511

*Question: What is your esteemed view of the one who avoids reading the books of the modern day callers, holding that to restrict themselves to the books of the first three generations is preferred, and so they take their methodology from such books? So is this perspective correct, or is combining the books of the first three generations, may Allaah have mercy upon them, along with the books of modern day callers and thinkers or writers?*

Answer:   I hold that one should take our call from the Book of Allaah and the Sunnah of the Messenger of Allaah, prayers and good mention be upon him, above any other source. And this is what is held by all of us without doubt. What is close to these two sources is that which comes from the rightly guided successors, and then from the Companions of the Prophet in general, and then the leading scholars from the first three generations. As for those matters spoken about by those from the latter times as well as our modern age, then they have taken up matters that have happened to them in their time and which they are more acquainted with.

So if a person takes from their books what benefits him considering this aspect then he has obtained a good portion. And we know that those of the modern times have taken what they have obtained from those who came before them, and so we are taking from them what they have taken from those before them. However, there are new events which have occurred that they have a better perception of, and this information was not known by the leading scholars of the first generations.

Due to this I hold that an individual should combine between these two sources of good. We rely firstly upon the Book of Allaah and the Sunnah of the Messenger of Allaah, praise and good mention be upon him, then secondly from the statements of the righteous predecessors from the first three generations- meaning from the rightly guided Successors of the Messenger of Allaah and his Companions in general, as well as the leading scholars of the Muslims. Then utilizing what has been written by the authors in our modern times who have written about events that have occurred in their time that were not known by the leading scholars among the first generation.

(74) The Eminent Guiding Scholar Muhammad Ibn Saaleh al-'Utheimeen-, may Allaah have mercy upon him, from 'Book of Knowledge': page 132 )

*Question: Does an individual have an excuse for neglecting the seeking of knowledge because they are busy with educational studies which are not related to Sharee'ah knowledge, or due to having to work, or because of other reasons?*

Answer:    Seeking Sharee'ah knowledge is a collective obligation, if it is established by some individuals to a sufficient level then to the remaining people it is recommended act. It can also in some cases be obligatory on a specific person becoming a personal obligation upon him. Therefore what is required from a each individual, meaning as an personal obligation; is such as when a person wishes to undertake a specific act of worship for Allaah then it is obligatory on that person to understand how to properly carry out this act of worship. So upon this we say that if the matters that occupy him from seeking Sharee'ah knowledge are related to the needs of his family and other similar affairs, while preserving that which is fundamental from his obligatory matters of worship; then certainly this is excused and there is no criticism his limits and ability.

(75) The Eminent Guiding Scholar Muhammad Ibn Saaleh al-'Utheimeen-, may Allaah have mercy upon him, from 'Book of Knowledge': page 150

*Question: Is it permissible for someone to leave working in order to devote himself to seeking knowledge, thus becoming a burden upon his father and his brother?*

Answer:  There is no doubt that seeking knowledge is from the best of deeds. Rather it is jihad in the path of Allaah. Especially in this age in which innovations in the religion have begun to surface and spread in Muslim societies, tremendous ignorance has become apparent in many of those who aspire to give rulings with out sufficient knowledge, and controversies and disputes have broken out amongst many of the people. These three matters together make it mandatory upon the young to be diligent in seeking knowledge.

Firstly, the evils effects of innovations in the religion emerging and becoming apparent.

Secondly, people aspiring to give rulings in the religion without knowledge.

Thirdly, the spreading of disputes in matters which are clear to the people of knowledge however the common people enter into them and dispute regarding them without knowledge.

Due to these facts we are in tremendous need of the people of knowledge who have a comprehensive and firm grounding in knowledge, who possess true understanding of the religion of Allaah, and wisdom in guiding to Allaah. Also because many people have acquired the ability to examine individual issues, however they do not give priority examining that which rectifies the character and enables their correct cultivation upon guidance. So they give a ruling in this or that matter it ends up as a means for a tremendous evil the extent of which is only known by Allaah. The Companions of the Messenger of Allaah, may Allaah be pleased with them, at times adhered to matters which the source texts in general indicated should not have be adhered to for the purpose of cultivating and educating peoples character. 'Umar Ibn al-Khattab, may Allaah be pleased with him, compelled the people to take the performance of three divorce pronouncements in one sitting as an irrevocable divorce. Whereas the divorce pronouncement three times simultaneously during the lifetime of the Messenger of Allaah, upon him be Allaah's praise and salutations, and the period of Abu Bakrs leadership, as well as two years when 'Umar was the Khalifah - when done in a single sitting was forbidden. Because it when outside of the bounds of the limits set by Allaah, the Most High, the Most Exalted.

'Umar, may Allaah be pleased with him, said: "*The people began showing laxity and indulging in the matter of three pronouncements which previously they had shown restraint.*" (narrated by meaning from Saheeh Muslim: 1472) As such if we are strict with them, so also was he strict with them. He made the pronouncement of three divorces in one sitting as a matter which was to be considered as three separate divorces, not a single divorce as it was considered in the past during the time of the Prophet, prayers and good mention be upon him, and the time of Abu Bakr, and the first two years of 'Umar's own period of leadership, may Allaah be pleased with them. He compelled the people to consider it as three separate divorces and therefore it was treated like a final irrevocable divorce. While if a man attempted to return to his wife after this type of pronouncement of divorce, during the time of the two previous leaders as well as in the first two years of his time as the Khaleefah- it was considered correct or a valid return or reconciliation. However he saw that the general societal good required the compelling of the people to consider the pronouncement of the three times simultaneously as an act which made returning to ones wife permanently prohibited.

Likewise in regard to the punishment for the drinking of intoxicants during the time of the Prophet, upon him be Allaah's praise and salutations, they would bring a man who drank intoxicants and strike him with forty blows with a twisted long strip of a fabric like a lash, a palm branch, or shoe close to forty times, and in the period of Abu Bakr it was also forty strikes. In the first years of 'Umar's time it was also forty strikes, however when the drinking of intoxicants spread he gathered the Companions and consulted them regarding this. 'Abdul-Rahman Ibn Auf said: "*The punishment is now considered light, there so make it eighty strikes.*" (narrated by meaning in Saheeh Muslim: 1706) So 'Umar then made the punishment for the drinker of intoxicants eighty strikes. All this was towards the goal of rectifying the character. So it is necessary for the Muslim, the scholar, or the one who gives a ruling in such matters to observe the existing conditions of the people and what will best rectify them.

**(76) THE EMINENT GUIDING SCHOLAR MUQBIL IBN HAADEE AL-WAADI'EE, MAY ALLAAH HAVE MERCY UPON HIM, FROM 'BRIDLING THE RESISTANT ONE': PAGE 590**

*Question: Some people say to the students of knowledge, "You are idle without work." So what should our reply to this be?*

Answer: The refutation against them is that the idler is the one who does not seek closeness to Allaah, the Most High, the Most Exalted through working and efforts. As for the student of knowledge, then he- all praise is due to Allaah, is one who is engaged in serving the religion of Islaam. And the Lord of Glory says in His noble book: ❖*Of every troop of them, a party only should go forth, that they who are left behind may get instructions in religion, and that they may warn their people when they return to them, so that they may beware of evil.*❖-(Surah Tawbah:122) The Prophet, Allaah's praise and salutations be upon him and his family, said as is found in the two Saheeh hadeeth collections from the hadeeth Mu'aweeyah, may Allaah be pleased with he: *{Whoever Allaah intends good for He grants him understanding in the religion}* [63]. And he said is is reported in Saheeh Muslim from the hadeeth of 'Umar, may Allaah be pleased with him: *{Allaah raised one people by this Book and lowers other people by it.}* [64].

The seeking of knowledge is considered from the best means of coming closer to Allaah, and the Muslims have a tremendous need for scholars, and this is an evident reality today, as well as for tomorrow and after tomorrow. Therefore, know that the students of knowledge are not from those who are squandering away their lives. The one who squanders his life is the regular drinker of alcohol, or the one who is occupied with movies and entertainment shows, or the one whose focus is watching or playing football or soccer, or the one always hanging around in the streets, and the one who is dedicated to musical and idle pleasures. But as for the student of knowledge he perseveres night and day, as truly seeking knowledge is a tremendous hardship. The student of knowledge is incredibly fatigued from being busy all day long hurriedly going back and forth in this effort. Thus this demands patience as was stated by 'Abdullah Ibn 'Umar when he said to a student of knowledge: "*You should obtain two shoes made of iron.*" Additionally, it was mentioned by Yahya Ibn Abee Kather, may Allaah The Most High have mercy upon him: "*Knowledge cannot be achieved through ease and comfort of one's body*"

Therefore it is not proper that you listen and comply with those of your fathers who scheme regarding you or others who devise similar plans. As Allaah the Most high and Most Exalted, says in His Noble Book: ❖*Obey not him whose heart We have made heedless of Our remembrance, one who follows his own lusts and whose affair*

[63] Narrated in Saheeh al-Bukhaaree: 71, 3116, 7312/ Saheeh Muslim: 1037/ Sunan Ibn Maajah: 221/ al-Muwatta Maalik: 1300, 1667/ Musnad Imaam Ahmad: 16395: 16404, and other narrations/ Musannaf Ibn Abee Shaybah: 31792/ & Sunan ad-Daaramee: 224, 226/- on the authority of Mu'aweeyah. And it is found in Jaame'a al-Tirmidhee 2645/ & Musnad Imaam Ahmad: 2786/ & Sunan ad-Daaramee: 270, 2706/- on the authority of Ibn "Abbaas. And it is found in Sunan Ibn Maajah: 220/ Musannaf 'Abdul-Razzaaq: 30851/- on the authority of Abu Hurairah. It was declared authentic by Sheikh al-Albaanee in Saheeh al-Aadab al-Mufrad: 517, Silsilat al-Hadeeth as-Saheehah: 1194, 1195, 1196, Saheeh at-Targheeb at-Tarheeb: 67, as well as in other of his books. Sheikh Muqbil declared it authentic in al-Jaame'a al-Saheeh: 9, 3123, 4650.

[64] Narrated in Saheeh Muslim: 817/ Sunan Ibn Maajah: 218/ & Musnad Imaam Ahmad: 233/ Sunan ad-Daaramee: 3360/-on the authority of 'Umar Ibn al-Khattab. It was declared authentic by Sheikh al-Albaanee in Silsilat al-Hadeeth as-Saheehah: 2239, Mishkaat al-Masaabeeh: 2115, & Saheeh al-Jaame'a as-Sagheer: 1896.

-*deeds has been lost.*-(Surah Kahf:28) And Allaah the Most High, the Most Exalted says in His Noble Book: *Therefore withdraw from him who turns away from Our Reminder and desires nothing but the life of this world. That is what they could reach of knowledge.*-(Surah an-Najm:29-30) *They know only the outside appearance of the life of the world, and they are heedless of the Hereafter*-(Surah ar-Rum: 7) So you deficient one, oh deficient one! Do you not know that the Prophet, prayers and good mention be upon him and his family, said: *{When a son of Aadam dies his deeds end except for three matters: a continuing charity, or a righteous child who supplicates for them, or knowledge by which others are benefited.}* [65]. Do you want to facilitate your son becoming a drinker of alcohol, or a homosexual, or a communist, or a Ba'athee socialist, or a Christian?!? *Verily, it is not the eyes that grow blind, but it is the hearts which are in the breasts that grow blind.*-(Surah al-Hajj:46) As your son if you do not ensure that he receives an Islamic education, then you can be viewing him as someone who is simple minded. And so due to this lack of education maybe he will eventually come to strike you upon your face, as well as strike your back. Yet if you had educated him with a proper Islamic education, then he would fear Allaah, the One free of all faults and Most Exalted. And he would know that Allaah, glorified and exalted said: *And your Lord has decreed that you worship none but Him. And that you be dutiful to your parents.*-(Surah al-Isra: 23)

And he would know that the pleasure of his Lord is to be found in pleasing his parents, the anger of his Lord is gained through angering his parents and that disobedience to ones parents is from the most serious of major sins. However, if you wipe out his perception and comprehension of such matters, and maybe he may become an alcoholic, or become a military general obsessed by acquiring more stars of higher rank. But if you have twenty stars to show your high rank and you have not established that which Allaah has made obligatory upon you then you are foolish. Allaah, the Most Perfect, the Most High says: *Let not the free disposal and affluence of the disbelievers throughout the land deceive you. A brief enjoyment; then, their ultimate abode is Hell; and worst indeed is that place for rest.*-(Surah Aal-'Imraan:196,197). It is upon you to fear Allaah, and to be diligent in guiding your sons towards seeking knowledge and to spend your wealth on your sons for this purpose. As assuredly if your son said to you: "*I will go to America to complete my education*", then some of the people would probably assist their sons by giving them 100 thousand riyals or an even greater amount! While saying: "*Go my son and complete your education so that you may return*". However after this "education" their thinking and beliefs will be corrupted and become that of a secularist, or Ba'athist socialist, or a communist, or some other brand of the various ideologies. And we have a cassette regarding this subject by the name: "*My Advice to Fathers & Mothers*"

---

[65]  Narrated in Saheeh Muslim: 1631/ Sunan Abu Dawud: 2880/ Jaame'a at-Tirmidhee: 1376/ Sunan an-Nasaa'ee: 3681/ Musnad Imaam Ahmad: 8627/ & Sunan ad-Daaramee: 559/-on the authority of Abu Hurairah. It was declared authentic by Sheikh al-Albaanee in Saheeh at-Targheeb at-Tarheeb: 78, 93, Mishkaat al-Masaabeh: 127, 203, & Saheeh al-Jaame'a as-Sagheer: 793, and the three 'Sunan' collections

**(77) THE EMINENT GUIDING SCHOLAR MUHAMMAD AL-'AMEEN ASH-SHANQEETEE, MAY ALLAAH HAVE MERCY UPON HIM, FROM 'VARIOUS QUESTIONS': ISLAMIC RULING NO. 9581**

*Question: If a student of knowledge receives discouragement regarding his efforts from his family, his wife, and some of his close relatives, what will assist him in shielding himself from this?*

Answer: In the name of Allaah, all praise is due to Allaah, prayers and good mention be upon the best of creation, and upon his family, Companions. and those who show allegiance to him. To proceed:

There is no true supporter except Allaah, the Most High and Exalted, and if Allaah grants success to His servant, leads him to that which is true, inspires him, guides him, and He blesses him to have the seeking the Hereafter his greatest priority, and endows him with knowledge, and blesses his desire and aspirations with the correct perspective and aims, and blesses him with insight by which he distinguishes truth from falsehood, and guidance from misguidance, and goodness from evil. Then if Allaah the Exalted confers these blessings upon His worshiper, how quickly they lead him towards the soundness and rectification of his religion, his worldly affairs, and his Hereafter. Know, may Allaah have mercy upon you, that there is not anything more treasured nor more noble than Allaah's revelation. This light which Allaah revealed to His Prophet, may Allaah's praise and salutations be upon him, and bestowed upon the people of knowledge of the laws of Islaam of previous nations, and made His Book dominant over all of the previously revealed laws.

The message of Islaam is the final of all the messages, this faith is the completion of the faiths, and there is not anything more noble in the sight of Allaah than knowledge. Due to the nobility of this knowledge Allaah has joined it with those matters which are beloved to Him, as He glorified and exalted said: ❲*Allaah will exalt in degree those of you who believe, and those who have been granted knowledge.*❳- (Surah al-Mujaadilah:11). There is no third matter that is joined with these two in status and value, never! There is faith in Allaah and then knowledge, there is nothing of higher in value to Allaah after faith than knowledge! So when an individual recognizes that his happiness, his rank, his nobility, and his honor are all due to his knowledge, then he will turn to gaining it with true devotion and he will love it with a true love. And he will then devote himself to that he loves and desires. When this occurs then Allaah will add to his knowledge even more. Because of this, it is said in the well known statement of wisdom: "*The one whose beginning is already strong- his outcome is a radiant one.*". The beginning which is strong is a beginning that starts with the individual, then proceeds to his wife and his children, and then his brothers and sisters, then his neighborhood, his extended family, and his community, then to the common people in general. Its conclusion only reaching a level that Allaah Gloried and Exalted has decreed it stops at. And certainly the people vary in regard to this.

Allaah has given you control over your every moment and instant, and your knowledge is a trial that you constantly tested by. This trial is one which when it reaches you and you truly trust in Allaah after having acquired knowledge, then you are raised in degree and increased in closeness to Allaah. As he has already paid its price, and he truthfully loves the signs of Allaah the Exalted in His Book, and the hadeeth narrations of the messenger of Allaah, may Allaah's praise and salutations be upon him,. The pious predecessors left their residences and were separated from their original lands, their beloved ones, their brothers, from the homes that they built and in which they lived, and from their beloved neighbors. If the wealth of the world was presented to them they would not choose it in exchange or as a substitute, nor in their path accept any change in course, as there is not anything from their people, or their companions, or their close relatives, or parents, or the people all together which is as vital as knowledge!! They carried the trust of their knowledge, and they left their own lands, and travelled, and encountered difficulties, hardships, and problems. They saw death in front of their very eyes, and were travelers far outside their own lands. They encountered difficulties, hardships, and poverty, such that some of the people of hadeeth would faint due to the extreme hunger they encountered while they were carrying this essential matter for the Muslim nation- the preservation of the narrations of the Messenger of Allaah, prayers and good mention be upon him. Such that they forfeited their food and drink. So we ask Allaah the Great, Lord of the Mighty throne that He bestows showers of His mercy upon those pure hearts which carried for this Muslim nation the most bountiful, noble, and complete matter which can be conveyed- knowledge.

If you desire to travel upon their way, and to follow their path, and to truly have a complete reliance that Allaah The Most High and the Most Exalted will recompense you with that which is better. As the one who leaves a thing for Allaah's sake, Allaah will present him with something better than it. So my brother in Islaam, I am not calling you to leave your family, nor to have hostility towards those in our community or your wife, no. But instead to give to everyone that has a right upon you -their right, thus placing matters in their proper place. The successful student of knowledge begins with the first priority - his individual needs. He give his body its right in regard to rest and relaxation, and what Allaah has obligated upon him before even that. Then he proceeds to those who rely upon him, by spending time with his family for rest and companionship.

On one side he makes a designated time for his wife and children, and on the other side he has a specific time for his effort to study. As the knowledge that he gains during this specific time is an indispensable fortress from the fortifications of the Islam and the Muslims. Especially in this age is which there is a scarcity of those who carry for this Muslim Ummah the proper Sharee'ah rulings, or those who bring to it the understanding of the religion of its Lord, those who cultivate it upon the truth, enlightening and guiding the Ummah to that which will rectify its religious affairs and its Hereafter. Therefore, when these specific hours arrive, and these designated times approach, then that time is not for your sons, daughters, brothers, sisters, your family members or your wives. Rather, turn to the study of knowledge wholeheartedly, and commit yourself to acquiring knowledge, give it your complete focus, until Allaah grants you success in that, as He is the best of those who grant success. This is the foundation of an individual's organizing his conditions and circumstances to the best of his ability- in order to realize the acquiring of knowledge as well as fulfill his obligatory duties and responsibilities.

Clearly his wife and family have a specific right, and the mistake which harms the student of knowledge is when his family and children overstep these guidelines regarding the times which are designed and sufficient for them. So if they go beyond the established guidelines of your time, stop them and say to them: *"You have such and such time."* This should be clearly established, except in particular circumstances and specific conditions, giving them this to the limit of your ability in order to bring them happiness. As being kind or lenient in some matters you control is a type of kindness from you. This is a matter that no one else can devise a plan that is suitable for you and your needs. But, be completely committed and firm regarding correcting and rectifying that which is between you and between Allaah, then Allaah will rectify that which is between you and between the people.

It often occurs with many a student of knowledge, that sometimes he is approached by worries, distress, and troubles in regard to his wife and children, and these troubles weigh upon him like a mountain, the extent of which is only truly known to Allaah. And by Allaah, they are dispersed or dissolved, just a smell or odor disperses, because Allaah specifically takes care of this. If the student frequently recites the Qur'aan, often remembers Allaah, holds close to Allaah with strong certainty in Him, nothing will descend or afflict him, except that it comes to be the concern of Allaah, and so Allaah will suffice him. And the student of knowledge may be lacking in the remembrance of Allaah, or deficient in his obedience of Allaah being overly occupied with knowledge, will distract him from nourishing his soul and perfecting his heart. So there will be worries that occur that are hard upon him, as these difficulties are of different levels upon the student of knowledge, and from them is that which is at the level of bringing him rectification and goodness. Whenever you learn the Sunnah, practice it, hold fast to it, act according to it, it will have an effect upon your behavior and your actions and upon your family. Because Allaah the Most High the Most exalted, will make for the believing righteous truly fearing worshiper love of him in the hearts of others; as the exalted said: *❧ Verily, those who believe and work deeds of righteousness, the Most Beneficent will bestow love for them in the hearts of the believers. ❧* -(Surah Maryam: 96) This love is that which will be the key to many forms of good for the worshiper in regard to his wife and children, as well as his relations among the people.

What is intended is that which is necessary for the student of knowledge is that he not put his family in position of a barrier between him and Allaah. Be from those who utilize their wealth for and keep their families engaged in the obedience of Allaah. And certainly Allaah blamed those people who opposed the Prophet, may Allaah's praise and salutations be upon him, when they staed behind the prophet, may Allaah's praise and salutations be upon him, in a time of goodness and righteousness while the believers were fighting for the cause of Allaah. They said: ❨*... Our possessions and our families occupied us.* ❩-(Surah al-Fath:11), rather they were preoccupied from a tremendous good and noble reward. So it is not proper for the Muslim to places his family in a position that they stand between him and Allaah, rather is upon him to place them behind his back. And to make the next life as the goal in front of his eyes, and to support Allaah, the One free from all faults. As the one who supports Allaah, and is satisfied with Allaah the Most High, and what is considers important, and what displeases him. Allaah suffices him and the most important matter to him. We ask Allaah, The Exalted, Lord of the Noble throne, by his beautiful names and lofty attributes to make us of those who support and have allegiance to Him, and those who love Him with a true love, as that permits his love and what he is pleases with.

(78) THE EMINENT GUIDING SCHOLAR MUQBIL IBN HAADEE AL-WAADI'EE, MAY ALLAAH HAVE MERCY UPON HIM, FROM 'A DEFENDING MISSION FROM AUDIO LECTURES UPON THE PEOPLE OF IGNORANCE & SOPHISTRY': VOL. I, PAGE 437

*Question: What is the ruling regarding the one who does not obey his mother in the issue of seeking knowledge if she will not give him permission to go to another land to seek knowledge? Is he considered from those who have fallen into a major sin as someone who behaved badly toward his parents? Or is he from those who are rewarded for his seeking knowledge even thought he disobeyed his mother in conformance with the statement of the Messenger (upon him be good mention and peace), "There is no obedience to the creation in disobedience to the creator."?*

Answer:   He should obey his mother if she had a need for him to financially support for or as a need for him to serve her and she does not have anyone else to do so. But if she does not require either one of these, and he does not fear for her that she would  grieve and cry to a degree that it would harm her eyesight or cry and grieve so much that her mind would be harmed, that it is not required to obey her. Because seeking knowledge is an obligation and the Messenger, may Allaah's praise and salutations be upon him and his family, said: *{ Obedience is in that which is permissible and good.}* [66]. Imaam Ahmad mention this as was transmitted from him by Ibn Haanee and which we've also transmitted from him in the book *((Makhraj min al-Fitnah)11-21)*.

---

[66]  Narrated in Saheeh al-Bukhaaree: 7145, 7257/ Saheeh Muslim: 1840/ Sunan Abu Dawud: 2625/  Sunan an-Nasaa'ee: 4210/ Musnad Imaam Ahmad: 623,726, 1021/ -on the authority of 'Alee Ibn Abee Taalib. It was declared authentic by Sheikh al-Albaanee in Silsilat al-Hadeeth as-Saheehah: 181, Mishkaat al-Masaabeh: 3665, & Saheeh al-Jaame'a as-Sagheer: 7319, 7519, and in his verification of al-'Emaan by Ibn Taymeeyah.

**(79) THE EMINENT GUIDING SCHOLAR MUQBIL IBN HAADEE AL-WAADI'EE, MAY ALLAAH HAVE MERCY UPON HIM, FROM 'BRIDLING THE RESISTANT ONE': PAGE 419**

*Question: Which of them has precedence: going forth in seeking knowledge or going forth for jihaad? Additionally, is it required to get permission from your parents in both situations?*

Answer:  As for asked related to jihaad then it is a requirement, as is found narration of 'Abdullah Ibn 'Amr, may Allaah be pleased with them both, that *{the Prophet saw a man who intended to go forth in jihaad so he said to him: "Are your parents were alive?" He responded: "Yes." The Prophet then said: "Then strive through serving them."}* [67]. This narration is found in the 'Saheeh' collections of Imaams al-Bukhaaree and Muslim. As for seeking knowledge that if they both have a need for you to support them or to serve them or both of them are advancing age and they do not have anyone else who would serve them, then is upon you to give precedence to them. And Allaah will make for you a means of escape or a way out from that situation. As perhaps Allaah will facilitate for you one who would teach you in your home or in your land. However if your parents do not have a need for you to support them, being self-sufficient financially. And I do not intend by "self-sufficient financially" this is what is commonly known as being rich, but that they possess what is sufficient for them from sufficient food and drink. Then it is not required to seek their permission.

Also, perhaps your father may be a communist or someone who's deficient in his religion. So if you said to him: "*I'm going to work in Saudi Arabia.*" He would say: "*This is good my son.*" But if you were to say to him: "*I am going forth to seek knowledge.*" He would say: "*No!*" raise his voice and your mother might do likewise. Therefore there is no obedience to them in this case, as the Prophet, upon him and his family be Allaah's praises and the best of salutations, said:*{ Obedience is in that which is permissible and good.}* [68]. And this is what was mentioned by Imaam Ahmad as is found in the book *((al-Masa'il)07-28)* transmitted by Ibn Haanee, as Imaam Ahmad was asked about this issue in regard to seeking knowledge.

---

[67]  Narrated in Saheeh al-Bukhaaree: 3004/ Saheeh Muslim: 2539/ Sunan an-Nasaa'ee: 3105/ Musnad Imaam Ahmad: 6508, 6726/ -on the authority of 'Abdullah Ibn 'Amr. It was declared authentic by Sheikh al-Albaanee in Irwa' al-Ghaleel: 1199, Ghaayat al-Maraam 281, & Saheeh at-Targheeb at-Tarheeb: 2480, 2483.

[68]  Narrated in Saheeh al-Bukhaaree: 7145, 7257/ Saheeh Muslim: 1840/ Sunan Abu Dawud: 2625/  Sunan an-Nasaa'ee: 4210/ Musnad Imaam Ahmad: 623,726, 1021/ -on the authority of 'Alee Ibn Abee Taalib. It was declared authentic by Sheikh al-Albaanee in Silsilat al-Hadeeth as-Saheehah: 181, Mishkaat al-Masaabeh: 3665, & Saheeh al-Jaame'a as-Sagheer: 7319, 7519, and in his verification of al-'Emaan by Ibn Taymeeyah.

(80) The Eminent Guiding Scholar Muqbil Ibn Haadee al-Waadi'ee, may Allaah have mercy upon him, from 'A Defending Mission from Audio Lectures Upon the People of Ignorance & Sophistry': Vol. 2, Page 378

*Question: How should the student of knowledge behave towards his parent who attempts to prevent him from seeking knowledge?*

Answer: He should deal with them gently and with mildness and say to them: The Prophet, upon him and his family be Allaah's praises and the best of salutations, said: *{When a son of Aadam dies his deeds end except for three matters:..}* and from them is *{...a righteous child who supplicates for him}* [69]. And the Lord of Might has said in His Book: ❖*And those who believe and whose offspring follow them in Faith, to them shall We join their offspring, and We shall not decrease the reward of their deeds in anything. Every person is a pledge for that which he has earned.*❖-(Surah at-Tur: 21) and he said: ❖*And those who say: "Our Lord! Bestow on us from our wives and our offspring who will be the comfort of our eyes, and make us leaders for the pious*❖-(Surah al-Furqan:74).

So it is required for them to praise Allaah the Exalted that their child is not an alcoholic, or a homosexual, or a fornicator, or one who behaves badly towards them. Exhort and remind your parents of these things so that they will agree. But if they still refuse then go forth to study and afterwards write and speak with them and treat them well as much as you can. And if Allaah wishes then He will guide them through the child, as how many fathers forbad their sons initially, and then after some days perhaps the father himself comes himself to study with us, when he saw the behavior of his son and his good treatment towards him.

(81) The Eminent Guiding Scholar Muqbil Ibn Haadee al-Waadi'ee, may Allaah have mercy upon him, from 'Bridling the Resistant One': page 219

*Question: Why is it not a condition to get permission from your parents when going to seek knowledge, but required when going for jihaad? Isn't there a distinction in this, that if they have a need for you that you do not go for knowledge, and if they do not have a need for you then you may go seek knowledge?*

Answer: Certainly, is has a necessary distinction and that distinction has been explained. As for jihaad in the path of Allaah it is a collective general obligation, whereas seeking knowledge is an individual obligation, seeking knowledge is an obligation upon every Muslim. And we specify that knowledge which is an individual obligation as that matters which you as an individual utilize in your worship and that which it is necessary for you to understand, such as the correct fundamental beliefs, how to pray the obligatory prayers, what obligatory charity you must give if you possess the required amount of wealth, and the obligatory pilgrimage once you have decided to make that pilgrimage, the regulations of buying and selling if this is your

---

[69]  Narrated in Saheeh Muslim: 1631/ Sunan Abu Daawud: 2880/ Jaame'a at-Tirmidhee: 1376/ Sunan an-Nasaa'ee: 3681/ Musnad Imaam Ahmad: 8627/ & Sunan ad-Daaramee: 559/ -on the authority of  Abu Hurairah. It was declared authentic by Sheikh al-Albaanee in Saheeh at-Targheeb at-Tarheeb: 78, 93, Mishkaat al-Masaabeeh: 127,203, & Saheeh al-Jaame'a as-Sagheer: 793 as well as in his verification of the three 'Sunan'.

profession, and the regulations of jihaad in the path of Allaah if you have decided to undertake it. Therefore seeking knowledge is an obligation upon every Muslim.

**(82) THE EMINENT GUIDING SCHOLAR MUHAMMAD IBN SAALEH AL-'UTHEIMEEN, MAY ALLAAH HAVE MERCY UPON HIM, FROM 'EXPLANATION OF RIYAADH AS-SAALIHEEN': VOL. 4- PAGE 3-4 )**

### Seeking Knowledge and Jihaad in Path of Allaah

There is no difference between the one who strives in the path of Allaah who prepares the arms of his archers bow, and between the student of knowledge who extracts knowledge based issues from the depths of books. All such are engaged in striving in Allaah's path and explaining the Allaah's Sharee'ah to worshipers of Allaah. For this reason the compiled follows the *'Chapter related to striving in the path of Allaah'* with the *'Chapter of Knowledge'*, to indicate that is is similar to what preceded it. Rather, some of the scholars give it preference over jihad in the path of Allaah, and what is correct is that in that there is a required distinction and explanation for this comparison.

From the people there are those for who physical striving in his case is preferred, and there are from the people those for whom seeking knowledge in their case is preferred for them. As if a man is someone of courage and strength, but in regard to knowledge he is not strong, As he has only a limited capability, possessing only a limited ability to memorize and very little comprehension, then it will be difficult for him to acquire significant knowledge. So in this case we say: Jihaad in his situation is preferable for him. However if the case is the opposite of this, where a man does not have a great deal of physical strength nor a courageous heart but he has good ability to memorize and understand and the capacity to strive in knowledge- then this is preferred for him. Moreover, if he has characteristics suitable for both of these endeavors, then some of the people of knowledge give the precedence to seeking knowledge as that is the foundation. Also because it benefits all of the people: those near to him as well as those who are distant, because it benefits those who are presently alive and those who will be born after them, and it benefits the one who possesses this knowledge when he himself is alive and after his death! As the Prophet, may Allaah's praise and good mention be upon him, said: *{When a person dies all of its deeds end except for three: a continuing charity, of knowledge by which people benefit, or the righteous child who supplicates for him.}* [70].

---

[70] Narrated in Saheeh Muslim: 1631/ Sunan Abu Daawud: 2880/ Jaame'a at-Tirmidhee: 1376/ Sunan an-Nasaa'ee: 3681/ Musnad Imaam Ahmad: 8627/ & Sunan ad-Daaramee: 559/ -on the authority of Abu Hurairah. It was declared authentic by Sheikh al-Albaanee in Saheeh at-Targheeb at-Tarheeb: 78, 93, Mishkaat al-Masaabeh: 127,203, & Saheeh al-Jaame'a as-Sagheer: 793 as well as in his verification of the three 'Sunan'.

(83) THE EMINENT GUIDING SCHOLAR 'ABDUL-'AZEEZ IBN 'ABDULLAH IBN BAAZ, MAY ALLAAH HAVE MERCY UPON HIM, 'COLLECTION OF RULINGS AND VARIOUS STATEMENTS': VOL. 7 PAGE 231

*Question: The statement has spread among the students of knowledge especially in the colleges and institutions of knowledge that: [Knowledge has left with the passing of the people of knowledge, and those who now study in the institutions of knowledge do so only for the purpose of obtaining degrees or the benefitting in this world]. So what is the response to them? Additionally, what is the ruling of combining the intention for a worldly benefit or receiving a diploma along with one's intention to seek knowledge to benefit oneself and one's society?*

Answer:   This speech is not correct, and it is not proper to make this statement or statements similar to it. The one who says [the people are destroyed], rather he he is the most ruined among them! However encouragement and motivation towards the seeking of knowledge is what is required, devotion to it, having patience and persevering upon it, having the good suspicion of the students of knowledge, except for the one you know who clearly differs from this. And when death came to Mua'dh Ibn Jabal it is said that he advised his students of knowledge around him saying: *"For the one who truly wants them, certainly knowledge and faith are here and available."* meaning:  Their location being the Book of Allaah the Mighty, and the Sunnah of His trustworthy Messenger, may Allaah's praise and salutations be upon him.

The scholar is taken with his knowledge and so knowledge is removed through the death of the scholars, however all praise is due to Allaah, there will never cease to be a group victories upon the truth. Due to this the Messenger, upon him be Allaah's praise and salutations, said:  *{Verily, Allaah does not take away knowledge by plucking it from the chests of the people but He takes away knowledge by the passing away of the scholars, so that when there is no scholar present, the people turn to the ignorant as their leaders; then they are asked to deliver religious verdicts and so they deliver them without knowledge, they go astray, and lead others astray.}* [71]. This is what one should be afraid of, being wrongly put forwards to give Islamic rulings and therefor teaching ignorance, such that you are from those who are astray and are sending other astray.

As for the statement which is made: [Knowledge has left. There is nothing left except for such and such] One should fear from making this statement due to possibly leading of some of the people towards being discouraged. But if one if steadfast and has insight one should not be discouraged from this statement. Rather, it should push you towards seeking knowledge, until that clear need of the Muslims is fulfilled. Additionally the sincere person of understanding, and the truthful person of insight are not disheartened by the likes of this statement. Rather, they step forward and take the initiative to strive hard, persevere, study, and move quickly due to the intense demand for knowledge, and to fulfill that need which is claimed by those who make this statement: [No one remains...] But what has actually occurred is that there is a clear deficiency of knowledge as well as the passing away of it people.

---

[71]   Narrated in Saheeh al-Bukhaaree: 100, 7307/ Saheeh Muslim: 4829 / Sunan at-Tirmidhee:  2576/ Sunan Ibn Maajah: 51/ Musnad Of Ahmad: 6222, 6498, 6602/ & Sunan ad-Daaramee: 239 from the hadeeth of 'Abdullah Ibn 'Umar Ibn al-'Aas.

However, all praise is due to Allaah, there has not ceased to be a group upon the victorious truth. Just as the Prophet, may Allaah's praise and salutations be upon him, said: *{There will not cease to be a group from my Ummah victorious upon the truth. They are not harmed by those who oppose them nor by those that leave them, until Allaah's command or judgment comes.}* [72]

It is upon us to strive in seeking knowledge, and to encourage others towards it, and be diligent regarding the significant need for it, and establishing its obligation in our land as well as others, acting upon the Sharee'ah evidences in this, desiring the benefiting and teaching of the Muslims. Also it is required that we should encourage others towards purity of intention and truthfulness in the seeking of knowledge. The one who desires a diploma, to strengthen his efforts to convey knowledge and call to goodness, then he does well in that. And the one who desires money in order to be strengthen by it - there is no harm if he studies, learns and obtains a diploma which will assist in the spreading knowledge, and by which the people will then accept from him this knowledge, and to take money that will assist him in that effort. As if it were it not for Allaah, glorified is He and then wealth, many people would not be able to call and invite and convey this call. So wealth helps the Muslim upon seeking knowledge, and upon fulfilling his needs, and conveying knowledge to the people.

As when Umar, may Allaah be pleased with him did some work for the Messenger of Allaah, may Allaah's praise and salutations be upon him, gave him some money. But 'Umar said *"Give it to someone poorer than me."* So the Prophet, may Allaah's praise and salutations be upon him, said: *{Take this wealth to increase what you have or give it in charity. That which comes to you from this wealth without your hoping for it nor without begging- take it, but in other circumstance's do not let yourself pursue or run after it.}* It is narrated by Imaam Muslim in his 'Saheeh' collection. The Prophet, may Allaah's praise and salutations be upon him, gave to some of them to unite their hearts, and encourage them such that they would enter into Allaah's religion in numbers. If it was prohibited he would not have given to them, and in reality he distributed wealth to them before and after the conquest of Mecca. And during the Day of Conquest of Mecca, he gave to some people one hundred camels, and he gave gifts to those whom he did not fear poverty for them, upon him be Allaah's praise and salutations, encouraging them towards Islaam and calling them towards it. Allaah, free from any imperfection has decreed that a portion from Zakaat be given for those who hearts would be be united through It. He decreed that from what was in the public treasury they had portion and others such as teachers and judges had a portion, as did other from among the Muslims. And Allaah is the Best Guardian and the source of success.

[72] Narrated in Saheeh al-Bukhaaree: 3641, 7460/ Saheeh Muslim: 1037/ & Musnad Imaam Ahmad: 16485/-on the authority of Mu'aweeyah. And it was narrated in Saheeh Muslim: 1920/ & Musnad Imaam Ahmad: 21897/-on the authority of Thawbaan Ibn Bujaddid. And it was narrated in Jaame'a at-Tirmidhee: 2192/ Sunan Ibn Maajah: 6/ & Musnad Imaam Ahmad: 19849/ --from the hadeeth of Qurrat Ibn Eyaas. It was declared authentic by Sheikh al-Albaanee in Silsilat al-Hadeeth as-Saheehah: 1957, and Sheikh Muqbil declared it authentic in al-Jaame'a al-Saheeh: 2384.

(84) The Eminent Guiding Scholar Saaleh Ibn Fauzaan, may Allaah preserve him, 'A Selection of Islamic Rulings': vol. 2, page 210)

*Question: We have noticed that in the present day the number of Sharee'ah universities, colleges, and institutes, and similar places of learning have spread. However along with this increase, we see that they are not able to produce scholars similar the those who came forth during the previous ages from the circles of learning in the masjids. This is in relation to their ability in regard to knowledge or in regard to their ability to discuss and debate matters. So what are the reasons for this?*

Answer:   There is no doubt that the general level of knowledge in the present age is less that found in previous ages. However we should not state absolutely that all of the people are at a weak level of knowledge. As all praise is due to Allaah, there are indeed present those people who are distinguished in both their knowledge and their practice.

As for the weakness of scholarship in the present age, then I believe that this doesn't reflect upon the method of study, as in most ways the present day method of study agrees with the past methods of study. The material for the curriculum of study is basically the same source material. However in my view the method of study is not the entire issue. As the method of study is only the initial key and the introduction to knowledge. And the scholars of previous ages -their lives, in their entirety were considered a period of learning and study. They did not restrict it to what they were able to obtain within the circles of knowledge. Rather, they continued and persisted in thier reading and studies.

In addition it is well known that one's knowledge increases through further investigation and study, and this is the opposite case of what commonly occurs in our presently time. As many students achieve a high level and excellent grades, but when they complete their studies- most of them end their relationship with works of knowledge and knowledge itself. This practice causes their understanding and knowledge to die and pass away. As knowledge is like a young planti if you cultivate it it thrives and bears fruit and if you neglect it then it withers away and dies. Additionally, in regard to the aspect of acting upon knowledge, then the scholars of the past where for the most part scholars committed to efforts which implemented their knowledge, striving solely for the sake of Allaah alone, fearing Him, the Most High and the Most Exalted. And so perhaps this characteristic has become something rare in our present age. As most students, and we do not have a poor opinion of everyone, do not act upon the knowledge they hold, and their knowledge does not develop into actual deeds. And Allaah the Most High say ❴*It is only those who have knowledge among His slaves that fear Allaah.*❵-(Surah Faatir:28) The scholars they are the ones who fear Allaah. It was said by some of those from the first generations: Knowledge is of two types, knowledge which is only upon the tongue, and it is a proof of Allaah against His worshippers. And that knowledge found reflected upon the heart, and this is true knowledge. Meaning that knowledge which cultivates and increases one in the fear of Allaah. This is what is derived from this verse- ❴*It is only those who have knowledge among His slaves that fear Allaah*❵-(Surah Faatir:28)

(85) The Eminent Guiding Scholar Ahmad Ibn Yahya An-Najmee-, may Allaah preserve him, from, 'Decisive Rulings on the Methodologies of Calling to Allaah': Vol. 2, pages 73 & 142)

*Question: Is it permissible for the proficient student of knowledge to declare someone a person of innovation or to declare that someone has abandoned Islam, or is this a matter exclusively for the scholars?*

Answer: It is not permissible for the beginning student of knowledge to make statements identifying someone as an innovator in the religion or a disbeliever except after becoming qualified and fit for this. He should refer the judgment in this specific case to the senior scholars. Because Allaah the exalted says: ❁*...if only they had referred it to the Messenger or to those charged with authority among them.*❁- (Surah an-Nisaa:83).

*Second question: Is it for the beginning student of knowledge to put forth criticism or praise regarding individuals, or to declare people to be innovators in the religion without relying upon evidence?*

Answer: It is not proper for the beginning student of knowledge to criticize or praise others, from his capacities as an individual. Rather he should take from the statements of the people of knowledge who views are considered reliable in these matters. Consequently it is acceptable to relate or narrate a criticism, if you are certain that it originates from one of the scholars. And the success is from Allaah.

(86) The Eminent Guiding Scholar Ahmad Ibn Yahya An-Najmee-, may Allaah preserve him, from 'Decisive rulings on the methodologies of calling to Allaah': vol. 1, page 27

*Question: Some of the minor students of knowledge have busied themselves with speech regarding the people of division and group partisanship towards their group, and have made that the focus of the majority of their time, thus neglecting knowledge- the opportunity to seek knowledge which will benefit them with their Lord and to seek knowledge which would explain and distinguish for them those matters which are hated and despised from those matters that are desired and good. They say that this is so that they understand the errors of the people of these groups of partisanship. However, it has come about that nothing has the level of importance to them as the asking: "What is your opinion of so-and-so, and what is your position regarding so-and-so?" Likewise, it has reached the point where the majority of their sittings are regarding these matters, and they have begun to accuse the people haphazardly. What is your advice to these youth, and your encouragement to them to give concern to that Sharee'ah knowledge which will protect them from innovation in the religion?*

Answer: The reality is exaggeration in these matters takes a student of knowledge from the bounds of truth into disputes and the wasting of their time with speech which will not result in benefit for them. Rather it causes a person to spend his time in gatherings which are absent of true benefit. So this is not proper, rather it is obligatory upon the student of knowledge that he occupy his time in the obedience of Allaah, the One free from imperfections and  the Most High and in study of knowledge and research and the attending of sittings of knowledge.

It is acceptable to listen to warnings regarding them and the clarification of their blameworthy characteristics until you are informed and thus safeguarded from them. However, if we use all of our time for speech regarding them and do not occupy ourselves with the acquiring of knowledge which benefits us- then no doubt this is a serious error and a significant mistake.

(87) THE EMINENT GUIDING SCHOLAR MUQBIL IBN HAADEE AL-WAADI'EE, MAY ALLAAH HAVE MERCY UPON HIM, FROM 'A DEFENDING MISSION FROM AUDIO LECTURES UPON THE PEOPLE OF IGNORANCE & SOPHISTRY': VOL. 2-PAGE 103

*Question: Esteemed sheikh, may Allaah preserve you, we hope that you would give advice to your sons from among the students of knowledge who live in Abu Dhabee and the United Arab Emirates as a whole.*

Answer:   That which I advise our brothers with a seriousness and diligence in acquiring beneficial knowledge, and that they do not busy themselves with that which does not truly help them. As differing and the separation arises from the lack of activity. It is said: so-and-so scholar is correct, and so-and-so scholar is wrong, and that so-and-so scholar you should not take knowledge from him, and for so-and-so scholar is such and such. So I say: it is obligatory that you say to yourself that you will be like the example of  so-and-so scholar or even better than him otherwise the only thing you will end up with is occupying yourself with is the going from this masjid to that masjid, and from this sitting to this other sitting with *"So-and-so scholar is correct and this other one is mistaken."*. Rather I advise you to be serious and diligent and likewise if it is easy upon you to travel; then if you are informed that in such and such place some of the brothers are benefiting, then it is fitting that you travel to them and benefit from them.

We also advise them towards to spread the Book of Allaah and the Sunnah of Messenger of Allaah, upon him and his family be Allaah's praises and the best of salutations, upon the understanding of the first generations, and to visit their brothers from the people of knowledge. And we advise them to seek out scholars from the scholars of the land of the two Holy sanctuaries and Najd as well those from any other lands. Additionally, to be with the general people who are 'Sunni' in order that they may explain to them the methodology of the people of the Sunnah. Also having lectures has benefit and an effect upon the people, all praise is due to Allaah the mighty. However the effect of individual lectures, it is not of the same degree of benefit as regularly held lessons. And all praise is due to Allaah Lord of all the worlds.

(88) The Eminent Guiding Scholar Muhammad Naasiruddeen al-Albaanee, may Allaah have mercy upon him From audio lecture no.288 of the 'Guidance and Light' Audio Tape Series

*Question: What do you say regarding the student of knowledge authoring works early on in his studies? Is it true that this sharpens the intellect of the student of knowledge?*

Answer: This is not correct. And by authoring works- I understand from your question is that the authoring that you are inquiring about means producing works which are to be printed and distributed. However, I say: Author it just for yourself, and compile it for it to remain in your library only with you. This until such a time that you perceive that you have achieved a maturity in knowledge; then at that time you can bring forth what your authored to the people. As without doubt, you will not be able to release the first or second or third of your initial works or writing until you have reexamined and revised them. For you will have matured along with the passing of time, and you will have differed with many of the matters that you previously thought and viewed as correct.

A perfect example of this is sitting in front of you. I have a book which was the first fruits of my efforts, and which I refer to in many of my other books. It is well know by the title "Rawdha an-Nadher fee Tarteeb wa Tarkheej Mu'ajam at-Tabaraanee as-Sagheer". I have it compiled into two large volumes, however I will not consent to be being printed. As when it occurs to me that doing so is something suitable, I return to it but in reviewing it say: *"How could I have stated that? What a strange statement!"* As knowledge does not progress except stage by stage, or stage after stage. I will present to you an example of the blessing of Allaah upon me, as an admonition to the Islamic world today, as I have experienced through a period that which contrasted with it.

As all of you, like most students of knowledge today, are aware that Ibn Hibbaan is an Imaam from the leading scholars of hadeeth, he is considered from those who are make judgments of praise or criticism of hadeeth narrators. And it has been stated that in this matter he is somewhat lax in the area of his statements of various narrators trustworthiness. But myself when I authored this work, I often relied primarily upon the ruling of trustworthiness of Ibn Hibbaan. The issue as it stood with me and others from the students of hadeeth in this age, and from those just before it- was that if Ibn Hibbaan declared a narrator trustworthy -then that was sufficient. However as time passed, its became clear to me that the declaration of trustworthiness of Ibn Hibbaan could not be absolutely or unrestrictedly relied upon. When this became clear to me I began to draw people's attention to this in all of my books. So now it is the general state today that the majority of my students specifically- those from the Islamic University of Medinah as well as those outside of it- have the understanding of this issue which I did not have. Knowledge that I was ignorant of, but which later became apparent to me. So I began to warn the people with knowledge that the declarations of trustworthiness of Ibn Hibbaan must be taken with caution; as he sometimes declares fully unknown narrators to be trustworthy. Then after some time passed I discovered that in specific situations, even when Ibn Hibbaan is the only hadeeth scholar declaring a narrator to be reliable, that such a narrator can indeed, under those conditions, to be considered trustworthy. So I wrote this is some of my final books.

How is that? If Ibn Hibbaan declares a narrator trustworthy while that narrator is found to have many narrations attributed to him; then by merit of those many narrators who transmitted from that specific narrator- who is in general considered unknown by other scholars- he is removed from the state of being absolutely "unknown" to being a narrator of a level or description of being "unknown" which is limited and restricted in its scope. Consequently, that narrator who is now at a level of being in restricted state of being "unknown" is viable for consideration and use in specific circumstances as acceptable. Because it is suitable for possibly being declared trustworthy as a narrator, if in addition to these many narrations he is also declared trustworthy by Ibn Hibbaan. So in this way it became clear to me. And the credit for that goes to someone other than myself, from the people of note. He was the Sheikh 'Abdur-Rahman al-Mu'alamee- may Allaah have mercy upon him, as found in his statement: "*The one stated as trustworthy by Ibn Hibbaan- if he is one of the scholars of Ibn Hibbaan, then he is to be considered reliable, as he declared him trustworthy upon direct knowledge of his state and condition.*"

As when he rules upon the trustworthiness of an individual from the Successors to the Companions or from those who came after them; then he states about some of them clearly: "*I do not know him nor his father!*" How can it be that such a narrator is considered reliable with him when in fact Ibn Hibbaan stated that he does not know that narrator nor his father. This is one from the narrator who narrates that which is not found in the narrations of others. So in summary, these are matters that I was unaware of for several years, perhaps for ten years, Allaah knows best the period. However with time, the reality of them became apparent to me. Therefore due to that I do not advise the students of knowledge to be hasty or quick to publish their books and works. It is upon them the write and compose, in those matters or areas that it is not prohibited for them, as this exercise of composing and writing will train them. They can preserve what they have studied in a book or a written work, and place it upon a shelf, just as I did with the work "ar-Rawdh an-Nathar". And in my belief this specific book of mine shall be as if it has died, and will always remain in the state that it is now. Why? Because I do not have the time in which it is possible to review and reexamine it from the beginning to the end, such that it would become suitable for publishing among the people.

Because to this, it is tremendously dangerous for the beginners in knowledge to author works and then distribute them. Rather, it is for their general benefit to produce those knowledge based writings and then store them away. Thus keeping his written works to himself until a time when he perceives that he has reached maturity of his comprehension of knowledge, if Allaah wills.

**(89) THE EMINENT GUIDING SCHOLAR MUHAMMAD AL-'AMEEN ASH-SHANQEETEE, MAY ALLAAH HAVE MERCY UPON HIM, FROM 'VARIOUS QUESTIONS: ISLAMIC RULING': NO. 9544**

*Question: I am a beginning student of the efforts to seek knowledge, and presently I am come close to the time for my vacation as generally known. And I hope that Allaah will grant me success in utilizing and taking full advantage of it. So I hope to receive from you, esteemed sheikh, an explanation and discussion of some of the guidelines that will assist me in accomplishing that.*

Answer: May Allaah love you as you loved me for His sake, and I bear witness in front of Allaah that you loved for His sake. I ask Allaah to join us by this shared love in His abode of honor.

In reference to your vacation, then the best way to take advantage of it is in seeking knowledge. The reason for this is that is Allaah has made is a path for you the path towards Jannah. As a student as well as others are often occupied with various matters during their ordinary schedule that prevents seeking knowledge. However, if Allaah grants him success in his vacation, he attends the circles of remembrance through knowledge, and memorizes the Qur'aan, and he memorizes what he is able to from the Sunnah of the Prophet, may Allaah's praise and salutations be upon him drinking from the spring of knowledge. If he does this then Allaah opens his breast to guidance, and illuminates his heart, and causes goodness to become beloved to him. As the Prophet, may Allaah's praise and salutations be upon him, said: *{The one who takes the path of seeking knowledge, Allaah makes easy for him the path to Jannah.}* [73] .Some of the scholars state that: "*This contains evidence that the student of knowledge will be granted success in righteous endeavors the consequence of which will be his entrance into Jannah.*"

So look towards the people of knowledge as they have achieved the mercy of Allaah, they are immersed into Allaah's mercy, because they are engaged in seeking knowledge and traveling for its sake. Traveling, the leaving of one's home country, staying awake at night, exhaustion and illness- if they find themselves confronted by all of these, then they have acquired reward and recompense from Allaah. If they achieve knowledge then it carries them towards its realization and practice. So they act according to what they have learned and so are they closer to the Sunnah, and the closer to the obedience of Allaah, general good and goodness. They learn what is pleasing to Allaah, the Most Perfect, and then act upon it, as well as what is hated by Allaah and then stay away from it. They are immersed in the mercy of Allaah, after He has given them knowledge and raised them to that level. Such that if they become from those who are considered scholars then they direct others towards good, and guide them to obedience of Allaah and general goodness, by Allaah's permission and through success granted by Him.

Allaah has increased their reward, and made heavier their scales of good deeds and He brings forth goodness and blessing in that which they say. He has ennobled them, and honored them and made them the inheritors of the Prophets and

---

[73] Narrated in Saheeh Muslim: 2699/ Sunan at-Tirmidhee: 2945/ Sunan Ibn Maajah: 225 / & Musnad Ahmad: 7379- from the hadeeth of Abu Hurairah. Declared authentic by Sheikh al-Albaanee in Saheeh at-Targheeb wa at-Tarheeb: 69, 89, as well as in other of his books

Messengers; those who establish the proof of Allaah's guidance upon His creation. So this noble goal and this tremendous position of honor is truly worthy or deserving of the Muslim striving to achieve it and seeking the means to achieve it, pursuing the causes that bring it about, and struggling and working diligently to attain this level and position. The content one who has been given success is the one whom Allaah has granted success in attaining the higher levels of knowledge; so he works hard and struggles specifically during the occasions of his free time. So the best goodness you can be advised towards is seeking knowledge, as certainly The Messenger, may Allaah's praise and salutations be upon him, said: *{Whoever Allaah intends good for He grants him understanding in the religion.}* [74]. So perhaps Allaah, the Most Perfect, will from His mercy facilitate this matter for you. As Allaah loves that the one who worships Him, should bring forth and manifest those things which He loves. And certainly Allaah loves this knowledge. He loves this knowledge because it is His revelation which He revealed through His Book, and upon the tongue of His Messenger, may Allaah's praise and salutations be upon him. So be devoted to this revelation, and hold fast to learning it, and devote your time and your existence, ending your life upon that. As there is no doubt this is for the benefit of the worshipers of Allaah and their own rectification. Certainly in each and every age Allaah has selected for this knowledge its upright and just individuals. He has selected in every era the best of its people; those who can bring about rectification and good. So good tidings for the one whom Allaah grants success and gives him the blessing of utilizing his vacation in seeking knowledge.

As for the first issue upon you: Organize your time, and your vacation as a whole towards seeking knowledge. Designate and arrange specific lessons for yourself and prepare specific knowledge based texts for you to memorize, learn, strive to fully comprehend, and establish the rights of that knowledge upon you. So that when your vacation has ended you will have found that you have produced good results. As there is no doubt that the one who seeks knowledge, and searches for knowledge, then what he attains is Allaah's raising his level and position due to that knowledge according to the degree of what he has acquired of knowledge. If you attend a single sitting of knowledge, and listen to a single verse from the Book of Allaah, then act upon the matters which it has indicated to be permissible as well as what is forbidden from within it, as well as all its legislated directives and orders- learning them well. So that your level after leaving that sitting should not be the same as your level when you sat down. Certainly, Allaah raises the people of knowledge by degrees and stages. So good tiding are for the one whom Allaah raises his level during these periods of vacation, and grants him success to best utilizing it is seeking knowledge.

---

[74] Narrated in Saheeh al-Bukhaaree: 71, 3116, 7312/ Saheeh Muslim: 1037/ Sunan Ibn Maajah: 221/ al-Muwatta Maalik: 1300, 1667/ Musnad Imaam Ahmad: 16395: 16404, and other narrations/ Musannaf Ibn Abee Shaybah: 31792/ & Sunan ad-Daaramee: 224, 226/- on the authority of Mu'aweeyah. And it is found in Jaame'a al-Tirmidhee: 2645/ & Musnad Imaam Ahmad: 2786/ & Sunan ad-Daaramee: 270, 2706/- on the authority of Ibn "Abbaas. And it is found in Sunan Ibn Maajah: 220/ Musannaf 'Abdul-Razzaaq: 30851/- on the authority of Abu Hurairah. It was declared authentic by Sheikh al-Albaanee in Saheeh al-Aadab al-Mufrad: 517, Silsilat al-Hadeeth as-Saheehah: 1194, 1195, 1196, Saheeh at-Targheeb at-Tarheeb: 67, as well as in other of his books. Sheikh Muqbil declared it authentic in al-Jaame'a al-Saheeh: 9, 3123, 4650.

The second matter, after the organization of your time in seeking knowledge- is righteous companionship. Therefore search for a righteous companion. Because this time period is somewhat long. If your vacation is a month long, or more than a month, than that is lengthy. As an individual may become bored, so he requires someone who will help and assist him. As such he should search for a righteous person who will assist him upon his seeking of knowledge. And if someone has the ability to establish this by himself, seeking knowledge with diligence, struggling and working hard in this along with this being easier and more convenient for him- then that is better.

Similarly from that which one is advised with related to utilizing his vacation well, especially for the one who wants Allaah to grant him success in his studies and in his seeking knowledge is standing in prayer at night and other good deeds. As a person who during his normal studies and during his general business is not able to perform a great deal of such acts of obedience. However when he is on vacation he has free time. Thus, he should strive to the limits of his ability to complete a section from the Book of Allaah while standing to recite at night. He should undertake during this vacation to complete a portion from the Book of Allaah; committing himself to reciting the entire Qur'aan every three days. He should realize and make apparent the Word of Allaah the Most Perfect, the Most High in all his speech and actions, both internally and externally; demonstrating in all the various affairs of his life, his priorities, and all his concerns- the perfect word of Allaah.

Glad tidings upon glad tidings for the one who Allaah makes the Qur'aan a renewing spring for his heart, a light for his chest, a means for the polishing away of his sorrows and dismay, and the means for removal of his worries and concerns. He makes it the pilot and driver which lead to his greater contentment as well as to Paradise. So glad tiding are for the one who places the Book of Allaah before his eyes and he takes joy or rejoices in its delights, and has sadness or sorrow in its grief and distresses it coveys. If it mentions Paradise- he longs for it, if it mentions the Hellfire -he stands in fright and dread of it. Glad tidings are for the one who fully takes advantage of these hours and times in reflecting upon the Noble Qur'aan. Certainly the happiness of the worshiper in his religion and the world, in the Hereafter lies in the book of Allaah. As by Allaah, the first generations, may Allaah have mercy upon them, were not truly fortunate and did not achieve that elevated status and lofty position except through the grace and blessings of Allaah, and then through this Qur'aan. ❧*Verily, this Qur'ân guides to that which is most just and right*❧-(Surah al-'Israa:9) This refers to the Qur'aan, but what is the Qur'aan? ❧*This is a Book, the Verses whereof are perfected in every sphere of knowledge, and then explained in detail from One (Allaah), Who is All-Wise Well-Acquainted with all things.*❧-(Surah Hood:1). So the successful righteous worshipper if the opportunity comes to him in the form of some unoccupied time, then he seizes it before he becomes occupied with something else.

If this vacation passes or is completed and within it you have completed the recitation of the Qur'aan every three nights, and within it you have fasted during each Monday and Thursday day of the week which are the praised recommended days for this, then when your vacations ends you have already gained enormous benefits. Because obedience invites towards that which is close to and related to it. As how many people when they had some free time began to use it for the obedience of Allaah, and then what occurs is that they do not have the ability to leave that activity for anything else! As Allaah has made their feet firm upon that deed. As some the scholars have said: "*Seclusion in the masjid during Ramadhaan is from blessing of the month of fasting, as from the matters which Allaah has legislated during the month of Ramadhaan is this recommended seclusion for a Muslim. Because through this seclusion a worshiper is strengthened upon the act of praying at night. Perhaps he would come out of his time spent in these days of seclusion and devotion and he has become one who now establishes the consistent standing in the night prayer, or one who regularly completes the recitation of the Qur'aan every three nights. Similarly, it is the same way with other acts of worship of Allaah.*"

Similarly, from those matters which I advise you to take the opportunity to do during your vacation is to look towards what deeds and endeavors are most beloved to Allaah. From the most beloved deeds and acts of obedience to Allaah that are of this type and from those which is the most valuable and noble after the worshiping Allaah alone without partners or associates- is good treatment of your parents. So the successful one, the righteous young man is devoted to be from those who are best in treatment to their parents. Thus the days of your vacation also utilize them in fulfilling the needs of your parents. Do not find out about a need of your father or your mother, except that you show your love and service to them through fulfilling that need in anything that Allaah is pleased with. As Allaah says: ❴**And lower to them the wing of submission and humility through mercy, and say: "My Lord! Bestow on them Your Mercy as they did bring me up when I was young.**❵-(Surah al-'Israa:34)

During the school year you are normally busy and pardoned with an excuse, may Allaah open their hearts to accept your excuse. But during your free time, you should not hear of a need of your father nor one of your mother- except that you knell at their feet receptive and responsive in their needs. This is from the greatest of the ways and means of coming close to Allaah and from the matters which He loves, meaning the good treatment of one parents by which Allaah spread forth His mercy and within which He places ease and success. As the one who acts in goodness does not endeavor to walk upon a path of benefit and good except that Allaah facilitates that for him, nor does he knock at the doors of good except that Allaah opens them for him within his face. as it is found that some brothers during their vacation act in a way which is a means for being undutiful and ungrateful towards their parents. This is when they use that period to travel and visit countries far away from their parents. So that their parents feel distress and sadness- as when the normal period for their studies arrives they are too busy with that to give attention to them, and then when the vacation comes he travels far away from them- so where is the good treatment!!

So when will there be the opportunity for the beautiful and notable compassion, the compassion which leads to your father and mother being pleased and content with you; if you are far away from your parents during your general schedule of study as well as throughout your vacation, and if you are occupied with other matters instead of them in your free time a well as your time of work and study? Thus the satisfied successful one aspires to make the period of his vacation an undertaking which leads to Allaah's mercy, and to righteous supplications for him from his father and mother.

And if they have already died- then he should exert himself in remembering them within his righteous supplications, asking that Allaah's mercy be upon them, asking Allaah to make their graves spacious, and that Allaah make easy for both of them the trials of the Day of Reckoning and Resurrection. So he constantly asks Allaah for goodness for them while he is not busy, for as long as he is on vacation and not occupied. *Oh Allaah forgive my father and have mercy upon him, oh Allaah forgive my mother and have mercy upon her." Look at how this is mentioned in the Qur'aan: "Say my Lord! Bestow on them Your Mercy as they did bring me up when I was young.*-(Surah al-'Israa:34). And some of the scholars have stated:  One is amazed at this verse, as Allaah the Exalted says: *My Lord! Bestow on them Your Mercy ...* but the verse does not stop there, because if you were to say: "My Lord! Bestow on them Your Mercy ..." then in this you acting well by yourself in this asking of good for your parents. So one says additionally: *My Lord! Bestow on them Your Mercy ...* Meaning: In that you do not have any merit over your parents when you are only returning to them their rights upon you, and your kindness to them is related to their previous kindness upon you. So goodness to ones parents is from the most beloved types of obedience, and it is made easy for the one whom Allaah grants success to look towards the needs of his parents. And if you know that your mother will not be present where you are -then travel to her, making the best of your vacation days. Turn your attention to her and bringing her happiness to, make her content, and fulfill her needs. Do likewise with your father, travel to him, present yourself to him, ask him about his condition, fulfill his needs. In this way making these vacation days a lessening and reduction of your normal absence from your parents.

Similarly, one of the most beloved acts of obedience, is seek to attend the sittings of those who are righteous, and devoting your time to sitting with the people of righteousness. So if you learn about some upright brothers the always strive to visit them and sit in their company. Upon them you have a right that they love you for Allaah's sake, that they aid you in the obedience of Allaah, and they help you be firm in every matter that Allaah is pleased with. Equally, they have a right upon you that you assist them in obeying Allaah, and that you have within your heart love for them, and that you have good relations between yourselves for Allaah's sake. You should want for them good, and love for them what you love for yourself. When the hearts are joined at such times, and you associate with the best of people, then you will find that you will have become tranquil, contented and satisfied. Then even when you are with your family and children Allah's pleasure will be upon you.

Furthermore, it is proper that the Muslim understand the various rights and obligations at their proper levels or priorities. Do not go on visits to the righteous people, utilizing the time that is actually the right of your sons, daughters, or wives. Rather, your should start with the most important of matters and then proceed level by level according to priority. Such that one of you also ensures that he makes his children happy. Even if this means taking them on a trip, a permissible outing or picnic. As this is from those matters which please Allaah, bringing happiness to them through permissible ways which do not contain prohibited matters and do not include that which is forbidden. So utilizing your vacation in endeavors such as these is from the success bestowed by Allaah upon His worshiper.

It is upon the Muslim to know that this world is a transitory and passing affair, and that the time is short, and an individual does not know when his appointed time here will come to an end. So good tidings for the one who places remembrance of his death right in front of his eyes! So make good use of your free time before you are occupied and your health before you are stricken with illness, and your youth before your coming old age. Good tiding are for the one who reaches the end of these vacation days having had good facilitated for him within them, while having his scroll of deeds rolled up after efforts which reaches towards the highest levels of those who strive, and upon righteous purifying deeds. They have made their pages of deeds glow white with their rewards, and made their scales heavy through upright deeds. While other people- and we ask Allaah for protection, health and safety- have filled their records with evil deeds and destructive and ruinous actions.

So we ask Allaah for protection, health and safety. As good acts invite and lead to their like, and sins invite and lead to further evils that spring from them. So it is upon an individual to be fully warned and cautious, and to act with true concern and diligence towards fully benefiting from this time of his, and to utilize all of that time fully- that being something that will not occur except being blessed with the success that comes from Allaah. So constantly ask Allaah for success by saying: "*Oh Allaah I ask You for success, oh Allaah do not prohibit from me the success that comes from you- due to the sins that I have committed.*"

We ask Allaah the Most High, Lord of the Tremendous Throne, to rectify for us our religion in which lies the protection and safeguarding of all our affairs. Oh Allaah rectify for us our religion in which lies the protection and safeguarding of all our affairs, rectify for us our religion in which we find our life, rectify for us our success in the next world to which our final return will be. Make for us a bountiful life in which there is every good, and make death a mercy for us as an escape from every evil. And Allaah, the Most High knows best.

**(90) The Eminent Guiding Scholar Muqbil Ibn Haadee al-Waadi'ee, may Allaah have mercy upon him, from 'A Defending Mission from Audio Lectures Upon the People of Ignorance & Sophistry': vol. 1, page 472**

*Question: Oh Abu 'Abdur-Rahman, we need for you to inform us how you organize your time in seeking knowledge. When do you do your research, when do you teach your brothers, and how many lessons do you have during a day and a night? And we ask Allaah for sincerity of intention for you and for ourselves.*

Answer: At present, after salatul-fajr I review the research related writings of my brothers which they hope to publish. Then a short while before the sun rise above the horizon, I go to an open area for a while to rest and recuperate my energy. Then a little while after the sun rises, we read from *((as-Saheeh al-Musnad Memaa Lasaa fee as-Saheehayn)02-35)*. Afterwards, we proceed to the library for research until the call to prayer of salatul-dhuhr. After the call to prayer of salatul-dhuhr we study from *((Tafseer Ibn Katheer)01-01)* or something related to the study of the proper recognition of dictation or to handwriting. Then after salatul-dhuhr, lunch, and the essential period of resting, if I have not done less than usual then I am not able to study more. So then I rest a while from that time until the time of salutul-asr. At that time, I go to the masjid for salutul-asr, and afterwards I teach from *((Saheeh al-Bukhaaree)02-01)*. Then after that lesson I instruct some of the brothers in the study of *((Sharh of Ibn Aqeel)10-06)*. After this lesson, depending on the time remaining, I rest until the sun sets then I make wudhu and proceed to the masjid. After salatul-maghrib I teach from *((Saheeh Muslim)02-02)*, and after salatul-isha I teach from the work *((as-Sunnah)06-22)* by 'Abdullah Ibn Ahmad Ibn Hanbal.

As for the research that I am presently working on, it is the study of *((Mustadraak of al-Haakim)02-25)*, and I am on the verge of completing it. In this I am examining all the hadeeth narrations which he declared where authentic, or in which there is possible disagreement regarding due to the possibility of error from al-Hakim when he states: "*Authentic according to the conditions held by the Imaams Bukhaaree and Muslim*", or "*Authentic according to the conditions of Imaam Muslim*". So I am investigating these and I consider those error that are considered to be from the mistakes of Imaam Haakim not from the errors of Imaam adh-Dhahabee in his review of the work, may Allaah have mercy upon him. Similarly, I am working on the book *((Hadeeth Narrations that have Hidden defects but which upon only a basic examination are considered authentic)02-36)*. The after some days, if Allaah wills, I will return to my work upon *((as-Saheeh al-Musnad Memaa Lasaa fee as-Saheehayn)02-35)*, when I have finished these other endeavors, Allaah wiling. In any case my time in these days is quite restricted, due the increased numbers of students. So I am not satisfied with the little time that remains to be given to my research. Yet on the other hand, in the beginning of my efforts there where only a few brothers; so that the majority of my time was able to be spent in research. And all praise is due to Allaah that resulted in tremendous good.

So I advise my brothers who are students of knowledge to study the life histories of 'Abdullah Ibn Mubaarak, Imaam Ahmad, Imaam al-Bukhaaree and Imaam Muslim, as well as those who adhered to and followed their path from the scholars of hadeeth- until you understand how to preserve your time. As I am not completely satisfied with my own efforts nor how I have been able to proceed, so the objective has not been realized completely nor fallen short of entirely. And all praise is due to Allaah, certainly a great deal of good has come forth from what was accomplished.

And I have forgotten to mention an important matter, that being the editing and correction of material that was previously only distributed on cassette tapes. We had spread tremendous good through these audio tapes, and they were received and well accepted by the students of knowledge. And some of them were prepared and willing to examine what those lectures contained and indicate any mistakes or errors, then correct the material of the tape as was required. So than after that stage, I further corrected them after the material was transcribed, and then these works were released. And there have come from these efforts tremendous benefit. The book ((al-Fawaakahu al-Jannah)12-34) was produced from some previous lectures, as well as the book ((al-Muqtarah)04-23); it being questions and answers related to hadeeth sciences and terminology. In addition the book ((Qirat al-'Ayn fee Ajweebat Qaa'ed al-'Alaabee wa Saahib al-'Adeen)12-18), the book ((al-Qawl al-'Ameen fee Bayaan Fadhaaeh al-Mudhabdhabeen)12-40) the book ((Maqatil as-Sheikh Jameel are-Rahman)12-35), rahimhu Allaahu ta'ala", the book ((al-Masaar'at)12-36) as well as a work composed of rulings in various matters which is named ((Ijaabatul-Saa'el 'An Ahemul Masaa'el)07-15),and the book ((Qamaa' al-Ma'aanid wa Zujur al-Haaqid al-Haasid)07-16) which encompasses various subject related to the situations that we find ourselves dealing with in present age. Issues and subjects such as voting and elections, and such as the issue of the many divisive groups of partisanship. As cassette tape is only a medium, which just like an individual- can considered foolish and ignorant, or otherwise.

In general, I hope that Allaah will bring benefit through these cassette lectures. And all praise is due to Allaah, they are easy and simple to benefit from, and the common people certainly have a need for their share of our efforts to call to the truth. So if we come to a common person and we say to him: "*Waleed Ibn Muslim is a 'mudallis' in hadeeth narrations and Ibn Laheeyah is 'mukhtalat', and Sha'bee did not hear naarations from Umm Salamah.*"; then he will nor understand what we are saying in the least and you are only wasting his time. On account of this we are eager to distribute these general audio cassettes. However this can occur after giving them proper attention and review, and that is the result of having the time, to give to it. But I am not an individual to be followed in this, as I am not satisfied with myself, by Allaah I am not truly satisfied with myself. As sometimes I will lose some of my time with the small children. As I myself have made mistakes in this, due to many problems that have reached me. Because of this, a person himself might simply sit down in the place of children to sometimes only play and joke with them.

**(91) The Eminent Guiding Scholar Saaleh Ibn 'Abdul-Azeez Aal-Sheikh, may Allaah preserve him, from 'Explanation of Kitaab at-Tawheed': Audio tape 3**

### The Personality of the Student of Knowledge and Attending Lessons

The subject of our talk today is about the personality of the student of knowledge in regarding to attending lessons. As those who attend to listen to knowledge are different types. They differ from the aspect of their desire and eagerness for what they hear, and they differ in regard to their preparedness and readiness. Their levels of desiring and being eager for knowledge are not all comparable, nor are their degrees of readiness and preparedness all similar. Firstly, eagerness for knowledge is found to be at varying levels:

1. From them there is the one who listens to knowledge truly desiring to acquire or obtain it. This is the majority of them, and all praise is due to Allaah.
2. And from them there is the one who listens only wishing to make an estimation of that individual scholar, or to comprehend his level of knowledge, and the capacity of his ability to teach, or the degree of his aptitude in the areas of knowledge in general.
3. And among them is the one who attends a single time and then is absent for ten other instances.

These are some of their types, and within them there are those possessing different levels of desire, and we are assuming that these all are approaching knowledge truly desiring it. Therefore secondly, when the student of knowledge approaches a class or series of lessons desiring to benefit; it is necessary that he do so with a specific frame of mind and specific state of his heart, as well as possessing a certain intellectual mindset. As for the state of heart and the frame of mind it is that:

His intention in seeking this knowledge should be to remove himself from a state of ignorance. This is having sincerity in ones knowledge. Because the seeking of knowledge is worship, and it is an obligation to have a pure intention when doing so. Having sincerity in ones knowledge is intending that through learning it you will remove ignorance from oneself. Imaam Ahmad was asked about the intention one has in regard to knowledge, how should it be? He replied: "*It should be intended to remove ignorance from himself.*" As if you undertake seeking knowledge with the desire to become a teacher, a caller to the truth, an author, or something similar to that; then the correct and righteous intention in this and true sincerity in that is based upon two matters: Firstly, that the purpose is to remove ignorance from oneself, and secondly, that the purpose is to remove ignorance from others.

If one does not intend one of these two purposes, or both of them together, then he is not someone who possesses the correct intention. As if one of us aims to seek knowledge, then it is required that it be based upon the intention to remove ignorance from himself. And if you have such an intention then it naturally, must encompass various matters. Such as that Allaah, the Most High and exalted created him, and placed upon him commandments and prohibitions in the matter of most essential of all fundamentals and foundations- that being the right of the Most High, the Most Magnificent that He be worshiped alone without any partners or associates. Similarly, it encompasses understanding His commands and prohibitions in the permissible and impermissible matters; as well as comprehending the issue of recklessness of entering into prohibited matters in issues of belief.

Likewise, what is related to ignorant behavior and poor manners, and from the reasons of that is ignorance as well as other causes. So if he learns, he thus removes ignorance from himself, then he becomes someone with knowledge of what by Allaah the Most High, the Most Magnificent desires from him in life. Then after this, he must seek the assistance of Allaah the Most High, the Most Magnificent in conforming to the aims of His Sharee'ah, this is a personal matter related to this- that is essential.

A second personal matter that is also essential: is that when he seeks to acquire knowledge, he does so certain of the soundness of the knowledge possessed by his teacher. By this meaning that he is personally convinced that the basic state or condition of his teacher is that he teaches what is correct and sound. As if it comes to him in his thoughts that what the teacher teaches in in error, or that the information he conveys is mixed up and confused, or that he has this or that issue which would weaken his position or rank in knowledge; then the student will not benefit from this. Because as he sits and listens, his listening will be like that of a person who is reluctant to accept, having some objections to the one speaking. And so what occurs is that when such a teacher makes statement, a minute or half a minute after hearing it the listener will think and say to himself: "*This is correct and from the matters this scholar has strong understanding in.*". But then he thinks of such and such information which contradicts that statement just made by the teacher. Yet by the time he will have realized this, that minute has passed and the teacher has moved on to other matters. Likewise when the teacher ends that part of his explanation, the student hears another sentence, which is also seen as confused to him. Therefore more objections come forth, and this makes it impossible for the listener to properly take knowledge.

Rather, if there is something which seems to be incorrect within that which the student of knowledge hears, then he should have a paper or notebook in his hands in which he can write down the problem or issue; but then no longer think about it or consider it, just continue to listen to the knowledge of the lesson. He should just write in his notebook: "*investigate the issue of- such and such- later*". Then when he is finished with that specific session, he should go that day or sometime afterwards and investigate this issue or ask regarding it. As from the matters which are well known is that it is not a required condition that a teacher be unquestionable and beyond mistakes, and it is not from the conditions that a teacher always be correct. As certainly he may take individual positions or views that differ from what is well known, or he may have recommendations or advice that he is mistaken in. However the issue or concern is that the teacher be witnessed or recognized to possess knowledge, connected to knowledge, having a sound understanding of what he speaks about.

As if he understands what he speaks about, as well as the various statements of the people, and teaching beneficial knowledge; then he may lack comprehension in an specific issue, ruling, or similar matter. He may have mistakes in one instance, or regarding this concept, or something similar to this. And this is not something strange. As a teacher is human, and humans make mistakes. Accordingly, what is important is to take knowledge from the one that you are confident of his knowledge and that within yourself you have no about reservations about or objections to him. As this deprives many from a tremendous amount of knowledge, when they take knowledge with a mind set that is dubious or uncertain towards the teacher. Due to this the majority of questions that arise during a circle of knowledge, will not be answered.

Once we were present in a sitting with Sheikh 'Abdul-Razzaq al-'Afeefee, the well known guiding scholar, may Allaah the Exalted have mercy upon him. There was one there with him was asking him regarding some of the issues related to Hajj or the obligatory pilgrimage. Whenever someone came forth and asked the Sheikh for a ruling in a matter and the Sheikh replied; then one specific questioner would then come forward and say, "*Well, what if it was like this?*" He was attempting to learn knowledge by putting forwards additional issues other than the one the questioner originally asked regarding. Therefore the Sheikh, may Allaah have mercy upon him-said to him: "*Knowledge does not come in this manner, rather knowledge comes through studying it.*" And this is correct. Because the student as he spends time with the people of knowledge listening, if he exposes or opens his mind to it then perhaps with every issue which is raised -he asks something about it or every matter which he hears he immediately questions something in relation to it. There have been many brothers and young men like this who passed along with us in the circles of knowledge. They put forth questions and problems that naturally come forth because of what they lack of knowledge. Due to this they put forward many such questions and problems, and if they had only been patient, that would have been better for them. This personality has an effect and influence upon ones intellect, and upon ones characteristics, and upon ones conception of areas of knowledge during lessons. Therefore it is required for us that when we take knowledge we take it with the mindset of someone who does not possess any knowledge. We must listen, and listen, and listen, and if a difficulty in understanding arises, then we write it down and then investigate or ask regarding it later. Again, this naturally should be in relation to the teacher we feel an secure regarding his knowledge, so we are able to take knowledge from him having confidence in what he generally brings forth.

(92) The Eminent Guiding Scholar 'Abdur-Rahman Ibn Naasir as-Sa'dee, may Allaah have mercy upon him, from 'Islamic Rulings of Sheikh Sa'dee': page 91

*Question: What are the proper manners for the scholar and the student to acquire and be molded by?*

Answer:  The foundation of manners for them both is having sincerity of intention solely for Allaah's sake and seeking His pleasure alone, along with the aim of reviving the religion and the following of the leader of the Messengers of Allaah, Muhammad. His intention should be the face of Allaah the Exalted, in seeking and conveying knowledge, in striving to understand as well as bringing understanding of it to others, in his reading, studying, and reviewing. As well as seeking to remove from himself and others the death of ignorance and its oppression by bringing the light to his heart and giving it life through beneficial knowledge. As certainly knowledge is light by which one is enlightened and guided through darkness and by which the different forms of ignorance are debased and subdued. Thus whenever his knowledge increases his light increases and enables him to distinguish the truth from falsehood, guidance from misguidance, the permissible from the forbidden, and that which is sound and complete from that which is corrupt and deficient. He will come to understand the proper places and positions of matters, and can distinguish the paths of good from those of evil.

Seeking knowledge is a form worship which gathers together a number of these ways of coming close to Allaah and one gains closeness to Allaah by being occupied with them. Indeed most of the scholars have said that seeking knowledge is preferable to some of the greatest of other acts of worship. And they said this in  those times which were illuminated by the presence of abundant knowledge among the people. So how abundant would that reward be in those eras in which knowledge has vanished or so diminished that is has come close to disappearing through the departure of those scholars who have inherited from the prophet, may Allaah's praise and salutations be upon him. The one who travels the path of seeking knowledge, Allaah makes easy for him the path to Paradise, and benefits him in acquiring knowledge as well as thorough his passing on to others, thus benefiting the possessor of knowledge while alive and after his death. As when the actions are cut off by death and the recording scroll of the worshiper's deeds is rolled up, the good deeds of the people of knowledge still continue to increase as others benefit from their guidance and are guided by their statements and deeds. So it is only appropriate that the successful one who, possessing intelligence, utilizes the most valuable of his time and his most precious years preparing for that coming day of his death and true need.

It is necessary that the teacher be patient upon his efforts at instruction and education, and that he make every effort to impart understanding to every student according to their intellectual capacity. He should not keep a student overly occupied with reading, or with matters that will not strengthen him intellectually. But he must encourage him to persevere by questioning and testing him often, causing him to become accustomed to discussing and properly investigating and considering issues, and the explaining of their benefits, wisdom, and sources, and from which principles of the Sharee'ah they has been derived from. As comprehension of the fundamentals and essential principles, and considering and weighing them in regard to various issues and their forms, is from the most beneficial paths of learning. The more a student of knowledge tastes the delight and pleasure of his understanding and comprehension, and corrects his misunderstandings; it increases and strengthens his desire and the depth of that understanding.

Similarly, it is fitting for him to awake and stir the student's comprehension of matters through questions and answers as well as frequent encouragement to investigate further. Such that he will be someone who shows pleasure when a question or problem is put to him, or when someone challenges what he has stated. As certainly the goal is to benefit, and to reach the truth, not to support and bring dominance to the statement which one has previously made, or the path which you are presently proceeding upon. Rather, if someone less than him in knowledge indicates to him a defect or deficiency in that which he has stated, he is grateful to him, and searches along with him -in an investigation whose goal is the arrival at the truth. Not simply giving victory to that method or way which he is upon.

For the teacher's returning to or accepting the correct understanding put forward by a student, due to the fact that it is actually closer to the truth, is from the most indicative signs of his merit, his elevated position in status, the goodness of his character, and of his sincerity towards Allaah the Exalted. So if he has not reached this state of acting in this way, then he must train and accustom himself to this. As engaging in a matter brings forth aptitude and capacity within it, and practicing a matter advances the practitioner in degrees of its perfection and proficiency. It is also necessary that the student beautify his manners with his teacher. He should thank Allaah, that Allaah has facilitated for him the study with someone who will educate him in his state of ignorance, who brought him 'life' when he was dead, and who awakened him from his state of slumber. Therefore he should seize every opportunity and chance to take knowledge from him, and frequently supplicate for him whether he is present or absent. As the Prophet, may Allaah's praise and salutations be upon him said: *{The one who does towards you an act of goodness then return it back to him, and if you do not find that by which to return it back to him by, then supplicate for him, until you have seen that you have compensated the good from him by this means}* [75].

---

[75] Narrated in Sunan Abu Daawud: 1672/ Sunan an-Nasaa'ee: 2568/ Musnad Imaam Ahmad: 5342, 5709, 6071/ & Mustradrak 'Alaa as-Saheehayn: 2424/- -from the hadeeth of 'Abdullah Ibn 'Umar. It was declared authentic by Sheikh al-Albaanee in Silsilat al-Hadeeth as-Saheehah: 254, Irwa' al-Ghaleel: 1617, Saheeh at-Targheeb at-Tarheeb: 967, Saheeh al-Jaame'a as-Sagheer: 6021, Saheeh Sunan Abu Dawud & Saheeh Sunan an-Nasaa'ee. Sheikh Muqbil did not state any difference with the ruling of authenticity given by Haafidh al-Haakim in his own verification of al-Mustadrak alaa Saheehayn- 'Pursuing the Errors of al-Haakim which adh-Dhahaabee Did Not Mention' regarding hadeeth numbers 2424.

And which act of goodness is considered greater than the goodness of his conveying knowledge to you? Every form of goodness ceases except for endeavors of knowledge, giving of advice, and guiding others. As in every subject or concern in which someone may benefit and those matters more significant than it, benefit comes about from its being taught as well as from other related matters. So its rewards reach the which the one engages in it.

Certainly one of my companions informed me that he himself gave a ruling in the matter of inheritance, and his sheikh was someone who previously had died. He afterwards saw him in his sleep reading in his grave: and his sheikh said to him: "*The issue of so and so that you gave a ruling in- the reward of that has reached and come to me*". And this is a matter well known in the Sharee'ah. *{The one who establishes a good sunnah or way of conduct, for him is the reward of it and the one who acts upon it until the day of Judgment}* [76]. Similarly, it is necessary for the student to behave thoughtfully in the matter of asking questions, and have gentleness towards his teacher. He should not put questions to him at times of fatigue, tiredness, or anger. Such that perhaps he may give a response that opposes the truth due to his unsettled state of mind; or which at a minimum would lead to him offering a response which is deficient.

And if you see him as mistaken in a matter, do not openly state that error. Rather, inform him through a refined and sophisticated manner. Not ceasing in this until what is correct becomes clear to him. As many people if you openly speak of their error, it only increases them in distance and likelihood of returning to what is correct. This returning to the truth becomes a difficult matter, except for the one who is truly master of himself and has molded himself towards having a noble character. As that mentioned type of individual will not be concerned at all that you came back to him with his own mistaken words, and stated openly that he was mistaken. However this virtuous character and condition is from the most unique of dispositions, yet nothing stands between the worshiper and his reaching this state of excellent temperament except the success that is given by Allaah and his struggling to reform and train his soul.

Likewise it is proper for the student, if he enters into the study of a subject or area from the various branches of knowledge, that he explores and looks into every area from that branch of knowledge. He should memorize or preserve from that effort -the issues of importance and beneficial researches, fortifying, conceiving and understanding them appropriately, thoroughly comprehending both its sources and the fundamentals which it is build upon. Then, you will continue to proceed in this way until you achieve tremendous good, and considerable knowledge. ❦*He to whom Hikmah is granted, is indeed granted abundant good*❧-(Surah al-Baqarah:269). We ask Allaah for success and continual guidance, as He is close and the One who responds. May Allaah's praise be upon Muhammad and His salutations.

---

[76] Narrated in Saheeh Muslim: 1017/ Sunan an-Nasaa'ee: 2555/ Sunan Ibn Maajah: 203/ Musnad Imaam Ahmad: 18718 and others/ & Sunan ad-Daaramee: 512, 514/ -on the authority of Jareer Ibn 'Abdullah. It was declared authentic by Sheikh al-Albaanee in Saheeh at-Targheeb at-Tarheeb: 65, 1222, Saheeh al-Jaame'a as-Sagheer: 6305, 6306, as well as in his verification of the Saheeh Sunan Ibn Maajah.

**(93) The Eminent Guiding Scholar 'Abdur-Rahman Ibn Naasir as-Sa'adee, may Allaah have mercy upon him, From 'Light Of the People of Insight and the Men of understanding': Page 75)**

### A Basic Summary of the Behavior and Manners of Scholars and Students

It is a duty upon the people of knowledge specifically that their endeavors of learning and teaching be established upon a firm foundation of complete purity of intention, seeking to come closer to Allaah through this act of worship which is from the most valuable and noted forms of worship. This will engage the best of the worshippers lifetime- striving to establish this required essential in every small or significant aspect of their affairs. Whether this be in relation to teaching or studying knowledge, researching and overseeing others, enabling other to hear their knowledge or listening to it oneself, sitting in circles of knowledge or directing the footsteps of others towards the circles of knowledge; whether this be through writing, memorizing, repeatedly studying specific lessons, or reviewing its subject or another's from different books, or purchasing books or anything else that assisting with acquiring knowledge. In all of these endeavors you are among those who will be counted and considered as those who are realizing his statement, may Allaah's praise and salutations be upon him: *{The one who takes the path of seeking knowledge, Allaah makes easy for him the path to Jannah.}* [77] As every path whether concrete and tangible or abstract and conceptual that a individual proceeds upon as part of the path towards knowledge, enters into the meaning of this hadeeth.

After this it is important to begin with the matters of greatest importance and then proceeding to matters a lesser importance in the various branches of Sharee'ah knowledge and its means of acquisition. And the detailed explanations of this fact are numerous and well known. However, the approximate path to accomplish this is that from branch of knowledge which you chose to focus and engage yourself in- you select from among its various authored works the work which is the most beneficial and highest in value, the one which possessing the greatest clarity and benefits for study. Then give this book the majority of you focus in terms of memorization if this is possible, and for frequent study; in order to reach a point where you have the substance, content, and meanings well preserved in your heart. Then always review and return to its study until you reach a sufficient degree of proficiency in it. Then proceed to utilizing the extensive works within that branch of knowledge, so that they will act as an explanation and commentary for you to the first work that you selected and gave priority to, as that priority indeed serves as a foundation and basis for your extending further in your studies.

It is upon the teacher to consider and look at the intellectual ability of the student, and his preparedness or lack of it. So that he does not call him to become occupied with a book that is not suitable to his level. As a little which he understands and benefits from in much better than a significant amount which he is presented simply to forget its wording as well as its meaning.

---

[77] Narrated in Saheeh Muslim: 2699/ Sunan at-Tirmidhee: 2945/ Sunan Ibn Maajah: 225 / & Musnad Ahmad: 7379- from the hadeeth of Abu Hurairah. Declared authentic by Sheikh al-Albaanee in Saheeh at-Targheeb wa al-Tarheeb: 69, 89, as well as in other of his books.

Just as it is upon the teacher to explain to the student and clarify and intended in what is being taught, according to the degree of his comprehension in order to broaden his understanding; without confusing various issues with each another, or moving from one issue to another until the first issue or matter is fully understood and comprehended. As this way brings full comprehension of the first matter, and enables the full focusing the mind upon the second issue or matter which comes after. And it is upon the teacher to advise the student, and to encourage him regarding every matter of benefit he can, and to be patient with the students' lack of understanding, or poor manners, as well as drawing the students attention to each matter which will correct and improves the manners of the student. Because the student has a right over the teacher, whenever he turns towards and comes close to that knowledge that will benefit him and benefit the people, and consideration that whatever of benefit he takes from his teacher is the true harvest and yield of the teacher, as the student preserves it, develops it, seeking through it a substantial profit. He is the true child of the teacher, and his inheritor.

Indeed the instructor is rewarded according to the value of his teaching, whether it is understood or not understood. As the understanding and comprehension encourage the continuing efforts of the teacher, and doesn't stop continuing to be beneficial. Certainly, this is a tremendous trade and bargain compared to similar pursuits, so let the competitors compete! As such it is upon the teacher that he revive and encourage this trade as this will be recorded among his deeds and the consequences of his deeds. ❖ *Verily, We give life to the dead, and We record that which they send before them, and their effects* ❖-(Surah Yaa Seen:12). So what is that which is sent before: it is your efforts and those endeavors which you have undertaken. And the meaning of ❖ *effects* ❖ is what results or comes from their efforts of goodness but from other peoples actions. There for it is upon the student to reverence and honor their teacher, and have good manner when interacting with him, due to what his teacher has over him in regard to a general as well as a specific right.

As for the general right: it is the good teacher who is prepared and undertakes what brings benefit for the people. So it is required that he has a right upon them, for what he carries out of teaching them what they are ignorant of, guiding them towards every matter of goodness, and warning them from every matter of harm and evil, and what comes from him of spreading knowledge and affairs of the religion. Furthermore this benefit is realized among the present people as well as among those who will come after them. So there is nothing equivalent to this tremendous benefit and gain from among various good works.

As for his specific right upon the student, then because he strives in his efforts to teach, and is diligent regarding every matter which will guide and bring his student towards a high level of achievement, that he utilized the best of his time and the core and heart of his intellect in striving to bring understanding to those who wish for guidance, as well as benefiting his students. This is along with his being patient with this effort by being of good character with kindness, and guidance related to worldly matters, and goodness in matters of worldly affairs. Therefore it is obligatory that he receive his full tremendous right from the one who received that matter of good from him. So what you think regarding the gift of many beneficial types of knowledge, whose benefit remains and have a tremendous effect. Through sitting at his hands your manners are perfected, and your full need for his knowledge becomes apparent, and through your frequently supplicating for him when he is present and absent. And if he brings forth an unusual knowledge related benefit, pay attention to it- listening intently with your mind and then take advantage of it.

And if the scholar is mistaken in a matter draw his attention to it with gentleness an kindness according to his standing and position and do not say: "*You are mistaken.*" or "*The matter is not as you have stated!!*" Rather bring forth a kind expression or statement which would indicate for the scholar his mistake without bringing about any confusion. Indeed this is from the right that must be adhered to. Additionally, this way of indicating a mistake invites to what is correct. And it is upon the scholar if he makes a mistake to return to what is correct, and he is not prevented by the statement that he first made, and he himself has a greater right to differ with it and return to the truth and be aware if it. Indeed, this is from the sign of justice and humbleness, towards Allah, al-Haqq as well as towards the creation. From the blessing of Allaah upon the scholar is that he finds someone from among his students who indicates his mistake to him, and directs him to what is correct in the matter.

This is certainly from the greatest obligations upon the teachers, scholars, and those who give Islamic rulings, if that they do not issue rulings or make an decisive statement regarding a matter which they do not fully have knowledge of. This refraining from speaking is from the signs of strength of one's religion and fairness, and its opposite signs are engaging in acts from the people to see and be aware of, as well as weakness in ones religion. Indeed, this withholding from issues a ruling without knowledge which is seen from the scholars is actually beneficial instruction from them, which brings about a good example. Such that the goal of both the scholars and students in all of their efforts of searching for knowledge be the seeking of truth, seeking what is right, and what is most correct according to the authentic evidences.

Be warned from, and far away from becoming occupied with knowledge for corrupt ends, such as boasting, bragging, so the people will see your actions, seeking leadership, or to achieve some worldly benefit. As the one who seeks knowledge for these aims, not have in the next world any reward. From the most significant matters which is a duty upon the people of knowledge from the scholars and students to fulfill: is to reflect and be characterized by that which they call to from knowledge in relation to having beautiful character, and abandoning despised character, as they are the most worthy of the people for that. They have been distinguished by knowledge and are examples, as general people are molded and shaped by following the examples of the people of knowledge among them, and because they are open to complaint or disapproval from them unlike others.

Knowledge if it is implemented, its blessings become established and apparent, as the spirit and life of knowledge is fulfilling it through actions, being molded by it, learning it, advising with it. It is proper that the memorization and proficiency of material by students is promoted and maintained by review and testing, and encouragement to study and review, and going back of one's present and previous lessons. As education has the role of the seed or the seedling in relation to planting and cultivation, and promoting it by study and repeated review is like giving it needed water, and removing harmful things from it increase its life and endurance. The people of knowledge warn about becoming preoccupied with the investigation about the condition of various people and their defects. As then he becomes worthy of punishment like the person in error, as he became preoccupied away from knowledge, and hinders every matter of benefit.

From the manners of the scholar and the student is: The giving of advice and the spreading of beneficial types of knowledge according to one's ability. This is such that someone learns an issue, spreads it, examining an discussing it with the ones who is relevant to - certainly this is from the blessing and goodness of knowledge. Likewise the one who is stingy with his knowledge, his knowledge dies before he dies himself; just as the one who spreads his knowledge it is if he has been given a second life, and Allaah rewards him in relation to the type of his knowledge.

For the most important matters which are a duty for the people of knowledge is to strive to unite their voices together as one and to unite their hearts. This is from the greatest of obligations, especially for the people of knowledge who are seen as examples for others, trough this tremendous good is reached and significant harm is averted. And be warned from jealousy of any of the people of knowledge, as this eats your good deeds just as fire consumes wood, and it is inconsistent with the giving of advice which is an essential aspect of the religion. And Allaah knows best.

**(94) The Eminent Guiding Scholar Muhammad al-'Ameen Ash-Shanqeetee, may Allaah have mercy upon him, from 'Various Questions': Islamic Ruling no. 9386**

*Question: Certainly, there is a need for the student of knowledge to learn the well known excellent manners that are enjoined by the Sharee'ah. So esteemed sheikh, if only you would counsel us as to what is proper for the student of knowledge to strive to achieve in relation to humbleness and the aspects of forbearance of character.*

Answer: Indeed humbleness of one's character is something praised by Allaah, the Most High, and if He wishes to show mercy upon his worshipper He removes pride as well as harshness from that worshipper's heart, and He makes his heart compassionate and compliant. Through this blessing of mercy Allaah the Most Exalted, brings ease to both his present religious and worldly affairs as well as those of his life in the next life. As mercy does not enter the heart of a worshipper nor find residence there except that the effects of that appear and can be seen upon the other parts of his body. Due to this, this significant aspect of one's character, meaning the characteristic of humbleness and modesty is that was revealed by Allaah to His noble Prophet, may Allaah's praise and salutations be upon him. As he said in what is affirmed upon him in an authentic narration: *{Indeed it was revealed to me that we should be humble and modest such that one of us does not dominate over another nor one of us oppress another.}* [78]. So humbleness is from the noble character of the Prophets and the domain of the righteous virtuous worshippers of Allaah. Allaah clothes them on the garment of humbleness, so the good of a worshiper is raised by this humbleness, and it raises his position and increases his rank. People believe that humbleness leads to lowness, and that if one is humble in front of the people that they will humiliate you and degrade you. But the Prophet, may Allaah's praise and salutations be upon him, indicated the falsehood of this belief and said in a narration with is affirmed upon him in Saheeh al-Bukhaaree. *{...Allaah does not increase a worshiper in the characteristic of pardoning others except that he is increases status and honor due to that, and Allaah does not make a servant humble except that He elevates his position.}* [79]. Therefore Allaah raises the standing of the worshiper in the affairs of his religion, his world, and his next life through humbleness. If Allaah gives importance to a person having good, and He wished to bless him in that goodness-He grants him humbleness. As being good natured and generosity is the foundation which similar to the branch, whenever it increases in goodness likewise he increases in humbleness and leniency.

The people most worthy of possessing humbleness are the scholars, the people of knowledge, the carriers of the Book of Allaah from its memorizers, and the students of knowledge. Those whom one hopes from them goodness in the affair of leading the Ummah and guiding the people to Allaah, they are deserving to reflect every good manner and aspects of noble character. It is necessary that the people look attentively towards Islaam in regard to the criterion of what their good qualities and characteristics should be, as the source for their noble manners which guide to the Sunnah and through its realization new life is given to the guidance of Messenger of Allaah, may Allaah's praise and salutations be upon him.

It is also necessary for a Muslim to seek the assistance of Allaah in achieving a humble character. As humbleness is not acquired simply by ones desiring it nor by merely wishing for it, rather it is a divine blessing and a merciful gift that Allaah gives to whom He wills. It is a merit by which he distinguishes with it whom He desires, from those individual he wishes to honor in this world and the next world. So frequently pray to Allaah to bless you with humbleness and to strip from your heart pride and to not make you conceited in regard to yourself. As Allaah the Most High if he wishes to make His servant wretched causes him to be deluded or deceived by the knowledge he possesses. Such that he becomes brazen and insolent when dealing with the worshipers of Allaah and disrespects and scorns the close associates of Allaah among His worshipers, perhaps acting impudently with the people of knowledge. Such a one then supposes that his precision in this issue or that, his knowledge of

[78]   Narrated in Saheeh Muslim: 2865/ Sunan Abu Daawud: 4895/ & Sunan Ibn Maajah: 4179/ -on the authority of Eyaadh Ibn Himyaar. It was declared authentic by Sheikh al-Albaanee in Silsilat al-Hadeeth as-Saheehah:570/ Mishkaat al-Masaabeh: 4898/ Saheeh at-Targheeb at-Tarheeb: 2890, Saheeh al-Jaame'a as-Sagheer: 1725, in his verification of the Saheeh Sunan Ibn Maajah, & and within Sharh al-'Aqeedah at-Tahaweeyah.

[79]   Narrated in Saheeh Muslim: 2588/ Jaame'a at-Tirmidhee: 2029/ Musnad Imaam Ahmad: 8782/ & Sunan ad-Daaramee: 1676/ -on the authority of Abu Hurairah. It was declared authentic by Sheikh al-Albaanee in Irwa' al-Ghaleel: 2200, Mishkaat al-Masaabeh: 1889 & Saheeh at-Targheeb at-Tarheeb: 858,2464,2891.

this narration, or his understanding of this or that matter - is greater than that of the scholar or is greater than that individual of knowledge, or better than such a such a recognized work of knowledge, or than the scholars who explained a certain work, and this makes it required to affirm the superiority of his ability. No by Allaah, rather if he believes this then he is someone is destroyed. There is no doubt that Allaah will seize him in a way that he does not anticipate. For if someone disrespect the scholars there will come to such an individual a time in which he stands unconcerned and uninterested in the knowledge they possess. We ask Allaah for health and safety.

As the one who supposes that his knowledge is substantial or significant, then Allaah permits its decline and the loss of the blessing which comes from his knowledge. So if is necessary that the student of knowledge always have humbleness, specifically towards the predecessors of this Ummah and the leading scholars of the early generations and that he not disdain their explanations of narrations, nor their knowledge in general. Rather he must give significant value this knowledge from them. As how often a brief statement which Allaah knows the truthfulness of the one who is speaks it- becomes significant and widespread due to his sincerity, truthfulness, and knowledge through Allaah. Similarly, how many there are who speak frequently, and write prolifically- but who have reflected in their words and in their deeds little sincerity of intention to Allaah and little thankfulness to Him. Certainly we ask Allaah the Tremendous to make us from those first mentioned, and to make us and you from them as He is the Most merciful of those with mercy.

The humble character is more deserving and worthy for the students of knowledge specifically within the sittings of knowledge and specifically for some students. As then the advanced student of knowledge does not place himself above a narration of the Messenger of Allaah, may Allaah's praise and salutations be upon him, nor does he attempt to give priority to his own words nor giving precedence to his own action or conduct. Because humbleness is found within his action and within his statements. Likewise, it is necessary for the advanced students of knowledge to have compassion for their brothers who are newcomers and who have recently become students, and to be humble with them, and become close to them, and to spread between them love and brotherhood, as Allaah gathers and unites between the people of knowledge by this knowledge and places mercy between them. So if this noble character spreads between the students of knowledge- Allaah will then love them. This is what is obligatory and required. And by Allaah, humbleness is furthermore required in your dealings with the general Muslims in addition to the students of knowledge, so do not look down upon anyone. As Allaah, the Most Perfect, is well aware of all hearts. They said *{Oh Messenger of Allaah, who is the best of people? He replied those who fear Allaah the most.}*-(Saheeh al-Bukhaaree 3353/ Saheeh Muslim:2378). So this fear of Allaah is something which resides in the hearts. As perhaps you may see a young insignificant student of knowledge that Allaah permits him to excel, and perhaps there will be a day when he will be a leading scholar from among the leading scholars of the Muslims.

This is the bounty of Allaah which he give to whomever He wishes, so be warned from disdaining or belittling anyone. This advice is for every student of knowledge, and it is upon him to be humble towards the truth, and humble towards the Sunnah. It is mentioned from one of the people of knowledge, may Allaah have mercy upon them have narrated the following account. One day he in his sitting of knowledge one of his students came forward. This student was extremely proficient in the Arabic language. So he asked the scholar regarding an issue from the issues of the Arabic language. So the scholar brought forth the most important of statements in the issues and summarized it. Then the student spoke privately to him and said to him that in this issue of the Arabic language there is some differences of opinion between the leading scholars in this branch of knowledge. Then he stated that which was the most sound or correct is such and such and mentioned the particulars of that position to him. Then the scholar said to him, "*Where did you get this knowledge from?*" He replied to the scholar, "*I have compiled a research regarding this issue.*", as he was knowledgeable of the Arabic language. So the scholar said, "*Give me this compilation or research what you have written regarding this subject.*" As this student compiled this work only after reaching a level excellence and proficiency.

It was not like in our present age where a student of knowledge may sit for a short time in a sitting of knowledge and then goes to *((al-Mughnee)07-07)* and *((al-Majmu'a)08-04)* to extracts a few sentences from their statements in order to compile some comments regarding them! It was not like this, we did not used to know this way nor practice it, no- we did not even know about it. And all praise is due to Allaah we have not seen this among the students of knowledge who are our students, and we do not purify anyone above Allaah. All praise is due to Allaah, the is just one characteristic, as the writing related to this matter of authoring extensive works, and the compiling researching about regarding details issue is not for anyone to enter into.

I mentioned this point so that someone will not suppose that anytime there is within a discussion of an issue put forward by a scholar, an aspect in he considers a mistake that should go and research and then come back with the results of the research. No this is not the case, the position of this individual was that he was someone who had excelled and was distinguished in his knowledge of the Arabic language, and then he came to study the principles of jurisprudence with that scholar, who was a leading scholar in the positions of fiqh issues, one of the scholars in this field in the area of Khurasaan. This scholar was someone who had standing in the knowledge of jurisprudence. So the student came and sought knowledge of jurisprudence from him, while he himself was distinguishes in knowledge of the Arabic language. So when that scholar mentioned this issue, the student mentioned to him that there was some differing in the issue among the scholars of language. Then he brought forth his own book regarding the issue. When he gave his book the scholar began to look through it, and he found that that student was highly proficient in this area of knowledge. He could not have imagined that the student possessed that level of knowledge! So when he turned the first page and then turned the second page, he realized that this student was a leading scholar with mastery in this branch and area of knowledge. He got down from his chair which he normally sat in for teaching, and swore that the student must sit in his place. Then he sat down and read to the assembly the students composition up to its conclusion, and the student felt as if he would melt from his embarrassment and self-consciousness because he was sitting in the sheikh's place. This is in light of the fact that the scholar of fiqh was older in age, and he himself had position of excellence and eminence due to his knowledge, however he was humble in regard to his knowledge and subservient and modest in regard to knowledge.

This is the position of the righteous devout and devoted scholars, they were humble and not arrogant and and disdainful of others. We ask Allaah, the Great, the Lord of the Noble Throne to place within us this characteristic seeking purely His Face alone, and make this humbleness the cause for achieving His pleasure, and He is the Great.

(95) The Eminent Guiding Scholar Muhammad Ibn Saaleh al-'Utheimeen, may Allaah have mercy upon him, from his explanation of the book 'Jewels for the Student of Knowledge': page 187-189

### *These are from the Distinguishing Signs of Beneficial Knowledge.*

Firstly, that is is acted upon. This is after the foundation of faith in Allaah, that you truly believe what you learned and then act upon it, as it is not possible to act upon good except upon having faith in Allaah. If an individual is not granted success in that, such that he learns certain matters however he is not able to act upon and realize them, then his knowledge is not beneficial. However it should be asked- is that knowledge harmful to him, or is it neither beneficial nor harmful? In reality it is indeed harmful to the one who does not act upon it. Because the Prophet, may Allaah's praise and salutations be upon him, said: *{The Qur'aan is a proof for you or against you.}*- (Saheeh Muslim: 223) He did not say neither for you and nor against you, therefore knowledge stands as either beneficial or harmful.

Secondly, from its signs is the aversion for commendation, praise, and pride and haughtiness over the people. This something which some of the people have indeed been tested with. As someone may have a very good opinion of himself and view that what he has stated is correct, and as for others if they differ with him then they must be wrong or something close to this. Likewise, having a love of being praised. You will find him asking or inquiring, what is said about him when he is discussed among them. If it is said: *"They have praised you."* He swells with pride, to such an extent and degree that his skin can hardly contain his enlarged body! Similarly pride and haughtiness over the people, as some of the people, and we seek refuge in Allaah from this, if Allaah gives him knowledge he becomes prideful. Just as the person who is financially wealthy may become arrogant. Due to this the Prophet, may Allaah's praise and salutations be upon him, stated that the arrogant beggar is from those individuals whom Allaah, the Most Glorified and the Most Exalted, will not speak to them, not look towards them, nor purify them on the Day of Reckoning, and they have a tremendous punishment. As they did not even posses the wealth that would have caused such arrogance.

So it is not fitting that that the scholar be like the wealthy man, such that when he is increased in knowledge he is increased in arrogance. Rather what is fitting is in fact the opposite, when he increases in knowledge he increases in humility and humbleness. Because from the forms of knowledge which are to be studied is the character of the Prophet, may Allaah's praise and salutations be upon him, and his character in its entirety, reflects humbleness to the truth, and towards the creation. Regardless, in any case- if there is a conflict or contradiction between humbleness to the creation and humility in face of the truth which one of them should take precedence?

Thirdly, an increase in your humility when you have increased in knowledge. And this is in reality a victory in regard to another issue, meaning that of arrogance in regard to the people. It is proper that when you increase in knowledge you likewise increase in humility.

Fourthly, distancing yourself from desiring leadership, prominence, and worldly pleasures. This one also can be seen as an aspect of the dislike of commendation and praise, meaning that you do not strive to be in a position of leadership because of your knowledge, nor do you attempt to use your knowledge as a vehicle for acquiring worldly things. As this means that you have in fact made the means your goal and the stated goal now only a means. However if you were to debate with individual in an effort to support and affirm the truth, it is fitting to consider yourself as above him or below him in understanding? Above him, because if you felt or considered yourself below him you would not be able to effectively debate and discuss with him, but if you considered yourself to be above him solely due to the truth that you possess, then you in this situation are able to prepare to debate with him.

Fifthly, to abandon being a claimant to great knowledge, the meaning of this, do not claim to possess knowledge, do not say [I am a scholar] or [I am someone well known, a person of prominence and position when I put on my turban, which shows who I am, you will indeed know me!] As the one who is like this, when he is in a sitting in a gathering he always wishes to head or direct that gathering, and if anyone else present desires to speak, he might say: [Be quiet, as I am more knowledgeable than you.].

Sixth, having the low opinion of oneself, and a good suspicion of the people, and yearning for that to be a reality for them. By this meaning, that he has a low opinion of himself because perhaps at times, he deceives himself or allows himself to be lead towards an evil matter, therefore he does not have a excellent opinion or perception of himself, and when he starts to have aspirations about his status he reminds and rebukes himself. As for the statement: "he has a good suspicion about the people" then this requires further clarification. The principle or rule is having a good suspicion about people, and when there is a viable interpretation or construction towards good that can be taken with the speech of others -then give it this meaning, without having the bad suspicion. However if you know that an individual from the people is generally held to actually deserve having the bad suspicion, then in this case there is no problem with having a bad suspicion of them in order to protect yourself from him. As if you were to hold the good suspicion in this situation it may cause you to trustingly and openly tell him everything that you held, while in reality he is not as you thought him to be.

# ENEFICIAL GUIDANCE FOR FEMALE STUDENTS OF SHAREE'AH KNOWLEDGE

*"The Muslim woman's position among the Muslims cannot be assessed with sufficient value, as she is more precious than everything found upon the face of the earth from material things. And how could this not be, when she brings our men into maturity and raises generations? From her hand comes forth the guiding sincere scholars who fear Allaah and who are the truthful strivers in Allaah's path, as well as the best of men, distinguished young men, and wholesome young women.*

*So if the Muslims sacrifice or suffer in relation to the Muslim woman, our institutions are corrupted at their very foundations, our pillars fall from their places, and in this lies a tremendous danger."*

(The noble scholar Abee Naasir Muhammad Ibn 'Abdullah al-Imaam, may Allaah preserve him, in the introduction of his book '*The Immense Plot Again the Muslim Woman*')

**(96)** The Eminent Guiding Scholar Muqbil Ibn Haadee al-Waadi'ee, may Allaah have mercy upon him, From 'A Defending Mission from Audio Lectures upon the People of Ignorance & Sophistry': Vol. 2, Page 459

*Question: There are many hadeeth narrations which are addressed to "believers" or "Muslims" without using the phrase "woman" (or women). Does this indicate that the Muslim "woman" is not intended by these specific texts, as there are other verses of the Qur'aan and hadeeth narrations which do specifically mention them and are directed towards explaining the rulings for women and clarifying them?*

Answer: The fundamental rule is that the entire Sharee'ah generally applies to everyone, male and female, just as Allaah, the Most Glorified and the Most Exalted, states in His Noble Book, *Never will I allow to be lost the work of any of you, be he male or female. You are one of another*-(Surah Aal-'Imraan:195)  So the fundamental rule is that the entire Sharee'ah generally applies to everyone. There is nothing specified to just men except those matters which there is exact evidence for that specification, and there is nothing specified to just women except those matters which there is exact evidence for that specification.

Indeed, some women came and mentioned to the Messenger, may Allaah's praise and salutations be upon him, that indeed Muslim men engage in jihaad, and that Allaah, the Most Perfect and the Most High mentions men in verses but not women. Then this verse was revealed, *Never will I allow to be lost the work of any of you, be he male or female. You are one of another*-(Surah Aal-'Imraan:195)  And Allaah, the Most High, also revealed, *Indeed, the Muslim men and Muslim women, the believing men and believing women, the obedient men and obedient women, the truthful men and truthful women, the patient men and patient women, the humble men and humble women, the charitable men and charitable women, the fasting men and fasting women, the men who guard their private parts and the women who do so, and the men who remember Allah often and the women who do so...*-(Surah al-Ahzaab:35) until the end of the verse. So the fundamental rule is that the entire Sharee'ah applies generally to all except where it specifies one gender.

**(97)** The Eminent Guiding Scholar Muqbil Ibn Haadee al-Waadi'ee, may Allaah have mercy upon him, From 'A Defending Mission from Audio Lectures upon the People of Ignorance & Sophistry': Vol. 2, Page 476

*Question: What is the Sharee'ah knowledge that it is obligatory upon a woman to learn?*

Answer: First, it is obligatory upon her to learn her fundamental beliefs from the Book and the Sunnah, and then her ritual prayers, knowing how exactly the Messenger of Allaah, may Allaah's praise and salutation be upon him and his family, prayed. If she is someone who possesses wealth she must learn what Allaah has made obligatory upon her from the obligatory charity or zakaat. If she is engaged in buying and selling she must learn the related rulings of that commerce. Likewise, if she is involved in any work, then it is obligatory upon her to learn the ruling related to that field or endeavor. This is what is meant by the hadeeth of the Messenger

233

of Allaah, may Allaah's praise and salutation be upon him and his family, *{Seeking knowledge is an obligation upon every Muslim}* [80]. Similarly, if she is a female doctor it is obligatory upon her to study the issues such as: is it permissible for her to mix with men, is it permissible to use as medication that contains forbidden substances? It is required that you understand the rulings of those matters related to the work you are engaged in from the guidance of the Book and the Sunnah. What I mean by this is that she gain an understanding of the relevant evidences from the Book and the Sunnah, not that she restrict herself to only those medical practices based upon the knowledge from the Book and the Sunnah.

**(98) THE EMINENT GUIDING SCHOLAR MUQBIL IBN HAADEE AL-WAADI'EE, MAY ALLAAH HAVE MERCY UPON HIM, FROM 'A DEFENDING MISSION FROM AUDIO LECTURES UPON THE PEOPLE OF IGNORANCE & SOPHISTRY': VOL. I, PAGE 92**

*Question: Esteemed sheikh, if our brothers desire beneficial knowledge they go to you and learn. But we are young women who have great ignorance of the affairs in our religion. Specifically, we need to be taught the rules of how to recite the Qur'aan; however we do not have the ability to have a teacher for this among ourselves or to conduct these lessons ourselves. So how can we seek beneficial knowledge?*

Answer: Allaah says, ❧*And whosoever fears Allaah and keeps his duty to Him, He will make a way for him to get out from every difficulty. And He will provide him from sources he never could imagine.*❧-(Surah at-Talaq:2,3) and He says ❧*So be afraid of Allaah; and Allaah teaches you. And Allaah is All-Knower of everything.*❧-(Surah al-Baqarah:287) and He says ❧*Oh you who believe! If you obey and fear Allaah, He will grant you a criterion to judge between right and wrong*❧-(Surah al-Anfaal:29) and He says ❧*Oh you who believe, Fear Allaah, and believe in His Messenger...* ❧ up until his statement, ❧*...and He will give you a light by which you shall walk straight.*❧-(Surah al-Haadeed:28) Therefore if we fear Allaah, then Allaah the Most Glorified and the Most Exalted will facilitate for us those who will help teach us, and make easy for us acquiring that book which is beneficial and that audio tape which is beneficial. And I praise and thank Allaah the Most Glorified and the Most Exalted, that we have among us young women who have reached the level of having authored works, that by the blessing and grace of Allaah, are beneficial. And in the coming days if Allaah wills, such a book will be made available which is entitled: *((My Advice to Women)12-31)*. It is presently being printed. Another example is that recently a book has become available from a sister which is a work that I do not know any comparison to in its subject area, that being the area of studying the distinguished characteristics of the Prophet. As there is known to be a *((small treatise)09-09)* authored by Imaam at-Tirmidhee in this subject, and I was informed that Imaam al-Baghawee has authored a similar work, but I have not read it. But it is hoped that a copy will be sent to us from the land of the Two Holy Places. This new

[80] Narrated in Sunan Ibn Maajah: 224/ -on the authority of 'Anas Ibn Maalik. It was declared authentic by Sheikh al-Albaanee in Saheeh at-Targheeb at-Tarheeb: 72, Mishkaat al-Masaabeh: 218, Saheeh al-Jaame'a as-Sagheer: 3813, 3914, & Saheeh Sunan Ibn Maajah.

work is by the grace of Allaah, as another book like it has not been compiled with the objective of carefully selecting only authentic narrations. It will have a verse of the Qur'aan placed at the head of every chapter, and will be entitled either "al-Jama'ah as-Saheeh fe as-Shamail al-Muhammadeyyah" or *((as-Saheeh al-Musnad fe as-Shamail al-Muhammadeyyah)09-04)*. When the book is completed it will be decided which of the two titles is more worthy. So the object of bringing up this issue is to point out how many students of knowledge have benefited simply from reviewing beneficial books individually. Therefore, if you are able you should have a library which contains such as: *((al-Lu'Lu wa' al-Marjaan feemaa Itifaq Aleeheh as-Sheikhayn)07-01)* and the work *((Bulugh al-Maraam)02-34)* and *((Nayl al-Awtaar)03-08)*, *((Fath al-Majeed Sharh Kitaab at-Tawheed)06-12)*, and the book *((al-'Uluu)06-45)* by Hafidh ad-Dhahabee or its summarized version from Sheikh al-Albaanee. This is because books commonly make reference to other works as the source of something within them, so that a researcher will be using a book and it will say in it, "*narrated by at-Tabaranee*". Therefore he then needs to purchase the work *((Mu'jam al-Kabeer)02-21)*. Or it may say "*narrated by al-Humaidee in his work Musnad,*" so that he then needs to purchase the work Musnad al-Humaidee. Indeed, at one time I possessed a library which was held in two or three large bookcases, and I used to think that my library contained the books of the world, until I was writing the work *((at-Talea'ah Fee Rad 'Alaa Gulaat as-Shee'ah)11-12)*. As when I had composed part of it, it became clear that there were several reference works that I did not possess. Then I began compiling *((as-Saheeh al-Musnad Min Asbaab an-Nuzul)01-10)* and after working on this I again realized that my library required additional works as references. So a researcher will often come across references to other books such that he then says, "*I will go and buy this book.*" Therefore I advise you, female students, to strive in acquiring knowledge, in acquiring beneficial books, and in the memorization of knowledge. So how excellent is your position if you were to sit in your home and memorize the Book of Allaah, and then memorize *((al-Lu'Lu wa' al-Marjaan feemaa Itifaq Aleeheh as-Sheikhayn)07-01)*, and memorize *((Riyadh as-Saaliheen)02-11)*! We are in true need of righteous women to establish the call to Allaah among the ranks of the women. There has entered among us evil matters that spread by way of some women. Indeed the enemies of Islaam have mislead her, lied to her, and deluded her, such that perhaps she comes to hold Islaam is disdain or contempt as a religion, and so washes her hands of learning anything about Islaam. Therefore it is required that you obtain a strong understanding of this religion of Allaah, and then spread it to the farthest degree of your ability from beneficial books.

I also advise those young women who adhere to the religion to give significant attention to marrying a man who also strives to adhere to the religion, as establishing and building a family that strives to hold fast to Islaam is something to be sought after. And the Messenger, may Allaah's praise and salutation be upon him and his family, said, *{The individual is upon the religion of his associate or friend}* [81]. And he also said, *{The example of the righteous companion and the evil companion is like the example of sitting with the musk seller and the blacksmith. So from the musk seller, either he will give you some as a gift, or you would buy some musk or at the least enjoy from him a good pleasing smell. But as for sitting with the blacksmith either your clothes with be burned, or at the least you will experience a bad nasty smell.}* [82]. Found in both of two most authentic hadeeth collections, Saheeh al-Bukhaaree and Saheeh Muslim, as narrated by Abu Musaa. But do not be fooled, as the saying goes about meat, "Not everything that is white is truly a piece of delicious fat." So do not suppose that every individual who allows his beard to grow, and wears an imaamah as a turban, and makes his thawb so that it only comes to the middle of his shin is someone who is now a Sunni Muslim. As perhaps he may be from the astray sect of the Mukaramah who are worse in their evil than the Christians and the Jews. Perhaps he may be someone who only resembles the people of the Sunnah in the affairs of practicing his religion and other matters. As such it is required that a woman know the condition of a man before she is married to him. But as for the case where she would learn well and then become someone who is a caller to Allaah and His religion, and then she is thrown into a situation by her greedy father, who "sells" her in marriage for a hundred thousand Yemenee Riyals, he sells her just like one sells a product! No, rather it is obligatory that one look for a righteous man who is suitable, and then in addition that he gives from his wealth. So if one is tested with the like of this circumstance, then it is better for her to temporarily put to the side the matter of marriage until Allaah makes it easy for her to marry a righteous man.

---

[81]  Narrated in Sunan Abu Daawud: 4833/ Jaame'a at-Tirmidhee: 2378/ & Musnad Imaam Ahmad: 7968, 8212/ -from the hadeeth of Abu Hurairah. It was declared authentic by Sheikh al-Albaanee in Silsilat al-Hadeeth as-Saheehah :927, Mishkaat al-Masaabeh: 5019, Saheeh al-Jaame'a as-Sagheer: 5858, his verification of al-'Emaan by Ibn Taymeeyah page 55, as well as in Saheeh Sunan Abu Dawud, & Saheeh Sunan at-Tirmidhee. Sheikh Muqbil declared it authentic in al-Jaame'a al-Saheeh: 4565, 4292.

[82]  Narrated in Saheeh al-Bukhaaree: 2101, 5534/ Saheeh Muslim: 2628/ -on the authority of Abu Moosa al-'Asha'ree. And it is in Sunan Abu Daawud: 4829/ -on the authority of 'Anas Ibn Maalik. It was declared authentic by Sheikh al-Albaanee in Silsilat al-Hadeeth as-Saheehah: 3214, Mishkaat al-Masaabeh: 5010, Saheeh at-Targheeb at-Tarheeb: 3064, 3065, Saheeh al-Jaame'a as-Sagheer: 2365, 5828, 5829, 5839, as well as in Saheeh Sunan Abu Dawud.

**(99)** The Eminent Guiding Scholar 'Abdul-'Azeez Ibn 'Abdullah Ibn Baaz, may Allaah have mercy upon him, From 'A Collection of Rulings and Various Statements': Vol. 4, Page 240

> *Question:  What do you say regarding women and calling to Allaah?*

Answer:    In relation to this she is similar to the man in that she should call to Allaah, enjoin everything good, and forbid wrongdoing. This is because the source texts of the Noble Qur'aan, and the pure Sunnah generally indicate this, and the statements of the people of knowledge directly state this. Therefore, she should call to Allaah, enjoin everything good, and forbid wrongdoing using the proper Islamic manners and etiquette, which are also desired from men. Along with this she should not allow herself to become discouraged from calling to Allaah due to hastiness or a lack of patience, nor by the contempt and disdain that some of the people have towards her or their speaking against her or mocking her. No. Rather, she should endure this and have patience, even if she see a kind of jeering and mockery from the people. In addition to this, it is upon her to consider and look at another matter, and this is that she should be a model of modesty and should shield herself from foreign men outside of her family, and distance herself from free mixing. Indeed, her endeavors of calling must be put forth along with diligent attention to preserving herself from every matter that they may pour blame upon her concerning. If she calls a man to what is correct then she calls him while she is properly wearing hijaab and without being secluded with any foreign man. When she calls and invites women she does so with wisdom and insight. She should be upright in her character and lifestyle so that they do not turn away from her, and do not say *"Why doesn't she begin with correcting herself!"* It is also upon her to stay away from wearing any type of clothes that which cause trials or problems among the people, and to be far away from every cause of strife and trials, from displaying aspects of her beauty or unwarranted softness in her speech, which are from those matters that she might be considered blameworthy for. Rather, she should be diligent in calling to Allaah in a manner that does not harm her practice of the religion nor harm her reputation.

**(100) The Eminent Guiding Scholar Muqbil Ibn Haadee al-Waadi'ee, may Allaah have mercy upon him, From 'A Defending Mission from Audio Lectures Upon the People of Ignorance & Sophistry': Vol. 2, Page 478**

*Question: What is the work of the female caller to Allaah, as you state that the Messenger of Allaah, may Allaah's praise and salutations be upon him and his family, said: "Narrate from me even if it is a single statement." And you mentions the statement, "The one who conceals knowledge, it will be a bridle upon him on the Day of Judgment." So is it upon a woman to teach every matter that you teach, or is it established that this is not permitted for her?*

Answer: Allaah the Most Glorified and the Most Exalted says, ❖*So keep your duty to Allaah and fear Him as much as you can.*❖-(Surah at-Taghaabun: 16). So I advise her to memorize *((Riyadh as-Saaliheen)02-11)* and from the book *((al-Lu'Lu wa' al-Marjaan feemaa Itifaq Aleeheh as-Sheikhayn)07-01)*, as well as from the different verses of the Qur'aan, and to engage in calling to Allaah among women even if that entails leaving some of her other work, especially if she sees that she has an effect upon the people. Indeed, the enemies of Islaam travel to the mountain tops and to wild and distant places just to call the Muslims towards apostasy from Islaam, or to Christianity, or towards some other way, path, or disbelieving ideology. Therefore it is suitable that we call and invite to Allaah, the Most Perfect and the Most High, and we strive hard and struggle in this. Still, it is not permissible that a woman stands up and gives a sermon among men, or is a teacher among men, as this is a societal trial, as has been previously mentioned. But she should teach her sisters, and young children whose ages reach seven or perhaps ten years old, who have not yet developed sexual desire towards women. But as for her standing among men and addressing them and inviting them then no, this is not something permissible. She can fulfill her obligation among and through women. As many Muslim women in different countries believe in supplicating to others than Allaah, thinking they may benefit them. This one supplicates to the one known as al-Khamsah. This one supplicates to 'Alee Ibn Abu Taalib. This one supplicates to al-Hasan. This one supplicates to al-Husayn. This one supplicates to this or that person from among Allaah's creation. In addition to this, there is the case where some Muslim women, if injustice is done to them, they look towards the sky and say, [I look towards Allaah and how spacious He is! ] Because she falsely believes that the sky and heavens are Allaah, the Most Perfect and the Most High. We generally are in great need, and you women are in great need, of striving hard and struggling in efforts of calling among women. In this there is tremendous good. And we seek Allaah's assistance in our affairs. Similar to this, is calling to Allaah by means of authoring and compiling works. It is proper that you delve into authoring works by taking from verses of the Qur'aan and authentic hadeeth narrations from the Prophet, may Allaah's praise and salutations be upon him and his family. As these other types of statements, meaning the speech and statement whose origin is from the people themselves, their intellectual meandering and philosophy, is not something which benefits and their popularity will not last.

Additionally, the woman must not call the people using a public microphone, and the voice of a woman may cause societal trials, as even now we hear on the radio the female announcers. May Allaah remove these female announcers from the Muslim radio programs. We fear for ourselves being put to trial, and so we disapprove of listening to these female announcers. So be those who simply invite women, as if you establish this obligation, then you all stand upon a tremendous good.

(101) The Eminent Guiding Scholar Muqbil Ibn Haadee al-Waadi'ee, may Allaah have mercy upon him, From 'A Defending Mission from Audio Lectures Upon the People of Ignorance & Sophistry': Vol. 2, Page 479

*Question: What is the Islamic ruling of a woman who fulfills all the conditions of seeking knowledge within her home, but despite this goes to the masjid to meet her sisters in faith or to convey to them knowledge that she has?*

Answer:  There is no harm in this, if she goes to the masjid and she believes that she is safe from falling into harm or trial, and safe from causing trials for men from outside of her family- then this is a good undertaking. Yet if the other women come to her in her own home then this is better and more of a safeguard for her. And in any case there is a tremendous obligation that is to be established by righteous women, and the responsibility upon them is a very significant burden indeed. Because it is in the area of the Muslim woman that tremendous corruption has entered into our Islamic societies, as the enemies of Islaam invite the Muslim woman towards the revealing and exposing of her beauty, as a tool being used to direct her and advance her towards other aims and objectives. Tremendous corruption has entered into our society in the area of women. The scholars of Somalia were not destroyed and burned except due to corruption that occurred related to women. Yet they have unnecessarily come out in Sana'a, in Riyadh, and in many other places- they have come out to participate in demonstrations which are something they have been pushed towards by those who are the enemies of Islaam. So I advise them strongly and severely, and we also ask Allaah to stop them from stop engaging in this practice, and that instead they engage in that which benefits Islaam and the Muslims.

NOTES

(102) THE EMINENT GUIDING SCHOLAR MUQBIL IBN HAADEE AL-WAADI'EE, MAY ALLAAH HAVE MERCY UPON HIM, FROM 'A DEFENDING MISSION FROM AUDIO LECTURES UPON THE PEOPLE OF IGNORANCE & SOPHISTRY': VOL. 2, PAGE 480

*Question: If a female seeker of knowledge studies in the masjid, she needs to review what she has learned while at the masjid when she returns home, and this takes considerable time. However, she understands that needed work in her home awaits her, as she needs to assist her mother in the home. The affairs of her home take all of her time and seeking knowledge needs full dedication from her. So if she is occupied in her home, she is not able to acquire a great deal of knowledge. How can we reconcile between her commitment to her home and her dedication to seeking knowledge?*

Answer:   If she is able to avoid some of the worldly activities that she has to do, then I advise her to do so. If it is not possible to do that, then she should organize her time and give a significant part of it towards seeking knowledge, and then a part toward her worldly activities. It is not possible for anyone to acquire knowledge unless worldly matters are placed secondary to knowledge. As for the case where knowledge is made secondary in importance to the worldly matters, then it will not be acquired. And we ask Allaah to assist us.

(103) THE EMINENT GUIDING SCHOLAR MUQBIL IBN HAADEE AL-WAADI'EE, MAY ALLAAH HAVE MERCY UPON HIM, FROM 'A DEFENDING MISSION FROM AUDIO LECTURES UPON THE PEOPLE OF IGNORANCE & SOPHISTRY': VOL. 2, PAGE 481

*Question: A woman studies in her home and prefers to remain in her home- not even going out to the masjid. Is she better, or the woman who seeks knowledge outside and visits different masjids?*

Answer:   The woman who stays within her home and learns within her home is better, because the Prophet, may Allaah's praise and salutation be upon him and his family, said: *{Do not prevent the maidservants of Allaah from attending the masjids, but their houses are better for them.}* [83].

---

[83] Narrated in Sunan Abu Daawud: 480/ & Musnad Imaam Ahmad: 5445, 5448/ -on the authority of 'Abdullah Ibn 'Umar. It was declared authentic by Sheikh al-Albaanee in Irwa' al-Ghaleel: 515, and Saheeh Sunan Abu Dawud.

**(104) THE EMINENT GUIDING SCHOLAR MUHAMMAD NAASIRUDDEEN AL-ALBAANEE, MAY ALLAAH HAVE MERCY UPON HIM, FROM THE TAPE SERIES 'GATHERINGS OF GUIDANCE & LIGHT,' TAPE NUMBER 19)**

*Question: Our sheikh, we have heard that there are, among those women who are present in some of the universities, schools, colleges, or who attend lectures- meaning those who are giving importance to such lectures, lessons or even those attending telephone lectures specifically held in the morning- we have heard that the husbands of these women are not at all pleased or satisfied with them because they are acting similar to men in these undertakings. We need a clarification from you regarding the subject of this question.*

Answer: The source of this particular issue is the deficiency in their proper Islamic education and upbringing, and from the reasons for this deficiency in education is the present state of degeneration of society, and the corruption of the methodology upon which they have based the educational system in which both men and women, or young men and young women, are being educated. This is something clear, because in regard to most of the female students present in the schools, I am almost positive that they have never heard a word similar to the statement of the Messenger of Allaah, may Allaah's praise and salutations be upon him, *{Allaah curses those women who act like men.}* [84]. Just as is found in another narration on the authority of 'Abdullah Ibn 'Abbaas, may Allaah be pleased with him, *{The Messenger of Allaah cursed those men who imitated women, and those women who imitated men.}* [85]. So it is my belief that when young female students graduate from secondary school, or even from the level above this, they have never ever heard any statement similar or reflecting this narration or the meaning of the narration that I first mentioned. Indeed even if at some time some brief mention of these two narrations had reached their ears; then it inevitably ended up like that which simply enters one ear and exits out of the other. The curriculums under which they study, or upon which the lessons they study are based upon, do not allow the teachers, even if it is restricted to the teacher designated to teach religious courses, to fully explain subjects such as this.

Yet it is a matter well-known in the Sharee'ah of Islaam, as well as among the people of knowledge, that the basic principle regarding the sphere of activity of men is that they generally are those who regularly go out of their homes to work for the benefit of their families, while the opposite side of this is that the basic principle regarding the sphere of activity of women is that they remain generally within the home, and that they do not go out regularly. This is the implementation of the statement from our Lord, the Blessed and the Most High, ❝ *And stay in your houses, and do not display yourselves like that of the times of ignorance*❞-(Surah al-Ahzaab:33). But when the woman becomes like a man, leaving in the morning and only returning to the home in the evening, then in this she has become someone

---

[84] Narrated in Sunan Abu Daawud: 3576/ -on the authority of 'Aishah. It was declared authentic by Sheikh al-Albaanee in and Saheeh Sunan Abu Dawud.

[85] Narrated in Saheeh al-Bukhaaree: 5880, Sunan Abu Daawud: 3574/ Sunan Ibn Maajah: 1894/ & Musnad Imaam Ahmad: 2901, 2150, 2983/-on the authority of 'Abdullah Ibn 'Umar. It was declared authentic by Sheikh al-Albaanee in Irwa' al-Ghaleel: 515/ Mishkaat al-Masaabeeh: 1062/ Saheeh at-Targheeb at-Tarheeb:363, Saheeh al-Jaame'a as-Sagheer: 7458, and in other of his verifications. Sheikh Muqbil declared it authentic in al-Jaame'a al-Saheeh: 226, 1437, 4058, 4500.

who imitates men, regardless of whether she understands this or not, regardless of whether she realizes this or not.

Due to this, we no longer see in these later times the young unmarried lady who is ashamed to openly look at a man. In fact, such a young lady, due to the strength and height of her modesty, would generally turn her sight downward in order to only see her footsteps when she walks. We no longer see examples of such a young lady, like this example which was well known even in the times before Islaam, before even mentioning the period in which the light of Islam appeared. This is something established, as is shown in what we find authentically reported as being from among the distinguishing characteristics of the Prophet, may Allaah's praise and salutations be upon him, that he was more modest that virgin woman in her private room. The example of this virginal young woman whom the best of Creation was compared to- as being similar to her in the nature of his modesty- we do not see or hear about one such as her in this latter age. This is because we find that in general, many women have come to imitate and emulate men.

Undoubtedly there are multiple reasons for this. From the most significant of these and from its fundamental causes, is the domination of the disbelieving systems of government and rule upon many of the Muslim countries and lands, such that the disbelievers have spread within these lands their own disbelieving customs, traditions, inclinations, and ways of character which are in fact deviated from the natural human inclination. An entire generation of people has taken on and inherited them, and they have been embraced by those "guided and enlightened" as they claim, male and female teachers. Such teachers have circulated among the generation of young men and women the concept which is known as "equality between men and women." Therefore, this is one of the reasons that has caused many women to have little modesty, and which has caused many from among them to act in a way similar to men in many of their manners.

There is no doubt that this change in a woman, in which she takes on male characteristics, makes her someone who oversteps what is proper in her personal relations with her husband. She raises her voice to him, and she may humiliate him in front of some of his close family or some of her close relations through her defiance, showing she is "dominant" in her relations with her husband. But where is the legitimacy of this example of this type of woman when compared to that which is found in the advice of the Messenger of Allaah, may Allaah's praise and salutations be upon him and his family, given to men regarding their women?! Rather he, Allaah's praise and salutations be upon him, has shown the falseness and deficiency of this way or example, putting forward a complete and total negation of this deficient upbringing and education of women that we see in the present age, in his statement where he, Allaah's praise and salutations be upon him, says, *{Treat women well as they are like prisoners in your hands.}* [86].

---

[86] Narrated in Jaame'a at-Tirmidhee: 1119, 3095/-on the authority of 'Amr Ibn Ahwaas. It was declared authentic by Sheikh al-Albaanee in Saheeh at-Targheeb at-Tarheeb:1930, Saheeh al-Jaame'a as-Sagheer, and other verifications.

There is an affirmation of this in that when the Prophet, may Allaah's praise and salutations be upon him and his family, ordered men to treat women in a good manner as found in this narration, he explained and justified this by his statement, *{As certainly, they are like prisoners in your hands.}* Meaning that they are in a state similar to prisoners. A prisoner is not able to truly act rebelliously against the one who has a position of authority over them. Likewise is the situation and position of the Muslim woman who has been raised and embraced the correct Islamic character; she stands in relation to her husband in a condition similar to a submissive prisoner.

Because of this general state and position of women concerning their husbands, the Prophet was afraid that men might take advantage of these attractive and suitable characteristics of women, and act in an arrogant manner with them, act as like a tyrant when dealing with them, or fall into treating them unjustly. Therefore, due to this, they were commanded to treat women in a good manner. So he explained with this explanation, meaning the specific statement of the Prophet, Allaah's praise and salutations be upon him, *{Treat women well as they are like prisoners in your hands.}*[87]. Yet the women of today do not desire for that way found in this advice with which the Messenger advised men to treat women. Rather, they have overthrown and turned the matter upside down! They have made the situation such that woman must remember to treat the men nicely, because they have now become independent from them and autonomous in their endeavors and affairs, as well as their way of conduct. Indeed, we very often hear from some of today's women, [There is no true difference between me and my husband. He is my husband, and I am his wife. He is a partner and I am a partner with him in this life...]

But indeed, it is upon this Muslim woman who truly and properly adheres to her religion, whenever she is put to trial and tested by any matter relating to her role and social interaction with her present day society, to strive to save and protect herself from being affected and harmed by those ways of deviation and separation from the truth that many women have fallen into. This has all occurred because of the causes which we have mentioned from corrupt and deficient educating and upbringing, as well as the corruption of society. And this is only a reminder, as indeed the reminder benefits the believers. Assalaamu 'aleikum.

---

[87] Narrated in Jaame'a at-Tirmidhee: 1119, 3095/-on the authority of 'Amr Ibn Ahwaas. It was declared authentic by Sheikh al-Albaanee in Saheeh at-Targheeb at-Tarheeb:1930, Saheeh al-Jaame'a as-Sagheer, and other verifications

(105) The Eminent Guiding Scholar 'Abdul-'Azeez Ibn 'Abdullah Ibn Baaz, may Allaah have mercy upon him, From 'Collection of Rulings and Various Statements': Vol.9, Page 337 & Vol. 8, Page 317)

*Question: I have left my studies and my mother is not pleased with this. Am I a wrongdoer due to this?*

Answer: Studying and learning contain tremendous good and significant benefits, and it is obligatory upon each Muslim man and woman to learn and understand the religion. It is required upon every Muslim to understand his religion and learn those matters in which ignorance cannot be accepted. From the causes of contentment and happiness is gaining an understanding of the religion. The Prophet, may Allaah praise and salutations be upon said, *{Whoever Allaah intends good for He grants him understanding in the religion.}* [88]. As such, from the signs of being granted contentment and satisfaction is having an understanding of Allaah's religion, and gaining understanding of the Sharee'ah such that a Muslim then understands what is obligatory upon him, and what is forbidden for him, and such that he worships Allaah upon understanding and insight. This is found in the statement of the Prophet, may Allaah praise and salutations be upon him, *{Whoever goes forth upon the path of seeking knowledge, Allaah makes easy for him the path to Jannah.}* [89]

Therefore it is obligatory upon you that you learn and gain understanding of the religion if that is facilitated for you in a good trustworthy Islamic school. Especially if your mother is encouraging and pushing you towards this, then that is something which just makes it more obligatory that you be concerned and diligent in gaining an understanding of your religion. She only wants good for you, and your true benefit in this world as well as the next. So it is not proper that you disobey her in this request except if the specific school is one that mixes the students of both genders together or which has some other characteristics which may harm your religion. In that case there is no harm in your leaving studying in that place even if your mother is not pleased with this, because the Messenger of Allaah, may Allaah's praise and salutations be upon him, said, *{Verily, obedience is only in that which is good and permissible.}* [90]. And he said *{There is no obedience to the creation in that which is disobedience to the Creator}* [91].

---

[88] Narrated in Saheeh al-Bukhaaree: 71, 3116, 7312/ Saheeh Muslim: 1037/ Sunan Ibn Maajah: 221/ al-Muwatta Maalik: 1300, 1667/ Musnad Imaam Ahmad: 16395: 16404, and other narrations/ Musannaf Ibn Abee Shaybah: 31792/ & Sunan ad-Daaramee: 224, 226/- on the authority of Mu'aweeyah. And it is found in Jaame'a al-Tirmidhee: 2645/ & Musnad Imaam Ahmad: 2786/ & Sunan ad-Daaramee: 270, 2706/- on the authority of Ibn "Abbaas. And it is found in Sunan Ibn Maajah: 220/ Musannaf 'Abdul-Razzaaq: 30851/- on the authority of Abu Hurairah. It was declared authentic by Sheikh al-Albaanee in Saheeh al-Aadab al-Mufrad: 517, Silsilat al-Hadeeth as-Saheehah: 1194, 1195, 1196, Saheeh at-Targheeb at-Tarheeb: 67, as well as in other of his books. Sheikh Muqbil declared it authentic in al-Jaame'a al-Saheeh: 9, 3123, 4650.

[89] Narrated in Saheeh Muslim: 2699/ Sunan at-Tirmidhee: 2945/ Sunan Ibn Maajah: 225 / & Musnad Ahmad: 7379- from the hadeeth of Abu Hurairah. Declared authentic by Sheikh al-Albaanee in Saheeh at-Targheeb wa al-Tarheeb: 69, 89, as well as in other of his books.

[90] Narrated in Saheeh al-Bukhaaree: 7145, 7257/ Saheeh Muslim: 1840/ Sunan Abu Dawud: 2625/Sunan an-Nasaa'ee: 4210/ Musnad Imaam Ahmad: 623, 723, 1021/ -on the authority of 'Alee Ibn Abee Taalib. It was declared authentic by Sheikh al-Albaanee in Silsilat al-Hadeeth as-Saheehah: 181, Mishkaat al-Masaabeeh: 3665, & Saheeh al-Jaame'a as-Sagheer: 7319, 7519, and in his verification of al-'Emaan by Ibn Taymeeyah.

[91] Narrated in Musnad Imaam Ahmad: 1098/ -on the authority of 'Alee Ibn Abee Taalib. It was declared authentic by Sheikh al-Albaanee in Silsilat al-Hadeeth as-Saheehah: 179, Mishkaat al-Masaabeh: 3696, & Saheeh al-Jaame'a as-Sagheer: 7520.

(106) The Eminent Guiding Scholar Muhammad Naasiruddeen al-Albaanee, may Allaah have mercy upon him, From the magazine 'al-Isaalah', Dhul-Qaedah 1419 Hijri Issue 19, Page 74

*Question: What is the ideal example of calling to Allaah by women?*

Answer:    I say to the women: Stay attached to their homes, as the matter of calling to Allaah (da'wah) is not for them. And I disapprove of the usage of the term "da'wah" as found between the young men, meaning by this that they are the "people of da'wah," such that "da'wah" has become something fashionable or trendy in the present time, with every individual who learns a small amount of knowledge then becoming a "caller." In addition, this phenomenon has not stopped at the young men, but has spread to the young women, until it has even reached those women who are responsible for their households. These women then begin to turn away from much of the commitment of time needed for the responsibilities of their homes, their husbands, and their children. They turn away from these obligations for that which is not obligatory upon them, in order that they can give "da'wah".

The basic rule for the woman is that she strives within her home, and it is not legislated for her to leave except for an urgent need, due to the statement of the Prophet, may Allaah's praise and salutation be upon him, *{...their homes are better for them}* [92] for prayer rather than prayer in the masjid. We see at the present time the widespread coming out of women. They frequently go out to the masjid for general congregational prayer rather than simply going to Friday congregational prayer, while their remaining in their houses is actually better for them. The exception is the case when there is a masjid where the one who leads the prayer is also a scholar who teaches those who attend matters from the knowledge of the religion. In this case, when a woman frequently goes out to pray in the masjid so as to listen to matters of knowledge, there is nothing to prevent this. But as for a woman busying herself with what is called "da'wah"; it is better that she remain in her home and read from the books which are provided for her by her husband, brother, or some of her close family members.

Additionally, there is nothing to stop her from specifying a day to invite other women to come and visit her, or that she go out to visit them at one of their homes. And the second case is better than a group of women leaving their home, meaning that she herself comes out individually to them is better than that they all leave their homes to visit her. But as for her rushing about and traveling, and possibly even traveling without a guardian, and this being considered permitted for her- that she travel around for "da'wah"- then this is from the innovations of the present age which is actually not only found among women. Indeed, it is also seen among young men who are captivated with speaking about "da'wah," after they have acquired only the barest illusion of knowledge.

---

[92]  Narrated in Sunan Abu Daawud: 480/ & Musnad Imaam Ahmad: 5445, 5448/ -on the authority of 'Abdullah Ibn 'Umar. It was declared authentic by Sheikh al-Albaanee in Irwa' al-Ghaleel: 515, and Saheeh Sunan Abu Dawud.

(107) The Eminent Guiding Scholar Muqbil Ibn Haadee al-Waadi'ee, may Allaah have mercy upon him, From 'A Defending Mission from Audio Lectures Upon the People of Ignorance & Sophistry': Vol. 2, Page 486

*Question: I am a female student of knowledge. I have been proposed to by close to 25 young men and I refused all of them during the past eight years. This was because I did not feel comfortable with any decision after making salat al-istikharah to Allaah the Most Glorified and the Most Exalted. However, my family has blamed me frequently regarding the failure to marry by saying, "What is important is any man who is acceptable." But I have promised myself that I would only marry a brother who adheres to the Sunnah, and strives in the way of Allaah with his wealth, words and his self. So is this permissible?*

Answer: This is permissible, if Allaah so wills, as the righteous companion assists you in doing good, as has been previously mentioned. A woman might be righteous and then marry a man who is a wrongdoer. In a very short time he will distract, distance, and busy her away from that previous good she was established upon. Rather, what I advise is choosing for marriage a righteous man, even if it requires spending of her own wealth for this, if she possesses it, or providing their housing even she didn't have wealth. So in light of this, she shouldn't intentionally choose a life of remaining unmarried, as, all praise is due to Allaah, the righteous people are many in Algeria and in other lands. Indeed there are those from among righteous people who are wishing and looking for righteous women. How excellent it would be if you were to marry a righteous man and establish a righteous Muslim family, establishing the call of inviting to the Book of Allaah and the Sunnah of the Messenger of Allaah, may Allaah's praise and salutations be upon him and his household. Therefore, all praise is due to Allaah, the righteous men are numerous.

I know of some brothers from Algeria, and all praise is due to Allaah, they are righteous men. Even from the students of knowledge who are here with us there are righteous men who are upright on Allaah's path from our students from Algeria, may Allaah preserve them, and they wish for and are seeking righteous women to marry, even to the degree that they might remain here in Yemen after marriage with her. Yet if Allaah so wills, they will travel to call to Allaah to places such as America and many other lands.

Regarding choosing a righteous woman for marriage, it is narrated in the two 'Saheeh' Collections of Imaam al-Bukhaaree and Imaam Muslim and the authority of 'Aishah, may Allaah be pleased with her, that the Prophet, may Allaah's praise and salutations be upon him and his household, said: {*A woman is married for four things: her wealth, her family status, her beauty and her religion. So you should marry the religious woman otherwise you will be from the losers.*}-(Saheeh al-Bukhaaree: 5090, Saheeh Muslim: 1466). So a man should choose a righteous woman and a woman should chose a righteous man. Otherwise, if this is not the case then the situation will be as found in the statement of the Messenger of Allaah, may Allaah's praise and salutations be upon him and his household,

{A person is upon the religion of his close associate so look closely at who you take as a close friend.} [93]. We do not make it a condition that the person be free of any mistakes or does not commit any sins, as perhaps such a person does not exist. But indeed how excellent is the statement of the one who said,

> As for the one who possesses that overall character and nature that you are pleased with,
>> Then content yourself with this noble one, and look beyond his minor shortcomings.

And another person said:

> I am not one who runs after the faults of my brother or gathers his faults,
>> As at the times which he is untidy and disordered, what man could be considered well mannered and cultured!

So it is required to overlook some matters. I am not saying that a woman should marry a man who is a wrongdoer, or marry the one whose heart is committed to seeking worldly wealth; but if a student of knowledge comes who loves knowledge then this is the one to choose. He might be one who has memorized the Qur'aan, or a caller, or one who writes that which invites to Allaah and His religion, and through such a righteous woman is blessed in this to be able to call to Allaah, the Most Perfect and the Most High. Such a situation should be considered the Paradise of this world. And we seek Allaah's assistance in our affairs.

(108) MUQBIL IBN HAADEE AL-WAADI'EE, MAY ALLAAH HAVE MERCY UPON HIM, FROM 'A DEFENDING MISSION FROM AUDIO LECTURES UPON THE PEOPLE OF IGNORANCE & SOPHISTRY': VOL. 2, PAGE 479

*Question: What is the Islamic ruling regarding organizing our Islamic efforts in regard to women, with those efforts being in the masjid? That being, for example, a sister who takes the responsibility of straightening the rows of the women, and a sister who takes the responsibility of making sure the menstruating women are separated in a different area, and a sister who takes the responsibility for the management of a library by using cards for its administration. These young women would remain later after the other women have left in order to avoid any disorganization.*

Answer: This is something good and there is no harm in it, insh'Allaah, as Islaam encourages organization which is not related to any innovation in the religion. Such library cards should be made without the images of living things, as the Messenger of Allaah may Allaah's praise and salutation be upon him and his family, said, {The angels do not enter a house within which there are images or a dog.}-(Saheeh al-Bukhaaree: 3225, 3322, 4002/ Saheeh Muslim: 2106)

---

[93] Narrated in Sunan Abu Dawud: 4833/ Jaame'a at-Tirmidhee: 2378/ Musnad Imaam Ahmad: 7978, 8212/ -on the authority of Abu Hurairah. It was declared authentic by Sheikh al-Albaanee in Silsilat al-Hadeeth as-Saheehah: 927, Mishkaat al-Masaabeh: 5019, & Saheeh al-Jaame'a as-Sagheer: 5858, and in his verification of al-'Emaan by Ibn Taymeeyah. Sheikh Muqbil declared it authentic in al-Jaame'a al-Saheeh: 4265, 4292.

# GUIDANCE FROM THE SCHOLARS REGARDING IMPORTANT BOOKS TO ACQUIRE FOR SEEKING KNOWLEDGE

*"Isn't the one who collects books of knowledge in some ways like the one who gathers silver and gold? Isn't the one with an ardent desire for them like the one who craves these other two? Isn't the one with a passion to store and preserve them like the one who treasures the other two? Similarly, just as there is no benefit in wealth that is not spent, likewise there is no benefit in knowledge except for the one who puts it into practice and fulfills its requirements.*

*So every individual must examine himself, and be concerned for his remaining time, as the time till his burial is short, his leaving of this world is close at hand. The path is treacherous and being mislead from it occurs frequently, and the danger is significant. The one who takes account is himself is the one who is wise…"*

(Imaam Khateeb al-Baghdadee, may Allaah Have mercy upon him, in his introduction to '*Adherence to Knowledge and Deeds*')

**(109) The Eminent Guiding Scholar Muhammad Ibn Saaleh al-'Utheimeen, may Allaah have mercy upon him, From 'Islamic Revival: Guidelines & Guidance', Page 125**

*Question: Is it permissible to learn the religion solely from books without the scholars, specifically in the situation where it is difficult to learn from the scholars because of their scarcity? In addition, what is your view regarding the one who says, "The one whose teacher is his book his errors are greater than that which he is correct in?"*

Answer: There is no doubt that knowledge is acquired by seeking it from the scholars as well as from seeking it from books. The book of the scholar is like the scholar himself, as he conveys knowledge to you by means of his book. So if it is difficult for you to acquire knowledge from the people of knowledge directly, then you should acquire it from books.

However, acquiring knowledge by way of the scholars is better than acquiring it by means of books. The one who acquires by means of books goes through more difficulties and needs to put forth tremendous effort. In addition to that, some matters such as important Sharee'ah principles and guidelines which are well understood by the people of knowledge will not be made clear to him. Therefore it is necessary that you refer to the scholars themselves as much as possible.

As for the one who says: *"The one whose teacher is his book, the issues he is wrong in will outnumber the issues he is correct in."* Then this is not completely correct nor is it absolutely wrong. As for the person who takes knowledge from any book he comes across, then without doubt he will have many mistakes. But as for the one who relies upon books from individuals well known for their knowledge, trustworthiness, and reliability, he will not make numerous mistakes. Rather, he will be correct in the majority of what he states.

**(110) The Eminent Guiding Scholar Muqbil Ibn Haadee al-Waadi'ee, may Allaah have mercy upon him, From 'A Defending Mission from Audio Lectures Upon the People of Ignorance & Sophistry': Vol. 1, Page 63**

*Question: We see that some people do not give importance to seeking knowledge from the hands of the scholars and are satisfied with studying books in their homes. They argue that Sheikh al-Albaanee (may Allaah the Exalted preserve him) was able to reach the level of knowledge that he possesses solely by means of reading, not by means of taking from the scholars themselves. Is this correct and with what do you advise the one who says this?*

Answer: That which I advise him is that if he is able to, then he should attend the gatherings of the scholars, because at times sitting with a scholar can be equal in its benefit to reading for an entire month. Yet if it is not possible for one to sit with the scholars, then he should have a library for his study and should correspond with the people of knowledge, consulting and seeking clarifications from them and striving in a good way. But how would this be implemented? If he has a book and he is sure that it is from so-and-so who is trustworthy then there is no harm in reading it and benefiting from it. As for the different meaning of statements and expressions of the scholars then these will eventually become clear in the mind of the individual reading them. I still recall some of the statements of my Sheikh, Muhammad Ibn 'Abdul-Wahaab as-Somaalee, may Allaah the Exalted preserve him, from his lessons in the sanctuary of Masjid al-Haram in Mecca.

However, if there are no scholars available or he is not able to attend, then he should have a library, and rely upon Allaah, the Most Perfect and the Most High to successfully learn. But be warned with a serious warning of the slips, unintentionally misleading statements, and those statements that conflict with what is correct that come from the established, well-known scholars that he may read. As such it is upon him to submit and compare his own thinking and ideas to that to the thinking and ideas held by the early scholars of this Ummah. And I am not inviting one to simply blindly follow them, as blind following is generally impermissible in the religion. Rather, he must seek to be guided by their understanding. Then in proceeding in this way a library is something good and is a blessing from Allaah, the Most Perfect and the Most High, and it makes the use of books easier. Perhaps this present availability of books were never this easy for many of the early Muslim scholars. If one of us was charged with having to copy *((Fath al-Baaree)03-01)* by hand, as perhaps they did, he would not be able to do so!

**(III) The Eminent Guiding Scholar Muhammad Ibn Saaleh al-'Utheimeen, may Allaah have mercy upon him, From 'Kitaab al-'Ilm': Page 209**

### Benefits of Studying Books with a Guiding Scholar

From what is proper for the student of knowledge is the practice of taking knowledge from the scholars, because many benefits are achieved from this:

1. The shortening of the path to acquiring knowledge. This is the opposite of the one who delves into the depths of the books, investigating the statements of the scholars for the most suitable position, and the reasons for its suitability, as well as determining the weaker statements or positions and the reasons for their weakness. All of this is replaced with the assistance of the teacher, facilitating the path to understanding by explaining the different positions found between the people of knowledge in various issues, in which there are found two or three differing positions, and clarifying which of them is strongest and the evidence for that. This undoubtedly benefits the student of knowledge.

2. Facilitating quicker comprehension. If the student of knowledge reads a work of knowledge along with a scholar, he understands more rapidly than if he went and read from the books himself. When he reads individually from books, he will find difficult phrases and ambiguous matters which require that he consider carefully and review the expressions repeatedly, which takes both his time and effort. Additionally, he may misunderstand something he read by himself and then proceed to act upon that misunderstanding.

3. Lastly, the establishment and maintaining of the relationship between the student of knowledge and the scholar, over a person reading individually.

**(112) THE EMINENT GUIDING SCHOLAR SAALEH IBN FAUZAAN, MAY ALLAAH PRESERVE HIM, FROM 'AN EXPLANATION OF THE MISTAKES OF SOME WRITERS': PAGE 18**

### Acquiring Knowledge from the Scholars

It is an obligation upon the Muslims to acquire knowledge from the scholars, and act according to their instructions and guidance. However, we have seen in recent years, with great regret, many who, although they desire knowledge- specifically among the youth- have turned away from this correct way. They have turned away from taking knowledge from the trustworthy scholars, to taking knowledge from either ignorant individuals, those who do not comprehend the guidelines related to Sharee'ah rulings, or the conditions related to determining permissible and prohibited matters, or from those who are not well-known for being reliable or distinguished for their sound understanding and beliefs. There is no doubt that turning to these unsuitable people will not lead to any praiseworthy outcome or any good result. Some of our pious predecessors have said, "*This knowledge is the religion, so look carefully from whom you take your religion.*" [94]. And Ibn Mas'ood, may Allaah be pleased with him, said, "*The people will remain successful while they continue to take knowledge from their scholars, leaders, and elders. But if they turn to taking knowledge from the lesser and foolish ones among them, then they are destroyed.*"

Oh Muslim youth! Oh students of knowledge! Connect yourselves to your scholars! Attach yourselves to them, and take knowledge from them. Attach yourselves to the reliable scholars well-known for the correctness of their beliefs and the soundness of their methodology in order that you may take knowledge from them and establish your connection with your Prophet, may Allaah's praise and salutations be upon him, as your pious predecessors did. The Muslims have never ceased receiving this knowledge from their Prophet through their scholars, generation after every generation.

So those whom we have just referred to as mistaken are from this first category. Then there is another category from those who seek to learn by acquiring knowledge from books without attaching themselves to the scholars. They claim that they have no need of the scholars due to their having books. This is a very serious error which leads to significant danger for them. All books with the exception of the Book Of Allaah and those of the narrations of the Sunnah of the Messenger contain what is right as well as what is wrong; they all contain correct matters as well as mistakes. Indeed, some works actually contain fabrications and deceptions regarding Islaam, and so spread their misconceptions among the people. Along with this, the beginning learner cannot distinguish between the beneficial and the harmful in the content of a book. Moreover, it may be that the harmful matter is that which becomes fixed in his mind. So it is essential that he have a teacher who possesses insight to examine the books he studies, in order to indicate to him both their beneficial and harmful

[94] Narrated in the introduction of Saheeh Muslim: 26 / & Sunan ad-Daaramee: 419, 424/ -from Muhammad Ibn Sireen.

matters, to indicate to him what they have of mistakes and what is correct. For this reason those who sought knowledge in the past ages usually traveled to distant lands to acquire it from the scholars and take beneficial knowledge from them. They were not satisfied with simply reading from books. Such that Imaam Ahmad travelled to the Hijaaz or the western area of the Arabian peninsula, to Yemen, and to other lands. Imaam al-Bukhaaree made long journeys for narrations of hadeeth. Imaam Muhammad Ibn 'Abdul-Wahaab traveled from Najd in the central area of Arabia to the Hijaaz or the western area of Arabia, to al-Ahsaa within Arabia, and to Basra in Iraq in order to take from the scholars. We see example after example,and the narrations of this type are lengthy. So if books were sufficient, then they would simply obtain a copy of a work while remaining in their homelands and not burden themselves by traveling to distant lands, especially in an age when there were no automobiles or airplanes. In summary, certainly books are only tools. They do not make it possible to do without a teacher.

The following is a description of a third type of seeker of knowledge who has recently appeared in our time. That is the beginner who says, [You should not go back to the various books nor refer to the scholars. Rather read the Qur'aan and ahaadeeth and derive the rulings directly from these two texts directly!] They say this, yet most of them are not even able to correctly recite a verse of Qur'aan, not to mention their inability to understand their correct meaning! This type is even more dangerous than the one we described previous to him, because he does not understand the established principles of deriving rulings properly.

It is well-known that the source texts encompass texts that have a single clear meaning and those that carry more than one possible meaning, those which are basic in context and those which are detailed in context, that which is specific and that which is general, that which is unrestricted in meaning and that which is restricted. Similarly, in hadeeth narrations there is that which as of the highest rank of authenticity, that which has acceptable rank of authenticity, that which contains unacceptable weakness, and that which is clearly fabricated in its origin. In addition to this, there are various types of evidence other than these two fundamental sources. There is consensus of the Muslims, the use of correct analogy, and other types of secondary evidence whose status is differed upon by the scholars in the specific field of knowledge related to this.

These principles of properly deriving rulings are truly only understood by those scholars deeply rooted in knowledge, not by every scholar. So how could they be understood by these beginners who rush to the source texts and haphazardly derive rulings without true understanding?!? Indeed, it is an obligation to seize their hands in order to prevent them, in their proceeding in this way, from harming themselves or others. Additionally, they have no proof for putting forth this way as a methodology to be followed except under the general call to abandon blind following. However for those of this level, the general Muslims, it is an obligation to blindly follow the scholars. As the only one who is required to completely abandon blind following is the scholar who is proficient in deriving rulings and utilizing independent reasoning.

He alone is the one who has satisfied the requirement by fully understanding the concepts and matters which were explained previously. As for the one who has not reached that level, then it is obligatory that he blindly follow. Allaah the Exalted says, ❊*...so ask the people of the knowledge if you do not know.*❊-(Surah al-Anbiyyah:7) So fear Allaah, oh seekers of knowledge, and fear Allaah oh scholars of the Muslims. Take the hands of such individuals and guide them to the proper way, direct their faces towards the correct orientation. Favor them with your time and knowledge in order to remove from them their defects. Satisfy their thirst for understanding so that they become satisfied with the Muslim societies in which they live, and then through these people will come gradual rectification of their nations and lands. We ask Allaah to guide us to joining beneficial knowledge and righteous action. Praise and salutations be upon our Prophet, his family, and all of his Companions. Lastly, all praise is due to Allaah, Lord of all the World.

**(113) The Eminent Guiding Scholar Muhammad al-Ameen ash-Shanqeetee, may Allaah have mercy upon him, From 'Various Questions': Islamic Ruling no. 9519**

*Question: Is it from the correct methodology in seeking knowledge, for the student of knowledge to combine taking from his scholar with additional study and research, or rather to concentrate on becoming proficient on what is gained from studying with his scholar without combining with it additional research?*

Answer: In the name of Allaah. All praise is due to Allaah. Praise and salutations be upon the best of Allaah's creation, and upon his household, his Companions, and those who follow him. To proceed:

The fundamental or general way is to take knowledge by sitting and learning from a single scholar who is considered reliable in relation to his knowledge and his practice of the religion. As if the student were to proceed in a scattered manner, coming to take knowledge from many scholars at once, their different statements may confuse him, and they may differ in their perspectives, such that this results in his beginning efforts of seeking knowledge being weak. Perhaps he might suppose that a specific matter is correct, but since he doesn't scrutinize it closely he fails to reach what is in fact the correct stance, and so remains on what is mistaken. So it is proper to take knowledge from a single scholar initially, and then afterwards to increase his scope of study to other scholars. This is the guidance of the first generations, may Allaah have mercy upon them. For this reason the Companions, may Allaah be pleased with them, as well as the leading scholars of the Successors to the Companions, also stood upon this way in which each of the major Companions who spread knowledge had students who were known to stay with and study with him specifically. Ibn 'Abbaass had as his students Sa'eed ibn Jubayr, and also 'Ataa' Ibn Abee Rabaah, and other students. And Ibn 'Umar had Naafi who was his freed client who took knowledge from him, and his son Saalim Ibn 'Abdullah Ibn 'Umar, as well as others, may the mercy of Allaah be upon them. The leading scholars of Islaam generally took knowledge on the path of remaining with a single scholar.

Yet it is not at all intended by this is to confine the people to only being allowed to take from one scholar- not at all. Rather, what is intended is undertaking the gaining of knowledge by means of the correct path, such that one avoids taking conflicting positions and being someone unsteady who wavers in matters- specifically in matters of understanding of how to implement the source texts and ruling, because there are many different independently derived rulings and numerous derived principles which you may encounter. Building upon this point, we find that when the leading biographical scholars and people of knowledge compiled the biographies of those scholars specializing in fiqh, they would commonly say, *"He gained his understanding of fiqh from so and so sheikh."* Meaning that they gained their understanding of the fundamental principles of that specific science from a specific scholar. If he remained with him and he was a scholar possessing knowledge and capable of issuing rulings, then he is someone who it is suitable to follow according to the evidences, without exaggerating or being biased towards him to the degree that one would turn away from evidence despite its being clear for the sake of holding fast to the statement of his scholar. Indeed, he takes knowledge from the scholar, and whatever is not clear to him from the statements of other scholars or differing evidences he presents to his scholar and asks him to respond to these matters which are not clear to him as a student. The scholar will clarify for him that which is soundest and most correct in that issue according to the correct sources and references.

As for the one who takes his basic understanding of how to implement the guidance of the source texts by reading with a scholar, but after those lessons proceeds to take a lengthy scholastic work or a work that discusses many differences, then this is someone who will take a position from one perspective but will contradict the same position in other stances, statements, and independent rulings which he has adopted. So in reality he is someone week and feeble in his understanding and comprehension. For this reason one finds that many of the students of knowledge, except those who Allaah has mercy upon in this matter, are from those who proceed upon this incorrect way. Not even one from among them is firmly established on the fundamentals of knowledge, not in the area of ritual worship or in the area of the guidelines related to everyday affairs.

Such a student will in one instance read a chapter relating to ritual prayer in one work and will adopt the independently derived rulings of "Zayd." Thereafter he studies the subject of zakaat, or obligatory charity, and in this area he will adopt the rulings of "Amr." Then he will go on to the study of obligatory fasting and he will adopt the rulings of a third individual, and will do likewise in the subject of a Hajj, such that the understanding of the fundamentals of these matters that he holds are unsteady and inconsistent. When he came to the book of ritual prayer and perhaps determined that what was the soundest in a matter was the position of "Zayd", and his evidence in this was his understanding of the word 'siffah.' Thereafter as was mentioned, when he comes to the study of obligatory charity he rejects the position of so-and-so based upon the understanding given to the same word 'siffah.' So the situation is that in some cases he considers the understanding of the word 'siffah' a proof established in the correct position, yet in other cases he does not consider it a proof. And perhaps he would encounter a single heading which is narrated in different forms. This hadeeth has a foundation within the chapters of obligatory charity in the hadeeth collections as well as in the chapters of ritual prayer. As for that narration which is found in the chapter of obligatory charity, then a scholar determines that what is soundest is that this narration is accepted as that which is correct from the specific narrator who transmitted, whereas in the chapter of ritual prayer the same scholar determines that in this case what has been transmitted by this narrator is not the strongest narration to be accepted. So he accepts the statement of this one in the chapter of ritual prayer and from a different one in the chapter on obligatory charity and both of them contradict each other completely such there is no way to reconcile them.

For this reason we advise the students of knowledge to hold to the path of the first generations in this, by taking knowledge by way of proceeding gradually in steps. So one should read in the subject of fiqh and its various rulings by studying with a scholar, with the condition of adherence to the evidence. In that way if you meet Allaah and He asks you, *"Why did you believe this was the correct ruling?"* you may mention the evidence which is found in the Book of Allaah and the Sunnah. In this way once you complete your study of the correct understanding of the mentioned source text within the work completely, and then the complete study of the mentioned hadeeth in its different chapters, and finish the complete explanation of the work, you will have extensively studied evidences as well as various independently derived rulings, such that you may eventually reach the level of being able to put forth independently derived rulings yourself. But as for the beginning- if you submerge yourself is the different statements of the leading scholars and eminent people of knowledge who had themselves reached the high level of being able to independently derive rulings from the source texts; then undertaking this when beginning to seek knowledge only leads to completely failing to become well-grounded. And I recognize this among my associates and contemporaries. We find this occurring and we recognize this phenomenon.

The scholars used to warn us against this way, wherein the student of knowledge merely reads from books or initially learns from several different men of knowledge, without completing his studies with any single one of them, as in this case he sways and wavers unsteadily. By completing his studies it is meant that he took his initial scholar as the foundation from which he viewed the positions of others, regardless of whether he accepts those differing positions or rejects them. As opposed to this we find that the one who studies the different texts systematically upon their evidences, then his understanding develops firmly and systematically, and this is the way which the leading scholars of Islaam have followed. If you study the distinguishing aspects of fiqh and different areas of knowledge with diligence and according to their evidence with a well-grounded scholar who freely accepts the truths without bias, taking from one whose knowledge you have confidence in, then you are connecting your own chain of narration back to the Messenger of Allaah, may the praise and salutations of Allaah be upon him. And when you are in this state, having developed your understanding gradually and systematically than when a question reaches you regarding any matter, whether in relation to ritual worship or the guidelines for everyday affairs, then you can put forth your efforts in clarifying this issue within its area, recalling its ruling and determining that according to evidences. Thereafter you might proceed to a different issue in the area of everyday affairs and affirm its ruling according to its evidences and upon that foundation about which there is no disagreement and no contradictions, doing so with correct guidelines and clear steadfast principles. This is knowledge. If an individual develops his knowledge according to this path he himself benefits and can benefit others, and can continue to develop within his knowledge, and grow within his knowledge from a small stage to one of significance.

For that reason some of the leading scholars from the first three generations, may Allaah have mercy upon them, stated in explanation to the statement of Allaah, the Most High, *Be you Rabbaneeyoon (learned men of religion who practice what they know and also preach others), because you are teaching the Book, and you are studying it.*-(Surah Aal-'Imraan:78) "The *Rabbaneeyoon* are those who teach the lesser fundamental aspects of knowledge before the difficult complex ones." The realm of independently deriving rulings is for those who have reached a significant degree of knowledge and delving into comparing the evidences, and debating and discussing them is also for those who have reached a significant degree of knowledge. If you attend a sitting of knowledge in which there is differing and various statements, then take the cream, or the best, by adhering to the evidence that is put forward. If we mention differing statements regarding an issue, then the beginning student knowledge takes the "cream" of what was stated and a summary of what was correct while he is in that sitting of knowledge. If he is someone who does not have the ability to understand how to refute assertions and engage in knowledge-based dialogue, then Allaah may facilitate matters for him from His bountiful favors.

Indeed we sat for a significant time with this book, meaning this hadeeth collection of at-Tirmidhee. I recall that indeed we sat with my father, may Allaah have mercy on him, along with a group of students of knowledge. Yet we were from the youth, and he was in the prime of life, may Allaah have mercy on him. I was close to 13 years old, yet still he was a beginner in this study of this collection of Imaam at-Tirmidhee, may Allaah have mercy on him. I continued until I reached the age of fourteen; but in spite of that many statements were incomprehensible to me. So I took the cream, or the most important of whatever was said. And my father, may Allaah have mercy on him, would say just take the summary of what was mentioned, and take that statement which has evidence. Then after this I proceeded gradually in the different areas of knowledge but I did not seem to be gaining understanding in the areas of ritual worship or that of the guidelines for everyday affairs. As in the beginning of sitting in the gatherings of knowledge we would sit down and not understand a single thing. Thereafter we were patient, and Allaah facilitated this matter for us from His bountiful favor.

Perhaps only a month or two will pass by, after which Allaah will facilitate these matters for you. You'll see linguistic definitions that are very strange and difficult for you to comprehend, but eventually they become matters which you are familiar with. You will see many derived points, explained aspects of matters, and benefits, and if Allaah facilitates for you recalling them and memorization, little bit by little bit. Allaah will open up the doors of His favor for the one who is patient and continually perseveres. Knowledge is mercy, and the mercy of Allaah, the Most Glorified, and Most Exalted encompasses every matter and everything.

The people are of different levels in relation to the mercy of Allaah; from them are those who receive little, and from them are those who receive a significant portion. So don't become daunted and overwhelmed by the matter of gaining knowledge. If you sit in a gathering of knowledge and see that what is discussed is far above your level, then simply take that which will help you and that which you are able to summarize, or end your time in that sitting with the most important of what was mentioned in that lesson or its most important conclusions. All this while asking for an excuse with Allaah for not knowing this ruling according to its evidences. Thereafter Allaah will facilitate matters for you in the future. As Allaah has favor, and his favor is not difficult upon anyone; Allaah's favor is given to whomever He wishes.

Do not allow Shaytaan to deceivingly magnify and exaggerate by saying to you, [How are you going to sit with them and you don't understand a single thing?] What is it that you would say in response? What is it that will assist you in answering such words? It is but by Allaah's permission you will always find some fruit in your efforts, even if that merely be- and this in itself is not a small thing- that afterwards when you leave the gathering you know that Allaah will give you rewards simply for being present. And certainly even in this there is tremendous good for the Muslim! Indeed the love of Allaah becomes obligatory upon those people who love each other for His sake, who sit with each other for His sake, and who visit each other for His sake. It is narrated in an authentic hadeeth that Allaah, the Most High, said, *{My love is obliged for those who love each other for My sake, and those who sit with each other for My sake, and those who visit each other for My sake...}* [95]. As such, then the sitting in a gathering of knowledge- even if it is above your level- is still considered beneficial for the person as he was in the sitting of goodness which receives Allaah's mercy. And if you find difficulty in understanding what is taught, then through this Allaah increases your reward, and makes more significant your compensation with Him, and raises your level if you struggle until you gain understanding, and ask about that which you are ignorant of. As certainly the path of knowledge is to ask and inquire.

The one whom Allaah has blessed with an intelligent heart and a tongue which asks has successfully gained from the favors of Allaah that which is hoped for and desired. So it is upon the Muslim to strive and diligently struggle in order to firmly comprehend that knowledge presented in this way, taking an overall summary of

---

[95]  Narrated in Musnad Imaam Ahmad: 21525/ al-Muwatta Maalik: 1779/ -on the authority of Mu'adh Ibn Jabal. It was declared authentic by Sheikh al-Albaanee in Mishkaat al-Masaabeh: 5011, and as-Saheeh at-Targheeb wa at-Tarheeb: 2581 & 3018

what was put forward in that sitting of knowledge. And how excellent it is that if one does not have the ability to firmly comprehend and record and write down a summary of the lesson, then in every sitting he should at least note down five or six beneficial points, writing these down as the most important benefits of his lesson or that "cream" of that information which was reached him. Then after this Allaah will facilitate affairs for him. Perhaps he will write down knowledge about a specific issue and then still be able to remember it after some time.

I swear by Allaah Who there is None Worthy of Worship besides Him that you will be amazed, and not cease being amazed, by that which Allaah makes easy for you in your sittings with the people of knowledge. I swear by Allaah, it is not due to our strong intellects, nor to our ability, strength, or our ability to memorize, as we are nothing. Every matter of goodness is solely by the favor of Allaah, who has no partner or associate. I swear by Allaah that if you intended to take from the many oceans of knowledge you would not take from them a single matter if Allaah prevents you from obtaining it. As perhaps a very simple and clear issue will be presented to you and it will be incomprehensible for you such that you fail to understand even a single aspect of it. And perhaps a very complex and difficult issue will be presented to you which requires significant effort, work, struggling and examination to understand. Yet if your Lord makes matters easy for you from His abundant favor, then such difficult matters will stand before you, easily understood like the sun in the middle of the day.

Because firstly this matter returns back to being the result of the favor of Allaah, in the beginning and in the end. Secondly it returns back to sincerity of intention and Allaah guiding you to that. Thirdly it returns back to your position of submissiveness between the Hands of Allaah Who was the One who taught Aadam and Who granted Dawud and Sulaymaan understanding. He is the one who grants wisdom to whomever He wishes, and likewise this is the case with humility. Therefore one should in every situation give importance to learning, not to seeking to raise his position. The student of knowledge who has been given knowledge, should likewise always be tolerant and gentle  and be close to the people such that they would experience from him behavior as if he was someone who had not gained knowledge, due to his humility. And if it comes, look closely at the favor and blessing of Allaah upon you. You should understand that Allaah has given you something which He has not given to someone else, due to your tremendous awareness of the favor and blessing He has given you. But also when knowledge comes to you consider your position among the people and so be humble and submissive, someone tolerant and gentle.

As consider the Prophet Musaa the son of 'Imraan, upon him and upon our Prophet be the praise and salutations of Allaah be upon him, whom Allaah said to him directly, ❖*...And I bestowed upon you love from Me that you would be brought up under My Eye.*❖-(Surah Taha:39). What a tremendous position he was told he had! ❖*I bestowed upon you love from Me that you would be brought up under My Eye*❖ And Allaah spoke with him directly without any intermediary in a voice which he actually heard, may Allaah's praise and salutations be upon him. Yet despite all this, that he reached the level of prophethood which he reached, and that he reached the position of knowledge which he reached, yet what occurred when he was asked who was the most knowledgeable? He indicated towards himself, and Allaah admonished him from above the seven heavens and commanded him to go saying to him, {"At the junction of the two seas there is a slave of Ours who is more learned than you."}-(as narrated from the hadeeth of Ibn 'Abbaas found in Saheeh al-Bukhaaree hadeeth no. 4725). Yet when he came to know that there was someone more knowledgeable than himself, look at how he became humble despite the knowledge he possessed and the fact he was one who had been given revelation and this was a tremendous good which Allaah had revealed to him directly! But despite all that, may Allaah's praise and salutations be upon him, his position when in front of al-Khidhr was one who was humble and submissive to greater knowledge: {"May I follow you?..."} So what would one say when seeing the poor manner of association and companionship which is found in the example of some of the students of knowledge? Such a one comes to the scholar and says, [Sheikh, let us sit together so that we can discuss something.] Who are you, such that you are able to discuss matters with the scholars?!? Look at the example of this prophet from among the prophets of Allaah, and he said {"May I follow you?..."} He treated al-Khidhr as an eminent person of knowledge, as well as acting as someone below and lesser than him, saying, {"May I follow you?..."} Then after saying this he continued on, saying, {"...so that you teach me of that knowledge which you have been taught."} By Allaah, this is the point of the matter, gaining that insight which will enable an individual to know his own capability, and the tremendous boundaries of this Islamic knowledge.

A scholar who truly comprehends the position of knowledge, that comprehension makes him humble. And the individual who seeks knowledge, then whenever he is raised a level in knowledge, it increases him in humility. And I summarize the following, as some have mentioned an incredible story which some of the scholars narrate regarding Imaam ar-Raazee, may Allaah have mercy on him. It is stated that he was sitting with one of his students in front of him, and he was a leading scholar in many areas of knowledge. He was discussing a matter from among the matters of Arabic grammar and mentioned this specific matter in summary. But one of his students, despite the fact that Imaam ar-Raazee was distinguished by considerable knowledge of the Arabic language, said the following to him. "Oh Sheikh, regarding this issue what is correct is such and such." And he mentioned to him that which indicated this. So Imaam ar-Raazee said to him, "Have you written something regarding this issue?" He replied, "Yes, I have written a work regarding it."

He then went and retrieved what he had written. And when Imaam ar-Raazee, may Allaah have mercy upon him, paged through the work, despite the fact that he was the scholar and its author was one of his students, when he turned to the first pages and saw the clear knowledge and recognized the wisdom and the merit which had been given to the student, he got down from his chair, and swore that the student should go and sit in his place. He said to him, "By Allaah, you have excelled *tremendously.*" He then sat the student down at his place, and sat down in front of him, listening to the student read, a student who had previously been sitting down listening to him. The one who understands his own limited capability, then Allaah facilitates for him knowledge by means of his humbleness. Knowledge grants an individual understanding of his limited capability such that he becomes humble in front of the people of knowledge and takes knowledge by means of the path of being informed by his own perception of the favor of Allaah and that he only stands beneath the Mercy of Allaah. We ask Allaah, the Tremendous, Lord of the Mighty Throne that He teach us beneficial knowledge, and that He grant us hearts that fear Him. Indeed He is the One Who is in Control of that and Most Capable Regarding it.

(114) The Eminent Guiding Scholar 'Abdul-'Azeez Ibn 'Abdullah Ibn Baaz, may Allaah have mercy upon him, From 'A Collection of Rulings and Various Statements': Vol. 6, Page 64

*Question:     We find that some of the common people and he students of knowledge make statements regarding Sharee'ah issues, while not being from the people possessing knowledge of these matters. Then their misguided statements spread among the general people and circulate among them. We need from you, our esteemed scholar, a clarification regarding this issue, so by Allaah what is your view of this?*

Answer: It is obligatory that the Muslim be cautious in regard to the affairs of his religion and not take rulings from just any person, regardless of whether this is taken from a written source, from a media broadcast, or any other way, which has not been verified. This is regardless of whether the person is a secularist or not; it is required that you verify whom you take rulings in the religion from. Not everyone who in fact issues rulings is truly of those with the understanding to properly understand rulings. Therefore is it required that you verify what is stated. What is meant by this is that the believer is cautious regarding the affairs of his religion, and does not hastily enter into matters, or take religious rulings from other than those known to be capable to issue them. Rather, verify this such that you stop at what is proper, and ask the scholars who are well known for their uprightness and the merit and high level of their knowledge such that you act cautiously in regard to the affairs of your religion. Allaah, the Most High, said, *Ask the people of knowledge if you do not know*-(Surah an-Nahl: 43), "the people of knowledge" are those people with knowledge of the Book of Allaah and the Sunnah. You do not ask someone who is accused of not being sound and steadfast in his religion, or the one whose knowledge you are not aware of, or the one who is known to have deviated from the methodology of the people of the Sunnah.

(115) The Eminent Guiding Scholar Saaleh Ibn 'Abdul-'Azeez Aal-Sheikh, may Allaah preserve him- From 'the Fruits of Knowledge': Question 4

*Question: Does the student of knowledge convey Islamic rulings to the people according to what he holds as most correct or by the prevailing rulings in that land?*

Answer: This is a very significant and important issue because the student of knowledge engages in considering and reconciling positions within himself, such that it will become clear to him that some statements are sounder and more correct than others. Meaning the statement of Sheikh so-and-so is sounder in light of the evidence that he brings forth, and so he is content with that opinion, meaning with that particular ruling as opposed to others or with that statement rather than others. This is something which commonly occurs. If this happens, then the scholars have stated that the one who this occurs to should act according to this conclusion individually. This is due to the statement of Ibn al-'Abbaas to Sa'eed, *"How excellent is the one who stands upon what he has heard of knowledge transmitted to him."* If he personally acts upon his knowledge, then he has fulfilled his personal responsibility to Allaah, as he has realized and affirmed that knowledge.

As for the matter of issuing rulings to other people, then the general way of the Companions was to shift the issuing of rulings towards others from among them. It is not permissible for the student of knowledge to compete in giving rulings and be pleased with the people coming to seek rulings from him. Because issuing a ruling is as if you are saying that a signature of Allaah the Most Exalted, the Most High is upon that matter and it is unquestionably from the religion, meaning that you are conveying what is the ruling and judgement of Allaah the Most Exalted, the Most High. Therefore the worshiper of Allaah does not need to give a ruling and should direct the people to those who are qualified to give rulings who are present within that land; refer those seeking rulings to those individuals capable of issuing rulings. This is fulfilling your responsibility and is closer to goodness in relation to knowledge, actions, and the matter of issuing rulings.

If he is compelled to state a ruling due to the need presented to him, then he should not state a ruling that differs with what the people who issue rulings have already stated- meaning the people well-grounded in knowledge in his land where he lives. As the people proceeding and acting upon a single way is something which is desired in order to avoid the people's efforts to act upon the Sharee'ah being confused. The people would mock or try to subvert and pull down the Sharee'ah if it is seen to have different conflicting positions. This has, in fact, already occurred.

For example, some of the people made independent judgements or rulings, perhaps within the different sunnahs of the ritual prayer or something similar. But the general people do not understand that in some matters there are acceptable differences based upon evidence; they don't understand this. So then they begin to doubt the general validity of the action itself, or the scholar who issued the general ruling, or this student of knowledge and what action he is doing, or they have doubts about the religion in general. He says in this area there is wide latitude so do whatever you want, this is not something crucial. There is no doubt that this result has many forms of corruption related to it. For this reason, the scholars of this land and the leading scholars of the call to adhere to the Qur'aan and Sunnah first and foremost, may Allaah the Most High have mercy upon them, prohibited an individual who has not been charged with giving rulings from issuing rulings generally for the people. But the one who, after consideration of the evidences, concludes for himself what he believes is the strongest and soundest position, can act upon this individually. But those who give ruling to others generally should only be those who are charged with putting forth rulings.

**(116) THE EMINENT GUIDING SCHOLAR 'ABDUL-'AZEEZ IBN 'ABDULLAH IBN BAAZ, MAY ALLAAH HAVE MERCY UPON HIM, FROM 'A COLLECTION OF RULINGS AND VARIOUS STATEMENTS': VOL.6, PAGE 430**

*Question: It is commonly said among some of the people that the one who does not have a scholar, Shaytaan is his scholar. So what is your guidance for them, Esteemed Sheikh?*

Answer: This is a mistake found from the average person, and is ignorance originating with some of the Sufees in order to encourage the people to attach themselves to them and blindly follow them in their innovations and false matters of misguidance. If an individual gains understanding by attending circles of religious knowledge, or contemplating the Qur'aan and the Sunnah and he benefits from that, then one cannot say his scholar is Shaytaan. Rather we say he has struggled in seeking knowledge and attained significant good.

However, it is necessary for the student of knowledge to attach himself to those scholars who are well-known for having sound beliefs and a good record, in order to ask regarding matters which he has difficulty understanding. If he does not ask the people of knowledge he will make many mistakes and many matters will deceive him. Whereas if he attends gatherings of knowledge and listens to the preaching and teaching of the people of knowledge, then through this he can achieve tremendous good and gather many benefits, even if he does not have a specific scholar he studies with. There is no doubt that the one who attends gatherings of knowledge and listens to the Friday sermon, the sermons on the days of 'eid, and the general lectures that are given in the masjids, has many scholars, even if he has not associated himself to one specific scholar whom he blindly follows and adheres to his opinions.

(117) The Eminent Guiding Scholar 'Abdul-'Azeez Ibn 'Abdullah Ibn Baaz, may Allaah have mercy upon him, From 'The Obligation of Enjoining the Good and Forbidding Evil': Page 22-27

### Gaining Knowledge of Good and Evil is Achieved Through Studying

So it is necessary, my Muslim brother, that you gain knowledge of what is good through studying and seeking to understand the religion. Likewise, it is necessary to comprehend evil by this same manner, and then to proceed to fulfill the obligation of enjoining the good and forbidding evil. Certainly, possessing insight and understanding in the religion is from the signs of being granted well-being and happiness, and from the indications that Allaah wants goodness for His worshiper. It is narrated in the two "Saheeh" collections of the Imaam al-Bukhaaree and Imaam Muslim on the authority of Mu'aweeyah, may Allaah be pleased with him, on the Prophet, may Allaah's praise and salutations be upon him, that he said, *{Whoever Allaah intends good for He grants him understanding in the religion.}* [96]. So if you see an individual who sticks closely to the circles of knowledge, and inquires about knowledge and gains understanding and insight in the matters of knowledge, then this is from the signs that Allaah intends good for him. He should hold fast to this way, and continue to strive, neither being diverted nor weakening in his effort. As the Prophet, upon him be Allaah's praise and salutations, stated in an authentic narration, *{The one who takes the path of seeking knowledge, Allaah makes easy for him the path to Jannah.}* [97]. So seeking knowledge has a tremendous position, and is from jihaad in the path of Allaah, and is from the causes of success, and is from the signs that one is upon goodness. This may be through attending sittings and circles of knowledge, or through reading and studying beneficial books if you are from those who can understand their content. It may be through listening to sermons and beneficial reminders, or through putting questions to the people of knowledge. All of these are beneficial means and paths. Also, it may be accomplished by memorizing the noble Qur'aan, as it is the foundation of knowledge. The noble Qur'aan is the head of every form of knowledge, it is a tremendous foundation, and it is the firm and solid rope of Allaah. It is the greatest book and the most noble of books and it is the most tremendous foundation leading to goodness, and the most significant barrier against evil reaching you.

[96] Narrated in Saheeh al-Bukhaaree: 71, 3116, 7312/ Saheeh Muslim: 1037/ Sunan Ibn Maajah: 221/ al-Muwatta Maalik: 1300, 1667/Musnad Imaam Ahmad: 16395: 16404, and other than these two/ Musannaf Ibn Abee Shaybah:31792/ Sunan ad-Daaramee: 224, 226/- on the authority of Mu'aweeyah, and it is found in Jaame'a al-Tirmidhee: 2645/ Musnad Imaam Ahmad: 2786 /Sunan ad-Daaramee: 270, 2706/- on the authority of Ibn 'Abbaas, and it is found in Sunan Ibn Maajah:220/ Musannaf 'Abdul-Razzaaq: 30851/- on the authority of Abu Hurairah. It was declared authentic by Sheikh al-Albaanee in Saheeh al-Aadab al-Mufrad: 517, Silsilat al-Hadeeth as-Saheehah: 1194, 1195, 1196, Saheeh at-Targheeb at-Tarheeb: 67, as well as in other of his books. Sheikh Muqbil declared it authentic in al-Jaame'a al-Saheeh: 9, 3123, 4650, may Allaah have mercy upon them both.
[97] Narrated in Saheeh Muslim: 2699/ Sunan at-Tirmidhee: 2945/ Sunan Ibn Maajah: 225 / & Musnad Ahmad: 7379- from the hadeeth of Abu Hurairah. Declared authentic by Sheikh al-Albaanee in Saheeh at-Targheeb wa al-Tarheeb: 69, 89, as well as in other of his books.

So it is my advice to every believing man and woman to give attention to and focus on the Noble Qur'aan, frequently reciting it and being diligent in its memorization, or whatever is easy for you in that regard, this being done along with the consideration and contemplation of its meaning. It contains guidance and light, and Allaah the Most Perfect said, ❴*Verily, this Qur'aan guides to that which is most just and right*❵-(Surah al-Isra:9) and from His statements, ❴*This is a Book which We have sent down to you, full of blessings, that they may ponder over its Verses, and that men of understanding may remember.*❵-(Surah Saad:29) And the Most blessed and Exalted says, ❴*Do they not then think deeply in the Qur'aan, or are their hearts locked up from understanding it?*❵-(Surah Muhammad:24). So it is upon us to live within the Book of Allaah, through recitation and memorization, through contemplation and consideration, and to ask about anything that is not clearly understood. Similarly the Sunnah of the Messenger of Allaah, may Allaah's praise and salutations be upon him, as it is the second source of revelation and the second foundation. It is that which explains the book of Allaah and makes clear what it intends. It is upon the student of knowledge and upon every Muslim to be concerned and devoted to the Sunnah to the limit of his capacity and the limit of his knowledge of it. This is through memorization and reading, such as the memorization of *((Imaam Nawawees' Forty Hadeeth))02-27)*, and the work which completes it by Ibn Rajab for total of fifty hadeeth. What are found in these two works are from the most comprehensive and beneficial narrations, and from the significant and comprehensive speech of the Messenger of Allaah, may Allaah's praise and salutations be upon him. So it is suitable that both men and women memorize these two books.

Also, the likes of the book *(('Amdatul-Hadeeth)02-29)* by Haafidh Abdul-Ghanee al-Maqdasee which is a tremendous book in which he has collected more than four hundred simple narrations which are from the most authentic narrations in the related areas of knowledge. So if is it possible for you to memorize it, then that is a tremendous blessing from Allaah. Similarly, the book *((Bulugh al-Maraam)02-34)* by Haafidh Ibn Hajr, is a wonderful summarized work, and a beneficial book. So if it is possible for the student of knowledge to memorize it, then this is a tremendous good. As for what is connected to the beneficial books of correct belief: there are two significant books by the leading scholar Sheikh Muhammad Ibn 'Abdul-Wahaab, may Allaah have mercy upon him: *((Kitaab at-Tawheed)06-01)* and the book *((Kashf ash-Shubahaat)06-04)* Additionally from the important books of correct belief are *((al-Aqeedatul-Wasateeyah)06-05)* by Sheikh al-Islaam Ibn Taymeeyah which is tremendous book, which although summarized contains significant benefits in summarizing the beliefs held by the people of the Sunnah and adherence to the Jam'aah. The book *(Kitab al-Emaan)06-39)* by Sheikh al-Islaam Muhammad Ibn Abdul-Wahaab is a tremendous book in which he has gathered a body of narrations connected to faith or emaan.

It is necessary for both the male and female student of knowledge to memorize as much as is possible from these beneficial books. They should combine this with the focus upon the Noble Qur'aan, spending significant time in its recitation and memorization, or what is feasible for him as has been mentioned; along with giving attention to reviewing what you have memorized with your associates. Along with this is always asking your teachers and those scholars whom you believe possess goodness and knowledge regarding those matters you encounter that you do not fully understand. Ask your Lord to grant you success and assist you, and do not slack in you efforts or become lazy. Properly utilize your time, dividing it into portions: a portion of the day and night for the recitation of the Qur'aan and its contemplation, a portion for seeking knowledge and seeking to understand the religion, memorizing texts and reviewing parts that you find difficult, a portion for the needs of your family, a portion for prayer and worship, and the various types of remembrance and supplication. Diligently adhere to every matter which facilitates holding firmly to these mentioned characteristics of excellence: ❁ *Help you one another in righteousness and the fear of Allaah, but do not help one another in sin and transgression. And fear Allaah. Verily, Allaah is Severe in punishment.* ❁-(Surah al-Maidah:2).

(118) THE EMINENT GUIDING SCHOLAR AHMAD IBN YAHYA AN-NAJMEE, MAY ALLAAH PRESERVE HIM, FROM 'DECISIVE RULINGS ON THE METHODOLOGIES OF INVITATION': VOL.2, PAGE 182

*Question: What are the books that you advise us to read in the subjects of worshiping Allaah alone and correct beliefs?*

Answer:   The first works I recommend are *((Kitaab at-Tawheed)06-01), ((Usul At-Thalathah)06-02), ((al-Qawa'idal-Arba')06-03), ((Kashfash-Shubahaat)06-04),* and the books of Sheikh al-Islaam Ibn Taymeeyah in understanding Allaah's names and attributes.  Additionally the writings of Sheikh Muhammad Ibn 'Abdul-Wahaab and his children, grandsons, and students. Then after these works books such as *((Kitaab at-Tawheed)06-36)* by Ibn Khuzaimah, *((Rad 'Alaa Jahmeeyah)11-10)* of Imaam Ahmad *((Rad 'Alaa Jahmeeyah)11-11)* of Uthmaan Ibn Sa'eed ad-Daramee, *((al-Ibaanah al-Kubraa)06-27)* and *((al-Ibaanah al-Sughraa)06-28)* of Ibn Battah, *((Sharh Usul 'Itiqaad Ahlus-Sunnah)06-29)* of Laalakaa'ee, as well as many other beneficial books.

(119) THE EMINENT GUIDING SCHOLAR SAALEH IBN FAUZAAN, MAY ALLAAH PRESERVE HIM, FROM 'AL-MUNTAQAA MIN FATAAWA': VOL.2, PAGE 308

*Question: What are the best books to study related to the subjects of worshipping Allaah alone and to that of correct beliefs?*

Answer:  Those books which you should study and examine in order to learn the subject of making our worship solely for Allaah alone and the other necessary authentic beliefs are numerous, all praise is due to Allaah, and accessible. I mention to you as an example the book *((Idtidhaa' as-Siraat al-Mustaqeem)11-02)* by Sheikh al-Islaam Ibn Taymeeyah, may Allaah have mercy upon him. It is printed with many copies in circulation, and all praise is due to Allaah. Similarly, *((Ighaathah al-Lahfaan Min Musaa'id as-Shaytaan)12-05)* by Imaam Ibn Qayyim, especially the second volume. Similarly *((Kitaab at-Tawheed)06-01)* and its explanation by Sheikh

Muhammad Ibn 'Abdul-Wahaab, and its explanation *((Fath al-Majeed)06-12)* by Sheikh 'Abdur-Rahman Ibn Hasan, or *((Tayseer al-'Azeez al-Hameed)06-20)* by Sheikh Sulaymaan Ibn 'Abdullah Ibn Muhammad Ibn 'Abdul-Wahaab. Also, there is *((Thalathatul-Usul)06-02)* and *((Kashf as-Shubahaat)06-04)* both by Sheikh Muhammad Ibn 'Abdul-Wahaab I will also mention to you *((Tatheer al-'Itiqaad An Idraan al-Ilhaad)06-30)* by Sheikh Muhammad Isma'eel as-Sana'aanee and *((ad-Durur An-Nadheed Fe Ikhlaas at-Tawheed)06-11)* by Sheikh al-Imaam Muhammad Ibn 'Alee ash-Shawkaanee. I also should mention a book which encompasses all the different areas and subjects of authentic beliefs, and that is the *((Aqeedah of Imaam at-Tahawee(06-08)* and *((its explanation(06-09)* by Ibn Abee al-Izz al-Hanafee. As *((al-Aqeedatul-Wasateeyah)06-05)* and this explanation of it are from the most expansive of books concerning authentic Islamic beliefs, as well as being from the best and the most comprehensive.

(120) The Eminent Guiding Scholar Muhammad Amman al-Jaamee, may Allaah have mercy upon him, From Audio Lecture entitled '27 Questions Regarding the Methodology of the First Three Generations of Muslims'

*Question: Which books do you advise us to read in the subject of correct beliefs, the explanation of the Qur'aan, hadeeth narrations and their related sciences, and in the subject of fiqh?*

Answer: The first work that I advise the one who wishes to begin seeking knowledge to study is that he memorize the works *((Usul Ath-Thalathah wa Adilaatuha)06-02)*, *((The work discussing the pillars of ritual prayer, the obligations of ritual prayer, the conditions of prayer)07-26)* there is a single work which includes all of this information, along with *((Qawaa'id al-'Arba')06-03)*. It also be excellent if one also memorized the conditions of the statement *{There is none worthy of worship other than Allaah}* and memorize those matters which negate this statement. It is proper that you memorize these matters very well. Then you should sit down with students of knowledge to take knowledge from the mouths of men, not simply from the bellies of books.

After this, if it is easy for you, then proceed to the memorization of *((Kashf as-Shubahaat)06-04)* This is good, yet the book which it is essential that you memorize, and should be studied by the student of knowledge in the subject of essential beliefs, especially regarding singling Allaah out alone for all worship, and for ruling and judgement in all matters, which is written in a new mode is *((Kitaab at-Tawheed Aladhee Hu Haq Allaah Alaa al-'Ebaad)06-01)*. It is a tremendous book, and is a worthy expression of various abridged verses from the Book of Allaah, the Most High, Prophetic narrations, and the transmitted statements of some of the people of knowledge. It is a book by which Allaah has benefited many people. I advise our youth to focus upon this book, in relation to memorization and striving to understand it, and by reading its explanations until he stands upon clarity and surety in this area from the area of essential beliefs.

Then after this matter in relation to the subject of worshiping Allaah alone through the understanding and affirmation His names and attributes, for that student who has a incredible hunger for knowledge to memorize the text of *((al-Aqeedatul-Wasateeyah)06-05)* or to study it to understand it. Thereafter to study those different smaller writings which are gather together in *((Majmu'a Fatawaa Sheikh al-Islaam)07-19)*, as this is a collection of very important different writings which it is necessary that the student of knowledge study. And if someone wishes to expand further in his study of books written on the subject of Allaah's names and attributes, he can further pursue this by studying the *((Explanation of Aqeedah at-Tahaweeyah)06-09)* because its author transmitted in his book entirely or significantly from the works of Sheikh al-Islaam Ibn Taymeeyah and his student Ibn Qayyim, as well as from the books of Ibn Katheer. So it is a book which collects a great deal together and is quite beneficial.

In regard to the area of the explanation of the Qur'aan, then it is suitable for the beginning student of knowledge to study the *((Explanation of Sheikh 'Abdur-Rahman as-Sa'adee)01-02)*, may Allaah have mercy upon him, as it is concise and his methodology is well known to be that of the first three generations of Muslims and those who adhered to their way. If the student of knowledge has good comprehension of the Arabic language and is proficient in it, and wishes to be directed to a teacher and commentator on the Qur'aan who is Salafee, adhering to the methodology of the first generations of Muslims, then he should study the work *((Fath al-Qadeer)01-05)* by ash-Shawkaanee. Yet certainly this must be carefully undertaken, with some conditions. Because Imaam ash-Shawkaanee despite his wide knowledge and the excellence of this writings, especially *((Fath al-Qadeer)01-05)* and *((Nayl al-Awtaar)03-08)* was not free from mistakenly falling into incorrectly misinterpreting some the source texts related to Allaah's characteristics. So the student might be deceived into accepting that statement which was incorrect from him.

This is what is proper, the selecting of a commentator on the Qur'aan who follows the way of the first three generations. Therefore he should study this commentary of the Qur'aan, because this will help him to appreciate the Book of Allaah the Most High. Thereafter his attention is drawn towards the direction of Iraab, and at times towards the points of eloquence. Then we have the well-known explanation of the Qur'aan is *((Tafseer Ibn Katheer)01-01)*, and there is no harm in studying the abridged versions so that afterward you can study other larger works of commentary. And all of this is, as is said, *"It is not proper that the student of knowledge merely rely upon reading, rather it is necessary to interact and taken with the people of knowledge."* As for the hadeeth narrations and its related sciences, but before we stop discussing the area of the explanation of the Qur'aan, it should be said that it is proper to also study some of the related sciences of commentary. From these sciences is the study of the proper rules of recitation, and from them is the branch of studying the Arabic language- these are from the related sciences of commentary of the Qur'aan.

Then there is the study of hadeeth, in relation to memorizing texts, as we mentioned last night you should start with *((al-'Arba'een an-Nawaweeyah)02-27)* then *(('Amdat al-Ahkaam)02-28)* then *((Bulugh al-Maraa'm)02-34)*. After this is the subject of the condition of authenticity for hadeeth narration, and gaining understanding of these mentioned works and studying them with the people specialized in these area, and with sound understanding of them. Furthermore, if a student of knowledge also wishes to study the different opinions of the scholars which are found within secondary matters, he should memorize a small work from each of the four well-known schools of jurisprudence. But he should do so without simply getting used to following the recorded positions of one specific school of jurisprudence, because truly sound and correct understanding is that which is studied in the works such as *(('Amdat al-Ahkaam)02-28)* then *((Bulugh al-Maraa'm)02-34)*, the understanding of the original Sunnah of the Prophet. After this he can study the mentioned work of fiqh of Imaam ash-Shawkaanee, upon the conditions we mentioned, without falling into biased allegiance and partisanship to any specific individual or specific school of jurisprudence; rather his goal should always be generally seeking knowledge.

(121) THE EMINENT GUIDING SCHOLAR SAALEH IBN FAUZAAN, MAY ALLAAH PRESERVE HIM, FROM 'AL-MUNTAQAA MIN FATAAWA': VOL. 2 PAGE 215

*Question: I hope that you would direct me to some of the beneficial books in the subject of understanding how to correctly practice the religion, as well as that of worshipping Allaah alone without associates.*

Answer: The books which are beneficial are, all praise is due to Allaah, numerous. This religion of Islaam is rich with beneficial books taken from the sources of the Book of Allaah and the Sunnah, and the understanding of them which the righteous first generations held, as seen in the four well known schools of jurisprudence. From the summarized books in the Hanbalee school of jurisprudence for use by the beginner in knowledge are books such as *(The Manners of Walking to the Prayer)07-18)* by Sheikh al-Islaam Muhammad Ibn 'Abdul-Wahaab may Allaah have mercy upon him. This work will clarify for you many of the rulings regarding ritual prayer, obligatory charity, and obligatory fasting, as these are all necessary for the establishment of your religion. And before even this, those concise shorter writing regarding the rulings of ritual purification and the water used for purification which can be found in the work *((Majmu'a ar-Rasaa'l wa al-Masaa'il)07-22)* compiled from the writings of the scholars of Najd- Saudi Arabia- and other trustworthy Muslim scholars who reliably verify matters. If you proceed beyond this level, then there is the work *(('Amdat -Ahkaam)02-28)* Muwaafiqudden Ibn Qudaamah. There is also *((Matn ad-Daleel)06-48)* by Mura'ee Ibn Yusuf al-Karee al-Hanbalee, which is concise, beneficial and simple. There is also the work *((Za'ad al-Mustaqna')07-01)*

As for the field of essential beliefs, then there is *((al-Usul ath-Thalathah)06-02)* by the leading scholar, the reviver of the religion, Sheikh Muhammad ibn 'Abdul-Wahaab, may Allaah have mercy upon him. And *((al-Aqeedat al-Wasateeyah)06-05)* by Sheikh al-Islaam Ibn Taymeeyah, may Allaah have mercy upon him, *((Kitaab at-Tawheed Aladhee Hu Haq Allaah Alla al-'Ebaad)06-01)* by Sheikh Muhammad ibn 'Abdul-Wahaab, may Allaah have mercy upon him. There is also *((Aqeedah at-Tahaweeyah)06-08)* and its *((explanation)06-09)*. All these books are beneficial in the subject of essential beliefs. There are also the books of the two well known scholars: Sheikh al-Islaam Ibn Taymeeyah and his student, the guiding scholar Ibn Qayyim in the subject area of essential beliefs as well as fiqh.

Certainly, the Muslim should act according to whatever is established upon evidence, giving consideration to whether it is stated by the adherents to the Hanbalee school of jurisprudence, or the adherents to the Shaa'fee school of jurisprudence, or the adherents to the Maalikee school of jurisprudence, or the adherents to the Hanafee school of jurisprudence. It should be from whoever had the best comprehension of the various evidences. If you are a beginner in knowledge then it is upon you to simply ask the people of knowledge and take from whatever rulings they give you. Allaah the Most High says, ❧ *Ask the people of knowledge if you do not know* ❧-(Surah an-Nahl:43), and his general path will be the school of fiqh of the one giving rulings to him, and the one whom he blindly follows from the people of knowledge.

(122) THE EMINENT GUIDING SCHOLAR MUQBIL IBN HAADEE AL-WAADI'EE, MAY ALLAAH HAVE MERCY UPON HIM, FROM 'A DEFENDING MISSION FROM AUDIO LECTURES UPON THE PEOPLE OF IGNORANCE & SOPHISTRY': VOL. 1, PAGE 275

*Question: What are the books related the subject of understanding how to correctly practice the religion that you advise me and those who are with me to read?*

Answer: The book which we advise you with is *((al-Muhalla)08-07)* from Abee Muhammad Ibn Hazm, may Allaah have mercy upon him, while putting aside and staying away from his severity and harshness with regard to those who differed with him, as well as his stubborn adherence to the 'Dhareeyah' school of fiqh. Likewise this also applies to the mistakes of Abee Muhammad (Ibn Hazm) in the matters of belief. After this work, then *((Nayl al-Awtar)03-08)* of Shawkanee, then *((al-Majmu'a)08-04)* of Nawawee, then *((al-Mughnee)07-07)* of Ibn Qudamah. Along with what will come of your many questions, you should not refer to the books of compiled rulings except when you have a definite need. I also say to you, I do not refer to such books of compiled rulings except when I have a clear need related to an issue that has come forward which requires this. Were we to spend so much of our time in such books, then we would not be able to gain beneficial knowledge in other branches of knowledge. There might be six, ten, or even twenty different opinions or positions regarding a specific issue. Due to this we advise a comprehensive commitment to referring first and foremost to the Book and the Sunnah, and then to acquiring the books of fiqh and benefiting from them in the situations in which you have a need.

NOTES

**(123) THE EMINENT GUIDING SCHOLAR SAALEH AL-FAUZAAN, MAY ALLAAH PRESERVE HIM, FROM 'AL-MUNTAQAA MIN FATAAWA': VOL. 2 PAGE 214**

*Question: What are considered the most authentic books after the Noble Qur'aan?*

Answer: Those book which can be considered the most authentic books after the Noble Qur'aan are numerous. From those which are often neglected or overlooked and those which are usually considered and referred to are: the *((Saheeh)02-01)* by the leading scholar al-Imaam al-Bukhaaree, may Allaah have mercy upon him, and the *((Saheeh)02-02)* by the leading scholar al-Imaam Muslim, may Allaah have mercy upon him. And similarly the four well known 'Sunan' books. *((Sunan Abu Dawud)02-04)*, *((at-Tirmidhee)02-06)*, *((an-Nisaa'ee)02-03)*, and *((Ibn Maajah)02-05)*. Certainly within this four 'Sunan' works there are narrations that are authentic as well as those that have weakness; yet those with weaknesses are not many, and their level of authenticity has been clarified by the scholars, all praise is due to Allaah. There are also works of collected hadeeth narrations related specifically to the rulings of Islaam such as the book *((al-Muntaqaa)07-13)* by the Imaam al-Majd Ibn Taymeeyah. He has collected within it narrations related to various rulings and guidelines of the Sharee'ah. It is two large volumes in which he clarifies the level of the different narrations for the reader, so that he can stand upon clarity in the matters of this religion. Likewise Imaam Ibn Hajr, may Allaah have mercy upon him, compiled a book of hadeeth narrations which is named *((Bulugh al-Maraam Fee Adilatul al-Ahkaam)02-34)* and is a remarkable single volume work. There is also *(('Amdatul-Hadeeth)02-29)* by Dheyaa'uddin al-Maqdasee al-Hanbalee, may Allaah have mercy upon him. He compiled in it hadeeth narrations which are found in both the collections of Imaam al-Bukharee and Imaam Muslim related to Sharee'ah rulings and guidelines, and entitled it *(('Amdatul-Ahkaam)02-28)*

There are also books which were compiled by some of the leading scholars which contain narrations related to acts of ritual worship, general deeds, character, and so on, such as *((Riyaadh as-Saaliheen)02-11)* by Imaam an-Nawawee, and *((Mishkaat al-Masaabeeh)02-30)* by Imaam al-Baghawee, and other general collected works in the sciences of hadeeth. There are also to be mentioned the books of Sheikh al-Islaam Ibn Taymeeyah and his student, the guiding scholar Ibn Qayyim, and the books of Sheikh Muhammad ibn 'Abdul-Wahaab and his students, as well as other beneficial books which were authored by the leading scholars of Islaam.

**(124) The Eminent Guiding Scholar Muqbil Ibn Haadee al-Waadi'ee, may Allaah have mercy upon him, from 'Bridling the Resistant One': Page 492**

### Books of Guidance and Books of Misguidance.[98]

All praise is due to Allaah Lord of all the worlds, may Allaah's praise and salutations be upon our Prophet, his household, and all his Companions. I bear witness there is none worthy of worship other than Allaah alone, having no partner. And I bear witness that Muhammad is his worshipper and Messenger. As for what follows: Indeed the Imaams al-Bukhaaree and Muslim have narrated within their two 'Saheeh' collections, on the authority of Mu'aweeyah, may Allaah, the Most High be pleased with him, that the Prophet, may Allaah's praise and salutations be upon him and his household, said, *{Whoever Allaah intends good for He grants him understanding in the religion.}* [99]. And it is narrated in their two 'Saheeh' collections on the authority of Abu Musaa al-'Asha'ree, may Allaah, the Most High be pleased with him, that the Prophet, may Allaah's praise and salutations be upon him and his household, said, *{ The example of guidance and knowledge with which Allaah has sent me is like abundant rain falling on the earth, some of which was fertile soil that absorbed rain water and brought forth vegetation and grass in abundance. Another portion of it was hard and held the rain water and Allaah benefited the people with it and they utilized it for drinking, letting their animals drink from it and for irrigation of the land for cultivation. A portion of it was barren, and could neither hold the water nor bring forth vegetation (so that land gave no benefits). The first is the example of the person who comprehends Allah's religion and gets benefit from the knowledge and guidance which Allah has revealed through me and learns and then teaches others. The last example is that of a person who does not care for it and does not accept Allaah's guidance revealed through me. (He is like that barren land.)}* -(Saheeh al-Bukhaaree: 79, & Saheeh Muslim: 2282). Muslim narrated in his 'Saheeh' collection on the authority of Abu Hurairah, may Allaah be pleased with him, that the Prophet, upon him and his family be Allaah's praises and the best of salutations, said:, *{When a son of Aadam dies his deeds end except for three matters: a continuing charity, a righteous child who supplicates for him, or knowledge by which others are benefited.}* [100].

---

[98] This extraordinary selection was the original heart of this compilation as well as the original map that was used to build the library of books for our household, and any success is from Allaah. An additional note to the reader is that the specifics related to the availability and preference of certain printings was specific to the original time of presentation and in many cases these have now changed quite significantly, as the availability of beneficial books has increased tremendously-alhamdulillah. Please refer to our website for current book information connected to the recommended book list which we hope to continually update insh'allaah.

[99] Narrated in Saheeh al-Bukhaaree: 71, 3116, 7312/ Saheeh Muslim: 1037/ Sunan Ibn Maajah: 221/ al-Muwatta Maalik: 1300, 1667/Musnad Imaam Ahmad: 16395: 16404, and other than these two/ Musannaf Ibn Abee Shaybah:31792/ Sunan ad-Daaramee: 224, 226/- on the authority of Mu'aweeyah, and it is found in Jaame'a at-Tirmidhee: 2645/ Musnad Imaam Ahmad: 2786 /Sunan ad-Daaramee: 270, 2706/- on the authority of Ibn 'Abbaas, and it is found in Sunan Ibn Maajah:220/ Musannaf 'Abdul-Razzaaq: 30851/- on the authority of Abu Hurairah. It was declared authentic by Sheikh al-Albaanee in Saheeh al-Aadab al-Mufrad: 517, Silsilat al-Hadeeth as-Saheehah: 1194, 1195, 1196, Saheeh at-Targheeb at-Tarheeb: 67, as well as in other of his books. Sheikh Muqbil declared it authentic in al-Jaame'a al-Saheeh: 9, 3123, 4650, may Allaah have mercy upon them both.

[100] Narrated in Saheeh Muslim: 1631/ Sunan Abu Dawud: 2880/ Jaame'a at-Tirmidhee: 1376/ Sunan an-Nasaa'ee: 3681/ Musnad Imaam Ahmad: 8627/ & Sunan ad-Daaramee: 559/-on the authority of Abu Hurairah. It was declared authentic by Sheikh al-Albaanee in Saheeh at-Targheeb at-Tarheeb: 78, 93, Mishkaat al-Masaabeeh: 127, 203, & Saheeh al-Jaame'a as-Sagheer: 793, and the three 'Sunan' collections.

NOTES

Therefore when we read from and listen to *((Saheeh al-Bukhaaree)02-01)* or *((Saheeh Muslim)02-02)* or *((Tafseer Ibn Katheer)01-01)* or *((Musnad of Imaam Ahmad)02-07)* or other works which are from the books of the Sunnah, then that author is rewarded for this, by the permission of Allaah the Most High, according to the evidence which we have just heard- that one's works cease after his death except for three. And from them is knowledge by which others are benefited.

A book is to be considered a sitting companion, so it is only proper that you select a righteous companion. al-Bukhaaree and Muslim have narrated in their two 'Saheeh' collections, on the authority of Abu Musaa al-'Asha'ree, may Allaah be pleased with him, that the Prophet, may Allaah's praise and salutations be upon him and his household, said, *{The example of the righteous companion and the evil companion is like the example of sitting with the musk seller and the blacksmith. So from the musk seller, either he will give you some as a gift, or you would buy some musk or at the least enjoy from him a good pleasing smell. But as for sitting with the blacksmith either your clothes with be burned, or at the least you will experience a bad nasty smell.}* [101].

In these days we often find there are book fairs, and the righteous people use and busy themselves at them for good, while the people of wrongdoing use and busy themselves at them for evil and wrongdoing. During one of the previous years there was found at one of the fairs a book entitled [[The Neighing Form]] which contained outright disbelief in Islaam, and cast false accusations against the Prophet Yusuf. Accusations that I am not even able to speak about, even worse accusations than adultery! Indeed a significant door of evil is opened by books of deviation and misguidance. But as for true books of goodness, then it is falsely said by some [The Wahaabee Books are dangerous!] They have no shame in expressing their ignorance such that they say,[Saheeh al-Bukhaaree is a Wahaabee book!] Oh you poor ignorant one, Imaam al-Bukhaaree is from the scholars of the third century, but as for Muhammad Ibn 'Abdul-Wahaab it has only been one hundred and fifty or two hundred years ago, or something similar to this, since he died, may Allaah have mercy upon him! So how many centuries are there between Imaam al-Bukhaaree and between Muhammad Ibn 'Abdul-Wahaab?!? And perhaps al-Bukhaaree's book might be that which delivers and saves you from entering Hellfire. How excellent is the speech of the poet who said:

*She said, "Oh you, you have spent upon books until your hands empty."*

*Yet I replied, "Leave me alone,*

*As perhaps I may find among them a book that will guide me,*

*So that tomorrow I will be able to take my book of deeds with my right hand*

---

[101] Narrated in Saheeh al-Bukhaaree: 2101, 5534/ Saheeh Muslim: 2628/ -on the authority of Abu Moosa al-'Asha'ree. And it is in Sunan Abu Daawud: 4829/ -on the authority of 'Anas Ibn Maalik. It was declared authentic by Sheikh al-Albaanee in Silsilat al-Hadeeth as-Saheehah: 3214, Mishkaat al-Masaabeh: 5010, Saheeh at-Targheeb at-Tarheeb: 3064, 3065, Saheeh al-Jaame'a as-Sagheer: 2365, 5828, 5829, 5839, as well as in Saheeh Sunan Abu Dawud.

And it has been said, "*The clever one in a matter is devoted to knowledge and dedicated to writings*". And it has been said,

*If we are the companions of rulers and kings they act arrogantly with us,*

*They belittle and undervalue the right of the sitting companion.*

*And if we sit as companions of the business men and traders we lean towards worldly matters,*

*becoming those concerned with counting money.*

*So we stick to our houses, and extract knowledge*

*and fill the blank pages of books with it.*

This was the case of our scholars from the first generations whose works benefited the Muslims and the non-Muslims. They wrote, may Allaah have mercy upon them, many volumes. Often they will compose an entire volume regarding a single issue, such as the question about when reciting as the imaam in certain prayers, should the verse "*Bismillah ar-Rahman ar-Raheem*" be recited aloud or recited quietly. And I am not trying to say that you will find one book on these issues, rather there are many scholars who individually wrote entire volumes discussing a single issue! For example Ibn Jawzee, Khateeb al-Baghdadee, ad-Darqutnee, and Ibn 'Abdul-Bar - each have written a work about this entitled, *((Insaaf fee Masi'alat ul-Khilaaf)07-24)*. These four scholars all wrote works about this single issue of how to recite the basmallah. What is correct in this issue is that it should be recited quietly. This is what is correct due to what is narrated by the scholars al-Bukhaaree and Muslim in their two 'Saheeh' collections, on the authority of 'Anas, may Allaah be pleased with him, where he said, {*I prayed behind the Messenger of Allaah, may Allaah's praise and salutations be upon him and his household, Abu Bakr, and 'Umar, and they all began their audible recitation with the verse "Alhamdulillahi rabbil 'Alaameen."*} Therefore this is what is soundest from among the various statements of the people of knowledge. But it is not this specific issue which I intended as my point, this was only put forward as an example.

The people differ in relation to the issue of benefiting from books, so it is proper for the common person to acquire the following books: *((Riyaadh as-Saaliheen)02-11)*, *((Tafseer Ibn Katheer)01-01)*, *((Bulugh al-Maraam)02-34)*, *((Fath al-Majeed Sharh Kitaab at-Tawheed)06-12)*, *((Ad-Dur an-Nadheed Fee Ikhlaas Kalamaat at-Tawheed)06-11)*, and this is the last work by ash-Shawkaanee, *((Tat-heer al-'Itiqaad 'An Adraan al-'Ilhaad)06-30)* by Sana'anee. These books are what it is proper that the general Muslim acquire, as well as *((Lu'Lu' wa al-Marjaan Feemaa 'Itifaaq 'Aleihi as-Sheikhaan)02-16)*.

As for the individual who is at a higher level of knowledge than the general Muslim, then it is proper that he acquire the following books:

*((Saheeh al-Bukhaaree)02-01)*

*((Saheeh Muslim)02-02)*

And similarly if you are able to acquire the remaining four hadeeth collections which are all together known as the "*Six Mother Collections of Hadeeth*" then this is good. These works are for the like of someone who is literate and reads and writes well; someone who simply loves knowledge. These books are, all praise is due to Allaah, easy to read works. As for the one who is a researcher, then it is proper for him to be diligent in trying to acquire all of the books of the Sunnah. It is not suitable that he neglect a single book from the acknowledged books of the Sunnah if he has the ability to get it. This is in view of the fact that our scholars, may Allaah grant them and us the success of attaining every good, are often occupied with their strictly scheduled work of livelihood and employment, such that their working hours are in the morning, after dhuhr, and they have a gathering between maghrib and 'ishaa' or after salatul 'ishaa'. One of them may be a judge, so that after his working hours it is necessary that he take with him cases that he must rule upon, so that he can read and review them after hours. This busy schedule is enough to make one go crazy, especially as the scholar does not have any time available to sit with his students or to review that which he has learned.

So considering that our scholars are often busy with their positions and employments and have left teaching, then it is only proper and necessary for the student of knowledge to be diligent and have significant concern for acquiring good books, which will repel from him misguidance and straying from the straight path. From the students of knowledge are those who have graduated from the Islamic University in Medinahh Munawarrah or from al-Azhaar University in Egypt, or from the Main University in Sana'a, or from al-Haadee University in Sa'ada, or other than these universities. But before you know it they have become one who chooses something over the reward found with Allaah, and so become as is said:

> *Concerned with gaining knowledge in every land are youth,*
>> *but when they have achieved it and gathered it,*
> *Then after having mastered the chains of the transmission and its principles,*
>> *and having become scholars, they then waste it and turn their backs on it.*
> *They lean towards worldly gains, milking them,*
>> *going against their knowledge, and ignoring it.*
> *So oh evil scholars where are your intellects and where now are,*
>> *your connected hadeeth narrations of the chosen prophet!*

And, all praise is due to Allaah, the books are available and present, may Allaah reward our scholars with good. We advise the students of knowledge to be diligent in acquiring books, even to the degree that he sells his car or his turban in order to purchase a book of guidance. Indeed, a single book of guidance may be equal to the contents of the entire world. For the student who is also a researcher it is also possible that he acquires the main well known hadeeth collections by means of buying their explanations such as:

*((Fath al-Baaree Sharh Saheeh al-Bukhaaree)03-01)*, and the best printing of this is the 'Salafeeyah' edition due to what it incorporated indicating the different location of hadeeth narrations.

*((Saheeh Muslim be Sharh an-Nawawee)03-02)*

*((Sunan Abu Dawud Ma' 'Awn al-Ma'bood)03-03)* this is printed in two different editions, one from Egypt and the other from India.

*((Tuhfat al-Awadha Sharh Jaame'a at-Tirmidhee)03-04)*; likewise, this is printed in two different editions, one from Egypt and the other from India. The Indian edition is most correct and is five volumes along with an introduction. But the Egyptian printing is printed such that it is easier for the student of knowledge to read.

*((Sunan Ibn Majaah)03-05)* with a concise and excellent commentary. It has now been printed with the verification of Muhammad Fouad 'Abdul-Baaqee

*((Sunan an-Nasaa'ee)02-03)* This is the smaller Sunan compiled by Nasaa'ee which has marginal notes by Sindee and Suyootee. It has been numbered and indexed by Abu Ghuddah

*((Musnad of Imaam Ahmad)02-07)*; if you are able to acquire the verification of this work by Ahmad Shaakir then do so. Otherwise the Musnad of Ahmad in six large volumes, and searching within it is difficult. But Allaah facilitates research in it thorough utilizing an index compiled for this printing.

*((Musannaf 'Abdur-Razzaq)02-15)*

*((Musannaf Ibn Abee Shaybah)02-14)*

*((Musnad Abee Ya'laa)02-18)*

*((Kashf al-Astaar 'An Zawa'id al-Zubaar)02-17)*

*((Musnad al-Humaydee)02-19)*

*((Saheeh Ibn Hibaan)02-13)* which is favored by some of the scholars

*((Saheeh Ibn Khuzaymah)02-20)*

The three Mu'jam collections by at-Tabaree: *((Mu'jam al-Kabeer)02-21)*, *((al-Awsaat)02-22)*, and *((as-Sagheer)02-23)*. Additionally, there are other beneficial books which it is proper to acquire, such as:

*((Talkhees al-Khabeer)04-03)* by Haafidh Ibn Hajr

*((Nasab ar-Raawee fee Takhreej Ahadeeth al-Hadaaeyah)04-05)* by Zayla'ee

*((Nayl al-Awtaar)03-08)* by Shawkaanee

*((Subl as-Salaam)03-06)* by as-Sana'anee. Also, all the books of Sheikh Naasirudden al-Albaanee should be acquired, as a researcher cannot do without the books of Sheikh Naasirudden al-Albaanee, may Allaah the Exalted preserve him.

And from the important books of fiqh, or understanding how to correctly apply the guidance of the source texts, are:

*((al-Muhalaa)08-07)* by Abu Muhammad Ibn Hazm

*((al-Ahkaam fee Usul al-Ahkaam)08-02)* by Abu Muhammad Ibn Hazm

*((Zaad al-Ma'ad Fee Haadee Khair al-Ebaad)09-05)*

*((al-Mughnee)07-07)* by Ibn Qudaamah

*((Tarh at-Tathreeb fee Sharh Taqreeb al-Asaaneed)04-06)* by Haafidh al-Iraaqee and his son.

*((Majma' az-Zawa'id)02-24)*

*((al-Mutaalib al-'Aleeyah)12-32)*

*((al-Mustradraak)02-25)*

*((al-Hilyaah)05-03)*

As for the one who enjoys reading and has a love of knowledge, I don't believe it is possible for him not to have a library. As perhaps he will be reading and come across a hadeeth and its source is another book. So he says, "*This is a book that I must purchase.*" Myself, when I was compiling the work *((at-Talea'ah Fee Rad 'Alaa Ghulaat as-Shee'ah)11-12)*, at that time I had a large bookcase and I used to suppose that I had gathered the books of the world within it. But when I began writing this book, I came to references to other source works which I did not possess. So then I was diligent in acquiring those specific source books I lacked. Then afterwards when I was compiling *((as-Saheeh al-Musnad Min Asbaab an-Nuzul)01-10)* I again came to realize that my library was still deficient. But it was Allaah, the Most Perfect and the Most High, was the One Who made it easy for me to raise the money for those books even if I had to borrow some of it. At one time I had wanted to buy the book *((Tadheeb at-Tadheeb)05-18)* by Haafidh Ibn Hajr, and it was around 200 Saudi Riyaals. I was living in Mecca and said to one of my companions, "*Loan me some money.*" He said, "*For what?*" I replied "*There is a book that I wish to buy.*" He said, "*No. If you have a need in relation to something for your household or family, or clothing, or something like this, then I will lend you money. But I will not lend it to you for a book.*" However, before he knew it, somehow I had purchased the book. Later he asked me, "*Where did you get the money from?*" I said, "*Allaah, the Most Perfect and the Most High made it easy for me.*" And this was our brother from the sake of Allaah, who we loved for the sake of Allaah. May Allaah reward him with good. So if a person gives importance to acquiring books, then Allaah, the Most Perfect and the Most High makes this easy. I do not mean that you should gather books just for appearance as some of the people do. We visit some of the people from Ahlus-Sunnah and find that they have a brand new library, yet his state is as is said:

> *There are a large number of volumes with the Sheikh,*
>
> *but in truth, he does not actually read them.*

Rather, acquire books and then devote yourself to reading them. Just as the wife of Imaam az-Zuhree said to him when she found him so engrossed with his books, and perhaps lacking in the time spent interacting with her. She said, *"By Allaah, your books are harder on me than if you had three more wives!"* In such a way this is necessary for the student of knowledge, if he makes the goal of gaining beneficial knowledge secondary to pursuing worldly aims then he will not gain significant knowledge. The same is the case if he makes knowledge merely a means to attain worldly benefits, or makes his efforts of calling to Allaah and His religion a means to worldly benefit

And we must go back to examine the books of criticism and commendation in the religion. These books are indeed important, and Allaah has given our scholars success. When you read the biographies contained within these books, you are always coming across important points of knowledge. This is if you read works such as *((Mizaan al-'Itidaal)05-19)*. As *((Mizaan al-'Itidaal)05-19)* has been said to be the best book written by Imaam adh-Dhahabee, such that some of the Hanafees, the Asha'rees, and the Shee'ah feel tormented by this work! They say, [If adh-Dhahabee writes the biography of a Hanafee scholar or an Asha'ree then he shortens his biography, but when it is the biography of a Hanbalee scholar he lengthens it extensively!!] But ash-Shawkaanee staes in *((al-Badr al-Talaa')05-29)*: *"No this is not correct. However this man, Imaam adh-Dhahabee, was a man whose heart drank deeply from the knowledge of hadeeth, such that if he writes the biography of a scholar of hadeeth he gives free rein to his pen in composing such a biography; but when he is composing the biography of someone who is not a scholar of hadeeth then he does not have the same concern."* As for the Shee'ah, then he protected *((Mizaan)05-19)* from being filled with their madness. To the degree that they said:

> In the scale the book al-Mizaan mostly inclines towards
>> the like of those mentioned in Surah ar-Rahmaan
> So (oh Shee'ah people) openly declare the deficiency of the one
>> who denies the rightful place of the prophet's family,
> While you raise their level and position, such that you break the thorn
>> which is the book al-Mizaan

But all praise is due to Allaah, in fact it is *((al-Mizaan)05-19)* which actually throws a tremendous blow and breaks them, while they have not struck any blow against it. The people have not ceased competing with each other to acquire *((Mizaan al-'Itidaal)05-19)* and *((Lisaan al-Mizaan)05-20)*, and other books by Imaam adh-Dhahabee may Allaah, the Most High, have mercy upon him. Additional beneficial books for the researcher are: *((Taarikh Baghdaad)09-03)* and *((Taarikh Ibn 'Asaakir)09-10)*, the copies of which the people of Sa'adah stole from me when the shipment reached there from al-Qaseem, Saudi Arabia. They consider it war booty in their conflict with us as Ahlus-Sunnah, so they always stall their release in hopes that we will simply leave the books to them in frustration. The individual who stole them is the one who is responsible for the various media and news in Sa'adah.

And this book is one you cannot do without, and is from those beneficial books about which it is said, "*If an individual is to acquire of the books of biography and information about men, he must acquire ((at-Taarikh al-Kabeer)05-21) by al-Bukhaaree.*" It is a book of history, biography, commendation and criticism of men, indicating the hidden defects of narrations, as well as declaring narrations authentic or weak. It is a valuable book which it is proper that you acquire. And the book *((Jarh wa at-Ta'deel)04-07)* by Ibn Abe Haatim, as perhaps there is a narrator which is mentioned in *((at-Taarikh)05-21)* of al-Bukhaaree without any commendation or criticism, but you will find that he has been mentioned and spoken about within *((Jarh wa at-Ta'deel)04-07)* by Ibn Abe Haatim. As for *((Taarikh Baghdaad)09-03)* then certainly it has been said about it that it is proper that it be named "*History of the World.*" This is because in its age and time it was the capital of the Muslim world, and scholars come to it from every single Muslim country of the earth. Therefore it is considered a biography of the majority of the Muslim scholars of that time. Also from the beneficial books in history are the *((History of Ibn Ma'een)09-06)* may Allaah the Most High have mercy upon him, and that of *((ad-Darqutnee)09-07)*, may Allaah the Most High have mercy upon him. Similarly, there are the books of biography from the Companions such as: *((al-'Isaabah)05-02)*, and this is a tremendous book! But as for the book [[Hayat as-Sahabah]] it contains what is authentic as well as that which is false or inaccurate, so it is not suitable that it be held as reliable.

Similarly the book *((Asad al-Ghaabah)05-01)* is from the valuable books, as is the book *((al-'Isteea'aab)05-05)* by Haafidh Ibn 'Abdul-Bar. Additionally from the beneficial general reference works which it is proper that the student of knowledge acquire are the books of Sheikh al-Islaam Ibn Taymeeyah and Haafidh Ibn Qayyim, may Allaah have mercy upon them both. Indeed there is no opportunity to list their numerous books right now, as if they were all listed that itself would be enough to fill several pages of a book itself!

From the books that we haven't mentioned yet is *((as-Sunan al-Kubraa)02-31)* by al-Bayhaqee. It is an excellent book regarding issues of ritual worship and general rulings to the degree that some scholars have even said, "If there was any book that I was not able to do without, I would not be able to do without *((as-Sunan al-Kubraa)02-31)* of al-Bayhaqee regarding the matters of worship and rulings, rather than other books." There is also *((Ta'dheem Qadr as-Salaat)12-47)* by Muhammad Ibn Nasr al-Maruzee and *((al-Muntaqaa)12-21)* by Ibn Jaarood *((al-Musnad)02-32)* which is attributed to Imaam as-Shaafa'ee, and *((al-Bidaayah wa an-Nihaayah)09-02)* in the subject of History *((at-Tamheed)07-29)* by Ibn 'Abdul-Bar. Then there are the explanations of the Qur'aan from the first generations of Muslims *((Tafseer Haafidh Ibn Katheer)01-01)* and *((Tafseer Ibn Jareer)01-04)*, and *((Tafseer al-Baghawee)01-07)*. It is proper that you are diligent in striving to acquire these books of commentary, not simply relying upon the available summarized versions of *((Tafseer Ibn Katheer)01-01)*. Also it is proper that you acquire *((Tafseer Ibn Katheer)01-01)* itself, as it is from the most significant of references in explanation of the Qur'aan. It often transmits from books which we no longer have as existing manuscripts or printed copies in our time, and we find that it is transmitted with the reports with the chain of narration, whether authentic or weak. So it is a valuable work that is only proper you strive to have.

As for the books of correct beliefs from those known as the fundamental and best of works in this area are: *((as-Sunnah)02-26)* by Ibn Abee 'Aasim which Sheikh Naasirudden al-Albaanee, may Allaah the Most High preserve him, verified its narrations and investigated their sources and chains. And from them is *((as-Sunnah)06-22)* by 'Abdullah Ibn Ahmad Ibn Hanbal. And from them is the book *((al-'Asmaa' wa al-Sifaat)06-35)* by al-Bayhaqee, and *((Kitaab at-Taheed)06-36)* by Ibn Khuzaymah. The book *((al-'Emaan)06-37)* by Ibn Munduh. Also the book *((Tahaweeyah)06-08)*, yet if you are able to study the works of the earlier scholars, then this is easier on you, as *((Tahaweeyah)06-08)* has within it the false statements of the sect of the Kilaabeeyah, the Bishreeyah, the Mariseeyah, and others who were misguided- so this might be difficult upon you. But the works of the early scholars are not tarnished by the statements of the people of false philosophical rhetoric and so are easier to understand.

From those books which are precious is *((Kitaab as-Sharee'ah)06-34)* by al-Aajooree and the book *((ar-Rad 'Alaa al-Jahmeeyah)11-11)*, and *((Khalq 'Afaa'al al-'Ebaad)06-33)* as well as the book *((Sharh Usul 'Itiqaad Ahlus-Sunnah)06-29)* by Laalikkaa'ee. Now we move onto the those books related to the specific terminology of the sciences of hadeeth. Perhaps it is possible to limit this to the book *((al-Ba'ith al-Hatheeth)04-37)* if there is no one available to teach you. And possibly *((Tadreeb ar-Raawee)04-08)* and I mention these two works as both of them are easy and simple. But as for the case where you find someone to teach you, then *((Muqadamah Ibn Salaah)04-38)* and *((an-Nukat)04-04)* by Haafidh Ibn Hajr, *((at-Taqyeed wa al-Islaah)04-09)* by Haafidh al-'Iraaqee, *((al-Kifaayah)04-10)* by Haafidh al-Khateeb *((al-Jaame'a Li Akhlaaq ar-Raawee wa as-Saame'a)04-11)* by Haafidh al-Khateeb, and the book of ar-Raamhazmuzee which is considered the first book of this kind written on the subject of hadeeth science terminology and is named *((al-Muhadeeth al-Faasel)04-12)*. Also the book *((Fath al-Mugheeth)04-26)* despite its printing mistakes. I have been informed that others are working on a verification of this book, may Allaah assist them in this endeavor. Also there is *((Ma'rifat Uloom al-Hadeeth)04-13)* by Haakim, it is from the best of books. And the book *((Sharf Ashaabul Hadeeth)06-32)* is also from the best of books in this area. Likewise *((at-Tankeel Bemaa fee Ta'neeb al-Kawtharee Min Abaateel)04-27)* is also from the most excellent of books.

Now we will go to the books of the Arabic language. From them are those works which one may benefit from even without sitting with the scholars and learning from the people of knowledge, such as: *((al-Qaamoos)10-01)*, *((Taaj al-'Aroos)10-02)*, and *((Lisaan al-'Arab)10-03)*. They only speak about the meaning of individual words and terms. However, regarding the matter of learning grammar, then it is required the you seek its knowledge from the people of knowledge, because you may read something but not understand it.

The area of usul al-fiqh, or the principles of jurisprudence, is similar; it is required that one benefit while learning it through some of the people of knowledge, as one may read something but not comprehend its full or correct meaning. Among the people there are those who gain understanding from significant reading and going over the various principles and guidelines found in works such as *((Nayl al-Awtaar)03-08)*, as you read over its discussion of such principles.

Now we move on to the books related to discovering hidden defects with hadeeth narrations, as this is a significant matter dealt with by the books of this science. Perhaps a hadeeth narration may have an excellent chain, clear in its soundness like the bright sun, but will nonetheless have a hidden defect. From the best of such books is *((Kitaab al-'Ilal)04-14)* by Ibn Abee Haatim which we have with us here. The book of hidden defect by *((ad-Darqutnee)04-36)* is considered the most comprehensive and excellent, but its printing has not been completed. The book *((al-'Ilal al-Kabeer)04-15)* by at-Tirmidhee has been organized and a commentary made of it. Also *((al-'Ilal as-Sagheer)04-16)* by at-Tirmidhee and which has an *((explanation of it)04-19)* by Haafidh Ibn Rajab which bears witness to his having traveled for knowledge. As for *((al-'Ilal)04-17)* by Imaam Ahmad it is restricted to hidden defects in biographies of narrators. As for *((al-'Ilal)04-18)* of 'Alee Ibn al-Madinee, there is only a small volume available from it. And from those books which are beneficial are *(('Awdhu' al-Bayaan)01-03)* which is a good book which can be benefited from as well as the book *((Jaame'a al-Usool)07-11)*. Likewise the book *((Sharh as-Sunnah)06-40)* by Baghawee is a good book which one can benefit from.

And also from the beneficial works in principles of jurisprudence are *(('Irshaad al-Fuhool)08-09)* and *((al-Mudhakirah)08-05)* by Sheikh ash-Shanqeetee. Sheikh al-Albaanee, may Allaah the Exalted preserve him said, "*The best of works in this subject is ((al-Ihkaam Fee Usool al-Ahkaam)08-02) by Ibn Hazm, may Allaah the Most High have mercy upon him.*" I am not calling you to become someone who adheres inflexibly to the Dhaaharee school, like Abu Muhammad Ibn Hazm was, but simply to benefit from his book, may Allaah reward him with good.

And from the valuable books is *((Tagleeq at-Ta'leeq FeeMaa Yata'leq Be al-Ahadeeth al-Mua'liqah Fee Saheeh al-Bukhaaree)02-33)* and *((ar-Risaalah)08-03)* by Imaam Shaafa'ee which is related to principles of jurisprudence, and *((al-Majmu'a)08-04)* by Imaam an-Nawawee, and *((al-Mughnee)07-07)* by Ibn Qudamah. Acquire these in order to benefit from them. But as for striving and struggling in some works over others, then this should be in the memorization of the Book of Allaah, and the memorization of the hadeeth of the Messenger of Allaah, may Allaah's praise and salutations be upon him and his household. But acquire these other books as references for yourself, so that if an issue is presented to you you can refer them.

There are hadeeth narrations which are well known and commonly said by the people. From them are narrations which are authentic at the highest level, from them are those which are authentic at an adequate intermediate level, from them are those which are weak, and from them are those which are fabricated or have no true basis to be considered hadeeth at all. Related to this are the following books: *((al-Maqaasid al-Hasnah Feemaa Ishtahar 'Alaa al-Alsanah)04-28)*, which is a valuable book. There is an author of a similar work, *((Kashf al-Kafaa' wa Mazeel al-Ilbaas 'Amaa 'Istahar 'Alaa Alsanah an-Nas)12-51)* who brings additional narrations and leaves some other mentioned narrations out. But *((al-Maqaasid al-Hasnah)04-28)* is better from the aspect that its author is an established scholar, whereas the author of *((Kashf al-Kafaa' wa Mazeel al-Ilbaa)12-51)* sometimes mentions a hadeeth narration which is completely false but doesn't mention anything further about this! An example of this is the false narration, [If difficult affairs come to you, then hold fast to the companions of the graves.] Similarly he mentions in his own introduction that it is possible for an individual to recognize the state of authenticity of a hadeeth- whether it is in fact authentic or whether it is weak- simply by mystical illumination or inspiration. Meaning that it will mystically become apparent to him that this narration is authentic, and this one is weak according to the scholars of hadeeth. That it will be revealed to him, just as Jibreel revealed revelation to the Prophet, may Allaah's praise and salutations be upon him and his household, and so that narration will be considered authentic or week! He also brings other corrupted beliefs in his introduction, corrupted beliefs that originate with the Sufees. There is also the book *((Asnaa al-Mutaalib fee Ahadeeth Mukhtalafahu al-Muraatib Min al-Ahaadeeth al-Mushtaharah)12-39)*.

We move on to the specific subject of books indicating fabricated hadeeth narrations, from among the most excellent of them is *((al-Maudhuaat)04-21)* by Ibn Jawzee, *((al-Abaateel)04-22)* by Jazqaanee, and *((al-Laa'lee al-Maudhuaat)04-20)* by Suyootee, which is a refutation of the assertions of the work *((al-Maudhuaat)04-21)* by Ibn Jawzee. Related to this last book is an examination of its own assertions entitled *((al-Fara'ed al-Majmu'ah)04-29)* by ash-Shawkaanee. However, this work almost does not clarify the conclusions of its investigations! How can this be? Consider an example: Imaam ash-Shawkaanee will mention the relevant hadeeth and then mention the stated position of Imaam as-Suyootee, but upon reading it an individual will not be able to determine whether ash-Shawkaanee agrees with as-Suyootee in his refutation of the claim of fabrication or agrees with the original assessment of Ibn Jawzee that the hadeeth is fabricated?!? However, Allaah allowed that an exemplary scholar, 'Abdur-Rahmaan al-Mu'alamee, may Allaah the Most High have mercy upon him, to comment and clarify the book by Imaam ash-Shawkaanee.

Also from the beneficial books is *((Dalaa'il an-Nabuwah)06-41)* by Imaam al-Bayhaqee, and *((Dalaa'il an-Nabuwah)06-42)* by Haafidh Abee Na'eem, may Allaah the Most High have mercy upon him. As for books related to the permissible abstinence from pursuing worldly goods, then from this works is *((Kitaab az-Zuhd)12-22)* by Imaam Ahmad, and *((az-Zuhd)12-23)* by Wakee'a *((az-Zuhd)12-24)* by Hinaad as-Saree *((Kitaab az-Zuhd)12-25)* by Ibn Mubaarak. And in the subject of Allaah's decree there is the beneficial book by Ibn Qayyim *((Shafa'a al-Aleel)06-28)*. As we have previously mentioned, you should be diligent in acquiring the books of Sheikh al-Islaam Ibn Taymeeyah and Haafidh Ibn Qayyim, within *((Majmu'a al-Fataawaa)07-19)* there is an entire volume related to this aspect of belief, meaning Allaah's decree. Now we proceed to the books which categorize the biographies of the different scholars, the works of tabaqat From them is *((at-Tabaqaat Ibn Sa'd)05-06)* as well as *((Tabaqaat al-Hufaadh)05-07)* by Haafidh as-Suyootee, there is also the book *((Tadhkirah al-Hufaadh)05-04)* by Haafidh adh-Dhahabee, from them is *((Tabaqaat ash-Shaafee'ah)05-08)* by as-Subkee and *((Tabaqaat al-Hanaabilah)05-09)* by Ibn Abee Ya'ala then *((Tabaqaat al-Hanaabilah)05-10)* by Ibn Rajab. There is also *((Minhaj al-Ahmad)05-16)* with biographies of those individuals upon the methodology of jurisprudence founded from the methodology of Imaam Ahmad. There is *((Tabaqaat al-Qura'a)05-11)* by Haafidh adh-Dhahabee, *((Tabaqaat an-Nahweeyeen)05-12)* *((Tabaqaat al-Mufassireen)05-13)* by Dawudee, and *((Tabaqaat al-Fuqahaa)05-14)*.

And from the generally important books is the book *((Shu'ab al-Emaan)02-10)* by Haafidh al-Bayhaqee, may Allaah, the Most High have mercy upon him, *((al-Umm)08-06)* by Shaafa'ee, *((Tabaqaat al-Khulafah)05-15)* by Ibn Khayyat, and the book *((al-Ba'ith wa an-Nashoor)05-22)*. Among the books of biography there is also the book *((al-Insaab)05-23)* by , and *((al-Kunyaa)05-24)* by Dawlaabee. Also from amongst the important books is *((Tufaat al-Ashraaf)04-30)* and *((al-Mu'ajam al-Mufahris)04-33)*.

As for those works which are books of heresy and misguidance, then those are the books of the Shee'ah, and the Ba'athees, and the books of Qadhafee, which may be found distributed at the book fair during some years. Unfortunately there is not the opportunity to enumerate them all and mention them completely. But also among the books of misguidance are those of the Sufis, and it is not proper that they be used and relied upon. The books of the Raafidhah, or the Shee'ah should also not be relied upon. Similarly those books which discuss general matters but which also excite and inflame people's nationalistic impulses and feelings should not be used or turned to. And the books written by those modern-day authors preceding upon new and recently devised ideas and concepts are not proper to be used or relied upon. Such as the book [[al-Aghaanee]] by Asfahaanee, which has been refuted by the work *((Sayf al-Yamaanee Fee Nahr al-Asfahaanee)11-33)*. And that explanation of the Qur'aan [[Tafseer al-Manaar]] is considered from among the books of heresy and misguidance. I mentioned some of these issues within the book *((Rudood Ahl-Ilm Alaa at-Taa'neen Fee Hadeeth as-Saher)11-25)* and have explained the great distance between the author of that explanation of the Qur'aan, Muhammad Rasheed Ridhaa, and the path of the first three generations, the Salaf. Additionally the books of Ibn 'Arabee such as [[al-Fusoos]], along with his explanations of the Qur'aan, are considered books of misguidance, as he is a deceiving Sufee who has committed a greater form of disbelief then the Christians and Jews. Therefore it is not proper that you use his books or the books of the later al-Ghazaalee, and I mean the present day Muhammad al-Ghazaalee, such as [[Dustoor al-Wahdah al-Thaqaafeeyah]], or such as the book [[Hummam ad-Da'eeyah]], and [[as-Sunnah an-Nabaweeyah Bayn Ahl al-Fiqh wa ahl-Hadeeth]]. Do not rely upon or use his books in any case.

And from the books of misguidance is the book [[Badaa'eea az-Zahoor]]; it is not a book to be used. Just as the book [[Tanbeeh al-Ghaafileen]] by Ibn Layth as-Samarkaandee also should not be. And the book [[Ayoon al-Mu'ajezaat]] by an evil wrongdoing Raafidhee, contains open and apparent disbelief in Islaam. The book [[al-Kaafee]] by Kulaynee is from this type of harmful book also, as well as the books [[as-Sunne al-Mutaalib fee Najaat Abee Taalib]], [[Saloonee Qabl In Tafqedoonee]], [[Matn al-Azhaar]], and [[Sharh alAzhaar]]. The book [[Tafseer az-Zamakhsharee]] is Mu'tazilee in nature and should not be used or relied upon. He is someone who is generally ignorant of the narrations of the Prophet. He authenticates those narrations which agree with his desires and he weakens those which do not conform to it.

And similarly the books of the people of biased partisanship; we have long been from those who warn against the books of such people. Hasan at-Turaabee is also someone who has produced books yet is an individual upon heresy and misguidance. Abu Rayyah, the author of [[Adhu'a Alaa as-Sunnah]]- and in reality this book is in fact "*darknesses upon the Sunnah*" not illuminations upon the Sunnah- is certainly astray and from the leading scholars of misguidance. The work [[Asha'aar al-Muqaaleh]] is not a book that should be relied upon; rather, within some of the poetry that he brings forth are statements of disbelief. Also from such books are the books related to sorcery such as [[Shams al-Ma'arif]] and the book [[ar-Rahmah]]. Therefore it is upon the student of knowledge to inquire and ask the people of knowledge which of the books he should purchase. From the harmful books are those of Ibn Alwaan, such as his book [[al-Mahjuraan]], as well as the publications by the author of [[Bayt al-Fiqh]], as he is a misguided false messiah from among the false messiahs. Certainly we've discussed some of his falsehood and nonsense within the work ((*Irshaad Dhuwa al-Fatan Lil Iba'ad Ghulaat ar-Rawafidh min al-Yemen*))11-17). Likewise the book [[Tabaqaat ash-Sha'raanee]] and [[al-Mizaan]] which he also wrote is from the books of misguidance and heresy.

Additionally those magazines which are published by the enemies of Islaam, or those works which are written by the people of biased partisanship- it is necessary that the student of knowledge distance himself from these books. The books of misguidance and harassment, as well as newspapers and magazines of a similar nature are not proper for the student of knowledge to busy himself with reading them. But as for the scholar who has the ability to refute their errors, then there is no harm in reading such works for the purpose of refuting them. And those books which advocate the celebration of the Prophet's a birthday in all the different forms and types- it is necessary to stay distant from them. Similarly the book [[Min al-Mahd Ilaa al-Lahd]] is from the books of heresy and misguidance. And from the books of disaster and calamity for the Muslims are those which are written by Yusuf Haashim ar-Raafa'ee which were printed by the people of Hudaydah, who consider themselves the 'Scholars of Yemen.' We say they are ignorant ones of Yemen, or the foolish ones of Yemen, we do not say or call them the scholars of Yemen. That statement is an insult and affront to all the people of Yemen, as thouigh they were upon such superstitious misguidance. Indeed the people of Yemen are free from any involvement in that misguidance which that book possesses. And it is necessary to bring forth a detailed explanation regarding such books; however the time does not permit that elaborate, detailed discussion

As for the books of Ibn Sinaa', then there is no harm in benefiting from those which are related to only medical science. But in relation to beliefs he is someone who denies the physical resurrection and so he is considered a heretical apostate. Indeed Sheikh al-Islaam Ibn Taymeeyah and Haafidh Ibn Qayyim stated that he was from among those who followed the worshipers of the ancient Egyptians. Additionally it should be said that the books of an-Nabahaanee are also from those books considered of misguidance and deviance from the religion. And now we will mention some of the beneficial books in the area of classical Islamic medical science, from among them is the book *((at-Tibb an-Nabawee)12-26)* by Haafidh Ibn Qayyim, which is a selection taken from his book *((Za'ad al-Ma'ad)09-05)*, as well as *((at-Tibb an-Nabawee)12-27)* by Haafidh adh-Dhahabee, and from them is *((at-Tibb an-Nabawee)12-28)* by as-Suyootee, as well as *((at-Tibb an-Nabawee)12-29)* by Abee Na'eem. There are also other general books of medical science from the Arabs which are proper to acquire and benefit from such as: *((al-Mu'atamid fee Tibb wa al-Hikmah)12-07)*. It contains some matters of misguidance as well as issues of deviation, but is suitable for the one who has the ability to distinguish between what is harmful and what is not. The work *((Mu'jiza'at as-Shifa'aa))12-19)* is also a good book.

And from the generally beneficial books is the book of our brother Muhammad Ibn 'Abdul-Wahaab al-'Abdalee al-Wasaabee *((al-Qawl al-Mufeed fee Adilat at-Tawheed))06-19)*... And from the beneficial books is the book *((Qaraa' Alasanah Fee Nafee at-Tataref wa al-Ghulu' wa aas-Shadhudh 'An Ahl Sunnah)11-19)* by our brother in Allaah's religion 'Abdul-'Azeez Ibn Yahya al-Bure'aa, may Allaah preserve him. And from the valuable books is the work *((al-'Itisaam)11-01)* by Shaatabee, and *((Bid'ah at-Ta'asub al-Madhhabee)11-15)* by our brother 'Eid Abbasee. And from the books which it is proper that you acquire is the book *((al-Ibtidaa' Fee Madhaar al-Ibtida'a')11-06)* And this is what Allaah has made easy for me to mention during this lecture and I was reminded of some of them by my brother in Allaah's religion, may Allaah reward him with good. And in closing, all praise is due Allaah, Lord of all the worlds.

(125) The Eminent Guiding Scholar Muhammad Ibn Saaleh al-'Utheimeen, may Allaah have mercy upon him, from 'Kitaab al-'Ilm': Pages 154-156

*Question: What are the books you recommend for the beginner in seeking knowledge, and specifically in the subject of correct beliefs?*

He answered saying: From among the best books which there are in the subject of essential beliefs, is the book *((al-Aqeedatul-Wasateeyah)06-05)* of Sheikh al-Islaam Ibn Taymeeyah as it is an outstanding summary of the beliefs of the people of the Sunnah and adherence to the Jama'ah. Yet it requires explanation, and so the beginning student of knowledge is in need of someone to explain its text to him. Likewise the work *(('Aqeedah as-Safaareenaa)06-47)* which is structured as a poem, however it should be noted that it contains some generalized statements which apparently contradict the methodology of the Salaf. For example his statement:

*Our Lord does not have any directions nor any measurements*

*Nor does He have any form, as He is the Highest in His sublimity*

This general statement conflicts with the methodology and position of the first generations of Muslims in this matter. Therefore if a student of knowledge is able to study this work of beliefs with a scholar who is well acquainted with the correct beliefs of Islaam, then such a scholar will clarify for him those generalizations which conflict with the methodology of the first generations regarding beliefs. If he is someone younger, and a beginning seeker of knowledge, he should begin with the memorization of *(('Amdat al-Ahkaam)02-28)* as it is a concise work, and includes general hadeeth from within the two well known 'Saheeh' collections, and so does not require from him any investigation about the authenticity of its hadeeth or need to inquire about the original sources of its narrations. In the subject of hadeeth terminology, from the most comprehensive books present is *((Nukhbat al-Fikr)04-01)* by Ibn Hajr, may Allaah have mercy upon him. It is equivalent in length to about three or four full sized pages and so it is possible for a person to memorize and have it stay in his mind such that he can use it after he gets older.

In the subject of explanations of the meaning of the Qur'aan there is *((Tafseer Ibn Kather )01-01)*. It is an excellent, beneficial, and reliable commentary. There is also the commentary of Sheikh 'Abdur-Rahman Ibn Naasir as-Sa'dee, which is easy to understand, as well as being both excellent and reliable. So begin with these two books, and then after studying them then progress into other works of commentary.

In the subject of fiqh, meaning the way to correctly implement what is found in the source texts, there is the work *((Zaad al-Mustaqna')07-01)* upon which there is the commentary *((Rawdh al-Maraba')07-02)*. This is a blessed book, both concise and comprehensive. It was explained to us by Sheikh 'Abdur-Rahman as-Sa'dee. And despite the fact that he himself had memorized the text of another similar work *((Daleel at-Taalib)07-23)*, he himself said to us *"You all should memorize ((Zaad al-Mustaqna')07-01)"*.

In the subject of Arabic Grammar begin with the work *((al-Aajroomeeyah)10-05)*. It is a concise, simplified book which is easy for a student to memorize and read; an excellent work. Then after completing your study of it, proceed to the memorization of *((Alfeeyah of Ibn Maalik)10-04)* as it summarizes every aspect of Arabic grammar and benefits a student. From the best of the works that I have read in the seerah, or the life history of the Messenger of Allaah, may Allaah's praise and salutations be upon him, is the book *((Zaad al-Ma'aad)09-05)* by Ibn Qayyim. It discusses the life history of the Prophet, may Allaah's praise and salutations be upon him and his household, in every different situation of his life, along with encompassing a derivation of many rulings and guidelines from the events of his life and the battles he fought.

As for the subject of the principles of jurisprudence, then this is difficult, but there has been written in this area a summarized book entitled *((al-Usul Min 'Ilm al-Usul)08-01)* which can open the door for the student in the study of this area.

Similarly in the subject of the guidelines of inheritance, there is the book *((al-Burhaneeyah)12-33)* it is a comprehensive book which is summarized yet beneficial regarding all aspects of the proper division of the wealth of inheritance. Its author is Muhammad al-Burhaanee.

(126) THE EMINENT GUIDING SCHOLAR MUQBIL IBN HAADEE AL-WAADI'EE, MAY ALLAAH HAVE MERCY UPON HIM, FROM 'ANSWERING THE QUESTIONER REGARDING THE MOST IMPORTANT ISSUES', PAGE 442

***Question regarding acquiring the books which are important for a student of knowledge***

Answer: Regarding the students of knowledge, than among their ranks there is the beginner who just has been mentioned by our noble brother, I ask Allaah, the Tremendous to grant him His blessings. And from among the students of knowledge there is also the one who has reached the level of researcher. As for the one who is a beginner, then we advise him to acquire the book *((Riyaadh as-Saaliheen)02-11)*, and to acquire *((Fath al-Majeed Sharh Kitaab at-Tawheed)06-12)* as well as *((al-'Ulu)06-45)* by Haafidh adh-Dhahabee, and its summarized version by Sheikh Muhammad Naassiruddeen al-Albaanee, as it is simpler to read, may Allaah reward him with good. As for the individual who is a beginner, I advise him to be diligent in striving to sit with the people of the Sunnah, as well as in asking them about the evidence of matters, asking them about anything that is not clear to him from the meanings of the Qur'aan, or which he does not understand from the hadeeth narrations of the Messenger of Allaah may the praise and salutations of Allaah be upon him, and that one mixes with the people who give importance to their religion. This will make him someone who is a student of knowledge and benefits from his efforts in a short amount of time; and that is something he would otherwise not know how to search for.

So attach yourself to your brothers from amongst the people of the Sunnah, either by means of the telephone, correspondence, or visiting your brothers. Because many of our brothers who fall short in traveling, they gather a number of questions and wait until one of their knowledgeable brothers comes to them. What is proper is that if an issue comes up they should travel in the path of Allaah for the sake of it. Then one is someone seeking knowledge even if it is for a single issue. This was the case of Jaabir Ibn 'Abdullah, who traveled to the land of Sham, north of Arabia, for the sake of a single issue, and for the sake of a single hadeeth narration. This hadeeth which he traveled for is well-known among our brothers who are students of knowledge. It is that of Riz Ibn Hubaish who asked Safwaan Ibn 'Asaal who said: "*There came this fountain of knowledge and asked him about a single issue!*" that being the matter of wiping over one's socks during purification. So what I intend by this is that if one travels for the sake of a single matter and that afterwards one achieves knowledge of that. After that, one would find another pleasure which also manifests itself within his mind as long as he is alive. But as for the likes of the books of those sects such as the Zaydeeyah, then I do not advise the beginner to get these and neither should the student of knowledge, whose time is limited and restricted.

Just take hold of the truths and do not worry yourself with those who oppose you. As for the one who wants to establish a library and wants to be able to research matters and write works, then it is still not for him to acquire such books, as he then takes them as a reference. However, the one who wishes to refute some of the innovations and contradictions to the truths which they contain within them should be the one to read them. A student of knowledge should give attention to that which will benefit him, as we have heard, such as the work *((Riyaadh as-Saaliheen)02-11)*, and *((Lu'lu wa al-Marjaan Fee Ma Itifaaq 'Aleihi ash-Shakhayn)02-16)*. Similarly, he should ask his brothers about beneficial books, just as it would be necessary for him to ask one who was an expert in a certain type of expensive merchandise if he wanted do purchase it from the market. The same is the case for books. One should ask the advice of the ones who have knowledge concerning them.

This is because in some books there are some matters which lie concealed like a poisonous scorpion, and that which is like a bloody death. So it is proper that one strives diligently to acquire those books which will benefit one and which will guide one upon the easiest way in the shortest amount of time. Do you not consider the one who reads and studies for twelve long years in the Haadee University? Their educational curriculum spans twelve years, yet even after that someone graduates and he himself admits that he is not able to stand in comparison to that student of knowledge who has studied the hadeeth sciences, because they simply repeat their various statements. They are not comparable to that student knowledge who studies in the Masjid al-Haram in Mecca. This is what day themselves say. But why? Because the one who studies by means of "*Allaah said,*" and "*The Messenger of Allaah said,*" may the praise and salutations of Allaah be upon him, gains significant benefits within a short time, in contradiction to the one who studies the various statements of men and studies the intricate issues upon which there are numerous

287

NOTES

disagreements, merely saying. [Muwedbillah says...] and [Abu Taalib says...], and [Abu al-Abbass says...] and [Yahya Ibn Hamzah says...] He has squandered his time, my brothers, especially if he was a beginner seeker of knowledge and especially if he was not someone with the ability to distinguish between the various evidences.

I will inform our brothers about myself, and I have told them of this on more than one occasion. In the beginning of my studies I would read from the book ((Rawdhat an-Naadher)08-08). I had resolved that I would not blame or take issue with any of those individuals mentioned in their differing. And I said, [Each of the people have some evidence, so why should you find fault with the people? Why should you do that when there are numerous statements?] I was someone who did not have the ability to distinguish between that which was evidence and that which was not considered evidence, or between that which was authentic evidence and that which was not authentic evidence. So I used to suppose that every statement I found had some evidence or, as is said amongst the people, that the [Differing among my Ummah is a mercy.] Indeed Allaah is sufficient for us, and the sufficient Guardian! At that time I believed that every scholar who strove to independently derive a ruling was in some way correct, and that each of them had some support from the Messenger of Allaah! So therefore it is necessary, may Allaah bless you, to be diligent in taking from strong, valuable books. As for the researcher, it is not necessary that he acquire the work [[al-Bahr al-Zakhaar]] or other similar books. And we will stop here, May Allaah bless you all.

(127) The Eminent Guiding Scholar ahmad Ibn Yahya an-Najmee, may Allaah preserve him, 'From Decisive Rulings on the Methodologies of Calling to Allaah': Vol. 2, Page 104

Question: Someone wishes to attend lessons in 'al-Aqeedat ul-Tahaweeyah'. However, when I asked him about his level in studying Sharee'ah knowledge; he replied, "I have read 'Thalatatul-Usul', 'Kitab at-Tawheed', 'al-Aajroomiyyah' and 'Milhat al-Iraab' and I did not have difficulty in understanding them." So does this person have the ability to study 'al-Aqeedat ul-Tahaweeyah' without having progressed gradually in his study of Sharee'ah knowledge? Similarly, what is the case in regard to other areas of knowledge? Please benefit us regarding this, so that we may be of those who are rewarded.

Answer: If this individual studied in an organized way and reached through these efforts a good level of understanding, or studied with a scholar, and perhaps studied some principles of the Arabic language, or studied from the books explaining the matters of worshiping Allaah alone, or from the sciences of assessing or explaining hadeeth narrations; then possibly he has come to understand certain matters and he may need to study other matters further with a scholar. ((Sharh Aqeedah at-Tahaweeyah)06-09) is complex, even to university students. However, the people differ in their levels of comprehension. Whatever the case may be, he needs to study with a scholar when reading the work ((Sharh Aqeedah at-Tahaweeyah)06-09). If there is no one suitable close to him to read and study with, then he can read it alone.

Afterwards he should note and write down those issues which were difficult for him to understand, and send those questions to one of the well-known scholars who has a firm and comprehensive understanding in the area of correct beliefs. Additionally, what he has taken and understood from his study needs to be examined, to see if it is indeed correct, or if it contains errors or misunderstandings. In any case, what is important in my view is that he does not miss the opportunity to read and review the work with a scholar. And from Allaah comes the success.

(128) The Eminent Guiding Scholar Muqbil Ibn Haadee al-Waadi'ee, may Allaah have mercy upon him, From 'Excellent Responses to Questions from those Present and those Absent': Page 156

*Question: What books should a student of knowledge should begin with, and then which should he proceed on to?*

Answer: As for the books that a beginning student of knowledge should start with- if he has the ability to read and write, he should read *((Fath al-Majeed Sharh Kitaab at-Tawheed)06-12)* as it is a tremendous book, as well as *((al-Aqeedatul-Wasateeyah)06-05)* of Sheikh al-Islaam Ibn Taymeeyah and *((al-Qawl al-Mufeed fee Adilat at-Tawheed))06-19)* of our brother Muhammad Ibn 'Abdul-Wahaab al-Wassabee. Likewise, he should read *((Bulugh al-Maraam)02-34)* and *((Riyaadh as-Saaliheen)02-11)* If he has read those books and wishes to proceed to other books, then if he has the ability he should begin memorizing the Qur'aan; this is better and preferable. Additionally, there is the issue of the Arabic language for our non-Arab brothers, which is essential. If a non-Arab is not strong in the Arabic language, then perhaps someone might go to him who has a pleasing form, outwardly reflecting Islaam, and explain the Qur'aan for him with other than its proper meaning and correct explanation. This is known to be what happened with the misguided sect known as the Mu'tazilah.

(129) The Eminent Guiding Scholar Ahmad Ibn Yahya an-Najmee, may Allaah preserve him, From 'Decisive Rulings on the Methodologies of Calling to Allaah': Vol. 1, Page 18 )

*Question: Oh sheikh, we would like you to name some of the books which are in conformance with the methodology of the first three generations of Islaam that the youth upon that clear way should acquire and place in his home library?*

Answer: Those books that it is necessary that student of knowledge acquires: from the books of hadeeth narrations, the "fundamental six" collections: *((Saheeh al-Bukhaaree)02-01),((Saheeh Muslim)02-02), (Sunan Abu Dawud)02-04), ((Jaame'a at-Tirmidhee)02-06),((Sunan an-Nasaa'ee)02-03), ((Sunan Ibn Majaah)02-05), ((Musnad of Imaam Ahmad)02-07)*, and also *((Saheeh Jaamea as-Sagheer)02-37)* and what has been added to it by Sheikh al-Albaanee, as well as his collection *((Silsilat al-Hadeeth as-Saheehah)02-38)*. Similarly, the books of the early scholars of hadeeth, the books of Sheikh Muhammad Ibn Abdul-Wahaab, his grandsons, and those related scholars in his time and after it.

Likewise, the books of the people of our time who adhere to the methodology of the first generations of Islaam, such as Sheikh 'Abdul-'Azeez Ibn 'Abdullah Ibn Baaz, Sheikh 'Abdul-'Azeez Ibn 'Abdullah Aal-Sheikh, Sheikh 'Abdullah Ibn 'Abdur-Rahman al-Ghudyan, Sheikh Saaleh Ibn Fouzan al-Fouzan, and Sheikh Saaleh al-Laheedaan. Also, the scholars of Medinah such as Sheikh Rabee'a Ibn Haadee al-Madkhalee, Sheikh Saaleh Ibn Saad as-Suhamee, Sheikh Alee Ibn Naasir Faqeehee, Sheikh Muhammad Ibn Haadee al-Madkhalee, Sheikh Abdul-Musin al-Abbaad and his son Abdur-Razzaq, and Sheikh Muhammad Ibn Rabee'a al-Madhkhalee, as well as other than them from the scholars who follow the way of the first generations. Also the books of Sheikh Zaid Ibn Muhammad al-Madhkhalee and works similar to them; all of them are excellent, beneficial books. The books of those who followed the way of the first generations in every age and time are beneficial books, and all praise is due to Allaah. However, as for the books of the people of division and groups and partisanship, then student of knowledge should be fearful of approaching such books.

**(130) The Eminent Guiding Scholar Muhammad Naasiruddeen al-Albaanee, may Allaah have mercy upon him: From the magazine 'al-Isaalah', Dhul-Hijjah 1423 h. Issue, Page 60**

*Question: Which books do you advise the developing youth to use in knowledge-based endeavors of his life?*

Answer: If he is a beginner, then we advise him to read from the books of fiqh such as the book *((Fiqh as-Sunnah)07-06)* of Sayyed Saabiq with the assistance of related references in his study such as *((Subl as-Salaam)03-06)*. In addition, he should refer to *((Tamaan al-Minnah)07-04)* as this is stronger than the original work. Additionally I recommend *((ar-Rawdhat ul-Nadeyyah)07-24)*. In regard to the books explaining the Qur'aan, he should make it his regular practice to read from the book *((Tafseer al-Qur'aan adh-Dheem)01-01)* of Ibn Katheer. Its explanation of some matters are somewhat lengthy; however it is the most correct of the books explaining the Qur'aan available today. After this, in regard to the works of admonition and softening the heart he should turn to the book *((Riyaadh as-Saaliheen)02-11)* of Imaam Nawawee. Then I advise, in relation to the books of correct belief, use of the book *((Sharh al-Aqeedatul Tahaaweeyah)06-09)* of Ibn Abee al-Izz al-Hanafee, with the assistance of my explanation and comments upon it.

Next he should make it his regular routine and practice to study the books of Sheikh al-Islaam Ibn Taymeeyah and his student Ibn Qayyim al-Jawzeeyah, may Allaah have mercy upon them both. I believe them to be from the rare and exceptional scholars from those the Muslims who have remained and proceeded upon the understanding of the religion according to the methodology of the righteous first three generation, along with the fear of Allaah and uprightness. And I do not purify or praise above Allaah anyone.

**(131) THE EMINENT GUIDING SCHOLAR MUQBIL IBN HAADEE AL-WAADI'EE, MAY ALLAAH HAVE MERCY UPON HIM, FROM 'A DEFENDING MISSION FROM AUDIO LECTURES UPON THE PEOPLE OF IGNORANCE & SOPHISTRY': VOL. I, PAGE 118**

*Question: In the name of Allaah, the Most Gracious, the most Merciful. I have come here only for a short trip and a short time I am not able to remain here and acquire knowledge from the hand our esteemed sheikh and from the hands of those others who teach here. For that reason I ask our sheikh with what he advises me in regard to books to read and study, and especially in the science of hadeeth?*

Answer: That which I recommend or advise the brother with is that if he reaches the point where he has a good understanding through reading, he should read works such as *((Saheeh al-Bukhaaree)02-01)*, *((Saheeh Muslim)02-02)*, and *((Tafseer Ibn Katheer)01-01)*. If his level of understanding is below this, than I advise him to frequently read from *((Riyaadh as-Saaliheen)02-11)* and *((Lu'Lu' wa al-Marjaan Feemaa 'Itifaaq 'Aleihi as-Sheikhaan)02-16)*, as well as *((Fath al-Majeed Sharh Kitaab at-Tawheed)06-12)*. In the subject of fiqh, to read from the book *((Bulugh al-Maraam)02-34)* of Haafidh Ibn Hajr. Knowledge is that which calls one and invites one further. When one reads from *((Bulugh al-Maraam)02-34)* it will indicate to him other reference works which he then refers to. Likewise, when you read from the work *((Lu'Lu' wa al-Marjaan Feemaa 'Itifaaq 'Aleihi as-Sheikhaan)02-16)*, at times they will indicate other reference works in some of its narrations mentioned without the full chain. I also advise the brothers to invite and facilitate attendance of a knowledgeable brother from among our brothers here who were students, so that perhaps they will instruct them in the religion, purely seeking Allaah's face and His reward for one, two, or three months. This time is like a school established by the favor of Allaah, in which his study for the sake of Allaah, and for the purpose that he might read from some works related to the Arabic language such as *((Tuhfat as-Sunneyah)10-07)* until his tongue becomes trained and he gains understanding of the meanings of words. Simply reading from books is not the same as taking knowledge from a scholar, even though those books which we of mentioned will benefit by the permission of Allaah, the Most High.

Before this there is the matter of memorizing what is easy for you from the Qur'aan, as the Qur'aan is considered to be that which heals and rectifies the illnesses and diseases of our hearts and our bodies. ❖*Verily, this Qur'aan guides to that which is most just and right*❖-(Surah al-Isra':9) The Companions of the Messenger of Allaah, may Allaah be pleased with them all, would learn the Qur'aan when they embraced Islaam. Some of them said, *"We use to learn emaan before the Qur'aan, and we would not proceed until we had fully learned ten verses..."* or a statement which carries this meaning. So one should first be fully engaged with the study of the Qur'aan and thereafter with the study of these other books.

Whenever different life matters occur, then it is possible for one to refer them back to the relevant books. For instance, the issue of divorce. Regarding this you would refer to *((Nayl al-Awtaar)03-08)* and *((Subl as-Salaam)03-06)* by Sana'anee. It strengthens and fortifies an individual when he searches for the guidance regarding a matter himself. Then he is confident and has assured himself that the ruling is not simply the statement of so-and-so, or the opinion of so-and-so. However, if you have searched and found the true ruling of a matter, then know that the Messenger of Allaah, may Allaah's praise and salutations be upon him, said, as was mentioned in the narration of Ibn 'Abbaas, *{Being informed of something is not like observing it oneself.}* [102] And as a poet once said:

> Oh Ibn al-Karaam, will you not draw close to observe, as reflecting upon,
>
> > that which has occurred in front of your own eyes is not like hearing about it.

The one who is able to go to the land of the two holy sanctuaries of Mecca and Medinahh, or to this place, in order to sit with the scholars of the people of the Sunnah, then indeed I advise them with such sittings with the people of the Sunnah. Sitting with the people of innovation in the religion does not result in or lead to anything other than misguidance. Similarly, sitting with the people of bias and partisanship to different groups and movements amongst the Muslims also does not result in or lead to anything other than misguidance. Indeed, sitting with these people of bias and partisanship causes destruction to knowledge, as perhaps an person was someone who had memorized the Qur'aan, but when he entered into this way of partisanship, he became forgetful of that which he had memorized, and his understanding and thinking became corrupted, when previously it was straight and steadfast. And we end with the praise of Allaah, Lord of all the Worlds.

**(132) THE EMINENT GUIDING SCHOLAR SAALEH IBN 'ABDUL-'AZEEZ AAL-SHEIKH, MAY ALLAAH PRESERVE HIM, FROM 'EXPLANATION OF AL-AQEEDATUT-TAHAAWEYAH': LESSON 42**

*Question: We require a good method for reading books. Is it enough to read them a single time or is it necessary to reread books? If this is indeed necessary, how is this possible considering the large number of books?*

Answer: The method of reading of books differs as some books are books of fundamental and essential knowledge, these perhaps should be read two or three times. While with other books this is not done, as they are simply reffered to once when needed. An example would be *((Tayseer al-Azeez al-Hameed Fath al-Majeed)06-20)*, this book is one that deserves be read a number of times, as it is a book of fundamental principles. And *((Sharh al-Waasiteeyyah)06-21)* by Sheikh Ibn Rasheed, may Allaah have mercy upon him, or for example *((Sharh al-Tahaweeyah)06-09)*. These works are important, so if you many times then that is fine. This is also the case with the explanation *(Sharh al-Badhur)03-07)*, or the explanations of *((az-Zaad)07-01)* or *((al-Hawasha)07-27)* there is no harm in rereading them, rather it is in fact better to read them several times. However works

---

[102]

such as *(Fath al-Baaree)03-01)* should be gone through in a similar way to *(al-Mughnee al-Kafee)07-07)* meaning until you reach its end, completing it fully once. But neither of this books are from those which needs to be read repeatedly. Therefore some of the books it may be possible for you to reread them, and some are turned to only when needed or used for reference, this is what is intended.

(133) The Eminent Guiding Scholar Ahmad Ibn Yahya An-Najmee, may Allaah preserve him-Decisive Rulings on the Methodologies of Calling to Allaah- Volume 2 page 103

*Question: Please benefit us, may Allaah reward you. Is it better to repeatedly study a specific text from the texts of Sharee'ah knowledge, or is it sufficient to study it a single time and then move on to a different text. Please benefit us regarding this, so that we may be of those who are rewarded.*

Answer: This depends on the comprehension of the student. If the student has acquired a strong understanding and understands the subject or text well, then it is better for him to proceed to another text of knowledge. However, if the student's understanding is somewhat weak and he does not properly or fully understand the text, then is is better that he review the text until he understands it well. And there is no doubt that reviewing a work a second time will strengthen your comprehension of it. And the success is from Allaah.

(134) The Eminent Guiding Scholar Muhammad Ibn Saaleh al-'Utheimeen, may Allaah have mercy upon him, from 'Explanation of the Book 'Jewels for the Student of Knowledge': page 200-202

### Gathering Beneficial Books for your Library

Gathering books which are necessary for the student of knowledge is something that should be given attention. However it is important to begin with most important works and book and then proceed to those of lesser importance. If someone only has a small income then it is not something good nor is it acting wisely to purchase many books, burdening himself with the financial burden of their cost. This is from disliked spending of wealth. Due to this understanding the Prophet, may Allah's praise and salutations be upon him, did not command the man who wanted to marry but did not posses any wealth, to borrow money and indebt himself in order to accomplish that. So first give importance to the most important and fundamental books, not including modern works as some of the modern authors do not have well established knowledge. Because of this if you read such a modern book it is often found to be somewhat superficial, perhaps transmitting something in its various words, and written using lengthy terms and expressions, but in the end is still considered something of little value.

Focus upon the early foundational works from the past, give precedence to the fundamental books, such as the books of the first three generations of the Muslims. As these are excellent and contain more blessing than the books of the later generations. Second, be warned against placing in your library books which do not contain good.

NOTES

And I do not speak of books that are clearly harmful. Rather, I refer to books that do not contain benefit for you, as books are divided into three categories: good books, bad books, and books which contain neither evident good nor bad. Always make sure your library is kept free from books which do not contain evident good. For instance, there are books that are known as books of literature. But they simply misuse your time and waste it without achieving any true benefit. So by this we mean books that are indistinct and unfocused lacking a clear and proper vision or a clear methodology. Do not place such books in your library.

Another matter which is also essential is that an individual select for his library the fundamental works from the early period of Islaam, as the majority of those who came later are short on beneficial meaning in what they express but prolific in number of words and length of writing. Within one of them, you may read an entire page which could be summarized within a line or two. Such a work meanders, has difficult passages, and impulsive statements within what is written, which cannot be understood except if you make assumptions. However the books of the first generations, they posses simplicity, flexibility, and steadiness of composition. You will not find a word present there except that it carries a contributing meaning.

(135) THE EMINENT GUIDING SCHOLAR MUQBIL IBN HAADEE AL-WAADI'EE, MAY ALLAAH HAVE MERCY UPON HIM, FROM 'A DEFENDING MISSION FROM AUDIO LECTURES UPON THE PEOPLE OF IGNORANCE & SOPHISTRY': VOL. 1 PAGE 387

*Question: What are the most authentic books through which we know from the transmitted accounts from the lives of the Successors of the Companions?*

Answer: Reading books in this subject requires that an individual have understanding of the sciences related to recognizing the reliability of individual who transmit reports and accounts. As these books mention hadeeth narrations and different stories with their original chains of narrations, such that it is them required that you read biographies in *((al-Hilyah)05-03)*, and *((Tareekh ad-Dimashq)09-10)*, and *((Taarikh Baghdaad)09-03)*, and within *((Kaamel)05-25)* of Ibn 'Adee, and *((adh-Dhua'faa')05-26)* of 'Uqaylee. So there is not present any such book that we can simply say:

[This is the most authentic book in this subject, and everything within it is authentic.] As you might find that there is a story that circulated, spread, and become widely known among the people, and the Khateebs all move their heads when mentioning it, yet it is not authentically verified as coming from that Sucessor to the Companions. I advice my brother who wishes to gain awareness of the life stories of the Successors of the Companions to read within books such as: *((Seyaar)05-17)* by Haafidh adh-Dhahabee and I refer to *((Seyaar 'Alaam an-Nubala')05-17)*. And read within the works such as *((Tadhkirat al-Hufaadh)05-04)*, and such as *((Taarikh al-Kabeer)05-27)* by adh-Dhahabee. As it was his practice, may Allaah have mercy upon him, to criticize the veracity of some narrated stories and accounts because of them not being affirmed and authentic, as such his books are considered from the best and most authentic of such works.

(136) The Eminent Guiding Scholar Muqbil Ibn Haadee al-Waadi'ee, may Allaah have mercy upon him, from 'The Final Travels of the Imaam of the Arab Peninsula' by Umm Salamah as-Salafeeyah: page 233

*Question: What is your view of the book 'Fiqh as-Sunnah' by Sayyed Saabiq?*

Answer: It is generally acceptable, however it often relies upon weak hadeeth. Additionally its discussion of the issue of shaving the beard shouldn't be given any consideration, nor the issue discussing the person whose work is strenuous- as he incorrectly allows him to eat and not fast and then perform an expiation for this. This is not correct. For in the time of the Prophet, may Allaah's praise and salutations be upon him, there were those who whose work was strenuous and it was possible for someone to work while fasting. We used to work strenuously in Ramadhaan while we were in Saudi Arabia.

They say that he is one those scholars of Egypt who many of the people follow and adhere to. However as for the book, it contains those shortcoming that are know to be within it. Also I have seen within it very good statements in regarding the matter of insurance, and he is to be thanked for this. As I have benefited from that discussion, may Allaah reward him with good. However in general it is not to be relied upon as a work. Superior in value to it is the book *((Nayl al-Awtaar)03-08)* or the work *((Subl as-Salaam)03-06)* of Imaam Sanaanee, or the book *((ar-Rabaa'ee)07-12)*. He is one of the scholars from the scholars of Yemen. Also a more excellent work is *((al-Muntaqaa)12-21)* by the grandfather of Sheikh al-Islaam Ibn Taymeeyah, who is named either 'Abdul-Haleem or 'Abdul-Salam.

(137) The Eminent Guiding Scholar Muhammad Ibn Saaleh al-'Utheimeen, may Allaah have mercy upon him, from 'Book of Knowledge': page 130

*A Question on Regarding the Book 'Fiqh as-Sunnah'.*

Answer: There is no doubt that it is from the good books, as it covers many issues presenting along with that related evidence. However it is not free from errors. As was mentioned by Ibn Rajab, may Allaah have mercy upon him in the introduction to the work *(al-Qawa'id al-Fiqeeyah)08-13)*, "*Allaah has refused that any other book than His Book -meaning the Qur'aan, be freed from all errors. Yet the one who is just and balanced overlooks the few mistakes when the majority of what is written is correct.*" So the book is without doubt beneficial, but I do not hold that it should be acquired except by the student of knowledge who can distinguish between the correct and weak within it. As it contains many issues discussed in a weak manner. And from them is the putting forth a ruling asserting the legitimacy of that form of ritual prayer known as "Tasbeeh". Yet regarding Salatul Tasbeeh, Sheikh al-Islaam Ibn Taymeeyah, may Allaah have mercy upon him, said: "*All of its various supporting narrations are fabricated.*" and that it was not recommended by any of the established leading scholars. When Imaam Ahmad was asked concerning it, he shook his hand dismissively to show his disapproval of its authenticity.

Accordingly, anyone less than a student of knowledge must refer back to a scholar in his country from what he sees of that which is contrary to what is known to be true from that which is in the book, and to not rely on it alone.

**(138) THE EMINENT GUIDING SCHOLAR MUQBIL IBN HAADEE AL-WAADI'EE, MAY ALLAAH HAVE MERCY UPON HIM, FROM 'ADVICES & CLARIFICATIONS': PAGES 63-66**

*Question: What do you say about a student of knowledge who encourages beginning students of knowledge to read the book [[Fee Dhilaal al-Qur'aan]] and to place it within their homes? I explained to this student that these students are only beginning students of knowledge and they do not have the ability to distinguish between the beneficial and harmful statements in this book, or discern what the author stated reflecting the concept of unity of the creator and the creation! I put forth that they should read books such as 'Fath al-Baaree', 'Sharh al-Muslim' and 'Riyaadh as-Saaliheen', but he challenged this saying, "These books also have mistakes and errors. So why can they read those books and not read this book?" I responded by saying: "But he has statements advancing the concept of the unity of the creator with the creation!" However, he replied: "What else is there other than this one thing?" As he does not see this issue as significant enough. So are the following actions he is doing correct?*

*Firstly, advising the students to read that book, meaning [[Fee Dhaleel al-Qur'aan]]. Secondly, making equal the author of that book to the two Imaams, Imaam an-Nawawee, and Imaam Ibn Hajr in regard to: a) mistakes in the issues of belief, as well as b) their position among the people of knowledge.*

Answer:   As for the book [[Fee Dhaleel al-Qur'aan]], and the other books of Sayyed Qutb, may Allaah have mercy upon him, then I advise that they should not be read. As some of the Muslim groups who have fallen into the innovation of declaring other Muslims as disbelievers developed, and some of the young Muslim men have become individuals with the same corrupt beliefs as those misguided groups, due to some of the incorrect  expressions and statements of Sayyed Qutb, may Allaah have mercy upon him. Yet Sayyed Qutb should only be considered a writer, but not a scholar capable of explaining the Qur'aan. As his explanation of the Qur'aan is a personal explanation coming from someone who for 11 years, lived in the state of disbelieving denial of Allaah! How could such a person be considered suitable  to write an explanation of the Qur'aan?!  However it is those callers from the organization of the "Muslim Brotherhood" whose practice it is to identify individuals as having an elevated status even if they do not in fact qualify for that status. For example: They say, [The professor said], and [The professor such and such…] Yet in reality he is only someone who falsely inflames and agitates the people's sentiments, and not in fact a professor.

When we attended the Islamic University in Medinah, even if you or someone who was highly distinguished in knowledge and understanding, they would say to you: "Have you read the book, [[Allaah]], [[ar-Rasool]], [[al-Islaam]] by Sa'eed Hawaa?" And if you had said that you had not read these books, then they would say to you: [You do not possess anything of knowledge.].

Yet we, all praise is due to Allaah, indeed embraced seeking knowledge from that knowledge which was truly beneficial. And I ask Allaah. the Tremendous to preserve our brother Rabee'a Ibn Haadee as he clarified and exposed the incorrect beliefs held by Sayyed Qutb, and those matters which he was upon a deviation from the truth. And similar to this was the clarifying effort of our brother, may Allaah have mercy upon him, 'Abdullah Ibn Muhammad ad-Duwaysh who was a strong memorizer in the sciences of hadeeth, the like of which I have not seen someone similar to him. As within his book ((al-Mawrood al-'Adhab az-Zalaal Fee Bayaan Akhtaa' adh-Dhalaal)11-26) he is indicated many issues which were mistakes by Sayyed Qutb.

So Sayyed Qutb should not be considered from those who could properly explain the meaning of Qur'aan, nor amongst those who have distinguished themselves in the level of knowledge they acquired. Rather he was an individual who had tremendous enthusiasm for Islaam, but without sound understanding. I advise the brothers to return to utilizing ((Tafseer Ibn Katheer)01-01) regarding which Imaam ash-Shawkaanee may Allaah have mercy on him, stated: "*He is explanation of the Qur'aan is from among the best of explanations, if not the best of them.*" And Suyootee, stated in his work ((Tabaqaat al-Huffadh)05-04) "*Certainly Tafseer Ibn Katheer is from among the best of explanations of the Qur'aan.*" As ((Tafseer Ibn Katheer)01-01) is an explanation of the Qur'aan through the Qur'aan itself, as well as the authentic prophetic narrations. It clarifies that which is authentic from the Sunnah from that which is not authentic, and that which has a hidden weakness from that which has been transmitted soundly without defect or having been altered by unsupported stories originating from the reports coming from previous nations of the Christians and Jews. And similarly I advise you to read those explanations which come from our first generations such as ((Tafseer Ibn Jareer)01-04) ((Tafseer al-Baghawee)01-07) and what is available from ((Tafseer Ibn Abee Haatim)01-08) and ((Tafseer Ibn Mardaweeh)01-09). As they contain tremendous benefit and good. But do not rely upon [[Fee Dhaleel]] as I fear that it will lead you into misguidance. And it it is somehow necessary that you read it then, I advise that you read it along with the books of clarification by the brother 'Abdullah Ibn Muhammad ad-Duwaysh and with the books written by Sheikh Rabee'a Ibn Haadee, may Allaah preserve him.

**(139) PERMANENT COMMITTEE FOR SCHOLASTIC RESEARCH AND ISSUING OF ISLAMIC RULINGS: ISLAMIC RULING NO. 9247**

*Third question from the ruling:  What is the Sharee'ah ruling regarding those explanations of the Qur'aan known as scientific explanations? What is the proper Sharee'ah-defined relationship between verses of the Qur'aan and matters of scientific research, as there is a great deal of controversy regarding these issues?*

All praise is due to Allaah, may Allaah's praise and salutations be upon His Messenger, the Messenger's family and companions. As for what follows:

If what is intended by this is that type of explanation which explains verses such as the statement of Allaah, the Most High, ❧ *Have not those who disbelieve known that the heavens and the earth were joined together as one united piece, then We parted them? And We have made from water every living thing.* ❧-(Surah al-Anbeeyah:30) to mean that the Earth was originally part of the sun and then separated from it, and that due to the forceful pull caused by the rotation of the sun this caused the earth to separate, and that after that its surface cooled and its inner core remained hot, or that there are bodies in heaven among the stars that rotate around the sun; if they are explanations of this type, then it is not proper that we place confidence in them or rely upon them. Included are those explanations of the Qur'aan from which their authors derive that the statement of Allaah the Most High ❧ *And you will see the mountains and think them solid, but they shall pass away as the passing away of the clouds.* ❧-(Surah An-Naml: 88) is an indication of the rotation of the earth. Indeed these explanations distort statements by taking them out if their proper context, and subject the texts of the Qur'aan to explanation through scientific views and perspectives. However, these views are actually speculations or human theories and concepts. Similarly, we consider all of those explanations that rely upon newly originated opinions having no foundation or origin in the Book and the Sunnah or in the statements made by the first generations of the Muslim Ummah, as those engaged with speaking about Allaah without knowledge. The success is from Allaah alone, praise and salutations be upon our Prophet Muhammad, his family, and companions.

(140) The Eminent Guiding Scholar 'Abdul-'Azeez Ibn 'Abdullah Ibn Baaz, may Allaah have mercy upon him, from 'Collection of Rulings and Various Statements': Vol. 9, Page 362

*Question: I am a student in an institute. I am twenty one years old, and from the blessings of Allaah upon me are faith in Allaah and the decision to reject that which I previously held, and I have abandoned these affairs and I ask Allaah's forgiveness. What is the best path for me to be guided to? May Allaah bless you with good.*

Answer:    I direct and encourage you towards firmly holding to repentance from the previous errors you engaged in, that you sincerely regret them, that you stand firmly upon the obedience of Allaah and His Messenger, and that you have a sincere resolve to not return to that sin and wrongdoing. I also advise you to frequently read the Book of Allaah, and to carefully consider its meanings, and that you frequently struggle to memorize collections of the hadeeth narrations of the Prophet such as *((Bulugh al-Maraam)02-34)* by Haafidh Ibn Hajr *(('Amdatul-Hadeeth)02-29)* by Haafidh 'Abdul-Ghanee al-Maqdasee *(('Arba'een an-Nawawee)02-27)* and that *((work)03-09)* which adds other narrations completing those forty narrations, as well as *((Kitaab at-Tawheed)06-01)* by Sheikh Muhammad Ibn 'Abdul-Wahaab, and *((al-Aqeedatul-Wasateeyah)06-05)* by Sheikh al-Islaam Ibn Taymeeyah, and also *((Kashf ash-Shubahaat)06-04)* by Sheikh Muhammad Ibn 'Abdul-Wahaab. We also advise you to review and refer to the book *((Zaad al-Ma'ad Fee Haadee Khair al-Ebaad)09-05)* by Ibn Qayyim, as it is a book of tremendous benefit. Similarly benefit from the work *((Fath al-Majeed Sharh Kitaab at-Tawheed)06-12)* by Sheikh 'Abdur-Rahman Ibn Hasan.

(141) The Eminent Guiding Scholar 'Abdul-'Azeez Ibn 'Abdullah Ibn Baaz, may Allaah have mercy upon him, From 'A Collection of Rulings and Various Statements': Vol. 5, Page 428

*Explanation of some of the matters and books which are important for calling to Allaah*

From 'Abdul-'Azeez Ibn 'Abdullah Ibn Baaz, our esteemed noble brother, may Allaah grant him success. Assalaamu 'aleikum wa rahmatAllaah wa barakatuhu. As for what follows:

Indeed we received your letter in which you acknowledged the benefit you gained from the books which were sent to you by the head of the Islamic affairs ministry, as well as your inquiries regarding some of the affairs which are essential to the effort of calling to Allaah.

Indeed you should know that it is obligatory upon the one who calls to Allaah to have insight and understanding of that which he is inviting to, and that he contemplate and consider the meanings of what is contained in the Qur'aan, the Sunnah, and the statements of the people of knowledge in relation to what every matter he intends to speak about. If one's speech is regarding the obligation to worship Allaah alone and to abandon associating anything or anyone with him, then he should consider and reflect upon those hadeeth narrations related to this issue; and refer back to the explanations and statements of the people of knowledge such as in *((Tafseer Ibn Katheer)01-01)*, *((Tafseer Ibn Jareer)01-04)*, and *((Tafseer Ibn Baghawee)01-07)*, until he achieves clarity in his understanding of the right of Allaah to be worshiped alone, and in his understanding the reality of associating others with Him in worship.

From the best specific books in this subject are the books of Sheikh al-Islaam Ibn Taymeeyah, Ibn Qayyim, and Sheikh Muhammad Ibn 'Abdul-Wahaab, as well as those who follow the methodology they proceeded upon from the other people of knowledge. From the beneficial books in this subject are *((Zaad al-Ma'ad Fee Haadee Khair al-Ebaad)09-05)* by Ibn Qayyim, and *((al-Qa'edah al-Jaleelah Fee at-Tawassul wa al-Waseelah)06-49)* Sheikh al-Islaam Ibn Taymeeyah, as well as his work *((al-Aqeedatul-Wasateeyah)06-05)*. Also there is *((Kitaab at-Tawheed)06-01)* by Sheikh Muhammad Ibn 'Abdul-Wahaab and *((Fath al-Majeed)06-12)* by his grandson Sheikh 'Abdur-Rahman Ibn Hasan.

And if his speech will be regarding ritual prayer, obligatory charity, or issues other than these from among the secondary matters, then one should work with those source texts which are relevant to that issue, and guide the one he is calling to that issue which he are teaching him by summarizing matters, having excellent behavior, and using comprehensive expressions in order to facilitate the attaining an understanding by the one he is calling and inviting. As for that which is related to translation, then it is possible for the student of knowledge to rely upon the one that he knows has sound beliefs and possesses knowledge along with an understanding of that foreign language into which he wishes to translate the desired statement. He should utilize some of the Islamic books which are in English and French languages along with volumes one and two of our book *(Collection of Rulings and Various Statements)07-17)*. I ask Allaah, the Most Perfect, to guide all of us together to the right path, and that He gives success to you and to us in being directed to that which He loves and is pleased with. Indeed He is the one who hears and is close Assalaamu 'aleikum wa rahmatAllaah wa barakatuhu.

(142) The Eminent Guiding Scholar Saaleh al-Fauzaan, may Allaah preserve him, From 'al-Muntaqaa Min Fataawa': Vol. 2, Page 212

*Question: I am a graduate from the college of Sharee'ah, and I now work as an employee. However I want to continue seeking knowledge and I fear being distant from beneficial books and studying. So which are the books, in your view, that I should continually read in important subjects?*

Answer:   You should read those books and works which enabled you learn that which you know, those which you previously studied in the Sharee'ah college. For example, the books which explain the Qur'aan, those which teach the necessary fundamental beliefs, those which properly explain the hadeeth narrations, the books of fiqh which explain how to implement the guidance of the source text and the fundamental principles of this branch of knowledge, the books of Arabic grammar, and the sciences of the Arabic language in general, as well as those books related to general Muslim culture which are beneficial.

Read whatever is easy for you from these books, especially *((Tafseer Ibn Katheer)01-01)*, *((Kitaab at-Tawheed)06-01)* by Sheikh Muhammad Ibn 'Abdul-Wahaab, and the commentaries on the works of Sheikh al-Islaam Ibn Taymeeyah and Ibn Qayyim. Also study the book *((Subl as-Salaam Sharh Bulugh al-Maraam)03-06)*, *((Nayl al-Awtaar Sharh Muntaqaa al-Akhbaar)03-08)*, *(Jame'a al-Uloom wa al-Hikaam Sharh 'Arba'een an-Nawawee)03-09)*, *((explanation of Za'd al-Musataqna')07-14)* [103] and *((Kaashif al-Qanaa')07-25)* in fiqh. Make your reading one which ensures understanding and give areful attention to your comprehension of what has been written. The success comes from Allaah.

Additionally, be diligent in first memorizing summarized works and reading their explanations, then progressing to longer text after this. Also you should read from the collections of different rulings such as *((ad-Durar as-Sanneyah Fee al-Ajwebah an-Najdeeyah)06-10)* and *((Majmu'a al-Fataawaa)07-19)* of Sheikh al-Islaam Ibn Taymeeyah, *((Majmu'a al-Fataawaa)07-21)* of Sheikh Muhammad Ibn Ibraaheem, *((Majmu'a al-Fataawaa)07-20)* of Sheikh 'Abdur-Rahman as-Sa'adee, and *((Collection of Rulings and Various Statements)07-17)* of Sheikh 'Abdul-'Azeez Ibn 'Abdullah Ibn Baaz.

---

[103]   The name of this commentary is not definitively indicated in the source text.

(143) The Eminent Guiding Scholar Muqbil Ibn Haadee al-Waadi'ee, may Allaah have mercy upon him, From 'A Defending Mission from Audio Lectures Upon the People of Ignorance & Sophistry': Vol. 2, Page 69

*Question:    What knowledge related benefits connected to understanding the religion properly can be found in the book 'Irwaa al-Ghaleel'?*

Answer: The work ((*Irwaa al-Ghaleel*)04-32) is a book containing rulings and explanations of how to implement the religion, and it contains criticism and praise of hadeeth narrators, as well as clarifying authentic narrations from weak ones. It is considered from the most valuable books of Sheikh al-Albaanee, may Allaah, the Most High preserve him. Additionally, it collects the various paths of narrations which the Sheikh found at that time, which is perhaps something which was not easy for someone in our age. Therefore it is from the most prized works. I do not say the most prized from the works of the Sheikh, rather from the most prized or valuable of all the books available. And how many different authors there are in this age who have benefited from the books of the Sheikh, may Allaah preserve him!

(144) The Eminent Guiding Scholar Muqbil Ibn Haadee al-Waadi'ee, may Allaah have mercy upon him, From The Expeditions for Sheikh Muqbil Ibn Haadee al-Waadi'ee When Calling to Allaah, Pages 121-123

*Notes Regarding the Best Books taken from the Statements of Sheikh Muqbil, May Allaah have Mercy upon Him (Points 70-90 only). He used to say:*

70- The best book after the book of Allaah, the Most High and the Most Exalted, explaining the matter of worshipping Allaah alone is the book ((*Fath al-Majeed*)06-12).

71- The best book in the area of various rulings derived from the source texts is ((*Nayl al-Awtaar*)03-08).

72- The best book which gathered rulings in the religion is ((*Majmua' al-Fatawaa*)07-19) of Sheikh al-Islaam Ibn Taymeeyah.

73- The best book in refutation of the matter of magic and witchcraft is (*Miftah Dar as-Saadah*)11-27) by Ibn Qayyim.

74- The best book related to the medicine of the Prophet is ((*Tibb an-Nabawee*)12-26) taken from the writings of Ibn Qayyim found within ((*Zaad al-Ma'ad Fee Haadee Khair al-Ebaad*)09-05) which can be purchased as an individual volume.

75- The best book dealing with and explaining the harms resulting from sins is the book ((*al-Jawaab al-Kaafee Liman Sa'ill An Ad-Duwaa' Ash-Shaa'fee*)12-30) by Ibn Qayyim.

76- From among the best books which deal with the merits of the Companions are ((*al-Ahaad wa al-Muthanee*)09-08) by Ibn Abee 'Assim, the book (*al-'Isaabah*)05-02), and the book ((*Fadhaa'il as-Sahabah*)05-30) by Mustapha al-Adawee.

77- The book ((al-Maqasid al-Husna')03-28) is better than the book ((Kashf al-Khafaa')12-09), as the writer of 'Kashf al-Khafaa' gathers narrations from different places of varying value, as well as even taking some from the work ((al-Maqasid al-Husna')03-28) itself.

78- The best book is the branch of knowledge in the Arabic language known as 'eloquence' is (('Aqood al-Jamaan)12-10).

79- The ((book of Ibn Azuuz)07-09) refuting of the some of the adherents to the Maalakee school of jurisprudence in the issue of raising one's hands in ritual prayer is from the best of books in its subject.

80- ((The best book)12-11) authored on the subject of major sins is by a modern day author whose name is Abu al-Bara' (Ghassan al-Philistinee), and after it the classical book ((al-Zuwaajir An Iqtiraaf al-Kabaa'ir)12-12) by al-Haithamee.

81- The best book authored in the matter of belief regarding our seeing Allaah on the Day of Resurrection is the ((book of Darqutnee)06-50), and after it take from what has been summarized of this from Ibn Qayyim, may Allaah have mercy upon him, in his book ((Haadee al-Arwaah' ila Balad al-Afraah)06-51).

82- The best book written in the subject of sending prayers when hearing the name of the Prophet Muhammad, may Allaahs' praise and salutation be upon him and his family, is the book ((Jalaa' al-Afhaam)12-15) by Ibn Qayyim, despite the fact that it does contains some weak hadeeth. Similarly, the ((book of as-Sakhawee)12-16). Yet it is to be considered as second in value to the book of Ibn Qayyim. It also contains weak hadeeth, yet contains good knowledge-related benefits.

83- The best book written regarding the subject of travelling specifically to the grave of the Messenger, may Allaah's praise and salutation be upon him and his family, is the book ((as-Saaram al-Mankee fee Rad alaa as-Subkee)06-52).

84- The best book authored regarding the detailed characteristics of the Hajj of the Prophet, may Allaah's praise and salutation be upon him and his family, is ((Hajj al-Wadaa'a)07-10) by Ibn Hazm, and likewise what is found in ((Zaa'd al-Ma'd)09-05) by Ibn Qayyim, as well as what Ibn Hazm related on the subject in his work ((al-Muhalaa)08-07).

85- The best book written in refutation of the sect of the Raafidhah is ((Minhaj as-Sunnah)11-09) of Sheikh al-Islaam Ibn Taymeeyah.

86- The Sheikh, may Allaah have mercy upon him, said, "The book of Sheikh al-Islaam Ibn Taymeeyah, may Allaah have mercy upon him, ((Iqtida' as-Siraat al-Mustaqeem)11-02) is a truly tremendous book."

87- The best reference source for the narrations from the first generations is ((Mussanaf Abee Bakr Ibn Abee Shaibah)02-14), then the ((Mussanaf of Abdal-Razzaq as-Sannanee)02-15), and then ((Tafseer at-Tabaree)01-04).

88- The best book dealing with the correct understanding of Allaah's name an-Nuzul, is the book of Sheikh al-Islaam Ibn Taymeeyah: ((Ismuhu An-Nuzul)06-53).

89- The book ((*ad-Dur al-Manthur*)*01-06*) by as-Suyutee is the best book in relation to what it gathers together of narrations explaining the Qur'aan. However, in regard to the overall level of authenticity of the narrations it contains, it includes accepted narrations, the highest grade of accepted narrations, weak narrations, and narrations that are actually fabricated.

90- The book ((*Makhraj Min al-Fitnah*)*11-12*) and the book ((*Sayyuf al-Baaterah*)*11-20*) contains that which I recommend to the students of knowledge.

(145) THE EMINENT GUIDING SCHOLAR MUQBIL IBN HAADEE AL-WAADI'EE, MAY ALLAAH HAVE MERCY UPON HIM, FROM 'A BASIC SUMMARY FROM THE LIFE OF ONE OF THE NOBLE ONES OF THE ARAB PENINSULA: THE MAJOR SCHOLAR AL-WAADI'EE': PAGES 68-75

### Some Beneficial Notes Regarding Books

The author Abu Hamaam said: Certainly Abu 'Abdur-Rahman, may Allaah have mercy upon him, was one who read extensively and he possessed subtle expertise in relation to books, their benefits, and their authors, and similarly the same insight regarding the books of the people of innovation in the religion. Certainly the student of knowledge loves to know those books which the scholars have warned us about, as well as those that they have advised us towards and recommended. So the following are the books that our sheikh warned from, or praised and recommended, or explained a matter regarding their authors or pointed out some of their benefits. So I say and the success is from Allaah. Abu 'Abdur-Rahman, may Allaah have mercy upon him said:

*Benefit:* The book of [[al-Munfalutee]] is not to be relied upon.

*Benefit:* The book which is an explanation ((*Riyaadh as-Saaliheen*)*02-11*) which is titled [[Daleel al-Faaliheen]] is an explanation based upon the beliefs of the innovated Asha'ree sect, so you should be warned from it.

*Benefit:* Imaam Nawawee included weak hadeeth narrations in his book ((*Riyaadh as-Saaliheen*)*02-11*) incorrectly relying upon the lack of comment of Imaam Abu Dawud or that of Imaam at-Tirmidhee as an affirmation of their authenticity, from that included in their own hadeeth compilations.

*Benefit:* The book [[Ilm as-Shaamekh]] which was written by al-Muqbilee supports and advocates the innovated views of the Asha'ree sect against the way of Ahlus-Sunnah, he has enmity towards those who raise up the way of Ahlus-Sunnah in opposition to the Shee'ah, and he does not restrict himself to the methodology of the people of the Sunnah. He falsely states: [Dhahabee had hatred towards members of the Prophet's household] and he says [And those people of hatred for the family of the Prophet from the region of Shaam- north of the Arabian peninsula- such as ad-Dhaabhee...] And attacks Imaam Bukharee severely, simply because he authored the book ((*Khalq Afa'al al-Ibaad*)*06-33*).

*Benefit:* The best printed edition of ((*Tareekh al-Kabeer*)*05-21*) by Imaam al-Bukhaaree is the one with the verification by Imaam al-Mu'alamee.

*Benefit:* The majority of *((explanation the Qur'aan)01-08)* from Ibn Abee Hatim has been lost to us, having not reached our time. However I viewed a surviving volume of it in the library in the Sanctuary in Mecca.

*Benefit:* If Ibn Adee mentions in his book *((al-Kamal)05-25)* hadeeth narrations from an individual narrator indicating his different narrations, and defends him as a narrator, then he considers him a reliable narrator. But if he mentions an individual and simply mentions that he is the only one who related this specific narration, then this is not considered an affirmation of reliability from him. As indeed Suyutee stated that "*The mentioning of a hadeeth of Ibn 'Adee in his work ((al-Kamal)05-25) is enough for it to be considered weak.*"

*Benefit:* The books of Sheebat al-Hamd are not to be relied upon.

*Benefit:* The books of Saaboonee, all of them, are not to be relied upon, as he is a sufi and a bigoted biased follower of the Hanafee school of jurisprudence. The people of knowledge have made clear his misguidance and deviation.

*Benefit:* As for the author of *((Tafseer Jalalayn)01-10)*, he is someone who lacks clarity of understanding. In once place he will explain 'Allaah's rising above his throne' with the false metaphorical meaning of "having conquered," and in another place he brings the correct understanding which has been transmitted from the first generations of Muslims in affirmation of its reality. He also has some aspects of the beliefs of the sect of the Mu'tazilah.

*Benefit:* book The book [[al-'Aql]] by Dawud al-Muhbar is one which has been criticized by the scholars.

*Benefit:* The book *((Aqeedatul as-Salaf)06-54)* by Abee 'Uthmaan as-Saboonee is one I advise reading.

*Benefit:* The book *((al-Qadr)06-55):* the people of knowledge differ as to whether its authorship is correctly attributed to Imaam Maalik or to the scholar Ibn Wahb.

*Benefit:* There is an *((excellent treatise)12-14)* by Sheikh Muhammad as-Sabeel discussing the prohibition of obtaining American citizenship for those who are not originally American.

*Benefit:* The book [[al-Mubaas fee Tafseer Ibn Abbaas]] cannot be affirmed to Ibn Abbaas, as within its chain of transmission there are several defects. There is a narrator, Muhammad Ibn Marwaan as-Sadee, who is accused of fabrications narrations, and he narrates on Muhammad Ibn as-Saa'ib al-Kalbee who was one who fabricated narrations, who lastly transmitted this work from Abee Saalah Baatham and he is a weak narrator.

*Benefit:* The first book to discuss the heretical sects who left Islaam by their deviation and expose them was the *((book)11-29)* by Abu Muhammad al-Yemenee, and it is its author's best work.

*Benefit:* As for the book [[Tooq al-Hamaamah]] attributed to Abu Muhammad Ibn Hazm, then we neither deny nor affirm this attribution. All we say is that the scholars mentioned n the book are in fact known to be the scholars of Abu Muhammad Ibn Hazm.

*Benefit:* The book [[Kashf]] by Zamakhsharee, ends the discussion of every surah of the Qur'aan with a weak, unauthentic hadeeth.

*Benefit:* The book *((Fadha'il al-Qur'aan)12-56)* mentions for every surah those hadeeth which discuss its specific merits. It has two chains of transmission. The first is through Maseerah Ibn 'Abd Rabuhu, and the second through Nuh Ibn Abee Marayam.

*Benefit:* As for the book [[Fee Dhaleel al-Qur'aan]] then Muhammad 'Ameen al-Misree has informed me that certainly those groups who indiscriminately declare the Muslims to be disbelievers discuss and debate with it, and that they derive rulings and understanding from it and from the other books of Sayyed Qutb, may Allaah have mercy upon him.

*Benefit:* The book of commentary of the Qur'aan *((Fath al-Qadeer)01-05)* has the best discussion of the separated Arabic letters found within the Qur'aan, to the best of my knowledge. And it is a remarkable explanation in that it challenges blind following, as its compiler states his evidenced position even when that clearly differs from what most of the people state.

*Benefit:* The book [[Tanaasiq Bayn al-Ayaat]] discusses the harmony of different verses of the Qur'aan. The first one to write a work in this subject was al-Bagaa'ee. Ash-Shawkaanee stated, "*This knowledge is not from the Sharee'ah of Islaam, and its discussion should not be entered into.*" And I say yes, his assessment of it is correct.

*Benefit:* The books of Sheikh Ihsaan Elaayhee Dhaheer exposed the truth of the sect of the Rafidhaah. It was asked of him that he should not publish his books. He said, "*I agree, upon the condition that you burn and destroy all those books (of misguidance) which I quoted from in my books.*" They said to him, "*That is not possible!*"

*Benefit:* The book [[Islaam and Christianity]] by 'Abdullah al-Qaseemee, contains a refutation of some of the claims of the Raafidhah. Its author had once been upon Islaam, and then he deviated, falling into apostasy.

*Benefit:* As for the book *((Kitaab at-Tawheed)06-36)* by Ibn Khuzaymah- he made it a condition of the work that he would only include authentic narrations, but it contains some weak narrations, as he is a scholar of hadeeth who was somewhat lax in his grading of hadeeth, both him and his well-known student Ibn Hibaan.

*Benefit:* The book [[Haqaa'iq al-Tafseer]] by Muhammad Ibn al-Hasan Abu 'Abdur-Rahman as-Salamee who was from the scholars of Imaam al-Bayhaqee. But the people of knowledge have stated, "*If he believed that which he stated in his explanation of the Qur'aan, then he has disbelieved, and what he has written is from misguidance.*"

*Benefit:* The book *((al-'Ilaal al-Kabeer)04-15)* by at-Tirmidhee, which is organized as part of his *((Jaamae')02-06)* collection. Whereas the separate work *(al-'Ilaal as-Sagheer)04-16)* is that which Ibn Rajab has written a *((commentary)04-19)* and explanation of.

*Benefit:* The book *((Hajjatul Wadaa')07-10)* by Ibn Hazm has been verified by 'Abdul-Majeed ash-Shamree with a good verification. Someone else verified this book before he did, but his verification is better that the first one.

*Benefit:* the book *((Shafaa' al-Ileel)09-01)* by Qadhee Ayaadh is a valuable book, even if he derives some matters from weak narrations, or fabricated narrations. Still, the book in its entirety is not weak or fabricated, because he was a scholar of the hadeeth sciences.

*Benefit:* I advise reading the Book *((at-Tawheed)06-56)* by Ibn Munduh.

*Benefit:* The book *((al-'Irhaab)11-30)* is a good book, and we were astonished at these books of refutation of the people of innovation in Islaam. As for the book *((al-Qutubiyyah)11-17)* then I say about it what I said about the first book. And we of heard good about the author of the first book, Zayd al-Madhkhalee, but as for the author of the second book- then I do not know him.

*Benefit:* Regarding the scholastic discussion surrounding the issue of reciting the "basmallah" aloud, then treatises have been written regarding it by al-Darqutnee, who adhered to the Shaafa'ee school of jurisprudence, and Khateeb al-Baghdadee, who did also. Likewise Ibn 'Abdul-Barr wrote regarding this issue, as did Ibn Jawzee.

*Benefit:* As for those mentioned books by Hasan al-Banna, as-Saba'ee, and Muhammad al-Ghazaalee, then we do not have time to read them even if they are said to be refutations against those who have innovated in the religion. Marwaan said, *"Do not place one's confidence in three: the innovator who refutes another innovator, the one whose focus is narrating stories, and the one who has adopted the innovated path of Sufism."*, as today they will criticize him, yet tomorrow they might praise him.

*Benefit:* If you read from all of the ignorant books of the twentieth century, you will not gain anything of significance. Rather, I advise you to take the book *((at-Tawasul wa al-Waseelah)06-49)* of Ibn Taymeeyah and its like.

*Benefit:* The book *((al-Qaa'edah Jaleelah fe at-Tawasul wa al-Waseelah)06-49)* contains some expressions and statements that require further clarification, but is considered one of the reference works in this subject of intercession between the creation and Allaah. The similar *((book by Sheikh al-Albaanee )06-57)* is easier to comprehend, while the work of Ibn Taymeeyah is more extensive and thorough in its knowledge-based discussion.

*Benefit:* The hadeeth narrations which come from the sect of the Zaydeeyah are not accepted, nor those of the sect of the Karamateh. And from their well-known works are [[al-Amaalee]] and [[Shams al-Akhbaar]], both of which originate with Yahyaa Ibn al-Hasan.

*Benefit:* I do not advise you to read the books of Sayyed Qutb, the books of Muhammad al-Ghazaalee, the books of Muhammad Qutb, or the books of Zaynab al-Ghazaalee. May Allaah reward our brother Rabee'a with good, as certainly he has advised and clarified that which is deviation from the truth and misguidance found in the books of Sayyad Qutb.

*Benefit:* The book *((ar-Ru'yaah)06-50)* by ad-Darqutnee: I do not know of a work comparable to it in this subject, because in it he proceeds upon the methodology of the scholars of hadeeth. Also his book *((Haadee al-Arwaah)06-51),* even though it is not specific to the subject of affirming that the believers will see Allaah. Its attribution to him is correct, because the scholars within the chains mentioned for it are the scholars of Imaam ad-Darqutnee.

*Benefit:* The work *((Meezaan al-'Itidaal)05-19)* by Dhahabee is one in which he compiles the biographies according to the standards of what was the truth and what was false; whatever was the truth regarding a narrator he accept and whatever was false regarding a narrator, he rejected.

*Benefit:* al-Haakim compiled his work *((Mustradrak)02-25)* at the very end of his life.

*Benefit:* As for the book [[al-'Elaan]] by Zarkulee, then its author has an inclination towards the organization the Muslim Brotherhood, and so he should not be relied upon. He praises them, and from what is apparent is from their ranks.

*Benefit:* The book of Sh. at-Tuwayjeree *((Fee Rad 'Alaa man Yaqool: In al-'Ardh Tadur)11-31)* is one which must be in the hands of the student of knowledge. It is a refutation against Mahmood as-Sawaaf.

*Benefit:* The work *((Fatawaa Umar Ibn- 'Abdul-'Azeez)07-08)* is from the best collections of the statements of the generation which came after the Companions of the Prophet, except in the matter of failing to distinguish what is authentically narrated from what is weak in narration.

*Benefit:* The book *((Jalaa' al-Afhaam)12-15)* by Ibn Qayyim is the best book written about the subject of the excellence of sending prayers upon him when hearing the name of the Prophet Muhammad, may Allaah's praise and salutation be upon him and his family.

*Benefit:* the Book [[ar-Rawdh al-Basaam Fee adh-Dhab 'An Sunnah Abee Qaasim]] by Ibn Wazeer is an abridged version of al-'Awaasem wa al-Qawaasim. In it he explicitly states his beliefs as a Muslim and indicates that he was afflicted by having been affected by having a brother from the sect of the Shee'ah.

*Benefit:* As for the book *((al-'Asmaa' wa al-Sifaat)06-35)* by al-Bayahaqee, then he was in some degree influenced by the incorrect beliefs of his sheikh, Ibn Farook, in what he wrote. But as for his book *((al-'Itiqaad)06-59)* then in this work he fully proceeded upon and explained the methodology of the first generations in essential beliefs.

*Benefit:* The work *((Ta'weel Mukhtalif al-Hadeeth)04-31)* is by Ibn Qudaamah, and at-Tahaawee has the work *((Mushkil al-Athaar)04-34),* and Imaam Shaafa'ee has *((Mukhtalif al-Hadeeth)04-25).* All these book gather together numerous hadeeth narrations that seem to contradict each other, and then explain according to the principles of the Sharee'ah and evidence why they in fact do not. However, they often wrongly try to reconcile between two hadeeth narrations which are weak and not accepted, and it is necessary that we leave both of those unauthentic narrations, and adhere to what is judged to be authentic.

*Benefit:* Imaam Muslim mentions in the introduction to his "Saheeh" collection that in presenting the hadeeth it contains, he has first put forth that which is most authentic and after this those authentic narrations of a slightly lower level. Yet this is not something he applied uniformly within the collection.

*Benefit:* From those hadeeth scholars who have compiled works about those narrators with the name 'Ataa is at-Tabaraanee.

*Benefit:* The best book written about those scholars from whom the scholars of the six principal hadeeth collections narrated hadeeth from- meaning so and so narrated from so-and-so- is the book of Ibn Asaakir *((Mashaaykh)05-28)*

*Benefit:* I came across a book by an evildoing Raafidhee, Saaleh al-Wardaanee, in which he ridicules and mocks Sheikh Ibn Baaz. This book is evidence that they were destroyed by his collected rulings and statements, because they were not able to respond with any knowledge-based refutations, only empty mocking. So this is an clear expression of their overwhelming spite and hatefulness.

*Benefit:* The book of Abu Haamed *((Darasatun wa Naqd)11-32)* is very beneficial. He is one of the students of al-Albaanee, named 'Abdur-Rahman ad-Dimashqee.

*Benefit:* The book *((Ajweebah Abee Mas'ood)04-35),* written in response to the specific criticism of some of the narrations of Saheeh Muslim by his own Sheikh ad-Darqutnee, is a response written with the highest degree of justice and fairness.

*Benefit:* The book *((Radd 'Alaa al-Jahmeeyah)11-10)* is attributed to Imaam Ahmad. I do not know that it has been affirmed to have authentically been authored by him.

*Benefit:* The book 'as-Sifaat' by Darqutnee, cannot be authentically attributed to him. There are other works which are more than sufficient for you such as *((as-Sunnah)06-26)* by al-Khilaal, the work of *((Lalaka'ee)06-29)*, *((at-Tawheed)06-36)* by Ibn Khusaymah, and *((al-'Asmaa wa as-Sifaat)06-35)* by al-Bayhaqee.

*Benefit:* The work *((Lisaan al-Mizaan)05-20)* does remove the need for *((Mizaan al-'Itidaal)05-19)* because even though Ibn Hajr added other additional narrators and criticized adh-Dhahabee's assessment of certain narrators, he removed from his work those narrators from the six principal hadeeth collections whom adh-Dhahabee discussed which he had already examined within his other work *((Tadheeb at-Tadheeb)05-18)*.

*Benefit:* The book [[al-Aghaanee]] by Abee al-Farj al-Asbahaanee contains a defense of the sect of the Shee'ah; therefore do not use or rely up it.

*Benefit:* The historian Muhammd al-Akwaa' has a verification of the book *((Qurrat al-Ayyun fee Akhbaar al-Yemeen)12-20)* which is a good historical verification.

# THE WARNING OF THE SCHOLARS FROM THE BOOKS OF THOSE WHO HAVE DEVIATED FROM THE SUNNAH & WARNINGS REGARDING WAYS OF GOING ASTRAY

*"...Likewise, there is no protection due to ownership against the destruction by fire of books of misguidance, and their elimination. al-Marwadhee said to Ahmad:*

*"I borrowed a book, and it contains matters of falsehood; do you hold that I should destroy it or burn it?" He replied, "Yes."*

*What is intended by this are books containing fabrications and innovations in the religion. It is an obligation to destroy and eliminate them. The destruction of such books has greater importance than the destruction of forbidden objects of amusement, musical instruments, or the breaking of containers of intoxicants. Certainly, the harm of these books is more significant than the harm of these other things. Therefore, there is no protection against their destruction, just as there is no protection from the breaking of containers of intoxicants and the shredding of wineskins."*

(Imaam Ibn al-Qayyim, may Allaah have mercy on him, in 'Turuq al-Hakimeeyah fee Seeyasah as-Sharaeeh', page 270)

(146) The Eminent Guiding Scholar Ahmad Ibn Yahya An-Najmee, may Allaah preserve him, From 'Decisive Rulings on the Methodologies of Calling to Allaah': Vol. 2, Page 73

*Question: What are the guidelines regarding reading the books of innovators in the religion or listening to their tapes, if they contain some benefit? Is it permissible for the common person to listen to the tapes of the preachers from among the innovators, or the people of division and group partisanship, or others similar to them?*

Answer:   It is not proper to read the books of those who innovate in the religion, or to listen to their audio lectures. They subtly conceal poison in the sweetness of the honey. So for one who does not possess the scholastic capabilities to discern, then he may hear something that he does not recognize as false, and then fall into this false understanding to whatever degree it affects him. What is important to establish is that one should not read the books of the people of innovation in the religion. The exception to this is the qualified, experienced scholar whose intent is to derive from the works what is necessary to compose a refutation against them. Moreover, it is even the case in regard to the scholars, as is it is not proper for them to frequently read from the books of the innovators in the religion, as this is dangerous even for them. And in the story of al-Qaseemee, who was upon the Sunnah and deviated, there is a lesson for every person of intelligence who fears Allaah and who firmly believes that the hearts are in His Hands and He turns them as He wishes.

(147) The Eminent Guiding Scholar Saaleh al-Fauzaan, may Allaah preserve him, From 'Beneficial Answers To Questions on New Methodologies': Page 125

*Question: What is the correct position regarding reading the books of the innovators in the religion, and collecting their audio tapes?*

Answer:   It is not permissible to read the books of the innovators in the religion or to listen to their audio lectures, except for the one established in knowledge who intends to refute them and clarify their errors and misguidance. But as for the individual who is a beginner, or the general student of knowledge, or the common person, or someone who only reads it for the sake of general information alone, not for the sake of refuting them and clarifying its misguided condition- then this is not permissible. It might influence his heart so that he accepts some of the falsehood in it and is harmed by it. Therefore, it is not permissible to read books from the people of misguidance except for those individuals from the people of knowledge who specialize in this area of refuting the misguidance of others, in order that they may refute it and effectively warn from it.

**(148) THE EMINENT GUIDING SCHOLAR MUHAMMAD IBN SAALEH AL-'UTHEIMEEN, MAY ALLAAH HAVE MERCY UPON HIM, FROM 'ISLAMIC REVIVAL: GUIDELINES & GUIDANCE': PAGE 127**

*Question: What is your advice, may Allaah preserve you, to one who advises the youth, or some of the youth, to read some of the books which contain errors in belief or methodology? However, they don't clearly explain that they contain mistakes, but only recommend reading them.*

Answer: As for those books which contain deviation in the area of beliefs or in general methodology, then it is not permissible to read them except for the individual who is well grounded in knowledge and can distinguish what is correct from that which is in error. But the student of knowledge who has just begun seeking knowledge at the initial stages and so cannot distinguish between what is correct and what is an error, then it is not permissible for him to read from such books. This is in order to prevent him from going astray. As for someone who is a scholar established in his knowledge who intends to read these books in order that he can clarify their errors from what is sound, then he does so and clarifies the mistakes contained within them. This is in fact a requirement from him, as he is unable to distinguish their specific errors except by reading them. But as for the one who doesn't have this level of understanding, then no. Rather, he must only distance himself from them. Due to this the Prophet, may Allaah's praise and salutations be upon him, said, *{The one who hears of the Dajjal should flee from him}* [104] meaning that he should endeavor to distance and keep himself far from him. Then this narration continues on to mention a man who comes to the Dajjal, and he considers himself a believer - confident of the faith within his heart before confronting the Dajjal. However, he proceeds to interact with him, and is confronted by doubts until eventually he comes to follow the Dajjal. In this narration there is an indication of the concept of cutting off the paths or means leading towards an evil, and an understanding that an individual is not safe from being put to trial no matter who he may be. Therefore it is obligatory upon those students of knowledge whom Allaah, the Most High, has blessed with knowledge, to explain to the people mistakes that are found in any book, or from any individual. However, regarding the one who made the mistake having his mistake explained to him privately, such that he may leave this error himself, then without doubt this is given priority. In the turning back from an error by the individual himself in this way, we gain two significant benefits.

The first benefit: This individual being rescued from the error he was upon.

The second benefit: It does not appear publicly that the people of knowledge have differed and separated, or that some of them unnecessarily say that others from them are misguided or that these others have errors. It is unquestionably beneficial that the scholars all come together in their statements, and make their word one.

---

[104] Narrated in Sunan Abu Dawud: 4319/ & Musnad Imaam Ahmad: 19374/ -on the authority of 'Imraan Ibn Husayn. It was declared authentic by Sheikh al-Albaanee in Mishkaat al-Masaabeh: 5488, & Saheeh al-Jaame'a as-Sagheer: 6301, and in his verification of Sunan Abu Dawud. Sheikh Muqbil declared it authentic in al-Jaame'a al-Saheeh: 334, 532, 3352, 3672.

**(149)** THE EMINENT GUIDING SCHOLAR MUQBIL IBN HAADEE AL-WAADI'EE, MAY ALLAAH HAVE MERCY UPON HIM, FROM 'EXCELLENT RESPONSES TO QUESTIONS FROM THOSE PRESENT AND THOSE ABSENT': PAGE 209

*Question: As for those who were previously considered to be upon the correct methodology and then deviated from it, is it permissible for us to listen to their tapes or to read their books which they wrote in the past, and similarly their recorded lectures?*

Answer: I do not advise reading their books or listening to their audio lectures. And I was once impressed by a tremendous statement from Sheikh al-Islaam Ibn Taymeeyah, may Allaah have mercy upon him. He said related to this issue, "If Allaah had not brought forth Imaam al-Bukhaaree or Imaam Muslim, still no harm would have reached this religion of His. Allaah, the Most Glorified and the Most Exalted, has certainly preserved and protected this religion. Allaah the Exalted says: ⟨*Verily It is We Who have sent down the Dhikr and surely, We will guard it (from corruption*⟩-(*Surah Hijr:*9) So I advise you to stay far away from their books, audio tapes, and their lectures where they stand as callers. They themselves are in need of being invited and called to the truth, and in need of returning back to the Book of Allaah and to the Sunnah of Allaah's Messenger, may Allaah's praise and salutations be upon him. They themselves need to repent to Allaah, the Most Glorified and the Most Exalted, from that which appeared from specific individuals from among them during the events of the Gulf War as well as concerning other matters.

**(150)** THE EMINENT GUIDING SCHOLAR AHMAD IBN YAHYA AN-NAJMEE, MAY ALLAAH PRESERVE HIM, FROM 'DECISIVE RULINGS ON THE METHODOLOGIES OF CALLING TO ALLAAH': VOL. 2, PAGE 75

*Question: The people of innovation in the religion have a masjid, and some of the people who utilize it are people of the Sunnah- as they do not have any other masjid other than that one. These people of the Sunnah are permitted to speak, teach, and have lectures with the condition that they attend the lectures held by the others who are the people of division and partisanship; and that these others will likewise attend the lectures held by the people of the Sunnah. Should they agree to this?*

Answer: I say that is not proper for the people of the Sunnah to attend the lectures of the people of biased partisanship and division, nor any classes they give, for fear of trials that would come from this. If they have allowed them and given them a specific time for classes, and given the people of parties and separation a specific time also, Then there is nothing to prevent this as everyone utilizes a separate time period specific for them. Just as we find that the people of partisanship towards different groups are cautious and wary from the people of the Sunnah, similarly it is required that the people of Sunnah be wary of the people of partisanship and warn others from them.

NOTES

**(151) The Eminent Guiding Scholar Saaleh Ibn Fauzaan, may Allaah preserve him, From 'Beneficial Answers to Questions on New Methodologies': Page 148**

*Question: Is explaining and clarifying some of the errors found in the books of the people of division and partisanship or of the numerous groups coming to our land considered to be harmful to the efforts to call to Allaah?*

Answer:   No, this is not considered harmful to the call to the truth and inviting to Islaam, because these books are not truly books calling to the truth and Islaam. Additionally these individuals, the authors of these books and concepts, are not from those who call to Islaam with insight into matters, with sound knowledge, and upon the truth. So when we explain the mistakes found within these books, or the mistakes of these individuals, it is not to be considered simply personal criticism. Instead, it should be considered from the aspect of advising the Ummah of that harm which is entering into it in the form of dubious concepts, which will eventually become a trial for us, and cause the loss of our united word and stance, and lead to divisions within our united ranks. So our objective is not the criticism of individuals. Our objective is the criticism of those false and deficient concepts and understandings found in the books brought among us in the name of calling to Islaam.

**(152) The Eminent Guiding Scholar Muqbil Ibn Haadee al-Waadi'ee, may Allaah have mercy upon him, From 'Advices & Clarifications': Pages 111- 117**

*Question: We observe that some of those who affiliate themselves with the methodology of the first three generations choose to occupy themselves with criticism and warning from the astray groups and sects, while neglecting the seeking of knowledge; whereas others who claim the same methodology do give priority to seeking knowledge yet turn away from the matter of warnings and criticisms. It has reached the state where those of the second group say, "Certainly, criticizing is not from the methodology of the people of the Sunnah at all." So what is correct in this issue?*

Answer:  As for those who occupy themselves solely with critically examining the mistakes of others and warning from them- they can be considered disproportionate in their affairs of seeking knowledge, as found in the answers to the questions of our brothers from the Emirates, as well as their being excessive in focusing on the realm of criticism. What is seen when one considers the lives of our previous scholars? If we look at the biography of Ibn Abee Haatim, we find that he was a tremendous memorizer; indeed he was even given the title of Sheikh al-Islaam. The same case can be seen with Imaam al-Bukhaaree, Imaam Ahmad Ibn Hanbal, Yahya Ibn Ma'een, Yahya Ibn Sa'ed al-Qahtaan, Abu Haatim, Abu Zura'ah, ad-Darqutnee, Ibn Hibaan, and Haakim. They wrote many beneficial books, such as in the subject of the explanations of the Qur'aan,as well as works in the various hadeeth sciences. They produced beneficial works and preserved for us the Sunnah of the Messenger of Allaah, may Allaah's praise and salutations be upon him and his household.

But in addition they also produced beneficial books related to criticism and commendation of individuals in the religion. Therefore it is necessary that we join between the first focus and priority and the second, as otherwise an individual will be deficient from one aspect, as well as being excessive from another.

I ask you, according to what criterion will we assess the state of individuals if we are ignorant of beneficial knowledge? Will we simply judge them by our desires or by following what has been said by sheikh so and so? Such that if Sheikh so-and-so recants a position we also recant it, and if he holds a position regarding a number of individuals then we also hold it. Therefore it can be seen that it is necessary that we combine the first matter and the second.

As for the second group which was mentioned, those who only give attention to knowledge without raising their heads towards commending or criticizing anyone, then in my view, of the two groups overall they are in a better state than the first group. The first group is attempting to enter into or concern themselves with an area which is not within their present ability to confront personally. Yet despite this fact, it is clear that this second group has itself torn down or subverted an important aspect of Islaam. Indeed, that work of our brother Bakr Ibn ʿAbdullah Abu Zayd [[*Categorizing the People between Doubt and Certainty*]] in this subject should be considered the worst book from those which he wrote. On the other hand, many of his works, all praise is due to Allaah, are from the best of those available, may Allaah reward him with good.

But as for the destruction of the role or position of criticizing and commending in the religion, then know that Allaah the Most Glorified and Most Exalted has Himself has said in His Noble Book, *And do not obey every worthless habitual swearer and scorner, going about with malicious gossip - A preventer of good, transgressing and sinful, Cruel, moreover, and an illegitimate pretender.*-(Surah al-Qalam: 10-13) And He said, *Perish the two hands of Abu Lahab and perish he! His wealth and his children will not benefit him! He will be burnt in a Fire of blazing flames! And his wife too, who carries wood. Around her neck is a twisted rope of fiber.*-(Surah al-Masad: 1-5). Allaah, the Most Perfect and the Most High, has criticized Abu Lahab and also criticized his wife. Likewise Musa, when he intended to strike the one with him from the previous incident of killing, said to him.*Indeed, you are an evident, persistent deviator.* These are all evidence of the permissibility of legitimate criticism of someone.

The Prophet, may Allaah's praise and salutations be upon him and his household, said regarding a man who came to sit with him, *{What an evil man of the tribe he is.}* But when that man entered, he sat with him and spoke with him nicely. ʿAishah then asked why he did that after having criticized him, and he replied, *{The worst people, in the sight of Allaah are those whom the people abandon to save themselves from their foul language.}.* This is narrated in both Saheeh al-Bukhaaree and Saheeh Muslim on the authority of ʿAishah.

It is also narrated in Saheeh al-Bukhaaree from the hadeeth of 'Aishah, that one of the women from the household of Abu Sufyan said, "*Abu Sufyaan is a man who is miserly, not giving us what is sufficient.*" The Prophet, may Allaah's praise and salutations be upon him and his household, remained silent regarding her criticism of Abu Sufyan. Moreover, in another instance the Prophet, may Allaah's praise and salutations be upon him and his household, asked, *{Who is your chief, oh Banu Salaamah?" They replied al-Jad Ibn Qays, yet we see him to be a miser." So the Prophet, may Allaah's praise and salutations be upon him and his household, said, "So which disease is worse than miserliness? Rather, your chief is 'Amr Ibn al-Jamooh."}* [105]. And the Prophet, may Allaah's praise and salutations be upon him and his household, said to Mu'adh Ibn Jabal, *{Are you a trial for the people, oh Mu'adh?!}* [106]. And he said to Abu Dhar, *{Indeed you are a man who has some aspects of those days of ignorance before Islaam still within him.}*-(Saheeh al-Bukhaaree: 30, 6050, Saheeh Muslim: 1661). And he said to some of the women of his household, *{Indeed, you are like some of the evil women who tempted Prophet Yusuf.}*-(Saheeh al-Bukhaaree: 664 & other narrations, Saheeh Muslim: 418). This was narrated by Imaam al-Bukhaaree in his Saheeh. And the Prophet, may Allaah's praise and salutations be upon him and his household, said, *{I do not believe that so and so and so and so understands anything at all from our religion.}*-(Saheeh al-Bukhaaree: 6068) Laith Ibn Sa'd explained this as referring to two of the hypocrites who did not truly embrace Islaam.

And the Prophet, may Allaah's praise and salutations be upon him and his household, said to Hamal Ibn Maalik Ibn an-Naabighah in judgment when it occurred that a woman from his people struck another woman with something which caused the other woman to abort the unborn child she was carrying, *{"They should be given a male or a female slave in compensation." So Hamal Ibn Maalik Ibn an-Naabighah said, "Oh Messenger of Allaah, why should we pay for that which has never eaten nor drunk anything, nor was even born. One such as this should not be considered." So the Prophet, may Allaah's praise and salutations be upon him and his household, said, "This one is from the brothers of the magicians"}* -(Saheeh al-Bukhaaree: 5758, 5760, Saheeh Muslim: 1681), due to his arguing using rhymed poetry.

And the Prophet, may Allaah's praise and salutations be upon him and his household, said, *{The extremists are destroyed, The extremists are destroyed, The extremists are destroyed.}* -(Saheeh Muslim: 2670, Sunan Abu Dawud: 4608). And he said regarding the sect of the Khawaarij, *{Indeed, they are the dogs of the Hellfire.}* [107]. He also said, *{Indeed, they will pass through the religion the way an arrow passes through the animal that was shot at.}* -(Saheeh al-Bukhaaree: 3344).

---

[105] Narrated in al-Adab al-Mufrad: 296/ & al-Mustadrak alaa Saheehayn: 4953/ -on the authority of Ab Hurairah. It was declared authentic by Sheikh al-Albaanee in Saheeh al-Adab al-Mufrad: 296.

[106] Narrated in Saheeh al-Bukhaaree: 705, 6106/ Saheeh Muslim: 465/ Sunan Abu Dawud: 790/ Sunan an-Nasaa'ee: 832, 836, 985, 998/ & Musnad Imaam Ahmad: 13778, 13895: -on the authority of Jaabir Ibn 'Abdullah. It was declared authentic by Sheikh al-Albaanee in Irwa' al-Ghaleel: 295, Mishkaat al-Masaabeh: 833, Saheeh al-Jaame'a as-Sagheer: 7966. Sheikh Muqbil declared it authentic in al-Jaame'a al-Saheeh: 240, 1026, 3628, 3630.

[107] Narrated in Sunan Ibn Maajah: 173/ & Musnad Imaam Ahmad: 18651, 18923: -on the authority of Ibn Abee 'Awf. It was declared authentic by Sheikh al-Albaanee in Dhelaal al-Jannah: 905. Sheikh Muqbil declared it authentic in al-Jaame'a al-Saheeh: 254, 645, 2349, 3305, 3954.

Therefore the one who is deficient in implementing criticism and commendation in the religion, is then deficient in implementing an aspect of the Sunnah. If criticism and commendation are not implemented then everyone speaks claiming to be a "*caller to Allaah*" or an "*esteemed scholar*," such as is seen in the speech of 'Alee at-Tantaawee, or the speech of Mahmood as-Sawaaf, or the speech of Muhammad al-Ghazaalee, or the speech of Hassan at-Turaabee, or the speech of as-Sharaawee, or the speech of the different Shee'ah and Rawaafidh, or such as the speech of the Sufee -Hasan Saqqaaf.

Therefore I say no one knowingly turns away from understanding of this branch of knowledge except an individual who is ignorant, or an individual with a spiteful heart, or an individual who comes to know that he has himself been criticized, so he then has an aversion to criticism and commendation in the religion due to the fact that he learns that he has been publicly criticized. Yet Allaah rejects anything other than what brings victory to His religion and makes supreme His word, and brings forth the truth. The people of the Sunnah have now given priority to criticism and commendation for the sake of the religion, while before it was as if some of them were sleeping, so Allaah brought forth those people those who would awaken them. Before, some of them didn't used to speak extensively in matters of commendation and criticism, as if this was something specific to the period of Imaam al-Bukhaaree and Muslim.

But I say clearly, shouldn't we criticize the one in this age who says, [Popular Democracy is compatible with Islaam.]? In reality, is not the correct way that we criticize the one who makes such a false claim and strive to explain to the people that the one who makes this claim is a deceiver from the many deceivers? Shouldn't we criticize those individuals who speak against and attack the scholars of the Muslims? Additionally, how could we, as we do, criticize our own esteemed scholars in some knowledge-based issues, yet consider it proper to remain silent about these more significant matters?!?

Therefore it is necessary that we join between these two matters, and focus both on seeking knowledge as well as criticism and warning against those who have opposed the truth. When we read the biographies of the Companions and read the biographies of the Successors to the Companions as well as those of the generation that followed them –the Successors of those Successors- we find that they often made statements that reflected this. Where do we stand when we hear the statements of Imaam ad-Dhahabee, "*Zatn, who is Zatn? He is only is a deceiver from among the deceivers, claiming that he is a Companion six hundred years after the year of the Hijra!*" Or when we hear the likes of the statements of Imaam as-Shaafa'ee who said, "*Narrating on Haram Ibn 'Uthmaan is itself haraam (forbidden).*" Or another statement from Imaam as-Shaafa'ee, "*The one who narrates on al-Bayaadhee (meaning a person of whiteness), may Allaah make his eyes white with blindness.*" Where do we stand when we hear such statements? Do we say that Imaam as-Shaafa'ee is from those who are harsh and unnecessarily severe, someone who was wrong in speaking against the Muslims or in speaking about those scholars?

We challenge you to prove with evidence that we have falsely spoken against any of the scholars, or against those advocating popular Democracy, or those who speak from this personal opinion or that personal opinion, or those who affirm the various mandates and resolutions of the United Nations or that of the Council of Nations, or those who say, [This age is not one of saying "so and so informed me" and "so and so narrated to me," or of stating that this narration is authentic or this one is weak.] And we respond to this last by saying, indeed this is certainly the age for this, as many hadeeth narrations presently circulating among the people are either weak or fabricated. I conclude what I have said with what was mentioned by al-Haafidh as-Sooree, may Allaah have mercy upon him, who said:

> Say to the one who opposes narrations of hadeeth and
>> comes forth blaming the people of hadeeth and those who adhere to them,
> Do you say this to me based upon knowledge, my son,
>> or does it come from ignorance, as ignorance is the character of a fool.
> Do you blame those who strive to preserve the religion?
>> from falsehoods, lies, and distortions,
> and find fault with their statements while what they narrate
>> is referred to by every true scholar and those with understanding of the religion?

And I do not intend by this that the one upon the Sunnah should unnecessarily occupy his time with this. Rather, one should occupy some of his time with clarifying the mistakes of the various sects and groups, and a good portion of his time for easy breathing and necessary rest, and also some time for eating and drinking, and so on. Indeed, what I intend is that one be as has been said:

> A man stands with his feet firmly upon the earth,
>> but indeed the highest of his goals is in the stars.

Some of our brothers in Islaam have written to me and said, [Do not preoccupy yourself with these matters.] They incorrectly believe that I am preoccupied with these matters, while in fact, all praise is due to Allaah, I am not. My efforts of composition and writing have their own time, as do my classes given in order to teach the people, and matters of criticism and commendation of individuals for the sake of the religion also has its place and time. Ibn Jawzee confronted the people of his time because of their using and narrating weak or fabricated hadeeth, and this practice is similarly present today. Likewise, others besides him from the scholars of the first generations confronted the people of their ages regarding the use of weak or fabricated narrations, and similarly people who engage in this are undoubtedly present today. Yet, all praise is due to Allaah, the knowledge of the Sunnah has spread tremendously, such that even the "Bankrupt Brotherhood" (the Muslim Brotherhood organization) is now teaching the science of hadeeth terminology! However as is said:

*They praise the efforts of the guard, yet he acts only for the sake of trying,*

*to retain in those young men already among them- so that they do not run away.*

Look at 'Abdullah Sa'tar from their group who has taken up the book ((Sharh at-Tahaweeyah)06-09) and it now teaching it. Oh 'Abdullah Sa'tar, you have certainly undertaken a difficult ascent! So what happened is that on the first night of those classes there was a large group of people attending, and the second night there were less, and on the third night even less. Thereafter, there were perhaps only seven people present, and then later maybe three.

Because in terms of knowledge, he actually doesn't have a firm grasp of matters except to know that such and such was said in the newspaper "al-Hayaat," and that such and such was mentioned by the "London Broadcast," and that such and such paper mentioned this or that. Therefore it is clear through their efforts that what they desire is only that their youth remain with them and not abandon them. So they announce: "We are teaching the issues of belief!" "We are teaching hadeeth terminology!" and so forth and so on. However we see regarding them, as it is said, "Eventually Haleemah just returned from her previous ways." So when they see that this way neither really profited them and their objectives, they will return once again to their way of lies and deception.

(153) THE EMINENT GUIDING SCHOLAR MUQBIL IBN HAADEE AL-WAADI'EE, MAY ALLAAH HAVE MERCY UPON HIM. FROM 'BRIDLING THE RESISTANT ONE': PAGE 326

**Question: Some people accuse the people of the Sunnah of being harsh. How should we respond to them?**

Answer: In truth we know our ownselves better than others know us. So the one who would accuse us of being those who have fallen short, and lax in what is necessary, then I bear witness to Allaah that He is the truthful! Otherwise we say that we wish to be of those who are moderate, neither falling short nor going to any extremes. I advise our brother to read the book ((Qaraa' Alasat fe Nafee al-Ghuluu wa at-Tatraf wa al-Ashadhudh 'An Ahl-Sunnah)11-14) until he understands the reality of this matter. So where is the required enjoining what is right and the forbidding what is wrong? Where is the self-sacrifice among us, where is the diligence in teaching others? In fact, we are those who have fallen short in what is required in this area, so I ask Allaah to forgive us, and accept our repentance. However, those who adhere to innovations in the religion contradict themselves regarding their claims about the people of the Sunnah. Sometimes they say, [They are extremists who are harsh!] and other times they say, [They just sit in their masjids reciting this and narrating that, and they have abandoned calling to Allaah and have left truly striving in the path of Allaah!] So in reality, the people of innovation are self-contradictory in their various conflicting claims about the people of the Sunnah.

**(154) THE EMINENT GUIDING SCHOLAR 'ABDUL-'AZEEZ IBN 'ABDULLAH IBN BAAZ, MAY ALLAAH HAVE MERCY UPON HIM, FROM 'A COLLECTION OF RULINGS AND VARIOUS STATEMENTS': VOL. 3, PAGE 68**

*Unity, Adherence to the Religion, and their Requirements: In discussing what was written by someone, it was mentioned to Sheikh Ibn Baaz that in his fourth article this person called to giving priority to attaining unity between the different Muslim groups and in cooperation upon jihad against the enemies of Islam. He also mentioned that this is not the time to criticize those who adhere to a specific school of fiqh with bigotry, or the sect of the 'Asharees, or the group known as "The Muslim Brotherhood," or even the followers of Sufism.*

In response he said: There is no doubt that it is an obligation upon the Muslims to unify their ranks and unite their voices as one upon the truth, and to cooperate among themselves in goodness and fearing Allaah against the enemies of Islaam, as Allaah, the Most Perfect has commanded them in His, the Most High and the Most Exalted, statement, ❖*And hold fast, all of you together, to the Rope of Allaah, and be not divided among yourselves*❖-(Surah Aal-'Imraan:103). He warned them against separating and division in His statement, ❖*And be not as those who divided and differed among themselves after the clear proofs had come to them*❖-(Surah Aal-'Imraan:105). However, the obligation to unite the Muslims and join their voices together upon the truth, and to hold fast to the rope of Allaah, does not require the abandoning of forbidding wrongdoing whether from actions or beliefs of the followers of Sufism or others. Rather, doing so is itself a requirement of the command to hold fast to the rope of Allaah and to enjoin good and forbid wrongdoing, and to make clear the truth for the one who has strayed from it, or who believes something which opposes the truth with evidences from the Sharee'ah until we are united upon the truth and have rejected that which opposes it. This is a requirement of the statement of Allaah, ❖*Help you one another in goodness and piety but do not help one another in sin and transgression.*❖-(Surah al-Maidah:2) and the statement of Allaah, the Most Perfect :❖*Let there arise out of you a group of people inviting to all that is good (Islaam), enjoining every matter of good and forbidding every matter of wrongdoing and evil. And it is they who are the successful.*❖-(Surah Aal-'Imraan:104).

When the people of truth are silent and refrain from explaining mistakes of those who have made them, and the errors of those who have fallen into them, then they have not fulfilled that which Allaah has commanded them from calling to good and enjoining what is right and forbidding wrongdoing. Furthermore, it is well known what results from this sin of refraining from forbidding evil; it is that the one who is in error remains in error, and the one who has opposed the truth stays upon his mistake. This contradicts what Allaah has legislated from giving advice and cooperation upon good and enjoining what is right and forbidding what is wrong. And Allaah is our guardian and the giver of success.

(155) The Eminent Guiding Scholar Muqbil Ibn Haadee al-Waadi'ee, may Allaah have mercy upon him, From 'A Defending Mission from Audio Lectures Upon the People of Ignorance & Sophistry': Vol 1, Page 71 )

*Question:  What is the difference between a statement of criticism and giving advice?*

Answer: The difference between a statement of criticism and the giving of advice is that in relation to advice it is possible that it be given privately, only between the one giving the advice and the one being advised. As Allaah says, ❧***And speak to him mildly, perhaps he may accept admonition or fear Allaah.***❧-(Surah Taha:44) " But as for a statement of criticism, most likely it is something written in books, or mentioned in public gatherings. Our scholars from the early centuries, may Allaah have mercy upon all of them, combined both of these matters. Imaam adh-Dhahabee, may Allaah have mercy upon him said, "*Ratan, and who is this Rattan? A lying deceiver from among the lying deceivers who falsely claims to be a Companion six hundred years after their period.*" And Imaam Sha'fee- may Allaah have mercy upon him said, "*Narrating on Haraam Ibn 'Uthma'n is haraam (meaning forbidden),*" and he also said, "*As for the one who narrated from al-Badhaee may Allaah whiten his eyes (as in blindness).*". In relation to the false hadeeth narration from Suwayd Ibn Saeed: [The one who loved passionately but remained chaste, and held back from his desires, dies the death of a martyr... ]Yahya Ibn Ma'een said: "*If only I had a horse and a spear with which to fight against this man Suwayd...*"  And it was requested from Shu'bah that he stop criticizing 'Abaan Ibn Abee Aeeash, as he 'Abaan- was an excellent individual occupied with worship and having little concern for worldly matters, but he was of those who confused matters when narrating hadeeth. So he initially said, "*I will consider this*". But later he replied to the one who gave him this advice by saying, "*This is related to the religion, and as such there is no possible course for me to follow except that I continue speak regarding the condition of 'Abaan Ibn Abee Aeeash.*" And Abu Haneefah, may Allaah have mercy upon him, spoke regarding Jaabir Ibn Yazeed al-Jaafee, "*I have not seen a greater liar than him.*" And Sha'bee may Allaah have mercy upon him, declared al-Harith Ibn 'Abdullah al-Hamdanee a liar. And we have mentioned some aspect of this issue in the introduction to the work ***(Makhraj min al-Fitnah)11-21)*** as found in the second and third editions, as well as the introduction to ***(Rudood Ahlul-Ilm Ala At-Taa'neen fee Hadeeth As-Sahr wa Bayan B'ued Muhammad Rasheed Ridha 'An As-Salafeeyah)11-25)***. And all praise is due to Allaah, both of these books are printed.

NOTES

**(156) The Eminent Guiding Scholar Saaleh al-Fauzaan, may Allaah preserve him, From 'Beneficial Answers to Questions on New Methodologies': Page 9**

*Question: What is your view of the book 'al-Qutubiyyah'? Do you advise that it should be read, and are such books of refutation from the methodology of the first three righteous generations of Muslims (may Allaah have mercy upon them)?*

Answer: The refutation of the one who differs from the truth is from the practice and way of the first three generations. Those of the first generations refuted those who opposed the truth, and their books containing these refutations are present and available. Imaam Ahmad refuted the corrupters who left he religion due to their beliefs and those Muslims who innovated in the religion. Sheikh al-Islaam Ibn Taymeeyah refuted the people of theoretical philosophy, the scholars of false rhetorical concepts, the people of the innovation of Sufism, and those who worshiped at graves. Additionally, Imaam Ibn Qayyim, as well as many of the leading scholars, refuted those people who opposed the truth in order to explain the truth and make it apparent to the people; in order that the Muslim nation not be lead astray and follow the people of error and those who had opposed the truth. This is from advising the Muslim Ummah.

As for the Book *((al-Qutbeeyah)11-16)* as well as other books, if what it contains is correct and true, then we must accept it. If those who composed the refutation of the one who opposed the truth accurately transmitted from that individual's statements found in his books and from his recorded lectures, mentioning the name of the book or cassette containing the false statements by page number and volume, and the statements which he brings forth are clearly in error, then what would prevent the one who brings forth a refutation of the one in error?!? The purpose is sincerely advising the people, not disparaging or criticizing individuals. Indeed the intent is advising the people and clarifying matters to them. As such the book *((al-Qutbeeyah)11-16)* or similar works do not bring forth lies against anyone, but simply transmit from the statements of those who have opposed the truth, not transmitting it by meaning only, or in a summarized form which distorts. Instead, they transmit it with the full text and specify the volume in which it is found and the page where it was found- indeed, even stating the line number where the statement was made. So what is wrong with this?! As for those of us who are silent regarding the errors of people, we are deceived by the people. Therefore, we say: These books which are commonly found in the hands of the youth and with general people- they contain concealed poisons as well as errors. They deceive the Muslim nation, and it is not permissible. It is necessary that it be explained and clarified, and that advice is given. It is necessary the good be enjoined and wrongdoing forbidden. These books of refutation have been present among us from the ages long past and no one found fault or discredited them, as all praise is due to Allaah, it is necessary to explain and clarify affairs.

(157) The Eminent Guiding Scholar Saaleh Ibn Fauzaan, may Allaah preserve him, From 'The Guidance of the True Belief': Page 383

### The Methodology of the People of the Sunnah and the Jama'ah in Refuting the People of Innovation in the Religion

The methodology of Ahlus-Sunnah wal-Jamaa'ah in refuting the people of innovation in the religion is based upon the Book of Allaah and the Sunnah. This is a methodology that is both convincing and persuasive, such that it refutes the doubts of the innovators and their misconceptions. We derive from the Qur'aan and Sunnah the obligation of holding firmly to the established practices of the Messenger, and striving against innovation in the religion and newly introduced matters. There have been many works written in this area. In the books related to correct beliefs there are general refutations of the sects of the Shee'ah, the Khawaarij, the Jahmeeyah, the Mu'tazilah, and the 'Ashareeyah, opposing their innovated statements in the fundamentals of the faith and belief. The people of the Sunnah wrote books specifically in this area of refutation, such as the book written by Imaam Ahmad ((Radd 'Ala Jahmeeyah)11-10); and other leading scholars composed work of this type. For example, that written by Uthman Ibn Saeed Ad-Daramee, as well as the books of Sheikh al-Islaam Ibn Taymeeyah and his student Ibn Qayyim. Additionally, there is Sheikh Muhammad Ibn Abdul-Wahaab and others who refuted these sects, as well as refuting those who worship at graves and followers of Sufism. So from the books specifically  written in refutation of the people of innovation in the religion, there are indeed many. For example among the earlier written works are books such as:

The book ((al-'Itisaam)11-01) by Imaam ash-Shaatabee.

The book ((Iqtidaa as-Siraat al-Mustaqeem)11-02) by Sheikh al-Islaam Ibn Taymeeyah, as he has devoted a significant portion of it to the refutation of the innovators.

The book (('Inkaar al-Hawaadith wa al-Bid'ah )11-03) by Ibn Wadhaah

The book ((al-Hawaadidh wa Bid'ah)11-04) by at-Tartooshee

The book ((al-Baaith Alaa Inkaar al-Bid'ah wa al-Hawadith)11-05) of Abee Shaamah

And from the modern works on this subject:

The book (al-Ibdaa' Fe Madhar al-Ibtidaa' )11-06) by Sheikh Alee Mafoudh

The book ((As-Sunnan wa Mubtadiaat al-Mutaliqat bi Inkar wa al-Salawaat)04-32) by Sheikh Muhammad Ibn Ahmad al-Shaqarah al-Hawandee.

The work ((at-Tadheer min al-Bid'ah)11-33) by Sheikh 'Abdul-'Azeez Ibn Baaz

So the scholars of the Muslims have not ceased, and all praise is due to Allaah, from criticizing innovation and refuting the innovators in the religion  by means of newspapers, magazines, and other media, as well as by Friday sermons, conferences, and lectures. Through such means as these there has been a significant enlightenment of the Muslims, and a suppression of innovation in the religion, and a subduing of those who innovate in the religion.

NOTES

**(158) THE EMINENT GUIDING SCHOLAR AHMAD IBN YAHYA AN-NAJMEE, MAY ALLAAH PRESERVE HIM, FROM 'DECISIVE RULINGS ON THE METHODOLOGIES OF CALLING TO ALLAAH': PAGE 80 )**

*Question: What are the reference books of the people of the Sunnah which are turned to in order to refute the people of innovation in the religion regarding those matters in which they have differed with the people of the Sunnah?*

Answer: These are such as the book *((Kitab at-Tawheed)06-36)* of Ibn Khuzaimah, *((ar-Rad Alaa Bishr al-Marisee)11-08)* by Uthmaan Ibn Saeed Ad-Daramee, *((Ibaanah al-Kubraa)06-27)* of Ibn Battah as well as *((As-Sughraa)06-28)* by him, *((Sharh Usul Itiqaad Ahlus-Sunnah wal-Jama'ah)06-29)* of Lalakaee, *((Kitab As-Sunnah)02-26)* from Ibn Abee Aasim, *((Kitaab As-Share'eah)06-34)* by al-'Ajooree, as well as *((Kitaab As-Sunnah)06-43)* by Abee Zamanayn, and *((al-Uluu)06-45)* of Imaam Dhahabee -as well as other works. As for the books of Sheikh al-Islaam Ibn Taymeeyah, Ibn Qayyim, Muhammad Ibn 'Abdul-Wahaab, as well as his grandsons and students, in all their works is found the explanation of the fundamentals and foundation of the correct beliefs.

**(159) THE EMINENT GUIDING SCHOLAR SAALEH IBN FAUZAAN, MAY ALLAAH PRESERVE HIM, FROM 'AN EXPLANATION OF THE MISTAKES OF SOME WRITERS': PAGE 13)**

### From Where Do We Obtain Beneficial Knowledge

Beneficial knowledge is obtained from the Book of Allaah and the Sunnah, through understanding them, contemplating them, and carefully studying them, seeking the assistance in this from the books written about worshiping Allaah alone, those which gather transmitted explanations the Book of Allaah, those containing explanation the meaning of hadeeth narrations, those books which have gathered the rulings in the religion and their principles, as well the books of grammar and the Arabic language. However, it is necessary that a warning be given about a grave deception and scheme which has spread among the youth from the hands of some of the people of bias and partisanship who have come to be known as "guides" and as "thinkers"; and many of the youth have been diverted and turned away from those beneficial books. This deception is found in their statements regarding the books which explain Allaah's right to be worshipped alone, those books which encompass and explain the methodology of the righteous first generations of Muslims and those who followed and adhered to their way in the matters of understanding Allaah's names and attribute, those books which contain refutations of the false negation of the sect of the Jahmeeyah and the Mu'tazilah and those that they gave rise to, those books which contain the explanations of the necessity of directing all worship towards Allaah alone, and what contradicts this completely and what diminishes it from different aspects of associating others in that worship.

Regarding these books they say: [These old books only refute people who have long since passed away and are now gone. They discuss misconceptions which have ceased to exist. We must abandon these books and occupy ourselves with refuting the new deviant methodologies such as Communism, Ba'thist Socialism...] until the end of what they mention. As they say regarding the books of ruling and jurisprudence what is similar to: [These are very complex books, and they incorporate suppositions which are far from reality, so we should abandon them and derive solutions to our problems directly from the Book of Allaah and the Sunnah ...] to the end of what they state. The response to that has several aspects:

1. Certainly, if we abandoned these books we would not have the ability to refute these newly emerging ideologies. These books instruct us in the proper methodology of refutation, and the correct way of reasoning and argumentation. Therefore if we abandoned them we would be in the position of the one who drops his weapon and then proceeds to meet the enemy without a weapon. Then what will result from this?! Truly, only your defeat and destruction or being captured.

2. Certainly the sects and groups which were refuted by the books of the early scholars which clarify the issues regarding Allaah's right to be worshiped alone have not ceased to exist. Rather, they have present day followers who embrace and adhere to what those first groups were upon, from the issues of negating Allaah's names and attributes, or the distortion of them, or engaging in actions which are associating others in the worship due to Allaah alone. These followers speak about these matters and spread them in their own publications as well as through comments on the printed works of others. So how can it be said that these sects have ceased to exist?!

3. As for the presumption and claim that these deviant groups have ceased to exist and there is no longer anyone who follows them, then the misconceptions and misinterpretations which caused them to go astray are present in the books they left behind; and what is feared is that one may come across these writings from the hands of those who do not understand their reality, and then go astray due to this, or this happens by the hands of those are clearly misguided and the people then are misguided by them. Therefore the study of what opposes these misconceptions and clarifies their falsehood from the early books of Ahlus-Sunnah wa'al-Jama'ah is something which is required.

4. The modern deviated methodologies and paths are descended from the early deviated methodologies and paths which the previous scholars have refuted in their books; therefore if we understand the earlier form of falsehood, then we also understand the falsehood which descended and was born out of it.

5. As for the assumption or claim that these new deviated methodologies do not have an origin in the past, then even if this was the case there is no conflict or contradiction between the refutation of the first forms of falsehood and refutation of the new forms of falsehood, in order that we not be deceived by either one of them! As it is obligatory to refute falsehood whenever one is able, the new and the old. And Allaah, the Exalted mentioned in the Qur'aan those aspects of disbelief the first people possessed as well as well as what was possessed by the first people, and refuted all of the them.

NOTES

6- As for their statements regarding the books of jurisprudence and fiqh, that "They are structured in a very complex way, and have strange suppositions." Then this is correct, if one speak truthfully about some of these texts due to being summarized, as they have been summarized in their explanations and clarifications, so the complexity is removed.

As for the strange suppositions, then these are regarding theoretical problems if they were to occur, a valuable resource for this Ummah, derived from the sources of the Book of Allaah and the Sunnah, which should not be undervalued or disdained.

So, the books of our predecessors of the first generations are resources which it is obligatory that we safeguard and that we must benefit from; not being deceived by the schemes of the enemies of Islaam and the partisans who are displeased and saddened by what is found within these books from clarification of the truth and the refutation of falsehood which they have inherited from their predecessors from the Jahmeeyah and the Mu'tazilah. So they begin stirring up the youth concerning them, instigating and working up amongst them an aversion and dislike for these books. ❧*They want to extinguish Allaah's Light with their mouths*❧-(Surah Tawbah:32) However, there has never ceased to be, and all praise is due to Allaah, those always present, the people of truth who were not deceived by this deceitful propaganda which opposes their illustrious history.

Allaah has decreed for these lands, and all praise is due to Allaah, Islamic universities which have been established upon teaching Islamic heritage, reviving and spreading it. They take as their model of educational methodology the verifying of the books which teach the methodology of the first generations of Muslims, as well as their printing and distribution. Examples are the Islamic university of Muhammad Ibn Saud, and the Islamic University in Medinahh, and the Islamic University Umm al-Quraa, and likewise what has been established through other universities in the kingdom of Saudi Arabia and other countries from praiseworthy efforts in this area.

(160) The Eminent Guiding Scholar Saaleh Ibn Fauzaan, may Allaah preserve him, From 'A Selection of Islamic Rulings': Vol. 2, Page 307)

*Question: Is it permissible to read some of the books which explain some of the religions other than Islaam, solely for the purpose of being familiar with these religions? Or to read some of the books regarding the communist system and methodologies similar to it? Not in order to be impressed by them or with the intent to act according to them, but simply for the purpose of familiarity as mentioned previously?*

Answer: First, it is upon an individual to comprehend the truth and to understand the true religion, and achieve a proficiency in beneficial knowledge. After this, such a one could read about what opposes the truth in order to warn from it and offer a refutation of it. But the ignorant person who has little education and his comprehension of Sharee'ah knowledge is limited, then it is not permissible for him to read from the books of false ideologies, as perhaps it will affect him and influence his belief without his realizing it- because he does have a firm understanding of that knowledge by which one distinguishes between the truth and falsehood. Therefore, it is required initially that he achieved a sound comprehension of that beneficial knowledge by which he can distinguish between truth and falsehood. After that then there is no problem with such reading.

(161) The Eminent Guiding Scholar Muhammad Naasiruddeen al-Albaanee, may Allaah have mercy upon him, From 'al-Isaalah' Magazine -Shawwal 1414 H. Issue, Page 38)

*Question: Is it permissible for book publishers to sell newspapers or magazines in which there are indecent pictures, which convey false stories, and which praise the hypocrites and wrong-doers? Moreover, is it permissible for them to print books that contain beliefs, concepts and understandings that do not agree with the way of the first three generations of Islaam, in order to facilitate the publication of its publications related to the methodology of the first three generations of Muslims?*

Answer: As for magazines which contain indecent pictures, then it is not allowed to waver or have misgivings in regard to not buying them, as purchasing them is not something permissible. As for other fiqh books, it is necessary for the one who desires to remain within the boundaries of the Sharee'ah to know that it is an obligation upon him to have knowledge of the views, rulings, and concepts contained within these books. At that time make a judgement according to what is generally found within them. If what is in them is acceptable then it is permissible to sell them; otherwise one cannot generally state that it is permissible to sell them. As there is no book other than the book of Allaah which if free from errors. So if we state that it is not permissible to sell any book that contains mistakes, then it would not be not permissible to sell any book. So look into the matter in order to assess the general state of the majority of its content.

# CLEAR STATEMENTS FROM THE ⬛ADVICE OF THE SCHOLARS REGARDING MEMORIZING KNOWLEDGE

*Abu Alee al-Haafidh said: "Ibn Khuzaimah used to memorize the understandings from the hadeeth he knew just as a reciter memorizes the recitation of a surah."*

('Seeyar 'Alaam An-Nubalaa' Vol. 14, Page 372)

**(162) The Eminent Guiding Scholar 'Abdur-Rahman Ibn Naasir as-Sa'dee, may Allaah have mercy upon him, From 'A Delightful Collection of Benefits & And the Pursuing the Desired Prey': Page 128)**

*The Types of Knowledge-Related Benefits from Studies of Knowledge. The benefits which gain from studying the various areas of knowledge are of two types:*

The first regards an issue that you did not previously understand; so you benefit by understanding after having been ignorant regarding it. The second regards an issue or subject that you previously learned and then forgot, so that you are then reminded regarding it. In relation to this Allaah mentions these two types in his speech, ❖ *An insight and a Reminder for every slave turning to Allaah.* ❖-(Surah al-Qaaf 8). So either it is the case of the general person who starts out ignorant, but then thinks and considers, so knowledge reaches him when he was previously ignorant; or it is the case that one who previously understood a matter is reminded of that which he previous knew but had forgotten.

And here is a second type of reminder from the types of reminder. When someone generally understands an issue, then he studies it, reaching a more detailed understanding of what he previously knew in general. So he achieves detailed knowledge after having a general understanding, and this is a tremendous occurrence. Then the way towards these two affairs of learned insights and beneficial reminders is to consider the limits of issues and to contemplate an issue in a way which distinguishes it from other issues, and then to derive a ruling from the evidences and proofs regarding it. So investigation and consideration are the initial stages of knowledge and from the keys to proceed within it. Then one proceeds to contemplating these matters and then to reaching a correct ruling upon them, so the one who was ignorant becomes enlightened in the issue and the one who had forgotten recalls and is reminded of it. The one who can truly benefit from this is the worshiper who sincerely turns to Allaah, turning his face to seeking the face of Allaah with the intention of adhering to the truth, and seeking the path to reach it. As for the one who in reality turns away from Allaah, or seeks other than the truth, then he cannot profit from the various signs and indications nor from the beneficial branches of knowledge. Rather, they become a proof against him. And Allaah knows best.

**(163) The Eminent Guiding Scholar Muhammad Ibn Saaleh al-'Utheimeen, may Allaah have mercy upon him, From 'Book of Knowledge': Page 160**

*Question: What is the correct way to seek knowledge? Is it to memorize the texts of the different Sharee'ah sciences, or simply to understand them without memorization? We hope for your guidance regarding this, may Allaah the Exalted preserve you.*

Answer:   If is for the student of knowledge to begin seeking knowledge step by step. So it is necessary for you to begin with the essentials and fundamentals, the basic principles and what is similar to that as found in the summarized works or texts. The summarized works are the ladder used to reach the longer works. However, it is necessary to understand the fundamentals and basic principles. "*The one who does not comprehend the fundamentals is prevented from reaching the objective.*" Many students of knowledge have memorized several individual issues, but they do not have an understanding of the principles behind them. If one unusual issue comes to him, then what he has memorized does not enable him to understand the nature of this new matter. But if he comprehended the guidelines and principles, then he would have the ability to judge upon any individual issue from such issues. So due to this I urge my brothers towards the understanding of the fundamental principles, guidelines, and essentials, as in this there are tremendous benefits. This is something that we have experienced and witnessed from others, that fundamentals are indeed essential and from this is the memorization of these summarized works. And clearly, I know that some of the people have tried to deceive us, as they have said to us: [Memorization does not possess any benefits, it is the meaning of the text which is fundamental.] However, and all praise is due to Allaah, we have been saved from accepting this false understanding and we have memorized what Allaah has wished for us from the texts of grammar works and those related to the principles of deriving rulings, and the works of the subject of worshiping Allaah alone. So due to this do not undervalue the issue of memorization. Memorization is the norm, and perhaps one from among you can now recall statements or passages which were read some time ago. So memorization is important to the student of knowledge despite being difficult. We ask Allaah, the Most Glorified and the Most Exalted, to make us of those who are on the way of our righteous first generations, and to make us guides among those who are guided. He is the Beneficent and the Generous.

**(164) The Eminent Guiding Scholar Saaleh al-Fauzaan, may Allaah preserve him, From 'Beneficial Answers To Questions on New Methodologies': Page 39**

*Question: It is known that calling to Allaah requires Sharee'ah knowledge. But is the knowledge that is necessary for that the memorization of the texts from the Qur'aan and Sunnah? And is the knowledge we study in the schools and the universities sufficient for calling to Allaah?*

Answer: Knowledge is memorization of the source texts in addition to understanding their meanings. So it is not enough to memorize the texts only. It is not sufficient for a person to simply memorize parts of Qur'aan or hadeeth narrations. It is also required that you understand their correct meanings. So as for merely memorizing the texts without understanding their meanings, then this is not sufficient for calling people to Allaah. Concerning what is studied in schools, if it consists of memorizing the texts in addition to understanding their meaning then there is no harm in that. But if that consists of memorization the source texts without also understanding there meanings, then that is not adequate for calling to Allaah.

**(165) The Eminent Guiding Scholar Muhammad Ibn Saaleh al-'Utheimeen, may Allaah have mercy upon him, From 'Islamic Revival - Guidelines and Guidances': Page 120**

*Question: Many students of knowledge are concerned with memorizing the Qur'aan and hadeeth narrations related to rulings but neglect the knowledge of "usul al-fiqh." They believe what they have memorized from the Qur'aan and hadeeth is enough, despite the fact that knowledge of "usul al-fiqh" is the branch of knowledge which explains how to correctly understand these source texts. So we hope for your guidance, Esteemed Sheikh, concerning this issue.*

Answer: My view is that when an individual begins seeking knowledge, specifically when they are young, they should start with the memorization of the Noble Qur'aan before anything else. This was the way used by the Companions of the Prophet, may Allaah be pleased with them. They used to learn the text of the Qur'aan, then its meaning, and then proceed to practice it or apply it. So the student of knowledge is in need of the Qur'aan. Can't you see that if you speak of a matter in a gathering and you need to derive something from a verse of the Qur'aan which you have not memorized it, then you will not be able to derive what is needed from the Qur'aan? So I urge the students of knowledge, specifically the young people, to memorize of the Word of Allaah, the Most High and the Most Exalted. After this, memorize what is easy for you from the hadeeth narrations such as the works *(('Amdat al-Ahkaam)02-28)* or *((Bulugh al-Maraam)02-34)*, if an individual has the ability to do so.

Then, after comes the subject of various understanding and rulings of the religion and the principles of how these are derived from the sources. There is no doubt that the principles of how rulings are derived is one of the best areas of knowledge. It contains satisfaction for the one who learns it, because if an individual understands the principles and guidelines, he is then someone who can train his intellect in the extraction of such correct understanding and rulings from the various evidences by means of utilizing these principles and guidelines.

(166) THE EMINENT GUIDING SCHOLAR SAALEH AL-FAUZAAN, MAY ALLAAH PRESERVE HIM, FROM 'A SELECTION OF ISLAMIC RULINGS': VOL. 2, PAGE 209

*Question: Which is better for the student of knowledge: to begin with the study of the explanations of the Noble Qur'aan, or the memorization of hadeeth texts, or the study of the various ruling of the religion and the fundamental principles of these two area of knowledge?*

Answer: The correct way for the beginning student of knowledge is memorizing texts while studying them with the scholars, in order to take the correct meaning and explanation of the texts from them. In this way, he will proceed by stages in seeking knowledge step by step. He begins with the summarized texts and then proceeds to those of medium length and finally to the longer books. Along with this is the necessity of sitting with the scholars in the circles of study or in the classroom. As knowledge is acquired by continually seeking it, not through reading by oneself. And Allaah knows best.

(167) THE EMINENT GUIDING SCHOLAR AHMAD IBN YAHYA AN-NAJMEE, MAY ALLAAH PRESERVE HIM, FROM 'DECISIVE RULINGS ON THE METHODOLOGIES OF CALLING TO ALLAAH': VOL.2, PAGE 101

*Question: All praise is due to Allaah, as for what follows : These questions come from one of our brothers in Qatar who follows the methodology of the first three generations. I ask Allaah to guide us and him to every goodness, and keep far from us and him every evil and harm. The questioner asks: "If a student of knowledge studies and reads a specific text from among the texts of knowledge with a scholar, and he then understands it but does not memorize it, is that sufficient? In this case is it then proper to go ahead and proceed to a different text for study or is it in fact necessary to first memorize the previous text and understand all its various issues from his scholar? Please benefit us regarding this, may Allaah make you of those who are rewarded.*

Answer: What is important is the understanding of that text of knowledge and comprehending its meaning. Yet if an individual combines between understanding and memorizing the text, then this is excellent; otherwise what is most important is the understanding. As from another direction, indeed the Messenger of Allaah, may Allaah's praise and salutations be upon him, stated, *{May Allaah bring light to the face of the person who hears my statement, fully retains it, and conveys it to one who has not heard it. As perhaps the one who carries it does not fully understand it, and perhaps the* *one who carries to another will convey it to one who understands it better than himself. There are three matters which the heart of the Muslim will never feel treacherous towards: Sincerely performing deeds for the sake of Allaah alone, offering advice to the Muslim rulers, and adhering closely to the body of Muslims united upon the truth, as Indeed their call is an all-encompassing one}* [108]. The third thing is that memorizing the text and words without understanding its meaning does not have any benefit. Certainly some time ago we heard that in Yemen there was a student of knowledge who had memorize *((ar-Rawdhah)07-27)* which is a work of Shaafa'ee jurisprudence. If you asked him regarding an issue he would not be able to explain or clarify it. So those students around him, whenever they differed in a matter of jurisprudence and they wanted to confirm the position stated within *((ar-Rawdhah)07-27)*, then they would call for that student. They would say to him, *"Tell us what it says in such and such chapter of ar-Rawdah."* So he would recite for them without missing a single letter. As such he was knows as the Donkey of Rawdhah.

Fourth, it is upon the student of knowledge to supplicate to Allaah, the Most Glorified and the Most Exalted, to bless him with understanding of the Book of Allaah and the Sunnah of His Prophet, may the praise and salutations of Allaah be upon him, and that he grant him understanding in the religion, as the Prophet, may Allaah's praise and salutations be upon him, said *{Whoever Allaah intends good for He grants him understanding in the religion.}* [109]

(168) THE EMINENT GUIDING SCHOLAR AHMAD IBN YAHYA AN-NAJMEE, MAY ALLAAH PRESERVE HIM, FROM 'DECISIVE RULINGS ON THE METHODOLOGIES OF CALLING TO ALLAAH': VOL. 2, PAGE 105

*Question: I am a young man who is almost thirty years old; however I have not completely memorized the Book of Allaah. I have not ceased being consistent in my efforts in memorization, and I ask Allaah for success. Is it better in my efforts to seek knowledge to memorize the book of Allaah completely, and after completing that, then to seek general Sharee'ah knowledge, or to combine between seeking knowledge and memorizing the Qur'aan?*

Answer: It is better in my view that you combine seeking knowledge and memorization, as you will not complete your memorization except that you will have also attained tremendous benefit from seeking knowledge, if Allaah so wills.

---

[108] Narrated in Sunan Abu Dawud: 3660/ & other hadeeth collections: -on the authority of Zayb Ibn Thaabit. It was declared authentic by Sheikh al-Albaanee in Silsilat al-Hadeeth as-Saheehah: 404, 1721 and within several other works. Sheikh Muqbil declared it authentic in al-Jaame'a al-Saheeh: 10, 162, 163, 1074, 3151,3801, 3802, 3916

[109] Narrated in Saheeh al-Bukhaaree: 71, 3116, 7312/ Saheeh Muslim: 1037/ Sunan Ibn Maajah: 221/ al-Muwatta Maalik: 1300, 1667/ Musnad Imaam Ahmad: 16395: 16404, and other narrations/ Musannaf Ibn Abee Shaybah: 31792/ & Sunan ad-Daaramee: 224, 226/- on the authority of Mu'aweeyah. And it is found in Jaame'a al-Tirmidhee: 2645/ & Musnad Imaam Ahmad: 2786/ & Sunan ad-Daaramee: 270, 2706/- on the authority of Ibn "Abbaas. And it is found in Sunan Ibn Maajah: 220/ Musannaf 'Abdul-Razzaaq: 30851/- on the authority of Abu Hurairah. It was declared authentic by Sheikh al-Albaanee in Saheeh al-Aadab al-Mufrad: 517, Silsilat al-Hadeeth as-Saheehah: 1194, 1195, 1196, Saheeh at-Targheeb at-Tarheeb: 67, as well as in other of his books. Sheikh Muqbil declared it authentic in al-Jaame'a al-Saheeh: 9, 3123, 4650.

(169) The Eminent Guiding Scholar Saaleh Ibn Fauzaan, may Allaah preserve him, From 'A Selection of Islamic Rulings': Vol. 1, Page 325

*Question:*   *What is your view, Esteemed Sheikh, of the one who is concerned with the important issues for the Muslims such as calling to Allaah, and educating the youth to adhere to the Qur'aan and pure Sunnah, but who does not find time to memorize the Qur'aan al-Kareem? What is your advice to someone like this?*

Answer: It is obligatory upon the caller to Allaah to become qualified before engaging in calling to Allaah. This is done through studying the Noble Qur'aan, its meanings and explanations, studying the Prophet's Sunnah and the basic matters from it, and reading those works that explain the various matters within it; as well as his learning the rulings of Islaam on various matters. It is an obligation upon the one calling to Allaah that he become qualified. No one is suitable for calling to Allaah except for the one who has knowledge. As Allaah the exalted said, *Say: "This is my way; I invite unto Allaah with 'baseerah', I and whosoever follows me*- (Surah Yusuf:108)This 'baseerah" is knowledge and wisdom. Allaah the Exalted said, *Invite to the Way of your Lord with wisdom and fair preaching*-(Surah An-Nahl: 125) So the ignorant person is not at all suitable for calling to Allaah, as perhaps he will actually harm the efforts to call to Allaah. He may declare the forbidden matters permissible, and the permissible matters forbidden, or overemphasize a subject or issue that should truly not have that much emphasis. It is necessary to have conditions for the one who would be a caller to Allaah. From the essential conditions is that he has studied and acquired that knowledge which will enable him to call the people to the religion of Allaah, the Most High and the Most Exalted. Additionally, sometimes there will be doubts or issues put forward to the caller to Allaah which require a response from him. If he is someone who is ignorant, how will he respond to these doubts and issues? How will he respond to the challenges from those who put them forth? How will he stand up to the people who have abandoned Islaam, corrupt individuals and those similar to them, if he is someone who does not have knowledge? Indeed, he would be defeated in front of them. So it is necessary that the caller to Allaah have knowledge of the Qur'aan, the Prophet's Sunnah, of hadeeth sciences, fiqh matters, and correct beliefs, and other than that from the branches of knowledge.

(170) The Eminent Guiding Scholar 'Abdul-'Azeez Ibn 'Abdullah Ibn Baaz, may Allaah have mercy upon him, From 'A Collection of Rulings and Various Statements:' Vol. 6, Page 374

*Question: Please guide me to the way that will assist me in memorizing the Book of Allaah.*

Answer:   I advise you to concentrate and be committed to this matter and to select the most suitable times for memorization, such as the later part of the night or after Fajr prayer or sometime during the night, or at the other times when you can feel comfortable, such that you can memorize well. Also I advise you to choose a good companion who will help and assist you in your memorization and study. Along with this, seek success and assistance in this endeavor from Allaah and humbly ask Him to help you, grant you success, and to guide you to the means of success. As the one who sincerely seeks assistance from Allaah, then Allaah will support him and facilitate his efforts.

(171) The Eminent Guiding Scholar 'Abdul-'Azeez Ibn 'Abdullah Ibn Baaz, may Allaah have mercy upon him, From 'A Collection of Rulings and Various Statements': Vol. 9, Page 416

*Question: What is the ruling of the one who recites Qur'aan but makes mistakes in the pronunciation of short vowels? Will he be rewarded for such a recitation?*

Answer:   It has been legislated that the believer strive to recite properly, and work to assess what is correct in his effort. He should recite to someone who is more knowledgeable than him in the knowledge of reciting Qur'aan until he benefits and is able to correct the mistakes he has. He is rewarded and he is indeed given two rewards if he struggles in reciting and works to correct his mistakes, as is seen in the statement of the Prophet, may Allaah's praise and salutations be upon him, *{The proficient reciter of the Qur'aan is associated with the noble and the upright, recording angels, and the one who makes mistakes and finds it difficult for him will have a double reward}* [110]. This is the wording of the narration as found in Saheeh Muslim.

[110]

**(172) THE EMINENT GUIDING SCHOLAR MUQBIL IBN HAADEE AL-WAADI'EE, MAY ALLAAH HAVE MERCY UPON HIM, FROM 'BRIDLING THE RESISTANT ONE', PAGE 434**

*Question:  Is it true that learning to recite with tajweed is obligatory upon every Muslim? The author of the book "The Study of Tajweed" states, "It is obligatory" and he derives this from the statement of Allaah the Exalted, ❴Recite the Qur'aan properly❵ .*

Answer: What is correct in this issue is that reciting with tajweed is not obligatory. The verse ❴**Recite the Qur'aan properly**❵-(Surah al-Muzammmil: 4) means to recite clearly and make the Qur'aan clearly heard, not mumbled and jumbled, mixing up the different letters together. As for the statement of al-Jazaree:

*Reciting with tajweed is an obligatory injunction,*

> *the one who recites the Qur'aan without it is a sinner.*

*Because he has lowered the station of his High Lord*

> *And so along with us that is what he has become.*

Then this is not correct. Rather it is found in the two well-known "Saheeh" collection of al-Bukhaaree and Muslim that 'Aishah, may Allaah be pleased with her said, that the Messenger of Allaah, may Allaah's praise and salutations be upon him, said, {*The proficient reciter of the Qur'aan is associated with the noble and the upright, recording angels, and the one who makes mistakes and finds it difficult for him will have a double reward*} -(Saheeh al-Bukhaaree: 4937, Saheeh Muslim: 798).

So this is in relation to the obligation reciting it correctly; but as for the matter of beautifying it with one's voice then this is only a matter which is desired and recommended. It is found in the 'Sunan' collections of hadeeth the narration of al-Baraa' Ibn 'Aazib, may Allaah be pleased with him, where he said that the Messenger of Allaah, may Allaah's praise and salutations be upon him, said, {*Beautify the Qur'aan with your voices.*} [111]. And as is found on authority of Sa'eed Ibn Abee Waqaas, may Allaah be pleased with him, the Messenger of Allaah, may Allaah's praise and salutations be upon him, said, {*The one who does not strive to beautify the Qur'aan with his voice, is not from among us.*} -(Saheeh al-Bukhaaree: 7527). Meaning the one who does not try to use his voice to recite the Qur'aan in a pleasing way, then he is not from us.

It is also found in the two well-known "Saheeh" collection of al-Bukhaaree and Muslim from Abu Hurairah, may Allaah be pleased with him, that the Messenger of Allaah, may Allaah's praise and salutations be upon him, {*Allah never listens to anything as much He listens to the Prophet reciting Qur'aan in a pleasant sweet sounding voice.*}- (Saheeh al-Bukhaaree: 5024, 7482, 7544, Saheeh Muslim: 792) Therefore reciting while beautifying one's voice is a recommended matter as indicated by the principles of Arabic language. One of those who takes an extreme position regarding tajweed used to teach us, and he would say, "The Arabs even used the rules of tajweed in their poetry," Then he would recite the line of poetry:

[111] Narrated in Sunan Abu Dawud: 1468/ & other collections: -on the authority of Baraa' Ibn 'Aazab. It was declared authentic by Sheikh al-Albaanee in Silsilat al-Hadeeth as-Saheehah: 771 and within other works. Sheikh Muqbil declared it authentic in al-Jaamee'a al-Saheeh: 347, 1019, 3845, 3846, 4668.

*Hold your tears from remembering your beloved and your home...*

And he said this verse of poetry with Qalqala on the Arabic letter baa, and joining the tanween and the Arabic letter waw of the following word together.[112] So it was said to him in criticism, *"Oh Sheikh, where is the chain of narration to Amr' al-Qays, (the poet of the above lines) which shows that he read this poetry as you have read it?!?"* Similarly, Haafidh Ibn Qayyim, mentioned in *((Ighathatul al-Lahfaan)12-05)* that this is considered from being among the traps of Shaytaan- unbalanced over-stringent focus upon reciting according to the rules of tajweed. He said, *"Some of the reciters will occupy a student of knowledge learning to recite for forty days over his recitation of Surat al-Faatihah alone."* And he also said, *"Some of them will be so thoroughly obsessed with trying to recite in this way that he recites it until it is as though he were vomiting; his veins become swollen, and his face reddens until it looks like he is about to vomit."* But the people should stand between both extremism and neglect. From among the people there is the one who does not give any concern to beautifying his voice when reciting the Qur'aan, and from among the people there are those who go to extreme lengths for the sake of beautification. And if you heard such a one reciting and you are far away from him, you could not be sure whether he was reciting the Qur'aan and or simply singing.

Yet the first generations of believers, may Allaah be pleased with them all, criticized this over-stringent focus on beautification of recitation. Some of them criticized Hamzah (one of the early Qur'aan reciters) regarding some of his recitation, such that some of our predecessors, may Allaah the Most High, have mercy upon them, stated, *"The method of recitation of Hamza is an innovation in the religion,"* as is mentioned in the work *((Mizaan al-'Itidaal)05-19)*. So over-stringent focus regarding beautification through tajweed is something blameworthy, just as a failure to give due consideration to reciting according to the guidelines of tajweed is considered neglectfulness in the religion. Therefore is proper that you sit and learn from one who will teach you the guidelines of tajweed and benefit from him, but as for considering it obligatory, then no, this is incorrect.

Rather this matter is as has been mentioned by ash-Shawkaanee, may Allaah have mercy upon him, in the biography of Muhammad Ibn Ibraaheem al-Wazeer, may Allaah have mercy upon him, as found in the book *((al-Badr al-Talaa')05-29)*. He stated, *"Some of the people overly praise in their writings an area from amongst the different areas of knowledge, because of their delighting in it, and they make it the embodiment of excellence in knowledge. Thereafter later scholars read their words, and come to consider that this matter is from the obligatory matters of Sharee'ah knowledge, and that is required to study it."*

So you should benefit from the one who knows how to recite according to the guidelines of tajweed, and be diligent and learning how to recite with tajweed, and hold fast to learning the Arabic language. The Qur'aan was revealed in the Arabic language, it did not come in a foreign language, or in the language of the people of Damaaj, or of 'Aden, or Hadhramaut, or America, such that you would want

[112] This is a reference to some of the specific guidelines of tajweed he used when reciting this poetry

NOTES

to recite the Qur'aan and that language. No, rather the Qur'aan is to be recited in the Arabic language just as it was revealed. This is what is proper. And some of the people say, [But the specific guidelines of tajweed are taken with chains of narration to their original reciters, and original reciters back to the Prophet, may Allaah's praise and salutations be upon him.] Then you should say to them, "*Where within these chains of narration are found the specific rules regarding elongation the letter 'aleef' here, with a single period of elongation, and in some places to periods of elongation, while in other places it is four or six.??*"

Yes it is true that it is affirmed on the Prophet, may Allaah's praise and salutations be upon him and his household, that he used to recite the letter 'aleef' with elongation in some places, therefore you should recite and beautify your recitation as Allaah has commanded you. But some of the people go to extremes, they make al-ikhfaa' (which is a concealing of the sound of letter accompanied by with a nasal sound to idgham (meaning here the full merging of a specific type of the letter into the letter that follows it when suitable), and they may extend the pronunciation of a word until it practically has been wrongly merged with that which follows it. Yet Allaah says, ❖*Say (Oh Muhammad): "Oh people of the Scripture (Jews and Christians)! Do not exceed the limits in your religion*❖-(Surah An-Nisa': 171)  So what is proper for us is that we engage in reciting, and that we gauge correctness according to the recitation of the Messenger of Allaah, may Allaah's praise and salutations be upon him and his household, and according to the recitation of the Companions, may Allaah be pleased with them all, and the recitation of the first generations in general, may Allaah be pleased with them all. There is a significant distinction between an individual improperly mumbling or jumbling together his recitation of the Qur'aan, and a different individual who recites clearly and beautifully. As a person is affected by the one who recites clearly and beautifully.

Indeed, as is mentioned in the 'Saheeh' collection of al-Bukhaaree, a man came to Ibn Mas'ood, may Allaah be pleased with him, and said, "*I recited the shorter Mufassal surahs at night in one rak'ah.*" Ibn Mas'ud said, "*This recitation is too quick, like the recitation of poetry.*" So the matter is undertaken in a middle way. And this verse is to be considered a ruling with ❖*Recite the Qur'aan properly*❖-(Surah al-Muzzammel:4) meaning, recite clearly and distinctly. Make sure that each letter and each word is distinct. And some of the imaams of prayer who lead the people in prayer, it is seen that there is no way that he could have recited the opening supplication in his prayer. He says, "*Allaahu Akbar,*" and then immediately he begins reciting al-Fatiha, and another Surah after it, without any break. This is playing with the religion, and certainly the best guidance is the guidance of Muhammad, may Allaah's praise and salutations be upon him and his household, in how he recited during the ritual prayer, as well as in the remaining matters of ritual worship, the guidance of every day affairs, as well as in our essential beliefs.

(173) The Eminent Guiding Scholar Muqbil Ibn Haadee al-Waadi'ee, may Allaah have mercy upon him, from 'Excellent Responses to Questions from those Present and those Absent': Page 157

*Question: What is the correct way to memorize the Qur'aan and ahadeeth?*

Answer: In regard to the memorization of the Qur'aan, then the people differ. Among people, one person may be able to memorize an entire page, and someone may be able to memorize several pages, and from them someone may only be able to memorize half a page or less. So everyone proceeds according to his ability and capacity. From those matters which aid and strengthen you in memorizing the Qur'aan is repetition and continual review, as well as standing in prayer in night, for the one who has the ability to stand at night. As Allaah, glorified be He, the Most High, said, ❃*Verily, the rising by night for Tahajjud prayer is very hard and most potent and good for governing the soul*❃-(Surah al-Muzzammel:6) and He said: ❃*And in some parts of the night also offer the salaat with it (i.e. recite the Qur'aan in the prayer), as an additional prayer for you*❃-(Surah al-Isra'a:79)

Also, take from the scholars in this area and memorize at their hands. If this is not possible for you then I advise you to obtain cassette tapes of precise narrators who recite with correct recitation. Not those reciters who stretch their recitation excessively as is done by such as the famous reciter 'Abdul-Baasset. No, only the one who recites in a moderate and balanced way, and not from those who do so in a manner that was hated by some of the first generations of Muslims. As for the memorization of hadeeth narrations then this is somewhat easier. If you can proceed without memorizing the chains of narration, then it may be possible to memorize a single hadeeth in one, two or perhaps three days. Then you should act upon and implement this hadeeth, as this will help the hadeeth become firmly rooted in your memory. Afterwords, be consistent to reviewing it with some of your brothers, as well as frequently repeating and reviewing it in general.

(174) The Eminent Guiding Scholar Ahmad Ibn Yahya An-Najmee, may Allaah preserve him, from 'Decisive Rulings on the Methodologies of Calling to Allaah': Vol. 2, Page 110 )

*Question: Is there a specific order in which we should memorize the texts and writings of Sheikh Muhammad Ibn 'Abdul-Wahaab; such as 'Thalathatul-Usul', 'Usul as-Sittah', 'Qawaid al-Arba '', 'Masaail al-Jaahiliyah', 'Nawaaqidh al-Islaam', 'Kitaab at-Tawheed', and 'Kashf as-Shubahat'? We hope that you would clarify the best order in which these texts should be memorized.*

Answer: Firstly, memorization requires a firm resolve and determination.

Secondly, it requires continuous reading for review.

Thirdly, one should start initially with smaller texts and then proceed to those that are larger and more advanced.

Fourthly, frequently make supplications to Allaah for Him to facilitate this effort for you. Through these means you will attain, if Allaah so wills, what has been written for you of success.

NOTES

**(175) The Eminent Guiding Scholar 'Abdul-'Azeez Ibn 'Abdullah Ibn Baaz-, may Allaah have mercy upon him, From 'A Collection of Rulings and Various Statements': Vol.6, Page 373**

*Question: I have often memorized verses of the Noble Qur'aan; however after some time passes I forget what I memorized. Similarly, when I recite I am not sure whether my recitation is correct or not. Afterward I discover that I indeed made mistakes in my recitation. So kindly offer me guidance regarding this.*

Answer:      The Sharee'ah guidance for you my brother is that you put forth your effort to memorize that which is easy for you from the Book of Allaah, and that you read back and review what you've memorized to some of your good brothers at school, in the masjid, or in your home. Additionally you should be diligent in this until your recitation is correct and sound. This is due to the statement of the Prophet, may Allaah's praise and salutations be upon him, *{The best of you are those who learn the Qur'aan and teach it.}* [113], as was narrated by al-Bukhaaree in his "Saheeh" collection of hadeeth narrations. Therefore the best people are those who are attached to the Qur'aan and have learned it, and then taught it to the people, and acted upon it, implementing its guidance. This is due to the statement of the Prophet, may Allaah's praise and salutations be upon him, *{"Which of you would like to go out every morning to Buthan and bring two large she-camels without being guilty of sin or without achieving it by severing the ties of kinship?" We said: "Messenger of Allah, all of us would like to do it." Upon this he said: "Does not one of you go out in the morning to the mosque and teach or recite two verses from the Book of Allah. the Majestic and Glorious? That is better for him than two she-camels, and three verses are better than three she-camels, and four verses are better for him than four she-camels, and so on in their number in camels."}* [114] or as the Messenger of Allaah, may Allaah's praise and salutations be upon him, has stated.

This makes clear to us the high merit of teaching the Qur'aan. So it is upon you my brother to learn the Qur'aan from those brothers who are knowledgeable of its proper recitation, until you benefit from this and are able to recite correctly. As for that which you've encountered of forgetfulness, then there is no blame upon you for this. Everyone forgets some matters. Just as Prophet, may Allaah's praise and salutations be upon his said, *{Indeed I'm a human being like you, and I forget as you forget.}* And once he was reciting and someone corrected him, and he said, *{May Allaah have mercy upon so and so, he reminded me of the verse which I missed or did not recall.}* -(Saheeh Muslim: 1353) What is intended by this is that an individual may forget certain verses and then later remember them, or someone else will remind him of what is correct regarding them. So what is better is that you say "I was made to forget." or "I was caused to forget.". This is due to what is narrated that the Prophet said "one of you should not saying I forgot that verse, rather he was made to forget by Shaytaan."

---

[113] Narrated in Saheeh al-Bukhaaree: 5027/ Sunan Abee Dawud: 1352/Sunan at-Tirmidhee: 2907/ & Musnad Ahmad: 414, 502/ from the hadeeth of 'Uthmaan Ibn 'Afaan. Declared authentic by Sheikh al-Albaanee in Silsilatul-Hadeeth Saheehah: 1173, and in Saheeh at-Targheeb wa at-Tarheeb: 1415, as well as in other of his works.
[114] Narrated in Sunan Abu Dawud: 1257/ -on the authority of 'Uqbah Ibn 'Aamr. It was declared authentic by Sheikh al-Albaanee in al-Albaanee in Silsilat al-Hadeeth as-Saheehah: 1456 and within other of his works.

As for that hadeeth narration which says [The one who memorizes the Qur'aan and then forgets it, will meet Allaah in a state in which he is mutilated.], then this narration is weak and not authentically affirmed as a saying from the Prophet. Forgetfulness is not something which one chooses or which one has the capacity to preserve himself from. So again what is intended according to the guidance of the Sharee'ah is that you memorize that which is easy for you from the Book of Allaah, the Most Glorified and the Most Exalted, and that you maintain and preserve that, as well as reciting what you memorize to one who has good recitation in order to correct your mistakes. And I ask Allaah to grant you success in this affair of yours.

**(176) THE EMINENT GUIDING SCHOLAR MUHAMMAD AMAAN AL-JAAMEE, MAY ALLAAH HAVE MERCY UPON HIM, FROM THE AUDIO LECTURE '27 QUESTIONS REGARDING THE METHODOLOGY OF THE FIRST THREE GENERATIONS OF MUSLIMS'**

*Question: What do you advise our youth who have memorized the Qur'aan but then have neglected to maintain that memorization?*

Answer: I fear that the reason for neglecting to maintain their memorization which some of the youth of Jeddah are asking about- as I reside in Medinahh- is because some of them say that for them, there is no benefit in simply memorizing the Qur'aan if they do not understand its meaning. This is a mistake, as it is for you to memorize the Book of Allaah whether you understand all of it or not. The recitation of the Qur'aan is from the highest forms of worship. Rather it is certainly from the best types of worship in general. If you do not understand its meaning, still for every single recited letter you receive ten rewards. The Prophet, may praise and salutations of Allaah be upon him said, *{I do not say that the word 'Aleef Lam Meem' counts as one letter in relation to your reward, rather 'Aleef' counts as one letter, 'Lam' as one letter, and 'Meem' as one letter.}* [115]. These are from the separated letters that are found in the beginning of some chapters of the Qur'aan, and only Allaah knows what is fully intended in their meaning; we don't have knowledge of this. But along with this fact we are rewarded for their recitation. So the young brothers should be firm regarding the memorization of the Qur'aan. As for the obstruction placed before them in the form of the false claim they do not understand the meaning of what is memorized, then this is an evil call or claim that it is not proper that you accept. Memorize the Qur'aan and that which you forget, review and strengthen it. Utilize those printed Qur'aans which have in the margins and explanation of some of the verses or some of the individual words or phrases, or from those small books that explain the meaning of the words in the Qur'aan, as well as asking the people of knowledge regarding their correct explanation, and then rely upon Allaah.

---

[115] Narrated in Jaame'a at-Tirmidhee: 2910/ -on the authority of 'Abdullah Ibn Mas'ood. It was declared authentic by Sheikh al-Albaanee in Silsilat al-Hadeeth as-Saheehah: 660, Saheeh at-Targheeb at-Tarheeb: 1416, Saheeh al-Jaame'a as-Sagheer: 1164, 7369, and within the notes of his verification of Sharh al-'Aqeedah at-Tahaweeyah.

**(177) The Eminent Guiding Scholar Muhammad Ibn Saaleh al-'Utheimeen, may Allaah have mercy upon him, From 'Book of Knowledge': Page 156**

*Question: What is your advice to the one who forgets what they have read or studied?*

Answer: The most important issue regarding the memorization of knowledge is that an individual acts upon that which he has memorized. Allaah the Most High has said, "While as for those who accept guidance, He increases their guidance, and bestows on them their piety" -(Surah Muhammad:17). Also He says: "And Allaah increases in guidance those who proceed upon what is right." -(Surah Maryam: 76). So when a person acts upon what he knows, Allaah increases him in memorization and understanding. This is indicted by the generality of His statement "increase their guidance." It is narrated from Imaam Sha'fee, may Allaah have mercy upon him, that he said:

*I complained to Wake'ah about my weak memory,*

*He guided me to abandon any sins.*

*He said, "Know that certainly knowledge light*

*and the light of Allaah is not given to the sinner."*

And from the reasons for that is being preoccupied with various distractions which occupy your thoughts from knowledge. An individual is human; if his concerns distract him then his ability to acquire knowledge is weakened. Additionally, one of the matters that benefits is extensive researching with your associates with the objective of reaching the truth of a matter and not for seeking the upper hand or victory, as without doubt one's purity of intention in a matter is from those things which will preserve your knowledge.

**(178) The Eminent Guiding Scholar Muqbil Ibn Haadee al-Waadi'ee, may Allaah have mercy upon him, From 'The Final Travels of the Imaam of the Arab Peninsula' by Umm Salamah as-Salafeeyah, Page 281**

*Question: What are the causes that assist the student of knowledge in memorization, may Allaah bless you with good?*

Answer: From the greatest of matters which assist a student of knowledge in memorizing are first: fearing Allaah, the Most Glorified and the Most Exalted as Allaah says, ❨*So have fear of Allaah; and Allaah will instruct you.*❩-(Surah al-Baqarah:282) and He said, ❨*Oh you who believe! If you obey and fear Allaah, He will grant you a criterion to judge between right and wrong*❩-(Surah al-Anfaal:29) and He said, ❨*Oh you who believe fear Allaah, and believe too in His Messenger, He will give you a double portion of His Mercy, and He will give you a light by which you shall walk straight*❩-(Surah al-Haadeed: 28). After this, having purity of intention in your acquiring knowledge for Allaah, the Most High and the Most Exalted's sake alone; Allaah, the Most Glorified and the Most Exalted says, ❨*Surely, the religion i.e. the worship and the obedience is for Allaah only*-(Surah az-Zumar:3). Indeed, we have seen that a person who has purity of intention will prevail over someone who possesses more knowledge than him. Then after this is a good deal of review and repetition, as this strengthens and assists memorization.

Also, distance yourself from problems; for an individual, if is he is overburdened with problems, then he is not able to memorize and if he does manage to memorize, he will often forget what was memorized. The matters above are the more abstract matters. Now as for more practical matters that will also assist you in memorization, from them is: eating foods that are considered of a sweet nature, such as dates, raisins, and honey, as well foods considered hot or spicy, such as black pepper and ginger- but do not consume too much of these two. If you have used them excessively then they may cause you to be depressed. Then after this fling far from you anxiety and whispered doubts and be strict in mastering the issues you are studying. Likewise from such beneficial foods is yogurt, as it strengthens one's efforts of memorization, with the condition that one not use it too much. If you use it excessively, perhaps you will become anxious and weaken your memorization. From the matters which lead to a weakening of your memorization are being preoccupied with your body, whether this is related to pursuing sexual relations or some other related matter. These matters weaken an individual, and may strip from him and what information or knowledge he possesses. Additionally, if you have memorized the Qur'aan, from those matter which will assist you in preserving that memorization is reciting while standing in the night prayer. *Verily, the rising by night (for Tahajjud prayer) is very hard and most potent and good for governing (the soul), and most suitable for (understanding) the Word (of Allaah).*-(Surah Muzammil: 6). This assists an individual in retaining that which he has memorized.

(179) THE EMINENT GUIDING SCHOLAR MUHAMMAD IBN SAALEH AL-'UTHEIMEEN, MAY ALLAAH HAVE MERCY UPON HIM, FROM HIS EXPLANATION OF THE BOOK 'JEWELS FOR THE STUDENT OF KNOWLEDGE': PAGE 136

### Preserving Knowledge by Means of Writing it Down

How many important and unique issues or points of benefit are not written down by the one depends on his statement, *"If Allaah wills I will not forget this matter."*. Then if they forget it, they wish that it had been written down! However, be careful regarding writing in your book in the margins or between the lines, as this may obscure the original printed text. Some people write in the margins or between the lines in a manner that obscures the original text. Rather, what is required is that if you need to write in your book you do so in the margins, some distance from the original text, in order that you do not obscure the original by your notes. If that is not easy for you, and you need to make notes which the margin is not sufficient for, then it is better that you take a piece of white paper and place it between the pages indicated to the original related area within the book, and write what you wish. The students of Sheikh 'Abdur-Rahman Ibn-Saadee, may Allaah have mercy upon him, used to narrate to us that they used to take small notebooks and keep these in their pockets so that when someone among them mentioned an important point they could write it down; regardless whether it was benefit from their thoughts or an issue or matter that the Sheikh was asked about, they wrote them down. So we benefitted from this tremendously.

(180) THE EMINENT GUIDING SCHOLAR SAALEH IBN 'ABDUL-'AZEEZ AAL-SHEIKH, MAY ALLAAH PRESERVE HIM, FROM 'EXPLANATION OF KITAAB AT-TAWHEED': AUDIO CASSETTE 2)

### Preserving Excerpts of Knowledge

All praise is due to Allaah, may Allaah's praise and salutations upon the Messenger of Allaah, and upon his family, his Companions, and all those who followed his guidance. As for what follows:

Indeed I ask Allaah, the Most Exalted, the Most Magnificent, for myself and for you - beneficial knowledge and righteous deeds, and that He bless us to work in those matters with which He loves and is pleased. And that He make our knowledge a proof for us and not against us on that final Day of Reckoning.

Certainly from among the important matters related to the student of knowledge proceeding in his studies is his giving attention to the preservation of knowledge through writing down notes and recording passages. What I intend by preserving knowledge through writing notes are those notes which one searches for in books, or which one hears from the scholars, the people of knowledge, or the students of knowledge. This latter is due to the fact that studying and taking knowledge from individuals has additional benefits which the majority of people will not find when simply studying books. For this reason it is necessary that you record them, and this means writing them down in a specific notebook. It is something rare that you would find one of the people of knowledge who did not have from his previous years of seeking knowledge a specific notebook for this, or collected papers where he had written down what he collected of important things which he read or heard from the scholars. As if you read you will always encounter many things which are not remarkable or which you do not have a significant need for which you simply leave it as it is. Yet sometimes when reading you will encounter points and benefits which are important, and similarly in what you hear from the scholars, or from your teachers.

There are matters which are important and there are matters which are general descriptions or explanations, and these general descriptions can be understood by referring back to available reference works or something similar. But as for that which is related to definitions, classifications, or conceptualizations, the mentioning of scholastic differences, what are the strongest position in various issues, the mentioning of the evidence of issues, or the direction of derivation of matters- then for these types of benefits it is required that you record them. Therefore, it becomes a requirement of study that you designate a specific notebook to write down such benefits which are heard from others or read. That which I mean should be written down in this notebook or note pad is that which you specifically use for writing down definitions and knowledge based precepts and principles, as knowledge is defined within definitions and knowledge based principles, so that one should be concerned with mentioning their restrictions and limits. If you hear mentioned a restriction in the application of a specific matter, then certainly that restriction has an essential importance like the importance of fundamental validity and basis of that issue. Without comprehending that crucial restriction your understanding of the foundation and basis of the issue will not be sound. It will likely be flawed and so you would apply it in other than its proper place. Similar is the matter of categorization, as you will find that in many of the books of the people of knowledge they state that this matter is divided into three categories, or this concept has three types of occurrences, or five, or it is mentioned that it has two categories which are each divided further into two more categories each. Ibn Qayyim may Allaah, the Most High have mercy upon him, said: *"Knowledge is comprehended through understanding it divisions and categories."*

Then your intellect can understand it well. Indeed, from verification is returning back to the correcting understanding of the basic definition, and reliably applying the boundaries upon properly understanding the divisions and categories in that area of knowledge. If you see in the statements of the people of knowledge that this matter is divided into this section and that section, then it is important that you write this down, or study it and preserve your understanding of this categorization.

Also among the important matters related to your proceeding in seeking knowledge regarding what you have recorded and written down is that you regularly reevaluate and review what you have written down in your notebook or notebooks. You will find, for example, that after a year of seeking knowledge some of what you had written down in that year will seem strange to you after the time has gone by. Why? Because at the time that you wrote them down, many of those issues were new and unfamiliar to you, so therefore you wrote them down in order to remember them. Yet after having remembered them, and then studying the subject, and previously repeatedly going over what you had written, the subject becomes as clear and understandable as your own name is to you. Subsequently, your understanding of matter increases, and whenever your understanding of that which you previously memorized increases, then it all becomes more clear to you, and there is no hardship in comprehending it. This is because it has become firmly imprinted and memorized in your mind, with all of its details and points.

For these reasons it is important that you train yourself to record and write down important notes about that which you hear or read in those aspects of knowledge which we have mentioned, either definition, or divisions and categorizations, or evidences, or the direction of how such evidences where derived. And this encompasses all the various areas and branches of knowledge, whether that be area of industrial and manufacturing sciences, or the fundamental religious sciences, which are what was originally intended. How excellent it would be if you started to undertake this way of preserving your knowledge this very day. So go and make for yourself a notebook for recording benefits, and then strive to memorize them. After some time you will find that these issues have become easy and understandable to you, and you can then proceed to other aspects or areas of study and so gather a good portion of knowledge after a time. I ask Allaah the Most Exalted, the Most Magnificent, to make us and to make you from among those whom he has made easy for use the gaining of knowledge and the building upon that knowledge with deeds. May the praise and salutations be upon our prophet Muhammad.

(181) THE EMINENT GUIDING SCHOLAR MUHAMMAD IBN SAALEH AL-'UTHEIMEEN, MAY ALLAAH HAVE MERCY UPON HIM, FROM BOOK OF KNOWLEDGE, PAGE 213

### Reviewing What You Have Learned Preserves Knowledge

From the affairs that it is befitting for the student of knowledge to be concerned with is reviewing. And reviewing is of two types:

The First Type: To review by yourself. For example that you sit alone examining or a matter from various issues that you have encountered. Then through examination and consideration of the presented statements, to reconcile the soundest opinion in the issue among the various positions. This is easier for the student of knowledge, and it helps you with issues that have been previously discussed.

The Second Type: The review with someone else. This is by selecting one of your brothers who can assist you in seeking knowledge and benefit you. So sit with him and read and review and read from what you both have memorized, each one reading a short time after the other. Or you both go over a matter or issue by reviewing it and seeing your level of understanding of it. This is certainly from the things that leads to a strengthening and increase in knowledge. But stay far away from causing problems or acting in a boastful way, because this will not benefit you.

 ISSUES RELATED TO THE VERIFIERS OF BOOKS IN OUR AGE

*Muhammad Ibn Seereen said:*
*"Certainly this knowledge is the religion, so look carefully from whom you take your religion."*

(Narrated by Imaam Muslim in the Introduction to his "Saheeh")

(182) The Eminent Guiding Scholar Muqbil Ibn Haadee al-Waadi'ee, may Allaah have mercy upon him, From 'Answering the Questioner Regarding the Most Important Issues': Page 564

*Question: Can we take from the book verifications of Shu'ayb al-Arnout and his brother?*

Answer: We benefit from the book verifications of these two, and there are not many remarks to be made in regard to them. So benefit from their efforts in verification of books. In most cases they have benefitted from the general verifications and hadeeth source verifications of Sheikh Naasirudden al-Albaanee, may Allaah the Exalted preserve him. And what I advise each of my brothers in Islaam is to strive to reach an assessment of authenticity of narrations yourself, and to be of those who have high goals and aspirations -as was said by the poet:

*A man stands with his feet firmly upon the earth,*

*but indeed the highest of his goals is in the stars.*

(183) The Eminent Guiding Scholar Muqbil Ibn Haadee al-Waadi'ee, may Allaah have mercy upon him, From 'Excellent Responses to Questions from those Present and those Absent': Page 118)

*Question: Along with the many people who verify the books from our righteous predecessors in this age, there are some verifiers who initially brought forth books in which are found beneficial points regarding general knowledge and correct belief. Then after they became well known among the ranks of youth, they began to bring forth strange statements and inconsistencies. How can the youth deal with this situation, when there is little or no warning from the scholars regarding these shortcomings? From these verifiers, as an example, is the Sheikh 'Abdul-Qaadir al-Arnaa'out and his verification of 'Aqaawel at-Thiqaat' of Karemee. We benefit from his introduction in relation to issues of correct belief and his refutation the distortion of the source texts by Asha'ree sect. However in contrast to this, in his comments in 'Saheeh Ibn Hibbaan', he brings forth similar distortions of them of some attributes of Allaah and legitimizes this. So we hope for a warning from these errors, and that you clarify for us the condition and level of some of the authors and verifiers in our time.*

Answer: It is an obligation upon the brother to write to him and advise him of this issue. Likewise, in truth, the brother Shu'ayb al-Arnaa'out has produced valuable books for the students of knowledge; so based on this fact take and benefit from his books. Certainly he produced works which were rare or unavailable that we were unable to acquire. Therefore it is necessary for the students of knowledge to write to him about this matter. And those who desire to refute him scholastically should do so. To Allaah alone we complain of many of the people today, how significantly they need to learn. How can this be? Because see that the early scholar Abu Haatim or Abu Zur'ah and other similar scholars have mentioned a hadeeth narration in their book *((al-'Ilal)04-14)*, then one of our companions today from the modern day verifiers of books says, [However, I say...] I say to him, who are you upon the scales of knowledge to come forth with [I say...]?!? Or they say, [In our view this impermissible.] Who are you to even have a view in this matter?!? And another such verifier says, [I differ with Imaam adh-Dhahabee.], or [I disagree with al-'Iraaqee.] or [I have a different opinion from as-Sakhaawee and Ibn Kaather.]! So if you differ with all of these leading scholars, then who stands with you upon your position?!

Such individuals need to gain deep understanding of and study the mentioned book *((al-'Ilal)04-14)*, which indicates the hidden defects in narrations. They are in need of understanding that there are only a limited number of scholars who specialize in this difficult branch of knowledge of hidden defects, such that you can count them upon your fingers. It is not simply anyone who has the ability to gain true competence in this field. One such verifier states, [I say, this addition to the narration is only narrated by such and such narrator but he is judged to be reliable and the addition to a narration of the reliable narrator is accepted.] But is the additional information from a reliable narrator always unconditionally accepted? Or is the proper position in fact that it is a condition that he does not contradict a narrator who is more reliable than him, and that it should be established that the early scholars who were masters of this specific branch of knowledge do not declare this specific narration of his to have a hidden defect?

# "These Diseases & Afflictions All Result from Ignorance & Their Cure is Knowledge"

A poet said:

*Some people die, but their knowledge always revives their memory,*

    *while when the ignorant die they only join the other unknown ignorant who have passed.*[1]

Imaam Ibn Jawzee, may Allaah have mercy upon him, stated in his book "The Deceptions of Iblees":

*"…Certainly Iblees (meaning Shaytaan) has deceived the majority of the common people to simply act according to their customs, and from this comes most of the causes of their ruin and failure. There are those who blindly follow their fathers and forefathers in their beliefs and what they were raised upon from general customs. So you may see a man who has lived to the age of fifty years, doing those things his father did. Yet he doesn't consider or investigate, were those practices which his father was upon correct or an error?*

*The Jews, Christians, and those in the period before the coming of Islaam blindly followed their forefathers. Likewise many of the Muslims in their prayer and other acts of worship simply follow the customs of their people. Therefore, you may see a man who has lived many years, praying only the way the general people are seen to pray. Perhaps he does not properly establish the recitation of Surah al-Fatihah nor does he understand the other obligatory matters of the prayer. Additionally, it is not easy for him to come to understand them! So he stands as someone disgraced in his practice of the religion."*

From what has been presented in this book from these well grounded scholars, it is hoped that the reader has come to understand the place and importance of knowledge, some of the paths of seeking it, and the characteristics of the people of knowledge. It has also shown the importance of our gaining a proper balanced understanding of the role of books, other media, and the internet as an important means of gaining knowledge but not a substitute from taking from the scholars directly. Indeed, a statement which summarizes the clarifying words from the scholars regarding this is from Imaam ash-Shaatabee, may Allaah have mercy upon him, where he explains,

*"Section: The ways of taking knowledge from its people*

*Since it is affirmed that it is necessary to take knowledge from the people of knowledge, then it should be known that this is accomplished in two ways.*

*The first of them is taking knowledge by hearing it from them directly. This is the most beneficial method and the soundest and securest of them, Due to the specific qualities and features of that relationship which Allaah, the Most High places between the teacher and the student. This is something which is witnessed by everyone who is involved in the realm of seeking knowledge and its scholars.*

[1]    al-Hafidh al-Khateeb al-Baghdaadee in his work, "Jaama'ee al-Akhlaaq ar-Raawee wa Aadab as-Sama'ee ", Page 422

*As how many issues does a student read from a book, memorize, and repeat within his heart, yet he does not properly understand it. But if he had taken the comprehension of that issue by learning from a teacher or scholar he would have understood it fully. When 'Umar Ibn al-Khattab said, "My Lord agreed with what I thought in three matters..." -(Saheeh al-Bukhaaree. vol.1: 504). Then indeed, this understanding which he possessed was from the benefits of sitting with the people of knowledge, meaning that there is a level of understanding facilitated and reached when the student places himself within the hands of the scholar to learn, which is not possible to gain from anyone less than him. The light from them then remains with the student, to whatever degree that the student adheres to what he was taught by his teacher, cultivates his manners through him, and follows their distinguished way. So through this first way one is brought benefit in every way that can be measured.*

*The second path is by reading authored works. This way is also beneficial in its place, if two conditions are met.*

*1. Firstly that the student achieves an understanding of what was the intended goal of that work of knowledge, as well as having a clear grasp of the specific terminology being used by the scholars in that area of knowledge; such that he can delve its relevant books. Yet this comprehension of the vocabulary of a specific area of knowledge is generally achieved by means of the first mentioned way of gaining knowledge, meaning verbally from the scholars or by those means which are similar to this. This is the meaning of the statement of the one who said,* **"Knowledge was first in the chests and hearts of men, then it passed on into books, but the keys to it still remain in the hands of men."** *As books alone will not benefit the student anything of the desired full comprehensive understanding, without such books being facilitated and made usable by the scholars. This is something regularly witnessed.*

*2. The second condition is that of turning to and utilizing the books of the early scholars within the intended area of study. As they are the leaders in the realm of knowledge who were foremost to be followed, as opposed to the others from among of knowledge from later centuries."* [2]

This balanced path to gaining knowledge in Islaam is something which is only made clear to those whom Allaah chooses to guide to success. There is no doubt that both the steadfast student of knowledge as well as the steadfast general Muslim both need a sound understanding of the most significant present ailment found among the Muslim today, that being ignorance of their religion in one or more aspects. Yet after coming to recognize this ailment as well as its remedy- beneficial knowledge, and they must also learn that there is a specific way in which the remedy is to be applied. If this is understood then it will become clear that the ones who administer this treatment for this ailment of the Muslims, can only be the guiding scholars. Consider the following words from the people of knowledge of different centuries all reminding and clarifying for us the importance of a living relationship with scholars in our lives, to whatever degree that is possible for us in our different circumstances.

---

[2] *Tadheeb al-Muwaafiqaat pages 49-50*

Ibn al-Qayyim al-Jawzeeyah, may Allaah have mercy upon him, in explaining the importance of the scholar in rectifying the worshipers and their lands and nations.

*"There is no cure for this illness except through knowledge, and due to this Allaah, the Exalted, has named His book ❁a cure for the illnesses of the hearts❁. The Exalted has said: ❁A healing for that (disease of ignorance, doubt, hypocrisy and differences, etc.) in your breasts, a guidance and a mercy for the believers.❁-(Surah Yunis: 57). Due to this, the scholars are associated with the hearts, just as doctors are associated with the body's organs. Or as is said regarding the scholars, they are the physicians of the hearts. This is from their ability to reconcile between hearts.*

*However, their place and position among us is actually greater than this. As indeed there are many able to do without physicians, and a doctor may not be present except in some distant area of a land- thus a man may live for many years or a considerable period without having need of a doctor; but as for Allaah's scholars and their position, then they are from the essence and spirit of our life, and it is not possible to do without them even for a limited time, as the need of the heart for knowledge is not like the need of having air to breathe, rather it is greater."* [3]

In our age the guiding scholar Sheikh al-Albaanee, may Allaah have mercy upon him- indicated the importance of the scholars in rectifying the Muslim ummah in this statement from him:

*"Certainly the wretched state of the Muslim world today, in consideration of all that is stated about the "Islamic revival"- is not the outcome of these present efforts of education upon Islaam. This is because as I believe that the influence of this revival- in relation to knowledge- will have to continue for a long time until the effects of that education start to become apparent within the younger generation. Presently, within the limits or bounds of the "Islamic revival", there are various behaviors of individuals which are considered something from mercy of Allaah, the Most High and the Most Exalted. Some of them are closer to what is correct and other are further from that.*

*Accordingly, from the aspect of individual understanding or knowledge, then you might not find anyone who differs or disputes with you that the basic fundamental in calling to Allaah is that it is to be carried forth with gentleness and the good reminder. However, what is essential is the actual practice or implementation of this, and the implementation of this requires a guide; it requires a scholar to act as one who cultivates and is responsible for the training of many students of knowledge. These students will then emerge from the training by the hands of this cultivating scholar as those who are then able to cultivate and train others. In this way the true Islamic education spreads gradually and slowly- by means of the education coming from these cultivating scholars of those students who are around them..."* [4]

---

[3]    Miftaah Dar al-Sa'aadah, Pages 370-371
[4]    From tape number 595 from the tape series *"Gatherings of Guidance & Light"*

Ibn al-Qayyim al-Jawzeeyah, may Allaah have mercy upon him, has said in describing this illness, the cure, and the proper one to treat the patient:

*Ignorance is a mortal disease which is healed,*

    *with two complementary sources combined,*

*A text from Qur'aan or from the Sunnah*

    *and the doctor overseeing this cure is the guiding scholar.*

These two lines of poetry were explained by Sheikh Muhammad Khaleel Haraas, may Allaah have mercy upon him:

*"There is no disease that afflicts like the disease of ignorance, as it damages the one it afflicts with the severest harm, and the only cure for this near incurable disease is from two medicines that are similar. They are the texts of the Book of Allaah, and the texts of the Noble Sunnah. But it is necessary that this remedy be administered by a skillful doctor. That being the guiding scholar who properly understands the relevant areas of the diseases and so can restore health and truly guarantee a cure."* [5]

These two verses of poetry were also explained by the eminent scholar Sheikh Saaleh Ibn Fauzaan al-Fauzaan, may Allaah preserve him:

*"Ignorance is without doubt a destructive disease. However, it has both a remedy and a doctor. The remedy by itself is not sufficient, it is necessary to receive guidance from the doctor as to how to use the remedy. And the remedy is already present- the Book and the Sunnah. Their examples are like medicines, one to be used along with another, that must be combined by a doctor into a complete prescription. Using this "prescription" is accomplished by referring to the scholars and asking them for guidance. So do not rely upon your personal understanding or what is found in your book alone. Rather, what is required is that you refer back to the people of knowledge and those who teach. Because just as medicine is not taken except with the supervision of a doctor, similarly it is necessary that this cure come only from the truly righteous guiding scholar, as from among those considered by some to be scholars, are those who in reality are only scholars of falsehood.*

*But, it is upon you to turn to the righteous scholar who has correct beliefs as well as a good goal and sound intention. This "guiding scholar" is the one who cultivates the people upon the truth. Ibn Abbaas stated, "The guiding scholar is the one who teaches the people the essential, simpler matters of knowledge before the larger, more complex ones.". The guiding scholar is the one who educates according to the best manner of teaching, level by level, and teaches the various issues, step by step. This is the correct methodology, because it is essential that you proceed by degrees in acquiring knowledge, advancing step by step."* [6]

---

[5]    Sharh Qaseedat an-Nooneyyah, volume 2 page 263
[6]    Summarized Notes upon the poem an-Nooniyyah, Page 1010

In addition to what was just stated Ibn al-Qayyim al-Jawzeeyah, may Allaah have mercy upon him, said:

*"Likewise, the jihaad related to one's self also has four stages: The first of them is that one struggles with himself to learn guidance, meaning the religion of truth without which there is no success nor happiness in this world or the hereafter except through it. As when one fails to learn it then his state in both worlds is undoubtedly wretched.*

*The second of them is that one struggles with himself to act upon his knowledge, after having learned and acquired it. As lacking this, he merely has knowledge without realization or practice, which neither benefits him nor harms him.*

*The third stage is that one struggles to call and invite to this way, and teach it to those who do not know it. Otherwise, he stands as one who conceals what Allaah has send down of guidance and proof, who has not fully benefits from his knowledge nor saved from Allaah's punishment.*

*The fourth stage is that one struggles to be patient with the difficulties of calling to Allaah, the injuries received from the creation, and that he tolerates that all for Allaah's sake alone. So if he completes this fourth stage, then he becomes from the guiding scholars. As the first generations of Muslims unanimously agree that a scholar does not merit being called a "guiding" scholar until he comprehends the truth, acts according to it, and teaches it to others..."* [7]

The guiding scholar Muhammad 'Amaan al-Jaamee (may Allaah have mercy upon him) stated:

*"In reality, ignorance is the type of disease which in practice the caller to Allaah must begin to cure by reforming himself and curing his own illness before entering the realm of calling to Allaah; and this is done by first attaining the correct and sound understanding.*

*Therefore, his high priority and his concern is towards acquiring knowledge from its fundamental sources- the Book of Allaah and the Sunnah. Indeed, these two are the fundamental sources of the Sharee'ah, for both its foundations and branches. Through studying them beneficial knowledge, guidance, supremacy in this world, and happiness in the Hereafter is achieved..."* [8]

Therefore, in closing I remind myself first and then my brothers and sisters in Islaam, to begin with the rectification of oneself and to return to the scholars themselves, to whatever degree Allaah makes this possible for you, to take general and specific advice and their guidance regarding all of his affairs. So that, with Allaah's permission, your affairs will be based upon a steady course of action and a deeply rooted foundation of beneficial knowledge and guidance from those scholars who truly correct and rectify our affairs. In our age this will almost always bring you into conflict with those around you who will oppose you because you choose this way which the guided Muslims have always followed in every century.

---

[7]    Zaad al-Ma'ad fee Haadee Khair ul-E'baad: volume 3, page 9
[8]    *Problems of the Call and the Callers on the Modern Age, Page 20*

Moreover, if your life becomes like that which is mentioned by Imaam al-Aajuree, may Allaah have mercy upon him, in his book, "The Strangers":

*"If the intelligent believer, the one whom Allaah, the Most High, Most Exalted, has given understanding of the religion and insight into his own weaknesses, has made clear to him what the general people are actually upon, has granted him the understanding to distinguish between the truth and falsehood, and between what is good and what is repulsive, and between the harmful and that which benefits, and given him the knowledge of which of these matters he is truly upon, if he aims for success, then he holds himself firm upon acting according to the truth in the midst of those who are ignorant of the truth.*

*As the majority of the people simply adhere to their desires. They do not show any concern for the shortcomings in their practice of the religion even if their evil deeds are openly presented to them. Because if they were to look closely at those who differ from them in their misguided ways, then this would in fact weigh heavily upon them, hating this, as it would surely trouble them severely, so they point out the others' shortcoming or weaknesses. Even one's family will become discontent with him, and his own brothers will put pressure on him. They will treat him in a way, which no one wishes to be treated. This is because the people of who adhere to desires are not upon the proper way of dealing with someone with whom you differ.*

*He, that believer, thus becomes like a stranger among his contemporaries and companions due to the spread of corruption in one's companionship and association among the people; a stranger in all of his worldly affairs as well as those of the Hereafter."*

Then know, may Allaah have mercy upon you, that 'Abdullah Ibn 'Amr, may Allaah be pleased with both of them, stated as narrated by Imaam Ahmad in his Musnad and at-Tabaranee:

**{..."Tooba" (and among its meanings is a tree in Jannah) is for the strangers." It was said, "Who are the strangers?" He said, "The few righteous people in the midst of the many who are not. Those who resist and disobey them are more than those who comply and obey them.}** [9]

And I end with all praise is due to Allaah Lord of the Worlds.

---

[9]    Authentic hadeeth by various routes as found in  "Saheeh at-Targeeb wa at-Tarheeb": number 3188 both from our sheikh the eminent scholar Muhammad Naasiruddeen al-Albaanee, may Allaah have mercy upon him

# Categorized List of Books Recommended within the Scholars' Statements Gathered in this Work

| | | Sh. 'Abdul-'Azeez Ibn 'Abdullah Ibn Baaz | Sh. Muhammad Ibn Saaleh al-'Utheimeen | Sh. Muqbil Ibn Haadee al-Waadi'ee, | Sh. Muhammad Naasiruddeen al-Albaanee | Sh. 'Abdur-Rahman Ibn Naasir as-Sa'adee | Sh. Muhammad 'Amaan al-Jaamee | Sh. Muhammad al-'Ameen Ash-Shanqeetee | Sh.Saaleh Ibn 'Abdullah Ibn Fauzaan al-Fauzaan | Sh. Saaleh Ibn 'Abdul-'Azeez Aal-Sheikh | Sh. Ahmad Ibn Yahya an-Najmee | Sh. Muhammad Ibn 'Abdul-Wahaab al-Wasaabee | Permanent Committee For Scholastic Research |
|---|---|---|---|---|---|---|---|---|---|---|---|---|---|
| The following is a key to using the list of recommended books from the different scholars. The scholar's name appears above that specific letter used to represent it within the general book list. Where ever there is a diamond icon under a letter this means that this specific scholar has recommended that book. | | | | | | | | | | | | | |
| Name of Book | Author | B | U | M | A | S | J | SH | F | Aa | N | W | L |

## 1. Books of Explanation of the Qur'aan and other Sciences of the Qur'aan

| | Name of Book | Author | B | U | M | A | S | J | SH | F | Aa | N | W | L |
|---|---|---|---|---|---|---|---|---|---|---|---|---|---|---|
| 01-01 | Tafseer Ibn Katheer | 'Isma'eel Ibn 'Umar Ibn Katheer | | | ♦ | ♦ | | ♦ | | ♦ | ♦ | | | |
| 01-02 | Tayseer al-Kareem ar-Rahman Fee Tafseer Kalaam al-Manaan | 'Abdur-Rahman Ibn Naasir as-Sa'adee | | | ♦ | | | | | | | | | |
| 01-03 | Adhuaa' al-Bayaan Fee Eedhaah al-Qur'aan Bil-Qur'aan | Muhammad al'-Ameen ash-Shanqeetee | | | ♦ | ♦ | | | | | | | | |
| 01-04 | Tasfeer at-Tabaree | Muhammad Ibn Jareer | | | | | | ♦ | | | | | | |
| 01-05 | Fath al-Qadeer al-Jaame'a Bayn Fee ar-Rewaayat wa'al-Diraayat Min 'Ilm at-Tafseer | Muhammad Ibn 'Alee ash-Shawkaanee | | | | | | ♦ | ♦ | | | | | |
| 01-06 | ad-Dur al-Manthur | Jalaaluddeen 'Abdur-Rahman as-Suyutee | | | | | | ♦ | | | | | | |
| 01-07 | Tafseer al-Baghawee | al-Husayn Ibn Mas'ud al-Baghawee | | | | | | ♦ | | | | | | |
| 01-08 | Tafseer Ibn Abee Haatim | Muhammad 'Abdur-Rahman Ibn Muhammad ar-Raazee | | | | | | ♦ | | | ♦ | | | |
| 01-09 | Tafseer Ibn Mardaweeh | Ibn Mardaweeh | | | | | | ♦ | | | | | | |
| 01-10 | as-Saheeh al-Musnad Min Asbaab an-Nuzul | Muqbil Ibn Haadee al-Waadi'ee | | | | | | ♦ | | | | | | |

## 2. Books of Hadeeth and other Narration Collections

| | Name of Book | Author | B | U | M | A | S | J | SH | F | Aa | N | W | L |
|---|---|---|---|---|---|---|---|---|---|---|---|---|---|---|
| 02-01 | Saheeh al-Bukhaaree | Muhammad Ibn Isma'eel | | | ♦ | ♦ | | | | ♦ | ♦ | | | ♦ |
| 02-02 | Saheeh Muslim | Muslim Ibn Hajjaj | | | ♦ | ♦ | | | | ♦ | ♦ | ♦ | | ♦ |
| 02-03 | Sunan an-Nasaa'ee | Abu 'Abdur-Rahman Ibn 'Alee | | | ♦ | ♦ | | | | ♦ | ♦ | | | |
| 02-04 | Sunan Abu Dawud | Sulaymaan Ibn Al'Ash'ath | | | ♦ | ♦ | | | | ♦ | ♦ | | | |
| 02-05 | Sunan Ibn Majaah | Muhammad Ibn Yazeed | | | ♦ | ♦ | | | | ♦ | ♦ | | | |
| 02-06 | Jaame'a at-Tirmidhee | Muhammad Ibn 'Esaa | | | ♦ | ♦ | | | | ♦ | ♦ | | | |
| 02-07 | Musnad of Imaam Ahmad | Ahmad Ibn Muhammad Ibn Hanbal | | | | | | ♦ | | | ♦ | | | ♦ |
| 02-08 | al-Muwatta | Maalik Ibn Anas | | | | | | ♦ | | | | | | ♦ |
| 02-09 | Sunan ad-Daaramee | 'Abdullah Ibn 'Abdur-Rahmaan | | | | | | ♦ | | | | | ♦ | ♦ |
| 02-10 | Shu'ab al-Emaan | Ahmad Ibn al-Husayn | | | | | | ♦ | | | | | | |
| 02-11 | Riyaadh as-Saaliheen | Yahya Ibn Sharf an-Nawaawee | ♦ | ♦ | | | | ♦ | | | ♦ | | ♦ | ♦ |
| 02-12 | al-Adhkaar | Yahya Ibn Sharf an-Nawaawee | | | | | | ♦ | | | | | | |
| 02-13 | Saheeh Ibn Hibaan | Ibn Hibaan al-Bastee | | | | | | ♦ | | | | | | |
| 02-14 | Musannaf Ibn Abee Shaybah | 'Abdullah Ibn Muhammad | | | | | | ♦ | | | | | | |
| 02-15 | Musannaf 'Abdur-Razzaq | 'Abdur-Razzaq as-Sana'aanee | | | | | | ♦ | | | | | | |
| 02-16 | Lu'Lu' wa al-Marjaan Feemaa 'Itifaaq 'Aleihi as-Sheikhaan | Muhammad 'Abdul-Baaqee | | | | | | ♦ | | | | | | |
| 02-17 | Kashf al-Astaar 'An Zawa'id al-Zubaar | 'Alee Ibn Abee Bakr al-Haythamee | | | | | | ♦ | | | | | | |
| 02-18 | Musnad Abee Ya'laa | Ahmad Ibn 'Alee at-Tameemee | | | | | | ♦ | | | | | | |
| 02-19 | Musnad al-Humaydee | 'Abdullah Ibn Zubayr al-Humaydee | | | | | | ♦ | | | | | | |
| 02-20 | Saheeh Ibn Khuzaymah | Abu Bakr Muhammad Ibn Ishaaq | | | | | | ♦ | | | | | | |
| 02-21 | Mu'jam al-Kabeer | Abu Qaasem at-Tabaraanee | | | | | | ♦ | | | | | | |
| 02-22 | Mu'jam al-Awsaat | Abu Qaasem at-Tabaraanee | | | | | | ♦ | | | | | | |
| 02-23 | Mu'jam as-Sagheer | Abu Qaasem at-Tabaraanee | | | | | | ♦ | | | | | | |
| 02-24 | Majma' az-Zawa'id wa manba' al-Fawa'id al-Mutaalib al-'Aleeyah | 'Alee Ibn Abe Bakr al-Haythamee | | | | | | ♦ | | | | | | |
| 02-25 | Mustadraak Alaa as-Saheehayn | Abu 'Abdullah al-Haakim | | | | | | ♦ | | | | | | |
| 02-26 | as-Sunnah | Ibn Abee 'Aasim | | | | | | ♦ | | | | ♦ | | |
| 02-27 | Arba'een an-Nawawee | Yahya Ibn Sharf An-Nawaawee | ♦ | ♦ | | | | | ♦ | | | ♦ | | |
| 02-28 | Amdaat al-Ahkam | 'Abdul-Ghanee al-Maqdasee | | | ♦ | ♦ | | ♦ | | ♦ | | ♦ | | |
| 02-29 | Amdatul-Hadeeth | 'Abdul-Ghanee al-Maqdasee | ♦ | | | | | | | | | | | ♦ |
| 02-30 | Mishkaat al-Masaabeeh | Waleeudden Ibn 'Abdullah | | | | | | | | ♦ | | | | |
| 02-31 | as-Sunan al-Kubraa | Abu Bakr Ahmad Ibn al-Husayn | | | | | | ♦ | | | | | | |
| 02-32 | Musnad ash-Shaafa'ee | Abu 'Abdullah Muhammad Ibn Idrees | | | | | | ♦ | | | | | | |
| 02-33 | Tagleeq at-Ta'leeq FeeMaa Yata'leq Be al-Ahadeeth al-Mua'liqah Fee Saheeh al-Bukhaaree | Ahmad Ibn 'Alee Ibn Hajr | | | | | | ♦ | | | | | | |
| 02-34 | Bulugh al-Maraam min Adilatul Ahkaam | Ahmad Ibn 'Alee Ibn Hajr | ♦ | ♦ | ♦ | | | ♦ | | ♦ | | | | ♦ |
| | NAME OF BOOK | AUTHOR | B | U | M | A | S | J | SH | F | Aa | N | W | L |

| | NAME OF BOOK | AUTHOR | B | U | M | A | S | J | SH | F | Aa | N | W | L |
|---|---|---|---|---|---|---|---|---|---|---|---|---|---|---|
| 02-35 | as-Saheeh al-Musnad Memaa Lasaa fee as-Saheehayn | Muqbil Ibn Haadee al-Waadi'ee | | | ◆ | | | | | | | | | |
| 02-36 | Ahadeeth Mu'alat Dhaaheruha as-Sehah | Muqbil Ibn Haadee al-Waadi'ee | | | ◆ | | | | | | | | | |
| 02-37 | Saheeh Jaamea as-Sagheer | Muhammad Naasiruddeen al-Albaanee | | | ◆ | | | | | | | ◆ | | |
| 02-38 | Silsilat al-Hadeeth as-Saheehah | Muhammad Naasiruddeen al-Albaanee | | | ◆ | | | | | | | ◆ | | |

## 3. Books of Explanations of Hadeeth

| | Name of Book | Author | B | U | M | A | S | J | SH | F | Aa | N | W | L |
|---|---|---|---|---|---|---|---|---|---|---|---|---|---|---|
| 03-01 | Fath al-Baaree Sharh Saheeh al-Bukhaaree | Ahmad Ibn 'Alee Ibn Hajr | | ◆ | ◆ | | | | | | | | | |
| 03-02 | Saheeh Muslim be Sharh an-Nawawee | Yahya Ibn Sharf an-Nawaawee | | | ◆ | | | | | | | | | |
| 03-03 | 'Awn al-Ma'bood Sharh Sunan Abu Dawud | Muhammad Shams Dheyaa' al-Haqq 'Abaadee | | | ◆ | | | | | | | | | |
| 03-04 | Tuhfat al-Awadha Sharh Jaame'a at-Tirmidhee | Muhammad Ibn 'Abdur-Rahman | | | ◆ | | | | | | | | | |
| 03-05 | Sunan Ibn Maajah be Sharh Mukhtasir | Muhammad Ibn Yazeed | | | ◆ | | | | | | | | | |
| 03-06 | Subl as-Salaam Sharh Bulugh al-Maraam | Muhammad Ibn 'Isma'eel as-Sana'anee | | | ◆ | ◆ | ◆ | | | | ◆ | | | |
| 03-07 | Sharh al-Badhur | - | | | | | | | | | ◆ | | | |
| 03-08 | Nayl al-Awtaar Shrk Munqataa al-'Akhbaar | Muhammad Ibn 'Alee ash-Shawkaanee | | | ◆ | | | | ◆ | | ◆ | | | |
| 03-09 | Jaame'a al-'Ulum wa al-Hikm | 'Abdur-Rahman Ibn Shehaabudden | ◆ | ◆ | | | | | | | ◆ | | | ◆ |

## 4. Books of the Various Sciences of Hadeeth

| | Name of Book | Author | B | U | M | A | S | J | SH | F | Aa | N | W | L |
|---|---|---|---|---|---|---|---|---|---|---|---|---|---|---|
| 04-01 | Nukhbat al-Fikr | Ahmad Ibn 'Alee Ibn Hajr | | ◆ | ◆ | | | | | | | | | |
| 04-02 | Nazhat an-Nadher Tawdheh Nukhbat al-Fikr | Ahmad Ibn 'Alee Ibn Hajr | ◆ | | ◆ | | | | | | | | | |
| 04-03 | Talkhees al-Khabeer fee Takhreej Ahadeeth ar-Raafa'ee al-Kabeer | Ahmad Ibn 'Alee Ibn Hajr | | | ◆ | | | | | | | | | |
| 04-04 | an-Nukaat Alaa' Muqadamah Ibn Salaah | Ahmad Ibn 'Alee Ibn Hajr | | | ◆ | | | | | | | | | |
| 04-05 | Nasab ar-Raawee fee Takhreej Ahadeeth al-Hadaaevah | Jamaaludden Abe Muhammad 'Abdullah | | | ◆ | | | | | | | | | |
| 04-06 | Tarh at-Tathreeb fee Sharh Taqreeb al-Asaaneed | Zaynudden al-Iraaqee | | | ◆ | | | | | | | | | |
| 04-07 | Jarh wa at-Ta'deel | Muhammad 'Abdur-Rahman Ibn Muhammad | | | ◆ | | | | | | | | | |
| 04-08 | Tadreeb ar-Raawee fee Sharh Taqreeb an-Nawaawee | Jalaaluddeen 'Abdur-Rahman | | | ◆ | | | | | | | | | |
| 04-09 | at-Taqyeed wa al-Idhaah lama Itlaqah wa Aglaqah Min Muqadamah Ibn Salaah | Zaynudden al-Iraaqee | | | ◆ | | | | | | | | | |
| 04-10 | al-Kifaayah fee Marifatul-Usul 'Ilm ar-Reewayah | al-Khateeb al-Baghdadee | | | ◆ | | | | | | | | | |
| 04-11 | Jaam'ee Ahlaaq ar-Raawee wa Aadab as-Saame'a | al-Khateeb al-Baghdadee | | | ◆ | | | | | | | | | |
| 04-12 | al-Muhadeeth al-Faasel Bayn ar-Raawee wa'al-Wa'ee | Hasan Ibn 'Abdur-Rahman | | | ◆ | | | | | | | | | |
| 04-13 | Ma'rifat Uloom al-Hadeeth | al-Haakim Abe 'Abdullah | | | ◆ | | | | | | | | | |
| 04-14 | al-'Ilal | Muhammad 'Abdur-Rahman Ibn Muhammad | | | ◆ | | | | | | | | | |
| 04-15 | al-'Ilal al-Kabeer | Muhammad Ibn 'Esaa | | | ◆ | | | | | | | | | |
| 04-16 | al-'Ilal as-Sagheer | Muhammad Ibn 'Esaa | | | ◆ | | | | | | | | | |
| 04-17 | al-'Ilal wa al-Ma'rifat ul-Rijaal | Ahmad Ibn Muhammad Ibn Hanbal | | | ◆ | | | | | | | | | |
| 04-18 | al-'Ilal | 'Alee Ibn al-Madinee book author | | | ◆ | | | | | | | | | |
| 04-19 | Sharh al-'Ilal at-Tirmidhee | 'Abdur-Rahman Ibn Shihaabudden | | | ◆ | | | | | | | | | |
| 04-20 | al-Laa'lee al-Maudhuaat | Jalaaluddeen 'Abdur-Rahman | | | ◆ | | | | | | | | | |
| 04-21 | al-Maudhuaat min Al-Ahadeeth al-Marfu'aat | 'Abdur-Rahman Ibn 'Alee | | | ◆ | | | | | | | | | |
| 04-22 | al-Abaateel wa al-Manaakir wa as-Sehaah wa al-Mashaaheer | al-Husayn Ibn Ibraaheeem | | | ◆ | | | | | | | | | |
| 04-23 | al-Muqtarah | Muqbil Ibn Haadee al-Waadi'ee | | | ◆ | | | | | | | | | |
| 04-24 | Mukhtasir 'Uloom al-Hadeeth | 'Isma'eel Ibn 'Umar Ibn Katheer | | | ◆ | | | | | | | | | |
| 04-25 | Mukhtalif al-Hadeeth | Muhammad Ibn Idrees | | | ◆ | | | | | | | | | |
| | NAME OF BOOK | AUTHOR | B | U | M | A | S | J | SH | F | Aa | N | W | L |
| | NAME OF BOOK | AUTHOR | B | U | M | A | S | J | SH | F | Aa | N | W | L |

| | Name of Book | Author | B | U | M | A | S | J | SH | F | Aa | N | W | L |
|---|---|---|---|---|---|---|---|---|---|---|---|---|---|---|
| 04-26 | Fath al-Mugheeth Sharh Alfeeyah al-Hadeeth | Muhammad Ibn 'Abdur-Rahman | | ♦ | | | | | | | | | | |
| 04-27 | at-Tankeel Bemaa fee Ta'neeb al-Kawtharee Min Abaateel | 'Abdur-Rahman Ibn Yahya | | ♦ | | | | | | | | | | |
| 04-28 | al-Maqaasid al-Hasnah Fee Bhayaan Katheer min al-Ahadeeth Al-Mastaharah | Test book author | | | | | | | | | | | | |
| 04-29 | al-Fara'ed al-Majmu'ah | Muhammad Ibn 'Alee Ibn Muhammad | | ♦ | | | | | | | | | | |
| 04-30 | Tufaat al-Ashraaf fe Ma'reefat ul-Atraaf | Abu al-Hajaaj Yusuf al-Mizee | | | | | | | | | | | | |
| 04-31 | Ta'weel Mukhtalif al-Hadeeth | 'Abdullah Ibn Muslim Qutaybah | | | | | | | | | | | | |
| 04-32 | Irwaa' al-Ghaleel | Muhammad Naasiruddeen al-Albaanee | | | | | | | | | | | | |
| 04-33 | al-Mu'ajam al-Mufahris al-Alfaadh al-Hadeeth an-Nabawee | Compiled by a group of non-Muslim western Orientalists scholars | | ♦ | | | | | | | | | | |
| 04-34 | Mushkil al-Athaar | Ahmad Ibn Muhammad Ibn Salaamah at-Tahaawee | | ♦ | | | | | | | | | | |
| 04-35 | Ajweebah Abee Mas'ood | - | | ♦ | | | | | | | | | | |
| 04-36 | al-'Ilal | ad-Darqutnee | | ♦ | | | | | | | | | | |
| 04-37 | al-Ba'ith al-Hatheeth | Ahmad Shaakir | | ♦ | | | | | | | | | | |
| 04-38 | Muqadamah Ibn Salaah | Ibn Salaah | | ♦ | | | | | | | | | | |

## 5. *Books of Biographies & the Sciences of the Determining the Condition of Narrators*

| | Name of Book | Author | B | U | M | A | S | J | SH | F | Aa | N | W | L |
|---|---|---|---|---|---|---|---|---|---|---|---|---|---|---|
| 05-01 | 'Asad al-Ghaabah fee Ma'reefatul-Sahabah | 'Izzuddeen Abdul-Hasan 'Alee | | ♦ | | | | | | | | | | |
| 05-02 | al-'Isaabah fee Tamyeez as-Sahaabah | Ahmad Ibn 'Alee Ibn Hajr | | ♦ | | | | | | | | | | |
| 05-03 | al-Hilyaah a'Awleeyah wa Tabaqat al-Asfeeyaa' | Ahmad Ibn 'Abdullah al-Asbahaanee | | ♦ | | | | | | | | | | |
| 05-04 | Tadhkirah al-Hufaadh | Muhammad Ibn Ahmad Ibn 'Uthmaan adh-Dhahabee | | ♦ | | | | | | | | | | |
| 05-05 | al-'Isteea'aab fee Ma'reefatu as-Sahaab | Yusef Ibn 'Abdullah al-Bar | | ♦ | | | | | | | | | | |
| 05-06 | at-Tabaqaat Ibn Sa'd | Muhammad Ibn Sa'ad Ibn Manee'a | | ♦ | | | | | | | | | | |
| 05-07 | Tabaqaat al-Hufaadh | Jalaaluddeen 'Abdur-Rahman | | ♦ | | | | | | | | | | |
| 05-08 | Tabaqaat ash-Shaafee'ah al-Kubra | 'Abdul-Wahaab Ibn 'Alee as-Subkee | | ♦ | | | | | | | | | | |
| 05-09 | Tabaqaat al-Hanaabilah | Muhammad Ibn Muhammad Ibn Abee Ya'ala | | ♦ | | | | | | | | | | |
| 05-10 | Tabaqaat al-Hanaabilah | 'Abdur-Rahman Ibn Shihaabudden | | ♦ | | | | | | | | | | |
| 05-11 | Tabaqaat al-Qura'a | Muhammad Ibn Ahmad Ibn 'Uthmaan adh-Dhahabee | | ♦ | | | | | | | | | | |
| 05-12 | Tabaqaat an-Nahweeyeen | Jalaaluddeen 'Abdur-Rahman | | ♦ | | | | | | | | | | |
| 05-13 | Tabaqaat al-Mufassireen | Dawoodee | | ♦ | | | | | | | | | | |
| 05-14 | Tabaqaat al-Fuqahaa | Abu Ishaaq ash-Sheeraazee | | ♦ | | | | | | | | | | |
| 05-15 | Tabaqaat al-Khulafah | Khalifah Ibn Khayyat | | ♦ | | | | | | | | | | |
| 05-16 | Minhaj al-Ahmad | Test book author | | ♦ | | | | | | | | | | |
| 05-17 | Seyaar 'Alaam an-Nubala' | Muhammad Ibn Ahmad Ibn 'Uthmaan adh-Dhahabee | ♦ | ♦ | | | | | | | | | | |
| 05-18 | Tadheeb at-Tadheeb | Ahmad Ibn 'Alee Ibn Hajr | | ♦ | | | | | | | | | | |
| 05-19 | Mizaan al-'Itidaal | Muhammad Ibn Ahmad Ibn 'Uthmaan adh-Dhahabee | | ♦ | | | | | | | | | | |
| 05-20 | Lisaan al-Mizaan | Ahmad Ibn 'Alee Ibn Hajr | | ♦ | | | | | | | | | | |
| 05-21 | at-Taarikh al-Kabeer | Muhammad Ibn Isma'eel | | ♦ | | | | | | | | | | |
| 05-22 | al-Ba'ith wa an-Nashoor | Ahmad Ibn al-Husayn al-Bayhaqee | | ♦ | | | | | | | | | | |
| 05-23 | al-Insaab | Abu Sa'd as-Sama'anee | | ♦ | | | | | | | | | | |
| 05-24 | al-Kunyaa wa al-'Asmaa | Abu Bashr Muhammad Ibn Ahmad Ibn Haamad | | ♦ | | | | | | | | | | |
| 05-25 | Kaamel de adh-Dhuafaa' ar-Rijaal | Abu Ahmad 'Abdullah Ibn 'Adee | | ♦ | | | | | | | | | | |
| 05-26 | adh-Dhua'faa' al-Kabeer | Abu Jaafir Muhammad Ibn 'Amr | | ♦ | | | | | | | | | | |
| 05-27 | Taarikh al-Kabeer | Muhammad Ibn Ahmad Ibn 'Uthmaan adh-Dhahabee | | ♦ | | | | | | | | | | |
| 05-28 | Mashaaykh | Ibn Asaakir | | ♦ | | | | | | | | | | |
| 05-29 | al-Badr al-Talaa' | ash-Shawkaanee | | ♦ | | | | | | | | | | |
| 05-30 | Fadhaa'il as-Sahabah | Mustapha al-Adawee | | ♦ | | | | | | | | | | |
| | NAME OF BOOK | AUTHOR | B | U | M | A | S | J | SH | F | Aa | N | W | L |

## 6. Books of Fundamental Beliefs

| | Name of Book | Author | B | U | M | A | S | J | SH | F | Aa | N | W | L |
|---|---|---|---|---|---|---|---|---|---|---|---|---|---|---|---|
| 06-01 | Kitaab at-Tawheed | Muhammad Ibn 'Abdul-Wahaab | ♦ | ♦ | ♦ | | | ♦ | | ♦ | | ♦ | | ♦ |
| 06-02 | Thalaathatul-Usul/Usul ath-Thalaathah* | Muhammad Ibn 'Abdul-Wahaab | ♦ | ♦ | | | | ♦ | | ♦ | | ♦ | | ♦ |
| 06-03 | al-Qawa'id al-Arba' | Muhammad Ibn 'Abdul-Wahaab | | | ♦ | | | ♦ | | | | ♦ | | |
| 06-04 | Kashf ash-Shubahaat | Muhammad Ibn 'Abdul-Wahaab | ♦ | ♦ | | | | ♦ | | ♦ | | | | ♦ |
| 06-05 | al-Aqeedatul-Wasateeyah | Ahmad Ibn Taymeeyah | ♦ | ♦ | ♦ | | | | | ♦ | | | | ♦ |
| 06-06 | al-Hamaweeyah | Ahmad Ibn Taymeeyah | ♦ | ♦ | | | | | | | | | | ♦ |
| 06-07 | at-Tadrumeeyah | Ahmad Ibn Taymeeyah | ♦ | ♦ | | | | | | | | | | ♦ |
| 06-08 | al-Aqeedatul-Tahaweeyah | Abu Ja'far Ahmad at-Tahawee | ♦ | ♦ | | ♦ | | | | ♦ | ♦ | ♦ | | |
| 06-09 | Sharh al-Aqeedatul-Tahaweeyah | Ibn Abee al-Izz al-Hanafee | ♦ | ♦ | | ♦ | | | | ♦ | ♦ | ♦ | | |
| 06-10 | ad-Durar as-Sanneyah Fee al-Ajwebah an-Najdeeyah | 'Abdur-Rahman Ibn Muhammad Ibn Qaasem | | | | | | | | ♦ | | | | |
| 06-11 | ad-Durur An-Nadheed Fe Ikhlaas at-Tawheed | Muhammad Ibn 'Alee as-Shawkaanee | ♦ | ♦ | ♦ | | | | | ♦ | | | | |
| 06-12 | Fath al-Majeed | 'Abdur-Rahman Ibn Hasan | ♦ | ♦ | ♦ | | | | | ♦ | | | | |
| 06-13 | Lama't al-Itiqaad | Muuwafiq Ibn Qudaamah | | | ♦ | | | | | | | | | |
| 06-14 | Usul as-Sittah | Muhammad Ibn 'Abdul-Wahaab | | | | | | | | | | ♦ | | |
| 06-15 | al-Qaseedat an-Nooneeyah | Muhammad Ibn Qayyim | ♦ | | | | | | | | | | | |
| 06-16 | Ijtimaa' al-Jawaish al-Islaameeyah | Muhammad Ibn Qayyim | ♦ | | | | | | | | | | | |
| 06-17 | Masi'al al-Jahiliyyah | Muhammad Ibn 'Abdul-Wahaab | | | | | | | | | | ♦ | | |
| 06-18 | Nawaqidh al-Islaam | Muhammad Ibn 'Abdul-Wahaab | | | | | | | | | | ♦ | | |
| 06-19 | A Beneficial Statement Regarding the Evidences of Tawheed | Muhammad Ibn 'Abdul-Wahaab al-'Abdalee al-Wasaabee | | | | ♦ | | | | | | | | |
| 06-20 | Tayseer al-'Azeez al-Hameed | Sulaymaan Ibn 'Abdullah | | | | | | | | ♦ | ♦ | | | ♦ |
| 06-21 | Sharh al-Waasiteeyyah | Ibn Rasheed | | | | | | | | ♦ | | | | |
| 06-22 | Kitaab as-Sunnah | 'Abdullah Ibn Ahmad Ibn Hanbal | ♦ | | ♦ | | | | | ♦ | | | | |
| 06-23 | ad-Durar as-Sanneyah min al-Fatawaa an-Najdeeyah | Muhammad Ibn 'Abdul-Wahaab, and other scholars | | | | | | | | | | | | ♦ |
| 06-24 | Hashiat Kitaab at-Tawheed | 'Abdur-Rahman Ibn Muhammad Ibn Qaasim | | | | | | | | ♦ | | | | |
| 06-25 | al-Qawl al-Mufeed Alaa Kitaab at-Tawheed | Muhammad Ibn Saaleh al-'Utheimeen | | | | | | | | ♦ | | | | |
| 06-26 | as-Sunnah | Abu Bakr Ahmad Ibn Muhammad al-Khilaal | | | | ♦ | | | | ♦ | | | | |
| 06-27 | al-Ibaanah al-Kubraa | Ibn Battah al-'Akbaree | | | | | | | | | | ♦ | | |
| 06-28 | al-Ibaanah al-Sughraa | Ibn Battah al-'Akbaree | | | | | | | | | | ♦ | | |
| 06-29 | Sharh Usul 'Itiqaad Ahlus-Sunnah | Hibuttullah Ibn Husayn Laalakaa'ee | | | | ♦ | | | | | | ♦ | | |
| 06-30 | Tatheer al-'Itiqaad An Idraan al-Ilhaad | Muhammad Ibn 'Isma'eel | | | | ♦ | | | | ♦ | | | | |
| 06-31 | ad-Durar an-Nadheed fee Ikhlaas at-Tawheed | Muhammad Ibn 'Alee ash-Shawkaanee | | | | ♦ | | | | ♦ | | | | |
| 06-32 | Sharf Ashaabul Hadeeth | al-Khateeb al-Baghdadee | | | | ♦ | | | | | | | | |
| 06-33 | Khalq 'Afaa'al al-'Ebaad | Muhammad Ibn Isma'eel | | | | ♦ | | | | | | | | |
| 06-34 | Kitaab as-Sharee'ah | Muhammad Ibn al-Husayn al-Aajooree | | | | ♦ | | | | ♦ | | ♦ | | |
| 06-35 | al-'Asmaa' wa al-Sifaat | Ahmad Ibn al-Husayn al-Bayhaqee | | | | ♦ | | | | | | | | |
| 06-36 | Kitaab at-Tawheed | Ibn Khuzaymah | ♦ | | | ♦ | | | | | | | | |
| 06-37 | al-'Emaan | Muhammad Ibn Ishaaq al-Asbahaanee | | | | ♦ | | | | | | | | |
| 06-38 | Shafaa' al-'Aleel | Muhammad Ibn Qayyim al-Jawzeeyah | | | | ♦ | | | | | | | | |
| 06-39 | Kitaab al-'Emaan | Muhammad Ibn 'Abdul-Wahaab | ♦ | | | | | | | | | | | |
| 06-40 | Sharh as-Sunnah | al-Husayn IBn Mas'ood al-Bagawee | | | | ♦ | | | | | | | | |
| 06-41 | Dalaa'il an-Nabuwah | Ahmad Ibn al-Husayn al-Bayhaqee | | | | ♦ | | | | | | | | |
| 06-42 | Dalaa'il an-Nabuwah | Ahmad Ibn 'Abdullah al-Asbahaanee | | | | ♦ | | | | | | | | |
| 06-43 | Kitaab as-Sunnah | Muhammad Ibn 'Abdullah Ibn Zamanayn | | | | | | | | | | ♦ | | |
| 06-44 | as-Saheeh al-Musnad min ad-Dalaa'il an-Nabuwwah | Muqbil Ibn Haadee al-Waadi'ee | | | | ♦ | | | | | | | | |
| | Name of Book | Author | B | U | M | A | S | J | SH | F | Aa | N | W | L |

*These two works are listed together despite being separate works, because of the fact that at times the title seems to be used generally for the other work without a clear distinction being made, as well as their related content, and not always being able to distinguish which work was specifically been referred to. This confusion in reference to the two works despite being different was indicated by Sheikh Saaleh Aal-Sheikh.

| | NAME OF BOOK | AUTHOR | B | U | M | A | S | J | SH | F | Aa | N | W | L |
|---|---|---|---|---|---|---|---|---|---|---|---|---|---|---|
| 06-45 | al-'Uluu lil 'Alee al-Ghafaar Fee Edhaah | Muhammad Ibn Ahmad Ibn 'Uthmaan adh-Dhahabee | | | ◆ | | | | | | | ◆ | | |
| 06-46 | Mukhtasir al-'Uluu lil 'Alee al-Ghafaar | Muhammad Naasiruddeen al-Albaanee | ◆ | | ◆ | | | | | | | | | |
| 06-47 | 'Aqeedah as-Safaareenaa | Muhammad Ibn Saalam | | | | ◆ | | | | | | | | |
| 06-48 | Matn ad-Daleel | Mura'ee Ibn Yusuf al-Karee | | | | | | | | ◆ | | | | |
| 06-49 | al-Qaa'edah Jaleelah fe at-Tawasul wa al-Waseelah | Ahmad Ibn 'Abdul-Haleem Ibn Taymeeyah | | | ◆ | | | | | | | | | |
| 06-50 | ar-Ru'yaah | 'Alee Ibn 'Umar Ibn Ahmad ad-Darqutnee | | | ◆ | | | | | | | | | |
| 06-51 | Haadee al-Arwaah' ila Balad al-Afraah | Muhammad Ibn Qayyim | | | ◆ | | | | | | | | | |
| 06-52 | as-Saaram al-Mankee fee Rad alaa as-Subkee | Ahmad Ibn 'Abdul-Haleem Ibn Taymeeyah | | | ◆ | | | | | | | | | |
| 06-53 | Ismuhu An-Nuzul | Ahmad Ibn 'Abdul-Haleem Ibn Taymeeyah | | | ◆ | | | | | | | | | |
| 06-54 | Aqeedatul as-Salaf | Isma'eel Ibn 'Abdur-Rahman | | | ◆ | | | | | | | | | |
| 06-55 | al-Qadr | Maalik Ibn Anas or his sheikh Ibn Wahb | | | ◆ | | | | | | | | | |
| 06-56 | at-Tawheed | Ibn Munduh | | | ◆ | | | | | | | | | |
| 06-57 | at-Tawassul Anwaa'hu wa Ahkaamuhu | Muhammad Naasiruddeen al-Albaanee | | | ◆ | | | | | | | | | |
| 06-58 | Sharh as-Sunnah | al-Barberhaaree | | | | | | | | | | ◆ | | |
| 06-59 | al-'Itiqaad | al-Bayahaqee | | | ◆ | | | | | | | | | |

## 7. Books of Fiqh - Explanations of How to Implement the Guidance of Source Texts

| | Name of Book | Author | B | U | M | A | S | J | SH | F | Aa | N | W | L |
|---|---|---|---|---|---|---|---|---|---|---|---|---|---|---|
| 07-01 | Zaad al-Mustaqna Fee Ikhtisaar al-Muqna' | Sharfudden Abu an-Najaa | ◆ | ◆ | ◆ | | | | | ◆ | ◆ | | | |
| 07-02 | Rawdh al-Maraba' | Mansoor Ibn Yunus al-Bayhutee | | | ◆ | | | | | | | | | |
| 07-03 | Amdat al-Fiqh | Muuwafiq Ibn Qudaamah | ◆ | ◆ | | | | | | | | | | |
| 07-04 | Tamaan al-Minnah | Muhammad Naasiruddeen al-Albaanee | | | | ◆ | | | | | | | | |
| 07-05 | al-Rawdhatul an-Nadeeyah Sharh ad-Durar al-Baheyyah | Sadeeq Hasan Khaan | | | | ◆ | | | | | | | | |
| 07-06 | Fiqh as-Sunnah | Sayyed Saabiq | | ◆ | ◆ | ◆ | | | | | | | | |
| 07-07 | al-Mughnee | Shamsudden Ibn Qudaamah | ◆ | | | | | | | | | ◆ | | |
| 07-08 | Fatawaa Umar Ibn- 'Abdul-'Azeez | - | | | ◆ | | | | | | | | | |
| 07-09 | (book refuting some adherents to the Maalakee school in the issue of raising one's hands in salaah) | Ibn Azuuz | | | ◆ | | | | | | | | | |
| 07-10 | Hajj al-Wadaa'a | Muhammad 'Alee Ibn Ahmad | | | ◆ | | | | | | | | | |
| 07-11 | Jaame'a al-Usool fee Ahadeeth ar-Rasool | Ibn al-'Atheer al-Jazree | | | ◆ | | | | | | | | | |
| 07-12 | ar-Rabaa'ee | - | | | ◆ | | | | | | | | | |
| 07-13 | al-Muntaqaa al-Akhbaar min Ahadeeth Sayyed al-Akhyaar | 'Abdul-Salaam Ibn 'Abdulluh al-Haraanee | | | | | | | | ◆ | | | | ◆ |
| 07-14 | Sharh al-Mumta' 'Alaa Za'd al-Musataqna' | Muhammad Ibn Saaleh al-'Utheimeen | | | | | | | | ◆ | | | | |
| 07-15 | Ijaabatul-Saa'el 'An Ahemul Masaa'el | Muqbil Ibn Haadee al-Waadi'ee | | | | ◆ | | | | | | | | |
| 07-16 | Qamaa' al-Ma'aanid wa Zujur al-Haaqid al-Haasid | Muqbil Ibn Haadee al-Waadi'ee | | | | ◆ | | | | | | | | |
| 07-17 | Majmu'a Fatawaa wa Maqaalaat Matanawa'h | 'Abdul-'Azeez Ibn 'Abdullah Ibn Baaz | ◆ | | | | | | | | ◆ | | | |
| 07-18 | Aadaab al-Mashee Ilaa as-Salaat | Muhammad Ibn 'Abdul-Wahaab | ◆ | ◆ | | | | | | ◆ | | | | |
| 07-19 | Majmu'a Fatawaa Sheikh al-Islaam Ibn Taymeeyah | Ahmad Ibn Taymeeyah | | | ◆ | | | | ◆ | ◆ | | | | ◆ |
| 07-20 | Majmu'a Fatawaa Sheikh 'Abdur-Rahman as-Sa'adee | 'Abdur-Rahman as-Sa'adee | | | | | | | | ◆ | | | | |
| 07-21 | Majmu'a Fatawaa Sheikh Muhammad Ibn Ibraaheem | Muhammad Ibn Ibraaheem | ◆ | | | | | | | ◆ | | | | |
| 07-22 | Majmu'a ar-Rasaa'l wa al-Masaa'il | | | | | | | | | | ◆ | | | | |
| 07-23 | Daleel at-Taalib | Sharfudden Abu an-Najaa | | | | ◆ | | | | | | | | |
| 07-24 | Insaaf fee Masi'alat ul-Khilaaf | Abu 'Umar Yusuf Ibn 'Abdul-Bar | | | | ◆ | | | | | | | | |
| 07-25 | Kaashif al-Qanaa' | al-Bahootee | | | | | | | | ◆ | | | | |
| 07-26 | Shurut as-Salaam | Muhammad Ibn 'Abdul-Wahaab | | | | | | | ◆ | | | | | |
| 07-27 | ar-Rawdhah | - | | | ◆ | | | | | | | | | |
| 07-28 | al-Masa'il | Ibn Haanee | | | ◆ | | | | | | | | | |
| 07-28 | at-Tamheed | Abu Yusuf Ibn 'Abdul-Bar | | | ◆ | | | | | | | | | |

## 8. Books of The Principles of the Science of Fiqh

| | Name of Book | Author | B | U | M | A | S | J | SH | F | Aa | N | W | L |
|---|---|---|---|---|---|---|---|---|---|---|---|---|---|---|
| 08-01 | al-Usul Min 'Ilm al-Usul | Abu Muhammad 'Alee Ibn Hazm | | | ◆ | | | | | | | | | |
| 08-02 | al-Ahkaam fee Usul al-Ahkaam | Abu Muhammad 'Alee Ibn Hazm | | | | ◆ | | | | | | | | |
| 08-03 | ar-Risaalah | Muhammad Ibn Idrees | | | | ◆ | | | | | | | | |
| 08-04 | al-Majmu'a Sharh al-Muhadhab | Yahya Ibn Sharf an-Nawawee | | | ◆ | | | | | | | | | |
| 08-05 | al-Mudhakirah | Muhammad al-'Ameen ash-Shanqeetee | | | | ◆ | | | | | | | | |
| 08-06 | al-Umm | Muhammad Ibn Idrees | | | | ◆ | | | | | | | | |
| 08-07 | al-Muhalla fee Sharh al-Jalee bil Hujajj wa al-Aathaar | Abu Muhammad 'Alee Ibn Hazm | | | ◆ | ◆ | | | | | | | | |
| 08-08 | Rawdhat an-Naadher | Muuwafiq Ibn Qudaamah | | | ◆ | | | | | | | | | |
| 08-09 | 'Irshaad al-Fuhool fee Tahqeeq al-Haq min 'Ilm al-Usool | Muhammad Ibn 'Alee ash-Shawkaanee | | | | ◆ | | | | | | | | |
| 08-10 | al-Usooleeyah | al-Qaraafee | | | | | | | | | ◆ | | | |
| 08-11 | al-Furu'a | Muhammad Ibn Muflih | | | | | | | ◆ | | | | | |
| 08-12 | I'laam al-Muwaqa'een | Muhammad Ibn Qayyim | | | | | | | ◆ | | | | | |
| 08-13 | al-Qawa'id al-Fiqeeyah | Ibn Rajab | | | | | | | ◆ | | | | | |

## 9. Books of the Biography the Prophet and General History

| | Name of Book | Author | B | U | M | A | S | J | SH | F | Aa | N | W | L |
|---|---|---|---|---|---|---|---|---|---|---|---|---|---|---|
| 09-01 | Shafaa' al-Ileel | Ayaadh Ibn Musaa al-Yahsebee | | | ◆ | | | | | | | | | |
| 09-02 | al-Bidaayah wa an-Nihaayah | 'Isma'eel Ibn 'Umar Ibn Katheer | | | ◆ | | | | | | | | | |
| 09-03 | Taarikh Baghdaad | al-Khateeb al-Baghdadee | | | ◆ | | | | | | | | | |
| 09-04 | as-Saheeh al-Musnad fe as-Shamail al-Muhammadeyyah | Umm 'Abdullah al-Waadeeyah | | | ◆ | | | | | | | | | |
| 09-05 | Zaad al-Ma'ad Fee Haadee Khair al-Ebaad | Muhammad Ibn Qayyim | ◆ | ◆ | ◆ | | | | | | | | | ◆ |
| 09-06 | Taarikh Ibn Ma'een | Ibn Ma'een | | | ◆ | | | | | | | | | |
| 09-07 | Taarikh ad-Darqutnee | ad-Darqutnee | | | ◆ | | | | | | | | | |
| 09-08 | al-Ahaad wa al-Muthanee | Test book author | | | ◆ | | | | | | | | | |
| 09-09 | ash-Shama'il al-Muhammadeeyah | Test book author | | | ◆ | | | | | | | | | |
| 09-10 | Tareekh ad-Dimashq | Test book author | | | ◆ | | | | | | | | | |

## 10. Books of the Various Sciences of the Arabic Language

| | Name of Book | Author | B | U | M | A | S | J | SH | F | Aa | N | W | L |
|---|---|---|---|---|---|---|---|---|---|---|---|---|---|---|
| 10-01 | al-Qaamoos | Qaasem 'Alee al-Hareeree | | | ◆ | | | | | | | | | |
| 10-02 | Taaj al-'Aroos min Jawaahir al-Qamoos | Muhammad Murtadhaa az-Zabeedee | | | ◆ | | | | | | | | | |
| 10-03 | Lisaan al-'Arab | Muhammad Ibn Mukaram Ibn 'Alee | | | ◆ | | | | | | | | | |
| 10-04 | Alfeeyah Ibn Maalik | Jamaaluddden Muhammad Ibn Maalik | | | ◆ | ◆ | | | | | | | | |
| 10-05 | al-Aajroomeeyah | Muhammad Ibn Daawood as-Sanhaajee | | | ◆ | ◆ | | | | | | | | |
| 10-06 | Sharh Ibn Aqeel Aala Alfeeyah Ibn Maalik | 'Abdullah Ibn 'Aqeel al-Aqeelee | | | ◆ | | | | | | | | | |
| 10-07 | Tuhfat as-Sunneyah | Muhammad Muhyeeuddeen 'Abdul-Hameed | | | ◆ | | | | | | | | | |
| | NAME OF BOOK | AUTHOR | B | U | M | A | S | J | SH | F | Aa | N | W | L |

## 11. Books of Refuting the Mistakes of Those who Innovate in the Religion

| Name of Book | Author | B | U | M | A | S | J | SH | F | Aa | N | W | L |
|---|---|---|---|---|---|---|---|---|---|---|---|---|---|
| 11-01 | al-'Itisaam | Ibraaheem Ibn Musaa ash-Shaatabee | | | ◆ | | | | | ◆ | | | | |
| 11-02 | Idtidhaa' as-Siraat al-Mustaqeem | Ahmad Ibn Taymeeyah | | | ◆ | | | | | ◆ | | | | |
| 11-03 | Inkaar al-Hawaadith wa al-Bid'ah | Muhammad Ibn Wadhaah al-Qurtubee | | | | | | | | ◆ | | | | |
| 11-04 | al-Hawaadidh wa Bid'ah | at-Tartooshee | | | | | | | | ◆ | | | | |
| 11-05 | al-Baaith Alaa Inkaar al-Bid'ah wa al-Hawadith | Abu Shaamah | | | | | | | | ◆ | | | | |
| 11-06 | al-Ibdaa' Fee Madhaar al-Ibtidaa' | 'Alee Mahfoodh | | | ◆ | | | | | ◆ | | | | |
| 11-07 | at-Taadher min al-Bid'ah | 'Abdul-'Azeez Ibn 'Abdullah Ibn Baaz | | | | | | | | ◆ | | | | |
| 11-08 | ar-Rad Alaa Bishr al-Marasee | 'Uthmaan Ibn Sa'eed ad-Daaramee | | | | | | | | | | ◆ | | |
| 11-09 | Minhaj as-Sunnah an-Nabaweeyah fee Naqs Kalaam ash-Shee'ah wa al-Qaadareeyah | Ahmad Ibn 'Abdul-Haleem Ibn Taymeeyah | ◆ | | ◆ | | | | | | | | | ◆ |
| 11-10 | Rad 'Alaa Jahmeeyah wa al-Zanaadiqah | Ahmad Ibn Muhammad Ibn Hanbal | | | ◆ | | | | | ◆ | ◆ | | | |
| 11-11 | Rad 'Alaa Jahmeeyah | Uthmaan Ibn Sa'eed ad-Daramee | | | ◆ | | | | | | ◆ | | | |
| 11-12 | at-Tale'ah Fee Rad 'Alaa Gulaat as-Shee'ah | Muqbil Ibn Haadee al-Waadi'ee | | | ◆ | | | | | | | | | |
| 11-13 | as-Seeyaasah ash-Shar'eeh | Ahmad Ibn 'Abdul-Haleem Ibn Taymeeyah | | | | | | | | | | | | ◆ |
| 11-14 | Qaraa' Alasat fe Nafee al-Ghuluu wa at-Tatraf wa al-Ashadhudh 'An Ahl-Sunnah | 'Abdul-'Azeez Ibn Yahya al-Bur'aee | | | ◆ | | | | | | | | | |
| 11-15 | Bid'ah at-Ta'asub al-Madhhabee | Muhammad 'Eid Abbasee | | | ◆ | | | | | | | | | |
| 11-16 | al-Qutbeeyah | Abu Ibraaheem Ibn Sultaan | | | ◆ | | | | | | | | | |
| 11-17 | 'Irshaad Dhuee al-Futan Lil Iba'ad Ghulaat ar-Rawwafidh min al-Yemen | Muqbil Ibn Haadee al-Waadi'ee | | | ◆ | | | | | | | | | |
| 11-18 | Riyaadh al-Jannah fee ar-Rad 'Alaa 'Adaa' as-Sunnah | Muqbil Ibn Haadee al-Waadi'ee | | | ◆ | | | | | | | | | |
| 11-19 | al-'Ilhaad al-Khomaynee fee 'Ardh al-Haramayn | Muqbil Ibn Haadee al-Waadi'ee | | | ◆ | | | | | | | | | |
| 11-20 | as-Suyuuf al-Baaterah | Muqbil Ibn Haadee al-Waadi'ee | | | ◆ | | | | | | | | | |
| 11-21 | Makhraj min al-Fitnah | Muqbil Ibn Haadee al-Waadi'ee | | | ◆ | | | | | | | | | |
| 11-22 | Iqaamat al-Burhaan 'Alaa Dhalaal 'Abdur-Raheem at-Tahaan | Muqbil Ibn Haadee al-Waadi'ee | | | ◆ | | | | | | | | | |
| 11-23 | Mutaabaqat Sareeh al-Mu'qal lesareeh al-Manqool | Ahmad Ibn Muhammad Ibn Hanbal | ◆ | | | | | | | | | | | |
| 11-24 | al-Jawaab as-Saheeh Leman Badala Deen al-Maseeh | Ahmad Ibn Muhammad Ibn Hanbal | ◆ | | | | | | | | | | | |
| 11-25 | Rudood Ahlul-Ilm Ala At-Taa'neen fee Hadeeth As-Sahr wa Bayan Bu'ed Muhammad Rasheed Ridha 'An As-Salafeeyah | Muqbil Ibn Haadee al-Waadi'ee | | | ◆ | | | | | | | | | |
| 11-26 | al-Mawrood al-'Adhab az-Zalaal Fee Bayaan Akhtaa' adh-Dhalaal | 'Abdullah Ibn Muhammad ad-Duwaish | | | ◆ | | | | | | | | | |
| 11-27 | Miftah Dar as-Saadah | Muhammad Ibn Qayyim | | | ◆ | | | | | | | | | |
| 11-28 | 'Ijmaa' al-'Ulema 'Alaa Hajr 'Ashaab al-Bid'ah wa al-Ahwa'a | Khaalid Adh-Dhaafaree | | | ◆ | | | | | | | | | |
| 11-29 | 'Aqaa'id ath-Thalathahwa Sabaaeen Firqah | Abu Muhammad al-Yemenee | | | ◆ | | | | | | | | | |
| 11-30 | al-'Irhaab | Zayd Ibn Muhammad al-Madhkhalee | | | ◆ | | | | | | | | | |
| 11-31 | Fee Rad 'Alaa man Yaqool: In al-'Ardh Tadur | - | | | ◆ | | | | | | | | | |
| 11-32 | Darasatun wa Naqd | 'Abdur-Rahman ad-Dimashqee | | | ◆ | | | | | | | | | |
| 11-33 | Sayf al-Yamaanee Fee Nahr al-Asfahaanee | Muqbil Ibn Haadee al-Waadi'ee | | | ◆ | | | | | | | | | |
| | NAME OF BOOK | AUTHOR | B | U | M | A | S | J | SH | F | Aa | N | W | L |

## 12. Books of Various Subjects in Various Branches of Knowledge

| | Name of Book | Author | B | U | M | A | S | J | SH | F | Aa | N | W | L |
|---|---|---|---|---|---|---|---|---|---|---|---|---|---|---|
| 12-01 | Jaame'a Bayaan al-'Ilm wa Fadhlihee | Abu Yusuf Ibn 'Abdul-Bar | | | ● | | | | | | ● | | | ● |
| 12-02 | 'Ilaam al-Muqa'een | Muhammad Ibn Qayyim | | ● | | | | | | | | | | ● |
| 12-03 | Tareeq al-Muhajareen | Muhammad Ibn Qayyim | | | | | | | | | | | | ● |
| 12-04 | as-Sawa'aiq al-Mursalah | Muhammad Ibn Qayyim | | ● | | | | | | ● | | | | |
| 12-05 | Ighathatul al-Lahfaan min Makaa'id as-Shaytaan | Muhammad Ibn Qayyim | | ● | | | | | | ● | | | | |
| 12-06 | al-Muqadamah | Abu Zayd al-Qeeruwaanee | | ● | | | | | | | | | | |
| 12-07 | al-Mu'tamad fee Tibb wa al-Hikmah | - | | | ● | | | | | | | | | |
| 12-08 | ar-Rihlah fee Talab al-Hadeeth | al-Khateeb al-Baghdaadee | | | ● | | | | | | | | | |
| 12-09 | Kashf al-Khafaa' wa Mazeel al-Ilbaas 'Amaa Ashtahar min al-Ahadeeth 'Alaa Lisanat an-Naas | 'Isma'eel Ibn Muhammad al-'Ajaloonee | | | ● | | | | | | | | | |
| 12-10 | 'Aqood al-Jamaan | 'Abdullah Ibn Muhammada | | | ● | | | | | | | | | |
| 12-11 | al-Kaba'eer | Abu al-Bara' Ghassan al-Philistinee | | | ● | | | | | | | | | |
| 12-12 | al-Zuwaajir An Iqtiraaf al-Kabaa'ir | al-Haithamee | | | ● | | | | | | | | | |
| 12-13 | Naseehatee Lil Ahl-Sunnah | Muqbil Ibn Haadee al-Waadi'ee | | | ● | | | | | | | | | |
| 12-14 | (book discussing the prohibition of obtaining American citizenship) | Muhammad as-Sabeel | | | ● | | | | | | | | | |
| 12-15 | Jalaa' al-Afhaam | Muhammad Ibn Qayyim | | | ● | | | | | | | | | |
| 12-16 | (book discussing sending salaam upon the Prophet when he is mentioned) | as-Sakhawee | | | ● | | | | | | | | | |
| 12-17 | Hadhaa Daw'atnaa wa 'Aqeedatnaa | Muqbil Ibn Haadee al-Waadi'ee | | | | | | | | | ● | | | |
| 12-18 | Qirat al-'Ayn fee Ajweebat Qaa'ed al-'Alaabee wa Saahib al-'Adeen | Muqbil Ibn Haadee al-Waadi'ee | | | ● | | | | | | | | | |
| 12-19 | Mua'jiza'at as-Shifa'aa | - | | | ● | | | | | | | | | |
| 12-20 | Qurrat al-Ayyun fee Akhbaar al-Yemeen | - | | | ● | | | | | | | | | |
| 12-21 | al-Muntaqaa | Ibn al-Jaarood | | | | ● | ● | | | | | | | |
| 12-22 | Kitaab az-Zuhd | Ahmad Ibn Muhammad Ibn Hanbal | | | ● | | | | | | | | | |
| 12-23 | az-Zuhd | Wakee'a Ibn al-Jaraah | | | ● | | | | | | | | | |
| 12-24 | az-Zuhd | Hinaad as-Saree | | | ● | | | | | | | | | |
| 12-25 | az-Zuhd wa al-Raqaa'iq | 'Abdullah Ibn Mubaarak | | | ● | | | | | | | | | |
| 12-26 | at-Tibb an-Nabawee | Muhammad Ibn Qayyim | | | ● | | | | | | | | | |
| 12-27 | at-Tibb an-Nabawee | Muhammad Ibn Ahmad adh-Dhahabee | | | ● | | | | | | | | | |
| 12-28 | at-Tibb an-Nabawee | Jalaaluddeen 'Abdur-Rahman as-Suyootee | | | ● | | | | | | | | | |
| 12-29 | at-Tibb | Ahmad Ibn 'Abdullah al-Asbahaanee | | | ● | | | | | | | | | |
| 12-30 | al-Jawaab al-Kaafee Liman Sa'ill An Ad-Duwaa' Ash-Shaa'fee | Muhammad Ibn Qayyim | | | | | | | ● | | | | | |
| 12-31 | Naseehatee Lil Nisaa' | Umm 'Abdullah al-Wada'eeyah | | | ● | | | | | | ● | | | |
| 12-32 | al-Mutaalib al-'Aleeyah be Zawa'id al-Musaanid al-'Aleeyah | Ahmad Ibn 'Alee Ibn Hajr | | | | ● | | | | | | | | |
| 12-33 | al-Burhaneeyah | Muhammad al-Burhaanee | | | | ● | | | | | | | | |
| 12-34 | al-Fawaakahu al-Jannah | Muqbil Ibn Haadee al-Waadi'ee | | | ● | | | | | | | | | |
| 12-35 | Maqatil as-Sheikh Jameel are-Rahman | Muqbil Ibn Haadee al-Waadi'ee | | | ● | | | | | | | | | |
| 12-36 | al-Masaar'at | Muqbil Ibn Haadee al-Waadi'ee | | | ● | | | | | | | | | |
| 12-37 | Ta'dheem Qadr as-Salaat | Muhammad Ibn Nasr al-Maruzee | | | ● | | | | | | | | | |
| 12-38 | al-Walaa' wa al-Baraa' Fee al-Islaam Min Mafaahem Aqeedatul as-Salaf | Muhammad Ibn Sa'eed Ibn Salim al-Qahtanee | | | ● | | | | | | | | | |
| 12-39 | Asnaa al-Mutaalib fee Ahadeeth Mukhtalafahu al-Muraatib Min al-Ahaadeeth al-Mushtaharah | - | | | ● | | | | | | | | | |
| 12-40 | al-Qawl al-'Ameen fee Bayaan Fadhaaeh al-Mudhabdhabeen | Muqbil Ibn Haadee al-Waadi'ee | | | ● | | | | | | | | | |
| | NAME OF BOOK | AUTHOR | B | U | M | A | S | J | SH | F | Aa | N | W | L |

# Index of Questions & Issues Organized by Scholar's Name

(**Q**-question number/**PG**-page number)

*Sheikh Muhammad Ibn 'Abdul-Wahab al-Wasaabee:*

Section 1:  Q23/PG95

Section 2:  -

Section 3:  -

Section 4:  -

Section 5:  -

Section 6:  -

Section 7:  -

*Permanent Committee For Scholastic Research & Issuing of Islamic Rulings:*

Section 1:  -

Section 2:  -

Section 3:  -

Section 4:  Q139/PG298

Section 5:  -

Section 6:  -

Section 7:  -

# Telephone Numbers for some of our Scholars

| Scholar's Name | Phone Number |
|---|---|
| Sheikh 'Abdul-'Azeez Ibn 'Abdullah Aal-Sheikh | 0096614582757<br>0096614595555 |
| Sheikh Saaleh Ibn 'Abdullah Ibn Fauzaan al-Fauzaan | 0096614588570<br>0096614787840 |
| Sheikh 'Abdul-Muhsin al-'Abaad al-Badr | 0096648475207 |
| Sheikh 'Abdullah al-Ghudyaan | 0096614113796<br>0096614580731 |
| Sheikh Muhammad Ibn 'Abdul-Wahaab al-Banna | 0096626930356<br>0096653604805 |
| Sheikh Saaleh Ibn Muhammad al-Luhaydaan | 0096612312266<br>0096614829657 |
| Sheikh Muhammad Ibn 'Abdul-Wahaab al-Wasaabee | 009673231399 |
| Sheikh Saaleh Ibn 'Abdul-'Azeez Aal-Sheikh | 0096614707942 |
| Sheikh Rabee'a Ibn Haadee al-Madkhalee | 0096625274450<br>0096625274419 |
| Sheikh Zayd Ibn Haadee al-Madkhalee | 0096655770551<br>009665770551 |
| Sheikh 'Abdul'Azeez Ibn 'Abdullah al-Raajihee | 0096614915930 |
| Sheikh Saaleh Ibn Sa'd as-Suhaymee | 0096648263897<br>0096648264197 |
| Sheikh Wasiullah al-'Abbas | 00966505526886 |
| Sheikh Muhammad Ibn 'Abdullah al-Imaam | 009676430521<br>009676430280 |
| Sheikh Muhammad Bazmool | 0096625274940 |
| Sheikh 'Abdul-'Azeez al-Burea' | 009674433245 |
| Sheikh Muhammad Ibn Ramzaan al-Haajaree | 00966505386236 |
| Sheikh 'Ubayd Ibn 'Abdullah al-Jaabaree | 0096648480637<br>0096655310086 |
| Sheikh Sulaymaan Ibn Saleem ar-Ruhaylee | 00966505307486 |
| Sheikh Muhammad Ibn Ahmad al-Afeefe | 00966505489848 |
| Sheikh Jamaal Ibn Farhaan al-Haarithee | 00966555704241 |
| Sheikh Hamd al-'Uthmaan | 009659638884 |
| Sheikh Falaah Ibn Isma'eel Mandakaar | 009653915630 |
| Sheikh Saalem at-Taweel | 009659830725 |

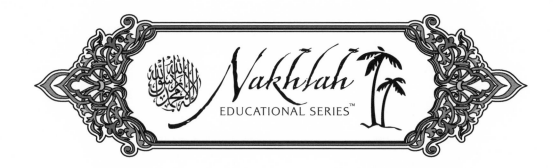

# The Nakhlah Educational Series: Mission and Methodology

## Mission

The Purpose of the 'Nakhlah Educational Series' is to contribute to the present knowledge based efforts which enable Muslim individuals, families, and communities to understand and learn Islaam and then to develop within and truly live Islaam. Our commitment and goal is to contribute beneficial publications and works that:

Firstly, reflect the priority, message and methodology of all the prophets and messengers sent to humanity, meaning that single revealed message which embodies the very purpose of life, and of human creation. As Allaah the Most High has said,

❖ *We sent a Messenger to every nation ordering them that they should worship Allaah alone, obey Him and make their worship purely for Him, and that they should avoid everything worshipped besides Allaah. So from them there were those whom Allaah guided to His religion, and there were those who were unbelievers for whom misguidance was ordained. So travel through the land and see the destruction that befell those who denied the Messengers and disbelieved.*❖—(Surah an-Nahl: 36)

Sheikh Rabee'a ibn Haadee al-Madkhalee in his work entitled, '*The Methodology of the Prophets in Calling to Allaah, That is the Way of Wisdom and Intelligence.*' explains the essential, enduring message of all the prophets:

"*So what was the message which these noble, chosen men, may Allaah's praises and salutations of peace be upon them all, brought to their people? Indeed their mission encompassed every matter of good and distanced and restrained every matter of evil. They brought forth to mankind everything needed for their well-being and happiness in this world and the Hereafter. There is nothing good except that they guided the people towards it, and nothing evil except that they warned the people against it. ...*

*This was the message found with all of the Messengers; that they should guide to every good and warn against every evil. However where did they start, what did they begin with and what did they concentrate upon? There are a number of essentials, basic principles, and fundamentals which all their calls were founded upon, and which were the starting point for calling the people to Allaah. These fundamental points and principles are: 1. The worship of Allaah alone without any associates 2. The sending of prophets to guide creation 3. The belief in the resurrection and the life of the Hereafter*

*These three principles are the area of commonality and unity within their calls, and stand as the fundamental principles which they were established upon. These principles are given the greatest importance in the Qur'an and are fully explained in it. They are also its most important purpose upon which it centers and which it continually mentions. It further quotes intellectual and observable proofs for them in all its chapters as well as within most of its accounts of previous nations and given examples. This is known to those who have full understanding, and are able to consider carefully and comprehend well. All the Books revealed by Allaah have given great importance to these points and all of the various revealed laws of guidance are agreed upon them. And the most important and sublime of these three principles, and the most fundamental of them all is directing one's worship only towards Allaah alone, the Blessed and the Most High."*

Today one finds that there are indeed many paths, groups, and organizations apparently presenting themselves as representing Islaam, which struggle to put forth an outwardly pleasing appearance to the general Muslims; but when their methods are placed upon the precise scale of conforming to priorities and methodology of the message of the prophets sent by Allaah, they can only be recognized as deficient paths- not simply in practice but in principle- leading not to success but rather only to inevitable failure. As Sheikh Saaleh al-Fauzaan, may Allaah preserve him, states in his introduction to the same above mentioned work on the methodology of all the prophets,

*"So whichever call is not built upon these foundations, and whatever methodology is not from the methodology of the Messengers - then it will be frustrated and fail, and it will be effort and toil without any benefit. The clearest proofs of this are those present day groups and organizations which set out a methodology and program for themselves and their efforts of calling the people to Islaam which is different from the methodology of the Messengers. These groups have neglected the importance of the people having the correct belief and creed - except for a very few of them - and instead call for the correction of side-issues."*

There can be no true success in any form for us as individuals, families, or larger communities without making the encompassing worship of Allaah alone, with no partners or associates, the very and only foundation of our lives. It is necessary that each individual knowingly choose to base his life upon that same foundation taught by all the prophets and messengers sent by the Lord of all the worlds, rather than simply delving into the assorted secondary concerns and issues invited to by the various numerous parties, innovated movements, and groups. Indeed Sheikh al-Albaanee, may Allaah have mercy upon him, stated:

*"...We unreservedly combat against this way of having various different parties and groups. As this false way- of group or organizational allegiances - conforms to the statement of Allaah the Most High,* **But they have broken their religion among them into sects, each group rejoicing in what is with it as its beliefs. And every party is pleased with whatever they stand with.** *–(Surah al-Mu'minoon: 53) And in truth they are no separate groups and parties in Islaam itself. There is only one true party, as is stated in a verse in the Qur'an,* **Verily, it is the party of Allaah that will be the successful.** *–(Surah al-Mujadilaah: 58). The party of Allaah are those people who stand with the Messenger of Allaah, may Allaah's praise and salutations be upon him, meaning that an individual proceeds upon the methodology of the Companions of the Messenger. Due to this we call for having sound knowledge of the Book and the Sunnah."*

*(Knowledge Based Issues & Sharee'ah Rulings: The Rulings of The Guiding Scholar Sheikh Muhammad Naasiruddeen al-Albaanee Made in the City of Medina & In the Emirates – [Emiratee Fatwa no 114. P.30])*

## Two Essential Foundations

Secondly, building upon the above foundation, our commitment is to contributing publications and works which reflect the inherited message and methodology of the acknowledged scholars of the many various branches of Sharee'ah knowledge who stood upon the straight path of preserved guidance in every century and time since the time of our Messenger, may Allaah's praise and salutations be upon him. These people of knowledge, who are the inheritors of the Final Messenger, have always adhered closely to the two revealed sources of guidance: the Book of Allaah and the Sunnah of the Messenger of Allaah- may Allaah's praise and salutations be upon him, upon the united consensus, standing with the body of guided Muslims in every century - preserving and transmitting the true religion generation after generation. Indeed the Messenger of Allaah, may Allaah's praise and salutations be upon him, informed us that, *{ A group of people amongst my Ummah will remain obedient to Allaah's orders. They will not be harmed by those who leave them nor by those who oppose them, until Allaah's command for the Last Day comes upon them while they remain on the right path. }* (Authentically narrated in Saheeh al-Bukhaaree).

We live in an age in which the question frequently asked is, *"How do we make Islaam a reality?"* and perhaps the related and more fundamental question is, *"What is Islaam?"*, such that innumerable different voices quickly stand to offer countless different conflicting answers through books, lectures, and every available form of modern media. Yet the only true course of properly understanding this question and its answer- for ourselves and our families -is to return to the criterion given to us by our beloved Messenger, may Allaah's praise and salutations be upon him. Indeed the Messenger of Allaah, may Allaah's praise and salutations be upon him, indicated in an authentic narration, clarifying the matter beyond doubt, that the only "Islaam" which enables one to be truly successful and saved in this world and the next is as he said, *{...that which I am upon and my Companions are upon today.}* (authentically narrated in Jaam'ea at-Tirmidhee) referring to that Islaam which was stands upon unchanging revealed knowledge. While every other changed and altered form of Islaam, whether through some form of extremism or negligence, or through the addition or removal of something, regardless of whether that came from a good intention or an evil one- is not the religion that Allaah informed us about of when He revealed, ❴ *This day, those who disbelieved have given up all hope of your religion; so fear them not, but fear Me. This day, I have perfected your religion for you, completed My Favor upon you, and have chosen for you Islaam as your religion.*❵–(Surah al-Maa'edah: 3)

The guiding scholar Sheikh al-Albaanee, may have mercy upon him, said,

*"...And specifically mentioning those among the callers who have taken upon themselves the guiding of the young Muslim generation upon Islaam, working to educate them with its education, and to socialize them with its culture. Yet they themselves have generally not attempted to unify their understanding of those matters about Islaam regarding which the people of Islaam today differ about so severely.*

*And the situation is certainly not as is falsely supposed by some individuals from among them who are heedless or negligent - that the differences that exist among them are only in secondary*

*matters without entering into or affecting the fundamental issues or principles of the religion; and the examples to prove that this is not true are numerous and recognized by those who have studied the books of the many differing groups and sects, or by the one who has knowledge of the various differing concepts and beliefs held by the Muslims today.*"(Mukhtasir al-'Uloo Lil'Alee al-Ghafaar, page 55)

Similarly he, may Allaah have mercy upon him, explained:

*"Indeed, Islaam is the only solution, and this statement is something which the various different Islamic groups, organizations, and movements could never disagree about. And this is something which is from the blessings of Allaah upon the Muslims. However there are significant differences between the different Islamic groups, organizations, and movements that are present today regarding that domain which working within will bring about our rectification. What is that area of work to endeavor within, striving to restore a way of life truly reflecting Islaam, renewing that system of living which comes from Islaam, and in order to establish the Islamic government? The groups and movements significantly differ upon this issue or point. Yet we hold that it is required to begin with the matters of tasfeeyah –clarification, and tarbeeyah -education and cultivation, with both of them being undertaken together.*

*As if we were to start with the issue of governing and politics, then it has been seen that those who occupy themselves with this focus firstly posses beliefs which are clearly corrupted and ruined, and secondly that their personal behavior, from the aspect of conforming to Islaam, is very far from conforming to the actual guidance of the Sharee'ah. While those who first concern themselves with working just to unite the people and gather the masses together under a broad banner of the general term "Islaam", then it is seen that within the minds of those speakers who raise such calls -in reality there is fact no actual clear understanding of what Islaam is. Moreover, the understanding they have of Islaam has no significant impact in starting to change and reform their own lives. Due to this reason you find that many such individuals from here and there, who hold this perspective, are unable to truly realize or reflect Islaam even in areas of their own personal lives in matters which it is in fact easily possible for them to implement. As he holds that no one - regardless of whether it is because of his arrogance or pridefulness - can enter into directing him in an area of his personal life!*

*Yet at the same time these same individuals are raising their voices saying, "Judgment is only for Allaah!" and "It is required that judgment of affairs be according to what Allaah revealed." And this is indeed a true statement. But the one who does not possess something certainly cannot give or offer it to others. The majority of Muslims today have not established the judgment of Allaah fully upon themselves, yet they still seek from others to establish the judgment of Allaah within their governments...*

*...And I understand that this issue or subject is not immune from there being those who oppose our methodology of tasfeeyah and tarbeeyah. As there is the one who would say, "But establishing this tasfeeyah and tarbeeyah is a matter which requires many long years!" So, I respond by saying, this is not an important consideration in this matter, what is important is that we carry out what we have been commanded to do within our religion and by our Mighty Lord. What is important is that we begin by properly understanding our religion first and foremost. After this is accomplished then it will not be important whether the road itself is long or short.*

*And indeed I direct this statement of mine towards those men who are callers to the religion among the Muslims, and towards the scholars and those who direct our affairs. I call for them to stand upon complete knowledge of true Islaam, and to fight against every form of negligence and heedlessness regarding the religion, and against differing and disputes, as Allaah has said, ﴾...and do not dispute with one another for fear that you lose courage and your strength departs ﴿—(Surah Al-Anfaal: 46).*

*(Quoted from the work, 'The Life of Sheikh al-Albaanee, His Influence in Present Day Fields of Sharee'ah Knowledge, & the Praise of the Scholars for Him.' volume 1 page 380-385)*

The guiding scholar Sheikh Zayd al-Madkhalee, may Allaah protect him, stated in his writing, 'The Well Established Principles of the Way of the First Generations of Muslims: It's Enduring & Excellent Distinct Characteristics' that,

*"From among these principles and characteristics is that the methodology of tasfeeyah -or clarification, and tarbeeyah -or education and cultivation- is clearly affirmed and established as a true way coming from the first three generations of Islaam, and is something well known to the people of true merit from among them, as is concluded by considering all the related evidence. What is intended by tasfeeyah, when referring to it generally, is clarifying that which is the truth from that which is falsehood, what is goodness from that which is harmful and corrupt, and when referring to its specific meanings it is distinguishing the noble Sunnah of the Prophet and the people of the Sunnah from those innovated matters brought into the religion and the people who are supporters of such innovations.*

*As for what is intended by tarbeeyah, it is calling all of the creation to take on the manners and embrace the excellent character invited to by that guidance revealed to them by their Lord through His worshiper and Messenger Muhammad, may Allaah's praise and salutations be upon him; so that they might have good character, manners, and behavior. As without this they cannot have a good life, nor can they put right their present condition or their final destination. And we seek refuge in Allaah from the evil of not being able to achieve that rectification."*

Thus the methodology of the people of standing upon the Prophet's Sunnah, and proceeding upon the 'way of the believers' in every century is reflected in a focus and concern with these two essential matters: tasfeeyah or clarification of what is original, revealed message from the Lord of all the worlds, and tarbeeyah or education and raising of ourselves, our families, and our communities, and our lands upon what has been distinguished to be that true message and path.

## Methodology:

*The Roles of the Scholars & General Muslims In Raising the New Generation*

The priority and focus of the 'Nakhlah Educational Series' is reflected within in the following statements of Sheikh al-Albaanee, may Allaah have mercy upon him:

*"As for the other obligation, then I intend by this the education of the young generation upon*

*Islaam purified from all of those impurities we have mentioned, giving them a correct Islamic education from their very earliest years, without any influence of a foreign, disbelieving education."*

*(Silsilat al-Hadeeth ad-Da'eefah, Introduction page 2.)*

*"...And since the Messenger of Allaah, may Allaah's praise and salutations be upon him, has indicated that the only cure to remove this state of humiliation that we find ourselves entrenched within, is truly returning back to the religion. Then it is clearly obligatory upon us - through the people of knowledge- to correctly and properly understand the religion in a way that conforms to the sources of the Book of Allaah and the Sunnah, and that we educate and raise a new virtuous, righteous generation upon this."*

*(Clarification and Cultivation and the Need of the Muslims for Them)*

It is essential in discussing our perspective upon this obligation of raising the new generation of Muslims, that we highlight and bring attention to a required pillar of these efforts as indicated by Sheikh al-Albaanee, may Allaah have mercy upon him, and others- in the golden words, *"through the people of knowledge"*. Since something we commonly experience today is that many people have various incorrect understandings of the role that the scholars should have in the life of a Muslim, failing to understand the way in which they fulfill their position as the inheritors of the Messenger of Allaah, may Allaah's praise and salutations be upon him, and stand as those who preserve and enable us to practice the guidance of Islaam. Indeed, the noble Imaam Sheikh as-Sa'dee, may Allaah have mercy upon him, in his work, *"A Definitive and Clear Explanation of the Work 'A Triumph for the Saved Sect'"* pages 237-240, has explained this crucial issue with an extraordinary explanation full of remarkable benefits:

*"Section: Explaining the Conditions for These Two Source Texts to Suffice You -or the Finding of Sufficiency in these Two Sources of Revelation.*

*Overall the conditions needed to achieve this and bring it about return to two matters:*

*Firstly, the presence of the requirements necessary for achieving this; meaning a complete devotion to the Book and the Sunnah, and the putting forth of efforts both in seeking to understand their intended meanings, as well as in striving to be guided by them. What is required secondly is the pushing away of everything which prevents achieving this finding of sufficiency in them.*

*This is through having a firm determination to distance yourself from everything which contradicts these two source texts in what comes from the historical schools of jurisprudence, assorted various statements, differing principles and their resulting conclusions which the majority of people proceed upon. These matters which contradict the two sources of revelation include many affairs which, when the worshiper of Allaah repels them from himself and stands against them, the realm of his knowledge, understanding, and deeds then expands greatly. Through a devotion to them and a complete dedication towards these two sources of revelation, proceeding upon every path which assists one's understanding them, and receiving enlightenment from the light of the scholars and being guided by the guidance that they possess- you will achieve that complete sufficiency in them. And surely, in the positions they take towards the leading people of knowledge and the scholars, the people are three types of individuals:*

*The first of them is the one who goes to extremes in his attachment to the scholars. He makes their statements something which are infallible as if their words held the same position as those of the statements of the Messenger of Allaah, may Allaah's praise and salutations be upon him, as well as giving those scholars' statements precedence and predominance over the Book of Allaah and the Sunnah. This is despite the fact that every leading scholar who has been accepted by this Ummah was one who promoted and encouraged the following of the Book and the Sunnah, commanding the people not to follow their own statements nor their school of thought in anything which stood in opposition to the Book of Allaah and the Sunnah.*

*The second type is the one who generally rejects and invalidates the statements of the scholars and forbids the referring to the statements of the leading scholars of guidance and those people of knowledge who stand as brilliant lamps in the darkness. This type of person neither relies upon the light of discernment with the scholars, nor utilizes their stores of knowledge. Or even if perhaps they do so, they do not direct thanks towards them for this. And this manner and way prohibits them from tremendous good. Furthermore, that which motivates such individuals to proceed in this way is their falsely supposing that the obligation to follow the Messenger of Allaah, may Allaah's praise and salutations be upon him, and the giving of precedence to his statements over the statements of anyone else, requires that they do without any reliance upon the statements of the Companions, or those who followed them in goodness, or those leading scholars of guidance within the Ummah. And this is a glaring and extraordinary mistake.*

*As indeed the Companions and the people of knowledge are the means and the agency between the Messenger of Allaah, may Allaah's praise and salutations be upon him, and his Ummah- in the transmission and spreading his Sunnah in regard to both its wording and texts as well as its meanings and understanding. Therefore the one who follows them in what they convey in this is guided through their understandings, receives knowledge from the light they possess, benefits from the conclusions they have derived from these sources -of beneficial meanings and explanations, as well as in relation to subtle matters which scarcely occur to the minds of some of the other people of knowledge, or barely comes to be discerned by their minds. Consequently, from the blessing of Allaah upon this Ummah is that He has given them these guiding scholars who cultivate and educate them upon two clear types of excellent cultivation.*

*The first category is education from the direction of ones knowledge and understanding. They educate the Ummah upon the more essential and fundamental matters before the more complex affairs. They convey the meanings of the Book and the Sunnah to the minds and intellects of the people through efforts of teaching which rectifies, and through composing various beneficial books of knowledge which a worshiper doesn't even have the ability to adequately describe what is encompassed within them of aspects of knowledge and benefits. Works which reflect the presence of a clear white hand in deriving guidance from the Book of Allaah and the Sunnah, and through the arrangement, detailed clarification, division and explanation, through the gathering together of explanations, comparisons, conditions, pillars, and explanations about that which prevents the fulfillment of matters, as well as distinguishing between differing meanings and categorizing various knowledge based benefits.*

*The second category is education from the direction of ones conduct and actions. They cultivate the peoples characters encouraging them towards every praiseworthy aspect of good character, through explaining its ruling and high status, and what benefits comes to be realized from it, clarifying the reasons and paths which enable one to attain it, as well as those affairs which prevent, delay or hinder someone becoming one distinguished and characterized by it. Because they, in reality, are those who bring nourishment to the hearts and the souls; they are the doctors who treat the diseases of the heart and its defects. As such they educate the people through their statements, actions as well as their general guided way. Therefore the scholars have a tremendous right over this Ummah. The portion of love and esteem, respect and honor, and thanks due to them because their merits and their various good efforts stand above every other right after establishing the right of Allaah, and the right of His Messenger, may Allaah's praise and salutations be upon him.*

*Because of this, the third group of individuals in respect to the scholars are those who have been guided to understand their true role and position, and establish their rights, thanking them for their virtues and merits, benefiting by taking from the knowledge they have, while acknowledging their rank and status. They understand that the scholars are not infallible and that their statements must stand in conformance to the statements of the Messenger of Allaah, may Allaah's praise and salutations be upon him. And that each one from among them has that which is from guidance, knowledge, and correctness in his statements taken and benefited from, while turning away from whatever in mistaken within it.*

*Yet such a scholar is not to be belittled for his mistake, as he stands as one who strove to reach the truth; therefore his mistake will be forgiven, and he should be thanked for his efforts. One clarifies what was stated by of any one of these leaders from among men, when it is recognizes that it has some weakness or conflict to an evidence of the Sharee'ah, by explaining its weakness and the level of that weakness, without speaking evilly of the intention of those people of knowledge and religion, nor defaming them due to that error. Rather we say, as it is obligatory to say, "And those who came after them say:* ◆ *Our Lord! forgive us and our brethren who have preceded us in faith, and put not in our hearts any hatred against those who have believed. Our Lord! You are indeed full of kindness, Most Merciful.* ◆ *-(Surah al-Hashr: 10).*

*Accordingly, individuals of this third type are those who fulfill two different matters. They join together on one hand between giving precedence to the Book and the Sunnah over everything else, and, on the other hand, between comprehending the level and position of the scholars and the leading people of knowledge and guidance, and establishing this even if it is only done in regard to some of their rights upon us. So we ask Allaah to bless us to be from this type, and to make us from among the people of this third type, and to make us from those who love Him and love those who love Him, and those who love every action which brings us closer to everything He loves."*

Upon this clarity regarding the proper understanding of our balanced position towards our guided Muslim scholars, consider the following words about the realm of work of the general people of faith, which explains our area of efforts and struggle as Muslim parents, found in the following statement by Sheikh Saaleh Fauzaan al-Fauzaan, may Allaah preserve him.

*"Question: Some people mistakenly believe that calling to Allaah is a matter not to be undertaken by anyone else other than the scholars without exception, and that it is not something required for other than the scholars according to that which they have knowledge of -to undertake any efforts of calling the people to Allaah. So what is your esteemed guidance regarding this?" The Sheikh responded by saying:*

*"This is not a misconception, but is in fact a reality. The call to Allaah cannot be established except through those who are scholars. And I state this. Yet, certainly there are clear issues which every person understands. As such, every individual should enjoin the good and forbid wrongdoing according to the level of his understanding. Such that he instructs and orders the members of his household to perform the ritual daily prayers and other matters that are clear and well known.*

*Undertaking this is something mandatory and required even upon the common people, such that they must command their children to perform their prayers in the masjid. The Messenger of Allaah, may Allaah praise and salutations be upon him, said, { **Command you children to pray at seven, and beat them due to its negligence at ten.**} (Authentic narration found in Sunan Abu Dawood ). And the Messenger of Allaah, may Allaah praise and salutations be upon him, said, { **Each one of you is a guardian or a shepherd, and each of you is responsible for those under his guardianship....**} (Authentic narration found in Saheeh al-Bukhaaree). So this is called guardianship, and this is also called enjoining the good and forbidding wrongdoing. The Messenger of Allaah, may Allaah praise and salutations be upon him, said, { **The one from among you who sees a wrong should change it with his hand, and if he is unable to do so, then with his tongue, and if he is not able to do this, then with his heart.** } (Authentic narration found in Saheeh Muslim).*

*So in relation to the common person, that which it is required from him to endeavor upon is that he commands the members of his household-as well as others -with the proper performance of the ritual prayers, the obligatory charity, with generally striving to obey Allaah, and to stay away from sins and transgressions, and that he purify and cleanse his home from disobedience, and that he educate and cultivate his children upon the obedience of Allaah's commands. This is what is required from him, even if he is a general person. As these types of matters are from that which is understood by every single person. This is something which is clear and apparent.*

*But as for the matters of putting forth rulings and judgments regarding matters in the religion, or entering into clarifying issues of what is permissible and what is forbidden, or explaining what is considered associating others in the worship due to Allaah and what is properly worshiping Him alone without any partner- then indeed these are matters which cannot be established except by the scholars"*

*(Beneficial Responses to Questions About Modern Methodologies, Question 15, page 22)*

Similarly the guiding scholar Sheikh 'Abdul-'Azeez Ibn Baaz, may Allaah have mercy upon him, also emphasized this same overall responsibility:

*"...It is also upon a Muslim that he struggles diligently in that which will place his worldly affairs in a good state, just as he must also strive in the correcting of his religious affairs and the affairs of his own family. As the people of his household have a significant right over him that he strive diligently in rectifying their affair and guiding them towards goodness, due to the statement of Allaah, the*

*Most Exalted,* ❴ ***Oh you who believe! Save yourselves and your families Hellfire whose fuel is men and stones*** ❵ *-(Surah at-Tahreem: 6)*

*So it is upon you to strive to correct the affairs of the members of your family. This includes your wife, your children- both male and female- and such as your own brothers. This concerns all of the people in your family, meaning you should strive to teach them the religion, guiding and directing them, and warning them from those matters Allaah has prohibited for us. Because you are the one who is responsible for them as shown in the statement of the Prophet, may Allaah's praise and salutations be upon him,* ❴ ***Every one of you is a guardian, and responsible for what is in his custody. The ruler is a guardian of his subjects and responsible for them; a husband is a guardian of his family and is responsible for it; a lady is a guardian of her husband's house and is responsible for it, and a servant is a guardian of his master's property and is responsible for it....*** ❵ *Then the Messenger of Allaah, may Allaah's praise and salutations be upon him, continued to say,* ❴ ***...so all of you are guardians and are responsible for those under your authority.*** ❵ *(Authentically narrated in Saheeh al-Bukhaaree & Muslim)*

*It is upon us to strive diligently in correcting the affairs of the members of our families, from the aspect of purifying their sincerity of intention for Allaah's sake alone in all of their deeds, and ensuring that they truthfully believe in and follow the Messenger of Allaah, may Allaah's praise and salutations be upon him, their fulfilling the prayer and the other obligations which Allaah the Most Exalted has commanded for us, as well as from the direction of distancing them from everything which Allaah has prohibited.*

*It is upon every single man and women to give advice to their families about the fulfillment of what is obligatory upon them. Certainly, it is upon the woman as well as upon the man to perform this. In this way our homes become corrected and rectified in regard to the most important and essential matters. Allaah said to His Prophet, may Allaah's praise and salutations be upon him,* ❴ ***And enjoin the ritual prayers on your family...*** ❵ *(Surah Taha: 132) Similarly, Allaah the Most Exalted said to His prophet Ismaa'aeel,* ❴ ***And mention in the Book, Ismaa'eel. Verily, he was true to what he promised, and he was a Messenger, and a Prophet. And he used to enjoin on his family and his people the ritual prayers and the obligatory charity, and his Lord was pleased with him.*** ❵ *-(Surah Maryam: 54-55)*

*As such, it is only proper that we model ourselves after the prophets and the best of people, and be concerned with the state of the members of our households. Do not be neglectful of them, oh worshipper of Allaah! Regardless of whether it is concerning your wife, your mother, father, grandfather, grandmother, your brothers, or your children; it is upon you to strive diligently in correcting their state and condition..."*

*(Collection of Various Rulings and Statements- Sheikh 'Abdul-'Azeez Ibn 'Abdullah Ibn Baaz, Vol. 6, page 47)*

## Content & Structure:

We hope to contribute works which enable every striving Muslim who acknowledges the proper position of the scholars, to fulfill the recognized duty and obligation which lays upon each one of us to bring the light of Islaam into our own lives as individuals as well as into our homes and among our families. Towards this goal we are committed to developing educational publications and comprehensive educational curriculums -through cooperation with and based upon the works of the scholars of Islaam and the students of knowledge. Works which, with the assistance of Allaah, the Most High, we can utilize to educate and instruct ourselves, our families and our communities upon Islaam in both principle and practice. The publications and works of the Nakhlah Educational Series are divided into the following categories:

*Basic: Ages 4- 6*

*Elementary: Ages 6-11*

*Secondary: Ages 11-14*

*High School: Ages 14- Young Adult*

*General: Young Adult –Adult*

*Supplementary: All Ages*

Publications and works within these stated levels will, with the permission of Allaah, encompass different beneficial areas and subjects, and will be offered in every permissible form of media and medium. As certainly, as the guiding scholar Sheikh Saaleh Fauzaan al-Fauzaan, may Allaah preserve him, has stated,

*"Beneficial knowledge is itself divided into two categories. Firstly is that knowledge which is tremendous in its benefit, as it benefits in this world and continues to benefit in the Hereafter. This is religious Sharee'ah knowledge. And secondly, that which is limited and restricted to matters related to the life of this world, such as learning the processes of manufacturing various goods. This is a category of knowledge related specifically to worldly affairs.*

*…As for the learning of worldly knowledge, such as knowledge of manufacturing, then it is legislated upon us collectively to learn whatever the Muslims have a need for. Yet If they do not have a need for this knowledge, then learning it is a neutral matter upon the condition that it does not compete with or displace any areas of Sharee'ah knowledge…"*

*("Explanations of the Mistakes of Some Writers'", Pages 10-12)*

So we strive always to remind ourselves and our brothers of this crucial point also indicated by Sheikh Sadeeq Ibn Hasan al-Qanoojee, may Allaah have mercy upon him, in: '*Abjad al-'Uloom*', (page 89)

*"…What is intended by knowledge in the mentioned hadeeth is knowledge of the religion and the distinctive Sharee'ah, knowledge of the Noble Book and the Pure Sunnah, of which there is no third along with them. But what is not meant in this narration are those invented areas of knowledge, whether they emerged in previous ages or today's world, which the people in these present times have devoted themselves to. They have specifically dedicated themselves to them in a manner*

*which prevents them from looking towards those areas of knowledge related to faith, and in a way which has preoccupied them from occupying themselves from what is actually wanted or desired by Allaah, the Most High, and His Messenger, who is the leader of men and Jinn. Such that the knowledge in the Qur'an has become something abandoned and the sciences of hadeeth have become obscure. While these new areas of knowledge related to manufacturing and production continually emerge from the nations of disbelief and apostasy, and they are called, "sciences", "arts", and "ideal development". And this sad state increases every day, indeed from Allaah we came and to Him shall we return....*

*...Additionally, although the various areas of beneficial knowledge all share some level of value, they all have differing importance and ranks. Among them is that which is to be considered according to its subject, such as medicine, and its subject is the human body. Or such as the sciences of 'tafseer' and its subject is the explanation of the words of Allaah, the Most Exalted and Most High, and the value of these two areas is not in any way unrecognized.*

*And from among the various areas there are those areas which are considered according to their objective, such as knowledge of upright character, and its goal is understanding the beneficial merits that an individual can come to possess. And from among them there are those areas which are considered according to the people's need for them, such as 'fiqh' which the need for it is urgent and essential. And from among them there are those areas which are considered according to their apparent strength, such as knowledge of physical sports and exercise, as it is something openly demonstrated.*

*And from the areas of knowledge are those areas which rise in their position of importance through their combining all these different matters within them, or the majority of them. Such as revealed religious knowledge, as its subject is indeed esteemed, its objective one of true merit, and its need is undeniably felt. Likewise one area of knowledge may be considered of superior rank than another in consideration of the results that it brings forth, or the strength of its outward manifestation, or due to the essentialness of its objective. Similarly the result that an area produces is certainly of higher estimation and significance in appraisal than the outward or apparent significance of some other areas of knowledge.*

*For that reason the highest ranking and most valuable area of knowledge is that of knowledge of Allaah the Most Perfect and the Most High, of His angels, and messengers, and all the particulars of these beliefs, as its result is that of eternal and continuing happiness."*

We ask Allaah, the most High to bless us with success in contributing to the many efforts of our Muslim brothers and sisters committed to raising themselves as individuals and the next generation of our children upon that Islaam which Allaah has perfected and chosen for us, and which He has enabled the guided Muslims to proceed upon in each and every century. We ask him to forgive us, and forgive the Muslim men and the Muslim women, and to guide all the believers to everything He loves and is pleased with. The success is from Allaah, The Most High The Most Exalted, alone and all praise is due to Him.

*Abu Sukhailah Khalil Ibn-Abelahyi*
*Taalib al-Ilm Educational Resources*

GENERAL ANNOUNCEMENT:

# Taalib al-Ilm Educational Publications is looking for

# *Distributors & Publication Contributors*

## Distributors:

We are working to make Taalib al-Ilm Education Resources publications available through distributors worldwide. As of 1433 h./2012 c.e. we offer local shipping from North America (United States), Europe & Africa (UK), & South East Asia (Australia), for soft cover, hardcover, as well as ebooks online. We offer quantity discounts worldwide including North and South America, Europe and U.K., Africa, and Asia, on all quantity printed purchases by individuals, masjids, Islamic centers, local study groups, Muslim homeschooling groups, conference vendors, and retail stores according to the following discount scale:

| | | |
|---|---|---|
| **10%** discount for order of | **USD** | **$100** or over |
| **20%** discount for order of | **USD** | **$200** or over |
| **30%** discount for order of | **USD** | **$500** or over |
| **40%** discount for order of | **USD** | **$1000** or over |
| **50%** discount for order of | **USD** | **$2000** or over |

All new distributors receive an additional **10% discount** on any of the above discount levels for their **FIRST OR INITIAL ORDER ONLY**. For further information, please contact the sales department by e-mail: ***service@taalib.com.***

## Publication Contributors:

Additionally, in an effort to further expand our publication library, we are seeking contributing authors, translators, and compilers with beneficial works of any area of Sharee'ah knowledge for submission of their works for potential publication by us. For details and all submission guidelines please email us at: ***service@taalib.com***

> **Referral bonus:** *Individuals who refer a new distributor or publication contributor to us can receive a **$25 PayPal payment**, upon a confirmed contract with a publication contributor or receipt of a newly referred distributor's initial order at the 40% discount level. Contact us for further information and conditions.*

# Fundamentals of Arabic Class for Women Only

## An Online Class for Muslim Women Taught by a Muslim Woman

*Developed and Taught by Umm Mujaahid Khadijah Bint Lacina al-Amreekiyyah*

[Available: **TBA**¦ Schedule: **Live Class Three times Weekly** ¦ price: **$60 Monthly** USD ]

Course Includes All Materials In EBook Format

## Course Features:

* Four Levels of Study & Supplementary Courses

* Limited class size

* Class meets online three times a week with the teacher

* Class moves at a moderate pace to ensure understanding of the concepts presented

* Begins with a short review of the Arabic alphabet, stressing correct pronunciation

* Grammar, morphology, and writing fundamentals

* Focus on understanding what is read and spoken

* Encompasses both speech and understanding

* Numerous exercises, both in class and out, to increase understanding and ability

* Practice in taking notes from Arabic lectures and simple translation

* Additional Out of class assignments and group projects

* Comprehensive reviews

* Periodic quizzes and tests

* End of class test will determine if one can advance to the next class

* Textbooks, dictionaries, and supplementary materials provided as ebooks

* Use of hadeeth texts and other Islamic material for reading,
understanding and translation exercises

* Class forum to make asking questions and doing group assignments easier

* The teacher will be available through email
to answer course questions and assist the students regularly

For more information about availability please visit
*arabicforwomen.taalib.com*

*Please visit **study.taalib.com** for information concerning other free and fee-based courses.*

BOOK PUBLICATION PREVIEW:

# *Thalaathatu al-Usool: The Three Fundamental Principles*

A Step by Step Educational Course on Islaam

Based upon Commentaries of 'Thalaathatu al-Usool' of Sheikh Muhammad ibn 'Abdul Wahaab
(may Allaah have mercy upon him)

*Collected and Arranged by Umm Mujaahid Khadijah Bint Lacina al-Amreekiyyah*

|Available: **Now Self Study/ Teachers Edition** pages: 350+ | price: (S) **$22.50** (H) **$29.50** | eBook **$9.99**
**Directed Study Edition** | price: (S) **$17** - **Exercise Workbook** | price: (S) **$10**]

## Description:

*A complete course for the Believing men and women who want to learn their religion from the ground up, building a firm foundation upon which to base their actions. This is the* **second** *in our* **Foundation Series** *on Islamic beliefs and making them a reality in your life, which began with* **"al-Waajibaat: The Obligatory Matters".**
*The course utilizes various commentaries of Sheikh Muhammad ibn 'Abdul Wahaab's original text from the following scholars of our age:*

*Sheikh Muhammad ibn Saalih al-'Utheimeen*
*Sheikh Saaleh Ibn Sa'd as-Suhaaymee*
*Sheikh 'Abdul-'Azeez Ibn Baaz*
*Sheikh Saalih al-Fauzaan*
*Sheikh 'Abdullah ibn Saalih al-Fauzaan*
*Sheikh Muhammad 'Amaan al-Jaamee*
*Sheikh Saalih Aal-Sheikh (and others)*

*In addition to various statements of scholars of the Sunnah throughout the centuries*

## Course Features:

*'Thalaathatu al-Usool' Arabic text and translation*
*Twenty-five lessons which discuss such vital topics as "Who is your Lord?"- "Who is your Prophet?"- "What is your religion?"- tawheed -shirk -the pillars of Islaam -the pillars of faith -having allegiance to the believers and how to deal with them, as well as the disbelievers -commanding the good and forbidding the evil -emigration to the lands of Islaam -and many many more.*
*-advice and insight on how to make Islaam a reality in your life -how to put into practice all that you learn in this course Review questions and vocabulary after each chapter as well as quizzes and tests A compilation of points of benefit found throughout the book*

*(Support and discussion group for students at www.taalib.com)*

SCAN WITH SMARTPHONE
PRINT
FOR MORE INFORMATION

SCAN WITH SMARTPHONE
EBOOK
FOR MORE INFORMATION

PREVIEW

BOOK PUBLICATION PREVIEW:

# Al-Waajibaat: The Obligatory Matters

**What it is Decreed that Every Male and Female Muslim Must Have Knowledge Of
-from the statements of Sheikh al-Islaam Muhammad ibn 'Abdul-Wahaab**

(A Step By Step Course on The Fundamental Beliefs of Islaam- with Lesson Questions, Quizzes, & Exams)

*Collected and Arranged by Umm Mujaahid Khadijah Bint Lacina al-Amreekiyyah*

[Available: **Now** - **Self Study/ Teachers Edition** pages: 290+ ¦ price: (S) **$20** (H) **$27**¦¦ eBook **$9.99**
**Directed Study Edition** pages: 190+ ¦ price: **$15** - **Exercise Workbook** pages: 100+ ¦ price: **$7**]

## Table of Contents:

SCAN WITH SMARTPHONE
FOR MORE INFORMATION

SCAN WITH SMARTPHONE
FOR MORE INFORMATION

BOOK PUBLICATION PREVIEW:

# *Fasting from Alif to Yaa:*
## *A Day by Day Guide to Making the Most of Ramadhaan*

By Umm Mujaahid, Khadijah Bint Lacina al-Amreekiyyah as-Salafiyyah With Abu Hamzah, Hudhaifah Ibn Khalil and Umm Usaamah, Sukhailah Bint Khalil

[Available: **1433** -pages: 250+ ¦ price: (S) **$20**   (H) **$27** ¦ eBook **$9.99**

## *Description:*

-Contains additional points of benefit to teach one how to live Islaam as a way of life
-Plus, stories of the Prophets and Messengers including activities for the whole family to enjoy and benefit from for each day of Ramadhaan. Some of the Prophets and Messengers covered include Aadam, Ibraaheem, Lut, Yusuf, Sulaymaan, Shu'ayb, Moosa, Zakariyyah, Muhammad, and more! -Recipes for foods enjoyed by Muslims around the world

## *Some of the subjects discussed include:*

*The Letter* أ : الإحتساب *(al-Ihtisaab) (consciously seeking the reward of Allaah with good deeds)*

*The Letter* ت : التراويح *(at-Taraaweeh) (the night prayer specific to Ramadhaan)*

*The Letter* ج : الجود *(al-jood) (generosity)*

*The Letter* ح : حفظ الجوارح *(hifdh al-jawaarih) (safeguarding the limbs)*

*The Letter* خ : الخروج من المنزل *(al-khurooj min al-manzil) (leaving the house)*

*The Letter* ذ : الذكر *(adh-dhikr) (remembrance of Allaah)*

*The Letter* ش : الشكر *(ash-shukr) (gratitude)*

*The Letter* ص : صيام الصغير *(siyaam as-sagheer) (the fast of the young person)*

*The Letter* ط : الطهر *(at-tahr) (purification)*

*The Letter* ظ : الظمأ الحقيقي *(adh-dhama' al-haqeeqee) (the true thirst on the Day of Judgment)*

*The Letter* غ : الغفلة *(al-ghaflah) (heedlessness)*

*The Letter* ق : قراءة القران *(qura'at al-Qur'aan) (reading and reciting the Qur'aan)*

*The Letter* ك : كظم الغيظ *(kadhm al-ghaydh) (controlling the anger)*

*The Letter* م : المفطرات *(al-maftooraat) (that which breaks the fast)*

*The Letter* ه : الهمة العالية *(al-hamat al-'aaliyah) (the high aspirations)*

*The Letter* ي : يمن الحسنة *(yumn al-hasana)*
*(the blessings of good deeds)*

*....And so on for all the days of this blessed month.*

*& A Few Words Concerning the Eid*
*from Sheikh Saalih Fauzaan*

SCAN WITH SMARTPHONE
FOR MORE INFORMATION

SCAN WITH SMARTPHONE
FOR MORE INFORMATION

BOOK PUBLICATION PREVIEW:

# My Home, My Path

## A Comprehensive Source Book For Today's Muslim Woman Discussing Her Essential Role & Contribution To The Establishment of Islaam – Taken From The Words Of The People Of Knowledge

*Collected and Translated by Umm Mujaahid Khadijah Bint Lacina al-Amreekiyyah*

[Available: **Now** ¦ pages: **420+** ¦ price: (S) **$22.50** (H) **$29.50** eBook **$9.99**]]

## Table of Contents:

*Publishers Introduction * Compilers Introduction*

The Role of the Woman and her Significant Influence in Life
by Sheikh 'Abdul-'Azeez Bin Baaz (may Allaah have mercy upon him)
The Role of the Woman in Building the Muslim Society
by Sheikh Muhammad ibn Saaleh al-'Utheimeen (may Allaah have mercy upon him)
The Role of the Woman in Educating and Raising the Family by Sheikh Saaleh Fauzaan
Islaam's Ennoblement of Women by Sheikh Saalih Fauzaan (may Allaah Preserve Him)
Warning against the Forbidden Display of Beauty and Uncovering
by Sheikh Muhammad ibn 'Abdul-Wahaab al-Wasaabee (may Allaah Preserve Him)
Rectification of the Households by Sheikh Muhammad al-Imaam (may Allaah Preserve Him)
My Advice to my Muslim Sisters by Sheikh Jamaal al-Haarithee (may Allaah Preserve Him)

### Islamic Ruling Section

*Rulings Regarding Beliefs • Rulings Regarding the Role of Women in Islaam*
*Rulings Regarding Education and Employment • Rulings Pertaining to Work*
*Rulings Regarding the Household • Rulings Regarding Marriage*
*Rulings Regarding Polygeny • Rulings Regarding the Children*
*Rulings Regarding Others*

### Obligations of the Believing Woman

Her Obligations Towards her Lord • Her Obligations Towards her Parents
Her Obligations Towards her Husband • Her Obligations Towards her Children
Her Obligations Towards her Extended Family
Her Obligations Towards her Neighbors and Companions

### Appendices

Appendix 1: Female Students of Knowledge (Parts 1-5)
Appendix 2: The Islamic Rulings Regarding
Free Mixing of Men and Women
Appendix 3: The Family & Principles
of Familial Conduct

SCAN WITH SMARTPHONE
PRINT
FOR MORE INFORMATION

SCAN WITH SMARTPHONE
EBOOK
FOR MORE INFORMATION

BOOK PUBLICATION PREVIEW:

PREVIEW

# My Hijaab, My Path

## A Comprehensive Knowledge Based Compilation on Muslim Women's Role & Dress

*Collected and Translated by Umm Mujaahid Khadijah Bint Lacina al-Amreekiyyah*

Available: **Now** ¦ pages: **190+** ¦ price: (S) **$17.50** (H) **$25** ¦ eBook **$9.99**

## Table of Contents:

SCAN WITH SMARTPHONE
PRINT
FOR MORE INFORMATION

SCAN WITH SMARTPHONE
EBOOK
FOR MORE INFORMATION

BOOK PUBLICATION PREVIEW:

# Whispers of Paradise (1): A Muslim Woman's Life Journal

## An Islamic Daily Journal Which Encourages Reflection & Rectification

*Collected and Edited by Taalib al-Ilm Educational Resources Development Staff*

*Abu Alee ath-Thaqafee said: Abu Hafs used to say:*

**"The one who does not each moment weigh his situation and condition against the scale of the Book of Allaah and the Sunnah, and does not question his very footsteps, then he is not to be considered worthy."**

(Seyaar 'Alaam an-Nubala: vol. 12, page 512)

[Available: **Now** | pages: **380+** | price: (H) **$32** ]

*[Elegantly designed edition is for the year 1434 / 2013]*

*Contents:*

*Publishers Introduction*

*12 Monthly calendar pages* with beneficial quotations from Ibn Qayyim

*Daily journal page* based upon Islamic calendar (with corresponding C.E. dates)

## Each daily journal page starts with one of the following:

-*A Verse from the Noble Qur'an*
-*An Authentic Narration of the Messenger of Allaah*
-*An Authentic Supplication*
-*A Beneficial Point from a Biography of the Early Generations*
-*A Beneficial Statement from One of the Well Known Scholars, Past or Present*

SCAN WITH SMARTPHONE

FOR MORE INFORMATION

## The Cure, The Explanation, The Clear Affair, & The Brilliantly Distinct Signpost

*A Step by Step Educational Course on Islaam*
*Based upon Commentaries of*

# 'Usul as-Sunnah' of Imaam Ahmad
### (may Allaah have mercy upon him)

Compiled and Translated by: Abu Sukhailah Khalil Ibn-Abelahyi

[Available: **TBA** ¦ price: **TBA** (Multi-volume) ¦ soft cover, hard cover, ebook]

A vital learning tool for striving, adult Muslims to learn their religion. The course is based upon various commentaries of Imaam Ahmad ibn Hanbal's original text, may Allaah have mercy upon him, from the following scholars of our age, may Allaah preserve them all:

- Sheikh Zayd Ibn Muhammad al-Madhlhalee
- Sheikh Saleeh Ibn Sa'd As-Suhaaymee
- Sheikh 'Abdul-'Azeez Ibn 'Abdullah ar-Raajeehee
- Sheikh 'Abdullah Al-Ghudayaan
- Sheikh Rabee'a Ibn Haadee al-Madhlhalee
- Sheikh Sa'd Ibn Naasir as-Shathree
- Sheikh 'Ubayd Ibn 'Abdullah al-Jabaaree
- Sheikh 'Abdullah Al-Bukharee
- Sheikh Hamaad Uthmaan
- Sheikh Falaah Ibn Ismaa'eel Mundaakir

In addition to various statements of scholars of the Sunnah throughout the centuries

## *Course Features:*

Study of text divided into chapters formatted into multiple short lessons to facilitate learning . Each lesson has: evidence summary, lesson benefits, standard & review exercises 'Usul as-Sunnah' Arabic text & translation divided for easier memorization. A tool to understandings many of the most important beliefs of Islaam, as well as how to implement them and avoid common mistakes and misunderstandings.

SCAN WITH SMARTPHONE

PRINT

FOR MORE INFORMATION

SCAN WITH SMARTPHONE

EBOOK

FOR MORE INFORMATION

# Additional Book Notes

# Additional Book Notes

Made in the USA
Middletown, DE
04 May 2021

38157613R00236